K   ES:

Information Technology for Sustainable Development

Robin Mansell and Uta Wehn

Editors

for the

United Nations Commission on
Science and Technology for Development

published for and on behalf of
The United Nations

D1471663

Oxford University Press 1998

Oxford Univ........................U...6DP

Oxford New York
Athens Auckland Bangkok Bogota Bombay
Buenos Aires Calcutta Cape Town Dar es Salaam
Delhi Florence Hong Kong Istanbul Karachi
Kuala Lumpur Madras Madrid Melbourne
Mexico City Nairobi Paris Singapore
Taipei Tokyo Toronto Warsaw

and associated companies in
Berlin Ibadan

Oxford is a trade mark of Oxford University Press

Published in the United States by
Oxford University Press Inc., New York

British Library Cataloguing in Publication Data
Data available

Library of Congress Cataloging in Publication Data
Data available

ISBN 0-19-829410-7

Designed and Produced by
Bank Design,
Brighton, East Sussex

Printed in Great Britain by
Butler and Tanner Ltd
Frome, Somerset

Foreword

At its second session, in May 1995, the United Nations Commission on Science and Technology for Development (UNCSTD) chose the topic of information technology (IT) and development as its main theme for the next session in 1997. A Working Group was established to study the particular problems of access to and use of IT by developing countries. The main task was to prepare a short report for consideration by the Commission.

In the course of its review, the Working Group commissioned a number of background reports and requested the UNCTAD secretariat to undertake a review of United Nations activities in this area. It convened a scenario-building workshop and benefited from other papers and reports made available to it by the United Nations University Institute for New Technology (UNU/INTECH) in Maastricht, the International Development Research Centre (IDRC) in Ottawa, and the Instituto Colombiano para el Desarrollo y la Ciencia y la Tecnología (COLCIENCIAS) in Bogota. The Working Group also became aware of many other studies and reports which are germane to the topic.

Initially, priority was given to the preparation of the short policy report. This document is summarised in Annex 3 of the present report. It soon became apparent, however, that the huge amount of relevant material could not be considered adequately in the short report. It was therefore decided to ask Professor Robin Mansell to take responsibility for preparing a report which would do greater justice to the wealth of accumulated knowledge. The goal was to produce a source book which would be useful for government officials, private sector firms, and academic researchers and which would provide a systematic review of available information on the topic. Professor Mansell was also encouraged to collect additional short statements from leading authorities to complement the available information.

The outline of this report was originally developed at a planning meeting in Cartagena, Colombia, modified and expanded by Ludovico Alcorta of UNU/INTECH, revised by Robin Mansell, and finally approved by the Working Group in Mumbai, India, in January 1997. Professor Mansell was given full responsibility for soliciting additional contributions and, together with her colleague Uta Wehn, for preparing the first draft of the report. This first draft was reviewed by an Editorial Board of the Commission in Ocho Rios, Jamaica, in April 1997, revised and made available for comments by UNCSTD members in May 1997, and further revised for submission to the Editorial Board in August 1997.

Major financial support for the project was provided by the Government of the Netherlands. The Governments of Colombia, India, and Jamaica financed meetings of the Working Group on IT and Development and of the Editorial Board. The IDRC, Canada, and the Government of Colombia provided further financial support for the project.

Although the Working Group has acted as an advisory group for the production of the report, full editorial responsibility rests with Professor Mansell and Uta Wehn. The views expressed in this publication are those of the authors/editors and do not necessarily reflect the views of the United Nations.

As befits a report prepared under the auspices of the United Nations Commission on Science and Technology for Development, it takes a deliberate science, technology, and innovation policy perspective on the topic. It is this perspective, plus the fact that it sets out to consider the implications of the IT revolution for developing countries and countries in transition, which provides its unique approach.

Where there are alternative viewpoints on key issues, the report attempts to present both arguments and, in particular, to ensure that the developing country perspective is clearly articulated.

Working Group Co-Chairs

Fernando Chaparro (Colombia)
Geoffrey Oldham (United Kingdom)

The Chapter Map

1

BUILDING INNOVATIVE KNOWLEDGE SOCIETIES

Harnessing ICTs to development goals

2

INDICATORS OF DEVELOPING COUNTRY PARTICIPATION IN 'KNOWLEDGE SOCIETIES'

What the indicators tell us about the spread of ICTs and capabilities for their use

3

INNOVATION SYSTEMS AND THE LEARNING PROCESS

How people in firms are learning to organise and manage ICTs and related services

4

STRENGTHENING THE SCIENCE AND TECHNOLOGY BASE THROUGH EDUCATION AND LIFELONG LEARNING

How people use ICTs to create, acquire, and share new knowledge

5

THE POTENTIAL USES OF ICTs FOR SUSTAINABLE DEVELOPMENT

Identifying potential applications for public and private sectors

6

IMPLEMENTING ICTs IN THE LEAST DEVELOPED COUNTRIES

Uses of ICTs when poverty is pervasive

7

ASSEMBLING THE COMPONENTS OF NATIONAL INFORMATION INFRASTRUCTURES

Lessons from ICT producers in developing countries – options for building infrastructure

8

NATIONAL INFORMATION INFRASTRUCTURE ACCESS – BUILDING SOCIAL AND MARKET VALUE CHAINS

Growing 'access gaps' and the impact of market liberalisation

9

FRIEND OR FOE? DEVELOPING COUNTRIES AND THE INTERNATIONAL GOVERNANCE SYSTEM

The global information infrastructure – emerging 'zones of silence'

10

INSTITUTIONAL INNOVATIONS FOR THE GOVERNANCE OF INFORMATION SERVICES

Enforcing intellectual property rights and protecting security and privacy

11

NATIONAL ICT STRATEGIES FOR KNOWLEDGE-BASED DEVELOPMENT

What processes are needed?

12

INNOVATIVE 'KNOWLEDGE SOCIETIES' – CONSEQUENCES OF ICT STRATEGIES

The benefits, risks, and outcomes

13

TOOLS FOR BUILDING 'KNOWLEDGE SOCIETIES'

Options for development

Table of Contents

Advanced microelectronics-based information and communication technologies (ICTs) are at the heart of recent social and economic transformations in both the industrialised and many developing countries. The costs of ICTs are continuing to fall. As their capabilities increase, they are being applied throughout all sectors of economies and societies. The increasing spread of ICTs opens up new opportunities for developing countries to harness these technologies and services to serve their development goals. In the last few years, there have been many initiatives at the highest levels of government and industry to promote the construction of a global information infrastructure. Developing countries are being encouraged to invest in their national information infrastructures so that they can participate in knowledge-based development and experience the predicted social and economic benefits.

Between 1995 and 1997, the United Nations Commission on Science and Technology for Development (UNCSTD) investigated claims and counterclaims about the benefits and risks of ICTs. Members of the Commission's Working Group on IT and Development examined the available evidence on the experiences of developing countries. They found that there are many instances where the use of ICTs is bringing widespread social and economic benefits. However, there are as many instances where ICTs are making no difference to the lives of people in developing countries or are even having harmful effects. They also found that the diffusion of these technologies is extremely uneven throughout the developing world. There is a very high risk that these technologies and services will deepen the disadvantages of those without the skills and capabilities to make the investments required for building innovative 'knowledge societies'.

The members of the Working Group concluded that although the costs of using ICTs are high, the costs of not doing so are likely to be much higher. They also recognised that developing countries are at very different starting positions in the task of building distinctive 'knowledge societies' to support their development objectives. The Working Group recommended that each developing country should establish a national ICT strategy. This recommendation was accepted by the United Nations Commission on Science and Technology for Development and, subsequently, by the United Nations Economic and Social Council.

This 'source book' synthesises views on the issues and controversies that were debated by members of the Working Group. It offers policy-oriented perspectives on three major sets of issues - constructing and accessing the ICT infrastructure, building capabilities and skills for producing or using ICTs and services, and preparing the framework of strategies, policies, and regulations that will help to ensure that developing countries can move towards innovative 'knowledge societies' that support their development goals.

The report is intended to be a resource for decision-makers and ICT producers and users, primarily in developing countries. The objective has been to gather together information to assist them in their debates and discussions about the social and economic impact of ICTs. It brings together the views of government policy-makers, industrialists, researchers, and other stakeholders in developing and industrialised countries and it draws substantially on the results of research in the field of science and technology policy studies.

The report is intended to be a 'source book'. It is structured to identify current knowledge about issues that are central to whether developing countries will be able to harness ICTs to meet their development needs. Readers will find that each chapter contains an overview of the issues on a particular theme, illustrations drawn from the experiences of both the wealthier and poorest developing countries, and a summary of priorities.

An overview of why it is important for developing countries to design and implement national ICT strategies is presented in Chapter 1. This chapter emphasises the fact that ICTs and 'digital' information must be combined with local human resources and tacit knowledge if they are to be helpful in addressing development problems. Major investments are required in both the social and technological infrastructure and, for the least developed countries, ways must be found to build on a very small base of existing ICT-related skills and competencies.

Chapter 2 introduces empirical evidence on the diffusion of ICTs and accumulation of capabilities for producing or using these technologies by people in developing countries. Existing data are used to develop an INEXSK (INfrastructure, EXperience, Skills, Knowledge) indicators approach which is used to map the strengths and weaknesses of those developing countries for which data are available and to compare the 'footprints' of selected countries. This approach was developed at the Science Policy Research Unit to assess what is known about the emerging 'gaps' in the ICT infrastructure and skills development between developing and industrialised countries. The chapter highlights the fact that available data do not allow us to measure the nature and quality of human 'capital', that is, the skills and capabilities that are essential for knowledge-based development.

Chapter 3 outlines our current knowledge about technological innovation and the learning process. The importance of organisational learning and creative responses to the challenges of managing technological innovation are emphasised. The importance of local knowledge, the understanding of user requirements, and the nature of upstream and downstream value chains are highlighted. The implications of new modes of knowledge generation for the education and science and technology research base in developing countries are also examined. Chapter 4 focuses on the formal and informal institutions where learning takes place. This chapter points to the major changes in education institutions that will be needed to support lifelong learning, as well as to the advantages and disadvantages of new forms of distance education which can be supported by ICT applications. It shows that governments and non-governmental organisations are playing an increasingly important role in empowering citizens by building new capabilities for using ICTs to participate more effectively in civil society. It also emphasises the potential threats associated with content that is unsuited to social and cultural traditions in developing countries and the factors contributing to the exclusion of people who are already disadvantaged.

Chapters 5 and 6 illustrate the potential applications of ICTs for sustainable development. Chapter 5 focuses on the leading developments in the application of ICTs to facilitate the provision of public services, achieve productivity gains, improve the quality of life for citizens, enhance access to information, and facilitate knowledge sharing. Applications in the manufacturing and public administration, transport, health, education, and agriculture sectors are highlighted, together with those aimed at supporting urban and rural development, people with special needs, and environment protection programmes. The growing importance of electronic commerce and the role of ICTs in the tourism and transport sectors are emphasised. The wealthier developing countries are investing in the human and technological infrastructure that is needed to unleash the potential of ICT applications for development. The least developed countries face a high risk of exclusion because they are less well-endowed with the human, physical, and financial resources needed to build capabilities and a widely accessible information infrastructure. Chapter 6 highlights the need for creative approaches to sharing limited ICT resources and the potential benefits of regional cooperation initiatives. It also emphasises the need for alternative models of providing infrastructure access in these countries.

Chapters 7 and 8 review the barriers and opportunities for developing countries in assembling the components of national information infrastructures and ensuring that they are accessible to as many people as possible. Chapter 7 shows that some developing countries have built up a considerable knowledge base for producing certain infrastructure components. Investment in science and technology research, programmes to stimulate ICT hardware and software production, and initiatives to promote electronic commerce and the use of information services are helping to build new capabilities. Telecommunication networks (including access to the Internet) are being upgraded, production capabilities for hardware and software are growing, and the generic skills for knowledge-based development are accumulating. Other countries are very far behind in developing the capabilities to assemble, maintain, and operate the underlying technological infrastructure.

Chapter 8 concentrates on arrangements for accessing local and global networks and 'digital' information sources. The opportunities and pitfalls of market liberalisation in the economies in transition, Latin America, India, China, and the ASEAN region show that policies and regulations are needed to ensure that market-led development does not produce new 'dualisms' or 'access gaps' between the wealthier and poorer people in developing economies. The need to couple market liberalisation, privatisation, and competitive entry policies with investment strategies that are responsive to each country's particular conditions is emphasised. The very great problems facing the least developed countries in attracting investors are highlighted.

Developments in the policies and the 'rules of the game' in the international ICT marketplace provide the focus for Chapters 9 and 10. Chapter 9 looks at the tensions between measures to open developing country markets to globally competing telecommunication companies and those aimed at retaining national control over the development of the telecommunication infrastructure. A large number of international institutions, including the International Telecommunication Union and the World Trade Organization, are setting the rules for trade in telecommunication services. This chapter assesses the risk that the poorest countries will be bypassed as new rules about market access are introduced and tariff barriers are reduced to encourage an expansion of trade in ICTs. Chapter 10 focuses on the role of the international governance system in shaping the global expansion of information services markets. Recent developments in intellectual property rights that aim to protect the economic interests of information service producers are also summarised. Electronic commerce which is leading firms to seek greater network security using measures to protect intellectual property and to secure networks from unwanted intrusions is creating challenges for national governments. This chapter reviews efforts to control criminal or destructive behaviour, to maintain national security, and to protect personal privacy.

Chapter 11 turns to the practical measures that developing countries can take to put national or regional ICT strategies in place. Some countries like Bermuda, with its 'Information Island of the 21st century' vision, and

Singapore, with its 'Intelligent Island' vision, already have national strategies in place. Chapter 11 shows that in some developing countries ICT strategies are proving to be very effective in strengthening human and technological capabilities. However, in other countries, visions are needed and these must be translated into action. This chapter offers practical guidelines for decision-makers who want to promote opportunities for innovative knowledge-based development. There are no simple recipes for success and investment in ICTs is not a panacea for development problems. However, there is evidence that social and economic resources can be mobilised to provide a basis for using ICTs to tackle development problems. The UNCSTD Working Group on IT and Development has suggested guidelines on how this can be achieved and these are summarised in Annex 3 of this report.

In Chapter 12, some of the social and economic outcomes resulting from investment in ICTs by some of the developing countries are reviewed. There is evidence of positive outcomes in terms of job creation, more effective ways of organising production, and enriched communication through ICT-based knowledge networks. However, the results are mixed. While some groups of people in developing countries are being empowered through their use of ICTs, others are being disempowered. There are gender biases in the ways the new technologies and services are being designed and implemented and these often favour men. The global information infrastructure is offering the potential to generate new sources of economic value for people in some of the developing countries. At the same time, new national information infrastructures threaten to erode the capacity of governments to generate public revenues to support development goals.

In Chapter 13, the main messages of the report are summarised. The principal conclusion is that national or regional ICT strategies can be designed and implemented in ways that maximise the potential of existing resources to use ICTs in support of development goals. They can be instrumental in ensuring that technological and social capabilities continue to accumulate. The specific combination of capabilities that is emerging in each country is a central issue for decision-makers. The least developed countries are at risk of being excluded from knowledge-based development. New approaches are needed to ensure that limited financial and other resources play catalytic and enduring roles in linking ICT applications to development needs.

The application of ICTs as 'tools' for development offers opportunities to reduce some existing disparities in income distribution and the quality of life. These tools are being developed and applied in social and economic contexts involving increasingly complex webs of interactions between policy-makers and those engaged in producing and using ICTs. Organisational and technical innovations are contributing to knowledge-based development and improving social, economic, and environmental conditions in developing countries. These interactions are occurring in the immediate presence of others, over the distance between one village and another, and across the globe. They are generating new social and technological capabilities - beneficial ways of learning, governing, conducting business, and occupying leisure time. However, they are also giving rise to new forms of exclusion by virtue of gender, religion, ethnicity, language, or illiteracy.

The material in this 'source book' emphasises that dynamic innovation processes are giving rise to the social and technological capabilities that could release the potential of ICTs for development. A global information infrastructure is taking shape, and ICTs are becoming more and more pervasive. If governments, businesses, and other stakeholders coordinate their actions, they will have a chance to amplify the social and economic benefits of these technologies and to reduce the risk of exclusion.

This 'source book' contains a synthesis of a wealth of information and commentary on the social and economic benefits and risks of ICTs for developing countries. We are extremely grateful to all the people who have contributed their knowledge and experience.

The members of the Editorial Board, the contributing authors, and the large number of other people who provided individual and institutional assistance in connection with this report are acknowledged in Annex 1. The contributing authors are listed in Annex 2.

We are entirely responsible for the views expressed in this report and for any errors or omissions. The report does not necessarily reflect the official views of any organisation or institution.

Professor Robin Mansell
Uta Wehn
Editors
Science Policy Research Unit
University of Sussex

CHAPTER 1

BUILDING INNOVATIVE 'KNOWLEDGE SOCIETIES'

Harnessing ICTs to development goals

1.1 INTRODUCTION - SCIENCE AND TECHNOLOGY POLICY FOR ICTs AND DEVELOPMENT

Recent developments in the fields of communications and information technology are indeed revolutionary in nature. Information and knowledge are expanding in quantity and accessibility. In many fields future decision-makers will be presented with unprecedented new tools for development. In such fields as agriculture, health, education, human resources and environmental mangement, or transport and business development, the consequences really could be revolutionary. Communications and information technology have enormous potential, especially for developing countries, and in furthering sustainable development (Annan 1997: 1).

United Nations Secretary General Kofi Annan emphasises the enormous potential of information and communication technologies (ICTs) for development in these remarks to the first meeting of the United Nations Working Group on Informatics. Is that potential being realised today? Are the benefits of the increasingly widespread, albeit uneven, diffusion and application of these technologies outweighing the risks for developing countries? Are the stakeholders in developing countries taking appropriate measures to minimise the risks of social and economic exclusion that could be associated with these revolutionary technologies?* These questions are central to understanding the social and economic impact of ICTs. The United Nations Commission on Science and Technology for Development's search for answers to these questions led to the establishment of a Working Group to assess the role of scientific and technological innovation as developing countries become more deeply engaged in building innovative 'knowledge societies'.

The United Nations Commission on Science and Technology for Development (UNCSTD) Working Group on IT and Development was set up in 1995. At that time the UNCSTD observed that:

Although the technological revolution in information technology and telecommunications has aroused much interest among policy-makers, the business sector, the media and the academic world in industrialised countries, little is known about the obstacles to accessing information technology and the diffusion and use of information technologies in developing countries, particularly the low-income economies. These issues, especially the impediments to the diffusion of information technology, need to be better understood (UNCSTD 1995: 9).

To develop a better understanding of the social and economic impacts of ICTs on all sectors of the economy, and on the social, cultural, and political lives of the citizens of developing countries, the Working Group was able to draw upon the insights of many experienced people. The United Nations Conference on Trade and Development (UNCTAD 1995a) had completed a special issue of the Advanced Technology Assessment System Report on 'Information Technology for Development' in the Autumn of 1995. The editors stressed that the social and economic characteristics emerging from the transformations associated with ICTs should benefit all people rather than the privileged few.

There is a consensus that the transition to the 21st Century will witness a quantum leap in the development and exploitation of information technologies, with corresponding ramifications for social and economic organisation, the environment, culture and the development of a global information infrastructure. The key issues of concern to policy-makers and international organisations are the extent to which this major transformation has benefited all aspects of society and the ways and means of achieving a truly global information infrastructure (Roffe et al. 1995: viii).

Since the Working Group began its assessment, debate over the potential of science and technology, and especially ICTs, to transform the lives of all the world's citizens has intensified. Positive impacts are being experienced widely in the industrialised countries and certain sectors of many developing countries are realising benefits. The Working Group reviewed more than sixty papers, solicited from experts, on different aspects of the implications of ICTs for development. Its members and consultants surveyed the enormous literature in the field; they talked with many experts, and engaged in debates in their home countries and abroad. They found substantial evidence that the new ICTs are transforming some sectors of some developing countries. Certain firms have dramatically improved their competitiveness by using ICTs and some developing countries are increasing their export strengths in the ICT sector. Some governments in the developing world are providing services to their citizens more efficiently using the new services.

The Working Group also found evidence that the positive impact of these technologies on developing economies and societies is not as deep or as pervasive as the debate about the benefits of the global information society some-

---

* In this report for the sake of brevity, it is not always indicated that statements apply to both developing countries or territories and countries with economies in transition. Where the distinction is important the text makes this clear.

times makes it appear. There are very many people, especially in the least developed countries, whose lives have been barely touched by ICTs. There are others whose lives are being negatively affected by their exclusion from the global information society or by the social or economic dislocations that can accompany the impact of these technologies. The problem is not simply that there is a lag in the diffusion of these technologies or in accessing the new technologies and services. There are substantial problems in ensuring that the capabilities for using these technologies creatively are embedded in new policy measures and firm strategies.

The UNCSTD Working Group reached two principal conclusions:

▌ Although the costs of using ICTs to build national information infrastructures which can contribute to innovative 'knowledge societies' are high, the costs of not doing so are likely to be much higher.

▌ Developing countries are at very different starting positions in the task of building innovative and distinctive 'knowledge societies' and in using their national information infrastructures to support their development objectives.

This source book is the third in a trio of documents representing the work and conclusions of the UNCSTD Working Group on IT and Development during 1995-1997. A first report summarising the Working Group's analysis of the key ICT issues for development and outlining guidelines for building national ICT strategies, contains recommendations for action by governments, other stakeholders, and the United Nations System (UNCSTD 1997a, see Annex 3).

The Working Group based its conclusions on the following observations.

▌ There is sufficient evidence of the potential of ICTs that all governments and other stakeholders need to build new capabilities for producing, accessing, and/or using these technologies. In order to build these capabilities each country should establish and implement a national ICT strategy that is responsive to sustainable development goals.

▌ As developing countries join the global information infrastructure, each country will need to find effective ways of maximising the benefits and controlling the risks from ICTs. This will involve coordinated action through national ICT strategies encompassing the technologies and services as well as many aspects of the institutional environment. Strategies are needed which help to build the necessary scientific, technical, and engineering knowledge as well as the management techniques and social and economic institutions that are consistent with creatively using ICTs to reap the potential social and economic benefits.

▌ Priority needs to be given to policies, regulation, educa-tion and training, and technology assessment programmes to enhance the capacity for creatively producing or using ICTs. The balance between producing and using the new applications will differ from country to country. Distinctions need to be drawn between producing ICTs for domestic consumption, especially where there is a requirement for divergence from standard commodity-type ICTs, and producing the technologies and services for export as a sector of the export economy. The ICT-using sectors in developing countries are highly differentiated and the relative benefits of encouraging use in the public and private sectors also need careful consideration. New coalitions of resources and partnerships among stakeholders, including the business sector, need to be encouraged in line with each country's development priorities.

▌ The roles of government and the public sector are very important in supporting new forms of market facilitation, introducing effective regulation, promoting 'stakeholder dialogues', and providing public services appropriate to local conditions. The creative, dynamic combination of government and private sector action in the context of each country's national or regional innovation system can offer opportunities to benefit from ICTs for all developing countries including the least developed countries.

▌ The coming decades will not see the eradication of the gap between the rich and the poor. However, if governments and other stakeholders design and implement effective national ICT strategies, the new technologies and services may help to reduce the gap for some of those who are disadvantaged or marginalised. Such strategies need to focus on the difficulties of using ICTs to transform data and information into useful knowledge that is consistent with development priorities.

▌ Special treatment will be needed for the least developed countries, and especially for countries in Sub-Saharan Africa and the rural areas of lower income countries, in order to provide the financial resources, physical infrastructure, and the knowledge base that is needed to achieve sustainable development goals.

A second report was prepared by the UNCSTD Working Group on IT and Development outlining several scenarios of the development and impact of ICTs on developing countries (Howkins and Valantin 1997). The scenarios highlight key certainties and uncertainties confronting decision-makers. The scenarios assisted Working Group members in assessing the impact of ICTs on developing countries under conditions where the global economy becomes more integrated and inclusive or, alternatively, more fractured and disintegrated. The scenarios provided a basis for considering whether national governments in developing countries could be expected to respond to the potential of ICTs very actively or relatively passively. The scenarios helped Working Group members to envisage alternative futures for developing countries in a global information society and to consider priority areas for action by all stakeholders. The report invites senior decision-makers to consider the implications of alternative 'knowledge societies' and to take action to devise strategies to ensure that the benefits of ICTs are broadly available and that the risks of social and economic exclusion are avoided or minimised.

This 'source book' is the third report prepared under the guidance of the Working Group. It stresses a theme neglected in the current debate about the benefits of devoting resources to building national information infrastructures in the developing countries. Effective national ICT strategies are most likely to emerge through creatively combining competencies in scientific, technological, and management fields related to ICTs in each country and recombining these strengths with externally available technologies, information, and knowledge resources. Key features of effective national ICT strategies are the capabilities to assess strengths and to target areas for more effectively producing or using ICTs that are responsive to development goals. This is especially important for the least developed countries. These countries will continue to face extremely difficult challenges in building and deploying human and technical resources that will enable them to benefit from ICTs.

The uneven diffusion of ICTs between the industrialised and developing countries, and disparities between and within the developing countries, raise concerns about how gaps in the accessibility and affordability of these new technologies can be reduced. More than a decade has passed since the widely circulated 'Missing Link' report of the Independent Commission for World-wide Telecommunications Development observed that 'neither in the name of common humanity nor on grounds of common interest is such a disparity [in telephony penetration] acceptable' (ITU 1984: 3). Some newly industrialised countries are investing heavily in the telecommunication infrastructure. The penetration of telephone services and advanced ICT-based services and applications is converging with the industrialised countries for these heavy investors. However, in other developing countries, and especially the least developed countries, the most basic telecommunication infrastructure is still absent, unreliable, and/or very costly. The 'missing link' is still missing in the 1990s for much of the world's population.

Since the 'Missing Link' report, innovations in ICTs have stimulated the technical convergence of telecommunication and computing hardware and software. The potential applications of ICTs also have blossomed in variety and in complexity. It has been realised that ensuring fair terms and conditions of access to national and global information infrastructures is only one, albeit important, part of the challenge of building innovative 'knowledge societies'. Knowledge principally resides in people rather than in ICTs, databases or services. Alliances and partnerships among stakeholders in developing countries and with organisations in the industrialised countries today need to address 'gaps' in a broad spectrum of ICTs and applications. They also need to recognise the importance of building social and technological capabilities among users.

Today's discussions of 'knowledge societies' emphasise the need to harness ICTs for development by enabling their use for empowering the poor and for scientific and technical capacity building that is consistent with development goals. The new technologies can be implemented to support democratic decision-making, more effective governance, and lifelong learning. The benefits are closely associated with establishing equitable policy and regulatory frameworks and with ensuring that understanding, sharing, and partnership-building are central components of national ICT strategies.

The World Bank argues that 'knowledge for development' is crucial for the future prospects for developing countries and that the capacities of these countries to apply the growing stock of global 'electronic' knowledge will be increasingly important. This UNCSTD report illustrates why this will present a major challenge for many developing countries. It stresses that by recombining local and external knowledge there are opportunities for developing countries, including the least developed countries, to benefit from ICTs.

The remaining sections of this chapter locate concerns about the ICT 'gap' in the wider context of the development process (section 1.2) and in the challenge of building social capabilities through individual and organisational learning within innovation systems (section 1.3). Section 1.4 introduces the main components of ICTs emphasising their role in the 'informatisation' process which is both a social and a technological process. Finally, section 1.5 considers the benefits and risks for developing countries as ICTs become increasingly important tools for building innovative 'knowledge societies'.

1.2 HARNESSING ICTs FOR DEVELOPMENT

Development has been understood since the second World War to involve economic growth, increases in per capita income, and attainment of a standard of living equivalent to that of the industrialised countries. This was to be achieved without incurring major social costs. This conception of development has been questioned because it gives too little consideration to the non-material aspirations of people in developing countries (Bezanson and Sagasti 1995).[1] There is no 'holy grail' offering a clear definition of the meaning of development, and each country must reach its own consensus on the changing meaning of development. It is much more widely recognised today that the social setting and people's capabilities are crucial

Box 1.1 – Building new social capabilities for ICTs and development

In their paper on the future of the ISDN Bandwagon for the OECD Tokyo/Osaka Workshop on information technology and new growth opportunities, Paul David and Edward Steinmueller (1988) pointed to the 'uneven and unintegrated development' of data communications and commented that this was often the case with technological change. It was indeed Schumpeter who first stressed this extremely uneven nature of technical change both with respect to timing and to location. He likened it to a series of unpredictable explosions.

Nowhere is this feature of technical change more apparent than in relation to the developing countries and ICTs. In the 1950s it was commonplace to regard the economic problems of Asia as almost insoluble. Outstanding economists such as Gunnar Myrdal were especially pessimistic about India. No less pessimistic about computer applications was none other than Thomas J. Watson, Senior, who as head of IBM still thought in the late 1940s that even in the United States, computers would find few applications in business and would be confined to a few machines in big science and government.

During the 1960s the Latin American countries were still regarded as 'miracle economies' because of their high rates of growth at that time. Even as late as 1965 Brazil still had more telephone lines per 100 inhabitants than either the Republic of Korea or Taiwan (Pr. China). Now these countries and territories have four or five times as many as Brazil and in every other area of ICT and its applications, the East Asian 'Tigers' have far outstripped Brazil and all other Latin American countries. Both Africa and Latin America had on average negative per capita income growth in the 'lost decade' of the 1980s while not only the countries of East Asia but increasingly those of Southern Asia too, enjoyed very high rates of growth.

In its report on the 'East Asian Miracle' in 1993 the World Bank (1993) attributed their astonishing success mainly to liberalisation, export orientation, high levels of investment and education.[2] However, it failed to mention that by the 1990s more than a quarter of all exports from the Republic of Korea, Taiwan (Pr. China), and Singapore were classified by GATT as 'ICT equipment' that is, telecommunication equipment, computers, office machinery, electronic goods and components. Since this category of equipment has a growth rate twice as high as commodity trade in general, it is clear that countries with an export structure of this kind are likely to perform fairly well in international trade. Again, although surely right in its emphasis on education, the World Bank also failed to address other forms of intangible investment such as research and development (R&D) and many other related scientific and technical services. It is in these areas that the achievements of the 'Tigers' have been particularly impressive, again far outstripping any comparable increase in Latin America or Africa, and again with a very heavy concentration on ICT industries and services.

In his seminal analysis of 'catching up, forging ahead and falling behind' in economic growth and development, Abramovitz (1986) emphasised above all the role of 'social capability' in catching up by less developed countries. Whilst no-one could or should make claims about any unique wisdom or forecasting capability residing in East Asia, it is evident that by a combination of good fortune and good judgement and by the lucky accident of proximity to Japan, the countries of East Asia have developed better than most a 'social capability' in dealing with information technology. It is this capability in relation to the most pervasive and dominant technology of the late 20th century that is above all responsible for the East Asian 'miracle'.[3]

However, this is a race in which all can have prizes. The applications of ICT are far more important than the production of super-computers, telephone switches, integrated circuits, or other equipment. It is of course an advantage to be able to design and produce some items of electronic equipment for local use and for the world market as the Tigers have learnt to do, but it is not essential. In the comparable technical revolution in the late 19th century in electric power, only a few countries had the capability to produce generators, transformers, and other expensive items of electrical equipment but far more countries learnt to use electricity in other industries and services in which they had some advantages. The same is likely to be true for many other countries catching up in world technology today. The one thing, however, that will be indispensable is the social capability to generate and promote intangible investment on the necessary scale, as well as, and complementary with, the tangible investment in infrastructure. Infrastructural development in telecommunications, as in the past in electric power, will be essential for effective participation in the world economy and above all for catch-up in economic growth. So too, will be intangible investment in education, research, development, and related scientific and technical services.

to the development process; knowledge and human capital are essential to all aspects of development.

...the capacity to acquire and generate knowledge in all its forms, including the recovery and upgrading of traditional knowledge, is perhaps the most important factor in the improvement of the human condition (Bezanson and Sagasti 1995: 5-6).

In this report development and scientific and technological progress are taken to mean the processes that lead to an 'evolution of shared perceptions of what humanity is and should be, and of devising the means of advancing, both individually and collectively, towards putting those values in practice' (Bezanson and Sagasti 1995: 9).

ICTs have an enormously important role to play in build-ing the social capability to generate information and to apply knowledge for sustainable development (see Box 1.1). 'Social capability' was the term used in the early 1970s by Kazushi Ohkawa and Henry Rosovsky to refer to the 'levels of general education and technical competence; the commercial, industrial and financial institutions that bear on their abilities to finance and operate modern, large-scale business; and the political and social character-istics that influence the risks, the incentives and the perso-nal rewards of economic activity, including those rewards in social esteem that go beyond money and wealth'.[4] Social capabilities complement technological capabilities and they combine in many different ways to generate economic growth.

The emergence of new capabilities is closely linked to the progress of scientific and technical innovation. Scientific discoveries and technological innovations in ICTs are moving at a pace and with impacts that are unprecedented. Those with access to these innovations - and those who have the capacity to absorb them and use them - will have opportunities to reap social and economic advantages. Those without access and the appropriate capabilities risk being marginalised in the 'knowledge societies' of the future.

Intense debates in recent years about the impact of ICTs emphasise capabilities for producing or acquiring hard-ware (telecommunication networks, personal computers, fax machines, etc.) over those for producing software and information content. In addition, the capabilities needed to turn information into useful knowledge are often neglected. Answers to questions such as whether there will be users for these ICT components depend as much upon economic conditions as upon the variety of social and cultural, systems (Collet et al. 1996). These social, cultural, and technological factors combine in building new user capabilities in very different ways. There is a growing need to understand how these interactions are affecting the characteristics of the 'knowledge societies' emerging in countries around the world.

The task for policy-makers, the business community, and representatives of civil society is to create conditions for building the knowledge base in a way that maximises the benefits of ICTs and reduces the risks. There is a risk that ICTs will contribute to a new 'global apartheid' because they are designed or applied in ways that are inconsistent with development goals (Bezanson and Sagasti 1995). The gap between the rich and the poor in terms of access to basic telephone service is being reduced, especially in the newly industrialising countries, but this experience is very unevenly distributed across the developing world (Saunders et al. 1994). However, if visionaries like Peter Drucker are correct, even if the telecommunication connections are in place to support global knowledge networks, developing countries will not be able to rely

upon lower cost labour for their comparative advantage. They will need to excel in the application of knowledge.

Developing countries can no longer expect to base their develop-ment on their comparative labor advantage - that is, on cheap industrial labor. The comparative advantage that now counts is the application of knowledge (Drucker 1994: 62, 64).

The generation and application of knowledge depends upon much more than access to a global information infra-structure. If developing countries are to experience 'empowerment through knowledge' they will need to build new partnerships and focus on capacity building.[5] They will need to focus on institutional and organisational change in the context of their development goals. New partnerships and networks are being formed around the world linking firms of all sizes into joint marketing, production and R&D. These networks of public and private sector partners are relying increasingly upon the use of ICTs (Mytelka 1995). However, little is known about the factors contributing to the success or failure of these partnerships.

The emergence of new partnerships between donor and recipient countries involves pragmatic approaches to the shared interests between firms and governments in indus-trialised and developing countries. Targeting poverty, social development, and sustainable development also means identifying and deepening capabilities for produc-ing and using information and communication services, promoting access to these services, sharing and exchan-ging information, and encouraging proactive local and national strategies for development. New forms of public and private partnerships, including concessions and sub-contracting arrangements, are characteristic of the 'new' approach to development (Dohlman and Halvorson-Quevedo 1997; Michel 1997).

The problem of achieving an appropriate, and changing, balance between producing and using ICTs is confronting developing countries and it is an especially difficult chal-lenge for the least developed countries. This is because opportunities for using ICTs creatively require technical and human capabilities that are built up through experi-ence with the new technologies and services. This does not mean that all countries must begin producing ICTs, but all countries need capabilities for maintaining ICTs and for tailoring them to their specific needs. The charac-teristics of the scientific and technical innovation systems in each country and region are central to encouraging the range of capabilities for effectively using ICTs.

1.3 ICTs, LEARNING, AND INNOVATION SYSTEMS

National scientific and technical innovation systems are the foundation for selecting areas of ICT production or use in which to concentrate scarce economic and know-ledge resources.[6] The concept of a national innovation system refers to the processes of technological and institu-

tional capability building and policy-making that enable effective choices to be made and implemented. The concept is closely associated with the notion of *social capability building* in the sense that it encompasses the social, political, and economic features of the institutional context in which learning takes place. Learning processes are important features of the innovation process. For example, as Bengt-Åke Lundvall, puts it,

... the most fundamental resource in the modern economy is knowledge and, accordingly, ... the most important process (of economic development) is learning. ... learning is predominantly an interactive and, therefore, a socially embodied process which cannot be understood without taking into consideration its institutional and cultural context (Lundvall 1992a: 1).

The national innovation system is the environment in which economic performance is shaped by learning processes. It is the system whereby knowledge is accumulated and distributed among each country's institutions (Gu and Steinmueller 1998 forthcoming). ICTs are important contributors to these processes because they provide improved access to information. They also offer opportunities for innovation when they are embedded in manufacturing and resource extraction processes as well as in services. 'Learning' takes place during routine activities associated with producing, distributing, and consuming ICTs and services. For example,

... the everyday experiences of workers, production engineers, and sales representatives influence the agenda determining the direction of innovative efforts, and they produce knowledge and insights forming crucial inputs to the process of innovation (Lundvall 1992a: 9).

Learning is not something that only people in firms do. Learning is also important for public and private sector organisations and institutions. Learning is as important for effective policy-making as it is for the competitiveness of firms or the effectiveness of local community groups. It is both a formal and an informal process and the outcomes of policy-making and the management of ICT innovations are 'designed and articulated not just in the formal "corridors of power" but in the everyday interventions and experiences of information and communication technology producers and users' (Silverstone and Mansell 1996: 225). Governments can contribute to learning processes by guiding or controlling the rate and direction of technical and economic change by identifying and filling important gaps in the institutional frameworks in which learning occurs. However, as in other sectors of the economy, the issue of where and how to intervene to strengthen ICT related capabilities is neither obvious nor straightforward. Governments can impede rather than promote more effective learning processes.

Choosing an effective national ICT strategy is difficult for developing countries because a key feature of the social and economic transition towards 'knowledge societies' is the opening of domestic economies to international trade. International trade brings major changes to the domestic economic environment including the creation of new incentives and competitive challenges. These changes are very important for the ICT industry, but the implications for developing countries as both producers and users of ICTs are very uncertain.

For some analysts, the global division of labour is largely asymmetrical, forcing developing countries to compete with one another in offering low wage assembly while denying them access to the design and process know-how (Ernst and O'Connor 1989, 1992). This means that the 'export led growth' strategy in the ICT industry, that contributed to the success of the Republic of Korea and some of the South East Asian economies, is unlikely to be reproducible in other countries, such as Thailand, Malaysia, Indonesia, or the Philippines. Adopting this strategy in the 1990s is constrained by the quality requirements of end-product markets in the industrial countries and by barriers to gaining access to key technologies.

Changes in international trade policy affecting ICT products and services and increasing vertical integration and horizontal networking are strengthening the market power of leading ICT companies. For example,

... market leaders have been forced to introduce a variety of entry deterrence strategies which aim to restrict the rate of technology diffusion ... major firms have become increasingly reluctant to license core technology to potential competitors and have aggressively sued those alleged to have violated their intellectual property rights ... entry possibilities for latecomers have become much more restricted for most sectors of the electronics industry (Ernst and O'Connor 1992: 263, 265).

Other observers reach different conclusions. For example, it has been argued that a rapid rate of international technology diffusion provides opportunities for newly industrialising countries to achieve 'world class' production of some ICT-related products and knowledge based services (Soete 1985). The prospects for the least developed countries are much less certain. The convergence in technological capabilities among industrialised countries makes them competitors in the sale of capital goods and knowledge to the newly industrialising countries, rather than controllers of an oligopolistic marketplace. Companies in the industrialised countries may seek restrictive arrangements such as those which favour the current owners of rights to intellectual property. However, this may be ineffective if technological change makes such protection difficult or costly, or if rival firms do not cooperate in restricting the market. As a result, competition among firms based in the industrialised countries may accelerate the transfer of ICT innovations to the newly industrialising countries. 'Leapfrogging' may still be a viable strategy for those developing countries where the absence of a scientific and technical education system consistent with innovations in ICTs is not a major bottleneck.

When this debate appeared in the literature in the mid-1980s there was little empirical evidence on which to base conclusions about either of these perspectives. By 1996 the World Bank gave a qualified 'yes' in answer to the question - 'Is the East Asian experience replicable?' (Hanna et al. 1996: 211) - based on its review of the experience of the East Asian countries and territories (Japan, Taiwan (Pr. China), Hong Kong, the Republic of Korea, and Singapore). But this report also emphasises that benefiting from ICTs requires 'intangible process re-engineering, managerial quality and leadership, flexible and multi-skilled labor, and institutional learning and experimentation' (Hanna et al. 1996: 190). Similarly, Christopher Freeman argues that 'the one thing, however, that will be indispensable is the *social capability* to generate and promote intangible investment on the necessary scale, as well as, and complementary with, the tangible investment in infrastructure' (see Box 1.1).

The prospects for entry into ICT production markets are unlikely to be available to all developing countries. Entry into the electronics industry for export, the strategy followed by the newly industrialising countries, may no longer be viable because automation has reduced the share of labour total cost, and competitiveness depends increasingly on quality and delivery time. Therefore,

... for many developing countries, local IT production may continue to be out of reach for some time to come ... For them the priority should be on using IT to revitalise and transform traditional, less technologically demanding industries, and to modernise their basic infrastructures and services (Hanna et al. 1996: 214).

One of the key insights of the experience of the past decade is that even if global markets are characterised by oligopolistic competition and the transfer of technological knowledge is limited, the negative impacts can be altered by active measures to stimulate learning and institutional change that lead to new ICT-using capabilities. This demands the innovative recombination of technological and social capabilities by ensuring that national (or regional) systems of innovation target and encourage effective use of ICTs and services.[7] If a process of 'innovative recombination' can be established, the resulting institutional restructuring is likely to release capabilities that can be recombined and improved to take advantage of domestic and international market opportunities. Recombining capabilities within a national system of innovation involves (Gu and Steinmueller 1998 forthcoming):

▮ The reallocation of previously accumulated capabilities in production, design, R&D, and testing in original and productive ways;

▮ The stimulation of market reform and trade liberalisation as a means of reallocating innovative capabilities and providing incentives to innovate;

▮ Identification of major gaps in the capabilities inherited

from previous systems and filling them as rapidly as possible;

▮ Institutional restructuring in many areas of the private and public sectors to support these initiatives and to ensure that policies and strategies are linked to broader development goals.

An important issue for developing countries is the strengthening of domestic demand. Although the diffusion of ICT hardware and software within the domestic economy is important, this also involves the innovation system as a whole including the public and private institutions and individuals who play a role in the innovation process. Because each country's resources, capabilities, and development priorities differ, national ICT strategies need to be tailored to specific technological strengths and social and economic development priorities. The ICT sectors and related capabilities of the national economies of the 1990s are very difficult to map or to measure. This presents a problem in assessing the relative strengths and weaknesses of developing countries. This is partly a reflection of rapid technological change in the ICT sector and partly of problems inherent in valuing information or knowledge assets.

1.4 Mapping and measuring ICTs for 'knowledge societies'

For three decades or more, people have been discussing the major transformations that are possible through harnessing electronic information processing technologies to the social and economic priorities of industrialised societies. These technologies are vitally important components of the new 'information economies' or 'information societies' (Machlup 1962; Porat 1984). More recently the term 'knowledge society' has been used to shift the emphasis from ICTs as 'drivers' of change to a perspective where these technologies are regarded as tools which may provide a new potential for combining the information embedded in ICT systems with the creative potential and knowledge embodied in people. ICTs are best considered as tools or facilitators which may substitute under certain conditions for other means of knowledge creation in innovative societies (OECD 1996a).[8] These technologies do not create the transformations in society by themselves; they are designed and implemented by people in their social, economic, and technological contexts.

Some observers mark the beginning of the ICT revolution by the production in 1969 of 'a computer on a chip' and the declining cost of semiconductor technologies and microelectronics. From this point onwards 'intelligence' has been built into products and this has been accompanied by the rise of more knowledge-intensive societies and global competition.

Although the information technology revolution represents a technological rupture that has produced significant qualitative changes in what is being produced, where, how and by whom, these changes build upon a cumulative and incremental process that had already begun to transform our system of production and the relationship between firms and states in the international economy (Mytelka 1995: 7–8).

The technologies, organisations, and capabilities that facilitate production and use of ICTs are called the national information infrastructure (NII) or the global information infrastructure (GII). Before the arrival of microelectronics and digital technologies, the technological components of ICTs generally were accounted for statistically as separate industries - computer hardware and software, microelectronics, telecommunications, broadcasting, etc. Today, convergence, which is sometimes very real and at other times only forecast, characterises all aspects of ICTs at least at the technical level.[9]

The technological convergence which is occurring throughout the ICT sector means that there are very few clear boundaries between these sectors on the supply side of the industry. ICTs are being used, and often produced or modified in the case of software, in virtually every segment of the manufacturing, services, and natural resources industries. This is the main reason for their pervasive and potentially revolutionary impact. ICTs are being used as control technologies leading to innovations in products and processes in the manufacturing sectors and resource extraction industries. They are playing an increasing role in computational activities supporting scientific and technological research and in the networks of communication research and development and business activity around the world. They are also being used by individual citizens to build new local and global communities as witnessed by the explosion of Internet applications and the connection of more than 16 million host computers and more than 50 million users over the past two or three years (ITU 1997).

To represent the components of ICTs and services it is helpful to use a map. To be useful a map should aid thinking about the potential for synergy and dynamic change among the components of ICTs. This is one of the features that gives the sector its very distinctive and challenging characteristics.

Another distinctive feature is that ICTs are centrally about 'informatisation' - the progressive application of ICTs to the input, storage, processing, distribution, and presentation of information. This term was used as early as the 1960s by the Japanese and it refers to a social as well as to a technological process. It requires changes in management processes, organisation, and skills as well as in the tools used in the production of goods and services. This idea links technical, organisational, managerial, and institutional aspects of ICTs. All these aspects must be considered if the social and economic implications of ICTs are to be understood. An 'informatisation' approach is consistent with an emphasis on the importance of technological

knowledge and social capabilities as well as on the hardware and software itself. The scientific, technological, and engineering disciplines and the management techniques used in information handling and processing are as important as the applications, hardware, and software, and their interaction with people and machines in social, economic, and cultural relationships.

Figure 1.1 shows the segments of the ICT sector organised around carriage-content and products-services axes. The sizes of the segments do not reflect the economic dimensions or relative importance of segments of the industry. The 'informatisation' process involves a mix of processes including input, storage, processing, distribution, and presentation of information. The axes in Figure 1.1 identify the dominant features of each of the segments.

▌ With respect to the horizontal axis, the business activities of the two segments at the right of the diagram, digitised content and broadcasting, are dominated by the costs of producing content, the 'input' of information. The costs of processing dominate four industries: computer equipment, software, enhanced voice and data services, and networking services. The added value of these segments is that they provide the tools for transforming or 'processing' information. At the left of the diagram, the emphasis is on providing products (broadcasting and network equipment) and services (basic network services) for the carriage of information.

▌ In the case of the vertical axis, above the horizontal axis are services and below are products. The software industry includes both products and services. 'Packaged software' and other means of selling software as a bundle closely conform to a 'product'. The adaptation of packaged software for particular applications more closely resembles a 'service'. These characteristics are changing as components of software packages are 'unbundled' and distributed through means such as data networks.

In addition to the eight segments shown in the circle in Figure 1.1, there are electronic components, consumer electronics, electronic measuring and scientific instruments, and professional services. Electronic components underlie two of the segments: computer equipment, and networking and broadcasting equipment. Most of the consumer electronics equipment is closely related to the distribution and presentation of information and is located adjacent to the broadcasting and networking segments. Computer equipment and electronic measuring and scientific instruments are closely related and professional services are available to all of the industry segments.

The recombination of all these components is giving meaning to the NII and GII concepts. The *time dimension* is important in terms of assessing the implications of further technological innovations for all the segments of the ICT industry. In addition, the process of 'informatisation' is resulting in changes in industry boundaries and

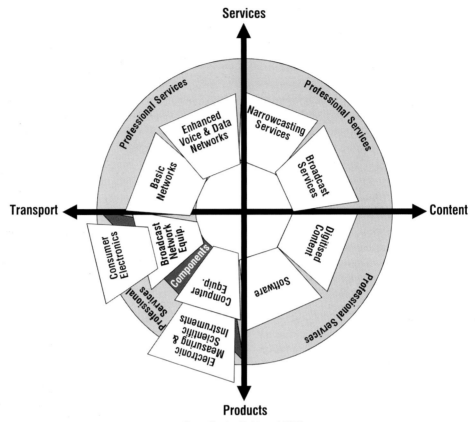

Source: Based on Hawkins et al. (1997).

providing opportunities for new entry by firms from within, and outside, the traditional ICT industry. This is creating turbulence in the competitive environment. Market instability has major implications for developing countries as uncertainty increases about which countries can develop the capabilities to produce the components of different segments of the industry.

The users of the components of the ICT segments shown in Figure 1.1 are as diverse as the suppliers. Increasing ICT product and service variety is characteristic of the applications for end-users as citizens who may be empowered to improve the quality of their lives (Bessette 1996). It is also characteristic of the range of applications where ICT components are embedded in services or manufactured products to support electronic commerce, new business information systems, or new product or process innovations to be employed by intermediate users. The array of ICTs around which the global inform-ation society is being built is enormous and it is constantly changing.

The principal concern of this report is with the social and technological capabilities, policy measures, and corporate strategies needed to acquire and use ICTs effectively to respond to development priorities.

Attempts to measure the impact of ICTs on the economies of industrialised and developing countries encounter severe problems of statistical classification and data avail-ability. The classification systems in use today do not capture the growing importance of services and inform-ation in the economy or changes at the boundaries of segments of the ICT industry. The lack of appropriate indicators of impact, combined with the absence of the financial resources in some developing countries to collect the relevant data, make it very difficult to measure 'impact' as such. However, the importance of improving measures of the impact of ICTs cannot be underestimated. The results of studies, for example, on the impact of tele-communication investment on productivity growth, have been influential in persuading some decision-makers of the economic importance of extending telecommunica-tion networks within developing countries (Cronin et al. 1993).

Demonstrating the returns on investment in ICTs more generally, including information technologies and systems, has proved to be at least as difficult and controver-sial (Berndt and Malone 1995). The diffusion of ICTs places heavy demands on all other aspects of the social and economic infrastructure and on existing organisational capabilities. Most of the research aimed at explaining the so-called 'productivity paradox' has needed to develop new tools and techniques for capturing and measuring the productivity impact of ICTs. For example, existing measures of service output are inadequate for tracing the impact of ICT diffusion on production.

One reason for the difficulty of productivity measurement is that ICTs are used to produce an intermediate good or product; information. The value of information in use varies dramatically depending upon the context. This context is likely to be dependent upon the level and nature of the development problem for which ICT are being employed. As Menou suggests, although it is logical to assume that information is an essential resource for developing economies, it is very difficult to demonstrate this empirically.

Although we have witnessed a steady growth in the provision of information services in developing countries, a number of fundamental questions remain unanswered. The people of these countries question the relevance and appropriateness of the services offered. Development assistance agencies are concerned about problems of sustainability. The extent to which information [and communication] services actually contribute to the empowerment of people and the accountability of the institutions concerned are subjects of controversy and debate. Logic dictates that information is an essential resource for the social and economic development of Third World countries, but how can this be demonstrated? How tangible is the linkage between information investments and the achievement of specific development goals? The limited status accorded to information in most developing countries suggests that its potential value is not self-evident (Menou 1993: ix).

There is a growing literature on performance indicators that seeks to assess the impact of ICTs from the perspective of specific user communities rather than attempting to quantify the overall impact of investment in ICTs on the economy.[10] This work is concerned with the specification of development issues, emerging patterns of operating and developing ICT or information service applications, and assembling base line data. The primary goals are to relate initial objectives of users to observed outcomes and to identify the important economic, social, cultural, and organisational factors that influence these outcomes. This work also suffers from a lack of consensus on the definition of 'information' and how it should be used in socio-economic impact studies. These studies are so costly to implement that there is considerable controversy over the interpretation of their results and the implications for decision-makers (Griffiths 1996). An additional factor which makes it difficult to assess the impact of investments in ICTs is the trend toward the liberalisation of markets. As competition increases in domestic markets, empirical evidence on the diffusion and use of ICTs tends to become more limited to protect commercial interests.

1.5 Conclusion - Maximising benefits and minimising risks

Wealth generation is becoming more closely tied to the capacity to add value using ICT products and services. The value of information and accumulated knowledge within developing countries is an important aspect of future growth potential. Only a very few developing countries have succeeded in narrowing the development 'gap' by harnessing the production or use of ICTs to their development goals. These technologies do not offer a magical potion that can be expected to provide a cure for the sick, to prevent environmental degradation, or to create jobs. However, if these technologies can be combined with domestic and external human resources, they can be instrumental in achieving major changes in the organisation of industrial activity and the conduct of everyday life in developing countries. If the changes are consistent with development goals, countries can gain advantages from ICTs and avoid the risks of exclusion and marginalisation. However, this requires national (or regional) ICT strategies that build upon the strengths of each country. Mapping and measuring the economic and social impact of ICTs, and the strengths and weaknesses of technological and social capabilities in developing countries will become an important tool for generating the information needed for informed policy choices.

The late 1990s and the first few years of the 21st century are likely to see major changes in the production and consumption of ICTs and related services in global markets. Until recently it has been mainly the industrialised and newly industrialising countries that have been actively involved in producing ICTs and in devising innovative applications. However, the rapid diffusion of ICTs in these countries is contributing to strengthened interest in the potential of markets in many of the wealthier developing country markets. The interest of major ICT suppliers in these markets is encouraging market liberalisation and an increase in international trade in ICT goods and services.

The completion of the multilateral trade negotiations on telecommunication equipment and enhanced telecommunication services at the end of the Uruguay Round of the General Agreement on Tariffs and Trade in 1995 represented a major step toward market liberalisation in the telecommunication sector. This was followed in February 1997 by further market liberalisation measures for basic telecommunication services. With forecasts of a trillion dollar telecommunication market, in the short term, the principal beneficiaries of the Geneva agreement will be the big carriers with a well developed international presence (Cane 1997a), and the new trade regime is likely to bring major changes in the pace of infrastructure construction in the wealthier developing countries (and selected areas of the poorer countries).

For example, as a result of these negotiations several Latin American countries are committed to wide-ranging market liberalisation. These countries are expecting to see the benefits of liberalisation in the wider accessibility of telecommunication and information services. Some Eastern European countries have offered to liberalise their national markets after the year 2000 and the Asian countries and territories, including Singapore, the Philippines, and Hong Kong, are planning to permit new entry and foreign investment in their domestic telecommunication markets. Other developing countries, such as Malaysia and India, already allow greater foreign investment than they were asked to guarantee in the recent round of trade negotiations. These market liberalisation measures are expected to boost foreign investment in the telecommunication infrastructure in developing countries but the capital requirements needed to achieve substantially improved access to domestic and international networks are enormous. The World Bank has estimated that about US$ 60 billion per year is needed (Williams 1997a). The liberalisation of these markets is being accompanied by the full or partial privatisation of national telecommunication operators (Ambrose et al. 1990). By 1995 some 44 public telecommunication operators world-wide had been privatised raising an estimated US$ 159 billion through domestic and international share offerings (ITU 1995a).[11]

In addition to the pressures to restructure and open the telecommunication markets in developing countries, tariff barriers restricting international trade in information technologies have become the subject of trade negotiations. In March 1997 an Information Technology Agreement covering 90 per cent of world IT markets was reached leading to tariff reductions on the import of computers, telecommunication products, semiconductors, software, and scientific instruments (Williams 1997b; WTO 1997a). Participating countries included Costa Rica, Estonia, India, Indonesia, Korea (Republic of), Macau, Malaysia, Romania, Singapore, and Thailand.

The developing countries who participated in these rounds of trade negotiation aimed at liberalising domestic markets have different profiles in terms of their strengths in producing and using ICTs and services. The negotiations are predominantly producer-oriented but they have major implications for the capabilities for using ICTs in participating countries as well as for countries that have yet to sign the new agreements and protocols. The impact on developing countries of these and other changes in the international governance regime, that is, changes in the scope and enforcement of intellectual property protection, are extremely difficult to predict. It is relatively certain, however, that they will lead to new market structures for ICTs on a global basis. Some developing countries will fare better than others in adjusting to the changes in the global economy. Developing countries will need to match their strengths to new opportunities and counter the negative impacts of changes in the global market. They will need to build new capabilities to use ICTs to complement other important aspects of the knowledge generation process.

The next chapter assesses the empirical evidence on the current and likely future participation of developing countries in the global information society. The analysis is limited by the absence of appropriate indicators for the production of ICTs (hardware, software, and services) and by the problems of capturing the social and economic value of electronic information and communication. The chapter emphasises several important points. First, the rate of diffusion of ICTs favours the industrialised, newly industrialising, and other wealthier developing countries. Second, the production of ICTs is highly concentrated in the industrialised countries and a small number of newly industrialising countries. Finally, the consumption of ICTs is heavily concentrated in the industrialised and wealthier developing countries.

Subsequent chapters in this report take the existence of a 'gap' in the rate of diffusion of ICTs and services as a feature of most developing countries, and especially the least developed countries, over the coming decade. However, the impact of this differential rate of diffusion should be expected to vary substantially depending upon the steps taken by stakeholders within these countries to improve the outcomes for citizens and businesses that may be threatened by new forms of social or economic exclusion.

NOTES

1   For a review of the debate in the communication sector on the definition of development, see Dordick and Wang (1993).

2   See also Hanna et al. (1996).

3   See, for example, Freeman (1987).

4   See Ohkawa, K. and Rosovsky, H. (1972) Japanese Economic Growth, Stanford CA: Stanford University Press, as discussed by David (1995: 25).

5   'Empowerment through Knowledge' was adopted as a corporate strategy by the International Development Research Centre, Canada, in 1993, see Valantin (1995).

6   National innovation systems have been discussed by Abramovitz (1986); Freeman (1987); Lundvall (1992b); and Nelson (1993).

7   The concept of 'innovative recombination of technological capabilities' is developed by Gu and Steinmueller (1998 forthcoming).

8   For a review of these discussions since the 1960s, see Hawkins et al. (1997); Nass (1987). In the early years, the focus was on the growing importance of services in the industrialised countries although some studies were undertaken on developing countries, see for example Jussawalla et al. (1988).

9   Convergence at the industry level has been forecast for many years, see for example Kelly (1989). Recent empirical studies in the European Union suggest that, although there has been evidence of horizontal integration across industry boundaries in the 1980s, there may now be a trend towards vertical re-integration among some of the largest players. Components of the segments of the ICT sector are being managed separately as lines of business even where they are present under the same corporate umbrella, see for example Micas (1997).

10 See for example Ang and Pavri (1994); Boon (1992); Stone and Menou (1994); Chataway and Cooke (1996).

11 These countries included Barbados, Belize, Bolivia, Cape Verde, Chile, Cuba, Estonia, Ghana, Guinea, Guinea-Bissau, Guyana, Jamaica, Latvia, Mongolia, Pakistan, Sao Tome and Principe, Argentina, the Czech Republic, Indonesia, Malaysia, the Republic of Korea, Peru, Singapore, Venezuela, and Mexico. Democratic Republic of the Congo, Ivory Coast, Ecuador, Nicaragua, Panama, Senegal, South Africa, Sri Lanka, and Zambia were expected to make offers for market liberalisation in the near future.

CHAPTER 2

INDICATORS OF DEVELOPING COUNTRY PARTICIPATION IN 'KNOWLEDGE SOCIETIES'

What the indicators tell us about the spread of ICTs and capabilities for their use

2. INDICATORS OF DEVELOPING COUNTRY PARTICIPATION IN 'KNOWLEDGE SOCIETIES'

2.1 INTRODUCTION - NEW MARKET OPPORTUNITIES

Markets have always been shaped by informational imbalances: traders who scanned 17th century port registers for signs of overdue ships are pretty much the same as arbitrageurs betting on coffee futures based on rainfall reports from Brazil. But in an advanced industrial - call it interconnected - world, much of that information advantage or disadvantage disappears. 'Information is transparent today', says Jon Corzine, CEO of the investment firm Goldman Sachs 'No-one really generates a long term competitive edge just because they know something that someone else doesn't. Anyone with a Reuters terminal and a phone is prowling the same level (and much less profitable) playing field as Goldman's highly trained, high octane traders ... So the ever-hungry marketeers are creeping out into less well-known but potentially more lucrative territory: the developing country world (Branegan et al. 1997: 34).

The world information technology market (including computers, software, peripheral equipment, and the customer interface) was estimated at US$ 514 billion in 1995. The market is highly concentrated in the G7 countries which account for about 88 per cent of the market (OECD 1996b). Although growth is widespread, it is uneven. For the economies in transition, middle eastern and African countries, the speed of global developments has been so rapid that even their 10.6 per cent annual growth rate was insufficient to prevent a decline in their share from 3.1 to 2.6 per cent in the past decade (see Table 2.1).

As the spokesman for Goldman Sachs, quoted above, makes clear, the major economic players in the world are pushing to extend their markets into the developing countries. Developing countries are often proving to be partners eager to extend the market by becoming suppliers and investors in ICTs. In becoming suppliers, countries are motivated by the possibility of following the dramatic export-led growth example of the newly industrialised Asian economies. As investors, developing countries are improving their capabilities to use ICTs to provide the infrastructure for modern global business. It is believed that such investments will assist domestic companies to integrate with the global economy and enhance the prospects for foreign direct investment.

These efforts are contributing to rapid growth. Even rapid growth, however, may not lead to convergence in the availability of ICTs for vast segments of the world's people, and particularly those in the poorest countries. The last decade's experience in the transition economies, the Middle East, and Africa illustrates that, for people in much of the developing world, these technologies may continue to be exotic and inaccessible well into the next century.

This chapter examines the usefulness and limitations of the available indicators of developing country participation in the creation of 'knowledge societies'. Among the many limitations of these indicators are their shortcomings in reflecting the human dimension of knowledge society developments. While it is comparatively easy to inventory physical capital and sales of tangible products, it is much more difficult to assess the nature and quality of human 'capital', the skills and capacities of individuals acting alone and in groups. Yet it is precisely the characteristics of human capital that are critical in the effective use of ICTs.

TABLE 2.1 – WORLD-WIDE INFORMATION TECHNOLOGY MARKET BREAKDOWN, 1985-1995

	1985	1995	1985-95 CAGR
By geographic area:	%	%	%
North America	59.2	43.5	9.4
Latin America	1.5	2.0	15.6
Western Europe	22.1	28.3	15.6
E. Europe, Middle East and Africa	3.1	2.6	10.6
Asia Pacific	14.0	23.7	18.9
	100.0	100.0	
By main segment			
PCs and workstations	20.9	30.5	17.2
Multi-user systems	29.5	13.0	4.0
Data communication equipment	3.0	4.3	17.0
Packaged software	13.5	18.4	16.3
Services	33.1	33.7	13.0
	100.0	100.0	

Note: CAGR means 'compound annual growth rate' [1]
Source: OECD Secretariat compiled from IDC data OECD (1996b).

2.2 CATCHING-UP, FORGING AHEAD OR FALLING BEHIND?

While ICTs can contribute to economic growth and competitiveness, they also introduce new challenges for developing economies. In thinking about the role of ICTs it is important to avoid the pitfall in reasoning called technological determinism. Growth in the use of ICTs is often thought of as a *cause* of economic growth but it may also be a *result* of economic growth. When ICT use is said to be a *cause* of economic growth, it is because ICTs are being used in the construction of larger human and physical systems that are capable of generating economic value. Adding equipment without adding physical and human capital is likely to increase electricity usage rather than economic growth. The challenge of mobilising the complementary investments in physical and human capital is often larger than that of raising the funds to invest in the technology.

ICT use is also the *result* of economic growth. In societies with higher levels of income, individuals employ ICTs to conserve the increasingly costly human inputs of their own and others' time. They also use ICTs to forge links between the growing number of information resources and to produce novelty in applications aimed at productivity, education, or entertainment. As ICT use increases as the result of economic growth, the challenge is to develop and exploit these emerging opportunities. This process often requires new methods of organisation and new investments in physical and human capital.

Given the economic significance of the use of ICTs, it is important to assess the desirability of producing them domestically. Recent history has demonstrated that the production of ICTs can provide a major source of export income and, in some cases, hasten the domestic deployment of these technologies. These observations raise questions about the contribution that ICT production may make to development. For example, does production of ICT products contribute to their effective use or, alternatively, is extensive use of ICTs a pre-requisite for effective production of ICT products and services? Recent history has demonstrated, for example, Korea and Taiwan (Pr. China), that it is possible to achieve a major position as an exporter of ICTs with lower than average rates of domestic use of these technologies. At the same time, however, the sustainability of this position may be vulnerable to the spread of production capabilities elsewhere in the world.

Because ICTs comprise a growing share of world manufacturing output, many countries will develop ICT production capabilities, even if these capabilities will often be confined to the assembly of imported components and subsystems. At the core of the issue of domestic production are the problems of identifying entry opportunities, potential paths for upgrading technological sophistication and opportunities for world class innovation, all of which are subject to increasingly vigorous competition. Thus, while domestic ICT production is likely to occur in many developing countries, its potential contribution to domestic growth and export earnings must be viewed with caution.

Growing ICT use is aided by persistent price reductions and quality improvements that are the result of improve-

ments in the science and technology of new materials. Foremost among these advances has been the progressive improvement of integrated circuit semiconductor fabrication methods and opto-electronics (fibre optic and semiconductor laser technologies).[2] Integrated circuits are the foundation for the personal computer while opto-electronics are responsible for dramatic increases in the capacity (and hence the potential for cost reduction) in the telecommunication network. The use of these new technologies in industrialised countries continues to expand while growth is now accelerating in the newly industrialising and some of the developing countries.

Analysing the possibilities for ICTs to contribute to knowledge-based social and economic development requires a systematic method for graphing indicators and making international comparisons. The task of assembling the appropriate indicators is hindered by the enormous variety of ICT applications. These range from expensive capital goods such as machine tools to the simplest portable calculators and watches. Similar problems exist in attempting to assess the comparative development of ICT-based services. Existing data for the industrialised countries do not provide a complete picture of the full size and nature of the ICT use. Data for the developing countries provide an even less complete picture. For many of the least developed countries, useful indicators are virtually non-existent. The absence of adequate statistics is particularly troublesome because of the impacts of these new technologies on new investment demands, application opportunities, and production possibilities. These impacts are large and are likely to become larger during the coming decade.

One approach to these data problems is to use some of the available indicators to create a coherent conceptual framework. If it is properly constructed, such a framework will suggest some of the key features by which ICTs, combined with the requisite human skills and organisational changes, may make significant contributions to economic development. The next section (2.3) outlines a conceptual framework. Sections 2.4, 2.5, and 2.6 examine several of the key indicators that can be used to implement this framework. They can also be used individually to analyse key issues about the relationship between ICTs and social and economic development. Section 2.7 brings these indicators together to illustrate how this framework can be implemented in practice and to assess its limitations and applications. The chapter concludes with a brief summary of the key issues for improving existing quantitative techniques.

2.3 THE INEXSK (INFRASTRUCTURE, EXPERIENCE, SKILLS, KNOWLEDGE) APPROACH

The aim of the measurement technique is to provide insight into how infrastructure, experience, and skills may contribute to knowledge-based economic growth and development. These factors can be displayed using a simple diagram as in Figure 2.1.

The base of Figure 2.1 displays the indicators of infrastructure development, a means of assessing how broad or narrow the foundation is for the development of experience and skills. A very undeveloped infrastructure provides a narrow base for the development of either production or consumption experiences and a similarly specialised foundation for the application of skills.

FIGURE 2.1 - THE BASIC INEXSK FRAMEWORK - BUILDING FROM INFRASTRUCTURE TO KNOWLEDGE

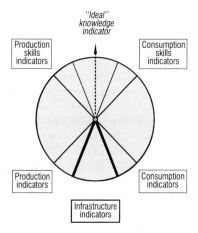

Production and consumption indicators are included next because of the consensus among experts that knowledge is accumulated through production or consumption experience. In principle, it would be desirable for these indicators to include production and consumption experience in *both* goods and services. In practice, however, adequate data on service consumption are often unavailable even for highly industrialised economies.[3] Next come indicators of production and consumption skills which accompany and reinforce the production and consumption experience indicators. At the top of Figure 2.1 is the 'Ideal' indicator, the development of improved knowledge and the application of knowledge for social and economic development. There is no existing indicator, or composite indicator, that can provide a satisfactory measure of the progress of knowledge.[4] Figure 2.1 shows a four-level grouping of indicators. The indicator groups at the bottom 'enable' and contribute to the indicators at the top of the figure.

This relatively simple arrangement allows comparison between experience and skills, a key feature of the development process for ICT production and use. Figure 2 illustrates these relationships.

Experience with production and consumption operates to push the new technologies into roles in the creation of knowledge, the first set of arrows (left and right) immediately above the experience indicators. Neither production

nor consumption alone, however, will bring infrastructure assets and experience into productive use in the creation of knowledge. This requires 'pull' influences from the production or consumption skills, represented by a second set of arrows leading to the skills level.

Finally, the diagram has a relatively larger gap between experience and skills indicators than between infrastructure and experience, or skills and knowledge. This gap reflects the difficulty in coordinating the 'push' of experience and the 'pull' of skills to achieve an effective outcome. This problem is highlighted by Figure 2.3.

Much of the challenge in harnessing ICTs to development objectives lies in the problems of mobilising tacit knowledge and organisational capabilities to effectively connect experience with skills in the construction of knowledge-based societies. This issue is taken up in Chapter 3 and subsequent chapters.

In the following sections the three levels that underlie the development of knowledge-based development - infrastructure, experience, and skills - are examined.

For infrastructure, the traditional measure is the size and growth of the telecommunication network (section 2.4). Telephone networks provide a broad base for building other types of infrastructure, such as data communication networks, but cannot serve as the only indicator of development. Unfortunately, few other indicators are as comprehensive as those associated with telecommunications. Where more detailed information is available, telecommunication indicators can be shown to be reasonably good proxies for other variables. For example, where it can be examined, the extent of data networking appears to be consistent with high levels of telephone access. More research is needed to explain variances in the rate

FIGURE 2.2 - DYNAMIC PROCESSES IN THE INEXSK FRAMEWORK

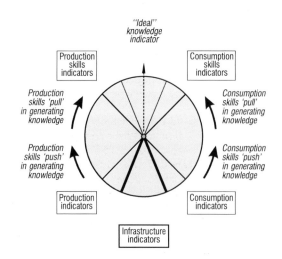

and direction of other forms of infrastructure development with the telecommunication indicators.

To understand the contribution of experience, electronics industry production and demand can be examined. These are indicators of the ICT production capacities of various countries, and of the domestic use and export or import of electronic products. Section 2.5 reviews levels and trends in production, consumption, and trade in electronics products. Although production and use of electronics products are only partial measures of the ICT revolution, they do provide insight into the vigour of the social and economic changes that are associated with the process of moving toward greater knowledge use in societies throughout the world.

FIGURE 2.3 – THE SIGNIFICANCE OF TACIT AND ORGANISATIONAL CAPABILITIES IN THE INEXSK FRAMEWORK

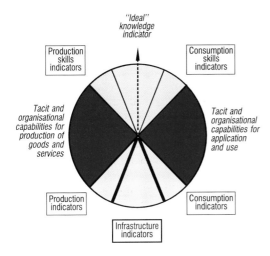

In examining skills, it is vital to develop measures that indicate the state of readiness to enlarge the use of information to develop knowledge (section 2.6). A principal indicator of such readiness is the literacy level. It is also important to develop measures of the skills that may be harnessed in producing or adapting ICTs. The stock of graduates with technical degrees in engineering, mathematics, and computer science is relevant here.

Section 2.7 brings together indicators from each of the categories, that is, infrastructure, experience, and skills, in a charting technique called the 'ICT footprint'.[5] The 'footprint' technique is developed from the INEXSK framework. It can be used to make inter-country comparisons and to benchmark the performance of different regions in preparing for, and participating in, the ICT revolution. It is also a means of organising the thinking about how other measures might be derived and used in the construction of international comparisons and strategic planning studies.

2.4 ANALYSIS OF TELECOMMUNICATION INFRASTRUCTURE AND INVESTMENT

Virtually all the statistics on ICTs focus on production in, and trade amongst, the most developed countries. There are major problems in charting the nature and extent of ICT infrastructure in the 'rest of the world', that is, the majority of the world's population. For a few developing countries, particularly those with significant electronic exports, it is possible to provide sufficiently detailed inventories of the production and consumption of ICT equipment to create a satisfactory measure of the nature of the ICT infrastructure. For most of the developing countries, and virtually all of the least developed countries, such inventories are unavailable. Subsequent chapters of this report provide detailed examinations of several of the countries that are part of this 'rest of the world' and section 2.5 provides some 'flow' measures of production and consumption experience in selected developing countries. This section focuses on the most complete available measures of the ICT infrastructure, telecommunication services. Although this is only one facet of development, it is a major one.

The statistics gathered by the International Telecommunication Union (ITU) on telecommunication services are the most comprehensive, in terms of country coverage, of any measure that is available to map the diffusion of ICTs. The most recent ITU database covers 209 countries and territories.[6] The database contains 102 indicators and 24 years,[7] making it theoretically possible to have 2,448 observations per country or 511,632 observations about the development of ICTs over the past 30 years. While very rich, the ITU database is not as complete as these numbers suggest. Any practical analysis of the ITU database must make a judicious choice of variables if an analysis of the least developed and developing countries is to be reasonably complete. The following analysis uses the most basic statistics on telecommunication infrastructure and investment, variables where the ITU database is reasonably complete for a very large number of countries for 1990 to 1995.[8]

Telephone main lines

One of the most comprehensively reported statistics in the ITU database is main telephone lines.[9] The ITU provides an analysis of the growth of main telephone lines which is summarised in Table 2.2.

The message of this table is very clear. Dramatic growth is occurring in the world telecommunication infrastructure in all countries except those with high income. In high income countries, the market for telephone service has matured and access to telephones is assured through

TABLE 2.2 – TELEPHONE MAIN LINES GROWTH BY ITU COUNTRY GROUPING

ITU income group	Main lines CAGR % 1990-1995	Main lines/100 CAGR % 1990-1995	% Share of global total of main lines 1995	Main lines/100 inhabitants 1995
Low income	27.4	24.9	9.3	1.98
Lower middle income	8.2	6.6	14.9	9.09
Upper middle income	8.2	6.4	10.1	14.51
High income	3.5	2.8	65.8	53.16

Note: Shares computed from reported data on total main lines.
Source: ITU (1997).

'universal service' regulatory policies. There are pockets where services are inaccessible and/or unaffordable in some regions or socio-economic groups. The maturity of the high income country markets is confirmed by the ITU indicator, residential main lines per 100 households, which was 101 for the high income countries or slightly more than one telephone line per household.[10]

The growth in main lines and main lines per 100 inhabitants for low income countries is a particularly striking feature of Table 2.2. During the 1990-1995 period, China made enormous strides in extending its telecommunication network, adding just under 34 million lines in only five years, a six-fold improvement on the 1990 base. This extraordinary performance lifts the estimated growth of the entire 'low income' group. Without China, the Compound Annual Growth Rate (CAGR) for the low income group is 13.8 per cent for main lines and 11.1 per cent for mainlines per 100 inhabitants or about half the reported figures. This change does not blunt the main

message of Table 2.2. Telecommunication infrastructure growth is pervasive and is occurring most rapidly in the lower income countries. The rate of catch-up of the lowest income countries, excluding China, with the rest of the world is somewhat slower than the table suggests.

Table 2.3 provides an analysis of regional performance to discern other significant differences in the pattern of growth in telecommunication infrastructure.

When considered on a regional basis, more variety is apparent in the pattern of growth in telecommunication infrastructure. Sorting by the rate of growth of main lines per 100 people, nine distinct patterns can be distinguished.

1 China is in a class by itself for the 1990-1995 period with extraordinary growth performance. The explosive growth of China, if it were possible to sustain it for another five years, would allow it to overtake the developed world in eight years. This is only partly a statistical illusion of growing from a small base. Between 1990 and 1995 China added nearly 34 million

TABLE 2.3 – PATTERNS OF TELECOMMUNICATION INFRASTRUCTURE GROUP BY REGION

Notes	Region	CAGR Main lines/100 inhabitants 1990-1995	Main lines/100 inhabitants 1990	Main lines/100 inhabitants 1995
1	China	40.9%	0.6	3.4
2	Asia NIEs Second Tier	18.6%	1.6	3.7
	Other Asia	15.3%	0.6	1.3
3	Mahgreb	11.4%	2.6	4.5
	West Asia	10.0%	7.2	11.5
4	Other North Africa	8.0%	2.3	3.4
	South America	7.5%	6.3	9.0
	Oceania Developing	7.5%	3.3	4.7
5	Europe Developing	6.5%	14.2	19.4
	Caribbean	6.0%	5.5	7.3
6	Asia NIEs First Tier	6.0%	32.3	43.1
7	Eastern Europe	4.9%	13.4	17.0
	Sub-Saharan Africa	4.0%	0.4	0.5
8	Developed	2.7%	45.2	51.5
9	Central Asia	2.6%	7.9	8.9

Note: The countries in each region are listed in the appendix to this chapter.
Source: Calculated from *ITU STARS Database* (1996).

main telephone lines or 20 per cent of a United States level accumulated over one century of development.

2 The Second Tier Newly Industrialising Economies (NIEs), Indonesia, Malaysia, and Thailand, are also growing very quickly, although they are likely to fall behind China at current expansion rates. In the Other Asia region, India, Philippines, Pakistan, and Viet Nam have been experiencing rapid growth rates of 13 per cent, 18 per cent, 20 per cent, and 51 per cent, respectively. If sustained, these rates applied to the current base of these countries will propel them to near parity with the older industrialised economies within a decade. The only other large country in this group, Bangladesh, is experiencing slow growth of 3.5 per cent.

3 The growth rate of countries in the Mahgreb region and West Asia is sufficient to attain convergence over a moderately long period of time. At these rates, the Mahgreb region, in 20 years will reach the level of Ireland, which at 36.5 was the country in the European Union with the lowest number of main lines per 100 inhabitants in 1995. Starting from a higher base than the Mahgreb region, West Asia, at a similar rate of growth, will reach Ireland's level in 13 years.

4 Although South American countries are growing more slowly than the Mahgreb and West Africa, they are growing from a larger base and the time to convergence is about the same, 19 years. For Other North African and Developing Oceania countries, convergence will be slower, requiring 31 and 29 years, respectively, to reach Ireland's 1995 level.

5 Although the growth rates of the European Developing countries (Malta and the republics formed from the former Yugoslavia) and the Caribbean are similar, they are on markedly different base levels. For the Caribbean, at current rates convergence with Ireland's level would take about 20 years. The higher base for the European developing countries will lead to this level in half that time, 10 years.

6 The First Tier NIEs have nearly converged with the industrialised world and their faster rate of growth suggests parity will be achieved in the next five years.

7 Although Eastern Europe and Sub-Saharan Africa's rates of growth are similar, they are occurring on entirely different base levels. The penalty of a slow growth rate on a moderate base for Eastern Europe is that it will take 15 years at current growth rates to reach Ireland's present level. The penalty of slow growth on a low base for Sub-Saharan Africa is that it will take over a century for it to reach the 1995 level of Ireland.

8 In the industrialised world, maturity means slow growth rates. The very high base level in industrialised countries means that significant additions are still occurring. In the United States, for example, more than 28 million lines were added between 1990 and 1995. This was almost three times as many as in Other Asia during the period and only slightly below China's exceptional performance.

9 Central Asia, the former Soviet Republics east of the Caucasus, have the misfortune to be growing very slowly on a small base level. At these rates, catching up to Ireland's 1995 level will take over 50 years.

This analysis can be used to recast the country groupings in terms of convergence. The basic message is that 'catch up' is occurring in the rapid growth of telecommunication infrastructure. However, at present rates this process will not be rapid for many countries. For a few, it is literally out of sight into the future (see Table 2.4)

TABLE 2.4 – CONVERGENCE AND 'CATCH-UP' IN TELECOMMUNICATIONS

Convergence criteria to the lowest level in industrialised countries	
Advancing at the frontier or nearly converged	Developed countries, First Tier NIEs
Convergence will take a decade	Second Tier NIEs, China (highly optimistic), European Developing Countries, West Asia
Convergence will take a generation (15-20 years)	Eastern Europe, China (more realistic), Other Asia, Mahgreb, Caribbean, South America
Convergence will take 30 years	Other Northern Africa and Developing Oceania
Convergence is out of sight (50-100 years)	Sub-Saharan Africa, Central Asia

Source: Calculated from *ITU STARS Database* (1996).

It is remarkable that, compared with other measures of convergence such as gross domestic product (GDP) per capita, the rates of growth of the telecommunication infrastructure are sufficiently rapid that convergence is foreseeable for the majority of the world's population.

Achieving and sustaining this pace of growth requires substantial investment and trade. At present, and for the foreseeable future, key equipment for extending the telecommunication infrastructure will originate in the countries with a highly developed telecommunication infrastructure. A considerable portion of the investment in telecommunication infrastructure will also be taken up by the costs of construction.

2.4.1 TELECOMMUNICATION INFRASTRUCTURE INVESTMENT

Extending or improving a telecommunication network requires equipment investment, particularly in central office switches and for building the copper or fibre-based grid used for carrying messages. Fibre optic cables have matured substantially in the past twenty years although their higher carrying capacity is partly offset by splicing costs. Thus, technologies for connecting switches remain divided among fibre, cable, or microwave links while most individual residence connections continue to be copper wire. In some developing areas, such as eastern Europe and China, significant additions to capacity are being made with the use of cellular telephone networks which have the advantages of reducing construction costs and time.

Historically, investment costs for equipment and construction were financed as very long term capital investments by government telecommunication administrations. Increasingly, these investments are made in a commercial framework where returns on investment are expected to be competitive with alternative investments. In both the industrialised and developing countries, demand for telecommunication service may be increased by reducing tariffs and by the process of economic growth.[11] Recent trends suggest that revenue growth and the potential economic returns to investment are strongest in those countries that are experiencing rapid economic development. Investment in the less rapidly developing countries is less likely to bring increases in revenue. If infrastructure development is based solely upon commercial returns, the rate and direction of investment may be insufficient to meet development and access goals.

Indicators of recent trends using telecommunication revenues and investment are shown in Table 2.5. The rows of the table are arranged by the 'convergence classes' discussed above so that the leaders are at the top and the regions for which convergence is 'out of sight' are at the bottom. The first column of this table indicates the percentage change of revenues received in the region in 1994 compared to 1990. This indicator, unadjusted for inflation, provides an estimate of the growth of the market in the region. Since most telecommunication networks were monopolies during the period observed, revenue growth is not necessarily closely linked to changes in cost. For example, fiscal requirements may dictate higher pricing and these may result in higher revenues if income is growing in a particular region.

In the Asia Developed countries revenue requirements appear to be driving the market. Revenues have increased

TABLE 2.5 – INDICATORS OF INFRASTRUCTURE DEVELOPMENT FOR DEVELOPING REGIONS FROM ITU DATA

Region (ordered by convergence group)	Revenue percentage change 1990-94	Revenue per main line percentage change 1990-94	Investment per main line (see text)	Percentage change in main lines 1990-1994	Percentage change in investment (see text)
Asia Developed	75.1	58.5	3,626	10.5	33.9
Asia NIEs First Tier	62.3	22.4	794	32.6	2.5
Oceania Developed	43.6	11.5	1,933	13.5	-17.0
Europe Developed	27.0	10.6	2,005	14.7	-3.8
Africa Developed	21.0	6.3	1,135	13.9	72.2
America Developed	10.6	-3.7	1,118	14.8	3.7
Asia NIEs Second Tier	92.7	-5.1	444	103.1	38.6
Europe Developing	28.2	-9.3	637	41.4	-40.9
West Asia	18.5	-31.0	179	71.7	-0.5
China	209.0	-22.3	204	297.5	207.6
South America	66.5	13.8	782	46.2	13.1
Other Asia	42.0	-26.2	417	92.4	22.9
Caribbean	21.2	-7.8	825	31.5	-9.6
Mahgreb	19.2	-31.4	477	73.7	-0.5
Eastern Europe	-26.2	-39.6	300	22.1	-25.9
Oceania Developing	64.7	26.5	943	47.7	-11.5
Other North Africa	-0.9	-35.4	288	53.3	32.9
Sub-Saharan Africa	16.4	-13.3	1,588	34.3	2.4
Central Asia	-67.7	-75.9	62	34.1	-34.5

Note: The countries in each region are listed in the appendix to this chapter.
Source: Calculated from *ITU STARS Database* (1996).

considerably faster on a total and per line basis than the increase in main lines. Some of this revenue growth was necessary to pay the very high costs of additional lines in these countries (to take account of the 'lumpy' character of investment, the total number of main lines added between 1990 and 1994 is divided by total investment in these years to give the values in column three of Table 2.5). Yet, since both countries are at a similar level of maturity to Europe and North America, the high investment cost per main line also raises questions about the level of efficiency of telecommunication operations.[12]

The performance of the second convergence group is particularly interesting. These countries are experiencing significant revenue growth in the face of declining revenue per main line, while the investment cost of adding main lines is one of the lowest in the world. This experience is the realisation of economies of scale during rapid growth which is also occurring in China and Other Asia (including India and Pakistan).

Toward the bottom of the third group, the decline in revenue per main line and modest total revenue growth become a constraint to the addition of telecommunication capacity. This is reflected in the decline in investment from the first to the second half of the period. In the fourth group, the performance of Developing Oceania is anomalous. A modest total, and per line, revenue growth seems to be consumed by the relatively high costs of adding main lines leading to a low rate of investment. Nevertheless, the number of main lines is increasing fairly rapidly on a small base, suggesting a targeted development effort. In Other North Africa (largely Egypt), the determination to push forward with development (the significant increase in main lines) is remarkable given stagnant revenue and a decline in revenue per main line. In Sub-Saharan Africa and Central Asia almost all the trends are negative. Particularly notable is the very high cost per main line of capacity additions in Sub-Saharan Africa. A number of factors contribute to these high costs, for example, cost allocation and reporting methodologies, geographic and climate conditions and distance factors, procurement practices of operators, and equipment design and architecture issues.

One means of addressing the problem of mobilising the investment required for improving the telecommunication infrastructure is to attract foreign investment in the telecommunication infrastructure. Such investments may be forthcoming if a number of conditions are met including an attractive rate of return on investment. Developing and newly industrialising economies are engaged in implicit and explicit competition to make such investments attractive. Vladimir Quintero has concluded that profit expectations, market size, required investment per monetary unit of revenue, and taxes on telecommunication income are important indicators of

the relative attractiveness of particular countries for foreign direct investment.[13]

In summary, the pattern of telecommunication infrastructure investment may contribute, or fail to contribute, to convergence. Investment trends may be constrained by available revenue, or buoyed up by rapid economic growth. By analysing investment in terms of 'convergence classes' it is possible to assess the magnitude of the 'catch up' effort. When revenue growth rates are related to investment, convergence opportunities and constraints, including the prospects for attracting foreign investment, to finance capacity additions can be estimated. It is not clear that convergence will be achieved in all cases solely through market-initiated or market-led processes because of revenue constraints. This is particularly so for the two slowest converging groups. Proactive policies also may be needed in the middle group of countries whose inhabitants constitute the majority of the world's population.

2.4.2 TELECOMMUNICATION AND DEVELOPMENT: REVIEWING THE RELATIONSHIP

The least developed countries do not appear often in this analysis because of the absence of meaningful data for measuring the nature and extent of activity in economies that are unable to make major investments in the communication infrastructure. For these countries, the process of developing an ICT capability is protracted. It is useful to examine a traditional measure, the relation between main telephone lines per 100 population and national income measured as GDP per capita. These are measures that have been shown to be closely related.[14] Both these measures are the result of long-term historical development. Therefore, neither is subject to the problems of short-term setbacks or detours in the development process.

Despite the fact that main telephone lines per 100 population is a measure of only one component of the knowledge and ICT infrastructure, it is a measure that may be correlated with other indicators in addition to GDP per capita. Although understanding of the levels of use of information technologies lags substantially behind understanding of the use of communication technology, it is generally believed that the two are closely related. There may be a country in the world in which the per capita use of computers is far greater than the use of the telephone. If so, it would be a major finding of great interest to the world. Because of the likely close correlation between investments in communication technology and investments in information technology in the long term, it is useful to look at the traditional measure in a new way.

The approach taken is to look at those countries that are performing substantially better and worse than the predicted relationship between main lines per 100

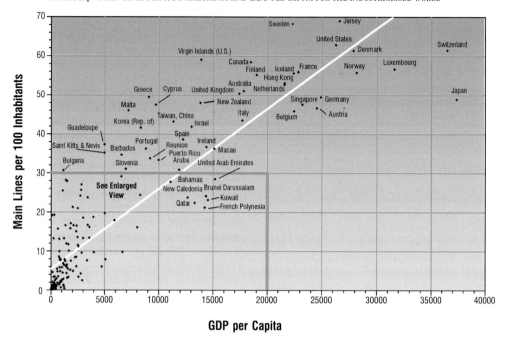

FIGURE 2.4 – MAIN LINES PER 100 INHABITANTS AND GDP PER CAPITA FOR THE INDUSTRIALISED WORLD

Note: Main lines per 100 inhabitants based on 1995 values for main lines in operation and population. GDP per capita based on most recent available values.
Source: Compiled from *ITU STARS Database* (1996).

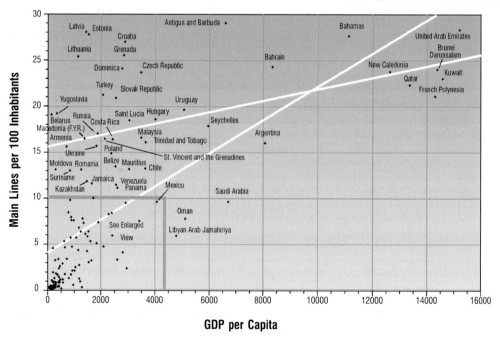

FIGURE 2.5 – MAIN LINES PER 100 INHABITANTS AND GDP PER CAPITA FOR COUNTRIES WITH LESS THAN 30 MAIN LINES PER 100 INHABITANTS

Note: Main lines per 100 inhabitants based on 1995 values for main lines in operation and population. GDP per capita based on most recent available values.
Source: Compiled from *ITU STARS Database* (1996).

inhabitants and national income. The basic picture is shown in Figure 2.4.

Figure 2.4 displays the countries for which measures of annual GDP per capita in US dollars (x-axis) and main telephone lines per 100 population (y-axis) are available for either 1994 or 1995. The relationship is that as income goes up, so does the number of main lines. At very high income levels (above US$ 20,000 per year) there is some saturation of demand, as in Japan. In the US$ 10-20,000 range, the less affluent industrialised countries, there is greater variation, but only seven countries in this income range have main lines per 100 inhabitants below 30, or about one phone for three inhabitants. All seven of these countries are notable for substantial concentration in the distribution of income. Some people are very rich while the standards of living of others are closer to the developing world. Of particular interest are two former socialist countries, Bulgaria and Slovenia, with exceptionally high telecommunication accessibility relative to their incomes. In general, however, there is little that is surprising in this figure. In industrialised countries, the relationship between income and telecommunication access is exceptionally regular. Some countries do somewhat better than their income would predict, while others do somewhat worse.

The more interesting stories are to be found in the mass of countries contained in the lower left hand box of Figure 2.4. Figure 2.5 shows the result if the lower left hand corner of Figure 2.4 is examined for the countries with numbers of main telephone lines per 100 population of less than 30.

Once again, a mass of countries appears in the lower left of Figure 2.5 representing those countries with less than 10 main lines per 100 inhabitants and annual GDP per capita below US$ 4,500. The steeper of the two lines in Figure 2.5 takes into account the unnamed countries in the box. The shallower line takes account only of those countries having 10 to 30 main lines per 100 inhabitants. These two lines provide two standards for examining the performance of the named countries. Falling below the steeper line is a likely indication of problems in the development of the telecommunication infrastructure. This issue was identified for the countries in the upper right hand portion of Figure 2.5. Income distribution issues also seem to be playing a role in Saudi Arabia, Oman, and Libyan Arab Jamahiriya. Argentina and Mexico (falling just inside the box in the lower left corner) fall below the steeper line (which defines an easier standard for infrastructure development). Numerous reasons, including financial crises during recent intensive investment periods in telecommunication infrastructure growth, may be responsible for this position. Nevertheless, the 'gap' in performance of both these countries indicates the conclusions that can be drawn from a careful reading of these data.

The striking feature of Figure 2.5 is the composition of the countries. Of the 20 countries above the shallow line, 10 are former socialist countries, 7 are island economies and 3 are left over (United Arab Emirates, Turkey, and Uruguay), all middle income countries. Of the 20, 13 have GDP per capita comparable to the countries in the box on the lower left of Figure 2.5. They are notable for

FIGURE 2.6 – MAIN LINES PER 100 INHABITANTS AND GDP PER CAPITA FOR COUNTRIES WITH LESS THAN 10 MAIN LINES PER 100 INHABITANTS

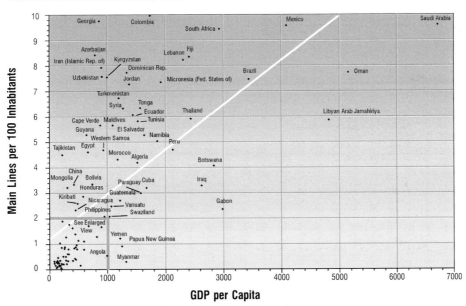

Note: Main lines per 100 inhabitants based on 1995 values for main lines in operation and population. GDP per capita based on most recent available values.
Source: Compiled from *ITU STARS Database* (1996).

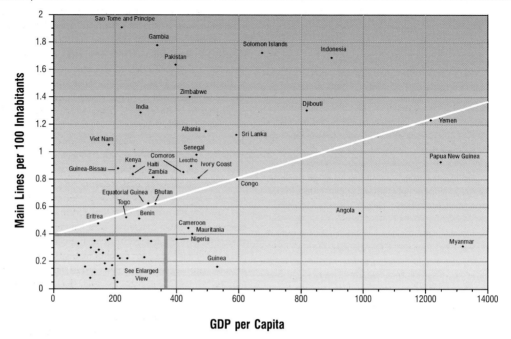

Note: Main lines per 100 inhabitants based on 1995 values for main lines in operation and population. GDP per capita based on most recent available values.
Source: Compiled from *ITU STARS Database* (1996).

FIGURE 2.8 – MAIN LINES PER 100 INHABITANTS AND GDP PER CAPITA FOR COUNTRIES WITH LESS THAN 1 MAIN LINE PER 250 INHABITANTS

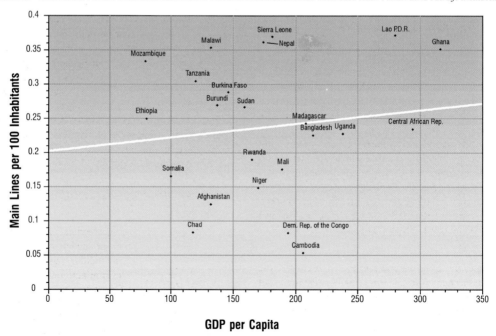

Note: Main lines per 100 inhabitants based on 1995 values for main lines in operation and population. GDP per capita based on most recent available values.
Source: Compiled from *ITU STARS Database* (1996).

having distinctly greater telecommunication infrastructure development as compared to that predicted by their income. One conclusion is that, under socialism, relatively more telecommunication infrastructure was constructed. Island countries, in some cases because of their financial and tourism connections, are likely to construct more extensive networks than other countries of similar income.

Figures 2.6 and 2.7 trace the relationship between income and telecommunication infrastructure, first for countries with between 2 and 10 main lines per 100 inhabitants, and then for countries with between 0.4 and 2. Most of the world's developing countries appear here as well as some countries that have achieved significant levels of industrial development, for example, Brazil.

In Figure 2.6 most of the identified countries are above the level of US$ 1,000 per year in GDP per capita. This is used as the definition of 'least developed' country. The diagonal line in the diagram is an estimate of the average relationship, taking into account all of the plotted points (including the unnamed countries in the box in the lower left hand corner). The fifteen countries appearing below this line have a less developed telecommunication infrastructure than would be expected from their income level. Saudi Arabia and Oman already have been mentioned. Libyan Arab Jamahiriya and Iraq are countries where international conflict has led to embargoes on key telecommunication equipment, a factor that may explain some or all of their current underdevelopment. Similar issues are likely to have influenced performance in Yemen and Gabon.

Botswana and Gabon are examples of countries that have achieved a higher level of economic performance with relatively undeveloped telecommunication infrastructure. Both countries have GDP per capita levels similar to South Africa and Thailand which have far better developed telecommunication infrastructures. Good prospects for further growth in the latter two countries are expected. Whether Botswana and Gabon will also continue to grow, and do so without catching up in telecommunication infrastructure, raises key questions about the relationship between development and telecommunication infrastructure for the next decade. Similar questions about growth potential may be asked about the relationship between countries around the US$ 2,000 GDP per capita level where Colombia, El Salvador, Peru, Cuba, and Paraguay are displayed.[15]

Turning to the lower income countries in Figure 2.7 the relatively strong performance of Indonesia, Pakistan, and Gambia are indications of the parallel development of economies and telecommunication infrastructure. Similarly, the economic growth of Cameroon, Mauritania, Guinea, Nigeria, and Angola has been weaker with civil turmoil and strife influencing the recent performance of the last two countries.

Finally, Figure 2.8 shows the countries with the very lowest state of development of telecommunication infrastructure, those with less than 0.4 main lines per 100 inhabitants or 1 main line per 250 inhabitants. All the countries displayed are among the least developed by most measures. Many of these countries have experienced civil strife in recent years and a number of the countries performing below the group average represented by the diagonal line in the diagram, share this characteristic (for example, Somalia, Cambodia, Uganda, Central African Republic). Of the 22 countries in Figure 2.8, 15 are in Sub-Saharan Africa, one of the regions having the worst prospects, based upon its growth history, for achieving convergence with the remainder of the world. For the people of these countries, telecommunication infrastructure is simply not part of everyday life or experience. Efforts to improve upon this infrastructure are likely to compete with other urgent social and economic needs. What, if any, strategy for developing telecommunication infrastructure in these countries will contribute to relieving poverty is an urgent question that is considered further in Chapter 6.

Telecommunication networks are only one aspect of the technological infrastructure needed for enhancing the relationship between ICTs and knowledge-based development. There are two reasons why telecommunication is central to the analysis of development. First, telecommunication infrastructure is more broadly dispersed and developed than other ICTs, such as personal computers. Second, measures of telecommunication development, such as main lines, are available for virtually all countries. Similar indicators for other ICTs are far less developed. Where available, they tend to be based on proprietary marketing studies or isolated reports on individual countries. This situation may change in the coming years as the significance of all components of the ICT infrastructure is better appreciated. Improved data would make a substantial contribution to providing an empirical basis for understanding the rate and direction of technological change. Broader measures of the ICT infrastructure would assist in the construction of knowledge-based societies throughout the world.

2.5 OVERVIEW OF THE GLOBAL PRODUCTION AND USE OF ICTs

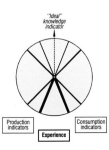

This section examines the role of production and use of ICTs in building upon the telecommunication infrastructure. Production and use are important in providing the impetus to build knowledge-based economic and social development. They are also important for the more familiar issues of stimulating economic growth and managing foreign trade deficits. This section provides a global overview of ICT production, followed by an examination of consumption patterns and the implications of production and consumption for foreign trade balances. An analysis of experience in some of the newly industrialising countries indicates a continuing distinction between export-led growth based on ICTs and the development of strong experience in ICT use as part of a knowledge-based growth strategy.

2.5.1 PRODUCING ICTs

Table 2.6 provides an overview of estimated production of the electronics industry for 1996 arranged according to nineteen regions:[16]

TABLE 2.6 – ELECTRONICS INDUSTRY PRODUCTION, 1996

	Region	1996 (US$ million)
1	America Developed	283,423
2	Europe Developed	193,351
3	Africa Developed	1,571
4	Asia Developed	260,787
5	Oceania Developed	3,909
6	South America	32,548
7	Caribbean	n/a
8	Mahgreb	n/a
9	Other North Africa	222
10	Sub-Saharan Africa	n/a
11	West Asia	2,362
12	Central Asia	n/a
13	China	33,369
14	Asia NIEs First Tier	121,419
15	Asia NIEs Second Tier	48,284
16	Other Asia	12,459
17	Oceania Developing	n/a
18	Europe Developing	552
19	Eastern Europe	6,710
	Total Electronics Production	1,000,966

Note: For country and territory groupings see the appendix to this chapter. The Elsevier data are based upon 50 countries of which only three, China, Egypt and India, are classified as least developed countries (LDCs) by the criteria of GDP per capita less than US$ 1,000 per year.
Source: Calculated from Elsevier (1996).

Although electronics production has begun to spread to the developing countries, it continues to be dominated by the industrialised countries. In 1996, 53 per cent of production was accounted for by Japan and the United States. An additional 20 per cent of production came from other industrialised countries. Thus, about one-quarter of production occurs in countries that are either newly industrialised or industrialising.[17]

The greatest amount of this production is performed in the newly industrialised economies of South East Asia where electronics production has become a key component of the industrialisation process. Table 2.7 provides details of 1996 production based on 27 countries and territories surveyed by Elsevier of which seven are newly industrialising economies (NIEs) (four in the First Tier and three in the Second Tier), twelve other industrialising countries (which include China, Egypt, India, and the Philippines as well as countries from South America and West Asia), two countries - Croatia and Slovenia - from 'developing Europe' and the eight eastern European countries. The three largest industrialising country producers Brazil, China, and Mexico, are reported separately from the total for 'other industrialising countries'.

In each of these sectors, manufacturing opportunities exist for technologically mature products in which developing countries can be competitive and for products in which labour-intensive assembly operations are required. The early growth of the electronics industries in Singapore, Republic of Korea, Taiwan (Pr. China), Malaysia, and Thailand, was based upon assembly operations for the world's largest producers in the United States and Japan. These last two countries remain active in this market in addition to their growing domestic capabilities. The production profiles of the First Tier NIEs is beginning to resemble that of more industrialised countries. There is a decline in their share of consumer electronics production as other industrialising countries improve their position.

2.5.2 MARKET DEMAND AND TRADE

One of the reasons that it has been argued that ICT production is essential to ICT *use* has been the close correlation until recent years between the level of production and internal demand for electronic production. On the supply side this pattern has changed as the result of the 'export-led' growth strategies of the NIEs. NIEs ran an export surplus in electronics production and, at least initially, appeared to be investing less in ICTs than would be expected from their growing income and wealth. This was a concern for some industrialised countries that lost market share for more mature ICT products. These losses, due to competition from the new producers, were not compensated for by added revenue from selling more innovative or 'state-of-the-art' products to the export-led countries during the 1980s. This trend contributed to bilateral trade tensions. Multilateral trade did not ameliorate the problem since demand in developing countries was also growing relatively slowly. Slow growth in imports in the developing countries was partially due to foreign exchange rationing and self-reliance policies as

TABLE 2.7 - ELECTRONICS INDUSTRY PRODUCTION, 1996 - SELECTED DEVELOPING COUNTRIES AND TERRITORIES (US$ MILLION)

	EDP	Office equipment	Control and instrument	Medical and industrial	Broadcasting radio and radar	Telecom. equip.	Consumer	Components	Total
First Tier NIEs									
Hong Kong	1,582	487	103	137	867	388	2,840	2,704	9,109
Singapore	21,298	305	534	89	1,087	558	2,835	12,410	39,117
Korea (Rep.of)	6,062	353	324	341	2,441	2,218	7,806	26,084	45,628
Taiwan (Pr.China)	15,216	156	142	281	852	1,573	1,083	8,261	27,565
Total First Tier	*44,158*	*1,301*	*1,103*	*848*	*5,247*	*4,737*	*14,564*	*49,459*	*121,419*
NIEs Share	*56.8%*	*34.4%*	*23.2%*	*23.9%*	*37.4%*	*35.8%*	*27.9%*	*55.7%*	*47.1%*
Second Tier NIEs									
Indonesia	731	81	151	169	461	309	2,917	1,282	6,101
Malaysia	7,085	156	194	150	1,082	1,011	8,622	10,698	28,998
Thailand	5,312	506	123	71	384	436	2,375	3,978	13,185
Total Second Tier	*13,128*	*743*	*468*	*390*	*1,927*	*1,756*	*13,914*	*15,958*	*48,284*
NIEs Share	*16.9%*	*19.7%*	*9.8%*	*11.0%*	*13.7%*	*13.3%*	*26.7%*	*18.0%*	*18.7%*
Other Industrialising									
Brazil	5,762	279	743	258	857	1,299	2,584	2,679	14,460
China	6,253	886	545	721	2,457	2,208	11,477	8,823	33,369
Mexico	3,282	300	339	591	1,139	832	4,740	2,957	14,180
Others	4,319	188	1,029	553	2,066	1,773	3,192	7,688	20,810
Total	*19,616*	*1,653*	*2,656*	*2,123*	*6,519*	*6,112*	*21,993*	*22,147*	*82,819*
Share	*25.3%*	*43.8%*	*55.8%*	*59.9%*	*46.5%*	*46.3%*	*42.1%*	*25.0%*	*32.1%*
Eastern Europe									
Total	*775*	*80*	*531*	*183*	*334*	*610*	*1,735*	*1,155*	*5,403*
Share	*1.0%*	*2.1%*	*11.2%*	*5.2%*	*2.4%*	*4.6%*	*3.3%*	*1.3%*	*2.1%*
Total All Selected	77,677	3,777	4,758	3,544	14,027	13,215	52,206	88,719	257,925

Source: Calculated from Elsevier (1996).

well as the weak growth performance of many of the developing economies.

These trends have changed over the past decade. The NIEs are investing at a much more rapid pace in ICTs. Many more countries without significant production capacities have begun to invest more aggressively in ICTs. They have developed significant sectoral balance of trade deficits in electronics as a result. These countries include developing countries that have both liberalised their economies and begun to experience economic growth, as well as countries like Greece and New Zealand. Table 2.8 shows the distribution of demand as of 1996 in terms of domestic

sales. The domestic production figures are subtracted from domestic sales to derive imputed imports (the numbers in parentheses) and exports (the numbers without parentheses) in the third column. The bottom number in the third column shows that countries that are not covered by the Elsevier data, had imputed imports of electronics of US$ 60 billion from the electronics producing countries.[18]

Japan's imputed net exports are approximately equal to the imputed net imports of the United States and Europe combined (see Table 2.8). Although these developed countries are important trading partners and the balance of trade favours Japan, the world is more complex than the numbers suggest.[19] In practice, Japan's trade surplus is spread over much more of the world than Europe and the United States. This is not only because other areas of the world are important trading partners for Japan, and because the First and Second tier NIEs have a combined trade surplus with the rest of the world approaching that of Japan.[20] What this illustrates is that the NIEs and Japan share the trade surplus in electronics with the rest of the world, including both industrialised and developing countries.

TABLE 2.8 - ELECTRONICS INDUSTRY TRADE BY REGION, 1996 (US$ MILLION)

	Domestic market consumption	Total production	Imputed (imports) or exports
America Developed	334,927	283,423	(51,504)
Europe Developed	228,145	193,351	(34,794)
Africa Developed	4,447	1,571	(2,876)
Asia Developed	174,882	260,787	85,905
Oceania Developed	11,113	3,909	(7,204)
South America	34,477	32,548	(1,929)
Caribbean	n/a	n/a	n/a
Mahgreb	n/a	n/a	n/a
Other North Africa	675	222	(453)
Sub-Saharan Africa	n/a	n/a	n/a
West Asia	4,994	2,362	(2,632)
Central Asia	n/a	n/a	n/a
China	30,199	33,369	3,170
Asia NIEs First Tier	67,919	121,419	53,500
Asia NIEs Second Tier	26,736	48,284	21,548
Other Asia	8,775	12,459	3,684
Oceania Developing	n/a	n/a	n/a
Europe Developing	809	552	(257)
Eastern Europe	12,232	6,710	(5,522)
Total	940,330	1,000,966	60,636

Note: See Table 2.6 for comments on the country groupings and the coverage of the Elsevier data.
Source: Calculated from Elsevier (1996).

This is the basis for 'export-led' growth in both the NIEs and Japan. It is a pattern that is continuing and it is an important source of rising living standards and Asian demand for non-ICT goods and services from both industrialised and developing countries. Finally, it is important to note that China is not, or at least not yet, following an export-led growth strategy. Instead, it is allowing domestic demand to develop at a relatively rapid pace. Although

China is a net exporter overall, it has major deficits in active components (semiconductors), telecommunication equipment, and control and instrumentation equipment, all important inputs to its rapid industrialisation.

According to the Elsevier estimates of consumption the market for all types of electronics products is widespread (Elsevier 1996). For the less wealthy countries, the market is of course smaller. The electronic data processing (EDP) market in India was only US$ 807 million in 1995 or less than 10 per cent of the market in France of US$ 10.5 billion despite the fact that India's population is about 16 times larger (Elsevier 1996). On a per capita basis, there are enormous disparities between the industrialised and developing countries.

The *use* of electronics in all forms is more widespread than the production. The overall size of the population in the industrialising and eastern European countries raises their share in consumption of electronics relative to their production. This is, of course, not true of all countries, for example, China's EDP market is smaller than its production. It does indicate that in many markets domestic production capacity is smaller than demand and net imports are a consequence. Growing domestic markets eventually will offer production opportunities for some electronic products.

The early phases of 'export-led' growth may involve low rates of domestic ICT consumption by exporters. Table 2.9 investigates this claim showing the per capita expenditure on EDP equipment for selected developing NIEs and industrialised countries.

Table 2.9 indicates that industrialised countries like Germany and France are investing in EDP equipment at a rate that is closely linked to their respective populations.[21] Among large countries, the United States and Japan lead, with almost one half of the world market and 75 to 100 per cent greater per capita demand than developed countries such as France and Germany.

Smaller countries or areas may also achieve very high rates of ICT use. It is useful to note the experience of Singapore, the country with the highest rate of per capita investment in computers, and Hong Kong, where a higher rate of investment in computers is occurring than in many industrialised countries. This investment reflects a 'catching up' process. However, it also reflects a growing specialisation in Singapore and Hong Kong in computer-*using* economic activities, such as finance and other ICT-intensive services.

Although the level of investment in the Republic of Korea falls between that of Hong Kong and Singapore, it is significantly smaller on a per capita basis than in either of the latter two areas. This indicates a less ICT-intensive investment pattern in the Republic of Korea which is similar to that of Taiwan (Pr. China). Although these countries are major producers of ICT equipment, their use of computers is more concentrated within their economies than in the industrialised countries. Nevertheless, it is important to note that Korea's investment rate is approximately double that of Taiwan (Pr. China). The patterns in the level and per capita rate of investment are consistent with theories of economic development based upon construction of more ICT-intensive public and private infrastructures. They are also consistent with a migration toward more ICT-intensive goods and services as development proceeds. This development process is occurring in both industrialised countries and NIEs.

TABLE 2.9 – EXPENDITURE ON ELECTRONIC DATA PROCESSING EQUIPMENT, 1995

	EDP sales (US$ million)	Population (US$ million)	EDP expenditure per capita (US$)
India	807	929	0.87
China	4,321	1,214	3.56
Rest of World	65,836	2,655	24.79
Thailand	1,727	59	29.07
Brazil	6,384	162	39.50
World	262,750	5,702	46.08
Malaysia	1,021	20	50.72
Taiwan (Pr. China)	1,249	21	58.64
Korea (Rep. of)	4,699	45	104.77
Germany	14,184	82	173.25
France	10,489	58	180.66
United Kingdom	12,947	59	221.20
Hong Kong	1,678	6	271.08
United States	82,946	263	315.24
Japan	50,045	125	399.69
Singapore	4,417	3	1,477.26

Note: World includes all people and world total electronic data processing equipment. Rest of World includes known production not absorbed by purchases of the above list of countries and territories and the population of countries and areas other than those listed.
Source: EDP sales calculated from Elsevier (1996); Population calculated from ITU (1997).

2.6 THE HUMAN DIMENSION AND INTER–COUNTRY COMPARISONS

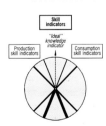

The human dimensions of the ICT revolution involve many aspects including the acquisition of new skills and the restructuring of work in ways that will support the productive use of ICTs. ICT use represents an augmentation of human skills and capabilities,

but there clearly is a hierarchy of skills. This hierarchy begins with the attainment of basic literacy. Virtually all of the work processes in which ICTs can make a contribution to economic growth require basic literacy. Literacy is therefore a first indicator of the attainment of the skill levels needed to use ICTs productively. Table 2.10 provides a summary of the level of illiteracy compiled by the United Nations Educational, Scientific, and Cultural Organisation (UNESCO).[22]

TABLE 2.10 – ILLITERACY IN THE DEVELOPING WORLD, 1995

	Illiteracy rate % total pop.	No. of men (million)	No. of women (million)
Latin America	13.3	26.6	33.0
Caribbean	20.9	2.4	2.6
Mahgreb	45.5	10.2	18.8
Other North Africa	49.2	16.6	28.7
Sub-Saharan Africa	45.3	83.8	139.4
West Asia	26.6	16.5	34.8
Central Asia	2.5	0.4	1.3
China	18.9	60.1	169.1
First Tier NIEs	3.1	0.3	1.3
Second Tier NIEs	14.2	12.2	26.6
Southern Asia	46.0	238.0	423.7
Pacific Islands	24.6	0.4	0.9
Eastern Europe	5.8	0.2	0.7
Developing Europe	1.9	0.8	4.2
Other	1.8	0.0	0.0
Total selected countries	**29.2**	**468.5**	**885.1**

Note: Data are included only for those countries and territories where data are complete. Industrialised countries are not included due to insufficient data. The total population of the 'Other' region is less than 100,000.
Source: Calculated from UNESCO (1995).

Illiteracy is a fundamental barrier to participation in 'knowledge societies'. It is possible to develop 'texts' and user interfaces based solely on pictographic information and audio-visual information. However, it seems likely that the vast majority of the illiterate population will be excluded from the emerging knowledge societies. This population amounts to at least 1.35 billion people or over 30 per cent of the world's population. For every illiterate male there are almost two illiterate females and the ratio of female to male illiteracy is relatively constant across different cultures. If literacy is a fundamental condition for the growth of knowledge societies, it appears that many of the world's people will not have the most basic skills for participating in it, and women will be more disadvantaged than men from the outset.

At the high end of the skills hierarchy are the professional skills needed to design and adapt ICTs to new uses. An indicator of the availability of these skills is the number of graduates of post-secondary education programmes in mathematics and engineering. Table 2.11 provides a summary of the number of graduates per million population.

TABLE 2.11 – GRADUATES IN ENGINEERING, COMPUTER SCIENCE, AND MATHEMATICS

	Region	Rate per million population
1	America Developed	851
2	Europe Developed	748
3	Africa Developed	n.a.
4	Asia Developed	974
5	Oceania Developed	583
6	South America	227
7	Caribbean	327
8	Mahgreb	151
9	Other North Africa	101
10	Sub-Saharan Africa	18
11	West Asia	247
12	Central Asia	665
13	China	238
14	Asia NIEs First Tier	1,735
15	Asia NIEs Second Tier	209
16	Other Asia	54
17	Oceania Developing	75
18	Europe Developing	452
19	Eastern Europe	1,440

Source: Calculated from UNESCO (1995).

There are immense differences in the extent to which various countries are participating in the technical education of their populations. The highest region on a rate per million basis is the First Tier NIEs (the Republic of Korea, Singapore, and Hong Kong; figures for Taiwan (Pr. China) are not included because of their absence from the UNESCO source). The highest individual country is Russia where the rate per million of engineering, computer science and mathematics graduates is 2,266. Even if this number is discounted for technical graduates who are not strictly comparable with engineering graduates elsewhere, it is still a very impressive performance. By comparison, the industrialised countries are not educating as many students as a proportion of their population. This suggests that the First Tier newly industrialised regions and eastern Europe (including Russia) will continue to have an ample supply of the skills needed for participating in future technical developments and this may enable them to accelerate their progress toward the frontier of technical development.

2.7 MAPPING ICT INDICATORS - A FOOTPRINT ANALYSIS

The INfrastructure, EXperience, Skills, Knowledge (INEXSK) approach can be used for inter-country comparisons by using indicators for each of its elements. Eight indicators are chosen based on data availability and their value in provoking thought about different patterns of development in knowledge societies.

Table 2.12 presents the indicators and how they are computed. Three factors were important in constructing the indices. First, it is desirable to adjust for population in measures of infrastructure and skills. A larger sized country will often have a larger infrastructure or a larger number of skilled individuals, but not necessarily higher levels per inhabitant. All the measures of infrastructure and skills as well as the two measures of 'outcome', Internet hosts and television sets, are adjusted for population. Second, in developing an indicator for production and consumption experience it is desirable to measure the relative specialisation of the economy in electronics. For these measures, the share of electronics in GDP is used to 'scale' the size of electronics experience in the total economy. Third, it is desirable to graph different countries on a common scale. Therefore, one country must be chosen as the 'extreme' or highest level against which to benchmark the level of other countries. Several of the values for the indicators are very high for a few countries, and it is not desirable to choose the country that is absolutely the largest in the world. This would mean that a great many countries would have very small values on the index. An approach was used to select the country 'taken to be 100' in the analysis. Some of the graphs show countries with index values exceeding 100.[23]

The available indicators are particularly deficient for developing and smaller countries. These limitations prevent the comparison of many countries for which useful insights might be developed using this technique. For those desiring to replicate the technique, different indicators might be chosen based upon the availability of data.

The indicators are presented in the following and Table 2.13 presents the index values for several industrialised countries.

The 'country taken as 100' is not the country with the highest value of the index in the world. This is apparent in the case of technical graduates in Table 2.13. Four of the five countries have index values (rates per 1,000 of technical graduates) exceeding that of the Netherlands, the country taken as 100. The United Kingdom is the country taken as 100 for the index of television sets and its value is 100, even though both the United States and

TABLE 2.12 – CONSTRUCTION OF INDICATORS FOR FOOTPRINT ANALYSIS

Indicator	Variables used to construct indicator	Computation used	Country taken as 100
❶ Personal Computer Index	Personal computers Population	Personal computers per capita	New Zealand
❷ Main Lines Index	Main telephone lines Population	Main telephone lines per capita	Sweden
❸ Electronics Production Index	Revenue from electronics production GDP	Share of electronics revenue in GDP	Ireland
❹ Electronics Consumption Index	Market for electronic products GDP	Per capita 'consumption' of electronics as a share of GDP per capita	Ireland
❺ Technical Graduates Index	Graduates in Computer Science and Maths plus all levels of Engineering Population	Total graduates per 1,000 population	The Netherlands
❻ Literacy Share	Percentage of population that is literate	Simple percentage	None (100% taken as 100)
❼ Internet Hosts Index	Number of Internet hosts Population	Internet hosts per 1,000 population	Denmark
❽ Television Set Index	Number of television sets Population	Number of television sets per 100 population	United Kingdom

Japan have higher numbers of television receivers per 100 population. The relative specialisation of the countries in electronics production is reasonably well reflected in the index values. The relatively high consumption value for the United Kingdom parallels its development as a leading European site for electronics production and foreign investment with the United States and Japan. This is because the 'consumption' measure includes the market for intermediate goods (used in the production of final electronic products). Ireland, the country taken as 100 for both the consumption and production indices, has a greater specialisation in electronics (relative to the total size of its economy) than any of the countries reported in Table 2.13. Like England, Ireland is an important site for foreign direct investment and has developed a strong specialisation in electronics assembly which increases the 'consumption' indicator.

TABLE 2.13 – INDEX VALUES FOR INDUSTRIALISED COUNTRIES

Index values for	France	Germany	UK	US	Japan
Personal Computers	60	74	60	147	68
Main Lines	82	72	74	92	72
Electronics Production	19	19	27	32	44
Electronics Consumption	32	32	46	54	43
Technical Graduates	114	87	165	104	121
Literacy	n.a.	n.a.	n.a.	n.a.	n.a.
Internet Hosts	27	60	78	238	22
Television Sets	95	90	100	127	101

Source: Computed from *ITU STARS Database* (1996); Elsevier (1996); and UNESCO (1995).

The graphs of the footprints are developed by connecting the available data points for the index values calculated for each country. Figure 2.9 demonstrates how these graphs are constructed. At the centre of the diagram, the value of each of the indices is zero and at the boundary of the circle the value is 100. The values for literacy are noted and correspond to the other indices. In the centre of the diagram is a small circle which is used as a means of graphing very low values (that is, less than five out of 100). When a line goes inside this circle, the corresponding

FIGURE 2.9 – GRAPHING METHOD FOR FOOTPRINT ANALYSES

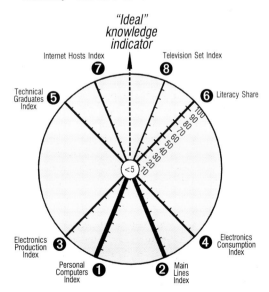

FIGURE 2.10 – REPUBLIC OF KOREA AND THAILAND FOOTPRINTS

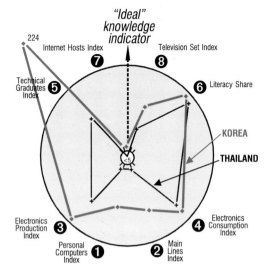

Source: Based on indices computed from *ITU STARS Database* (1996), Elsevier (1996) and UNESCO (1995), by the method described above.

FIGURE 2.11 – CHINA AND INDIA FOOTPRINTS

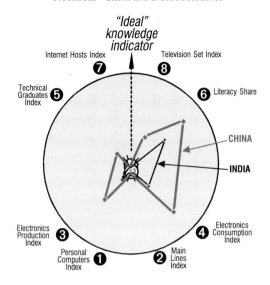

Source: Based on indices computed from *ITU STARS Database* (1996), Elsevier (1996) and UNESCO (1995), by the method described above.

value of the index is less than five. Throughout, the 'Ideal Knowledge Indicator' is included to signify that this analysis is provisional. Better measures of the knowledge consequences of infrastructure, experience, and skills are needed. In the following diagrams the scales are removed to enhance readability.

In Figure 2.10 the footprint analysis is used to compare the Republic of Korea and Thailand. These countries are

often referred to as members of the First and Second Tier NIEs. Both countries have a relatively high degree of specialisation in electronics production and consumption as indicated by the relatively high (over 50) values of these indexes. The narrower gap between the consumption indicators reflects the fact that Thailand continues to perform a substantial amount of electronics assembly, and imported components are included in the 'market'

FIGURE 2.12 – RUSSIA AND BRAZIL FOOTPRINTS

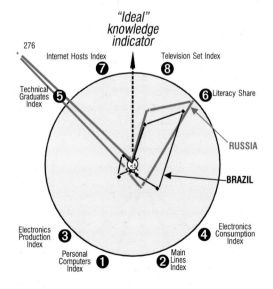

Source: Based on indices computed from *ITU STARS Database* (1996), Elsevier (1996) and UNESCO (1995), by the method described above.

FIGURE 2.13 – POLAND AND SPAIN FOOTPRINTS

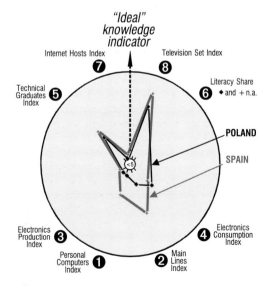

Note: n.a. = data not available.
Source: Based on indices computed from *ITU STARS Database* (1996), Elsevier (1996) and UNESCO (1995), by the method described above

FIGURE 2.14 - TURKEY AND SOUTH AFRICA FOOTPRINTS

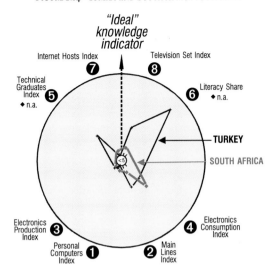

FIGURE 2.15 - PHILIPPINES AND PUERTO RICO FOOTPRINTS

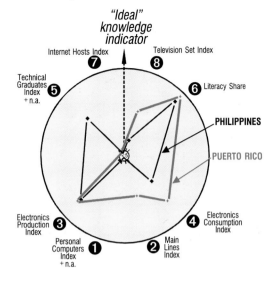

Note: n.a. = data not available.
Source: Based on indices computed from *ITU STARS Database* (1996), Elsevier (1996) and UNESCO (1995), by the method described above.

Note: n.a. = data not available.
Source: Based on indices computed from *ITU STARS Database* (1996), Elsevier (1996) and UNESCO (1995), by the method described above.

size figures that are based on revenues.[24] An important feature of the footprint is the far greater infrastructure development that has occurred in the Republic of Korea as the result of its longer history of industrialisation and higher income (Hong 1997). The Republic of Korea is also advantaged by having a very high number of technical graduates relative to its population, a rate over twice that of the Netherlands, a country with relatively strong technical education among developed countries (compare the developed countries reported in Table 2.13). The relative strength of the Republic of Korea in these areas highlights the achievements of Thailand in constructing its electronics production capabilities.

The footprint analysis can be applied to the case of large developing countries. In Figure 2.11, China and India are mapped. In this comparison, virtually the only strength that India brings to the ICT-related development of its knowledge society is its relatively literate population. China is making major strides despite the fact that its very large additions to the infrastructure are insufficient to bring its performance on this indicator very much above that of India. This reflects the enormous scale of infrastructure improvement that will be required for 'catch up' in the larger developing countries. Despite the continuing weakness of its infrastructure across its huge population, China is making major strides in developing the electronics sectors of its economy. One reflection of this is the strong diffusion of consumer electronics including television.

Figures 2.12 and 2.13 illustrate that the footprint technique can suggest similarities between countries which are not often compared with one another. In Figure 2.12, Russia

and Brazil look remarkably similar. This is significant because, historically, it has been common to compare Brazil with Korea. A comparison of Figures 2.10 and 2.12 indicates that Korea has forged ahead in virtually every indicator employed in the footprint analysis. In Figure 2.12, the most significant difference between Brazil and Russia is the extent of technical education. The inability to translate this high level of technical education into any other indicator of knowledge societies development is striking and reflects the enormity of Russia's transition challenge. For Brazil, the relatively low levels of infrastructure development may be contributing to the difficulties in developing further specialisation in electronics.

Figure 2.13 compares Poland and Spain, another two countries that are not often directly compared with one another. Here, there is even greater similarity except in the extent of infrastructure development. It seems that Poland and Spain face very similar challenges in development of the ICT foundations for building their knowledge societies. They also bring very similar assets to the task in terms of technical graduates.

Developing countries and territories at low levels are compared in Figure 2.14 (Turkey and South Africa), and at medium levels in Figure 2.15 (Philippines and Puerto Rico) of ICT development. In terms of electronics consumption experience, South Africa is leading Turkey, but both countries have relatively weak infrastructure development and very little specialisation in electronic production. Turkey has the opportunity to employ its relatively high number of technical graduates. However, as in the case of Russia, technical graduates alone cannot create a strong electronics capability. These people

FIGURE 2.16 - AUSTRALIA AND MALAYSIA FOOTPRINTS

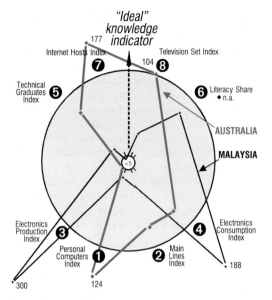

Note: n.a. = data not available.
Source: Based on indices computed from *ITU STARS Database* (1996), Elsevier (1996) and UNESCO (1995), by the method described above.

cannot contribute their skills directly to the construction of knowledge-based activities.

Figure 2.15 illustrates the similarity between the Philippines and Puerto Rico on several important measures. What distinguishes these two economies, whose income per capita is very different, is the extent of Puerto Rico's infrastructure development. This is a feature, along with its proximity to the United States, that has aided its electronics industry development. Despite this, the Philippines has managed to achieve comparable levels of electronics specialisation. A more negative view of this situation is that the Philippines economy's weakness in other sectors is responsible for its comparable specialisation in electronics, where much of the industry continues to be based upon assembly operations.

Finally, Figure 2.16 demonstrates that there is some value in considering the Internet Hosts Index as a measure of the development of the production and consumption relationship. The two countries that are compared, Australia and Malaysia, are engaged in vastly different strategies for constructing 'knowledge societies'. Both countries are world leaders based upon several of the indices where they exceed the 100 mark by substantial margins. Malaysia is clearly following a production-oriented strategy and is among the leaders of the Second Tier newly industrialising countries. Its rate of production, three times that of Ireland, indicates a very strong degree of specialisation of the Malaysian economy in electronics production. Malaysia has succeeded in achieving this

despite relatively weak performance on the infrastructure and technical education indicators. In contrast, Australia is almost as strongly specialised in the consumption of ICTs which are being employed to build a strong information production capability. This is reflected in the very high rate of Internet hosts, the high level of technical education, and the high level of personal computer usage. For countries that have achieved a relatively high level of income, electronics production may be unnecessary to achieve many of the advantages of the 'knowledge societies'.

The footprint analysis has a number of possible applications that can lead to thought-provoking and useful insights into the development of 'knowledge societies'. What is remarkable about these diagrams is the absence of a strong causal relationship between the development of different features of ICT production and use. Countries with both relatively weak and relatively strong infrastructures are successful in developing a specialisation in electronics. The extent of electronics specialisation has a relatively weak influence on the extent of technical education, literacy, or other measures of skills and knowledge. This suggests that there are a number of possible combinations of infrastructure, experience, and skills that can be used to further develop 'knowledge societies'. It would be incorrect to conclude that these 'inputs' are irrelevant, however. Many countries of the world conform to the pattern observed in Russia, India, Turkey, and South Africa. Low levels on many of the indicators coincide with persistent problems in mobilising for knowledge-based development.

2.8 CONCLUSION - LINKING TELECOMMUNICATIONS AND PEOPLE'S SKILLS FOR DEVELOPMENT

While developments in telecommunication networks, the available skills for using ICTs, and comparative international indicators provide a reasonably comprehensive view of trends in the development of the ICT revolution, the picture is still incomplete. This cannot be remedied using current statistical sources. The difficulty is fundamental to the problem of measuring the 'output' of services from the use of ICTs for producing, transmitting, storing, and processing information. For example, even if the huge task of measuring the installed base of computers in all the countries and regions of the world could be accomplished, this would tell us very little about how they are being used. It would not tell us whether they are sitting idle, performing at a small fraction of their capacity, or at work night and day. Nor would it tell us how well they are being used, whether they are being used productively, or are contributing to confusion and disorder.

Even with the statistics available on telecommunication services, such as international minutes of telephone connection, we do not know which of these minutes are being used to converse with relatives and which are being used to arrange for the financing or production of goods and services. This is a fundamental reason for enhancing our detailed knowledge about the *actual use* of ICTs in developing countries. This will be vitally important in adding value to currently available statistics and indicators.

The indicators approach does provide a technique to focus thinking about the relationship between development and the use of ICTs. These indicators show that convergence, as a result of current rates of telecommunication investment, will enable most of the world's population to follow a path that will provide access to the national information infrastructure. It also shows that many countries run negative balances of trade in ICTs. The prospect of doing so should not discourage countries from developing the technological component of their knowledge infrastructure. The nature and extent of these imbalances should be viewed as a stimulus to local economic activity in selling and servicing this equipment and, for some countries, becoming active producers. The fact of a trade imbalance should be weighed against the gains that can be expected. Countries may be willing to take out loans to upgrade their stock of ICTs if they are confident that returns will accrue from such investments as are comparable with other possible investments. If these returns from investment in ICTs cannot be achieved, due to absence of local skills or other complementary factors, loans might better be sought for investment in other development-related purposes.

The least developed countries face the most stringent requirements in justifying investments in their ICT infrastructures. In these countries, the focus of effort is likely to be extremely important. This is because these countries cannot afford to move the major indicators very much or very quickly. For these countries, the problem is to identify the activities where the expected benefits can be achieved with limited resources, relying on spill-overs and the positive influences of these first steps to achieve greater gains in the future.

The process of accumulation for these countries is protracted, but unless they begin the process, they will have little foundation for further development. The governments of these countries and international organisations need to take seriously the issue of what can be done cheaply and reliably to begin the process of building knowledge capabilities and the technological infrastructure. If good starting points are chosen, greater social and economic benefits are likely to be obtained with a larger spillover effect. Some of the social and economic considerations in identifying these opportunities are discussed in the following chapters.

NOTES

1 $CAGR = (V_{final}/V_{initial})^{(1/n)}] - 1$. The values V for final and initial must be known as well as the number of periods over which the growth is to be evaluated. In this table the CAGR is computed over ten years and the result is expressed as a percentage, that is, the arithmetic result is multiplied by 100. The CAGR is a refinement of the percentage growth measure. It recognises that growth is a cumulative process with each year's growth building on what has been achieved in previous years. For example, between 1990 and 1995 the number of main lines in the low income countries increased from 19 to 64 million, so that the 1995 value is more than triple that of 1990. On an annual basis the rate of increase appears to be over 60 per cent if a 300 per cent growth is spread over 5 years, proportionately. However, this would fail to capture the fact that each year begins from the base of the previous year, so the actual growth rate is a smaller value, 27 per cent per year, for a compounding period of one year.

2 Braun and Macdonald (1982) provide an excellent introduction to the history and impact of semiconductor electronics.

3 For example, in the United States the majority of computer systems analysts and programmers are employed outside the computer and software industries in 'user' companies. The flow of services provided by these professionals is included as part of the 'overhead' costs of these organisations. The value of their output is accounted for in the 'value added' by the business employing them in whatever sector their employer is classified. See Steinmueller (1996) for further discussion of this issue.

4 The problem of creating an 'ideal' knowledge indicator is that knowledge is embedded in individuals and in networks of individuals in extremely complex ways. In complex work processes, the knowledge of one individual may not be a substitute for that of another and the result of a group effort may reflect knowledge (or at least competence) that cannot be clearly identified with any single individual. Even with regard to 'simple' knowledge, efforts to assess the extent of public knowledge of common scientific facts, for example, that the earth rotates about the sun, indicate that little can be taken for granted about the 'commonality' of knowledge. Knowledge of all types is gained and lost. It would be difficult to design a census for determining the stock of knowledge in a society, and whether this stock is rising or falling over time.

5 The charting technique is known by several different names including the 'spider' graph for its resemblance to the spider's web.

6 Although not all the areas included in the database are countries, for convenience this term will be used to refer to all 209 of the countries and territories covered.

7 1960, 1965, 1970 and 1975-1995.

8 Although the 1996 ITU database includes 1995, the observations for this year are not as complete as for earlier years. Despite this, one of the analyses does include 1995.

9 The number of main telephone lines in a telecommunication network is the number of activated circuits capable of carrying telephone traffic. In practice, some of these lines are used for system maintenance and internal communication by the network operator. This measure overestimates the number of business and residential telephone subscribers plus pay phones in the network.

10 This indicator was 6.9 for low, 27.4 for lower middle, and 44.1 for upper middle income countries in 1995. Sweden, the country with the highest number of main lines per 100 population, has more than 115 main lines per 100 households. The excess is accounted for by extra lines to households, business lines, pay phones, and main telephone lines used by the network operator. The last three categories account for an average of 30 per cent of main lines for all four ITU income groupings. In the low and lower-middle income countries, however, there are many countries where less than one half of the main lines is residential.

11 In economic terms, telecommunication services are often both price and income elastic, particularly in developing countries. This means that either a modest percentage reduction in price or an increase in income, will result in an expansion in total revenues. The reason for this elasticity is that public telecommunication administrations in developing countries often rely on telecommunication revenue as part of the tax base. They set tariffs at a level that will increase revenues from existing capacity rather than reducing prices and being forced to incur additional expenditures on infrastructure investment. This pattern is now changing as there is some relaxation of foreign exchange constraints and a marked increase in international direct investment in telecommunication infrastructure.

12 A possible explanation is that revenues are needed for network upgrading. Although for some years Japan has been planning a much more sophisticated infrastructure based upon extensive installation of a fibre network, most of the actual building of this infrastructure has occurred in heavy traffic areas that would, in other industrialised countries, also be constructed using fibre. As yet, there is little evidence that Japan is forging ahead in the development of a telecommunication infrastructure that could be employed in the widespread delivery of advanced telecommunication services.

13 Quintero concluded that these four indicators were of different importance and suggests the relative weighting of 4 for profit expectations, 3 for market expectations, 2 for investment requirements per unit of revenue, and 1 for taxes on telecommunication revenue. He also suggests using 'waiting times' for telecommunication service as a measure of unmet demand for assessing profit expectations.

14 Saunders, Warford, and Wellenius (1983) were among the first authors to systematically use this measure. As noted, there are serious problems in inferring that telecommunication infrastructure causes, rather than accompanies, economic growth.

15 In the case of Cuba international trade embargoes continue to affect performance

16 The definition of the electronics industry used by Elsevier is based upon eight sectors, electronic data processing, office equipment, control and instrumentation, medical and industrial, communications and radar, telecommunication equipment, consumer, and components. Each of these sectors is defined in greater detail in the source publication. One important area is office equipment, where it is clear from the size of production in developed countries that what is included is office equipment in which electronic systems are very important, for example, copying machines will be included while paper cutters will not.

17 As stated in the table note, the coverage is for 50 countries, and there is certainly some electronics production in areas for which n/a (not available) is noted on the table and for some of the countries not listed by Elsevier in the listed regions (for example, neither Luxembourg nor Argentina is included in the Elsevier data, although both produce electronics products).

18 The fact that some US$ 60 billion in exports is left over after including the vast majority of production and many of the world's largest importing countries means that the unlisted countries must be absorbing these exports. There is some room for error in this imputation. To the extent that the non-included countries are exporters to those countries that are included in the table the imbalance will be smaller. The imputed value is based upon the assumption that all internationally traded production is included in the table, that is, that the total world production of electronics was, as reported in the table, just over US$ 1 trillion in 1996.

19 For example, a significant fraction of American semiconductor imports was fabricated in the United States and sent abroad for packaging, test, and assembly operations. If there are significant profits from the manufacture of these semiconductors most remain under the control of United States firms. Until Intel's success in becoming the standard microprocessor for the majority of the world's personal computers, semiconductor manufacturers' profits were below the average profits of United States manufacturers.

20 The size of NIE exports, particularly those of the Second Tier countries, is somewhat overstated. One reason is that 'transfer prices' between related companies may be set either to avoid tariffs or to realise profits in countries with favourable tax laws. Even the more accurate international trade statistics based upon value added rather than product shipment and purchase data do not completely reflect all the

complexity in the international division of labour in electronics production.

21 *Although domestic EDP sales are only provided for a single year, 1995, if other recent years are chosen, a similar ordering of the countries results.*

22 *UNESCO's report does not cover the rate of illiteracy for many of the developed countries. It should not be concluded from this that problems of illiteracy have disappeared in the developed world but, instead, that the issue of illiteracy in these countries is only studied sporadically.*

23 *From a technical viewpoint, the graphing problems arise from the fact that a number of indicators are skewed to the right (higher values) with only a few countries having very high values. The approach chosen was to arbitrarily select the 'cut-off' point for the country taken as 100 as either one or two standard deviations in excess of the mean. The indicators based on a one standard deviation cut-off are electronics production, electronics consumption, Internet hosts, and technical graduates. No country is chosen as 100 for literacy as a number of countries have literacy rates above 95 per cent and choosing any of them would make little difference to the index for other countries. The three other indicators, television sets, main lines, and personal computers are all based on a two standard deviation cut-off for selecting the country taken as 100 for constructing the index. The index for any country is computed from the value calculated from the 'Computation used' column in Table 2.12.*

24 *The use of revenue figures tends to overstate the size of markets with lower levels of vertical integration (where a supplier sells intermediate products) compared to markets with higher levels of vertical integration (where intermediate products are transferred within a company and are therefore not recorded as revenues). The 'double counting' resulting from including revenues and the sensitivity of the revenue measure to changes in industry structure are the primary justifications for using value added in the measurement of national income. Unfortunately, while countries are interested in value added, companies are interested in revenue, so many of the available measures are revenue-based.*

AMERICA DEVELOPED
Canada
United States

EUROPE DEVELOPED
Austria
Belgium
Denmark
Faroe Islands
Finland
France
Germany
Greenland
Greece
Iceland
Ireland
Italy
Luxembourg
Netherlands
Norway
Portugal
Spain
Sweden
Switzerland
United Kingdom

AFRICA DEVELOPED
South Africa
Asia Developed
Israel
Japan

OCEANIA DEVELOPED
Australia
New Zealand

SOUTH AMERICA
Argentina
Bolivia
Brazil
Chile
Colombia
Costa Rica
Ecuador
El Salvador
French Guiana
Guatemala
Guyana
Honduras
Mexico
Nicaragua
Panama
Paraguay
Peru
Puerto Rico
Surinam
Uruguay
Venezuela

CARIBBEAN
Antigua & Barbuda
Aruba
Bahamas

Barbados
Belize
Bermuda
Cuba
Dominica
Dominican Rep.
Grenada
Guadeloupe
Haiti
Jamaica
Martinique
Netherlands Antilles
Saint Kitts & Nevis
Saint Lucia
St. Vincent and the
Grenadines
Trinidad and Tobago
Virgin Islands (US)

MAHGREB
Algeria
Morocco
Tunisia

OTHER NORTH AFRICA
Egypt
Libyan Arab Jamahiriya
Sudan

SUB-SAHARAN AFRICA
Angola
Benin
Botswana
Burkina Faso
Burundi
Cameroon
Cape Verde
Central African Rep.
Chad
Comoros
Dem. Rep. of the Congo
Ivory Coast
Djibouti
Equatorial Guinea
Eritrea
Ethiopia
Gabon
Gambia
Ghana
Guinea
Guinea-Bissau
Kenya
Lesotho
Liberia
Madagascar
Malawi
Mali
Mauritania
Mauritius
Mozambique
Namibia
Niger
Nigeria

Reunion
Rwanda
Sao Tome & Principe
Senegal
Seychelles
Sierra Leone
Somalia
Swaziland
Tanzania
Togo
Uganda
Zambia
Zimbabwe

WEST ASIA
Bahrain
Cyprus
Iran (Islamic Rep. of)
Iraq
Jordan
Kuwait
Lebanon
Oman
Qatar
Saudi Arabia
Syria
Turkey
United Arab Emirates
Yemen

CENTRAL ASIA
Armenia
Azerbaijan
Georgia
Kazakhstan
Kyrgyzstan
Tajikistan
Turkmenistan
Uzbekistan

CHINA
China

ASIA NIEs FIRST TIER
Hong Kong
Korea (Rep. of)
Singapore
Taiwan (Pr. China)

ASIA NIEs SECOND TIER
Indonesia
Malaysia
Thailand

OTHER ASIA
Afghanistan
Bangladesh
Bhutan
Brunei Darussalam
Cambodia
Korea (D.P.R)
India
Lao (P.D.R.)

Macau
Maldives
Mongolia
Myanmar
Nepal
Pakistan
Philippines
Sri Lanka
Viet Nam

OCEANIA DEVELOPING
Fiji
French Polynesia
Guam
Kiribati
Marshall Islands
Micronesia (Fed. States of)
New Caledonia
Northern Marianas Islands
Papua New Guinea
Solomon Islands
Tonga
Vanuatu
Western Samoa

EUROPE DEVELOPING
Bosnia Herzegovina
Croatia
Malta
Slovenia
Macedonia, (Former
Yugoslav Rep.)
Yugoslavia

EASTERN EUROPE
Albania
Belarus
Bulgaria
Czech Republic
Estonia
Hungary
Latvia
Lithuania
Rep. of Moldova
Poland
Romania
Russia
Slovak Republic
Ukraine
American Samoa

OTHER
Andorra
Cayman Islands
Gibraltar
Guernsey
Jersey
Liechtenstein
Mayotte

CHAPTER 3

INNOVATION SYSTEMS AND THE LEARNING PROCESS

How people in firms are learning to organise
and manage ICTs and related services

3.1 INTRODUCTION - SOCIAL AND TECHNOLOGICAL COMPONENTS OF LEARNING

A central observation about ICTs is that these technologies offer new opportunities for social and economic transformation. In the industrialised countries, these transformations are evident in the way that new forms of learning are giving rise to innovative knowledge networks which facilitate the creation and exchange of information. This chapter discusses some of the changes affecting the management of technological innovation within firms and public sector establishments concerned with the scientific and technological innovation process. This chapter is concerned mainly with questions about how people in firms and public sector organisations are learning to organise and manage ICTs. It focuses on how ICTs are affecting the production of knowledge and its distribution, and on the impact of ICTs embedded in product and process innovations in the manufacturing sectors.

Illustrations are drawn from the experiences of both industrialised and developing countries. This chapter offers insight into the process of organisational learning and the importance of user-producer linkages in building social and technological capabilities. These linkages and the learning process are changing with the application of ICTs. The organisation of knowledge production is undergoing changes which may have profound consequences for established institutions as well as for the management of organisational change. In spite of the increasing use of ICTs to enable access to formal (codified) information, this chapter stresses the continuing importance of informal (tacit) knowledge in the innovation process.

The first main section (3.2) looks at the new modes of scientific and technological knowledge production which are beginning to emerge in the industrialised countries and considers their implications for developing countries. Section 3.3 considers the growing importance of linkages between users and producers and the way these are being affected by the application of ICTs. Section 3.4 examines the nature of the learning process for people in organisations when codified and tacit forms of knowledge are combined to generate new knowledge. Section 3.5 moves on to look at organisational learning processes in the context of the introduction of advanced manufacturing technologies and Section 3.6 illustrates some of the forms of industrial organisation which seem to be related to the effective use of ICTs. Section 3.7 takes up the important issue of skills and capabilities that firms need to acquire for productive use of these technologies giving special emphasis to skills involved in the management of technological innovation. The importance of trust is the subject of section 3.8 because of its role in alliances and partnerships among organisations that are providing the basis for people to learn and develop new capabilities. Section 3.9 provides a country case study (China) of the management of organisational change and technological innovation. The final section of the chapter, section 3.10, emphasises the types of knowledge that are needed to assess technology options, select innovative ICT applications and ensure that capabilities are built up to use them effectively.

3.2 CHANGES IN THE SCIENTIFIC AND TECHNOLOGICAL R&D PROCESS

The capacity to acquire and generate knowledge in all its forms is a critical aspect of the development process regardless of how that process is defined. The type of knowledge differs depending on whether a social, political, economic, technological, or scientific perspective is adopted. For example, some models of development concentrate on raising the average general level of education of a population, others stress the importance of a strong science base, while still others focus on technology transfer, that is, on adopting knowledge produced by others. Scientific and technological knowledge plays a very important role in the innovation process. It has been argued in recent years that the way in which scientific and technological knowledge are produced is changing quite radically (Gibbons et al. 1994). If there is a fundamental change in the 'mode' of knowledge production it is likely to lead to a reorientation of R&D practices and organisation. If the changes are pervasive across fields of scientific and technological activity, they will affect the research and innovation systems of both industrialised and developing economies, albeit in different ways.

The emergence of a new mode of knowledge production has profound implications for developing countries because of the tensions it creates with respect to the viability of existing institutions of science. In adopting the form of science which predominates in the industrialised countries, most if not all, developing countries have in some way embraced their institutional structures as well. As a consequence, many developing countries may find themselves 'locked in' to a mode of knowledge production which is increasingly less relevant to their specific technological and economic requirements.

The idea of a new mode of knowledge production is multifaceted and, therefore, difficult to describe briefly. According to Gibbons et al. (1994) the key change is that scientific and technological knowledge production is becoming a less self-contained activity. In many leading-edge areas of research, several different skills are required in order to solve problems. In addition, scientific knowledge production is no longer the exclusive preserve of special institutions such as universities from which knowledge is expected to spill over, or spin-off, to the benefit of other sectors. Knowledge production, its theories, models, methods, and techniques, has spread from academia and is now carried out in many different types of institutions. It has become a much more socially distributed process. Knowledge production has always had this characteristic to an extent, but the key feature of today's 'knowledge societies' is the rapid broadening of the production process on a spatial and institutional basis. The number of sites actively engaged in generating knowledge resources is multiplying rapidly. The new mode of socially distributed knowledge production has five principal characteristics.

▌ There are an increasing number of places where recognisably competent research is being carried out. This can be demonstrated by consulting the addresses of the authors of scientific publications. Change is taking place so quickly that the full extent of the social distribution of knowledge production is probably no longer fully captured by the printed word.

▌ These sites communicate with one another and, through this process, broaden the base of effective interaction. The stock of knowledge is derived from an increasing number of flows from various types of institutions that contribute to, and draw from, the stock of knowledge.

▌ The dynamics of socially distributed knowledge production lie in the *flows* of knowledge and in the shifting patterns of *connectivity* amongst these flows. Although the connections may sometimes appear to be random, in the new mode of knowledge production they move with the problem context rather than according either to disciplinary structures or the dictates of national science policy.

▌ The number of interconnections among knowledge producers is accelerating, apparently unchannelled by existing institutional structures, partly because these connections are intended to be functional and to survive only as long as they are useful. The ebb and flow of connections follow the paths of problem interest.

▌ The socially distributed knowledge production system is growing but it does not appear to be following the institutional patterns that have characterised science in the past. New sites of knowledge production are continually emerging and, in their turn, providing intellectual points of departure for further combinations of researchers. The emerging socially distributed knowledge production system appears to be characterised by a potentially exponential increase in the density of communication.

Research practices are changing fundamentally but the changes are not uniform across the whole range of research activities. However, when the changes described above occur together, the new practices have sufficient coherence to define a new mode of knowledge production called Mode 2 (Gibbons et al. 1994). Research practices in Mode 2 knowledge production differ from those that operate in the disciplinary structure of science which can be labelled as Mode 1. In Mode 2, problems are formulated and research is carried out in the problem solving context involving a complex interplay amongst specialists, users and funders. Research continues to be carried out in universities and in government and industry laboratories, but it is also, and increasingly, underway in research institutes, think tanks, consultancies, and in small firms supported by venture capital, for example, biotechnology and software firms.

Expertise in Mode 2 is configured around a particular problem, but the expertise itself may be drawn from a much wider range of backgrounds and institutions than in Mode 1. Mode 2 configurations tend to be organised in flat hierarchies and to have a relatively transient existence. The most interesting and intellectually challenging problems tend not to emerge from within disciplines, and research findings are less likely to be reported through the channels of communication that operate in Mode 1. The new ways in which research agenda are constructed and results communicated have major implications for all universities because generally they see themselves as the guardians of Mode 1. They define 'good science' in the terms that characterise Mode 1. The emergence of Mode 2 sets up different criteria of problem definition and of excellence in performance.

The new mode of knowledge production implies special problems for research in the developing world because the institutions which support science tend to be modelled on those of a former colonial power where it was assumed that there is a separation of the production of knowledge from its application and that 'open science' generates knowledge which can be passed through open exchange. For example, in Mode 1, specific types of institutions, universities and government laboratories are seen as producers of knowledge, while firms and other public institutions, such as the health services, are regarded as users of knowledge. In Mode 1 it is often assumed that difficulties in connecting the producers with the users of knowledge should be overcome by setting up technology transfer institutions of various kinds.

But in Mode 2, much leading-edge research is carried out in the context of application. In this process knowledge producers and users interact intensively in a process of negotiation. Until this process of negotiation occurs, no research is initiated. Access to this negotiation process is mainly the result of a recognition of specific expertise. For most industrialised countries, the problem is to access this process using whatever modes of communication are feasible including ICT-supported knowledge networks. In addition, in Mode 2, there may be a greater tendency for knowledge generation to pass from organisations committed to disclosure, to those committed to appropriating knowledge for profit, suggesting a factor which may exacerbate the exclusion of researchers in developing countries.

Researchers operating in the science systems of developing countries may be at a disadvantage in accessing various problem solving contexts. On the positive side, research in the context of application (Mode 2) may release developing countries from the need to create huge establishments of human capital devoted to pursuing a research agenda that has been set by others and structured along disciplinary lines. Mode 2 knowledge production requires a smaller, more specialist, scientific establishment which is skilled at making contributions to collective problem-solving efforts. On the negative side, problem contexts are more complex and developing countries may not be perceived as having sufficient expertise.

There is a tension here for developing countries because participation in Mode 2 requires both more and less specialisation. It requires more in that scientific and technological expertise within a country must be able to accommodate a wide range of contexts. It requires less specialisation in the sense that researchers need a wide range of generic skills. This is a difficult balance to maintain and it requires the identification of teams and partnerships to enhance the prospect of generating useful research results.

There is little evidence that Mode 2 is emerging in the developing world. Mode 1 remains dominant, in part because many national economic development plans that depend on foreign aid require countries to establish the types of Mode 1 scientific institutions that exist in the industrialised world. Many donor organisations insist that developing countries continue to build up establishments to match the 'best in the West'. This is an expensive option and it is not clear that this strategy is in tune with the changes in knowledge production which characterise Mode 1.

One locus for change consistent with Mode 2 knowledge production may be the universities. Meeting demand for higher education in the developing countries in the standard way through discipline-based universities is very expensive and governments are looking for less expensive alternatives. In a situation in which demand for higher education is fragmenting, no university is likely to be able to meet this demand entirely from within its own resources. Universities in developing countries are likely to need to seek partnerships of the Mode 2 kind to support teaching as well as research.[1]

If the scientific and technological base in developing countries is to engage in effective knowledge production in the context of application, people will be needed with the expertise to work in the way that characterises Mode 2. This process may be helped by efficient use of ICTs to enable researchers in these countries to develop a greater awareness of the range of expertise that exists world-wide and the partners with whom they might effectively combine to generate new knowledge. 'Knowledge networks' are increasingly spanning national boundaries and linking researchers in the industrialised and developing countries. Those who can engage in the new mode of knowledge production and who have access to global networks at relatively low cost are likely to be advantaged over those for whom such access is unreliable or costly. All these changes in the knowledge production process, and especially the trend toward knowledge production in the context of application, mean that the scientific and technical communities in developing countries need access to appropriate network infrastructures. They also need incentives to engage in international collaboration so that they can access the vitally important negotiation processes that lead to research.

The impact of ICTs is affecting the foundations of the 'culture' of scientific and technical knowledge production (Hawkins 1996). The use of ICTs to support scientific and technological research is influencing the way scientific and technical work is organised, the way it is operationalised, and the way it is evaluated. The potential exists for ICTs to be used to encourage diversity in the scientific and technical community by permitting more people to work in their own localities, and to develop research agenda that draw on local perspectives, experiences and conditions. For this to occur, however, institutional structures must evolve in a favourable way. Observers have pointed to the potential for conflict between the scientific community's interest in open networks and industrialists' interests in the protection of technological knowledge through the intellectual property rights regime. Others have noted that ICTs themselves do not create jobs, educate people or generate new knowledge. They can only contribute to the broader processes of learning, changes in work organisation, scientific and technological education, and the quality of life.

For the scientific and technological communities in developing countries, ICT-based research networks raise issues including: the balance that should exist between the requirements of the scientific and technological research community for open access to the most current scientific information and the rights to intellectual property held by various stakeholders; how to ensure that the knowledge generating communities in all countries have access to knowledge resources on reasonably equitable terms; how to allocate the costs of access to national, regional and global networks among various parts of the scientific and technological community; and how to ensure that scientific and technological research policies are linked with those for telecommunications, education, and industrialisation.

There is little dispute that scientific and technological research training is essential for the development process. Today, 'highly efficient technologies, even low cost technologies and technologies adapted for local use, tend to contain a large amount of research based knowledge' (Thulstrup 1994: 2). This is particularly so in the case of advanced ICT-based systems. The initiation of new learning processes in the public and private sectors is a prerequisite for effectively using these technologies.

3.3 BUILDING LEARNING CAPABILITIES

The full economic benefits of information technology depend on a ... process of social experimentation and learning which is still at an early stage (Freeman and Soete 1994: 42).

The diffusion of ICTs is being accompanied by major changes in the systems of relationships between the producers and users of goods and services. These changes go beyond the changes in the mode of scientific and technological knowledge production discussed in the previous section. They reach into every branch of industrial production. Advanced digital ICT-based systems appear to be strongly associated with a 'paradigmatic' shift from older to newer modes of production of goods and services. Table 3.1 shows a comparison of the main characteristics of the older 'Fordist' or mass production mode with the emerging new ICT-based production mode. The widespread diffusion of advanced digital technologies and the availability of cheaper and growing computing capacity are speeding up a major shift in the 'techno-economic paradigm' (Perez 1983; Perez and Soete 1988).

The social and economic impacts of this shift to the new 'ICT paradigm' are very uncertain for all countries (Freeman and Perez 1988). The changes in the organisation of production in local and global markets that are accompanying this shift are occurring at different speeds and with different consequences in the industrialised and developing world. Since ICTs are only beginning to be used in the least developed countries, the social conditions and modes of organisation necessary to produce benefits cannot be inferred directly from empirical studies in these countries. The best option is for these countries to look at the experiences of countries that are further along the learning curve in the context of their own particular circumstances. Insights can be derived from the experiences of suppliers and users in their organisational settings in other developing countries.

ICT diffusion and implementation require complex interactions between technological, economic, social, and political forces and selection from combinations of innovations. Knowledge and learning capabilities are strategic resources in this context (Cassiolato 1996). The traditional literature on the diffusion of technological innovations tends to overlook the tendency for suppliers to benefit from the learning experiences of users (Clark and Staunton 1989). Recent research has shown that new

technology diffusion and development processes are closely intertwined (David and Olsen 1984; David 1985; David and Bunn 1988). Technology diffusion rates can be explained by signals that motivate firms to overcome information asymmetries and to acquire the knowledge essential for the adoption of an innovation. In many cases, advanced users help to pull through innovations and generate further innovations that improve the new technology (von Hippel 1988). Thus, diffusion and development often occur simultaneously within competitive market economies (Metcalfe 1986).

TABLE 3.1 – CHANGES IN TECHNO-ECONOMIC PARADIGM

'Fordist' Old	'ICT' New
Energy-intensive	Information-intensive
Standardised	Customised
Rather stable product mix	Rapid changes in product mix
Dedicated plant and equipment	Flexible production systems
Automation	Systemation
Single firm	Networks
Hierarchical management structures	Flat horizontal management structures
Departmental	Integrated
Product with service	Service with products
Centralisation	Distributed intelligence
Specialised skills	Multi-skilling
Minimal training requirements	Continuous training and re-training
Adversarial industrial relations; collective agreements codify provisional armistices	Moves towards long-term consultative and participative industrial relations
Government control and planning and sometimes ownership	Government information, regulation, coordination, and 'Vision'
'Full employment'	'Active Society'
Emphasis on full-time employment for adult (16-65) male workers	More flexible hours and involvement of part-time workers and post-retirement people

Source: Based on Perez, C. and Boyer R. in Freeman, et al. (1991).

Social, economic, and political selection processes linked to the diffusion process shape the use of innovative technologies. The interactions between suppliers and users, and a relatively sophisticated pool of technical skills in the surrounding environment, are important elements in the technology development process. The interactions between suppliers and users have two major implications. First, collective learning arising through inter-firm links in the early stages is more likely when open (rather than proprietary) systems are emerging. Second, the competitiveness of suppliers is linked closely to the competitiveness of the technology-using firms (Perez 1988).

The technology user as a creative contributor to the innovation process is very important in the case of ICTs. Users of ICTs in developing countries need to be able to imaginatively develop and modify the technologies they use. If user-producer interaction is essential to the innovation process, then there is a need for a growing presence of creative producers (not just users) in developing countries. Although, many developing countries, and particularly the least developed, are unlikely to play the role of producers of ICTs, the network character of ICTs means that to be an effective user, these countries do need to acquire skills and capabilities that go beyond those received through the import of sophisticated machinery and hardware (Freeman 1994). In order to become an efficient user of ICTs, firms (or countries) also have to acquire the relevant knowledge through an interactive process of learning-by-innovating. Raphael Kaplinsky has observed that, in the case of the use of automation technologies, the adoption of ICTs by firms in developing countries may be hampered by the absence of any local capacity to produce them.

... unless all, or most of the "electronic jigsaw" is in place, the systemic advantages of automation are difficult to capture. In the IACs [industrialised advanced countries], the diffusion of these jigsaw pieces is occurring for a number of reasons, including product-enhancing characteristic (as in the development of CNC machine tools), factor price considerations (word processors save on expensive secretarial time) and material savings (energy control devices). In LDCs [less developed countries], the factor price considerations are of muted importance ... [and] hence ... in some parts of the Third World only those technologies associated with product characteristics are diffusing. This obviously poses obstacles for longer-run systemic competitiveness (Kaplinsky 1988: 8).

In addition, because proximity to local markets continues to be crucial for the successful development and diffusion of many ICT products during the initial take-off period, the requirements of developing country markets are likely to be addressed only after the new technologies have matured (Cassiolato 1992).

In spite of the disadvantages facing many developing countries, a shift in the emphasis of national ICT strategies away from diffusion and toward the build-up of user capabilities is likely to permit 'user' innovation to occur. This kind of shift in technology policy has been characteristic of policies in the industrialised countries since the late 1980s: 'IT diffusion actions were in place (in the early 1980s), but they commanded modest resources and limited attention. In the latter part of the 1980s, however, the policy focus shifted increasingly to the diffusion (use) side' (Hanna et al. 1995: 48).

As a result of user innovation, ICT-using firms and institutions in the developing countries may be adopting ICTs

in ways that are more efficient than some of their more developed counterparts (Cassiolato 1992), or at least at the same efficiency level (Coutinho 1995; James 1994; OECD 1993a). For example, strong user-producer relations led to very efficient production of banking automation goods and systems in Brazil. Achieving technological capabilities through a process of innovation/diffusion fostered by user needs also proved to be cost-effective (Cassiolato 1992). Even critics of Brazilian ICT policies acknowledge that the banking automation systems developed in Brazil are less expensive than their equivalents available internationally (Frischtak 1990). Case studies in Brazil show that banks successfully incorporated specialised personnel in their business, that is, electronics engineers who gradually acquired the skills to design and implement automation strategies. Institutional learning occurred as banks perceived the importance of ICTs and the engineers acquired the tacit knowledge of banking activities. They were able to transform this tacit knowledge into knowledge embedded in ICT systems. In contrast, retail firms in Brazil regarded specialised human resources as a cost. Automation decisions were taken by people with tacit knowledge about the retail business but no capacity to maintain a dialogue with technical people, and, as a result, interaction was impossible.

The successful diffusion of ICTs involves a process of collective and multidisciplinary, and dynamic learning. This encompasses the capabilities to use and to produce the technologies since relationships between users and producers are defined at the local level. Therefore, the domestic capacity to exploit ICTs lies in the particular mix of capabilities that it is able to generate for producing or using the technology. This defines a country's potential for exploiting *learning-by-doing* and *learning-by-using* processes. The learning processes are dependent on local action related to planning and organisational capabilities, 'managerial skills and entrepreneurship', human capital development, and strategies for generating large investments in telecommunications (Mody and Dahlman 1992).

Most developing countries cannot expect to cover all the components of the ICT sector. However, this is not crucial since the components, such as PCs, are becoming standardised. The critical issue for a national ICT strategy is to assess the importance of certain kinds of user-producer linkages in key segments of the industry and to encourage selected new capabilities in these areas.

3.4 THE 'LEARNING ECONOMY', ICTs, AND TACIT KNOWLEDGE

The capacity of a national (or regional) system of innovation for building the capabilities required to take advantage of ICTs is a reflection of the nature of the 'learning economy' that exists in developing countries. Learning capacity is related not only to the sophisticated use of ICTs to access global stocks of knowledge, but to the characteristics of the communication process among people involved in the innovation process. For example:

… studies … uniformly demonstrate that the way in which technical information gets communicated to those charged with solving technical problems is neither through formal computer-based scientific information or data retrieval systems, nor through news releases or technical briefings. Rather it is through people-to-people communication (Roberts 1980: 7).

ICTs should not be regarded as a potential substitute for human skills or tacit knowledge. Nevertheless, the use of ICTs can offer an important complementary component of the national information infrastructure leading to capability building and enhanced learning throughout the economy. Bengt-Åke Lundvall and others have suggested that the current phase of economic development is one in which knowledge and learning are more important than in any other historical period (Lundvall 1996a). This is because, regardless of the current capabilities of industrialised and developing countries, in the 'learning economy', individuals, firms, and even countries will be able to create wealth and obtain access to wealth in proportion to their capacity to learn.[2] This perspective holds that 'there is no alternative way to become permanently better off besides the one of putting learning and knowledge-creation at the centre of the strategy' (Lundvall 1996a: 2).

This means that broad definitions of knowledge and learning are needed. Wealth-creating knowledge includes practical skills established through learning-by-doing as well as capabilities acquired through formal education and training. It includes management skills that are learned through practice and insights generated by R&D efforts (see Box 3.1). In the 'learning economy', tacit knowledge is as important, or even more important, than formal, codified, structured and explicit knowledge.[3] Learning processes occur within all economic activities including R&D, marketing, production, and development.

Between the extremes of generic (codified) knowledge formulated in ways that can be accessed by anyone assuming a certain level of literacy and tacit competence that can be shared with others only through social interaction, there are mixed forms of knowledge.

How do these mixed forms of knowledge change with the ICT revolution? It is conceivable that the limitations on the transferability of tacit knowledge might be overcome by embodying it in products, process equipment and software systems such as business information systems and expert systems. However, the automation of human skills has proved to be successful only for relatively simple repetitive tasks that take place in a reasonably stable environment. There is also some evidence that firms which have over-emphasised the use of automated business information systems in their decision-making processes have been less than successful (Eliasson 1990).[4]

BOX 3.1 - WHAT IS TACIT KNOWLEDGE?

Should firm A take over firm B or should it leave things as they are? To make such a decision involves the processing of an enormous amount of information and attempts to analyse a multitude of relationships between ill-defined variables. Guesstimates and hunches about future developments are crucial to the outcome. Evaluating the human resources in the other firm is a complex social act. There is no simple arithmetic to refer to (depending on future developments $1+1$ may sum up to -2, $+2$ or even $+10$). It is obvious that the competence needed in this case is not easily transferred either through formal education or through information systems. It should also be observed that the decision is unique rather than one in a series of very similarly structured problems. Attempts to design formal decision models to cope with this kind of problem will not be meaningful and the knowledge remains tacit and local. The competence of business leaders can be learned but the learning will typically take place in a kind of apprenticeship relationship where the apprentice or the young business administrator learns by operating in close cooperation with more experienced colleagues (Lundvall 1996a).

The introduction of partially automated systems does not necessarily lead to the disappearance of tacit knowledge (Nonaka and Takeuchi 1995). The main impact of these applications is a speeding-up of specific phases of the innovation process rather than any reduction in the importance of tacit knowledge. This speed up may, paradoxically, increase the demand for tacit skills because there is a greater need to analyse and to react to a complex and rapidly changing flow of information.

ICTs can be used to reinforce human interaction and inter-active learning. For example e-mail systems connecting people with common local knowledge can have this effect, and broad access to data and information for employees can further the development of common perspectives and objectives for the firm. Information can be reduced to 'bits' and put into a computer but tacit knowledge cannot be transformed into information, at least not without changing the content of the knowledge. The introduction of tacit knowledge, including shared tacit knowledge rooted inside firms or in local knowledge-intensive networks of firms, has an impact on global competition and firms are increasingly exploiting their specific knowledge assets all over the world (Lundvall 1996a).

An optimistic scenario for developing countries in the face of the diffusion of ICTs envisages a massive transfer of tacit knowledge into information systems giving these countries access to new process technologies and products developed in the industrialised countries both rapidly and at low cost. In theory, this would lead to an acceleration of the catching-up process and a reduction in global inequalities. However there are two less optimistic

Problems in manufacturing	Potential contributions of AMT
Introducing new products on schedule	CAD/CAM shortens design lead time - tighter control and flexible manufacturing smooths flow through plant and cuts door to door time
Producing to high quality standards	Improvements in overall quality via automated inspection and testing, better production information and more accurate control of processes
Inability to deliver on time	Smoother and more predictable flow through design and manufacturing stages makes for more accurate delivery performance
Long production lead times	Flexible manufacturing techniques reduce set-up times and other interruptions so that products flow smoothly and faster through plant
High and rising material costs	Integrated production management systems (MRP2) reduces inventories of raw materials, work-in-progress and finished goods
Poor sales forecasts	More responsive computer-based systems can react quicker to information fluctuations. Better database permits more accurate forecasting

Source: Bessant (1996).

scenarios (Lundvall 1996a). The first is that access to the new knowledge is limited by the absence of capabilities to master the language and codes associated with ICTs. In this case access would be gained only by countries and firms with an appropriately trained labour force. The second scenario is more complex. In this case, tacit knowledge would play a major role but the application of ICTs would speed up the rate of economic change and stimulate the need for rapid learning, that is, the development of a 'learning economy' would be essential for developing countries. In this case the strategies for organisational learning, managing inter-firm relationships, and entry into the international or Global Information Society would be crucial.

There are likely to be different approaches depending on the institutional conditions in each developing country. A strategy which attempts to emulate the success of the newly industrialising countries in South East Asia often appears to be attractive as a basis for establishing a 'learning economy' because of their economic success in recent years. However, as noted in Chapter 1, it is not clear that this experience is replicable today. Organisational learning is possible if there is a substantial movement of people between the developing countries and the countries with some experience in practising strategies appropriate to the learning economy. Even when this is achieved, however, the importance of the local knowledge base and its integration with development strategies involving the application of ICTs should not be underestimated. Successful strategies in developing countries are likely to be those which give the greatest attention to the combinations of learning strategies that are promoted and to the way ICT applications are used to complement, rather than to replace, informal learning and technological and social capability building.

Information does not just "flow". Information must be coded, decoded, transmitted, comprehended. In an international economic, S&T, and socio-environmental setting this transmission and communicative requirement is very complex and not well understood (Whiston 1997: 8).

Learning occurs on an economy-wide basis and within, and across, organisational boundaries. The following section draws lessons about the learning process from the application of ICTs in advanced manufacturing technologies. Section 3.6 looks at some of the characteristics of the industrial organisation of the use of ICTs.

3.5 ORGANISATIONAL LEARNING AND ADVANCED MANUFACTURING TECHNOLOGIES

Successful adoption and implementation of AMT requires considerable learning on the part of organisations. Whilst some of this can be facilitated by the provision of traditional training inputs, such as those offered by equipment suppliers, the general message is that a much broader spread of support is required (Bessant 1996: 40).

Advanced manufacturing technologies (AMT) refer to a 'bundle of technological opportunities which are opened up by the application of information technology but ... include in this bundle the organisational "good practices" which have emerged in parallel with IT developments' (Bessant 1996: 1). Organisational learning on a continuous basis is needed to benefit from these technologies as well as investment in hardware, software, and human resource development (Leonard-Barton 1995; Pisano 1996). The increasing globalisation of manufacturing and services is accompanied by changes in competitive priorities away from non-price factors and there are strong pressures to offer a wide range of products at low cost and of high quality. Global markets are also characterised by increased numbers of suppliers and declining trade barriers in many sectors (Bessant 1996). AMTs are expected to contribute to strengthening firms' competitiveness and the expected contributions are shown in Table 3.2.

AMTs offer opportunities to replace manual monitoring and control functions by automated processes. They enable integration by linking functions into systems, offering the potential for producing a greater variety of products, and a basis for the introduction of organisational innovations leading to greater flexibility, quality, and customer focus. They also can be used to support networking among locally and globally cooperating firms.

Early experiences with AMTs such as computer-aided-design/computer-aided-manufacturing (CAD/CAM), flexible manufacturing systems (FMS) and other applications, such as robotics and integrated computer-aided production management, have demonstrated that they must be located within a coherent business strategy and accompanied by relevant parallel organisational changes if they are to be implemented successfully.

The roles of people and organisational processes are critical to the successful introduction of manufacturing innovations. Organisational learning is the process through which organisations acquire tacit knowledge and experience. This occurs through individuals and their beliefs and actions which shape the organisation's view of the world and give rise to particular forms of action. Organisational learning involves a continuous cycle of searching leading to new experiences, the diffusion of these experiences, and the emergence of shared understandings.

The learning process also involves experimentation, experience, reflection, and conceptualisation. When the cycle of learning is incomplete, the benefits of AMTs are very difficult to capture. Many firms in the industrialised countries have been successful in completing this cycle and firms are now giving priority to the need to build a 'learning capacity' within the organisation (Cohen and Levinthal 1990). The necessary knowledge is unlikely to be available in formal (codified) form and so it cannot be acquired by formal education and training, for example, using ICT supported education tools.

The cycle of 'continuous improvement' provides a means of strengthening learning capacity through a repeated cycle of action, experience, and review; evaluations building on measurable performance parameters; the capture of information resulting from experiments; the presence of an experimental climate that does not punish failure; the display and communication of the results of success; encouragement of continuous challenges to the status quo; and the high valuation of alternative perspectives on problems (Bessant and Caffyn 1997).

Organisational learning can take the form of a simple adaptation of existing skills and organisational behaviours or radical changes when integrated production information systems are introduced (see Table 3.3). Integrated systems can reduce lead times, stimulate quality improvements, allow greater flexibility, and generate cost-savings in terms of inventory stock.

If these types of organisational learning are introduced in isolation they may result in an initial period of enthusiasm, but this is likely to be followed by abandonment. Alternatively, if the changes are introduced as part of a cycle of learning they are more likely to produce major cultural shifts across the whole organisation.

At the firm level, successful organisational learning to benefit from AMTs requires (Bessant 1996): learning and adaptation on a continuous basis; training and development to be treated as an investment rather than as a cost; time and resources being devoted to developing an organisational context which permits innovation; establishing and reinforcing a learning cycle linking codified knowledge with tacit knowledge; formal training by equipment

TABLE 3.3 - TYPES OF ORGANISATIONAL LEARNING

Technique	Description
Total Quality Management (TQM)	Collection of techniques aimed at high involvement in monitoring and assuring quality, with emphasis on zero defects, customer focus, and continuous improvements.
Lean manufacturing	Collection of techniques focused on low/no waste manufacturing. Emphasises team working, continuous improvement, waste reduction.
Continuous improvement	Techniques designed to enable high involvement in incremental innovation.
Cellular/focused manufacturing	Grouping of operations focused on particular customer/product segment. Emphasises team working and continuous improvement.
Just-in-time	Originally based on Toyota Production System, the term refers to low waste techniques aimed at delivering the right quantity and quality just in time for it to be used in the next stage in the manufacturing process.
Concurrent engineering	Early involvement approaches designed to reduce problems due to inter-functional barriers.
Supplier partnerships	Close, cooperative relationships with suppliers can yield benefits in terms of faster, more reliable deliveries, lower inventories and improved quality. Emphasises joint problem-solving, lean principles.

Source: Modified from Bessant (1996).

suppliers complemented by common understandings of why changes are being introduced; training using class-room and 'on the job' opportunities; training 'just in time' to ensure connections are made between theory and practice; and an emphasis on core skills and enabling abilities (working cross-functionally, team working, monitoring, measuring and engaging in continuous improvement). These factors in successful organisational learning are found in case studies of different types of firms across industrial sectors. They point to the importance of lifelong learning, a feature that is central to the capacity to cope with challenges presented by ICTs.

Training at the firm level needs to be complemented by continuing education opportunities to upgrade and broaden skills and enabling abilities; the provision of opportunities for experiential learning through secondment programmes; awareness programmes raising support for companies; incentives for learning rooted in local cultures and firms; the use of bench-marking programmes to facilitate the transfer of knowledge between firms and sectors; and the encouragement of new 'knowledge' or 'learning networks'. The next section looks at the introduction of ICTs in manufacturing sectors in the context of industrial reorganisation over the past two decades.

3.6 Industrial organisation for the productive use of ICTs

The 'ICT paradigm' (see section 3.3) represents a major shift in industrial organisation. In the earlier period of mass production, enterprises survived and flourished by focusing on cost reduction as the key objective. This was achieved through the standardisation of final output, the use of special-purpose machinery, the development of work organisation, and tiered managerial structures built on a fine division of labour, and arms-length relationships with suppliers. The new forms of competition entail flexible customisation characterised by volatile and demanding final markets. Firms require the capability to compete not just on price, but also on a range of other features such as flexibility, quality, product variety, and time-to-market.

ICTs are playing an important role in meeting the multiple requirements of contemporary markets. Generally, they are implemented in ways that are flexible, highly fault-tolerant, and provide the capacity for meeting diverse and complex market requirements. The preceding section has emphasised the need for internal organisational learning to make the best use of the potential of these technologies. New principles of production flow have to be introduced that support operational flexibility, such as cellular plant layouts, the use of production-pulling techniques, and kanban control systems.[5] Quality at source has to be substituted for traditional end-of-line quality inspection and re-work. In addition, 'world class

manufacturing' involves the endogenisation of incremental technical changes through processes of 'continuous improvement'.[6]

Further changes are needed in the firm's relationship within its 'productive chain' (with both suppliers and customers). The firm's inter-firm relationships become characterised by greater trust-intensity which substitutes for arms-length relationships. This involves long-term relationships with fewer suppliers, 'open-book' costing negotiations, and participation of many supply-chain firms in the technological innovation process, for example, simultaneous engineering. Extensive international experience has shown that these organisational techniques are a necessary precursor to the productive utilisation of ICTs not only in the automobile industry (Womack et al. 1990), but in a range of other sectors (Bessant 1991; Schonberger 1986). For example, it was only after these organisational techniques were adopted that Japanese automobile firms invested heavily in ICTs (Hoffman and Kaplinsky 1988).

These experiences are drawn from the industrialised countries. Are there obstacles which disadvantage developing countries in the adoption of these human resource-intensive organisational techniques?

In most developing countries production has occurred in relatively closed import-substituting markets, often in the context of significant supply-constraints. The pervasive shift towards more open trading conditions has left many enterprises ill-equipped to meet the needs of increasingly more demanding domestic customers, and especially external markets. A second factor that potentially disables the adoption of these organisational techniques in developing countries is the weakness of the supplier base, particularly for small and medium-sized enterprises. Supply-chain development is often a more daunting task. New forms of organisation (and indeed the productive use of ICTs) also require adequate physical infrastructures including the traditional roads and ports and the new 'information highways'. Finally, low levels of education in many developing countries may undermine the capacity to introduce the new forms of organisation (Jaikumar 1986).

The shift required in organisational structures and processes generally is larger in developing countries than in the industrially advanced countries. This suggests that developing countries are significantly disadvantaged in their ability to introduce the organisational techniques that are necessary in today's global markets and are essential precursors to the successful adoption of ICTs. There is insufficient evidence to make an overall assessment, but there is evidence that enterprises in a growing number of diverse developing countries are making successful use of new forms of organisation.

New forms of layout and production control, for example, have allowed a Zimbabwean enterprise to reduce its costs significantly (see Box 3.2). In India, changes in organisation on both the shop floor and especially in white collar work have allowed an electrical firm to slash its lead times (see Box 3.3). The same Indian enterprise has demonstrated its capacity to upgrade its supply chain in order to improve the overall efficiency of its productive cycle. Similar stories can be told for Brazil (Fleury and Humphrey 1992), the Dominican Republic and Mexico (Kaplinsky 1994), and for a range of other low-income countries.

These experiences of using new forms of organisation result in the emergence of what economists call a 'superior technique'. They provide the capacity not only to enhance quality and product variety, but also to reduce costs and meet the requirements of small markets more effectively. As firms in developing countries increasingly operate in open markets, it is likely that the introduction of such organisational techniques will become more widespread. It is unclear whether ICTs represent a 'superior technique' or whether they simply offer a new form of mechanisation in which (expensive) capital is substituted for (cheap) labour. If the latter is the case, this could be a reason for the slower diffusion of ICT-related changes in the manufacturing sectors in many developing countries than in the industrially advanced countries.

3.7 SKILLS FOR CAPABILITY BUILDING

The availability of appropriate skills is central to the successful deployment of ICT-based innovations that enable organisational learning. Compared to earlier technological systems, such as steam power or electricity, ICTs are unique in that they affect every function within a firm as well as every industry in the economy (Freeman et al. 1995). Even in the poorest countries, the rate of diffusion of ICTs is increasing partly as a result of the rapid growth of international electronic networking. Against this background, ICTs may offer opportunities for 'catching up' by developing economies primarily as effective users of the new technologies and services. This depends on an increase in the capacity to learn new techniques (Cooper 1998 forthcoming). The catching-up process requires certain technological capabilities in order to absorb and make the best use of the revolutionary technology. One of the most important prerequisites for building technological capabilities is the accumulation of the skills needed to use ICTs.

If the necessary human resource base is present in developing countries, this can give them an initial entry into the global economy. Changing skills requirements are altering the pattern of trade between the industrialised and developing countries and opening up new opportunities for those countries that can offer the necessary expertise (see Box 3.4). It is becoming easier to locate certain information processing services and some

BOX 3.2 - APPLYING JAPANESE TECHNIQUES IN AFRICA

Many of the new industrial organisation techniques have emerged from high-tech industries in Japan. But they can be adapted to more straightforward industrial applications, as demonstrated by results from a Zimbabwean firm producing agricultural carts. They made a number of changes in factory layout, introduced just-in-time production and total quality control, and involved the workforce in continuous improvement activities. The result was a 35 per cent reduction in costs, with higher quality and more reliable delivery.

	Before changes	After changes
TIME TAKEN TO PASS THROUGH FACTORY	8 DAYS	80 MINUTES
DISTANCE TRAVELLED BY WORK-IN-PROGRESS	3.2 KM	100 METRES
LABOUR INPUT PER ITEM	23 HOURS	13 HOURS
OVERALL REDUCTION IN PRODUCTION COST		35%

Source: Compiled from Kaplinsky (1994).

BOX 3.3 - UNDERSTANDING THE MARKET: CUTTING LEAD TIMES TO MEET CUSTOMER NEEDS

An Indian producer of low-tension electrical switch gear found that a gap in the market lay in meeting customers' needs rapidly. By changing its internal organisation and its links with its suppliers, it slashed its lead-time from 57 to 24 days, and substantially increased its market share.

ACTIVITY	1995	END 1996
		Lead time (days)
ORDER PROCESSING	10	1
MANUFACTURING LEAD TIME	28	18
WAITING TIME IN DISPATCH	7	1
TRANSPORT	12	4
TOTAL	57	24

Source: Humphrey, et al. (1998 forthcoming).

BOX 3.4 - GLOBAL KNOWLEDGE

At a conference co-hosted by the World Bank and the Government of Canada with the governments of Switzerland and the United States, the UN Development Programme and other partners asked the question: '*How can developing countries, and particularly the world's poor, harness knowledge for development, participate in the global information economy, and gain access to the new tools for lifelong learning?*' (Global Knowledge 1996).

'service components' of manufacturing production such as inventory control in low-wage economies. As a result, a substantial part of routine services, for instance data entry, is increasingly being re-located in developing countries such as India or the Philippines. More highly skilled jobs, such as computer programming, are also being re-located to these countries. It is not the absolute cost of labour that attracts transnational companies to locate their information processing work in developing countries, but the relative cheapness of the requisite skills.

The absorptive capacity based on appropriate technology related skills needs to be measured against both the demands of the international economy and the local environment where a skills base for using ICTs is even more important. Training geared predominantly to the needs of the global economy can lead to a massive 'brain drain', as can be seen from the experiences of India, South Africa, and the Mahgreb (Djeflat 1998 forthcoming; Kaplan 1996). It has been claimed, for example, that the cost of training computer programmers who have migrated from India to the United States has, to a large extent, counterbalanced the aid India received from the United States in the last decade (Pundit 1995).

The dramatic shifts in skills requirements in domestic and international markets have led to an adjustment lag, resulting in macro-economic and micro-level skills mismatches in developing countries. At the macro-economic level, the 'knowledge intensive' economy is experiencing rapid growth in information-intensive services and manufacturing and the borderlines between manufacturing and services activities are becoming blurred. For example, inputs of information-processing services have reached 70 per cent or more of the total production cost of automobiles. In this and other manufacturing sectors 'over three-quarters of the value of a typical "manufactured" product is already contributed by service activities such as design, sales and advertising' (The Economist 1996: 44). This clearly creates a major challenge for formal and informal education and training systems in developing countries.

At the micro-organisational level, the diffusion of ICTs is characterised by a transition to new types of work organisation that are giving rise to increasing reliance on 'lean management' and to outsourcing of activities. Traditional centralised manufacturing based on assembly line types of mass production are shifting to decentralised production modes based on networks of subcontractors. Changes in management philosophy are giving opportunities to the small and medium-sized enterprises that cater to the demands of national and internationally operating companies. However, the businesses that fare well under the new management organisational scenario are those which acquire the necessary business, commercial, and technological skills.

Capacity building to develop appropriate skills is a dynamic process. As technologies change at increasingly dramatic speeds, so do the skill requirements of people in businesses and in their everyday lives. Lifelong learning is becoming the essential prerequisite for lifelong employability and there is growing emphasis on multi-skilling and the ability to learn new skills (OECD 1992). Education and training systems and labour market institutions are core elements in overcoming skills mismatches and adjusting to the characteristics of knowledge production. The problems of structural adjustment are even greater for developing countries which lag far behind the advanced industrialised economies in their flexibility to cope with these challenges.

Women's training is a crucial aspect of skills availability in developing countries. Access to certain cognitive skills is becoming one of the main determinants of both productive efficiency and distributive justice. It is very important to ensure that the contribution which women can potentially make to emergent knowledge-intensive economies is fully mobilised. Therefore, the inadequacy of current training systems to meet the educational and vocational aspirations of women should be at the core of policy-oriented research in order to improve existing training for the benefit of women and their countries (Mitter 1993, 1995).

3.8 ALLIANCES, PARTNERSHIPS, AND TRUST

The skills base is central to building the competencies to manage the technological innovation process. The transformation of the skills base is especially visible in the management of very large-scale projects that are involved in constructing the national information infrastructures in developing countries. The available skills must be appropriate for handling complex products and systems integration in the telecommunication, computing, and software sectors. While the industrialised countries may be able to outsource service sector work to some developing countries, there is evidence that this will not necessarily be the case for the management and organisation of highly complex manufactured product systems (Mitter and Efendioglu 1998 forthcoming).

The production of complex products and systems (CoPS) includes high value products, capital goods, control systems, networks, and civil engineering projects for example, air traffic control systems, aircraft engines, bridges, chemical plants as well as electronic commerce systems, intelligent buildings, supercomputers, and telecommunication switching systems and mobile radio infrastructure (Miller et al. 1995; Hobday 1998 forthcoming). Large production projects in these sectors focus on systems design, engineering and integration skills. Some of the key characteristics are shown in Table 3.4.

Advanced ICT systems are essential to the coordination of CoPS projects as well as to the design of innovative products and systems. It may be that the skills required for managing and organising the production of CoPS will be retained in the industrialised countries because they are high value knowledge assets, while the skills more closely associated with back-office services and international capital flows migrate to some of the developing countries.

Questions about the whether developing countries should have the capability for producing ICTs in order to use them effectively in applications such as the design of complex products have been central to debates about the need for capital goods production capabilities in developing countries (Cooper 1998 forthcoming). Developing countries have answered these questions in different ways. However, if people are to be able to take advantage of the availability of national information infrastructures they will need the skills to manage and operate increasingly complex systems.

TABLE 3.4 - COMPLEX PRODUCTS AND SYSTEMS, AND PRODUCT ORGANISATION

Product characteristics	Complex component interfaces Multi-functional High unit cost Product cycles last decades Many skill/knowledge inputs (Many) tailored components Upstream, capital goods Hierarchical/systemic
Production characteristics	Project/small batch System integration Scale-intensive, mass production not relevant
Innovation processes	User-producer driven Highly flexible, craft based Innovation and diffusion collapsed Innovation paths agreed *ex ante* among suppliers, users, etc. People embodied knowledge
Competitive strategies and innovation coordination	Focus on product design and development Organic Systems integration competencies Management of multi-firm alliances in temporary projects
Industrial coordination and evolution	Elaborate networks Project-based multi-firm alliances Temporary multi-firm alliances for innovation and production Long-term stability at integrator level
Market characteristics	Duopolistic structure Few large transactions Business to business Administered markets Internalised/politicised Heavily regulated/controlled Negotiated prices Partially contested (markets)

Source: Adapted from Hobday (1998 forthcoming)

One means of acquiring these skills is as a result of technology transfer which is increasingly regarded as desirable to parent companies and to recipient countries. Frequently manufacturing technology transfer involves operational technologies, maintenance, and inspection of technologies. Motivations for undertaking foreign direct investment range from wanting to take advantage of cheap labour, to business partners who invest because subcontracting a production system is important. A study of Japanese multinational parent companies that have expanded their activities by investing in East Asian countries has shown that the transfer of manufacturing technologies seems to improve with the length of operation in the host country. However the transfer of very sophisticated technology and skills depends to a greater extent on the ability of local management to exert pressure on the parent company, a high share of local workers, and the managerial status of local employees in the host country (Urata 1997).

Joint ventures and other types of alliances are potentially important means of building appropriate skills for using ICTs. Strategies based on competition are giving way to strategies that explicitly incorporate cooperation. Collaborative agreements are important sources of competitive strength and the importance of collaborative agreements is growing on a global scale. The promotion of cooperation by policy-makers in developing countries is crucial if they are to cope successfully with industrial and technological change in a turbulent international environment (Hillebrand 1996).

Joint ventures involving multinational companies are an increasingly common form of cooperative arrangement in industrialising economies (Freeman and Hagedoorn 1994). Government policy-makers often encourage joint ventures as a mechanism for transferring advanced technology and modern managerial practices to local firms. Despite their widespread occurrence, the management of joint ventures has proved to be problematic because multiple ownership increases the scope for potential conflicts between joint venture partners.[7] In addition, joint ventures may not meet parent company expectations. For example, the performance of nearly two-thirds of joint ventures in the developing countries examined in one study was considered to be unsatisfactory by the managers of multinational corporations (Beamish 1984). Joint ventures will not offer a particularly effective mechanism for technology transfer or a way of strengthening skills in developing countries unless their dynamics are better understood.

Empirical studies on the successful formation and operation of cooperative relationships highlight the crucial importance of intangible factors such as trust (Faulkner 1995; Schaan and Beamish 1988). Trust is a key factor in cooperative strategies (in contrast to competition) and involves mutual obligations (Buckley and Casson 1988; Thompson 1967). An explicit focus on trust, and concepts such as forbearance and commitment, is helpful in understanding the impact of different forms of business organisation and behaviour (see Box 3.5). It provides a basis for the formulation and implementation of development strategies by national governments, companies and other participants within and outside developing countries.

Box 3.5 – Trust and cooperative partnership strategies

Over the last decade or so, interest in trust has increased dramatically as its crucial social and economic importance has become more apparent (Fukuyama 1995). In the context of partnerships, trust is a mechanism for reducing uncertainty and increasing the predictability of desired outcomes. Trust can be placed in individuals (personal trust) or in institutions (impersonal trust) and each of these consists of promissory, goodwill, and competence components (Granovetter 1985; Shapiro 1987).

Promissory based trust is the degree of confidence with which a party can be relied upon to carry out a verbal or written promise (Rotter 1967). Goodwill based trust is the degree of confidence that a party can be relied upon to engage in actions which benefit the other party or refrain from actions which would disadvantage or damage the interests of the other party. This component of trust is related to the concept of forbearance, the situation where one party to a transaction will accept a time lag between fulfilling another partner's expectations and having their own expectations fulfilled in return. An essential aspect of trust is being open to the risk of parties reneging on a deal. Competence based trust is the degree of confidence with which a party can be relied upon to have the knowledge, skills, or expertise they claim or are believed to have (Sako 1992).

Personal and impersonal trust are likely to develop in different ways. Personal trust emerges in networks in which individuals engage in complex bartering of favours to build up mutual obligations. Processes of personal trust require intensive social interaction starting with minor exchanges whereby actors test each other before moving to bigger transactions (Blau 1964; Butler 1983; Shapiro 1987). Impersonal trust develops in institutions involving well defined rules and is thus closely related to the processes of decision-making.

Trust can be examined as a central mediating variable between the *context* of the joint venture arrangement (the interdependence between the parties, competition and ambiguity) and the *outcome* or performance. The results of case studies of joint ventures in the United Kingdom and Malaysia in sectors including automobile components, textiles, and natural resource consultancy between private and public sector organisations, show that trust is extremely important (Butler and Gill 1996, 1997; Gill and Butler 1996).

▌ Partner choice and the success (or failure) of partnerships are crucially affected by trust between the parties and contextual factors. Key contextual factors are the perception of mutual benefits between the organisations and whether competition is endogenous or exogenous in the cooperative arrangement.

▌ Symbols of trust and the interpretation of trustworthy behaviour are affected by the culture of the organisations in the partnership. There are variations within firms of the same nationality arising from different historical experiences or developments. Ownership type is important since organisations from the public sector or NGOs have different cultures from those in the private sector.

▌ Personal relationships are at the core of trust between organisations. Although instability in joint ventures arises from changes in personnel and the environment, the joint venture form is better suited to the transfer of the tacit component of knowledge (Teece 1981; Millar et al. 1996).

In the ICT sector the outsourcing of software development has led to countries like India and China generating software code for firms in industrialised countries, in some cases, through joint ventures. Trust is important because customers in industrialised countries require credible suppliers. Mechanisms for enhancing trust are needed so that policies aimed at building this kind of tele-trade are successful.

In general, industrialisation strategies have focused on the macro-level aspects of technology transfer where the crucial choices are the transfer mechanisms (for example, licensing, joint venture, technical assistance), rather than on the inter-organisational dynamics and trust. Analysis of the latter micro-level issues is needed to understand the processes underlying the (un)successful transfer of knowledge, skill and ICT applications between organisations.

ICTs increase the technology-intensity of manufacturing and services because information-processing becomes more central to their production and use. Expenditure on technology for services is growing rapidly in the industrialised countries and a greater proportion of investment is being directed towards equipment rather than fixed plant and other physical assets (Miles et al. 1990; OECD 1993b). Services are users of ICTs and some are highly innovative in their use of new ICT system configurations and applications while others play a substantial role in helping to diffuse ICTs via marketing, training, and consultancy (Miles 1996).

The features of the new electronic services are affecting the organisation of the innovation process in the manufacturing and service sectors. Services present additional challenges for developing countries because the innovation process in services differs rather substantially from that in the manufacturing sectors and natural resource industries. The relationships between service suppliers and clients and the modes of service delivery are very important in the production and use of services. Innovation in services involves a learning process where firms use ICTs for more than the support of routine information processing applications. ICT-based services, such as advanced management information systems, become strategic

TABLE 3.5 – FACTORS IN ICT ADOPTION SUCCESS AND FAILURE

Core factors	Symptoms	Consequences
Institutional weaknesses	Insufficient planning	Inadequately designed systems
	Unclear objectives	Cost over-runs
Human resources	Shortage of qualified personnel	Insufficient support
	Lack of professional training	Isolation from sources of technology
Funding arrangements	Underestimated project costs	Unfinished projects
	Lack of recurring expenditure	Higher costs for software development and repairs
Local environment	Lack of vendor representation	Lack of professional to solve technical problems
	Lack of back-up equipment and spares	Implementation problems and delays
Technology and information changes	Limited hardware and software availability	Incompatible hardware-software
	Inappropriate software	Over-reliance on customised applications

Source: Adapted from Miles (1996).

assets that underpin other activities in the manufacturing process and in public and commercial service delivery. The recombination of these knowledge assets with intangible, tacit knowledge helps firms to compete in global markets.

Table 3.5 shows that the institutional environment in the public and private sectors, the skills base, the availability of financing, and the technological capabilities in the local environment, together with the rate of innovation in ICTs, are contributing factors to the success or failure of the adoption of ICT-based services.

The evidence on the factors contributing to the success or failure of the adoption of ICTs and services by firms in developing countries is very limited. However, case studies of successful and unsuccessful applications suggest that: large firms often act as drivers in the introduction of ICTs; financial service firms are the prominent early adopters; competition in telecommunication service supply has a positive influence on the rate of diffusion of ICTs; a modern telecommunication infrastructure is important for the successful introduction of ICT-based services; network externalities are important for the rate of expansion of the use of ICTs; product champions have a decisive impact on speeding the introduction of ICTs in firms; and innovative firms or individuals are important in the diffusion of new technologies (Miles 1996).

Systematic evidence on how these factors interact with the social and economic conditions in developing countries, and especially the least developed countries, is needed if these countries are to develop effective strategies for improving their use of ICTs in all sectors of the economy. The following section provides a case study of the factors influencing the management of technological innovation in the ICT sector in China. This case study illustrates how this country has developed strategies to build capabilities for using ICTs to strengthen the economy.

3.9 MANAGING TECHNOLOGICAL INNOVATIONS IN CHINA

The production and use of ICTs in China are characterised by rapid increases in the volume and range of both domestic and imported ICT products. This rapid increase on the supply side has been triggered by fast-expanding domestic demand from industrial and private users. Table 3.6 shows that the increase in the quantity of ICT products consumed over the past 15 years has been phenomenal.

TABLE 3.6 - CONSUMPTION OF ICT PRODUCTS IN CHINA, 1980-1995 (IN '000S)

Consumption	1980	1986	1990	1993	1995
Total no. of computers	2.0	190		1,014	1,600
- of which domestically produced				93	800
Communications:					
No. of office program-controlled exchange lines			13,000	35,670	70,000
No. of mobile phones			18	421	3,500
No. of pagers					25,000
No. of telephones					54,000
Internet (no. of users)				6	50

Source: Data compiled from various issues of *Computer World* (1997) and *China Computer Daily* (1997) (Chinese).

Rapidly increasing demand for high-technology products in a developing country like China has substantial implications for the management of the innovation process. For example, escalating demand is raising questions about the evolutionary path of growth, the means of technology acquisition and the diffusion processes within Chinese organisations.

The western literature on China has been concerned primarily with issues such as the process of industrialisation in developing countries (Baark 1986), how to do business with China (Adler et al. 1992), and cross-cultural issues involved in international technology transfer (Minkes 1995; Tsang 1995). Despite their contributions to a better general understanding of China-related issues, there is a very great need for interdisciplinary analyses that grasp the extremely diverse nature of China's economic, technological, industrial, and market development. Concepts such as sectoral or regional systems of innovation are useful. However, the application of these concepts needs to reflect the diversity and radical nature of China's economic and technological development. The concepts must be adapted to reflect the different experiences of China as compared to countries like the Republic of Korea or Taiwan (Pr. China).

3.9.1 The evolutionary path of rapid growth in China

Several growth models have been used to explain the evolution of ICTs in the western industrialised countries including the 'three-era model' where ICT applications evolve from data-processing in the 1960s, to information systems in the 1970s, and to strategic information systems in the 1990s (Ward et al. 1990). In the 'three phase model', the hardware constraints of the 1960s are followed by software constraints in the 1980s, and user relationship constraints in the 1990s (Friedman 1990).

In China, the development of ICTs differs from the evolutionary paths suggested by these two models. Although China made its first computer in 1958, only a few years later than the western industrialised countries, the production and use of computers were restricted to research in the field of military technologies. The production of the first computers drew upon China's large resource endowment in basic science. The first civil ICT applications were for word-processing and technical calculation and they were used in national administrative departments and in a large vehicle manufacturers.

In the 1980s China began to pursue a new ICT policy - 'Import, Digest, Develop, and Create'. ICTs were identified as a key high-technology in China's '863' plan. In 1993, the State Council set up an organisation called the Joint Meeting of National Economy Informatization to promote further development and use of ICTs.

With the opening of the country's economy and its rapid growth, the orientation of scientific and technological development has shifted dramatically from 'defence-push' to 'market-pull'. The disadvantages of the old strategy with its exclusive emphasis on basic science and military technologies have become obvious. These include the absence of technologies that can be applied as a result of the slow speed of early technology development, low cost effectiveness, and weak understanding of the market. The result has been a heavy reliance on imported goods and technologies, poor quality domestic products, and low success rates in efforts to bring superior technologies to the market. For instance, of total PC sales of 1,600,000 units in 1996, and only 50 per cent were produced by domestic companies, such as Great Wall and Legend. Most of these were sold to home users who are much less quality-conscious than industrial users.

A distinctive feature of the evolution of China's ICT capabilities since economic reform in the 1980s is the overlap of the phases of the growth models developed in industrialised countries. For instance, although Chinese organisations have yet to master the use of information management systems, the Internet has entered the market and use of it is increasing.

3.9.2 Technology acquisition by Chinese businesses

The development paths of China's technologies, such as ICTs, are heavily conditioned by past historical and political situations. For more than 40 years, the strategy of the Chinese government in technology development was one of technological self-reliance rather than imitative learning, as in the case of countries and territories like the Republic of Korea and Taiwan (Pr. China), or technological dependence, as in the case of Hong Kong and Singapore (Kim and Ro 1995). Technology self-reliance depended heavily on indigenous development as the typical acquisition mode for new technology with a strong focus on the accumulation of in-house technical capability. Consequently, China is behind other East Asian countries in most fields of commercial goods manufacturing and application technologies, although it has substantial technological capability in military satellite and microwave transmission systems (He 1997).

China has been one of the largest importers of technology in the world since the 1980s. Among the various channels for absorbing foreign technology, the Chinese government has a strong preference for joint ventures (Tsang 1995). During the initial years of economic reform, China maintained tight control over inward foreign investment. Laws governing wholly foreign-owned enterprises were promulgated only in 1986, eight years after the start of reform. At that time, the Chinese government already had abundant experience in handling foreign investment and so was more confident about its ability to direct foreign-owned subsidiaries. Other means of technology transfer, such as turnkey projects, licensing, etc., have been played down. First, importing a complete production unit is very costly and often includes components that can be purchased domestically at lower cost. Second, these approaches did not yield the know-how expected by the Chinese and failed to spread the technology. There is substantial evidence to show that licensing in isolation is efficient for transferring only older, codifiable knowledge (Hennart 1988, 1989). As China's purpose in importing technology has been to develop its export capability and to compete in international markets, interest has focused more on complex technology at the cutting edge than on older generations of technology. When knowledge is tacit, close interaction between the transferor and the transferee is required and, as a result, licensing alone is insufficient.

Joint ventures have been the primary means of technology transfer in China for four reasons: the Chinese partner has a say in the management of a joint venture; the commitment of the foreign investor to make the project a success is secured; the transfer of sophisticated technology requires close interaction; and the transfer of much-needed managerial know-how is included.

There has been a rapid increase in the number of joint ventures since the start of the reform. For example, in 1996 a Mitsubishi-Stone joint venture was initiated in Beijing with total investment of US$ 2 billion and a capacity of 20,000 8-inch chips per month. Another joint venture company, Saiyifa, was set up in Shenzhen with a total investment of US$ 7.7 million. However, the technological element of these joint ventures is low since most of the equipment needed for the production of integrated circuits and chips, etc., is imported, and the main activities of these joint ventures are concerned with the final stages of production.

There are two categories of joint venture, Original Equipment Manufacturers (OEM) and production of goods, predominantly for domestic consumption (Hobday 1995). The extent to which Chinese partners in joint ventures in each of these categories can build up their own technological and managerial capabilities through cumulative learning is an important issue for China.

3.9.3 THE DIFFUSION OF ICTs WITHIN CHINESE ORGANISATIONS

Although the Government has been trying hard to push Chinese organisations to use ICTs, the results have not been promising. Three factors need to be considered to understand this: culture, technical skills, and the management structure in Chinese organisations. First, there is a potential contradiction between the implementation of ICTs and the organisational culture in China. The 'power-distance dimension' describes the extent to which a country accepts the fact that power is distributed unequally (Hofstede 1980). Chinese organisations are modelled on the family and are operated under a highly unequal distribution of power. The application of ICTs has two kinds of impacts. The installation of information systems increases the degree of transparency and information sharing across the organisation; and the use of computers tends to marginalise older, more senior people in the organisation (Zhao and Grimshaw 1991). This helps to explain the reluctance of some Chinese managers to introduce computers and information systems.

The second factor is concerned with the lack of technically skilled workers. The labour market in China has two tiers with an over-supply of unskilled workers and a corresponding shortage of professionals and managers (Tsang 1995). The huge population accounts for the excess of unskilled workers while two main factors are responsible for the shortage of professionals and managers: higher education cannot keep pace with the country's rapid economic development; and the destruction of education which was brought about by the Cultural Revolution (1966–76). During those ten years, intellectuals were sent to farms to undertake manual labour and the universities were closed down. This shortage of technical personnel is detrimental to technology transfer and diffusion. Organisations often purchase the latest computers and information systems as their first ICT investment because of a strong desire to catch up. However, neither the skills nor the organisational structures are adequate to handle the new technology. On the other hand, technical personnel in China are renowned for their quality. A survey of joint ventures located in Shanghai found that Chinese engineers and technicians were praised by both Japanese and US managers as hard-working and creative (Stavis and Gang 1988). Also, salaries are much lower than for their counterparts in the industrialised and newly industrialising countries, and this is regarded as an advantage for establishing high-technology industries such as ICTs.

The third factor concerns the organisational structures and the lack of managerial skills. Under the previous, centrally-planned economic system, a Chinese enterprise was a production unit inside the vast planning system. Each year, it was assigned a production output quota, and all its products were sold to the state at a predetermined price. Any profit was handed over to the state and any loss incurred was automatically absorbed by the state. Investment decisions could not be made independently, and the enterprise had little say in personnel matters, including salary scales, recruitment, dismissal, etc. Such modern management skills as marketing, corporate planning, finance, and human resource management were alien to Chinese managers until the mid-1980s, when more authority and responsibility were given to them under the 'manager responsibility system'. Since then, Chinese managers have been undergoing a period of adjustment and re-training. However, this is a slow and painful process, and the lack of competent and qualified managers in Chinese organisations remains one of the biggest obstacles to promoting and enabling the diffusion of ICTs at firm level. As a result, ICT applications are generally restricted to data-processing, calculation, accounting, etc., despite some successes in other areas such as the application of computer-integrated-manufacturing systems (CIMs) (Wu 1995).

3.9.4 Building capabilities in China

The demand for ICTs in consumer and industrial markets has expanded rapidly in China but the production capabilities of domestic producers are being marginalised by foreign producers and as a result of joint ventures. The volume of production is considerable but this is mainly for home use and is of relatively low quality. Many domestic producers are spin-offs from research institutes, originally with the aim of commercialising their research results. So far their performance has been limited by lack of experience in market environments.

In the longer term, domestic producers will continue their struggle to upgrade the quality of their products, to introduce new models, and compete head-on with foreign producers and joint ventures in both domestic and global markets. The likelihood of success depends on their ability to transform basic technologies into commercial products, to form strategic alliances with other East Asian countries, such as the Republic of Korea, to obtain application technologies, and to master modern management techniques through a process of learning-by-doing. In the meantime, the majority of the current joint ventures are for OEM production. They remain the primary focus for technology transfer and have assisted Chinese organisations in the acquisition of managerial skills.

The use of ICTs in Chinese organisations is characterised by a mismatch between the highly advanced technologies that are often adopted and the low level of managerial and technical skills within the organisations. Diffusion of ICTs has been limited to a relatively narrow range of sectors and functions, and the development of ICT systems in China is extremely uneven throughout industrial sectors and regions. Most of the organisations which have intensive investments in ICTs are in the aeronautics, telecommunication, chemicals, and manufacturing sectors. The ICT intensity is much lower in the agriculture, transportation and health-care sectors. There is also a considerable gap in ICT intensity between big cities like Beijing, Shanghai, and Guangzhou and small towns and villages, and between the developed Southeast regions and under-developed Northwest regions. The problem of how to reduce these gaps remains a big challenge for the country.

This challenge is being taken up by the State Science and Technology Commission by their appointment of an international team to undertake a comprehensive review of China's experience over the last decade in the reform of its science and technology system. The team concluded that 'there is not an explicit policy in China for international collaboration in science and technology that fully embraces the implications of today's realities in technological development' (Oldham 1997: 6) and recommended that more emphasis be placed on international collaboration in science and technology in order for China to learn about other international experiences.

3.10 Conclusion - Technology choices, selection, and capability building

The scientific and technological innovation process always brings challenges for policy-makers. Decisions must be made about whether or not new technologies should be adopted. The future of 'legacy' technologies when a new ICT good or service emerges needs to be considered and the appropriate balance between the old and the new options is subtle. There are often limitations on the financial and knowledge resources available, that help in making these choices. A decision to adopt a particular technology can limit the 'degrees of freedom' of decision-makers and users in the future.

The way in which Brazil chose to adopt earth station technology for its satellite communication system in the 1960s illustrates the complexity of the technological assessment process that is needed to choose between competing ICTs and to ensure that management and other skills are built up in order to use the new system effectively (Ferreira Silva 1996). In the case of Brazilian satellite technology, the existing technical options were the continued provision of international telecommunication services using high frequency (HF) radio or submarine cables. Both these technologies had limitations. Telecommunication circuits were limited in quantity and the quality of transmission was relatively poor. New satellite communication technologies appeared to provide a solution to many of the technical constraints.

The process of decision-making leading to investment in satellite communication technology involved the recognition by policy-makers that the selection of a new technical system should be based upon a comparison of the technical features of available alternatives, and that it needed to take account of constraints on decisions originating in the domestic and international environment. In the 1960s there was a shortage of financial resources, very limited technical knowledge, and an almost complete absence of technological and institutional organisational capabilities relevant to the development of satellite communication systems. A detailed assessment of the technical and economic features of competing systems, the political issues, and the required competency base, led to the successful adoption and development of a satellite communication system in Brazil.

This Brazilian case illustrates the importance of techno-economic factors relating to the scale of investment, the level of profitability, the learning processes, the market competition expected, the speed of technical innovation, and the productivity gains. Political factors were important including the willingness of countries leading in the production of the new technology to share technological knowledge with a developing country. It was also necessary to participate in, and comply with, an emerging international regulatory regime which was affecting the design of satellite systems and the technology transfer schemes available to Brazilian firms. The technology selection process involved a high degree of uncertainty and unpredictability, but the technology assessment process gave rise to opportunities for learning-by-using and learning-by-doing.

Developing countries need to acquire capabilities for a wide range of technology assessment practices in order to encourage effective technological learning by firms. As the global economy is transformed and the locus of power and the capabilities for action are re-distributed, there is a need for associated changes in management practices, new forms of organisational learning, and to develop effective partnerships that can lead to the accumulation of both technological and social capabilities.

The generic policy remedies that are available to developing countries to improve the links between technological innovation and development priorities include incentives introduced through macro-economic policy measures, increased role of competition in domestic markets, and measures to foster the competitiveness of domestic firms in foreign markets. Policies addressed to the skills base in management, technical, production engineering, design and development, scientific research, and organisational and marketing fields are also important. Policies which generate financial resources and focus directly on building technological capabilities can be combined with those which focus specifically on building up information on the range of technological options. Access to collaborating researchers who are producing new knowledge, standards, metrics and testing advances, support for basic research, and access to external sources of technology are important, but access to knowledge (with or without ICTs) is not sufficient. The remedies for weaknesses in these areas put a high premium on clearly identifying learning opportunities, strengthening knowledge in key areas, and selectively supporting priority sectors (Lall 1995; Reddy 1996).

Although production capabilities are important for creating technological capabilities, they are not the only pathway to effective use of ICT hardware. It also is not yet clear whether developing countries need to be able to produce software in order to use it effectively. It does appear that developing countries need to be able to provide ICT application support services and this implies the need to ensure that the population has a range of skills that are in some cases very similar to those needed for the development of software (Cooper 1998 forthcoming). Informal learning processes in firms will remain vitally important as this chapter has shown. Chapter 4 turns to the institutions of formal education and their use of ICTs to enable new forms of learning.

NOTES

1 For example, a decision to establish a new degree programme in one developing country might involve four partners; one providing the bulk of the teaching; a second providing experimental sites for thesis work; a third (in the industrialised world) assisting with course design, providing some teaching, and accrediting the whole programme; and a fourth providing pump-priming funds.

2 See Lundvall and Johnson (1994); Lundvall (1996a, 1996b); Foray and Lundvall (1996) and similar perspectives such as Drucker (1993).

3 The concept of tacit knowledge was developed by Michael Polanyi in the late 1950s and early 1960s, see Polanyi (1966). For a review of recent discussions on tacit (heuristic, subjective, internalised) knowledge as compared to knowledge that can be transmitted using a formal, systematic language (codified knowledge), see Senker (1995). Note that there is debate about the distinctions between the two types of knowledge.

4 The problems experienced by IBM, whom one might have expected to master the use of advanced business information systems, illustrate the point.

5 The 'kanban' control system refers to just-in-time production systems and organisational techniques developed by Japanese companies which originally were making very little use of ICTs. Such systems ensure that work in progress is pulled rather than pushed through the plant.

6 'Endogenisation' refers to the process of creating and embedding local capacities within domestic firms through processes of continuous improvement and learning.

7 Killing (1983) recommends forming joint ventures in which one partner has dominant equity control, but the understanding of joint ventures is incomplete (Parkhe 1993).

CHAPTER 4

STRENGTHENING THE SCIENCE AND TECHNOLOGY BASE THROUGH EDUCATION AND LIFELONG LEARNING

How people use ICTs to create, acquire, and share new knowledge

4. STRENGTHENING THE SCIENCE AND TECHNOLOGY BASE THROUGH EDUCATION AND LIFELONG LEARNING

4.1 INTRODUCTION - APPLICATIONS FOR FORMAL AND INFORMAL EDUCATION

Major transformations are occurring in the formal education sector and other organisations that play a key role in enabling people to develop new capabilities. These changes are partly the result of the increasing use of ICTs as enabling technologies for education and learning. The extension of more affordable communication networks enables networks among communities of interest supporting the exchange of scientific and technical information as well as sharing knowledge about all aspects of business and everyday life. The application of ICTs is leading to more flexible learning environments. The feasibility of interactive learning (between teachers and learners, between computer-based software applications and learners, and among teachers and learners themselves) is becoming a reality for some people in developing countries. In other countries, it is a technical possibility that may become a cost-effective alternative to traditional forms of education in the future. The possibility of continuous informal education and lifelong learning is growing with the increased availability of ICT applications and creativity in their application to address development problems.

In developing countries, the potential of the application of ICTs in these areas is only beginning to be realised. For example, there are now sufficient examples of both successful and unsuccessful initiatives to allow some lessons to be drawn. The use of ICTs in support of formal and informal education offers the potential to strengthen the capabilities of the populations in developing countries with the expectation that this, in turn, will strengthen the science and technology base. However, this potential can only be exploited if the formal and informal education processes in developing countries allow people to acquire the skills that are necessary to use new technologies creatively and productively. This task cannot be left solely to the education and training opportunities offered by the manufacturing and services firms in the business sector (see Chapter 3).

Major changes in formal education systems and institutions as well as the organisations that contribute to informal learning are needed to build new capabilities. The introduction of lifelong learning strategies require that the foundations of learning be strengthened and changed. It also implies that there must be flexibility for movement between education, training, and work, and new roles for public and private sector institutions that contribute to the learning process. Questions need to be asked about whether governments are moving to conceptualise the education that will be needed. These questions include whether there is an appropriate balance between investment in skills related to the use of ICTs and in the generic competencies for participating in future 'knowledge societies' (Rutanen 1996).

The explosion of Internet activity and the increasing use of ICTs to support distance education as well as interactive learning in the classroom has suggested to some observers that these applications will help to overcome problems of cost and location in the provision of education and training. For example, the content of education curricula can be delivered on CD-ROM, on diskette, or via satellite links developing software programmes and audiovisual programming from distant centres. Video productions can be circulated more easily among local and international communities. Subject databases can be accessed remotely. In principle, education institutions and informal community-based initiatives could become 'virtual'. Many new opportunities could exist to include students and citizens in developing countries in the informal and formal education process. Section 4.2 assesses the extent to which these opportunities are becoming a reality for developing countries.

The knowledge networks that support science and technological innovation are becoming increasingly international. They are involving a growing number of types of research and education institutions, not only institutions of higher education (Gibbons et al. 1994; Ziman 1994). Recent empirical evidence suggests that in the 1990s scientific research has generally involved teams of people working in different institutions in the same country or around the world. Science and technology research networks are becoming the norm, rather than the exception. Researchers working independently cannot hope to have the full range of skills, equipment, and materials needed to carry out modern scientific research (Hicks and Katz 1996). Scientists are engaged in a continuous learning process involving the recombination of codified information and tacit knowledge to generate new knowledge. The changes in the research process are enabled by ICT applications in a wide range of fields of expertise and they require specific skills in the use and application of ICTs by the research community. The strengthening of the overall science and technology base in developing countries is closely associated with the capabilities of the general population. The broader diffusion and effective use of ICTs to address development problems requires the development of new competencies throughout all areas of society to enable the creative application of ICTs. Section 4.3 highlights the roles of trade unions, vocational training programmes, governments, and non-governmental organisations (NGOs) in encouraging learning and the build-up of new capabilities to take advantage of the potential benefits of ICTs.

Although ICTs offer considerable potential, there are questions about the potentially negative impacts of greater access to the world's stocks of information as a result of connection to global networks. If this information is to be combined effectively with local knowledge, there will be a high cost in terms of investment in new forms of education and in achieving greater computer literacy in the business community and civil society. When there are inequalities in both access to networks and in the distribution of the relevant competencies, there is a risk that the introduction of ICT applications will be divisive. Disempowerment, rather than empowerment may be the result (Hamelink 1996). As Charles Cooper suggests:

These [possibilities of exclusion] are maldistributions of income and wealth, on the one hand, and (often closely related) inequities arising from the way the education system works, on the other. The risk is therefore quite clear, that if the introduction of information technology in fact leads to important economic and social advantages, i.e., if information technologies are in that sense a "good thing", they may nevertheless reinforce an already existing system of inequalities. Indeed, if they are applied without attention to the potential exclusions which existing income distribution and educational bias may introduce, we could face an outcome where the more successfully the new technologies can contribute to human welfare at the individual level, the more decisive they may be in deteriorating the distribution of welfare and generating socially damaging exclusions (Cooper 1998 forthcoming).

The recent attempts by some of the developing countries to strengthen their education systems by using ICTs provides insufficient evidence to reach any clear conclusions about whether the benefits will include the reduction of social and economic inequities. However, the evidence does suggest that much greater attention needs to be given to the organisation of education and training when ICTs are introduced and to the associated infrastructure (for example, electricity, transport, updating and currency of education and training content, responsiveness of content to local economic, cultural, and political settings, etc.). ICT applications for education in many cases have been over-specified in terms of their technical sophistication, have been unsuited to the organisational and technical infrastructure in developing countries, and insufficiently tailored to the problem-solving environment.

4.2 EDUCATION, LIFELONG LEARNING, AND INSTITUTIONAL CHANGE

The formal institutions of education that exist today, and even many of those in the planning stages in developing countries, are becoming less relevant to the requirements of emergent 'knowledge societies'. It is important for these countries to reshape education institutions in a way that is consistent with their development priorities. There are supporters of the ICT revolution who insist that conferences and small discussion groups around computers, surfing the Internet, etc., are all that is necessary to prepare students for the 'knowledge societies' of the future. This will be a 'world in which most problems, whether scientific or corporate, are addressed by teams. Students prepare papers collectively and they can log onto networks to confer with other students located in foreign countries' (Rutanen 1996: 7-8). The experience in Pakistan described in Box 4.1 emphasises the access element.

BOX 4.1 - NETWORK APPLICATIONS IN PAKISTAN

In Pakistan, the Education Support Trust uses networking facilities (EDUNET) to provide communication access to schools, teachers, and students and access to relevant educational material on the Internet and from the Trust's CD-ROMs and database. There is a fee for obtaining electronic material from EDUNET (Byron and Gagliardi 1996).

However, others argue that the Internet carries an abundance of poor quality information. In addition, they suggest that the ICT-based learning tools are culture-bound and produced mainly by, and for, the industrialised countries: 'The dry and inhuman information will be confused with worthwhile knowledge if people are not equipped with the ability to analyse the information flow from cyberspace. We might end up in a world where instead of soul we have membership in the crowd, and instead of wisdom, merely data and digits' (Rutanen 1996: 9).

The range of ICT applications in the education sector that is being developed to tackle problems in the development context is substantial (Byron and Gagliardi 1996). For example, computer-aided instruction is being used to assist in self-learning not only in the classroom but at a distance from the formal classroom. ICTs are being applied to help overcome teacher shortages. Serving as a teaching tool for students and for teachers, ICTs are used to develop and upgrade teaching skills. In some cases, this process is enhanced when electronic communication opportunities exist for teachers, enabling them to exchange both experiences and teaching material. ICTs and network access can be used to create repositories of study materials that can be transmitted and reproduced at very low cost.

In most developing countries the education systems are resource constrained as shown in the left-hand column of Table 4.1. The right-hand column shows some of the ways in which the potential benefits of the application of ICTs can help to alleviate these constraints.

TABLE 4.1 - THE POTENTIAL OF ICTs FOR EDUCATION

Constraints	Technological solutions
Time Teaching and learning have to take place at a particular time, repeated for different groups.	Different forms of recording and storage permit access on demand.
Place The same teaching module has to be repeated in several locations. Students have to congregate in a designated space.	Communication is made possible over considerable distances. Learning can take place in many locations, including the home.
Cost Well-presented, teacher-intensive education is costly.	Although the claim is often exaggerated, the use of communication technologies can lead to economies of scale.
Age Many educational processes, structures and opportunities are age-related, favouring the young.	The new technologies can provide learning opportunities for all ages.
Dimension Much of the teaching is confined to the individual and the teacher, with limited hands-on experience and exposure to other information.	Technology can enhance visualisation and sensory perception.
Environment Learners are inhibited by many barriers: ethnic, cultural, linguistic, physical, etc.	Learning through the new technologies can be customised, drawing on the best planning and teaching resources and a wide range of illustration.
Access Much information is inaccessible (in archives, remote locations, laboratories).	The new technologies can increase accessibility by making information available in user friendly settings and formats.
Creativity and Freedom of Expression Constraints on expression, endemic in many societies, can seriously impair educational processes.	The new technologies encourage creativity and freedom of expression, by exhibiting a variety of models and learning experiences, and by-passing many frontiers which restrict the circulation of ideas.

Source: Hancock (1997).

However, each of the technical solutions in Table 4.1 assumes that resources are also invested in organisational innovations on a continuous basis. In the absence of widespread institutional change, ICTs are likely to be applied within inflexible traditional education programmes. Under these circumstances they are unlikely to become the basis for lifelong learning opportunities for many of the marginalised people in the developing world.

There is a risk that new technical solutions that are intended to enhance learning will be biased in ways that disadvantage learners in developing countries. This may occur, for example, if software-based learning materials reflect only the cultures and values of the countries in which they were produced. The vast majority of education software is produced in English and originates from the industrialised countries. There is also some evidence that the ICT-based learning environments that are responsive to women's needs differ from those which are attractive to men. In designing software-based learning products, these differences need to be taken into account (Cockburn 1985). Software products also need to be consistent with the cultures and values of students.

4.3 ICTs FOR TEACHING AND LEARNING IN THE INDUSTRIALISED COUNTRIES

There is a growing amount of experimentation with the use of ICTs in the classroom and to support 'virtual' or 'distant' education systems in both the industrialised and developing countries. In the industrialised countries, concerns are emerging that the increasing application of ICTs in education and training may result in the emergence of communities of 'Intimate Strangers' who never meet within the traditional confines of the school or workplace. As Christopher Freeman has noted:

Schools are extremely important for socialisation and communication. ... one of the major needs of the future workplace is communication skills. It is difficult, if not impossible to acquire these in isolation or purely through ICT. Not only in work but also in social and political life, communication and socialisation are extremely important. Schools have a major role in social cohesion and in national culture (Freeman and Soete 1994: 157).

Evidence is accumulating in the industrialised countries to demonstrate the importance of efforts to ensure that the use of ICTs in education does not create new social divisions, especially among school children. Box 4.2 illustrates a network that extends to some developing countries which is attempting to avoid new forms of social exclusion. The relative accessibility of ICTs in schools and the home, and differences in access among income groups, the special needs of individuals in both urban and rural areas, the handicapped and elderly, and men and women also need to be given special attention as ICT-based learning opportunities are introduced.

Since the 1970s, the introduction of computers in schools has been an objective of government policy in Europe. The European Commission Task Force on Educational Software and Multimedia has estimated that investment in Europe of around 6 per cent of the European Union's total estimated expenditure on education in 1994 is needed to reach its targets for providing adequate access to computers in schools.[1] The experience of the United Kingdom offers an illustration of the problems that are encountered as schools make greater use of ICTs and some of the policy solutions (see Box 4.3).

In the United Kingdom, as in other industrialised countries, experimentation with new applications is revealing the crucial importance of how the new applications are introduced in terms of teacher and student training and organisation and equity issues. Most of the industrialised countries, apart from the United States, are finding that there is a 'content gap' and Britain is several years behind the United States in producing appropriate content for ICT-based applications in British schools (Macdonald 1997). The United Kingdom, like the United States, and several other countries in the OECD area, sees its strengths in the production of content for the international export market.

4.4 DISTANCE EDUCATION AS AN OPTION FOR DEVELOPING COUNTRIES

World population growth poses a tremendous challenge for the ideal of education for all and, even more so, for the provision of opportunities for lifelong learning. Even in the year 2025 about 100 million children world-wide will not be in a school. In the year 2000 the young age dependency ratio in developing countries will be 56 per cent compared to 31.2 per cent in industrialised countries. The old age dependency ratio will be 8.3 per cent compared to 20.3 per cent. The youthfulness of the population in developing countries has significant implications for the demand for teachers who are needed regardless of whether formal or informal education is provided. In many developing countries education efforts are expected to be directed to incorporating young people in first and second level education (Laaser 1998 forthcoming).

In developing countries it is estimated that nearly one-third of the children who start the first grade will drop out before completing grade four. In the least developed countries, overall public expenditure per pupil declined from US$ 50 in 1980 to US$ 45 in 1988 while increasing from US$ 1,862 to US$ 2,888 in the industrialised countries and from US$ 106 to US$ 219 per student in developing countries generally (UNESCO 1991: 37).

BOX 4.2 - THE KIDLINK PROJECT

The KIDLINK project provides the means for on-line communication for children between the age of 10 to 15 in any country with access to the Internet. Started in 1990 in Norway by the KIDLINK Society, the project consists of mailing lists, web sites and real-time online chat facilities. It aims to prepare children for the global information society and to increase their awareness of responsibility for shaping the future by allowing them to interact and learn in a multi-cultural, multi-lingual environment regardless of geographical boundaries. There are mailing lists for schools and the parents and teachers of registered children. On-line activities are targeted at classroom participation within the formal education system (Berg 1998 forthcoming).

Government policies are needed which take account of the advantages of the use of ICTs in education and seek to minimise the risks of becoming overly-dependent on imported training materials that cannot be customised to local conditions. The implementation of ICTs in the education system in developing countries is often dependent on contributors outside the public sector, that is, NGOs, commercial firms, parents, and other agencies acting as donors who introduce the technology into schools. The role of private sector involvement is controversial in many countries because of concerns about the potential clash of interests between the socio-cultural values embedded in training materials and the profit-driven interests of the private sector.

Universities can be valuable contributors to the successful implementation of ICTs in the education system because of their own experience of including ICTs in their curricula and their accumulated technical expertise. When equipment maintenance and other infrastructure barriers (that is, teacher training, electricity) have been overcome in the university context, this experience can be useful for the extension of ICT applications into the lower levels of education.

Developing countries began introducing computers in schools in the mid-1980s and many now are able to offer post-secondary, and some secondary, school access to the new technologies.[2] The biggest challenge is to provide schools with the necessary equipment.[3] Once this challenge is met, however, countries are faced with new issues concerning the selection of appropriate educational content and digital products. The costs of introducing computers in education institutions on a widespread basis are beyond consideration for most developing countries, even those at middle income level. The costs

Uniquely among the G7 industrialised countries, all young people in British schools have an entitlement to use ICTs in the course of their learning because of the national curriculum requirements (Blamire 1996). From age five to 16, young people can expect to use ICTs to help them learn subjects like history and English and at the same time to develop their ICT skills in, for example, handling information, and word processing. In secondary schools there is one computer for every eight pupils. The proportion of pupils to computers is one of the highest in the world. About 20 per cent of schools have Internet access but this includes approximately 85 per cent of secondary schools and no more than 5 per cent of primary schools.

Children who have been through the education system are able to use computers to access, select, assess, and apply information. They also develop the skills and motivation for lifelong learning so that they can continue to be employable as jobs demand new skills and abilities. They acquire the confidence and attitudes essential for successful use of ICTs.

Within the home the situation is very different. One-third of children are in families with an income of below half the national average. Some technology is ubiquitous: 99 per cent of the 22 million British homes have a colour television, 96 per cent of couples with children have a video cassette recorder and 91 per cent of all households have a telephone. In two-parent families with children, 48 per cent have a computer at home. In homes with a lone parent with children this figure drops to 24 per cent. Children from homes with computers tend to dominate the use of computers in schools, requiring compensatory measures to be taken. Over 3 per cent of homes (635,000) are on-line and in 1996, 5 per cent of the British population tried to access the Internet.

In Britain public funding has been used to support a number of schemes based around multimedia. Over 35 per cent of primary schools in England and Wales are equipped with multimedia PCs and a tool kit of CD-ROMs. Three initiatives illustrate recent approaches.

▌ Schools-On-Line. With industry partnership and the Department of Trade and Industry matching funding, over 60 secondary schools have had access to the Internet for over 18 months and the evidence shows, despite problems with the technology, time, training, and costs, that the benefits have been considerable, particularly for science and languages, and in increasing motivation (Department for Education 1996). Most schools report initial concerns from staff about access to undesirable content on the Internet but in almost all cases these concerns were addressed as a result of measures taken by the schools. Using the Internet is expensive for schools; and Schools-On-Line is developing a model of public

and private sector partnership to open up opportunities for young people.

▌ Special Educational Needs Co-ordinators. A project managed by the National Council for Educational Technology (NCET) enables over 300 special needs co-ordinators in schools to communicate in a managed discussion group on the Internet. Legislation requires each school to nominate a coordinator and to deal with a multitude of needs. The model could be adopted by other agencies whose effectiveness is constrained by the cost of bringing people together and publishing guidance and information.

▌ The Department for Education's Superhighways Initiative. The National Council for Educational Technology is managing the evaluation of over 20 projects, many of which address the issues of community access and equity of access. Evaluators are looking particularly at equity issues including gender, special needs, and rural and urban schools.

Policy measures continue to be needed to reduce barriers to accessing information networks and education services.

▌ *Increasing access*. Regulatory bodies seek to ensure universal affordable access to telecommunication services and digital television. Discussions are underway to explore how a universal service obligation might be extended to education. It may be that special initiatives and regulations will apply at least to primary schools because their small size means most are not able to meet the costs of even the most basic connection to the 'superhighway'. Many schools have access to the Internet but evidence suggests that the unpredictable and high costs of using the telephone are proving a significant inhibitor to greater uptake. In crude cost terms, the Internet is 12 times as expensive as other resources for a class of 25 using the Internet for ten minutes per group of three.

▌ *Educating and training*. Economic survival in the coming years will depend on knowledge workers and their ability to contribute and add value to the information society. Any service which can be delivered over a screen and computer can reach a world-wide market of tens of millions; any site on the World Wide Web is as accessible as any other. Education, at least for some learners, has always provided a passport to employment. Training and support for teachers who provide the education and training opportunities is a prerequisite.

▌ *Changing attitudes*. Schools can change attitudes to learning, other people, oneself, and technology. With careful supervision, contracts of conduct and acceptable use policies, location of computers in public places such as resource areas and libraries, most worries about unwanted content on the Internet can be allayed.

involved in establishing a computer lab including Internet connections, for example, have been estimated at US$ 50,000 in Brazil, and this does not include the costs of training and recurring expenses. Monthly expenditure including telephone charges has been estimated to represent 20 per cent of the fixed costs (Barros 1998 forthcoming). The challenge for the education system in South Africa is described in Box 4.4.

Education by correspondence has been common in Australia and Europe since the beginning of this century, but various forms of distance teaching reached developing countries only after World War II (Laaser 1998 forthcoming). Many of these were based on radio programmes supported by printed material. Later, distance teaching institutions were established including:

■ University of Nairobi Correspondence and Mass Media Unit (1968)

■ Tanzanian National Correspondence Institute (1970)

■ Mauritius College on the Air (1972)

■ Free University of Iran (1973)

■ Everyman University in Israel (1974)

■ Allama Iqbal Open University in Pakistan (1974)

■ Universidad Estatal a Distancia in Costa Rica (1977)

■ Universidad Nacional Abierta in Venezuela (1977)

■ Sukothai Thammathirat Open University in Thailand (1978)

■ China Central Radio and TV University (1978)

■ Andhra Pradesh Open University in India (1982)

As a result of the high cost of introducing computers and an appropriate infrastructure throughout education institutions in developing countries, the introduction of distance education continues to suffer from limited access to the necessary technologies and from the poor quality of technology.

By the mid-1990s, distance teaching institutions were located in many industrialised countries as autonomous institutions (for example, The Open University in the United Kingdom, Fern-Universität in Germany) or as departments of traditional education institutions. Distance education systems are also emerging as networks connecting a variety of education providers (for example, National Technological University in the United States). Distance education in the industrialised countries tends to be a highly individualistic concept and, until recently, has been based largely on printed texts.

By contrast, in Africa and Latin America, there is a much greater emphasis on community learning and oral traditions. Group learning, face-to-face tutorials, and audio or audiovisual information are very important. In many developing countries the education system has been inherited from the colonial powers bringing centralised structures and rigidities that can limit participatory

approaches to learning. Distance education systems also need continuous restructuring and adaptation to changing needs and this creates difficulties for developing countries where resources are scarce.

BOX 4.4 - EDUCATION MANAGEMENT INFORMATION SYSTEM IN SOUTH AFRICA

In South Africa a White Paper on Education has announced the intention to create an Education Management Information System (EMIS) linking all schools and provincial education departments. The system will contain an index of need which will provide a basis for allocation of resources. The use of ICTs in schools, with the exception of well-endowed private schools, is very limited, but the government sees distance education, and media and technical services as forces for social participation and economic development for all communities. Whereas the United States penetration rate is 35 per cent for PCs in households, in South Africa the rate is only 2.4 per cent. If the education system does not take the lead many learners will simply not gain access to information resources and learning opportunities (Hodge and Miller 1998 forthcoming; Butcher and Perold 1996).

The global information infrastructure offers new access to external learning resources. Access to education networks can enable students to participate in lectures with the 'best teachers'. In theory, oral communication and learning traditions can be emphasised via video-conferencing, and group learning via computer conferencing and e-mail. Access to the Internet provides one means of connecting with these new learning resources but it is relatively costly for learners in many developing countries. For instance, for a Russia/United States joint course development project funded by foreign aid, a fee of US$ 20 has been considered too high by the participants (Laaser 1998 forthcoming).

Donor countries often provide the model for distance education in developing countries. For example, the Open University in the United Kingdom provides a model for similar institutions in many countries and territories including India, Pakistan, Thailand, Indonesia, and Hong Kong. These institutions follow an autonomous centralised organisational pattern with some tutorial services at local study centres. The two large Latin American distance teaching universities in Costa Rica and Venezuela were modelled after the European Open Universities. These models are not necessarily responsive to the needs of developing countries. In the context of education,

The Commonwealth is fast evolving into two camps: those who need and hope to receive but are constantly frustrated; and those who have and give - but what they give and how they give is influenced primarily by their own trade and international political interests and their determination to control

Box 4.5 – Centralised and decentralised network models in China

The use of networking facilities for education and research in and between schools in China is the aim of the China Education and Research Network Project (CERNET), funded by the Chinese government. It involves a nation-wide backbone, regional networks, and Internet connectivity. From an organisational point of view, there are centralised and decentralised structures. The planning of the project and the implementation of the backbone are managed by the Chinese State Education Commission whereas the management and operational control of the regional networks are decentralised. Once complete, CERNET will connect all schools, other education and research institutions in China and constitute the largest network of its kind in the world (Byron and Gagliardi 1996).

The China Radio and TV University covers a wide area due to its use of satellite and TV broadcast stations, complemented by video and audio tapes, to train primary and secondary teachers. Participation rates are high, but estimates of the number of drop-outs are equally high. The necessary infrastructure of local TV stations and study centres is provided by local governments. Due to public ownership of the broadcasting medium, few constraints are imposed on the quantity of air time but there is room for improvement regarding the teaching methods employed in the transmitted programmes (Laaser 1998 forthcoming).

Box 4.6 – Public and private sector collaboration in Costa Rica

The use of ICTs in the education sector in Costa Rica can claim to have achieved partial success. Initiated during the late 1980s by the government, the Educational Telecommunications Network of Costa Rica (STNCR) was established through a collaboration between public and private sector institutions contributing computing equipment, infrastructure, and extensive teacher training. Targeted at public primary schools in rural areas, the aim was to create a student-centred learning environment, accomplished by staff training and collaboration at all levels. Contrasting with this approach is the use of ICTs in private primary schools where computers are treated simply as another medium for acquiring knowledge. To some extent, social conflict is anticipated between students from these different learning environments.

Despite a favourable ICT infrastructure with Internet access at universities, ICTs have not yet been integrated into curricula and learning processes at the higher education level. Network connections and infrastructure improvements originated in the scientific community. The digital network, CRNet, now links the academic research community as well as some government and private sector institutions (Flores 1996).

their own funds. For the present and as far as I can see into the future, Commonwealth Co-operation if not an outright shame, is an undernourished and sickly infant and I join with those who predict perhaps irreparable damage to the Commonwealth connection (Christodolou 1992: 29).

There are numerous examples of coordinated international education programmes, but there has been little cooperation at national or regional levels in developing countries. Lessons have begun to emerge from the experiences of distance education in developing countries. Projects should mainly support ongoing national projects and cooperation should lead to administrative and organisational support for an extended period rather than one-off translations of course materials. Projects should train local staff to develop their own teaching materials to address local education needs and be related to labour market demand. They should emphasise self-organised group learning and respect cultural patterns of learning which foster cooperation and specialisation among local distance learning institutions as well as cooperation with local conventional institutions. Low cost technology approaches such as audiocassettes and print media should be used in addition to the most advanced technologies. The mass media may provide support and publicity for new programmes as well a tool for learning (Laaser 1998 forthcoming). The alternative models for implementing new programmes and the use of the mass media to broaden the reach of education programmes is illustrated in the case of China (see Box 4.5).

In the 1990s there have been major initiatives to extend distance education in the higher education sector. Visions of the 'global classroom' with opportunities for all learners are gaining currency in the press and influencing policy-makers in some developing countries. For example, the University of the World is an initiative in the United States which seeks to exploit economies of scale to provide a global production centre for tele-education products.

... in the light of the tremendous needs for both the developed and the developing world, tele-education may be the only means for long-term human survival ... From a management viewpoint, creating one or even two global production centres for tele-education to serve the entire world would be highly efficient and desirable, especially distribution, billing, scheduling and marketing (Pelton 1991: 3, 8).

Until very recently, distance education institutions were the only institutions experimenting with ICTs. However, distance and traditional education institutions, pressured by budget constraints and incentives to change, are both experimenting with ICTs. Some aspects of the learning experience in both conventional and 'virtual' learning environments are likely to continue to need to be supported by face-to-face activities if they are to be successful. If ICTs are to be effective, transformative tools for development, they cannot simply be appended to schools. In Costa Rica and Chile, for example, efforts have been made to integrate ICT applications and to provide the necessary training (see Boxes 4.6 and 4.7).

Timely and competent partnerships are needed among educators, corporations, researchers, and politicians at national, regional, and global levels to support changes in education. The responses of education systems to people's learning needs and the use of ICTs have not been nearly as creative as they will need to be. Some observers fear that formal education is losing its ability to enable the development of the specialised human resources that will be needed or to supply the whole population with the intellectual skills to be able to operate in knowledge intensive societies (Bastos 1998 forthcoming).

Preparing the young and re-adapting the adult population with quality knowledge and skills for a fulfilling and productive life in this new reality, and offering the young and the adults the opportunities for continuous learning are the biggest challenges to be faced by education systems all over the world (Bastos 1998 forthcoming).

Global partnerships are evolving rapidly in a bid to meet these challenges. They can help education institutions to become better equipped to handle education needs, but they also bring potential dangers of cultural domination and local irrelevance. This may be avoided by the careful selection of partners and through international cooperation in setting up criteria to be met by international delivery of education programmes. Some observers argue that the trend is not towards the globalisation of cultures; it is in the direction of ethnic and cultural identity and the protection of national cultures (Tiffin and Rajasingham 1995). The skills required of managers, professionals, and workers include abstraction, problem-solving, systems thinking, and experimentation - together with adaptability, flexibility, and the ability to manage complexity, and to work as part of a team. To acquire these skills, learning-to-learn is the most basic skill that must be developed.

Unfortunately, many of the networks that exist today in support of education and learning, support only one-way communication as in the case of the Latin American experience in Box 4.8. In addition, some programmes offer little or no opportunity for interaction during the learning process although there are many variations. Even if these shortcomings could be overcome, the costs of maintaining communication links are a substantial burden for many education institutions in developing countries. The content and organisation of distance learning programmes need careful consideration to ensure that they do not reproduce the traditional education models which are themselves becoming inflexible and unresponsive to the needs of learners in the industrialised countries. Many of the new initiatives concentrate on high level teaching and research. These need to be complemented by initiatives that address literacy across the populations in developing countries where, particularly in the least developed, literacy rates are very low as compared to over 90 per cent in the industrialised countries, the newly industrialising countries of Asia, and some of the economies in transition (see Chapter 2).

BOX 4.7 - NETWORKS FOR EDUCATION IN CHILE

The Link Project (Proyecto Enlaces) in Chile connects teachers of basic and secondary education to improve their teaching methods and to encourage collaborative projects between schools. Apart from the necessary equipment for electronic communication, and educational software, the teachers receive training in person and through self-study material. Run as a collaboration between the Ministry of Education and universities, the secondary education project also accommodates educational computing centres to assist with planning, support, and training in schools connected to the network (Byron and Gagliardi 1996; Institute on Governance 1996).

BOX 4.8 - INTER-AMERICA DISTANCE EDUCATION

In Latin America, CREAD, the consortium of distance education throughout the Americas, has a mission to develop inter-American distance education through inter-institutional cooperation, resource sharing and partnerships. CREAD runs an electronic discussion forum called the Latin American and Caribbean Electronic Distance Education Forum (‹CREAD@YORKU.CA›) (Bourdeau et al. 1996). A spontaneous initiative, QuipuNet, was established for Peruvians linking them to nationals located outside the country. The result is a 'virtual campus' which is run as a non-profit corporation registered in Washington State in the United States and whose member contributors are volunteers.

Classroom-based teaching in primary schools relying on radio programmes is in place in Nicaragua, Honduras, Bolivia, Costa Rica, and Ecuador. The model used in Mexico, the Dominican Republic, Colombia, and Argentina is closer to distance education where participants have no traditional education and meet in homes, community centres or schools in addition to listening to the radio programmes. The limitations of the programmes are the fixed listening hours and restricted interaction due to the one-way communication of the radio programme (Laaser 1998 forthcoming). The Brazilian Telecurso 2000 distance education programme relies on television and video equipment to reach its audience. This is complemented by printed materials and personal tuition. Employees who lack formal education are targeted. Implementation and funding of Telecurso 2000 are provided by a partnership between the FIESP, a regional industry federation, and the FRM, an institution for social and educational projects (Azevedo de Paula Guibert 1998 forthcoming).

Some observers fear that developing countries will have to discover uses for the latest educational gadgets that the industrialised countries want to sell. 'I have a bridge, where is the river', said an engineer visiting a developing country in the past (Murphy 1993). Today, the engineer is often replaced by the telecommunication network operator, the satellite company representative, or the computer manufacturer who is looking for a market in overcrowded and inadequate schools. In order to avoid this scenario, developing countries need to decide when to introduce and where to place the new 'electronic bridges' (Theobald 1996). ICT applications must respond to local needs and development goals.

Although there are risks involved in using the global information infrastructure to access education materials, the risks of not doing so are high. In the industrialised countries, and particularly in the United States, the education sector is one of the fastest growing employers (Freeman and Soete 1994). If developing countries can acquire the software and related skills to produce software education products that are responsive to their local needs, they may substitute imported training packages with domestic products over time. The costs associated with this strategy are high in terms of training and skills, but the long term results could be significant. In addition, there may be opportunities for the customisation of training materials that are produced for other markets in the same region.

4.5 IMPLICATIONS OF ICTs FOR HIGHER EDUCATION AND TRAINING CURRICULA

Knowledge accumulation and the accumulation of skills for using ICTs will occur increasingly outside the traditional institutions of formal education. Learning in the workplace, and through collaborations that sometimes span the globe and at other times involve tightly knit local communities with similar interests, will become more common. Institutions of formal education, and especially higher education, will continue to play an important role. However, unless these institutions are closely linked to new ICT strategies, they are likely to slow down, rather than assist in, the task of building the new capabilities for 'knowledge societies'. The challenge for the formal education sector is especially great because of the uncertainty about what specific skills and training will prove to be necessary when ICTs diffuse more widely within developing countries.[4]

ICTs are one of the most pervasive technologies in the world, second only to 'human intelligence' or the human brain. ICTs can apply to almost anything: any product, process, system or organisational feature, from an application or development point of view. There is a theoretical and conceptual dimension as well as the information transmission characteristic, to be considered. ICTs are superseded by the human brain only in one sense - in terms of

intelligence or creativity. Even this may be removed if the field of artificial intelligence develops as some proponents forecast. The speciality of human information processing (which through pattern-recognition leads to perception) is being toppled by innovations in relation to automatic visual-scanning, voice keys and speech recognition. For example, it has been claimed that before the year 2000, the limited word-set at present capable of automatic recognition will be extended to full vocabulary range. If that stage of automatic speech recognition is achieved, a new era of computer mediated communication would be revealed. If it is assumed that wide diffusion of ICTs will occur and that developing countries will possess extensive and well-functioning higher education sectors, then there is a need to consider what kinds of skills and training will be essential.

As ICTs become more widely available in developing countries, there will be a need for a range of associated skills and training necessary to utilise, diffuse, maintain, and benefit from them. This has implications for managerial and administrative staff in higher education, and especially for those responsible for organising courses and planning curricula, for teaching and research faculty, for the students themselves, and for the wider support and maintenance staff (relating both to hardware and software).

Any taxonomy of skills and training needs must take into account the different *types* of equipment, for example, computational, data-transmission, word processing, audiovisual, database and related networking facilities. ICT equipment and facilities may range from a telephone to the most advanced satellite communication system coupled with local computational power. This may be supplemented by regional university networks and databases.

There is an enormous range of skills (and associated training) which is relevant to effective use of ICTs. The starting point with respect to existing skills is very important. For example, India has considerable software training expertise and Brazil has strong infrastructure capabilities. South Africa has quite substantial private sector and public sector (research councils and certain universities) capabilities already in place in comparison to several less developed African or Latin American countries. Cultural as well as technical capabilities must be considered in assessing education needs.

Despite the very great differences in conditions in the higher education sectors in the developing countries, there are several general observations that can be made about the requirements of students in the formal education sector.

▌ At undergraduate level, students must be able to use PCs and mainframe facilities, and understand databases and networking requirements. Engineering and science students will require more specialised simulation, experimental, and computational skills, and some will require more intimate knowledge of software programming. Arts and humanity students may require less specialised skills but they will need to be able to utilise standard packages.

▌ At the postgraduate level, many of the skills/training programmes that are implicit or indicated in the above need to be extended.

▌ If it is assumed that the international language will be either English or French, then subsidiary linguistic instruction may be needed, depending upon the language dominance of a particular culture.

▌ All of the above may require specific training of teaching faculty depending upon local conditions and facilities in the higher education sector. Whether or not this is undertaken in the home country or abroad is often a controversial issue relating, in part, to the desired rate of indigenous capability development. It is also related to the capabilities which exist locally to provide such training.

▌ Various forms of inter-university linkages generally are needed leading to the utilisation of centralised databases and international networking. This generates a need for a whole range of systems management skills and training.

▌ Cutting across all of the above are various programming and software skills, and maintenance and systems updating skills, creating a demand for more limited, specialised individual training.

▌ Many professionals require specialised training (for example, in the health, social services, government services, transport, accountancy, and agriculture sectors). The skills base required for most arts and humanities students is likely to be of a general, more universal nature, but there will be a growing need for computerised skills and training, database use and modification, for these students as well.

Many of the same skills are needed for students participating in distance learning schemes in order to use packaged ICT information supplement systems. Training is also needed in the informal education sector. As Christopher Freeman and Luc Soete have argued the balance between specialised skills and generic learning skills is difficult to achieve. They suggest that the latter have greater enabling potential.

The inherent contradiction in education is one between a broadening of the knowledge base with the aim of keeping learning options open as long as possible and specialisation with the acquisition of particular technical skills. While the latter are generally speaking an integral part of professional or occupational "skills", their introduction in education requires a much closer interaction with the labour market. Without this, the acquisition of such technical specialised skills can sometimes amount to investment in "evaporating wealth". Generalised learning, information and communication skills have a more

FIGURE 4.1 - SKILLS AND TRAINING MODES

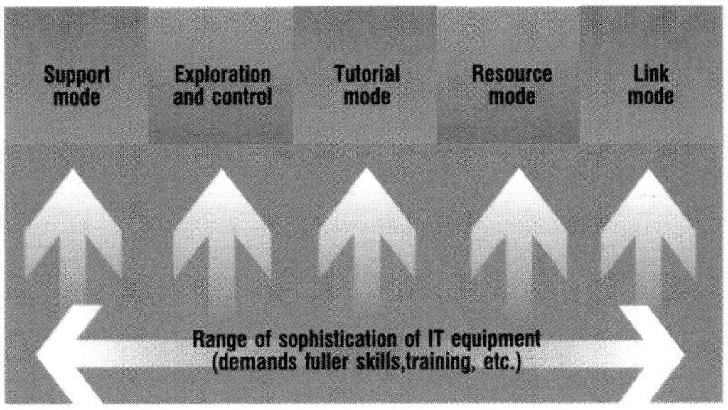

enduring value, enabling individuals to adapt to changing patters of demand (Freeman and Soete 1994: 156).

Whatever balance is selected, the functions and modes of teaching and learning also need to be considered. Figure 1 suggests that there are five basic functions or modes of using ICT resources. Each of these is associated with its own skills and training requirements.

The relationship between the function and mode of ICT use depends on the sophistication of the equipment used. For example, in the support mode, technology is used to increase accuracy and enhance presentation of work (including word processing packages, computer aided-design, and desk-top publishing), while in the exploration and control mode, the student is able to explore, examine, experiment with and build situations, for example, simulation, databases, expert systems, and statistical analysis packages. In the tutorial mode, information is presented at an appropriate level, paced with feedback (useful for maths, science, and literacy), while in the resource mode, ICTs can be used to access information and other resources (for example, Internet or off-line CD-ROMs). The link mode is present when ICTs are used for communication between individuals (electronic mail, video-conferencing, etc.) (Australian Computer Society and the Australian Council for Computers in Education 1996).

Many of the changes needed in the higher education sector could be undertaken in a piecemeal fashion. However, this would be wasteful and would involve considerable 're-inventing of the wheel'. Overly 'top-down' programmes of change are rigid and unresponsive to local needs (within a particular country), but national programmes can be instituted to good effect because they can enable coordination and sharing of experiences. An overall systems requirement for restructuring the formal education sector in developing countries to take advantage of ICTs is the setting up of appropriate coordinating bodies and training for those with responsibility for developing and implementing new strategies. This requires that people develop the managerial, strategic, and wide analytic skills encompassing a national and international dimension, and that there is both public and private sector input.

The capabilities for participating in all aspects of civil society are changing with the diffusion of ICTs. A growing amount of interaction with ICTs is becoming characteristic of the way that governments provide information and services for the public. Countries in the industrialised world are finding that the initial use of ICTs to provide timely and relevant public information services leads to a growing interest on the part of citizens in government information. There are also many debates about the extent to which the growing use of ICTs is leading to more 'direct' electronic interaction with public authorities (Bellamy et al. 1996). For example,

... PERICLES NETWORK developers and supporters argue that it is feasible to realise a system for regaining the immediacy that present "Democracy" lacks. It is possible to develop and implement a system which will allow the citizen an active and frequent participation on most matters which affect community, region, national or European Community life and policy making (Kambourakis and Nottas 1996: 2).

In the industrialised countries there is increasing debate about what kind of democracy is emerging. In the developing countries, and particularly in the newly industrialised countries where access to networks is rapidly becoming more widely diffused, there are a growing number of experiments with ICT applications to support governance activities. Many of these initiatives involve partnerships with the private sector and, in the least developed countries, the role of non-governmental organisations is growing in importance.

The application of ICTs is regarded as a way to enhance the development capabilities of countries by strengthening their governance systems. Initiatives are being undertaken world-wide to encourage more open government, to support local community initiatives, and to encourage greater efficiency in the provision of public services (Institute on Governance 1996) (see Box 4.9).

In Europe the view that the Information Society will offer new fora for public opinion formation and expression is gaining popularity. The organisation of interest groups and lobbying organisations is already benefiting as new electronic fora are opened through which citizens and interest groups can participate in decision-making processes (Arterton 1987). During a 1996 European Information Society Forum meeting it was observed that 'the information society is bringing about an enrichment of democratic life by giving citizens a new support for free expression and discussion of ideas. These new public spaces have no spatial limits (the 'global village') as do traditional fora such as public halls, churches or the market place' (European Commission 1996a: 6).

Similar developments are occurring in the developing countries. For example, the Tampines Web Town in Singapore encourages interaction between community members through the use of electronic networking facilities. Both the infrastructure and Tampines Web Town are funded by the government. The technical features include e-mail, a website, on-line booking of facilities and on-line chatting, and news groups. They also give community members access to political leaders and to information not generally easily available (Institute on Governance 1996).

ICTs are facilitating the rise of many new internationally operating interest groups as well. Some observers in the industrialised countries envisage a world divided between a minority which is connected to the global information infrastructure (some 900 million out of 5.3 billion) and a majority which is not (Stanbury 1995). ICTs reduce the costs of finding people with similar interests over wide geographic areas, communicating of large volumes of text, acquiring information, alerting constituents to a threat or opportunity, and raising funds. Highly specialised interest groups can organise and participate in the political arena. However, the skills necessary to create and engage with the emerging global interest groups reside mainly among the existing policy and economic elite. It is unclear whether the influence of these groups will grow because their increasing numbers may lead to greater competition among them and, therefore, to their declining influence on decision-making (Stanbury 1995).

The divergent views about the impact of ICTs on democratic processes and governance parallel controversies about the social and economic implications in other areas. As advanced ICTs have become more popular, high expectations about their potential benefits for society are being generated just as they were in the case of the telegraph in the 19th century and broadcasting in the 20th century. The expectations are that the new technologies will enable changes in existing ways of organising society with a qualitative improvement. The application of ICTs can make horizontal, interactive communication processes possible and there is an enormous amount of discussion about how this will empower people (van de Donk et al. 1995). The debate oscillates between the optimistic view that ICTs will bring the Greek Agora back to life and the pessimistic view that George Orwell's fantasy about the complete, although subtle, control of society is finally coming alive.

This debate is largely restricted to the western industrialised countries and there is little research on this topic in the developing countries. Nevertheless, the potential of ICTs for democracy in developing countries is being assumed implicitly. It is expected that investment in a good communication system and ICT applications will contribute to the development process and a 'leapfrogging' toward greater democracy. For example, during the G7 meeting in South Africa in 1996, the debates about the impact of the Internet referred frequently to a democratic South Africa, the country which scored the highest of all developing countries in Internet connectivity. However, this high degree of connectivity is the result of the sophisticated and relatively accessible telephone system for city dwellers and the white population. South Africa also built a strong backbone connecting most remote (white) areas of the country. In the 'new South Africa' there are concerns that liberalisation of the telecommunication industry will favour the urban regions and the affluent users. Of the Internet users in South Africa, 97 per cent still come from the affluent part of its society (Naidoo 1996) and the vast majority of the population has no access to the telephone. For some 40 per cent of the population (the unemployed), telephone bills simply are not affordable.

This reality means that in order to improve democracy and empower people, the physical telecommunication network must be reasonably available and affordable in terms of time and money. For example, one province in South Africa is introducing a 'one-stop-shop' concept where basic development information, statistics, and transactions relevant to citizens are being computerised and made accessible via kiosks and terminals located in communities (Hodge and Miller 1998 forthcoming).

What drives the use of ICTs in the industrialised countries will not necessarily hold for developing countries. Bulletin board services, the World Wide Web, news groups, and the other forms of electronic communication the use of which has inspired scholars in the industrialised countries to forecast radical changes in democracy has one thing in common: all these modes of communication are text-based and require a high degree of literacy. Given the high rates of illiteracy in the developing countries, improving governance systems using ICTs in these countries is likely to require a very different approach. As a representative of a South African non-governmental organisation expressed it, 'how is it possible to explain the mechanisms of a PC to people who can hardly read and don't even understand the principles of electricity due to its non-availability'.[5]

In some developing countries there is little of the information society 'hype' that is present in the industrialised countries and there is little or no 'culture' of ICTs. Education in the broadest sense has an enormous role to play here and the socio-cultural aspects cannot be neglected. In most developing countries the culture of individualistic use of communication technologies is absent because, for example, it runs against the culture of the power of the extended family. The predominant view in the industrialised countries about democratisation and ICTs, that is, defined mainly in terms of how can I serve my interests better while sitting at my desktop, is not likely to be appropriate for people in some developing countries.

The assumption that more Internet use necessarily equals more democracy is a potentially misguided one. A perfectly wired society could be an autocratic society. The difficulties the media have in some developing countries with 'freedom of expression' suggest that governments may be unwilling to 'open up' to provide more 'open

BOX 4.9 – ICTs FOR GOVERNANCE

ICTs and open government - The Canadian and United States governments have embarked upon plans to ensure that a wide variety of government documents and other material are available through electronic means. These types of initiatives raise legal and structural concerns. Transparent governance is not usually a legal requirement, and may be considered undesirable by some governments. Parameters should be defined about what types of documents are to be made public and at what point in the legislative process it is deemed appropriate to make them available (Institute on Governance 1996). While many governments of industrialised countries are developing home pages and elaborate sites on the World Wide Web (Kluzer and Farinelli 1997), few governments in developing countries have the capacity to disseminate information and documentation electronically.

ICTs and community networking - Community networking is an application that holds promise for linking ICTs to governance. A community network is a local computer-based system that allows people, and groups within a community, to share information, knowledge, and experience. These applications include systems ranging from the huge Freenets of North America (with user populations counted in the tens of thousands) to the 'telecottages' being developed in many parts of Asia and Africa. Community networks often feature public access points in locations such as schools, libraries, community centres, or churches allowing anyone to use the system (Institute on Governance 1996).

Government efficiency and economic benefits of ICTs - Governance is a highly information-intensive and expensive activity. ICTs are being seen as offering an efficient way of cutting the costs associated with generating and disseminating this information. In Brazil and Morocco attempts have been made to use ICTs to contribute to efficiency. Morocco's Public Administration Support Project uses ICTs to enhance the efficiency of its Ministries of Finance and Planning by supporting tax administration, auditing, public investment planning, and monitoring, using computers and computer modelling to assist with expenditure management, resource allocation, and collaboration between different ministries involved in economic management. Since the project began in 1989, the time required to prepare the budget is estimated to have been halved. Similar uses of ICTs have been documented in a wide variety of countries, including Colombia, the Philippines, India, Egypt, and Chile (Institute on Governance 1996).

government'. Making government more responsive to citizens by introducing ICT applications involves changing ways of governing and major changes in the political culture. ICTs may have the potential for building horizontal links in vertically organised political processes, but this is no guarantee that more democratic processes will emerge. ICTs alone cannot make governments more efficient or empower people; political will and vision are needed to change government styles in ways that will empower people. There is no single clearinghouse in which the efforts of people working with the problems and opportunities relating to the use of ICTs in the governance process can be compared.[6] Coordinated efforts at the administrative and national policy-making levels are needed if changes in the governance processes are to be implemented.

There is a need for coordinated initiatives that link people together in new ways to address development problems. For example, the Worldview International Foundation, established in 1980, has consultative status with the United Nations Economic and Social Council (ECOSOC) and the United Nations Educational, Scientific and Cultural Organisation (UNESCO). It is an independent, non-profit service organisation which focuses on participatory communication for democracy and sustainable development (Worldview 1997). Its goals are to use new communication technologies and methods in support of the environment and sustainable development via grassroots projects and networking. Training and education are central to the programme which operates a network of Media Centres in Asia, Africa and the Middle East. It claims to reach 10 million people and hopes to expand this to 100 million over the next 15 years. Projects focus on basic needs such as health and nutrition, the environment, population concerns, AIDS prevention, empowerment of women, child survival, crop replacement, and community development, and are located in 12 countries. The fundamental aim of the organisation is to support human rights, freedom of expression, and democracy activities.

NGOs have come increasingly to the fore in the last decade, particularly those which campaign, lobby, and deliver research and education around social justice and environmental issues. These organisations are beginning to give attention to how ICTs might be used to strengthen democratic decision-making in the developing countries. Their roles have increased dramatically not only in major fora such as international conferences, but also in activities that challenge the actions of public and commercial institutions, such as campaigns aimed at bringing pressure on the corporate sector and public multilateral institutions. At the same time, both large and small NGOs work across an ever-broader spectrum of community-based initiatives. These range from support for the community visioning and planning processes envisaged by *Local Agenda 21* following the Earth Summit, to the development and promotion of innovative initiatives in areas such as social enterprises, local currencies, and community-based banking, through to large-scale social service provision resulting from the withdrawal of state activities in the delivery of public services and 'development aid'.

NGOs have developed rapidly to meet these new roles and challenges. They have grown in size, become more professional, and, in many cases, moved entirely away from their original, voluntary roots towards a fully professional institutional base. At a time when many mainstream education institutions are in varying states of decay, more and more NGOs are building research capacity that combines action-research with more formal academic-style and quality work. Non-profit, civil institutions have always existed in all countries representing key groups in order to bring particular issues to the public notice. What has changed is that NGOs are doing work that is now seen as an integral part of the formal process of societal governance. It is increasingly unthinkable that a major piece of legislation could be passed in many developing countries without it being seen that 'consultation with the NGOs' had taken place. In some countries NGOs are seen as the most important actors for securing social justice and ensuring that responses to environmental vandalism are put in place. Their role in linking communities of ICT users is also growing in importance especially as new coalitions come to the fore and build partnerships.

The commercial sector, particularly the large-scale corporate sector, is assumed to have a major role in moulding societies at local, national, and international levels. However, there is growing concern over the degree of power that the corporate sector has and the growing inability or unwillingness of the public sector to mediate much-needed new social contracts. NGOs are seen as having a key role in mediating such new social contracts. They are well-positioned to mediate in decisions about the introduction and use of ICTs because of their ability to mobilise citizens through consumer action. NGOs are contributing to the process of reinventing the 'welfare state', offering insights into innovative ways of using ICTs to mobilise action, and playing an integral part in constructing the 'knowledge societies' in the developing world.

4.7 CONCLUSION - ICTs CONTRIBUTING TO SOCIAL INCLUSION

How ICTs can be most effective will depend upon the context in each developing country. Access to ICT-based education and training is only part of the challenge. The new ICT-based systems need to be maintained and the gaps between pedagogy and technology will need to be bridged (Patel 1997; Hall 1987). The content and styles of learning embedded in ICT-based learning resources are as important as investment in infrastructure (telecommunications and computing). The usefulness of ICTs in education is evident in overcoming obstacles such as geographic remoteness and scarcity of teachers. But there are major problems associated with ICT use in developing countries. Cost is an inhibiting factor in terms of the expense of hardware and software, maintenance, and infrastructure costs, including electricity (see Box 4.10) to support new knowledge networks.

Conflicting agenda with regard to the content of education curricula may arise as a result of private sector involvement in compiling software and multimedia-based teaching tools. In developing countries there are also concerns about the cultural and linguistic dominance of the Western, English-speaking world on the Internet and in the content of available teaching material. Collaboration between education professionals and commercial organisations producing content particularly for distance learning needs to be carefully managed to ensure that standards are not compromised by profit-seeking ambitions, and that content is customised to local needs.

The proficiency of teachers in using ICTs to enable them to integrate ICT-based content effectively into the curricula is an essential consideration. The large investment in terms of capital, time, and research that is needed to achieve this often clashes with the basic requirement of ensuring an adequately equipped teaching staff. The steep learning curve for incorporating ICTs effectively in the education system has implications for the way teachers perceive the technology. The introduction of ICTs into their professional environment may be seen as a threat to their status, and the time and effort demanded in addition to their usual professional commitments, may be unacceptable. The lack of technical expertise in most developing countries is constraining successful implementation of ICTs in education. Both education policy-makers and professionals lack the information necessary both for informed decision-making and for dealing with the practicalities of implementation.

The issue of gender as it pertains to the use of ICTs in education has hardly been touched upon in developing countries (Byron and Gagliardi 1996). However, differences have been observed with regard to the amount of time spent by boys and girls using computers. These may be attributed to the 'male dominated' image of the technology leading to a reluctance on the part of girls. Issues of access to computing facilities seem to play a role, particularly in the home environment which is more likely to be dominated by male ownership of the equipment. The use of ICTs by girls has been described as goal-oriented as compared to the process-oriented approach of boys. Integrating ICTs into all aspects of education rather than restricting the curricula to teaching computing skills may alleviate these gender differences and help to overcome access barriers and the reluctance of learners to use the advanced applications.

Overall, studies of the role of ICT in the education process point to the critical importance of the quality of skills and inequality of access to applications. Two additional issues are important for the design of training and education programmes relevant to people's needs in developing countries (Hodge and Miller 1998 forthcoming): quality of skills (that is, the match of the informal and formal education system with the demand for short and long term capabilities); and the mode of learning (that is, flexibility encouraged by all the institutions of education and training).

BOX 4.10 - THE INFRASTRUCTURE COSTS OF EDUCATION

Electricity is needed for many of the technologies which can be used to enhance teaching and learning. There are 16,400 schools in South Africa that will not be sufficiently close to an electrical grid point to be economically connected to the electricity supply. They are being connected to solar-panel generated electricity which is sufficient to supply lighting for four hours per evening. In addition, 220 VAC power is being provided to run a television/video and an overhead projector for two hours per day, as well as a personal computer for some hours. The cost per school is R56,000 and by 1999 all such schools are expected to have electricity to enhance their teaching and learning (Department of Education 1996: 40).

Broadly-based skills development is the foundation of 'knowledge societies'. Skills development in the workplace, via formal education, or through local community action, is essential if developing countries are to achieve their goals. Formal education using ICTs is resulting in the inclusion of increasing numbers of people in the developing countries and there are many successes. Although they are more difficult to document, there are instances of failures and concerns about the content of the new teaching materials. The use of ICTs is likely to be more successful when it augments, rather than replaces, existing locally developed education systems. The models introduced in developing countries for distance education need to be sensitive to cultural patterns. The 'global' or 'virtual' classroom offers new possibilities, but the importance of schools where people meet, socialise, and build social networks should not be overlooked. Distance learners will continue to need opportunities to meet in a physical place as a necessary complement to ICT-based exchanges.

There is a growing need to ensure that initiatives at all levels of education and in generic and specialised fields are coordinated. Uncertainty about the future demand for skills points to the need for continuous review and updating of curricula. Policy-makers will need to take every opportunity to encourage flexibility in institutions that provide formal education and training. They will also need to promote other institutions as sites of learning, problem-solving, and knowledge creation.

Lifelong learning means that people must be able to move into and out of formal education institutions at different stages of their working lives. New forms of certification and accreditation that are not based on hierarchies among institutions of education (for example, higher education, vocational training, etc.) will be necessary. New systems that are responsive to the needs of each developing country will need to be set up. If people are to benefit from the opportunities created by ICTs to enable greater empowerment and new forms of participation in civil society, the organisation of governance systems will need to become an issue for governments. If governments are to become more responsive to citizens through their use of ICTs, they will need to introduce major changes into their ways of governing and into the political culture in some countries. NGOs will play an increasing role in helping citizens and businesses to extend their capabilities for participating in 'knowledge societies'. They are well-positioned to contribute to the build up of new knowledge networks.

Chapter 5 looks more closely at the potential offered by a range of ICT applications across sectors of the economy. Chapter 6 focuses on the recent experiences of the least developed countries and the implementation of ICTs. These two chapters together illustrate in qualitative terms the very wide gap that exists between the promise of the new technologies and the necessary resources and capabilities in the poorest countries.

NOTES

1 For example, the National Development Programme in Computer Assisted Learning (NDPCAL) in the United Kingdom and the French experiment with minicomputers in 58 secondary schools in the mid-1970s. See also Hebenstreit (1992); Meyer and Berger (1996); European Commission (1996 b,c).

2 The introduction of computers in schools in developing countries occurred mainly in the mid-1980s either with the government leadership (for example China, Singapore, Sri Lanka) or stimulated by donations and initiative of individuals (for example Zimbabwe, Kenya, Malawi, Tunisia, Pakistan, Philippines) followed by government support (India).

3 Quantitative information on the current level of computer penetration in schools in the developing world is not available. However, it can be estimated that post-secondary teaching institutions in most middle-income countries are equipped with mainframes and terminals for limited access by learners. Telecommunication links are a very recent addition in post-secondary institutions. Networked applications are moving down the education system and reaching some secondary schools. In lower-income developing countries, many universities still do not have connectivity (as is the case of the University of Zimbabwe and others), but in some it is possible to develop school-to-school cooperative projects in the United States, Canada or Europe with counterpart schools in Latin America, Eastern Europe or Africa.

4 The following sources give several hundred references in relation to education policy, related technical change issues, and developing country problems, see Bowden and Blakeman (1990); Byron and Gagliardi (1996); and Whiston (1992, 1994).

5 Burgelman, J.-C., personal communication with representative of a South African NGO, 1996.

6 For American views on the role of ICTs and governance see Gilder (1994a); Mitchell (1995); Schuler (1996).

CHAPTER 5

THE POTENTIAL USES OF ICTs
FOR SUSTAINABLE DEVELOPMENT

Identifying potential applications
for public and private sectors

5. THE POTENTIAL USES OF ICTs FOR SUSTAINABLE DEVELOPMENT

5.1 INTRODUCTION – THE SOCIAL AND ECONOMIC IMPACTS OF ICTs

This chapter focuses on some of the ICT applications that are expected to assist developing countries to reap the social and economic benefits associated with extremely rapid innovation in advanced ICT-based goods and services. In the industrialised countries, there is a rapidly growing literature on the potential of innovative ICT applications and on the organisational, social, political, and economic conditions that are likely to support their effective use.[1] This literature is playing an important role in generating interest in the ICT revolution. It is helping to bring representatives of the policy, supplier, and user communities together to discuss policy issues and to seek new ways of capturing the potential social and economic benefits of ICTs.

In the developing countries, there is also a growing literature but it is more fragmented, and often restricted to sector applications or to country specific interests. It is difficult for decision-makers in developing countries to access systematic information about the potential applications that are being developed and implemented and to consider how they could be applied to meet their own development needs.

This chapter highlights some of the more advanced ICT applications that are in the development phase. In some cases, these are being implemented in the industrialised countries and in some of the wealthier and larger developing countries. With appropriate policies and ICT strategies these applications could become available to all developing countries. To a limited extent, they are already in use to strengthen the prospects for sustainable development. The review focuses on applications that are facilitating public and private services in public administration, urban and rural development, and transport sectors (section 5.2). Section 5.3 addresses the potential benefits of ICTs in improving the quality of life for citizens, especially in the health, special needs, education, environment, and agriculture sectors. Section 5.4 turns to the role of ICTs in improving access to public information. ICT applications are transforming the business sector and developments in this area are examined in the fields of manufacturing, electronic commerce, and the travel and tourism industry, in section 5.5. Section 5.6 concludes with an overview of the potential social and economic impact of the new applications and considers the extent to which this potential might be turned into a reality for the developing countries.

5.2 FACILITATING PUBLIC AND PRIVATE SECTOR ACTIVITIES

Public administration

Public administrations are playing a central role in the new 'knowledge societies'. They provide a range of services to citizens and industry, and engage in functions as diverse as economic development, environmental monitoring, and the provision of public information.

ICTs have considerable potential to cut administrative costs through the reorganisation of internal administration and through alternative provision of services. Electronic delivery points of access which can be made available from homes, schools, and libraries include audiotex, voice and data information services, teletext and interactive television services, fax, and state-provided terminals (similar to the French Minitel system). Multimedia customer-activated kiosks combine text, sound, video, and graphics. These multimedia and multilingual service delivery tools can be located in public places and provide information to meet the particular needs of citizens using video, audio or multiple languages. Kiosk access cards, similar to those required for automated teller machine access, control access to personal services. An advance in this area is the use of smart cards for additional functionality such as electronic fund transfer and state benefits. Remote areas can be served by cellular telephones, satellite receivers, and laptop computers and the range of benefits potentially available to citizens include social security, pensions, unemployment payments, and public assistance. ICTs can constitute tools for citizen involvement, soliciting feedback, and promoting private sector partnerships in development and testing of delivery mechanisms (Tang 1997a).

The electronic availability of public information can be of major assistance to small and medium-sized enterprises (SMEs) in administrative procedures for export, import, tax filings, and business opportunities. So-called 'one-stop' government service kiosks can further increase efficiency of service for SMEs. The benefits of these delivery mechanisms include user-friendly interfaces and advice for administrative procedures such as completing electronic forms; efficiency gains in claims processing time; and reduced cost of operation compared to paper-based systems. These services can be used in the prevention of fraud and abuse provided that adequate security measures are built into the system. Government-wide directories of government services and contact details facilitate citizens' access to an organisation.

Cooperation between government and the private sector to implement ICTs to provide citizen access to government information and services, such as the availability of public information, stimulates interaction between business and government. ICT applications can strengthen regional cooperation and support information sharing once interoperability of various information networks is achieved. Copyright on public information needs to be reconciled with the goals of information sharing and dissemination.

Urban and rural development

ICT applications are supporting development programmes in many urban and rural areas in developing countries. Databases and drawing facilities, simulation and modelling tools, form integral decision-support tools on which the planning, management, and development process can be based. Diverse current and historical data sets on health, education, water supplies, sanitation, and population growth and movement can be captured, collated, manipulated, and presented. Moreover, the visualisation of real-world situations assists in the analysis and identification of options such as land use plans for rural areas, and infrastructure and utility plans for urban areas. The comprehensive collection and analysis of seasonal and diurnal population demands and of physical and environmental factors in management information systems are useful in establishing development priorities. The successful implementation of these monitoring tools requires considerable time and resource investment in the data capture, complemented by sound training.

Economic development can be fostered by tele-working and tele-services in some of the developing countries. These applications can help to increase the competitiveness of rural and remote areas and tele-services in future may provide opportunities for tele-shopping, on-line reservation services, entertainment, and commercial information.

Transport

In the transport sector, advanced transport telematics (ATT) are being introduced to improve road safety, to maximise road transport efficiency, and to contribute to environmental problems of congestion, pollution, and resource consumption. ATTs affect vehicle and fleet operations, traffic monitoring, control and enforcement, safety, fee payment, and travel and traffic information. Applications appropriate for all transport modes and their interconnections, including road, air, rail, and water, are being developed to create integrated transport services through strengthened public-private partnerships. ATTs can measure the current level of traffic in networks, prioritise public transport vehicles by adjusting traffic signals, assess the level of congestion in real-time and re-route vehicles by communicating with them. Automatic vehicle location giving priority to public transport vehicles by adjusting signal timings renders the level of investment for the dissemination of these ATTs a matter for transport policy and strategy.

Economic losses through traffic delays and accidents are very costly and ICT applications are being developed which can help to reduce the levels of accidents. On-board vehicle control systems can assist a driver in hazardous driving situations. The development of electronically guided autonomous vehicles is based on the principle that if all vehicles are centrally controlled, the distances between them can decrease and their speed can be increased, resulting in less congestion and enforcing better driving behaviour and efficient route selection. Only small areas of land would be required for the infrastructure to host traffic management centres with which the vehicular guidance equipment communicates.

ATTs are expected to improve traveller support services, enabling citizens to make better choices for their daily journeys by taking advantage of the seamless availability of information across passenger transport modes (see Figure 5.1). Travellers could use portable personal traveller assistants or access networks of multimedia-enhanced public transport information terminals for timetable, route, and service and ticket information. On-line availability of real-time travel information relies on distributed information management for traffic data acquisition and its real-time processing. Smart cards offer travel services, such as bookings and payment, to the traveller while giving traffic network operators accurate information on passenger flows and routes chosen. In view of the congestion and pollution caused by ever-increasing traffic volumes, the scope for personalised travel using public transport may eliminate the disadvantages of public relative to private transport, giving rise to significant economic, environmental, and social benefits (Technology Foresight Panel on Transport 1995).

There are a number of applications for smart cards in the operation of transport, including payment for parking meters, identification of authorised parking space occupants, as well as recording and payment of travel along toll roads. Furthermore, airline travel benefits from smart card-assisted ticket vending and checking, and boarding public transport may be accelerated. Combicards are advances on smart cards which allow both contact and contactless card transactions, greatly increasing the fields of application of smart cards. Advances in the multifunctionality of smart (or intelligent) cards mean that functions can be changed or updated without re-issuing the card (see Box 5.1).

Urban freight transport is affected by changes in the supply chain as upstream relationships with suppliers and downstream relationships with customers are reconfigured. This results in requests for frequent deliveries. Flexible responses to customer requirements and supply chain interactions rely on sharing real-time information with

FIGURE 5.1 – THE DEVELOPMENT TRACK TO THE INFORMED TRAVELLER

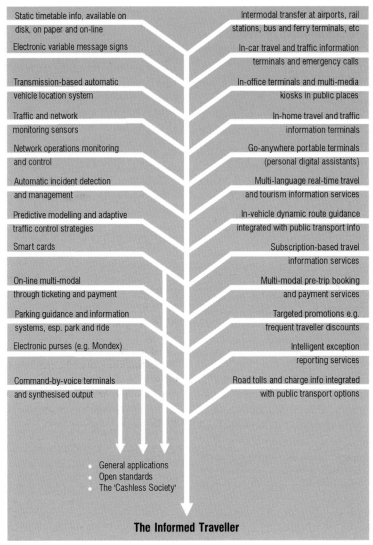

Static timetable info, available on disk, on paper and on-line

Electronic variable message signs

Transmission-based automatic vehicle location system

Traffic and network monitoring sensors

Network operations monitoring and control

Automatic incident detection and management

Predictive modelling and adaptive traffic control strategies

Smart cards

On-line multi-modal through ticketing and payment

Parking guidance and information systems, esp. park and ride

Electronic purses (e.g. Mondex)

Command-by-voice terminals and synthesised output

Intermodal transfer at airports, rail stations, bus and ferry terminals, etc

In-car travel and traffic information terminals and emergency calls

In-office terminals and multi-media kiosks in public places

In-home travel and traffic information terminals

Go-anywhere portable terminals (personal digital assistants)

Multi-language real-time travel and tourism information services

In-vehicle dynamic route guidance integrated with public transport info

Subscription-based travel information services

Multi-modal pre-trip booking and payment services

Targeted promotions e.g. frequent traveller discounts

Intelligent exception reporting services

Road tolls and charge info integrated with public transport options

• General applications
• Open standards
• The 'Cashless Society'

The Informed Traveller

Source: Buhalis (1995)

suppliers. Relevant ATTs include and support the following; fleet management traffic control systems, automobile on-board computers, real-time travel and traffic information, databases, and road management and logistics. The envisaged improvements to freight operation are expected to have positive gains in terms of efficiency and environment protection, yet they also have implications for mutual investment in hardware and software within the supply chains.

Examples of ICT applications for transport operations in the developing countries include the following initiatives undertaken by UNCTAD (1997). The Advanced Cargo Information System (ACIS), developed and implemented by UNCTAD, provides information on transport operations concerning the whereabouts of goods to facilitate

day-to-day management and decision-making as well as long term planning based on compiled statistics. In enabling operators in different regions to communicate, the system facilitates inter-regional trade and increases the efficient use of existing infrastructure and equipment capacity. Apart from automating the services, the system introduces advanced communication equipment to operators in participating countries.

UNCTAD has also responded to the problem of loss of revenue by developing countries arising from the lack of efficient customs management and procedures by developing an Automated System for Customs Data (Asycuda) and assisting with its implementation. Apart from altering customs procedures, the software allows trading formalities to be simplified and harmonised. ICT applications are being used to enable electronic registration and transfer of the transport documents that accompany cargo shipments. The software, which is installed in over 60 countries, consists of a number of pre-defined modules and, in addition, enables user-defined modules.

In India, funding provided by the United Nations INTERACT initiative enabled the establishment of the government-owned Computer Maintenance Corporation (CMC). In the early stages, the company concentrated on the assembly of imported computer components, and maintenance and requirement specifications for low end manufacturing of components. With the combination of technical knowledge and relevant experience gained from operating in the private sector, CMC was able to diversify into software development and consultancy. It now provides systems implementation and training for a diverse range of complex computer systems world-wide which have contributed substantially to the developing world. In Singapore, the software costs for implementing a computer-controlled airfield lighting system were recovered within two years of its inception. Computerised freight management in ports and handling of container traffic in a number of industrialised and developing countries also rely on CMC. Through automation of the passenger reservations of Indian Railways which transports numbers equivalent to the population of Belgium every day, the ticket-issuing procedure was reduced to a matter of minutes per reservation - a process which previously took several days (Narayan 1997).

Barriers to intermodal traffic optimisation include the high cost of the implementation of the technical and organisational infrastructure, and public acceptance. There is also a strong need for harmonisation and coordination of the technological components in this sector to avoid the development of technological islands. Major challenges are posed, firstly, by the need for open sharing of service information between competing transport operators and other providers, and, secondly, the need to develop open standards to ensure the shareability of information and the interoperability of systems (Technology Foresight Panel on Transport 1995). The actors involved in the implementation include public administrations, freight operators, public transport and commercial fleet operators (buses, taxis, trucks, etc.), public organisations, computer firms and software developers, travellers, traffic controllers, businesses, drivers, pilots, telecommunication operators, local, regional and national authorities, airlines, railways, shippers, and service providers.

5.3 IMPROVING THE QUALITY OF LIFE FOR CITIZENS

ICT applications have the potential to improve the quality of life for citizens in developing countries. A particular focus is on the areas of basic human needs (health, education, water, food) in the broader sectoral context of health

and special needs, education and lifelong learning, and environment and agriculture.

BOX 5.1 - USE OF SMART CARDS IN PUBLIC TRANSPORT

The world's largest user of contactless smart card technology is the Seoul Bus Union which represents 89 bus companies. At total of 8,700 buses are using contactless smart card terminals, and about 1,700 card reloading stations have been installed. By early January 1997 the number of contactless bus cards issued in Seoul had already risen to 2.5 million with approximately 2 million transactions per day.
The fully operational system has already been extended to the surrounding Kyung Ki Province and the Korean island of Cheju. Current plans and trials are intended to extend the functionality of bus cards to Seoul subways, ID, access control, retail and customer loyalty schemes, and an estimated 10 million cards will be issued within the next 12 months (Frotschnig 1997).

Health

In the health care field advances in medical science are putting a strain on health care resources and the task of managing these scarce resources continues to be a major economic and ethical challenge. ICT applications are supporting the more efficient exchange of information between health professionals thus saving time and money. They enable the transfer of patient records between sites and help to improve the response of the medical staff. ICT applications can improve clinical effectiveness, continuity, and quality of care by the full range of healthcare professionals.

The application of ICTs to provide medical care on demand and independent of person-to-person contact is referred to as tele-medicine. Tele-medicine can provide medical care to people in their homes, in isolated places or in times of emergency, and permits remote consultations between health professionals. Physician distribution and access issues for medically underserved and geographically remote areas of the developing world may be overcome by this way of extending the reach of specialists and general physicians. The successful implementation of tele-medicine is not only reliant on the availability of the necessary technology but also upon the willingness and ability of health care professionals to adopt ICTs.

Owing to the graphical and image-based nature of radiology, this is an area where significant applications of ICTs have been developed. Tele-radiology refers to the storage, retrieval, and transmission of medical images. Apart from overcoming geographical barriers to the access of diagnostic images - such as an emergency, or situations where the patient is far removed from the source of the image - tele-radiology also incorporates the time reduction and material saving characteristics generally attributed to ICTs. Thus delays in patient treatment due to misplacement, retrieval, and delivery of medical images may be eliminated. Tele-radiology places high demands on technical aspects such as adaptability and interoperability of implemented systems, complemented by comprehensive user training.

At a technologically even more sophisticated level, the combination of image processing, high performance computing, object-oriented distributed computing, advanced networking, and multimedia can be employed for advanced patient record systems. Virtual patient records may be created by combining information from geographically separate databases. Although individual health care facilities own and manage their own data, records can be made available to allow the integration of multiple databases including lab reports and radiographic data. The interface features of the virtual records include multimedia presentations, 3D-volume reconstruction, and visual navigation through complex data sets and query-by-example search through image databases. The advantage of such a patient record system is that it can provide the local physician with relevant and extensive quality information from distant specialists at low cost (Los Alamos National Laboratory 1996).

Although the potential of all aspects of tele-medicine has received much attention, the success of actual implementations has yet to be demonstrated on a large scale, even in the industrialised world. So far, much research has focused on the medical potential and the barriers to successful implementation due to low actual utilisation of telemedicine (Moore n.d.).

Expert systems which are designed to solve complex problems in well-defined domains are another means of supporting health care services. The initial construction of such medical knowledge-based systems is facilitated through the use of specialised software to allow the medical expert to model medical reasoning. Subsequently, the use of the medical expert system itself by many other practitioners involves inputting collections of ontological elements into the system and extracting task descriptions specifying the solution to the particular case under examination. The advances in this area are twofold: firstly, there is much focus on the simplification of the compilation procedure of medical expert systems so that they may be easily built and maintained by specialised physicians; and secondly, attention is paid to accessibility and usability of the medical expert systems. In order to ensure a wide audience of practitioners, both technical interoperability across numerous system platforms and user-friendly interfaces are important.

The modelling capabilities of ICTs have a number of medical applications such as simulation of surgery and endoscopy, image-guided surgery and endoscopy, and more general computer-based realistic visualisation of the living human body. Multimedia anatomical atlases, for example, display precomputed images and are based on a collection of planar images. Advanced methods of interactive anatomy viewing are now becoming feasible based on 3D imaging methods. These advanced atlases provide the user with individualised viewing of anatomy, giving choice over direction, focal length, and illumination and with simulated X-ray images of actual views (Priesmeyer 1997). Computer-based visualisation facilities comprise an important part of medical student education in dissection, proceeding beyond real-life operations by allowing reassembly of anatomical parts. Furthermore, they are points of reference for practising surgeons and radiologists.

Outside the medical profession, tools such as the World Wide Web are being used to educate health care and government workers in developing countries, to eliminate the isolation of health workers in rural areas, and to provide information to other members of the public with an interest in health care. Policy decisions about technical standards for databases containing medical records, and about the procedures for the protection of individual privacy, are especially important.

Special needs

ICT applications for the disabled and elderly can help to increase opportunities for independent living, and provide greater autonomy and improved social integration.

ICT applications, which can help with mobility and interpersonal communication, include computerised Braille and acoustical displays, robot arms for wheelchairs, and a wide range of other innovative services. Examples which can be found in the technical trade press include 'smart homes', multimedia medical files, graphical user interfaces, computerised drug prescription systems, 'smart prostheses', networks of organ donor banks, more accessible telecommunication terminals, biological signals, personal communicators, tele-diagnosis systems, alarm systems, remote expert consultation, and intensive care networks.

For many people with disabilities and learning difficulties, ICTs can be their route to independence by giving access to communication, education curricula, and informal learning, opening up opportunities that otherwise would be inaccessible. The choice and management of appropriate technology, balancing priorities, and monitoring progress require careful consideration and planning. Those involved in the development of these applications ideally should include as wide a range of stakeholders as possible, including citizens, the disabled and elderly themselves, family doctors, service providers, therapists, hospital workers, social workers, pharmacists, telecommunication operators, psychologists, social security organisations, computer firms, physicians, health care authorities, carers and families, and clinical laboratories.

For visually impaired or blind people, ICTs can alleviate some of the most common literacy and numeracy problems by allowing people to read and record their work. Large print, contrast print, choice of fonts, high quality resolution, and picture steadiness can be adjusted by using a word processor. Adjustable peripherals, such as colour or texture keyboards, Braille keyboards, and Braille printers, speech synthesisers, standard applications with built-in speech, and more advanced sound technology, such as digital speech recorders, are also important components. While ICTs can assist visually impaired people in gaining access to information and education curricula, the way in which generally available digital information is displayed is still too often a cause of exclusion. For example, the design of widely available CD-ROMs and multimedia materials has to build in sufficient flexibility for users to be able to adjust it to their needs. The successful use of ICTs by the visually impaired also relies on continuity of contact, owing to the difficulty for users to retain a mental map of the system, and this can be ensured by regular access to the system (NCET 1997). Learners with physical disabilities may have problems in recording their work in which case ICTs provide alternative means. Peripherals such as tracker-balls, microphones, and joysticks in addition to overlay keyboards can often prove useful. Advanced applications facilitating data entry include predictive word-processors, built-in word lists providing instant access to specialised vocabulary, whole phrase insertion, and keyboard displays on screen. Poor fine motor control can be compensated for by a touch screen and manual or sound activated switches in connection with switch-operated software, rather than a keyboard.

The main benefit of ICTs for people with hearing impairment is the acquisition of effective information handling skills such as the description, comparison, and contrasting of objects. Immediate and visual access to information on CD-ROMs and the opportunity to be creative with multimedia presentations, coupled with sound amplifiers, all offer learning opportunities without reliance on the spoken word. Speech impediments may be compensated for by digitised speech facilities, pointing devices or scanning systems which rely on user selection from a choice of displayed options. Hand-held spell checkers give people with dyslexia immediate access to an electronic dictionary, overcoming alphabetic searches and increasing their confidence. While portable tape recorders have proved to be useful for note taking, recorded speech or text-to-speech synthesis provide instant feedback to what has been typed. The quality of computerised speech is constantly improving and is commercially available in a variety of available voices, pitch and speed (NCET 1996).

The use of ICTs for people with emotional and behavioural difficulties creates a non-threatening environment in terms of personal interaction. For students, the pace and level of study can be controlled by the user, overcoming fears associated with poor handwriting, drawing, and spelling, while adding to their confidence and sense of achievement. More advanced ways of using ICTs for emotional and behavioural difficulties are modelling techniques, multimedia and sensor-based information capturing, for example, about the weather, all aimed at developing problem-solving capabilities. Software applications such as adventure programmes, interactive video, CD-ROMs, and video cameras used with digitisers all allow users to experiment with different strategies, experience simulations of real-time situations in role play, and to practise cooperation and teamwork with other students.

Combinations of impairments require a mixture of, and adaptation to, of a range of ICTs. Apart from changes in technical specification, English language-based software applications need to be adjusted to local languages and dialects. Encouraging reports from developing countries that have successfully adapted ICTs for the integration of people with special needs suggest that realisation of the potential of ICTs is feasible and does pay off. In Brazil, for example, voice synthesisers used in connection with speech software featuring Portuguese in high quality local 'carioca' accent enable the visually impaired to word process (DosVox) and even enjoy full Internet access (DISCAVOX). The scope of this application manifests itself in the wider application beyond its initial academic environment in helping blind students. It also allows blind people to take up employment in areas such as programming and telemarketing, as well as to manage their own companies (Barros 1998 forthcoming).

Education

In Chapter 4, this report reviewed developments in the adoption of ICTs to enhance learning and capability building and looked at the implications of ICTs for education and training. Education and training are no longer expected to stop when children leave school since it is now recognised that people continue to learn throughout their lives.

The use of ICTs for educational purposes has been described as a paradigm shift in education owing to the focus on learning, rather than on teaching, the latter being a model which concentrated on the teachers and their knowledge. Instead, emphasis on the learner means that they can devise a 'personal learning action plan' (Bargellini 1997: 30) to tailor knowledge and training to their own pace and style. Artificial intelligence is used by intelligent tutoring systems for tailored learning approaches. With this, the learning path, instructions, and feedback can all be geared to the individual student's knowledge, skills, and error patterns. Multimedia applications are providing new interactive materials and applications for learning at home, at school, and in the workplace. The advent of mobile-code, such as Sun Microsystems' Java programming language, presents the possibility of processing multimedia data locally on the user's machine, similar to off-line CD-ROMs, with the added advantage that the 'remote' teacher is able to control the flow of information according to the student's progress (Perdigao 1997).

High speed communication networks are enabling teachers to work together and develop courses jointly. Video-conferencing and computer conferencing is already providing some learners in rural and remote regions of developing countries with access to teachers in the heart of their own and other countries (mainly in the industrialised world). Adult education, employee improvement, and industrial training can also benefit from interactive digital video and CD-ROMs. On-line training using the Internet to deliver courses has the advantage of allowing full flexibility regarding the time of study although improvements still need to be made to peak time access.

Digital satellite radio services, incorporating high quality digital radio channels, text, and even photographs are envisaged to reach more than 4.6 billion people in the developing world (Snoddy 1997). The vast number of channels that can be transmitted offer a range of talk radio, mono-music, FM stereo sound, and CD-equivalent quality and provide much scope for educational content originating both in industrialised and developing countries. Digital television channels, whether satellite, cable or terrestrial, improve the quality of the broadcast image and are another means by which educational material can be broadcast. Digital terrestrial television (DTT) eliminates the need for satellite dishes and cable television lines as DTT can be broadcast from conventional land-based transmitters and received via ordinary metal aerials and a decoder box.[2] Hybrid products combining digital TV, personal computers, and Internet access are envisaged to succeed interactive television providing users with one comprehensive set of on- and off-line sources of information.

Advanced forms of virtual reality are synthetic environments that can be applied to education for training, operational planning, and analysis. These distributed interactive simulations are based on a technique in which the behaviour of mathematical models, real equipment, and people can be examined and their interactions observed (Moulton 1996). Major companies employ synthetic environments for company training in which a common computer-generated environment is the basis for assessment. School-specific applications are being developed.

Despite the declining costs of ICTs the costs of introducing major changes in education and training that take place in the school, the workplace, and the home continue to be very high. Owing to the new didactic approaches enabled by these technologies it is important to ensure a focus on the development of common basic knowledge assets and interpersonal skills. It is crucial to integrate teachers with their pedagogic expertise, into the introduction of innovations in education and learning (Bastos

1998 forthcoming). The implications of this change for the role of the teacher also have to be taken into account. Providing all people with equal access to lifelong learning is a major social challenge for developing countries.

Environment

In the environment field, ICT applications can facilitate improved access to environmental information for citizens, local, regional and national authorities, and businesses. Facilitating information flows between different actors is fundamental to improving environment protection and the effective management of emergencies. ICT applications can help in collating environment data in a form suitable to particular groups of users and mobile services, and can allow access to up-to-date information and provide real time decision support to speed up and increase efficiency in environmental monitoring. Examples of applications include multimedia public information kiosks, air and water quality monitoring and warning systems, labour market information, prediction of local air quality leading to control of traffic, rural-based teleworking, environmental emergency management systems for floods, forest fires, and industrial risks, home-based teleworking, public environment information services for cities and regions, etc. Those involved will often include citizens, environment agencies, local authorities in cities, towns and regions, service providers, environment protection agencies, chambers of commerce, firms, information providers, telecommunication operators, fire services, harbour authorities, computer companies, the police, etc.

Geographic information technology is the branch of geography that focuses on collection, storage, analysis, and display of geographic data and the application of these data to decision-making in every area of human endeavour. This rapidly growing field applies a combination of fundamental geographic principles and cutting-edge information technology to a wide array of problems facing humankind. Specific implementations are Geographic Information Systems (GIS) and Global Positioning Systems (GPS). A GIS is an automated system that enables the capture, storage, checking, integration, manipulation, analysis, display, and modelling of complex spatial data. It comprises hardware, software, and certain procedures to solve complex planning and management problems and to formulate coherent management strategies. A GIS may be considered an advanced equivalent of a traditional map from which different sets of information can be extracted more easily and as required, for example, for the purpose of famine prevention, forecasting plagues, and modelling of global warming. The integration of information on climate, soils, and terrains from a number of different sources (remote sensing, earthbound surveys, and cartography) permits the modelling of the potential and constraints of different areas under different management options. A

GPS is a space-based radio positioning system that provides 24 hour three-dimensional position, velocity and time information to suitably equipped users anywhere on or near the surface of the planet. Global Navigation Satellite Systems (GNSS) are extended GPS systems, providing users with sufficient accuracy and integrity information to be usable for critical navigation applications.

Allied to the use of a GIS is remote sensing for data gathering. This deals with the detection and measurement of phenomena - without being in contact with them - using devices sensitive to electromagnetic energy such as light (cameras and scanners), heat (thermal scanners), and radio waves (radar). Remote sensing provides a unique perspective from which to observe large regions and global monitoring is possible from nearly any site on earth. In practice, satellite remote sensing has been put to use to estimate atmospheric water vapour, trace gases, aerosol particles, clouds and precipitation, and to monitor and quantify changes in territories that are otherwise not accessible. The use of remote sensing means changes can be observed and merged with the other data layers of a GIS. These changes can be analysed, for example, as in the case of degradation of the rainforests around Maraca, a large land-locked riverine island situated in the northern part of the Amazon Basin (Gittings et al. n.d.). Owing to the low availability of topography and thematic maps, many developing countries rely on satellite images as a primary data source (GISL Ltd 1996a).

Another type of remote sensing device generating input for a GIS is videography, an advance on aerial photography. Video techniques using portable equipment produce georeferenced aerial video images in analogue (hardcopy) or digital format. Airborne videography does not rely on special aircrafts and incorporates visual, infra-red, and thermal imaging. The advantages of this technology lie in its customisation flexibility, the possibilities for data integration with other digital data such as scanned or digitised maps and satellite data, and its low cost compared with conventional aerial photography.

The combination of these technologies provides important means of analysis and access to environmental information. The United Nations Environment Programme (UNEP) contributes to the Global Resource Information Database (GRID), compiling and archiving georeferenced data. The GRID centres use specialised ICT applications, such as remote sensing, and geographic information systems, and are building the expertise to prepare, analyse, and present environmental data. UNEP's Environmental and Natural Resources Information Networking (ENRIN) programme is supported by a satellite telecommunication system (Mercure). With full Internet connectivity, Mercure provides a high capacity means of delivering environment data and information for other UNEP initiatives such as

GRID. The project is financed by a number of donor countries and implemented in collaboration with UNEP and the European Space Agency (ESA).

The Indonesian forestry sector has benefited from two separate initiatives using ICTs. A public sector initiative is funded and implemented by the Forestry Ministry to aid in sustainable forest management. The programme involves identifying and coding trees, optimising forest maintenance, and training in the use of laptop computers using the specialised software. A private sector initiative, the Forestry Resource Information System, has been introduced by the Forestry Management Association and incorporates a Geographical Information System; a database linked to remote sensing data, aerial photography images and digital mapping technologies (Talero and Gaudette 1995).

Owing to the large areas which can be covered with remote sensing and advances in image resolution, ever-increasing volumes of data are generated that need to be stored and analysed which require large amounts of processing time and power. Advanced parallel processing technology provides a means of coping with this data-intensive system. Aside from hardware considerations, the use of GIS and remote sensing techniques requires expertise in collating knowledge in the design and use of computerised geographic information systems for manipulating spatially referenced data, concepts of map design, and the use of computerised methods for designing and producing maps, the use of satellite and aircraft data and imagery for analysis of the earth's surface, the use of Global Positioning Systems and other appropriate technologies for data acquisition, and fundamental concepts of physical, cultural, and economic geography. The adoption and utilisation of these tools means that local environment stakeholders are an integral part of the data collection process and the principal analyst in the data processing and manipulation procedure (GISL Ltd 1996a).

The complexity, size and unpredictability of environment systems means that computer-aided, scientifically applied, modelling techniques are particularly useful in simulating behaviour and predicting outcomes. A wide range of environment and multimedia modelling techniques is available with the emphasis shifting to the facilitation of integrating separate but related models, such as air quality and water quality models, by removing extensive data reformatting requirements.

Environment conservation initiatives in all parts of the world greatly benefit from the networking and information exchange facilitates enabled by the use of ICTs in their aim to encourage compliance with environment clean-up and pollution prevention. The Sustainable Development Networking Programme (SDNP) was established in 1989 to facilitate information exchange between users and suppliers of information in developing countries. National network nodes assist all sectors and policy-makers by disseminating information on sustainable development. Building up national capabilities to implement and maintain information sharing networks and structures is the aim of a comprehensive training strategy organised by SDNP. Incorporated in the UN Development Programme 'Agenda 21', SDNP relies on local funding in addition to UNDP resources (Byron and Gagliardi 1996).

The United Nations Environment Programme (UNEP) also incorporates ICT applications in its projects. For example, the International Network on Information Referral System (INFOTERRA) is a specialised on-line system for scientific, technical, bibliographic, and institutional sources. The network currently consists of 173 national, government designated focal points that are collaborating with the UNDP's Sustainable Development Networking Project. Other ICT facilities are employed in the UNEPnet initiative to make environmental information products and services from UNEP and partner institutions globally accessible. UNEPnet consists of network nodes in several continents linked to the Internet and was a collaborative effort by experts from developed countries and UNEP. The Grito de Alerta em Defesa da Floresta Amazonica project was initiated by a college in Brazil with the aim of raising global awareness about the need to protect the Amazon region against environmental degradation and ICTs have been used as a facilitating tool. The technologies include video-conferencing equipment, multimedia applications, and a home page on the World Wide Web (Byron and Gagliardi 1996). The World Wide Weather Watch programme of the World Meteorological Organisation uses high speed data links to transmit data and weather charts throughout the world for private, public, and commercial use. ICTs facilitate the monitoring and diffusion of information on climate change and enable national governments to anticipate climate changes and to develop social and economic plans that are more responsive to climate change (UNCTAD 1997).

Agriculture

Further endeavours towards sustainability are focusing on the agricultural use of resources. Sustainable food systems benefit from the responsible use of resources by farmers who perform a wide variety of tasks in their crop management: planting date selection; water utilisation and management; pest and disease monitoring, identification, and remediation; and harvest management. These tasks can be facilitated by expert systems which increasingly adopt an integrated problem-solving approach to all aspects of crop management. Capturing local expertise, the systems improve with advances in the design of the interface to ensure easy knowledge acquisition and representation of knowledge within the expert system.

The basic infrastructure needed by agriculturists includes access to roads, inputs, and markets. At the land resources planning, land management, and administrative levels, information required is about markets, high level decisions on food movement, pricing, imports and exports, tariffs and quotas, under- and over-production, which can be provided by land information systems (LIS). Consisting of a database with spatially referenced land-related data, an LIS incorporates techniques for data collection (such as remote sensing), updating, processing, and distribution (GISL Ltd 1996b). Land information systems collate physical information on soils, hydrogeology, and rainfall with socio-economic information on rateable value, communications and utilities to support decision-making and planning activities at various administrative levels. Functioning as early warning and food security information systems they can play a part in strategies to alleviate hunger. In supporting decision-making and the re-examination of rural development policies, LIS can assist the process of reform of land tenure, land registration, urban planning, and local control over resources.

Regional development strategies for rural areas where livelihoods depend on agriculture, benefit from mechanisms to impart information directly to farmers and within the farming community, about new practices and systems from national and international agriculture research centres. In the agriculture sector information sharing using ICTs is being promoted, for example, by SIMBIOSIS, an Organisation of American States (OAS) project which is developing an international information system for the biotechnology and food technology sector. The long term goal is to use ICTs to provide access to regional resources for technicians and researchers. Another project in the Latin American region supports a Network on Natural Products Research (REDPRONAT in Latin America and CANNAP in the Caribbean) developed jointly by the OAS and the University of Chicago at Illinois. An electronically accessible hemispheric database on Thenobotany (MEDFOR) has been developed.

5.4   SHARING KNOWLEDGE AND IMPROVING ACCESS TO INFORMATION

ICT applications provide new tools for improving access to information and sharing knowledge. The competitiveness of industrial sectors in developing countries depends on the quality of research and the ability of firms to transform the results of research into marketable products. Researchers in the developing countries require easier access to up-to-date scientific and technical information as well as opportunities to communicate with other researchers. Networking services, e-mail, and multimedia conferencing are essential 'life-lines' for many researchers in the industrialised countries and researchers in the developing world must also be included in these networks.

In many developing countries, the technical networks supporting research activities have been developed piecemeal, resulting in a patchwork of technically diverse networks. A major challenge will be to create a regional research environment based on higher capacity networks which interconnect national networks and support state-of-the-art software based applications.

Libraries fulfil many of the cultural, educational, and professional needs of citizens and workers and with the emergence of the global information society there has been an explosion in resources, generating new demands and fuelling higher expectations. ICT applications for libraries are being developed to provide new tools and systems to improve and expand networked library services although this process is in its infancy in practical terms. In the future, networks will link library resources providing access to published information from a variety of sources. There is a growing number of alliances between publishers, distributors, and librarians which provide new services, accessible from libraries themselves and in some cases from homes, schools, and offices. Examples of applications include: computer based training, high speed research networks, open library systems, tele-education, tele-operation of experiments, tele-training, remote access to research results, cooperative learning, multimedia e-mail, electronic access to books, journals, documents, and multimedia resources, electronic production and delivery of multimedia learning materials, databases of course materials, interactive learning with student support and feedback, and distributed learning over the World Wide Web.

Language is an essential element of cultural identity which is a critical issue if information is to be shared by electronic means. As electronically based 'knowledge societies' emerge in the developing countries, the lives of those people who are connected to networks will become increasingly intertwined. Linguistic differences can be substantial barriers to communication and knowledge sharing. ICT applications are being developed that will help to improve information access and interchange across language barriers. Language engineering innovations are providing a basis for integrating written and spoken language processing technologies and improving their ease of use. New applications such as voice-controlled inquiry systems, multilingual information services, and computer assisted translation may provide greater possibilities for communication among the many dialects and linguistic traditions within and between developing countries. At present, however, most of the available systems are rudimentary.

ICT applications can be used to strengthen opportunities for sharing and exchanging information relating to sectoral applications and successes and failures in implementation. Initiatives are underway that may contribute to enhanced information sharing among dispersed communities with common interests. For example, networks sponsored by the World Bank and Volunteers for Technical Assistance (TechNet) and the Institute for Global Communications (LaborNet, PeaceNet) are allowing interaction and exchange of experiences within a widely dispersed community using e-mail and the World Wide Web to organise discussions in an orderly fashion (Institute on Governance 1996).

In March 1997, the World Bank announced its support of a 'data exchange' for infrastructure investment in Latin America. It is hoped that the exchange idea will be extended to Asia, eastern Europe, and possibly Africa. The proposal is supported by the Multilateral Investment Guarantee Agency arm of the World Bank and it is expected to give Latin American partners a 51 per cent controlling interest. Members would pay US$ 25,000 initially for a seat and the number of Latin American seats would be limited to 204. Twenty-six private and public sector companies have committed to become founder members with a further 39 agreeing to consider membership. The exchange would be managed by CG/LA, a Washington consultancy company, and would use the Internet to provide information about investment projects, business conditions, e-mail, and conferencing facilities (Financial Times 1997).

5.5 USING ICTs IN THE BUSINESS SECTOR

This section looks at sectors where ICT applications can produce major changes in the economies of developing countries. The manufacturing sector is witnessing the widespread adoption of ICTs in planning and control, factory automation, and general business management. Electronic commerce is widely regarded as an essential prerequisite for the 'knowledge societies' of the future. Those countries that do not implement the new electronic forms of business conduct will almost certainly find themselves disadvantaged in the conduct of trade and in their financial affairs. Tourism is another sector in which there have been major changes as a result of the application of advanced ICTs.

Manufacturing

In manufacturing, rather than accelerating single steps in the production process, now whole process chains are being targeted for elimination or speeding up (Freund et al. 1997). Supported by ICTs using database transaction processing, all-encompassing approaches to managerial and work-based organisational integration in manufacturing are being made. Broader definitions of computer integrated manufacturing (CIM) capture this notion (Senker and Senker 1994) while other sources refer to virtual manufacturing (Tang et al. 1997). Apart from automating the manufacturing process, ICTs facilitate the systematic capturing of information at all stages of design and marketing. This supplies important inputs to general business management, control and logistics, strategic planning, and total quality management. In particular, the systematic capturing of cost details is expected to have implications for investment owing to the detailed audit records of investment performance (Tang et al. 1997). Further improvements extend to waste, pollution, and energy reduction, and the efficiency of a manufacturing plant by making it more reliable, repeatable, and maintainable (Technology Foresight Panel on Manufacturing, Production and Business Processes 1995).

The design stages of both machine tools and manufactured parts benefit greatly from computer-aided-design (CAD) and interactive graphics. Virtual reality and simulation can be used to explore design alternatives in an easily manipulated model world. CADs can limit designers to working on manufacturable parts and eliminate time-consuming unfeasible designs. Further, it is possible to achieve reductions in the product development cycle with design-to-prototype services which allow the designs of manufacturable parts to be sent to a computer controlled milling machine for immediate fabrication (Integrated Manufacturing Lab Research n.d.). Simulation tools also allow a degree of customer participation in the design process and demonstration models can be made available to end users for comment on a company's web site. The potential of virtual reality simulation reaches far beyond industrial use for rapid product test methods in electrical, electronic, and mechanical engineering, textiles, clothing, architecture, and construction, to other sectors such as media.

Important stages of the production process are served by direct numerically controlled (DNC) machine tools which are an advance on computer numerical control (CNC), whereby multifunction machine tools in a production cell are computer controlled. Advances in this area are flexible manufacturing systems (FMS) in which the movement of workpieces between production stations is also computer controlled, leading to more flexible processes. Client/Server technology combined with expert systems for on-line analysis based on an individual manufacturing cell, allow a simulated 'look ahead' thereby reducing bottlenecks and maximising throughput in complex manufacturing environments such as aircraft manufacturing (The Quality Observer 1996). In addition, computer-aided-manufacturing (CAM) incorporating robotics is spreading rapidly, linking material handling machines, lathes, grinders, sprayers, and assemblers, to computers. Advances in mobile robot path planning and navigation, reactive robot navigation, vision and haptic-based object recognition, and knowledge-based grasping with dextrous hands, will allow the scope of robotic applications in manufacturing to increase further (RIM Lab n.d.). Facilitating the change of material from steel to aluminium, computer simulated guidance through the sheet metal stamping process lets employees adapt quickly to the new material (The Quality Observer 1996).

Controlled process sensor technology incorporates ICTs for evaluating the sensor data and processing the final result, taking inputs from optical and capacity sensors, additional laser interferometers and thermal compensation. This leads to remote and more accurate process control.

Supply chains are also affected by ICTs. Suppliers' real-time access to a manufacturer's CAD, CAM and/or CIM facilities can greatly improve product development, reducing time-to-market for new products. Reducing the travel time to suppliers of designers and engineers results in significant cost savings (Harvey and Gavigan 1996).

The range of skills required for these advanced manufacturing technologies includes electronic and mechanical engineering, mathematics and physics, software engineering, robotics, hydraulics and pneumatics, programming, and process control which need to be complemented with knowledge about internal processes. As Senker and Senker (1994) have argued, the choices in the skills requirements and organisational aspects presented by the application of ICTs in manufacturing defy a single solution. The introduction of ICTs into some or all stages of the manufacturing process necessitates changes in organisational structures (see Chapter 3). The high costs involved mean that the potential is out of reach for most small companies and developing countries. High levels of expertise and investment are required for the adoption of these technologies (Tang et al. 1997).

Electronic commerce

Electronic commerce can be defined as 'the use of documents in electronic form, rather than paper, for carrying out functions of business or government (such as finance, logistics, procurement, and transportation) that require interchanges of information, obligations, or monetary value between organisations and individuals' (Ferné 1996: 7). It includes activities that could be replaced by electronic media such as the exchange of documents, telephone calls, faxes, etc., and also includes standards for procurement of manufactured goods by governments and the private sector and the participation of firms and individuals in the electronic marketplace. In an era of electronic commerce, size of assets or capital has increasingly less bearing on competitiveness. Electronic commerce is developing in response to the need to build a technical and service infrastructure that will sustain commercial transactions in the 'knowledge societies' of the 21st century. To achieve this goal there is a growing need for cooperation between governments and the private sector (Mizuno 1997).

There is some dispute about the current role of electronic commerce in the economy. Some surveys (see Box 5.2) have suggested that electronic commerce of all kinds will be slow to take off for financial reasons or because of lack of training, while others see available networks as offering too little security for all sectors of the economy to engage in extensive world-wide trading by electronic means.

However, there is virtually no dispute about the potentially profound changes which the global information infrastructure, including the Internet, could bring to the traditional model of relationships between buyers and sellers in the marketplace (Information Infrastructure Task Force 1996). New models of commercial interaction are developing as businesses and consumers participate in the electronic marketplace. World trade involving computer software, entertainment products (motion pictures, videos, games, sound recordings), information services (databases, on-line newspapers), technical information, product licences, and professional services (businesses and technical consulting, accounting, architectural design, legal advice, travel services, etc.) has been growing rapidly over the past decade, and now accounts for well over US$ 40 billion worth of United States exports alone (US Department of Commerce 1996).[3]

Once the global information infrastructure is fully in place it will have the potential to radically alter commerce in these and other areas by accelerating the growth of trade. Use of the Internet, intranets, and other computer networks could lower transaction costs dramatically, and facilitate new types of commercial transactions. Based on the Internet protocol, intranets are accessible only to users of a corporate network (running on public or private networks) and rely on firewall security to shield them from unauthorised access. The main benefits are improvements in internal communication and information flows by facilitating the distribution of information access across a company, and features such as remote access and teleworking.

Extranets also use Internet technology - browsers and web servers - to link company-specific Intranets enabling business partners and suppliers to share corporate data. There is no necessity for a closed set of standards with additional large investment requirements in infrastructure. This is a major benefit for companies with Internet access, particularly for small companies upstream in the supply chain who can participate in electronic trading at low cost. Although extranets have the potential to widen the number of electronic commerce partners, companies with no previously established relationship need to authenticate their communications (Chappell 1997).

New arrangements between buyers and sellers will make commerce easier for those who have access to the global infrastructure. For example, in the information technology sector computer manufacturers can bypass retailers to supply equipment directly to individuals and businesses. Commerce on the Internet could reach several billions of dollars by the turn of the century and sales were estimated at US$ 200 million in 1995 (American Electronics Association/American University 1996). This is despite concerns about the legal environment for inter-national transactions, for example, enforcement of contracts, liability, intellectual property protection, privacy, security, and taxation (see Chapter 10).

Electronic commerce is growing in some sectors of developing countries and particularly in the newly industrialising countries such as Singapore which has promoted the use of electronic data interchange (a component of electronic commerce) for several years.

Box 5.2 - The Internet, not exactly the high street for doing business

Only one in 20 companies is dealing on the Net, a poll has found. Security and a lack of cost-benefit analysis are just two factors. A survey by Deloitte and Touche Consulting Group of almost 1,500 companies around the world has found that the overwhelming majority has no plans to use the Internet for business transactions. Other factors include the financial and human resources needed to respond to the technological issues (Rowan 1997).

Since the 1960s, the finance sector in Brazil has also made use of ICTs to automate its procedures. Owing to its favourable financial position but also to a lack of producers to respond to the specific ICT requirements of the banking sector, subsidiaries and spin-offs were created to provide electronic solutions. The strong user-producer relations established in hardware and software design specifically for banking, ensured that companies could compete successfully with foreign firms after the liberalisation of the economy in the early 1990s. The lack of a widely available telecommunication infrastructure encouraged banks to invest in private satellites to allow wide coverage to remote branches (Cassiolato 1996).

UNCTAD has supported a large number of projects in this area including debt management systems, information on laws, 'one-stop-shop' services, and information on markets and environment protection standards (see Chapter 10).

Tourism and travel industry

The travel industry has proved to be one of the fastest growing segments of the Internet. *Jupiter Communications* projects that on-line spending for travel services will reach US$ 1 billion by the end of 1997 - almost 50 per cent of the US$ 2.3 billion that will be spent on-line in 1997 - and will continue to grow to the US$ 3 billion mark by the year 2000. Consumer preferences for flexible travel and leisure services provide a strong impetus for a new tourism that is heavily dependent on ICTs (Poon 1987). ICTs are playing an important role in engineering new, more flexible, and quality driven tourism. A whole system of ICTs is being diffused rapidly throughout the tourism industry and it is unlikely that any developing country or economy in transition will escape its impact. These technologies are associated with frequent-flyer programmes, flexible holidays, ticketless

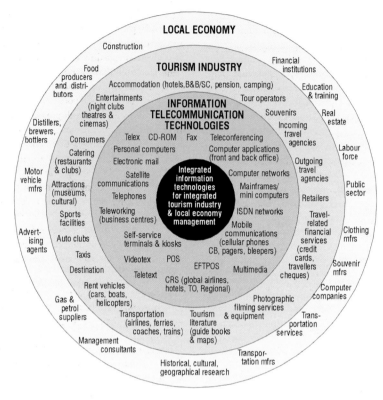

Source: Buhalis (1995).

travel, cyber offers, video brochures, web sites, on-line travel agency services, and more.

International tourism is a very information-intensive activity. Tourism's critical dependence on information flows can be illustrated by the information needs of a company such as American Express. This company needs rapid, unimpeded global communications to carry out its routine transactions, which include authorisation of more than half a million American Express card transactions daily all over the world, with an average response time of less than five seconds, and the number of transaction authorisations increasing at between 25 and 35 per cent annually. ICT systems are used for verification and speedy replacement of lost or stolen traveller's cheques sold by over 100,000 banks around the world, and for accessing reservations systems and travel related service databases from offices in over 125 countries.

In the travel and tourism industry, a whole system of inter-related computer and communication technologies is being employed (see Figure 5.2). The components consist of computerised reservations systems, teleconferencing, videotex, videos, video brochures, management information systems, airline electronic information systems, electronic funds transfer systems, digital telephone networks, smart cards, satellite printers, mobile communications, e-mail, Internet, etc.

Computerised reservations systems (CRSs) have emerged as the dominant technology and the Internet is also a very powerful emerging technology in the industry. The experience of CRSs and travel agencies in the United States provides clear evidence of the speed of diffusion. By 1988, a mere 10 years after deregulation, 96 per cent of travel agencies in the United States were automated. The rapid diffusion of a system of ICTs throughout the travel and tourism industry is having four major impacts. It is improving the efficiency of production; it is helping to enhance the quality of services produced for consumers; it leads to the generation of new services; and it enables the engineering and spread of a whole new industry set of practices.

For SMEs, and peripheral and remote destinations, the implications of ICTs for the tourism industry, are twofold. On the one hand, ICTs can reduce reliance on tourism intermediaries. On the other, if companies are unable to adopt ICTs, the intermediaries' power increases. For example, they are able to forecast demand levels, foster consumer relations, and influence the negotiation process in their favour (Buhalis 1995).

The cost reducing potential of ICTs is suggested by internal airline studies which have estimated that CRSs reduce the cost to an airline of making a reservation from approximately US$ 7.5 to US$ 0.50. A survey of travel agents reported that installing a CRS raised their productivity by 42 per cent and as a result, the direct social costs of airline reservation and ticketing have fallen dramatically by as much as 80 per cent (Poon 1987). The ICT impact on quality depends upon how different technologies are conceived and whether they are strategically used to render competitive advantages. One hotel may use computers simply as a tool to lay off workers and to reduce wage costs. Another hotel may use ICTs to improve efficiency and to release valuable person hours to add a 'high touch' element to the services offered. ICT adoption will have the effect of improving the quality and 'personal touch' of the services.

The future growth of the travel and tourism industry is taking place within the context of a new socio-institutional framework (limits to growth, environmental consciousness, deregulation, more planning and development of 'green' or 'soft' tourism services and facilities). These conditions create an excellent match with ICTs to develop a more flexible industry. The extent of the benefits and rate of diffusion of the new practices depends on the actions of the firms, consumers, host countries, and governments (for example, airline deregulation and environmental limits to growth). Developing countries face high up-front investment costs in ICTs if they are to compete effectively for the growing international tourist trade.

5.6 CONCLUSION - KNOWLEDGE SHARING FOR EFFECTIVE ICT USE

ICTs have many revolutionary implications, but in order to achieve their potential benefits it is necessary to focus on user-oriented and cost-effective applications rather than on technology-driven applications. The analysis of users' needs is essential as is consideration of the factors that may exclude them from participating in the design and implementation of applications. User representatives must be involved in all stages of ICT application development if the users themselves cannot be involved directly. The range of capabilities among potential users must be taken into account in the process of designing and implementing new applications. Resources sufficient for technology assessment and evaluation of the benefits of applications throughout their development must be allocated. Funds to support the wide dissemination of the results of experimental and commercial applications are also necessary. Cross-sectoral and vertical coordination between suppliers, users, and policy-makers is important

to ensure that the benefits of ICTs can be made available to potential users.

Many of the applications described in this chapter are the focus of experiments, trials, and demonstrator projects in the United States, the European Union, Japan, and the newly industrialising countries. Some of the earlier generations of the these applications are proving their commercial viability and their capacity to support research, business, and social activities on a limited basis within the wealthier developing countries. Since most of these applications are being developed initially in the industrialised countries, there are additional costs associated with adapting the software and hardware designs to the needs of developing countries. Policy measures are needed to address the key areas within each country's overall development strategy that could benefit from the use of ICT applications and to promote initiatives that will generate financial resources (see Chapter 11). These resources are needed not only to assemble the necessary hardware and software, but also to build new capabilities for effective use.

An analysis of project partners involved in the European Commission's Telematics Applications Programme suggests that the types of partnerships which emerge to develop ICT applications are a good indicator of the type of research that is performed (European Commission 1997a). Information about these partnerships is helpful in addressing questions about how closely R&D programmes are related to commercially viable applications and whether they are responsive to the requirements of users. The analysis of partnerships also provides a means of tracking the evolution of collaborations within countries and across national boundaries.

Given the difficulties and costs of establishing coordinated information on ICT applications, it is not surprising that few if any systematic analyses have been undertaken in developing countries. Nevertheless, such information would provide an important source of information for policy-makers within developing countries. It would provide a basis for observing changes in the profiles of organisations that are actively engaged in developing new ICT applications. It would also provide a means of benchmarking progress toward the greater inclusion of under-represented economic and social groups.

From the perspective of those within developing countries a continuously updated and systematic source of information of where the knowledge and expertise resides for launching innovative ICT applications inside and outside their countries is essential. Therefore, such information needs to be coordinated across ministries within countries and across the various development oriented agencies of the United Nations system and other international bodies that are active in this area.

Table 5.1 provides an overview of the potential social and economic impacts of ICT applications based on a study

TABLE 5.1 – THE POTENTIAL SOCIAL AND ECONOMIC IMPACT OF ICT APPLICATIONS

ICT trends	Technology capabilities and applications	Social, economic, and political impacts
Increased performance at greatly reduced cost, for example microelectronics, fibre optics, voice and video compression, fast-packet switching, very high-density storage technology.	Permits developing countries and the least developed countries to 'leapfrog' to advanced technology; maximises advantages of existing technology. Technologies also provide greater geographical coverage.	National political/economic integration; more efficient markets and more effective political control and administration. Potential for the erosion of national boundaries due to reinforcement of global ties, for example PeaceNet, EcoNet, etc.
Technology convergence due to digitalisation, wideband transmission, compression technologies, and standards developments.	Cost efficiencies in services due to economies of scale and scope and greater networking versatility. Greatly enhanced applications, such as real-time video transmission, videoconferencing, and multimedia applications for the home, the desktop, or (less expensively) public point-of-sale terminals.	Greater support for the low cost provision of public services such as health care and education. Multimedia is especially useful in developing countries given their high illiteracy rates. Supports business applications, such as computer-aided-design, desktop fax, videoconferencing.
Unbundling of communication functions and services due to the emergence of competing technologies, the dispersal of intelligence throughout communication networks, the demands of large users, and market liberalisation policies.	Permits users to purchase communication functions and services separately. Allows for greater flexibility in network design and architecture. More networking options and freedom to customise networks to minimise costs or to match specific needs. Lower costs also due to greater competition among vendors and service providers. Interoperability, network integration, and network management likely to require greater technology expertise.	Democratic process likely to benefit from greater diversity of communication sources and network designs. Allows developing countries to manufacture low-end components and gain technology expertise. Less elaborate and expensive systems may provide more 'appropriate' technology to meet developing country needs. On the other hand, problems of interoperability and increased complexity can create new information bottlenecks with consequences for politics and the economy. Technology experts and system integrators become new information gatekeepers.
Increased ease of use as a result of advances in storage, microelectronics, speech recognition, and search engines. Applications include simple to use graphic user interfaces (such as Windows), network browsers (such as Netscape), and intelligent agents.	Supports greater network access and usage, promotes deployment, and reduces the level of expertise required to take advantage of information technologies.	Reduces access barriers with positive benefits for both competitive markets and democratic politics.
Decentralised intelligence throughout communication systems due to software-driven and software-defined communication networks.	Provides for two-way interaction and greater user control. Applications include interactive television, personal digital assistants, desktop publishing, intelligent networks, and expert systems. Provides a platform for creating value-added services, such as 'free phone' services, point-of-sale services, and credit authorisation.	In many developing countries, two-way, interactive media can support local grass-roots participation, thereby enhancing democratic processes. Provides an opportunity to develop specialised or local content to reinforce community ties. Value-added services provide or substitute for a lack of an information infrastructure (banks, insurance, legal, etc.)
Increased networking capabilities due in part to advances in integration and switching technologies such as routers, intelligent hubs, and asynchronous transfer mode, frame relay, together with advances in wideband transmission technologies and software support applications such as CAD-CAM, EDI, groupware, as well as the development of standards and networking protocols such as TCP/IP (Internet) and application programming interfaces.	Supports distributed client-server computing and cooperative work applications such as e-mail, EDI, computer-integrated manufacturing, teleworking and groupware. Provides support for the development of specialised functional networks, such as financial services networks or special interest group networks such as EcoNet.	Supports democratic politics by helping individuals locate information, identify like-minded people, deliberate, and voice opinions. Networks help businesses and firms reduce their costs by integrating processes and information, and to gain a strategic advantage by developing exclusive networks that lock in customers and suppliers. Without access to advanced networking technologies, developing countries may become locked out.

TABLE 5.1 CONTINUED – THE POTENTIAL SOCIAL AND ECONOMIC IMPACT OF ICT APPLICATIONS

ICT trends	Technology capabilities and applications	Social, economic, and political impacts
Increased mobility and portability due to distributed intelligence and advances in wireless technologies such as satellite receivers, cellular telephony, personal communication services, radio paging, digital radio, wireless local area networks, wide area networks, and private branch exchange equipment.	Low cost alternative to fixed wireline technologies for use in difficult to reach, high cost areas. Greater ease and speed of deployment. Allows for greater network flexibility and support for remote information access and processing. Applications include wireless networks based on a mesh rather than hub architecture. When combined with unbundled intelligent peripherals, wireless networks support the widespread distribution of information and 'intelligence' to all areas. Applications include CD-ROM libraries or expert health care systems.	Facilitates open markets and democratic politics by supporting access to political and economic information and communication networks as well as to expertise and 'intelligence' from and to anywhere. Facilitates network configuration and shared information systems, which support the competence of local governments, and reinforces community ties.

Source: Adapted from US Congress OTA (1995a).

by the United States Office of Technology Assessment in 1995 (US Congress OTA 1995a). It is not certain that the potential benefits of ICT applications for developing countries will be the same as those described here. The outcomes for developing countries depend on public policy actions, and private sector management and strategic priorities.

Effective ICT policies and initiatives to take advantage of the new applications must be embedded in the local environment and in the organisations which expect to benefit from them. There is substantial evidence that if applica-

tions do not reflect user needs or involve them in the process of development, they simply will not bring the expected benefits. They are likely to create new problems that will be costly to address. If the specific social, cultural, and economic conditions, the expertise and commitment of users, and components of the infrastructure are not assembled together, ICT applications will fail to yield benefits.

The need for 'appropriate adoption, adaptation, and transfer', and the selection of ICT applications as a result of informed choices and the development of user capabilities

BOX 5.3 – PRINCIPLES FOR ENABLING ICTs AND DEVELOPMENT

▮ Work with the newest and best ICTs.

▮ Support research that is practical and result oriented.

▮ Place emphasis on generalisable outputs, rather than those specific to a particular country or institutional situation.

▮ Support quality research work.

▮ Link technologies and tools to past investments in the information content of existing systems.

▮ Establish specialised programmes to support ICT R&D and applied research.

▮ Support projects that can stimulate interest on the part of other potential donors and agencies.

▮ Support developing country capacity-building, through a mix of technology transfer, partnerships and local R&D activities.

▮ Foster international collaboration in ICT.

▮ Support activities based upon both identified user needs and technological opportunities.

▮ Support a variety of types of activities relevant to needs and real conditions in the countries that are to carry them out.

▮ Explore the usefulness of a new application in solving development problems in the industrialised countries, and promote the adaptation of the application for developing countries.

▮ While promising applications are still being tested and developed, their usefulness can be explored.

▮ Provide support for R&D in the software and hardware areas.

▮ Encourage sensitisation, evaluation, and dissemination activities.

▮ Support policy research to provide a framework for decision-making and allocation of resources.

▮ Consider carefully local factors and conditions when designing projects.

Source: Adapted from Valantin (1995).

should not be underestimated (Durant 1997). A key issue for developing countries is the enabling mechanisms for smaller firms and organisations. There is a need for strategic planning, increased commitment on the part of owners and managers, stronger efforts to achieve user participation, a willingness to change working procedures and to make provisions for building worker capabilities through training, retraining and education (Girvan 1994a).

The effective use of ICT applications provides the opportunity to harness the benefits of these technologies to national and regional development goals. To achieve this, education, lifelong learning, and attention to both technical and social capabilities must become central issues for policy-makers, firms, and the non-governmental organisation sector.

Two decades of experience in providing technical assistance to developing countries to extend capacities using ICT applications permits general lessons to be drawn. The principles shown in Box 5.3 can be tailored to the specific needs of developing countries. These principles can be used as a guide to actions that could enable greater empowerment of people through the appropriation of ICTs to meet their development goals.

A major goal of initiatives to implement ICT applications in developing countries is to help to alleviate poverty. Another is to ensure that the applications are perceived by their users as being useful. If these goals are not achieved there is little point in investing enormous amounts of money in the infrastructure for innovative 'knowledge societies' in developing countries. Chapter 6 looks at the constraints facing the least developed countries. In these countries the challenge to invest extremely scarce financial resources in ICTs and in people's capabilities to use them is enormous because of strong competing claims on those resources. However the promise of ICTs to assist in ameliorating pressing development problems means that efforts need to be made to give priority to strategic investments.

NOTES

1 For example Dutton (1997); Drake (1995); Kahin and Keller (1996); Branscomb and Keller (1996); Information Highway Advisory Council (1995); Dumort and Dryden (1997).

2 Separate decoder boxes are necessary until the electronics have been integrated with television sets.

3 The estimate covers 1995 and does not include transactions between affiliated companies which could add as much as US$ 47 billion in additional exports.

CHAPTER 6

IMPLEMENTING ICTs IN THE LEAST DEVELOPED COUNTRIES

Uses of ICTs when poverty is pervasive

6. IMPLEMENTING ICTs IN THE LEAST DEVELOPED COUNTRIES

Decision-makers in the least developed countries (LDCs) and regions of the world are becoming more aware of the potential benefits of ICTs. For many of these countries, widespread access to these technologies for people on an individual basis is simply out of the question in the time-frame within which policy and strategic actions are taken. Analysis of the relationship between the rate of investment in the telecommunication infrastructure and the penetration of telephones shows that convergence between the industrialised countries and some of the LDCs is decades away (see Chapter 2). Some countries in Eastern Europe, Asia, the Caribbean, South America, and the Mahgreb regions - and China - will take 15 to 20 years at current rates of investment to reach the telephone penetration rates of industrialised countries. For countries in northern Africa and the Oceania region, convergence will take some 30 years. Sub-Saharan Africa and central Asian countries will wait 50 to 100 years.

Plans for investment in ICTs bring the best results when they are embedded in, or informed by, a vision of the future that is consistent with the local or national environment. If the LDCs implement investment strategies that emulate the 'one person - one telephone - one Internet access point' model that is predominating in the industrialised countries, they are likely to experience frustration and disappointment. Even in the industrialised countries there are illustrations of the use of 'telecottages' and local learning centres to broaden access to ICTs, deepen the skills base, and build new competencies. Alternative models are emerging in the rural and less advantaged areas of wealthy countries (Gillespie and Cornford 1997, Taylor et al. 1997). It is essential that the LDCs devise innovative models of their own.

In the newly industrialising countries where access to communication networks is becoming relatively widespread, governments and the private sector are also investing in people. There is little to be gained from access to global, or even local, digital information resources if the skills to select, interpret, and apply the information are absent or very poorly developed throughout the population. The capacity to generate, distribute, and share information about local resources and activities is as important as access to distant digital information. LDCs need to develop models for 'access' and 'information content'. These models need to create incentives for cost-effective sharing of information resources as well as the hardware and software that facilitates access to networks. Similar considerations apply to ICTs embedded in production systems where there is a need to share knowledge about how to obtain the full benefits of new process and control technologies.

A synergistic relationship between investment in the technical components of the national information infrastructure, and in people, enables learning to take place which can benefit all sectors of the economy and society. The LDCs encounter these potential synergies from a position of poverty and existing wide inequities in the distribution of technology, access to electronic networks, and the capabilities to use them. Innovative models are needed that institutionalise and coordinate action leading to the targeting of key areas in which to build capabilities.

The constraints to achieving the goal of harnessing ICTs to development priorities in the LDCs in terms of building the national information infrastructure are different from those in the industrialised countries or the wealthier developing countries.

For example, some LDCs such as Djibouti, Rwanda, the Maldives, and the Solomon Islands, have very sophisticated digital telecommunication infrastructures (de Cuellar 1995). If the costs of usage could be kept at an affordable level, new technologies, such as multi-point multi-channel distribution systems and cellular radio, could be used to alleviate congestion on older terrestrial networks in other countries. A serious problem for network availability is the absence of reliable power sources. As the Internet becomes a more important mode of information exchange, the configuration of stand-alone Intranet and Internet usage to optimise available terminal and network use, needs to be considered (UNESCO 1996).

The use of ICTs relies on electricity and, in this respect, most of the LDCs - and particularly their rural areas - are at a disadvantage because of the limited extent of their national grids (de Oliveira 1991). Although alternatives, for instance solar power, are being explored (see Box 6.1), their viability is hampered by their cost. In addition, electricity prices often do not reflect actual costs because of the use of cross-subsidies. The reliance of ICTs on electricity further adds to the complexity of the 'trade-off between the utilities' financial viability and social, economic, and environmental objectives, each of which has to be carefully assessed' (de Oliveira 1991: 85). Challenges are posed by having to devise an integrated planning mechanism for infrastructure provision.

They [critics of ambitious electrification goals] argue that although electricity is a key factor in economic development, it can do little for it if transportation, banking and other infra-structures are not provided as well. ... Nevertheless, access to modern life is almost impossible without access to electricity (de Oliveira 1991: 78).

The integration of projects, such as those in Box 6.1, is necessary. This could avoid 'the risk that these schools may be deprived of the benefits of the so-called information age for which fast digital telecommunication lines are a prerequisite' (Butcher and Perold 1996: 16). The power requirements of ICTs will continue to increase and electricity costs will form a considerable part of education and other budgets allocated to the provision of ICTs.

The costs of using networks once they are in place are frequently prohibitive for citizens, businesses, universities, and other scientific research establishments, and schools. Measures are needed to introduce pricing structures that encourage greater use. For example, in the Dominican Republic, there is a promotional and reciprocal traffic agreement that provides for free connection of the research and academic community to the public data network and to the Internet. In Colombia, discounts for use of the public data network of 15 to 35 per cent are offered to the higher education sector, and fees for some connections to the Internet are reduced for these institutions. Other ways of reducing the costs to the user may include tax exemptions for selected user groups on network usage or hardware or software purchases (UNESCO 1996). Promoting second-hand markets in user equipment, a practice common among students especially in universities in some industrialised countries, and providing incentives for producers to offer content for older ICT platforms, may help LDCs to build competencies in using new applications (d'Orville 1996).

The costs of using ICTs are generally discussed in terms of infrastructure, hardware, network usage, and content. There are additional 'user' costs that also need to be taken into account. These include maintenance and hardware upgrading, the costs of software and software modification to user requirements, the costs of training and skills development, and the cost of language training.

Although the costs of ICT hardware are falling, the costs of software development for many applications are rising and they will continue to do so as systems applications become more complex. This is a significant problem in the industrialised countries (Quintas 1996). Cost reduction requires organisational and social knowledge of the design and implementation process, as well as software engineering skills, making it necessary to incur costs in these areas. In addition, despite increasing competition in the modes of delivery of information services and entertainment and education programming, the costs of information are increasing. As information that has been freely available to the user, for example, government information, education products, scientific information held in public libraries, etc., begins to be converted to digital form, it is often sold in the commercial market. Although the Internet is a growing source of 'free' inform-

ation, there are moves to introduce many more electronic commerce services. Information providers are seeking to boost their revenues from sales in global and regional 'electronic markets'. The extension of intellectual property rights to software and other information products, including compilations of multimedia products, also adds to the cost of information for producers and users.

Box 6.1 - ALTERNATIVE ELECTRICITY PROVISION IN RURAL SOUTH AFRICA

Shortage of electricity is a major deterrent to the use of ICTs, and in rural South Africa this problem is addressed by two particular projects. One is implementing digital telephone services as digital 'post office/telephone exchanges' in rural areas and uses solar-panel generated electricity that is stored in batteries. The other project introduces ICTs for enhanced teaching and learning in those schools that are not sufficiently close to an electrical grid point to be connected to electricity supply at an affordable cost. Therefore solar power is used to service the schools and their computing equipment. The project aims to supply all 16,400 remote schools by the year 2000 (Butcher and Perold 1996).

These factors leading to cost increases are complemented by efficiency gains in terms of time-savings, reduced transportation costs, energy savings, and product and process innovations. However, experience shows that these gains do not accrue unless the organisational system and institutional infrastructure is consistent with the new ways of working or learning that ICTs introduce. For LDCs this means that a systematic approach to the introduction of ICTs in key sectors of the economy and civil society is essential to ensuring that the benefits of networks, services, and ICT applications in the public and private sectors outweigh the costs.

These considerations are important for the models devised by LDCs to develop and implement ICT systems in ways that are responsive to their needs and priorities. There is no 'ideal-type' model that will fit the requirements of each country. However, as governments and other stakeholders in the LDCs develop plans for strengthening their national information infrastructures, three key issue areas are important. The first, examined in section 6.2, is the infrastructure 'access' issue. The second is the 'information content' issue (Section 6.3), and the third is the capabilities or 'skills base' issue (Section 6.4). Section 6.5 looks at the advantages of regional cooperation between LDCs that is attempting to address these issues. The final section looks at the linkages between these issue areas and processes that may assist LDCs in selecting their priorities.

6.2 THE LEAST DEVELOPED COUNTRIES AND 'ACCESS'

The countries classified as LDCs by the United Nations General Assembly in 1995 are shown in Table 6.1. The poverty of these countries means that there is an absence

TABLE 6.1 – LEAST DEVELOPED COUNTRY INDICATORS RANKED BY GDP PER CAPITA

	GDP per capita US $ 1995	Percentage of people in absolute poverty 1980-1990	Infant mortality per 1000 live births 1992	Percentage of population with access to safe water 1991	Telephone main lines per 100 population 1995
Developed market economy countries	***21598	n/a	10	99	–
All developing countries	***906	n/a	70	70	–
Least developed countries	376	n/a	113	51	0.93
Liberia	n/a	20	146	50	n/a
Uganda	n/a	*80	111	21	n/a
Mozambique	80	59	167	22	0.33
Ethiopia	81	60	123	25	0.25
Somalia	101	60	125	37	0.17
Chad	119	54	123	57	0.08
Togo	121	*30	86	60	0.30
Afghanistan	133	53	165	99	0.12
Malawi	133	82	143	56	0.35
Burundi	138	84	108	57	0.27
Eritrea	144	n/a	123	n/a	0.48
Burkino Faso	147	*90	101	68	0.29
Sudan	160	*85	100	48	0.27
Rwanda	166	85	131	66	0.19
Niger	171	*35	191	53	0.15
Nepal	175	60	90	42	0.36
Sierra Leone	182	*65	144	37	0.37
Mali	190	54	122	41	0.17
Dem. Rep. of the Congo	195	70	121	39	0.08
Cambodia	207	n.a.	117	36	0.05
Guinea-Bissau	209	*75	141	41	0.88
Madagascar	209	43	110	23	0.24
Bangladesh	215	78	97	85	0.22
Sao Tome and Principe	221	*50	65	n/a	1.91
Tuvalu	235	n/a	40	n/a	0.52
United Rep. of Tanzania	239	58	111	49	0.23
Haiti	257	76	87	39	0.84
Benin	278	*65	88	**55	0.52
Lao People's Dem. Rep.	281	*85	98	36	0.37
Central African Republic	295	*90	105	24	0.23
Equatorial Guinea	308	67	118	35	0.63
Zambia	323	64	113	53	0.82

TABLE 6.I CONTINUED – LEAST DEVELOPED COUNTRY INDICATORS RANKED BY GDP PER CAPITA

	GDP per capita US $ 1995	Percentage of people in absolute poverty 1980-1990	Infant mortality per 1000 live births 1992	Percentage of population with access to safe water 1991	Telephone main lines per 100 population 1995
Bhutan	331	*90	131	34	0.62
Gambia	337	*85	133	77	1.78
Comoros	422	*50	90	69	0.85
Lesotho	447	54	108	47	0.90
Mauritania	451	*80	118	66	0.41
Kiribati	485	n/a	60	73	2.60
Guinea	531	*70	135	53	0.16
Congo	594	*65	170	41	0.81
Solomon Islands	674	*60	27	61	1.73
Djibouti	817	*70	113	84	1.31
Cape Verde	880	*40	44	74	5.68
Samoa	933	*60	45	82	4.70
Vanuatu	1,070	n/a	65	71	2.49
Maldives	1,092	*40	56	69	5.67
Yemen	1,217	*30	107	36	1.24
Myanmar	1,319	35	83	32	0.32

Note: * Rural population, ** nearest year to column heading, *** 1993
Source: Compiled from UNCTAD (1995b), and *ITU STARS Database* (1996).

of 'buyer power' in the potential ICT-using population. In 1995, per capita GDP ranged from US$ 80 in Mozambique to US$ 1,319 in Myanmar. The reported percentage of the rural population living in absolute poverty varied from 30 per cent in Togo and Yemen, to 90 per cent in Burkino Faso, Bhutan, and the Central African Republic. Where the percentage of the whole population living in absolute poverty is reported, the figures ranged from 20 per cent in Liberia to 85 per cent in Rwanda. The infant mortality rate per 1000 live births ranged from 27 in the Solomon Islands to 191 in Niger. All but eight of these LDCs have higher rates of infant mortality than the 70 per 1,000 live births average for all developing countries. The percentage of people with access to safe water varied from 21 per cent in Uganda to 99 per cent in Afghanistan. Once again, only eight countries exceeded the average of 70 per cent for all developing countries.

The penetration rates for telephony are also shown in Table 6.1. Catching up from a position of as few as 0.05 telephone main lines per 100 population in Cambodia or just under 5.68 in Cape Verde is an enormous investment challenge. This is especially so when the income levels of major segments of the population are extremely low and many people are living outside the money economy.

These indicators illustrate that people in the LDCs need 'access' to many things - medical facilities, water and

other resources, jobs, and money. Where should 'access' to the telephone or the Internet be placed on the list of priorities for development? How important is it to link into the global information infrastructure, to acquire 'digital literacy', or to develop indigenous electronic information resources? What emphasis should be given to using ICTs to modernise manufacturing processes or public and private sector management decision-making? What emphasis should be given to using ICTs to address health, education, environment, and other problems?

LDCs, like other countries, need to build the capabilities to assess and evaluate their own priorities and to devise strategies that are responsive to their development goals. The weight of evidence shows that developing countries run very high risks of social and economic exclusion if they do not take steps to implement a national information infrastructure. For LDCs there is less evidence upon which to base a conclusion. However, experience of ICT applications appears to indicate that, under the right circumstances, the benefits of investment in ICTs can outweigh the risk that scarce resources diverted from other development problems will worsen conditions. This will be so, however, only if the circumstances are right, that is, if the emphasis is placed on people first; their needs and concerns.

'Knowledge societies' will bring the need for new models for ICT access, information generation, sharing and use, and capability building. Each of the LDCs faces the challenge of developing the national information infrastructure from a very different starting position and with very different capacities to attract external financing. The quantitative characteristics of the network access gap between LDCs and the industrialised countries are examined in Chapter 2 of this report at the aggregate national level. This section considers whether networking technologies - the Internet and its applications - will begin to reduce the 'access' gap for LDCs.

▮ NGONET provides e-mail access via Fidonet throughout Africa.

▮ ESANET (Eastern Southern African Network) links researchers in eastern and southern Africa by e-mail.

▮ HealthNet, a satellite network for exchange of medical information developed by Satlife (US).

▮ PADISNET (Pan African Documentation Centre Network), a data and information exchange for planners in 34 countries.

▮ WEDNET is a women's project network for the management of natural resources.

▮ MANGO (Microcomputer Access for NGOs) is an electronic billboard in Zimbabwe.

▮ ARSENATE is a Fidonet network supported by Canadian International Development Agency.

▮ CABECA (Capacity Building for Electronic Communication in Africa) is funded by the International Development Research Centre and implemented by the Pan Africa Development Information System of the United National Economic Commission for Africa (UNECA).

▮ RINAF (Regional Informatics Network for Africa) is supported by UNESCO's Intergovernmental Information Programme and financed by the Italian and Republic of Korea governments.

▮ COPINE (Cooperative Information Network Linking Scientists, Educators and Professionals in Africa) is funded by the UN Office for Outer Space to support satellite network connectivity.

The Internet's explosive growth is a very important 'driver' of the global information infrastructure vision. In the OECD countries a strong association has been found between telecommunication market liberalisation, competition, and growing numbers of Internet Access Providers and users. For example, Finland led the world in January 1996 with 41.2 Internet hosts per 1,000 inhabitants (as compared to the United States with 23.5, and Mexico with 0.2). In Finland and the United States there are competitive prices for the use of well-developed infrastructures. In Mexico, market liberalisation is beginning to take effect (OECD 1996c). From this experience it could be assumed that LDCs would see substantial growth in the use of the Internet if they opened their markets to competition and introduced a radical restructuring of prices for network access and use. However, market liberalisation on its own is unlikely to spark the massive increases in Internet use that have occurred in the industrialised countries and some of the newly industrialising countries. Several additional factors need to be addressed including the relevance of the information available on the Internet (see section 6.3).

First, in many LDCs there is diversity in the public and corporate networks and protocols already in limited use. Second, the base of installed PCs is generally not current generation technology. These two factors raise network interoperability and interconnection issues. These need to be addressed through policy measures with respect to standardisation and procurement specification for network operators. This means that regulatory authorities must possess an adequate amount of technical knowledge and that there need to be incentives for cooperation among all those who are responsible for managing networks.

Second, the lower prices resulting from competitive pressures still must be high enough to provide a commercial return to private sector information providers. These prices may be out of reach for potential users in already marginalised segments of the population. Third, in some countries moral and ethical traditions encourage governments to suppress access to the World Wide Web using 'intelligent agents' and to control the use of various kinds of bulletin boards and Internet-based discussion groups (see Chapter 10).

The mix of network providers offering connectivity in African countries is shown in Box 2. The history of the build up of these networks using different protocols is an illustration of the first point. Until the end of 1995, the majority of African countries were relying on non-governmental organisations (NGOs), such as GreenNet in London, for Internet access (with basic FIDOnet - store and forward - networking technique) (Holderness 1998 forthcoming).

Public telecommunication operators in a number of African countries (Benin, Central African Republic, Djibouti, Mauritius, Madagascar, Senegal, and South Africa) are establishing full Internet services, and others are in the preparatory stages (Angola, Ethiopia, Gambia, Gabon, Guinea, Mali, Sierra Leone, Tanzania, and Zimbabwe) (Jensen 1996[a]). NGOs continue to be important providers of minimal communication facilities, but commercial Internet Service Providers are beginning to establish a base in some of the larger cities in Africa (Holderness 1998 forthcoming). Table 6.2 shows the types

TABLE 6.2 - ELECTRONIC NETWORKS IN AFRICA

Country	FIDO[2]	Hnet	UUCP[3]	Co. IP	Comm. IP
Algeria	x		x	x	
Angola	x				
Botswana	x	x	x	x	
Burkina Faso			x		
Cameroon	x	x	x		
CAR	x				
Chad	x	x			
Dem. Rep. of the Congo		x	x		
Ivory Coast	x		x		
Egypt				x	x
Eritrea	x	x	x		
Ethiopia	x	x	x		
Gambia	x	x			
Ghana	x	x			x
Guinea				x	
Kenya	x	x		x	
Lesotho	x	x	x		
Madagascar	x		x		
Malawi	x	x			
Mali	x	x	x		
Morocco	x			x	
Mozambique	x	x	x	x	
Namibia			x	x	
Niger			x		
Nigeria	x		x		
Senegal	x		x	x	
Seychelles			x		
South Africa	x		x	x	x
Sudan		x			
Swaziland			x	x	
Tanzania	x	x		x	
Togo			x		
Uganda	x	x	x		
Zambia	x	x			x
Zimbabwe	x	x		x	

Note: Fidonet = public store and forward network, the largest user base in Africa; Hnet = HealthNet, Fido based system supported by SatelLife; UUCP = store and forward using packet switching in many French speaking countries; Co.IP = Cooperative TCP/IP for universities and other cooperative institutions; Comm. IP = full Internet Protocol connections for profit.
Source: Adam (1996), updated for 1997.

of protocols and network providers supporting connections in African countries during 1996 (Ajayi 1995). Full Internet connections were available in only a very few countries meaning that use of applications, such as the World Wide Web, was very restricted. The number of e-mail hosts in Africa in 1996 was also relatively small (Holderness 1998 forthcoming).[1]

BOX 6.3 - FALLING BEHIND AGAIN?

Internet II, a Very-High-Performance Backbone Network Service (vBNS), is sponsored by the National Science Foundation and is being built by MCI. The new network will operate at 622 Mbit/s (Gallivan 1997). In October 1996 the Internet II initiative was launched by 34 universities concerned about the privatisation of the existing network, its congestion, and its inability to continue to support world class research (Peters 1996). Partnerships with government agencies and the private sector, including IBM, Cisco Systems, AT&T, MCI and Sun Microsystems are at the core of the initiative to build an end-to-end broadband infrastructure among the participating universities. The aim is to introduce a common bearer service to support new and existing services and provide the capability to tailor the network to specific applications (Nairn 1997a).

A study in 1996 showed that the growing feasibility of full Internet connectivity has not been generating substantial interest. At that time the number of estimated users was small as compared to the explosion of Internet activity in other regions of the world. For example, in Ghana, Morocco, Algeria, and Uganda there were less than 100 users, in Zimbabwe and Mozambique less than 300 users each, in Zambia there were 380 users, in Tunisia 310, and in Egypt about 900 users (Adam 1996).

While the LDCs struggle with absent or inadequate infrastructure and user equipment, the United States is racing ahead with the next generation infrastructure to support advanced ICT applications. For example, the design and implementation of Internet II is getting underway (see Box 6.3). While one part of the world begins to build highly sophisticated 'next generation' Internets and applications, large parts of the world are struggling to achieve full connectivity to 'first generation' networks to support telephony or basic e-mail connections often using older generation PCs and software.

The affordability of services offered on a commercial basis is the second major factor for LDCs to consider in the 'access' context. Even where networks are accessible, they may simply be unaffordable, even for professional people, as illustrated by the prices for subscriptions in Ghana (see Box 6.4).

In developing country regions such as Latin America and the Caribbean, Internet usage growth rates have been among the highest in the world since full Internet access was established in 1994 with Organisation of American

States assistance (Bourdeau et al. 1996). However, the costs of accessing and using the Internet are not as low as they could be because many Internet Access Providers are located outside the countries. For example, Jamaica's main access route to the Internet is through Internet Service Providers in the United States, resulting in high access rates (Bennett 1995). This phenomenon is characteristic of many other developing countries. These countries are discussing arrangements for reducing the costs by 'cashing' information at Internet sites within their regions and by negotiating new Internet interconnection arrangements with providers based mainly in the United States. If the LDCs are to reduce costs arising from the geographical configuration of their access arrangements they will need to do so on a regional and coordinated basis.

BOX 6.4 - AFFORDABILITY OF INTERNET ACCESS

In Ghana in the Spring of 1995 there were only ten 14,400 kbit/s leased lines linked to the United Kingdom costing about US$ 7,500 per month each. One was used by the interbank clearing system, SWIFT, and another by the air-traffic control network, SITA. By early 1996, a private network computer systems host in the capital city had 140 subscribers paying US$ 1,300 each a year - the annual income of one Ghanaian journalist.[4]

In general, the overall use of ICTs remains very limited in the LDCs. In Ethiopia, for example, the application of ICTs in the health sector is localised mainly in libraries that are using CD-ROMs for database searches. Infrastructure constraints limit information sharing among organisations and e-mail exchange is very difficult. New applications are out of reach due to cost, absence of appropriate infrastructure, or the specialised capabilities necessary for their effective use. There are severe shortages of up-to-date, relevant information sources, and skilled employees, coupled with inadequate infrastructure. As of 1996, access to international networks was only available to a few specialised networks with a limited number of users. These included SITA, the airlines cooperative network, and the 1,000 e-mail users connected through the Pan African Development Information System (PADIS) using a telephone-based FIDOnet store and forward technique (Alemu 1996).

6.3 THE LEAST DEVELOPED COUNTRIES AND INFORMATION CONTENT

The extent to which national information infrastructures offer access to useful information for LDCs depends on the type of information that is accessible and affordable from a variety of electronic sources. The Internet is a potential outlet for governments and other stakeholders in the LDCs to 'publish' information and share the results of ICT applications. There is a growing number of sites with information about LDCs.

A search of the World Wide Web in mid 1997 for pages of information concerning LDCs suggests that this mode of information exchange has yet to become a source of information produced by businesses, citizens, or governments in LDCs about their own experiences. Many information pages are produced by observers from other countries or by intergovernmental organisations. Where information is provided by governments and others within LDCs (in this sample), it is top level information of a very generic nature, frequently offering basic contact information for government departments, or tourism information likely to be of interest to external searchers. The links to more detailed information are often 'dead' or they link the 'surfer' to very outdated sources of information. In addition, many of the commercial sites are managed by Webmasters in the United States, the United Kingdom, or Australia. Those sites originating in LDCs tend to contain outdated information. Table 6.3 illustrates the characteristics of some of these Web sites.[5]

If people are to use indigenous and external sources of digital information to contribute to lifelong learning and to implement ICT applications that alleviate development problems in the LDCs attention must focus on the needs of the information user and on the types of information that are becoming available as a result of commercial activity and public sector initiatives. In the education field in the United States, the home education software market was estimated in 1996 to be worth US$ 1.4 billion and the school courseware market was estimated at US$ 290 million (McKinsey & Company 1996). However, efforts to use digital stand-alone or networked distance learning products in the LDCs encounter problems with language teaching, different pedagogical methods, diplomas and curricula, and legal problems concerning copying and use of audiovisual materials (UNESCO 1996).

Libraries provide a potential source of information of local relevance for LDCs but there are very few libraries, especially on a per capita basis, and so access is limited. Mobile libraries provide one solution and 'global digital libraries' are being discussed. Current efforts include those by the Global Information Alliance of the International Federation for Documentation, a proposed 'Global Digital Library Initiative' under consideration by the International Federation of Library Associations and Institutions, and the G7 pilot project, Biblioteca Universalis (UNESCO 1996). Telecentres that are networked with libraries offering information and media access, social services such as education and telemedicine, and fora for public discussion and meetings of business people, could help to address the 'information content' challenge (UNESCO 1996).

Sources of information include the existing stocks of books, databases, and films that potentially could be made available via electronic information services although the costs are considerable. The UNESCO *World*

TABLE 6.3 – WORLD WIDE WEB PAGES WITH LDC INFORMATION

Country	Type of Information	Source of Information	Comment
Afghanistan	Travel/tourist information	External, private sector US	
	Aid organisations	French NGO	
	Human rights	Amnesty International	
	Local governance	UN Office for Project Services	
	War history	Afghan and US Army	
Bangladesh	Bangladesh Online Government information	Proshika Computer Systems – NGO	Contact links to government departments and contact details.
Bhutan	Gov./politics/society	Asiaworld UK	'Dead links'
	Thunder Dragon Kingdom of Bhutan	Personal website	
Cambodia (Kampuchea)	Khmer Neutral Party	Political party	
	Cambodia Times on the Net	Newspaper publisher	Only 3 March, 17-23 March 97
	Human rights	UN Economic & Social Council	February 1996
	Human rights	Human Rights Watch/New Cambodian Press Law	September 1995
	Internet		'Dead link' to information
Haiti	Newspaper scanned information	University of Florida	
Kiribati	Basic facts and statistics	Tohoku University	Last updated June 1996
	Who's Who in Telecommunications		Some information 'not available'
Laos	Government information		'Dead link'
	Transportation		'Dead link'
	Communication		'Dead link'
	Human rights	Lao Human Rights Council, US	
	Teaching English	NGO	
Maldives	General information, Tourist information	UN, UNICEF	
Myanmar	General information	Asia World UK	
	General information	University of Tokyo, Japan	
Nepal	General information	NGO	
	Project listings	NGO	
	Nepal Report to UNCED	NGO	
	Tourist information	Mainly US sources	
Samoa	General government and tourist information	Website of American Samoa Government	
Solomon Islands	Tourist information	CCC Inc.	
	Government Media Press	Ross Mining Web Site	
Tuvalu	Various tourist, general information	Commonwealth Online Webmaster, UK	
	Microstate Micronesia Sustainable development interchange	Microstate Network Inc. US	
Vanuatu	General country information and comment on impact of broadcasting	Vanatu On Line Content by a Canadian	September 1996
Yemen	General information	ArabNet	
	Public counter telecoms service information	General People's Congress and TeleYemen	
Asian Countries	Asian Studies WWW Virtual Library	Maintained by Australian National University, network of Asian, Australian, and US institutions	

Source: Various WWW sites, July 1997.

Information Report 1997/98 offers a comprehensive region by region survey of archival, library, and information services and databases produced by countries throughout the world. The capacity of many LDCs to publish in the print medium information that reflects their cultures, their technological, economic and political histories, and their current problems, is limited. For example, in 1993 the number of books published in the United Kingdom was 1,490 per 1 million inhabitants. The equivalent figure for Ethiopia and Senegal was five, four for Mozambique, 21 for Ghana, and Viet Nam produced 27 books per 1 million inhabitants (Dumort and Dryden 1997 based on UNESCO data).

In terms of book titles in the science and social science categories reflecting the scientific and technical research capabilities of LDCs, available data show that while India produced 7,465 titles in 1991 and Thailand 5,167 titles in 1992, Pakistan produced only 32, Brunei Darussalam 13, and Lao (P.D.R.) 22.[6]

In the central and east European countries the information generated in the science and technology fields is relatively well developed. Table 6.4 shows the number of electronic information services produced in the region in 1993 and 1995. The number of databases compares well with those produced in the European Union but many are not comparable in terms of quality and data reliability. Most of the databases included in Table 6.4 are produced by small outfits which has a negative affect on quality, and makes it difficult to maintain the continuity of data sets. In 1995 only 16 per cent of the 2,936 databases could be accessed on-line and more than 80 of the databases were marketed only locally. Although the telecommunication system is improving, the cost of the scientific and technical information has increased significantly since a price system was introduced. The 429 on-line databases are produced by 118 vendors, the biggest of which are Russian, Hungarian, Czech, and Bulgarian. Only one host, VINITI in Moscow, provides more than 30 databases and these are accessible via the Internet.[7]

TABLE 6.4 – ELECTRONIC INFORMATION SERVICES IN EASTERN EUROPE AND THE COMMONWEALTH OF INDEPENDENT STATES

	1993	1995
Vendors	145	118
Producers	779	1146
Electronic media/databases	1,918	2,936

Source: UNESCO (1997).

Print is only one of several media that capture the cultural, scientific, and technological history of countries. Audio-visual media record musical performances, oral histories, news, and current affairs. Audiovisual materials include visual recordings and sound recordings and are produced using a very wide range of formats and playback systems causing incompatibility problems. It is important to note, however, that the life expectancy of these materials is dependent on chemistry, and storage and handling conditions. Preservation and conservation are very costly.[8]

Print based materials, electronic databases, and audio-visual materials are all sources for the development of multimedia products. These are regarded by many as providing the foundation for new modes of interactive learning in the next century. The concept of multimedia goes back as far as 1945 when it was introduced in an article by Vannevar Bush. The idea was extended in 1963 in the form of NLS (oNLine System) by combining concepts of hypertext with other computing tools.[9] Multimedia extends the idea of hypertext to all forms of material that can be digitally encoded for storage and retrieval using a computer system including images, sound, graphics, and animation. Multimedia products include CD-ROM titles. Although the software and hardware tools for production are declining in cost, they are still not cheap from the standpoint of the LDCs (for example, Macromedia's Director software costs about US$ 900; a PC Pentium multimedia system ranges from US$ 1,500 to US$ 4,000 in the United States). In order to work with many CD-ROM titles a reasonably powerful PC is necessary.[10] Other costs include payments to copyright holders for use of copyrighted materials in order to produce compilations, whether in multimedia or single electronic medium format.

Excitement about the potential of multimedia and other computer-based products and services in connection with the global information infrastructure is intense. This is because, if the high capacity highways can be put in place (with 'off-ramps'), all these products, in principle, could be distributed worldwide, regionally or locally using the digital 'information highways'. The Internet has navigation tools such as Yahoo!, Lycos, WebCrawler, OpenText, AltaVista, Inktomi, InfoSeek, and Magellan, which offer free access to top level information, or charge on a subscription or per-search basis. In industrialised countries the costs of information are often subsidised by universities or covered by advertisers using a 'broadcast' model. However for LDCs, even if a reliable telecommunication system were to exist together with a software support system, the Internet and its information resources may be inconsistent with their rhythms of life.[11]

In contrast to the visionary expectation that national information infrastructures will enable people to use locally produced digital products and a vast stock of external information, the reality is very different in many of the LDCs. For example, in January 1996 there was one Internet host in Ethiopia compared to the 6,053,402 hosts in the United States, 22,769 hosts in Singapore, 2,351 in Indonesia, 93 in Zimbabwe, and 58 in Uganda (UNESCO 1997).

For most of the rural community in Ethiopia, radio and television broadcasting are the major means of communication. The diffusion of radio and television sets in 1991-1992 was estimated at 7.2 per 100,000 inhabitants and 0.4 per 100,000 inhabitants, respectively. As an economy based on agriculture, access to information is needed to increase productivity in Ethiopia. Specialised library databases have been introduced, but these tend not to be up-to-date and are of limited use due to the lack of staff training. Although indigenous capacity for generating specialised agricultural information is growing, this is hampered by the absence of linkages between R&D activities and information services. Remote research stations are particularly limited in their access to information and electronic communication. Similarly, the health sector requires much better access to scientific information (Alemu 1996).

In Tanzania, a national science and technology database has been created for researchers, planners, academics, and entrepreneurs. An e-mail node in Dar es Salaam is supporting efforts to implement e-mail and Internet connections to improve communication between institutions within and outside the country. In Nigeria a project called COPINE (Cooperative Information Network Linking Scientists, Educators, Professionals and Decision-Makers in Africa) is helping to improve the collection, transmission, distribution, and exchange of information. Twelve African countries are collaborating with five European centres in this project (UNCSTD 1997b).

There are many other initiatives to create databases relevant to development issues. For example, the United Nations University Institute for New Technologies (UNU/INTECH) in Maastricht, has developed a global technology and economic development (GLOB-TED) database containing entries for indicators in over 130 industrialised and developing countries. The data mainly concern foreign direct investment and licensing activities for foreign firms in developing countries. It is expected that eventually the database will be accessible externally.

Other information sources include the Zero Emissions Research Initiative (UNU/ZERI) initiative and the Integrated Biosystems Network run by the United Nations University in Tokyo enabling 210 experts to participate in debate. The UNU International Institute for Software Technology (UNU/IIST) provides software development and postgraduate training and fellowships for advanced software projects including design techniques for real-time, reactive and hybrid systems, railway computing systems, manufacturing industry information and command infrastructure systems, multilingual script systems, air traffic control support systems, and digital multiplexed telephone systems. In 1996, eighteen courses were organised in Macau, China, Viet Nam, India, the Philippines, Mongolia, Belarus, Russia, Romania, Poland, Brazil, Argentina, and Gabon (UNCSTD 1997b).

In Bolivia there was no public support for the creation of information networks and no access to the Internet in 1995. By 1996 access to the Internet was provided through the intervention of the National Council and networks such as the Sustainable Development Network providing environmental information (UNCSTD 1997b).

These illustrations demonstrate that, despite difficulties, ICTs are enabling more and more information, especially with regard to science, technology, and the economy, to circulate via electronic means. However, these developments bring benefits and risks. The information generated by satellite remote sensing and geographical information systems in Africa offers an illustration which emphasises the importance of assessing the social and economic impact of innovative information systems. Assessment is needed from the perspective of as many of the stakeholders who may be affected by the new systems as resources permit. Questions need to be asked not only about the direct effects of the systems but also about the pervasive impacts on the social and political fabric of society.

The first column in Table 6.5 shows the upward trends in the sophistication of ICTs and the decreasing costs. The effects of these trends are shown in the second column. Columns three and four highlight some of opportunities and the risks associated with these technological and economic trends. The benefits take the form of improvements in planning to alleviate famine and in managing ground water reservoirs and energy use. But the use of these systems also brings the risk that, by virtue of better access to remotely sensed data and capabilities for analysis, foreign firms may exploit this knowledge to their own economic benefit and to the disadvantage of LDCs. Access to remotely sensed data may also support government surveillance activities that are not in the interests of citizens. The adoption of ICT applications means that information becomes an even more important social and economic resource because of its improved timeliness, quantity, or quality. It benefits those who have the financial resources and knowledge to use it effectively.

Information sharing is occurring in LDCs to raise awareness about environmental problems in Africa. For example, the UN Institute for Training and Research (UNITAR) is encouraging Internet discussion groups where members share remotely sensed data and the analyses produced by geographical information systems and other sources. Training on the use of these systems is also provided using specially designed software for exercises and case studies (UNCTAD 1997).

In Sub-Saharan Africa, ICT applications are being used to disseminate policy-related information and to share technical information on, for example, the use of a geographic information system for mapping malaria in Africa (Council for Scientific and Industrial Research 1996).

Building new capabilities for using ICTs effectively involves a recognition that information is about people and that the information infrastructure is about hardware,

TABLE 6.5 – THE CONTRIBUTION OF ICT TOOLS TO SUSTAINABLE DEVELOPMENT

Trend	Examples of effects	Examples of opportunities related to these effects	Examples of risks related to these effects
Sensors improve data acquisition	Remote sensing provides data on large scale land use.	Improved planning as in the African Famine Early Warning System.	Foreign mining firms through greater mastery of technology will have greater knowledge of mineral resources, and will exploit that advantage unfairly in dealing with developing countries.
	Sensors available to provide industrial process control data.	Improved process control for least developed country industry, and thus higher productivity, better quality products, and less waste.	Industrialised countries through greater mastery of the technology will gain commercial advantage over developing countries in manufacturing.
Lower cost of computation	Design automation costs are reduced.	Taking advantage of cost reductions to improve design and thus improving manufacturing efficiency, improving product quality, and improving customer satisfaction.	ICT advantage of industrialised countries centralises design activity in these countries.
	Computer analysis more affordable, allowing more complex problems to be solved and more accurate approximations to be made.	More accurate analyses of water management issues such as exploitation of ground water reservoirs or management of river waters.	Improved analytical capacity used for inappropriate purposes, such as improved logistic management for coercive government actions.
	Simulation more affordable.	Improved weather and climate prediction through application of greater computer power (and improved data).	More accurate simulations allow for greater manipulation of public opinion for anti-democratic purposes.
Lower cost point-to-point communication	Development of the Internet and Intranets.	Improved enterprise efficiency achieved by taking advantage of improved communications.	Countries destabilised by minorities who utilise the Internet for subversive purposes.
Reduced cost and size and greater resistance to adverse conditions in microprocessors	Application of electronic control in motor vehicles, equipment control, etc.	Improved energy and resource use efficiency, as motors run more efficiently, irrigation controllers make more efficient use of water, etc.	Increased military spending if military forces are able to capture a greater portion of GDP to take advantage of these technological opportunities.
Lower cost and greater power of information storage and retrieval	Paperless office.	Improved access to electronic data will improve management of enterprises, natural resources, etc.	Countries with low capital to labour ratios will fall behind technologically because they will not be able to capture the benefits of automated data storage and retrieval as well as richer countries.
Improved human machine interface	Greater user access to computational power, electronic communication, and information.	Reduced demands on human resource development for dealing with information technology, and greater effectiveness of ICT users at whatever level of training possible.	Increased deleterious cultural impact of ICTs in some countries.

Source: Daly (1997).

software, and organisation. The most important and difficult issues are often as much about knowledge, information content, and values, as about the detailed technical design of ICT systems (Nostbakken and Akhtar 1995; Gilbert et al. 1994). Technology selection leads to priority areas for action but this requires technical and managerial skills and organisational learning. User-oriented strategies (including early, low-cost experience by large parts of the user community) are essential to building a critical mass of local users who can trigger a cumulative learning process within the LDCs.

6.4 ENHANCING THE SKILLS BASE

The use of ICTs to support development goals does not need to be considered only in terms of the extension of telephony networks to every household. Alternative modes of access may be preferable in some circumstances and the choice of radio, television or telephony as a means of connection of citizens to networks of information is dependent on each country's circumstances. The skills base that is built up must be compatible with the mix of ICTs available and provide a basis for continuous learning.

It is helpful to draw distinctions between generic skills and three specific types of skills that are particularly important and relevant for the LDCs (Enos 1996).

▌ *Participatory skills* are necessary for involvement in networked communication and information sharing. These incorporate computer literacy and fluency in the English language for use of the Internet, databases, and most software until more content is provided in local languages. Although there is considerable variability, English is widely spoken in these countries; it is used as the instruction language in schools for at least part of the population or for some subjects such as science and engineering.

▌ *Facilitating skills* for the design, implementation, and maintenance of networks involve a number of essential technical skills for installation, user training, and maintenance. In addition, software and computer systems engineering skills are desirable. As these skills demand fluent English in order to cope with the technical aspects and informational potential of the equipment, they constitute the greatest barrier for LDCs. Even more emphasis needs to be placed on *vocational training* to provide a large number of people with the ability to ensure the functionality of networks.

▌ Finally, *control skills* imply the allocation of funds for the acquisition of appropriate ICT equipment in order to manage access to networks in some countries to achieve public or private control. As these skills are based on the authority of governments rather than on specific training, this places fewer constraints on the existing skills base of least developed countries.

Much of the responsibility for enhancing the skills base in LDCs falls to the public sector. The provision of an adequate education system to compensate for the lack of informal learning opportunities and to provide the necessary participatory and facilitating skills base with technical and English language qualifications is becoming increasingly important. Bottlenecks are often experienced due to the high demand for facilitating skills from the private and public sectors. The public sector may not be able to attract technical personnel and may be dominated by senior officials, leading to a 'brain drain' to the domestic private sector.

Another factor to the advantage of LDCs is the age structure of the population and the presence of a significant number of younger people who are very adaptable (Patterson 1995). In many LDCs and smaller or island developing countries, there is a high proportion of skilled young professionals who have substantial innovative potential. However, as these younger workers acquire skills that are in demand in the industrialised countries, there is a risk of a 'brain drain' from developing to industrialised countries placing additional pressure on the educational infrastructure in developing countries.

The low level of skill availability in some countries forms part of a vicious circle whereby local contracts, commissioned mainly by the government as, for example, in Jamaica and Brazil, are given to outside experts rather than to local businesses (Hamilton 1995; Barros 1998 forthcoming). This is often due less to the absence of local capabilities, than to the restrictions imposed by lending agencies. The result is that local businesses are missing out on the opportunities as they arise. It may be possible to commission nationals living outside the country thereby enhancing opportunities for knowledge and expertise to be shared more effectively among a close community of professionals.

The experience of vocational training in Southern Africa illustrates some of the problems and options for building the skills base in LDCs. The lack of adequately trained people to meet demand is experienced by all member states of the Southern African Development Community (SADC). The problem is compounded by the lack of capacity within member states to develop the human resource base to meet this demand.

At the tertiary level of education, undergraduate programmes in computing are offered by universities and colleges in the majority of member states, either as a single subject or in conjunction with another subject, such as mathematics or statistics. Typically, the aim of these programmes is to prepare graduates for employment as computing professionals, taking responsibility for the analysis, design, and management of computer-based information systems. In a number of member states sustaining these programmes has proved difficult due to the relatively high cost of acquiring and maintaining up-to-date ICT equipment, and the poor remuneration of computing professionals in the public sector.

The relevance of these programmes can also be questioned. They are modelled on the undergraduate programmes in computing offered by universities and colleges in western Europe and North America. The programmes tend to focus on the technology and, in particular, on the design and implementation of software to control hardware components. They do not focus sufficiently on the use of the technology to meet organisational needs. Thus graduates of these programmes may be inadequately prepared for employment because they lack experience in the design of computer-based information systems that use readily available PC software packages, such as spreadsheets and databases. They also may have little or no understanding of the socio-political context within which these information systems will be used.

Rather than importing undergraduate programmes from western Europe and North America with aims and objectives that are more consistent with the needs of industrialised countries than of the LDCs, it may be more appropriate to devise programmes with aims and objectives that clearly address local requirements. Because of the lack of adequate resources it is also unlikely that graduates of other programmes will have been able to acquire competence in ICTs sufficient to access, analyse, and disseminate information. Without additional training, non-computing professionals will lack the experience and confidence to use ICTs as a tool in activities such as planning and management. This is particularly problematic for graduates of programmes in subjects such as business administration and public administration who will be expected to manage information within organisations.

Between 1989 and 1993, the Overseas Development Agency (ODA) funded a project to strengthen the teaching of computer science in the University of Malawi. A British Council-funded academic link in computer science was established between Malawi and the University of Abertay Dundee. The aims of this link were to increase the understanding of technical and non-technical constraints to the use of ICTs within the government, NGOs and small business sectors so that ICTs could be more effective in these sectors to enable users. The goal was to make use of ICTs for the retrieval, analysis, and dissemination of information through the provision of short courses, and to provide relevant and appropriate education experiences in the use of ICTs to undergraduate students (both computer science majors and non-computer science majors).

BOX 6.6 - ICTs IN PAPUA NEW GUINEA

The correspondence education system in Papua New Guinea which covers small numbers of students, makes only very limited use of ICTs in its teaching programme. Nevertheless, audiocassettes are available to accompany the printed study material. The two institutions running this programme rely heavily on study centres where tutorials take place at fixed times and assignments are submitted. Rural areas are not covered well by the distribution of study materials or study centres (Laaser 1998 forthcoming).

At the primary and secondary levels of education there is very little provision within the state sector, reflecting the low level of resources available in many member states to support universal access to primary and secondary education. The majority of school leavers are unlikely to have encountered ICT equipment during their schooling, much less to have acquired the competence to use PC software packages, such as word processors, to prepare even the most simple document. While the situation may change over the next five years as a result of a UNESCO-funded project to place ICT equipment in state secondary schools, the competence of secondary school teachers to integrate the use of ICT equipment into the curriculum will be crucial. This competence will itself depend on the provision of staff development for existing teachers and the revision of teacher training programmes to include the use of ICT equipment as a medium for teaching, learning, and assessment (see, for example, Box 6.5).

Vocational training in the use of specific ICT equipment is available in all member states, typically through the vendors of ICT equipment. Attendance at vocational training courses is popular as possession of certificates of attendance is often regarded by the possessor as a means towards career progression. Unfortunately, lack of awareness among some managers may lead to unrealistic expectations that competence in the use of specific ICT equipment is sufficient for analysing and designing computer-based information systems. The quality of the training provided varies considerably depending on the resources available to support such training. For example, the currency and the quantity of the ICT equipment and the competence of the trainers to deliver courses efficiently and effectively, affect the relevance of the training to meet the needs of employers and the resulting competencies of those who have attended such courses. The variable quality of vocational training available in the SADC member states has been a considerable problem for the public sector.

The SADC Council of Ministers agreed in 1994 that member states should be encouraged to work towards a community-wide scheme of certification of the non-academic providers of training courses and accreditation of the training courses (Mundy and Nyirenda 1995). Models for certification and accreditation already exist in western Europe and North America, most notably in the United Kingdom with the system of National Vocational Qualifications (NVQs) devised by the National Council for Vocational Qualifications (NCVQ) in conjunction with industry-led bodies and administered by the Business and Technical Education Council (BTEC). NVQs define national levels of competence that can be expected of those in the workplace. Achievement of NVQs is primarily through compilation of a portfolio of evidence generated in the workplace. Only those training organisations meeting the quality standards of BTEC are permitted to assess candidates for NVQs.

Human resource development for ICTs is not a once-in-a-lifetime process. As advances are made in ICTs and in our understanding of the process by which ICTs are introduced and used effectively in organisations, there is a continuous need for professional development. The driving force for continuous professional development might be expected to reside within the professional bodies representing the interests of computing professionals. However, with the notable exceptions of South Africa, Zambia, and Zimbabwe, the professional bodies in most SADC member states are inactive. There is little recognition among professionals that it is necessary to keep up-to-date, particularly with non-technical developments.

There are other examples throughout the LDCs of the application of ICTs to enhance learning opportunities and information sharing but many continue to make little use of available ICTs. For example, the biggest correspondence education system in Papua New Guinea makes very limited use of ICTs (audiocassettes), while in South Africa, the Internet and radio-based networks are providing a basis for collaboration between the public and private sectors to provide training (see Boxes 6.6 and 6.7).

Informal and formal training are essential components of innovative 'knowledge societies' and ICTs are being used increasingly to support learning in the wealthier developing countries. There are examples of initiatives in the LDCs as well, although there are many advantages and disadvantages to the models for learning that are being applied. A major issue is to maintain local diversity while simultaneously capturing social and economic advantage for the people in these countries. Regional initiatives may provide a 'middle ground' between the force of global developments and the missing capabilities at the local level.

6.5 COOPERATING REGIONS

Regional economic cooperation is a major theme for a growing number of intergovernmental organisations that represent LDCs or embrace LDCs within networks that include wealthier countries. These organisations are giving ICTs a high priority. In some cases, there are clear signs of action leading to jointly developed plans to build up regional information infrastructures. The plans emerging in Africa and the Asia Pacific region demonstrate the potential of these regional initiatives to provide a basis for active policy measures and new partnerships with the private sector.

6.5.1 AFRICA AS A COOPERATING REGION

ICT initiatives to strengthen cooperation between countries in Africa provide a good illustration of measures that can be taken to develop ICT strategies. A UN Economic and Social Council Economic Commission for Africa (UNECA) initiative is aimed at achieving integration of ICTs into all aspects of development. ICTs are seen as crucial to support decision-making at all levels (UNECA 1996a; Knight 1995). By 1995 an Action Plan had been produced by a high-level working group on ICTs (UNECA 1996a). The over-riding goal is to realise the African Information Society Initiative (AISI) for a sustainable information society by 2010. This vision is outlined in Box 6.8.

The Action Plan states that 'Africa has great potential to "leapfrog" development stages by adopting new strategies to build capabilities' (Economic Commission for Africa

1996: 1). The feasibility of technological 'leapfrogging' into a new era of development has been criticised because of its emphasis on a strong 'technology push' orientation and the tendency for ICTs to be treated as a panacea for development problems (Hobday 1994). The new Agenda for Action is an attempt to put information and knowledge at the centre of the strategy and to treat the technologies as tools that can help to strengthen endogenous capabilities. The plans for the national information infrastructures in African countries are driven by problems in areas such as debt management, food security, health services, education, population growth, unemployment and job

BOX 6.7 - DISTANCE EDUCATION FOR AFRICAN DEVELOPMENT

The Telematics for African Development Consortium focuses on distance education for the disadvantaged who were previously excluded from education either due to the Apartheid regime or financial constraints. Developing specific applications for distance education using the Internet and wireless wide-area bandwidth, the project makes use of the many collaborators from a range of private and public sector organisations including a telecommunication operator, a broadcaster, and a distance education university (Byron and Gagliardi 1996; Mbeki 1996).

BOX 6.8 - THE VISION FOR THE AFRICAN INFORMATION SOCIETY INITIATIVE

▮ Information and decision support systems are used to support decision-making in all the major sectors of the economy in line with each country's national development priorities.

▮ Every man and woman, school-age child, village, government office, and business can access information and knowledge resources through computers and telecommunications.

▮ Access is available to international, regional, and national 'information highways', providing 'off-ramps' in the villages and in the information area catering specifically to grass-roots society.

▮ A vibrant business sector exhibits strong leadership capable of forging the build up of the information society.

▮ African information resources are available which reflect the needs of government, business, culture, education, tourism, energy, health, transport, and natural resource management.

▮ Information and knowledge are disseminated and used by business, the public at large, and disenfranchised groups such as women and the poor, in particular, to make rational choices in the economy (free markets) and for all groups to exercise democratic and human rights (freedom of speech and freedom of cultural and religious expression).

creation, industrialisation, land reclamation, water management, and sectors such as tourism, trade, and textiles.

In the health sector in Africa there are a number of initiatives by foreign and local organisations. Although these do not fully exploit the potential of ICT applications, the projects are using ICTs to combat the isolation of health workers by providing information and e-mail discussion groups to help, for example, in disease control. There is a very great need to use ICTs in support of telemedicine initiatives to help to improve the reproductive health of women and to combat HIV and AIDS itself (Council for Scientific and Industrial Research 1996).

Governments, private sector firms, NGOs, and the media all have roles to play as stakeholders in implementing the Action Plan. Governments are expected to provide a vision, strategy, and an enabling environment. They are expected to promote the use of ICTs in government and society to improve the effectiveness of government service delivery and to stimulate local ICT industries. Governments also are expected to provide special support for less well resourced sectors such as the academic and research organisations. National governments are being encouraged to play a crucial role in coordinating ministries and forming joint boards involving government, industry, labour, and consumer associations. Mechanisms are being put in place to enable liaison with other countries, international organisations, and regional bodies to ensure coordinated development of ICT initiatives. The development of a legislative/regulatory framework addressing issues of cost and accessibility of telecommunication services, intellectual property protection, personal privacy, the free flow of information, and the convergence of broadcasting and telecommunication networks, are additional areas for public sector action.

The private sector's contribution is essential to the success of the Action Plan. The private sector is expected to stimulate growth and assume leadership in developing national information infrastructures, to seize new business opportunities arising from the implementation of a new infrastructure, and to support smaller enterprises in devising new applications. Voluntary organisations are playing a vital role in making known the needs of poor and disenfranchised groups such as rural communities, the homeless, aged, and sick, and by helping them to make use of the services. Consumer associations are involved to voice public concerns and the establishment of user groups is encouraged to help in the definition of priorities for ICT applications. Labour associations are responsible for promoting the concerns of the workforce.

The media are expected to help to create awareness about the national information infrastructure and to provide and support opportunities for communication which reach out to all citizens. Case studies demonstrating the use of ICTs and services in Africa have highlighted the

shortage of funds, difficulties in communicating over substantial distances, the shortage of trained personnel, the lack of resources to support the collection and dissemination of indigenous information, and the absence of an environment that enables innovative ICT applications (National Research Council 1996). The Action Plan is intended to reduce the impact of these and other barriers to making more extensive use of ICTs.

When governments have been reluctant to become involved in supporting the introduction of new ICT applications, the diffusion of ICTs often becomes reliant on donors who assume a very influential position (Wangwe et al. 1998 forthcoming). New regional initiatives are encouraging national policies focusing on local information needs by making available government information, increasing access to government documentation and activities, and encouraging a bigger role for NGOs in decision-making (Levin 1996). New projects are focusing on the delivery of government information, networking and sharing information (for example, e-mail), the distribution of legal information, new services for government departments and public sector organisations, information con-cerning human rights issues, services supporting election management and monitoring, and creating fora where issues concerning freedom of information and expression can be discussed.

The International Development Research Centre (IDRC) is involved in a major project to circumvent barriers to knowledge and capabilities development in Africa through the use of ICTs (IDRC 1996, n.d.). The Acacia Initiative will provide about CAN$ 8 million in its first year to encourage the use of ICTs to enable poor communities in Sub-Saharan Africa to access information and services to address their specific development problems. New models for overcoming barriers to community access are being considered focusing on policies promoting universal service as well as technological and organisational measures to adapt services to local community conditions. The project emphasises the training and tools necessary for effective ICT use together with the close collaboration of all the stakeholders. An evaluation process is integrated within the Acacia programme to achieve real-time learning about the factors contributing to the success or failure of ICT applications.

6.5.2 COOPERATING IN ASIA AND THE PACIFIC REGION

The United Nations Economic and Social Commission for Asia and the Pacific (UNESCAP) has taken steps to use regional economic cooperation as a platform to develop and promote advances in ICTs for industrial and technological applications (UNESCAP 1997). The ESCAP action programme in investment-related technology transfer is focusing on information technology because 'no country today can escape the ever-growing influence of information technology. It brings massive change to markets, production, service, and skills requirements. It also expands educational opportunities, improves the quality of life and creates jobs' (UNESCAP 1997: 1).

The countries represented by the Association of South East Asian Nations (ASEAN) have an information technology market which is of the same order of magnitude as China and Korea (Rep. of). However, the market is dominated by hardware (54 per cent) and services (29 per cent) suggesting that it is dominated by a few large corporations. In 1995, software accounted for only 13 per cent of the market and data communication for only 4 per cent (UNESCAP 1997). In this region it has been recognised that LDCs, including the Pacific Island countries and the Central Asian republics, will have problems in building up the absorptive capacity for ICTs because of pricing, restrictive terms and conditions on technology transfer, low technical capabilities of users, and continuing dependence on a narrow set of suppliers. Some LDCs have substantial numbers of qualified workers who can learn to use ICTs, for example, Kazakstan which has 28,000 university graduate scientists working in 287 research institutions.

Initiatives in the ICT field are leading to various forms of regional and subregional initiatives. In the computer field, the South East Asia Regional Computer Confederation (SEARCC) has been formed, and the Asia and Pacific Centre for Transfer of Technology (APCTT) and the Centre for International Cooperation in Computer-isation (CICC) have been set up. The regional group is able to distribute information about the benefits of ICT applications although many of the examples are drawn from the wealthier countries in the region (see Box 6.9).

An example of mass computerisation is Singapore's civil service computerisation programme. Every dollar spent, has generated US$ 2.7 in returns or more than US$ 100 million every year. The programme has reduced employment by 1,500 posts and made an additional 3,500 jobs unnecessary, which is beneficial in Singapore because of its labour shortage (UNESCAP 1997).

Regional cooperation aims to initiate joint projects addressing poverty, illiteracy, environmental degradation, urban decay, and health. ESCAP has recommended that regional library networks be created and that efforts be made to develop regional technology system standards and to introduce machine translation projects. Electronic commerce services are being targeted including the further development of a regional electronic data interchange network and the use of Computer-Aided

Acquisition and Logistics Support (CALS) standards to integrate technical and management information. Public sector computerisation activities are also being supported. Regional cooperation means that countries can share hardware, software, and knowledge resources and help to build both the technical infrastructure and human capabilities.

6.6 Conclusion - Identifying priorities for ICT initiatives

ICT initiatives must be linked to development goals in a way that leads to action and widespread social and economic benefit if they are to be successful. This requires substantial coordination, organisational change, and new partnerships. It is especially difficult for the LDCs, given their lack of financial resources and adequately trained personnel, to devise and implement ICT strategies. Cooperation leading to knowledge sharing, and coordinated initiatives to secure capital, are emerging through regional initiatives. The African Action Plan and the Asia Pacific regional initiatives show the steps that can be taken. The task of building national information infrastructures involves both people and technologies. It involves creative approaches to reconfiguring financial and human resources. The institutional set up is crucial to whether new initiatives are successful and the learning process is an ongoing one. Not all development problems can be addressed simultaneously in the face of competing claims on very scarce resources. Nevertheless, the LDCs which take some action on both the technological and human resource fronts will be better positioned to benefit from ICT applications and to reduce the impact of exclusion from emergent 'knowledge societies'.

Effective use of ICTs and services involves more than the expansion of telecommunication systems. Overemphasis on 'access' to links in the information 'highways' means that insufficient attention may be given to other crucial matters. Development needs, preparedness, affordability, and skills development all need to be considered systematically. Applications for economic sectors, the public sector and for individual citizens, need to be at the centre of national and regional ICT strategies (Melody 1995, 1996; Sanatan and Melody 1997). Table 6.6 illustrates some of the institutional links that need to be constructed between people's needs and the design of the ICT system.

Decisions are needed about which sectors of industry and government activity should receive priority for ICT applications. The aim should be to identify those sectors where the greatest benefit can be achieved for the least cost. This approach to assessment can lead to an operational plan for relevant components of the infrastructure and training. In Table 6.6 the columns identify the major markets and activities that make up the information infrastructure and the rows identify the major players, the essential resources, and the issues requiring government

TABLE 6.6 – CHECKLIST FOR POLICY-MAKERS TO IDENTIFY NII PRIORITIES

Markets/activities	Equipment supply	Network development	Content/value added services	Demand/applications
Players	Telecoms	Public telecoms operator	National	Industry
	Computing	Others	Regional	Government
	Media		Global	Households
	Electronics			
Resource requirements	Technology	Capital	Skills	Integration
	Capital	Skills	Management	Skills
	Skills	Management	Marketing	Capital
Policy/regulation	Industry development	Telecoms reform	Access	Sectoral reform
	Purchasing policy	Universal service	Intellectual property	Skill changes
	Import/export	Spectrum management	Standards	Transition policies
		Privacy/security		
Products/services	Transmission/switching	Public services	Databases	Designer networks
	Terminals	Designer networks	Value added services	Specialised content
	Software	Leased capacity	Media	Network management
Strengths/weaknesses/ opportunities/threats	By product line By technology development By skills base	Network coverage New service deployment Productivity impact	Local content Access Skills	Leading and lagging sectors Commitment to reform Relevance of services to needs

Source: Melody, W.H. (1996) 'Toward a Framework for Designing Information Society Policies', *Telecommunications Policy*, Vol. 10 (4) p.256, with kind permission from Elsevier Science Ltd, Oxfordshire, UK.

policy or regulatory direction. The priority given to the cells in this checklist will differ for each country.

For the ICT sector as a whole, structural and institutional reforms are needed to enable effective responses to unmet demand.

In the *telecommunication* sector the principal concerns are market access, interconnection, and interoperability rules enabling competition in services and infrastructure, radio frequency spectrum management, and the establishment of effective regulatory agencies. Privatisation of the main public telecommunication operator is often regarded as the best means of ensuring that telecommunication services are provided on a commercially efficient basis. Care must be taken to ensure that unregulated private monopolies do not replace the former public monopolies. In the LDCs that do not attract sufficient foreign investment to meet their targets for infrastructure development, innovative institutional structures are needed. The practice of using revenues generated by long distance operations to subsidise general government revenues tends to lead to under-investment in the extension and modernisation of the telecommunication infrastructure and to problems in attracting foreign investor interest.

The introduction of competition within national markets brings the need for changes in telecommunication and,

often, foreign investment legislation, new ways of managing the radio frequency spectrum, new specifications of technical compatibility standards, and policies to ensure equity through universal service development over an extended timeframe. New 'access' models, which must be financed, are needed. These must take account of the capabilities and requirements of users and the overall development strategy to create a dynamic learning process.

In the *computing and software* industries the import of computer and software technologies into domestic markets involves high tariffs in most LDCs. These have been introduced to encourage the build up of domestic capabilities. Pressures to reduce and, ultimately, eliminate these tariff barriers are growing. LDC governments will need to give consideration to areas where the capabilities to modify ICT system components are crucial.

In the *information services* and *audiovisual* sectors the potential for the generation of indigenous 'digital' content relevant to scientific and technological research, business requirements, and social and cultural communities, needs to be assessed in the light of the availability of externally produced content. In the 'cultural industries' a number of countries maintain import restrictions on foreign programming and films to strengthen their own industries. This practice, which is also used in some industrialised countries, such as Canada and, in the European Union, is subject to pressures from other industrialised countries for 'open skies' policies and market access for cultural products delivered by satellite and terrestrial modes of distribution. As the industrialised countries, including the United States, the United Kingdom, and several continental European countries, build market share in trade in 'digital information' products and services, the complementary products that can be produced by LDCs through regional initiatives need to be promoted and financed. These countries will need to concentrate attention as much on 'information content' as on 'access' policies.

The *ICT-using* sectors, including the public and commercial services, manufacturing, and natural resource industries, present major challenges for skills and training as well as technology acquisition and maintenance. User training is costly and the range of technical and organisational skills needed to maintain, customise, and use ICT applications is growing. Policies need to take into account the 'user costs' of the expansion of national information infrastructures. It is necessary to ensure that a growing cost burden does not fall on the end-user thus preventing the harnessing of ICTs to the development process.

An emphasis upon sharing ICT systems, the information they generate, and knowledge about how to use them effectively, is important to reduce the risks of exclusion for LDCs from the global information society. The risk of exclusion of firms and citizens is much greater here than in the wealthier developing countries. 'LDC firms tend to be smaller and less well endowed financially than developing country firms; and operate under macroeconomic conditions which increase the cost, risk and uncertainty of investment. With capital costs rising steeply, finance-based sources of exclusion will be of greater significance to LDC firms than to developing country firms' (Girvan 1997: 11).

As Norman Girvan argues, in the LDCs there is a 'dualism' emerging between firms that use ICTs extensively and those that are unable to do so. While the external environment is critically important to changes in firms' 'capability curves', the role of firms' financial, management, organisational, and human resources cannot be overlooked. Surveys of LDC firms have shown that finance is perceived as the most important obstacle to ICT acquisition in LDCs. This is a major paradox for countries as they seek advantage from these revolutionary technologies that are reducing the unit costs of information storage and processing (Girvan 1996).

LDC initiatives are likely to be successful if they avoid promotion of ICTs as a panacea for complex social and economic problems (Roode and du Plooy 1994). Effort is necessary to encourage the transfer of ICTs from industrialised countries to the developing world in a form that is compatible with the skill levels of the recipients. If the satisfaction of fundamental human needs is the 'driver' of the introduction of ICTs there is a greater chance of success than if the technology is permitted to 'drive' applications. This means that ICT strategies must recognise that social and economic development go hand-in-hand. The design of the implementation of ICTs (networks and software applications) should seek a 'good fit' between the technology and the culture of the recipient country. Special attention should be given to devising strategies by which LDCs can acquire training and experience in their use. Important social considerations include personal data privacy, approaches to the protection of information, and to sharing knowledge and ensuring equitable access to information.

NOTES

1 The total number of e-mail hosts was 53, 7 providing Internet and Bitnet access in Egypt, Tunisia, Algeria and Zambia, 21 providing GreenNet/gnfido access, 3 providing other FIDOnet access, 14 supporting ORSTROM UUCP (Dakar has Internet Protocol access using an X.25 packet data switched network), and 8 supporting other UUCP.

2 A store and forward network based on cheap PCs. Selected computers dial hosts which have full Internet connections to exchange messages with the rest of the world.

3 Unix to Unix Copy Program, faking an Internet connection over an intermittent UUCP link, a more advanced store and forward link than FIDO.

4 Holderness (1998 forthcoming) citing M. Mulligan, Financial Times, and a Dutch journalist, Michiel Hegener, p. 16.

5 The search was carried out for LDCs excluding African countries in July 1997 by the editors of this report. The survey method was informal and is not presented as comprehensive. Sites may have been overlooked. The aim was simply to gain an impression of the quality and type of information that is beginning to be located on the Internet for LDCs.

6 Lahiri, A., 'South Asia' in UNESCO (1997).

7 Butrimenko, A.V. 'Eastern Europe and the Commonwealth of Independent States' in UNESCO (1997).

8 Harrison, H.P. 'Audiovisual Archives Worldwide', in UNESCO (1997).

9 Vannevar Bush argued in 'As we may think', Atlantic Monthly, 1945, that the computer would be used to mechanise scientific literature using a device called 'memex'. The NLS system was developed by D.C. Englebart at Stanford Research Institute and T. Nelson of Xanadu in the United States and it included hypertext (non-sequential reading and writing that links different nodes of a text), windows, a mouse, electronic mail, and a hypertext-like ability to link and annotate documents. See C.-C. Chen, 'Multimedia Technologies' in UNESCO (1997).

10 For example, the minimum requirement of a PC system is an 80386 CPU, EGA/VGA or VGA Aplus Graphics, 2 MB RAM, double-speed CD-ROM Drive and Microsoft Windows 3.1. Some products will run properly only with a 486 or Pentium processor with at least 16 MB of RAM and four-speed CD-ROM.

11 See Danowitz et al. (1995) and Cronin and McKim (1996), and Cronin and McKim, 'The Internet' in UNESCO (1997).

CHAPTER 7

ASSEMBLING THE COMPONENTS OF NATIONAL INFORMATION INFRASTRUCTURES

Lessons from ICT producers in developing
countries - Options for building infrastructure

7 ASSEMBLING THE COMPONENTS OF NATIONAL INFORMATION INFRASTRUCTURES

7.1 INTRODUCTION - PRODUCING AND EFFECTIVELY USING ICTs

The first six chapters of this report focused on the uneven diffusion of ICTs throughout the world, the learning processes involved in the scientific and technological innovation process, and the potential of ICTs for developing countries, as well as the experiences of the least developed countries. The UNCSTD Working Group on IT and Development concluded that the costs of not building national information infrastructures in developing countries are likely to be very high and that each country is at a different starting point in this task (see Chapter 1).

Stakeholders and the governments in the developing world have very difficult choices to make about how to strengthen their capabilities in the ICT field. This first arises in deciding how to allocate their limited resources most effectively to gain some of the benefits of ICTs and to use them to build innovative and distinctive 'knowledge societies'. The economic, political, and social conditions as well as the cultural mores in each country differ substantially. Many of the advantages of ICTs will depend on the availability of an advanced national information infrastructure and on the human capabilities to integrate and use it effectively.

There is debate about how to strengthen ICT production capabilities and it is being recognised that effective use of ICTs depends upon knowledge of how they are designed, how they can be tailored to local conditions, and how they can be maintained. Even when the choice must be to buy, rather than to produce, the necessary technologies and services, an understanding of the range of alternatives is needed if ICTs are to be harnessed to development goals.

Some developing countries have built up a considerable knowledge base for producing components of their national information infrastructures and they are developing export markets for these products. Other countries are building their capabilities to select and implement ICT systems and services without necessarily engaging in local production activity. This chapter uses the experiences of countries that have achieved a combination of technological, institutional, and human capabilities to enable them to assemble the technological components or the content for the national information infrastructure.

Assembling the technological components and the capabilities involves measures to strengthen the science and technology base (section 7.2). It may, in some countries, also involve building capabilities in the hardware industry such as the case of semiconductors (section 7.3).

Opportunities may be created for the wider accessibility of communication networks through technical innovations as in the case of Low Earth Orbiting Satellites (LEOS) (section 7.4) and by entry into the software development market (section 7.5). The information content industries are considered together with the cultural implications for developing countries of the increasing flows of international programming and services in section 7.6.

All the experiences reviewed in this chapter involve countries that have started to assemble their national information infrastructures based on a relatively high level of pre-existing literacy and formal education. Each has moved relatively quickly along a learning curve and considerable investment has been necessary. The least developed countries do not have the technological components, the necessary capabilities in place, or the financial resources to invest in assembling the infrastructure on a large scale. For the most part, these countries will be 'buyers' of ICTs and services. However, this does not mean that they must simply be recipients of goods and services developed elsewhere, or necessarily be excluded from benefiting from the new technologies. There will be opportunities for them to become creative, innovative users if policies and private sector strategies encourage the development of key assembly capabilities.

7.2 SCIENCE AND TECHNOLOGY POLICY IN THE BRAZILIAN ICT INDUSTRY

An important aspect of the national information infrastructure in developing countries is the strength of R&D capabilities in firms, and their propensity to invest in R&D to enable them to participate in construction of the infrastructure. Brazil has the largest information and telecommunication industry in Latin America, and the second largest in the Americas, with a market of US$ 10 billion in 1994. The number of professionals working in the sector whose levels of education include undergraduate and postgraduate degrees is greater than the sum of all other Latin American countries. The size of the Brazilian market, combined with a competitive environment, has offered a challenge to Brazilian firms operating in the ICT sector. Firms have invested increasingly in R&D and employed the highly skilled workforce to innovate and compete, initially in the domestic market and subsequently, in the international market. Brazilian science and technology policies are aimed at strengthening and expanding R&D activities in the ICT sector. Brazil offers an example of the stimulus to investment that can be achieved as a result of policies that employ economic incentives to raise the level of investment and to target it in specific areas.

In 1991 the Brazilian government sought to create conditions whereby firms could benefit from investing in R&D activities. A new law established policy tools to promote R&D in the ICT sector and required complementary actions by firms.[1] First, fiscal benefits available until 1999 consisted of a waiver of the Industrialised Goods Tax resulting in a reduction of 15 per cent in the final cost of production. Until 1997 a discount of 50 per cent on the income tax on expenditures on R&D activities was available and support was provided for new capital investment as a result of a discount of 1 per cent on the income tax payable by companies investing in ICT firms. Second, government procurement policy was changed to favour the purchase of ICT goods with larger proportions of local industrial content.

In order for firms to take advantage of the fiscal benefits and procurement conditions, the legislation required complementary actions by firms. These actions include investment of at least 5 per cent of after-tax revenues from sales of ICT products and services in R&D activities of which 2 per cent must be through joint projects with universities, research institutes, and the main government programmes for the ICT sector. Firms have also been required to comply with a minimum use of advanced technologies in each class of product enabling companies to operate in production chain niches and to select products, parts or components for local production. Firms were required to achieve certification for meeting ISO 9000 quality standards within a period not exceeding two years. By 1997, 248 firms with a total net revenue of approximately US$ 5 billion in 1995, had benefited from these legislative measures and the government was projecting intra- and extra-firm investment of more than US$ 1 billion in R&D by 1998.

The Brazilian Ministry of Science and Technology is responsible for implementing current policy and approving joint projects that bring the private sector into close interaction with academic researchers. The Ministry of Science and Technology verifies compliance with legislative measures supported by the Ministry of Industry, Trade and Tourism and the Ministry of Planning. It also investigates R&D investments by firms benefiting from the legislative provisions supported by the Federal Treasury and Ministry of Treasury and observes compliance with the quality assurance standard. The objective of these actions is to ensure consistency and continuity of the industrial and technology policy.

In addition to these policy tools, the National Bank for Social and Economic Development (BNDES) opened a credit line of US$ 150 million to finance the acquisition of goods and services for the information and automation sectors of domestic firms. This credit line is intended to provide favourable financing conditions for the purchase of locally produced software and hardware. The objectives are to support the modernisation of the local ICT industry and to stimulate the diffusion of ICTs throughout Brazilian society.

The fiscal benefits for firms and their compliance with the complementary actions are linked to their eligibility for R&D projects and the Ministry of Science and Technology's priorities for R&D programmes. The impact of the ICT policy on each programme is monitored by the Ministry. The main programmes are shown in Table 7.1.

TABLE 7.1 – MINISTRY OF SCIENCE AND TECHNOLOGY, MAIN R&D PROGRAMMES, 1996

Programme	Responsible agency
National Research Network (RNP), Internet Brazil	CNPq
National Programme of Software for Export (SOFTEX-2000)	CNPq
Multi-institutional thematic programme in computer science	CNPq
Advanced technologies for industrial automation	CTI
Quality and Productivity in Software	CTI
Micro- and macro-structures	CTI
High performance processing	CTI
Support for the development of the software industry	FINEP
Support for technological capability of the tele-information industry	FINEP

Key: CNPq - National Council for Scientific and Technological Development; CTI - Foundation Technological Centre for Informatics; FINEP - Financing Agency for Studies and Projects.
Source: Ministério da Ciência e Tecnologia (1996).

The growing availability of funding for R&D in the ICT sector in Brazil, whether within companies, through joint projects with research centres and universities or within the framework of a large government programme for ICT R&D is linked directly to fiscal policy. The results of the policy are shown in Table 7.2 indicating the fiscal benefits received by firms and their R&D investment over the period 1993-95 (estimated for 1996 and 1997).

Table 7.3 shows the distribution of investment within firms, and collaborative R&D investment. The fiscal benefits granted to firms increased almost fourfold between 1993 and 1995 and were expected to continue growing throughout 1997. The most attractive fiscal benefit is the waiver of the Industrialised Good Tax. Firms appear to be willing to make cost reductions in order to become more competitive. Total investment in R&D grew almost fivefold from 1993 to 1995. On average within-company R&D investment comprised more than two-thirds of the total during this period. The data also indicate substantial growth in the allocation of funding for joint projects with universities and R&D centres suggesting a tendency for Brazilian firms to expand their R&D activities in the ICT sector into extra-firm activities.

TABLE 7.2 – FISCAL BENEFITS FOR THE BRAZILIAN ICT SECTOR, 1993-1997

Items	1993 US$ m	1994 US$ m	1995 US$ m	1996* US$ m	1997* US$ m
Eligible firms, total	151	217	248	271	290
Gross revenue in the domestic market	8,430	9,795	11,299	12,700	14,100
Gross revenue of supported firms	3,845	5,680	7,500	8,400	9,400
Net revenue during the period	1,401	4,128	4,900	5,400	6,100
Fiscal benefits, total	74	226	278	300	320
Investment in R&D, total	63	241	293	320	350
- within firm	56	181	178	192	208
- joint projects with universities and R&D centres	7	57	111	121	133
- programmes	-	3	4	7	9

Note: Under Law 8248 of 23/10/91; *Estimates
Source: Compiled from various sources.[2]

TABLE 7.3 – SCOPE OF INVESTMENT IN R&D IN THE BRAZILIAN ICT SECTOR, 1993-1997

Scope	1993 %	1994 %	1995 %	1996* %	1997* %
Within-firm	88.9	75.1	60.8	60	59.4
Joint-projects with universities and R&D centres	11.1	23.7	37.8	37.8	38.0
Programmes	0.0	1.2	1.4	2.2	2.6
Total	100.0	100.0	100.0	100.0	100.0

Note: * Estimates
Source: Compiled from various sources, see note 2.

The competitive environment in Brazil and in the international market is forcing firms to reduce costs and improve quality and this, together with the fiscal incentives, is resulting in an increase in investment in R&D activities. Firms are seeking to enhance their products and services to compete globally in the ICT market.

7.3 THE REPUBLIC OF KOREA'S SUCCESSFUL SPECIALISATION IN MEMORY CHIPS

The development of the semiconductor industry in the Republic of Korea is a dramatic instance of success in building new capabilities for a newly industrialising country. In little more than a decade, Korean *chaebol* firms such as Samsung have been able to catch up and move to the frontier of semiconductor production, specifically in the memory chip segment of the market and in Dynamic Random Access Memories (DRAMs). This is a highly technology-intensive industry and success was achieved in a very short time. Korean firms are now becoming major global players in the world memory chip market.[3] This section highlights the factors which have contributed to success in assembling the capabilities to exploit the export market for semiconductors.

Samsung became the world market leader in Metal Oxide Semiconductor (MOS) memories and the DRAM segment by 1993 (Integrated Circuit Engineering 1995) from a virtually zero market share in memory chips in 1984. Hyundai and LG Semicon (formerly Goldstar) also have been very successful in the world DRAM market, attaining fourth and fifth place, respectively, in the DRAM segment in 1996 (Electronic Business Asia 1997).

Many structural problems, including the highly fragmented industrial structure, remain to be addressed (EIAK 1995) if the growth of the Korean semiconductor industry is to be sustained over the longer term. Korean successes have been limited largely to the DRAM-segment, the low value-added mainstay of the semiconductor industry. The performance of the Korean semiconductor industry is very impressive (Kim 1998 forthcoming). Successful specialisation by Korean firms and export sales on the world market may be attributable to a clever state industrial targeting policy, to luck, and to timing to market, an instance of *chaebol* success in pursuing the strategies that were timely to achieve export market success by the second half of the 1980s. In fact, the evidence suggests that success is attributable to many factors including the politics surrounding state actions.

7.3.1 THE IMPORTANCE OF CHAEBOL GOVERNANCE AND THE STATE

The Korean state was important to the success of Korean firms in the semiconductors market but in an indirect way. Korean chip producers, especially during the second half of the 1980s, were fortunate to be able to capitalise on the gap in the world market which opened up after the US-Japan Semiconductor Agreement of 1986 (renewed and extended five years later). In addition, the strategy of narrowly focusing on DRAMs was a singularly appropriate one with Samsung acting as the DRAM 'pathfinder' while Hyundai concentrated on static RAMs.

The success of the *chaebol*-firms depended on the *will* as well as the *ability* to succeed. An explanation of their success requires consideration of the *chaebol-governance* process and the political institutional arrangements for the state-firm relationship based on the 'politics of reciprocal subsidy'. These subsidies have been conducive to the emergence of effective *chaebol-governance*,[4] and the structure of the governance system is well matched by the technological and economic competitive conditions in the memory chip segment of the semiconductor market.

The development process of Korea's semiconductor industry took place over two periods before and after 1983. Until 1983, Korean firms were merely specialised within the international division of labour, while world market dynamics and the 'visible hand' of foreign investors, played an important role. The dominant form of governance was the firm-hierarchy of foreign investors, resulting in limited development of Korea (Rep. of) as an assembly site for foreign semiconductor firms. The state remained relatively passive between 1965 and 1972, with limited interest in a general export-promotion policy (Kim 1991; EIAK 1989).

Between 1973 and 1979 there was a state-led push into the heavy and chemical industries (HCI) (Haggard and Moon 1986; Leipziger 1987), but no similar promotion policy was pursued for the semiconductor industry. Among the State incentives and measures after 1983, the most important and most frequently used policy instrument for encouraging large firm entry into the HCI industries was credit. The firms, and above all the *chaebol*s, that invested in targeted industries such as steel and petrochemicals received so-called 'policy loans'. The share of these policy loans amounted to as much as 60 per cent of the total lending by the big Korean banks (Hahn 1993).

An important condition attached to the policy loans was that the receiving firms should export their products almost from the outset and demonstrate their strength in export markets. This condition amounted to a 'reciprocal subsidy' between the state and the firms and worked as a positive incentive for the subsidy-receiving firms to increase their production efficiency and to sell their products on the export market (Amsden 1989). The implementation of the HCI policy based upon the 'politics of reciprocal subsidy' also had significant implications for the development of semiconductors.

From 1983, the Korean semiconductor industry attained momentum mostly as a result of the strategic initiatives of the *chaebol*-firms. The Very Large Scale Integrated (VLSI) chips era was initiated in 1983 by the *chaebol*s that had grown enormously during the preceding HCI-drive era and now recognised the economic potential of the semiconductor industry. The breakthrough came in 1987 with favourable world market conditions induced mainly by the international semiconductor politics between the United States and Japan. The world market dynamics provided an important 'window of opportunity' and the DRAM 'boom' rewarded the Korean firms for the

DRAM trajectories they had established. The three large *chaebol* chip producers had decisive structural advantages in terms of capital and human resource mobilisation as well as the opportunity for cross-financing. Without these advantages, they would not have been able to start their new DRAM businesses as quickly or to sustain huge financial losses until 1987 when the 'window of opportunity' in the world market finally opened (Korean Semiconductor Industry Association 1993; Samsung Electronics Co. 1994).

Korean *chaebol*-firms are hierarchically structured and centrally organised. The member companies are grouped around the chairperson and a central office which is responsible for resource allocation and often for personnel decisions at the *chaebol* group level. This structure enables quick and unified support for new business areas. *Chaebol*-governance implies a combination of a 'hierarchy' (built around the Chief Executive Officer and central office) and a 'network' (consisting of a *chaebol*-level network organisation). Resources can be mobilised very quickly through internal transactions and cooperation within the *chaebol* on a non-price basis. This permits focused and effective investment in the new semiconductor business. *Chaebol*-governance was an important institutional factor in the rapid entry of Korean companies into DRAM production, a market characterised by very high entry barriers.

Chaebol-governance fits well with the technological innovation characteristics of DRAMs and the 'technological regime' (Malerba and Breschi 1995). DRAM technical advances proceeded through ever-increasing integrated circuit capacity and a continuous series of product and process innovations. The incremental process innovations and learning effects from manufacturing (for example, learning-by-doing) were important sources of technological innovation and productivity gains. High yield rates were achieved through experimentation over details in the manufacturing process at which DRAM producers like Samsung and Hyundai proved very adept (Howell et al. 1988; Tyson and Yoffie 1991).

These technical innovations and the associated technological capabilities resulted in firm-specific patterns of knowledge. Each firm's capability to learn-by-doing was a decisive determinant of its competitive success. In the case of DRAMs, the Korean producers do not seem to have been penalised by the relatively low quality of the national system of innovation which existed at the outset. As long as they were capable of maintaining their firm and *chaebol*-level learning-by-doing and manufacturing efficiency, they were successful. However, in the case of Application Specific Integrated Circuits (ASICs), a closer degree of interaction between the large chip producers and small and medium-sized user firms was required and the implications for governance of a different product segment for effective technological innovation were different.

The 'politics of reciprocal subsidy' in the 1970s were important for the emergence of *chaebol*-governance, and the lack of interventionist regulation by the state in the 1980s was conducive to the continuation of this form of governance. The Korean state did not pursue a targeted sectoral policy for the semiconductor industry because of internal and external economic conditions and the largely politically motivated withdrawal from extensive policy intervention in the 1980s (Hong 1992). The government began to commit itself to promotion of the industry only after Samsung's success in DRAM development. The 'leapfrogging' by Korean firms' occurred initially as a result of state actions and politics, but it was the private firms who were forging ahead. The government's DRAM project promotion policy was an addition to the focused DRAM strategies of Korean firms and was successful only to a limited extent. The coordination of the technological and economic activities was left to the *chaebol*s, establishing *chaebol*-governance as the dominant governance mechanism.

Korean success in memory chips has been the product of neither the 'Korea Inc.' model nor 'free' market dynamics. State versus market explanations predominate in the literature on Korean/East Asian industrialisation,[5] but success was the result of complex interactions between regulations underpinning the world market, corporatist state policies, and *chaebol*s strategies. The Korean state indirectly played an important role as a result of the politics of reciprocal subsidy. The state set the scene for the *chaebol* firms' entry into VLSI chip production by supporting the *chaebol* structure. This experience illustrates the importance of politics as well as economic policy. This point is often overlooked in analyses of the factors determining the success of the newly industrialising countries in achieving production capabilities.

7.3.2 The lessons from East Asian strategies in microelectronics

Emulation of the Korean successes in the microelectronics industry is likely to be extremely difficult for other countries. However, there are lessons for other developing countries in the genesis and dynamics of sectoral governance and their effects on the growth dynamics of the ICT sectors. A form of 'institutional engineering' is likely to

be needed supporting the emergence of appropriate governance processes for different industry segments (Hollingsworth and Streeck 1994). By focusing on existing governance arrangements it may be possible to influence the evolution and operation of firms and to permit them to develop their own strategies rather than to impose general blueprints on them. The human resource aspects are as important for success as the technological aspects as demonstrated by a study of the East Asian electronics industry (Heeks and Slamen-McCann 1996). This study found that industrial targeting policies have been extremely broad in all the stages of the development of the microelectronics industry in East Asian countries (see Table 7.4).

Each of the newly industrialising countries in East Asia has relied on a different mix of skills as it has moved along the learning curve to establish international competitiveness in distinctive ways and, as discussed, education has played a crucial role (see Box 7.1).

An analysis of Japanese investment strategies in East Asian markets over an extended period by Dieter Ernst (1997) highlights the importance of regional resources in the building up of the production capabilities of both Japanese firms and their partners in the electronics industry in other countries. The concept of an 'international production network' is used as a basis for understanding how Japanese firms have selected international production sites for different stages of the value chain and how their strategies have changed over the years. Ernst argues that over time the focus of investments has shifted twice from Northeast Asia (Republic of Korea, Taiwan (Pr. China), and Hong Kong) to the ASEAN region (mainly Singapore, Malaysia and Thailand), and from about 1992, from the ASEAN region mainly to China. Expansion to Indonesia and India from the 1990s and currently into Viet Nam, Myanmar and the Asian republics of the former Soviet Union has also occurred. This recent analysis shows that Japanese firms have moved from earlier relatively closed and Japan-centred production networks to more open regional supply networks. The result is that there have been large swings in Japan's strategies corresponding to changes in the Japanese domestic economy. In the 1990s the tendency is now towards greater decentralisation of production in the region, and local embeddedness. As a result, Asia is now the most important source of Japanese electronics

TABLE 7.4 – Stages of growth in a dynamic environment

	Infantile stage	Growth stage	Maturing stage	Declining stage
Physical factor	Endowed resources	Business environment	Related and supporting industries	Domestic demand
Human factor	Workers, politicians, and bureaucrats	Politicians, bureaucrats, and entrepreneurs	Entrepreneurs, professional managers, and engineers	None

Source: Cho (1994) adapted in Heeks and Slamen-McCann (1996).

The micro-electronics-based industry production of the four East Asian newly industrialising countries and territories - Hong Kong, Singapore, the Republic of Korea, and Taiwan (Pr. China) - displays commonalities including the significance of electronics production to all the economies, especially exports, and an initial reliance on building the industry on foreign investment, foreign infusions of technology, and low local wages. Nevertheless, there are emerging differences between these countries. In terms of firm type, foreign investors dominate in Singapore; small local entrepreneurs are most common in Taiwan and Hong Kong; while in the Republic of Korea, the chaebol conglomerates take by far the largest share of production. In terms of industrial development, Singapore still appears to rely heavily on its labour pool as a basic factor of production; the Republic of Korea is increasingly focused on investment in its well-developed local industries; while Hong Kong and Taiwan (Pr. China) lie somewhere between the two. Not only have these countries followed a path somewhat different to that of industrialised countries, but in some instances, they can also be considered 'ahead' of the game compared to the industrialised countries.

In terms of the necessary skills base, the national technology infrastructure, with the exception of Hong Kong, is well in place and gaining in global recognition. It supports further expansion of the electronics industry, ensures ongoing skill changes and presents a structure to support positive technology and skills management. At the micro level, the best firms in these areas have retained a constant commitment to training and to learning, with clear strategies for raising their level.

There has been no clear evidence, at an organisational or industrial sector level, of employment diminishing in the electronics industries of these countries through the use of new manufacturing technologies. Even where automation has created labour displacement, continuing increases in investment and output have more than compensated, assisted by government action and managerial strategies. The latter often involve using technology differently to typical 'leader' strategies, with less emphasis on labour saving and more on improving product quality or breaking into new markets.

Slowly but steadily, firms in certain sectors seem to be emerging from a phase of catching-up to a phase of leadership. This is accompanied by an apparent adoption of Western characteristics of electronics industry leadership such as globally competitive R&D and use of leading-edge technology.

East Asian electronics industries have been, and are likely to remain, significantly export-oriented. Nevertheless, these countries' domestic markets are growing, especially certain consumer markets, driven on by the rising level and relative equality of incomes. In the future inequality between export- and domestic-oriented production is less likely to emerge. Although the attention of foreign producers will be drawn increasingly to these domestic markets, the overall outcome for production, income, and jobs is still likely to be positive.

The electronics industries of Hong Kong, Republic of Korea, Singapore, and Taiwan (Pr. China) are constantly maturing. The signs in the late 1990s point towards a declining strategic role for government, after nurturing sections of the electronics industries in their infancy, and towards an increasing role for industrial managers and entrepreneurs. Future success is still likely to depend on government action to support the industrial infrastructure, local R&D, easy access to new technology, and, perhaps most importantly, education.

Source: Heeks and Slamen-McCann (1996).

imports and this has been achieved so far without a decline in quality, speed or reliability of delivery. At the same time, most key electronics components are still sourced from Japan, from other Japanese firms producing in the region, or non-Japanese producers in the region.

The capabilities of subcontracted firms have been built up to the point that East Asia has become a leading supply base for an increasing variety of information products. Ernst (1997) suggests that although the initial focus was on manufacturing excellence and supply chain management using imported designs, this is changing and design and market development capabilities are emerging that seek to tailor products to the heterogeneous demand patterns in the East Asian markets, that is, products that are used for computing, communicating and multimedia purposes. This recent study is particularly interesting because of the emphasis it gives to the shifts in the location of production networks over time. As Ernst (1997:

57) puts it: 'nothing is automatic about the benefits from participating in international production networks. Periodically, there may be important reversals in the distribution of such benefits'.

Another recent study focusing specifically on the semiconductor industry shows how important it is to take account of all the factors contributing to production capabilities in order to assess the likelihood that the newcomers will be successful, whether their success will be sustained, and whether other countries will be able to 'forge ahead' into new areas of ICT production. Richard Langlois and Edward Steinmueller (1997) argue that discussions about the most appropriate structure of an industrial sector and its form of governance (whether by corporatism or state-corporatism for instance) often miss the fact that the competitive success of each country's industry is dynamic and demand-related as well as supply-related. They argue in the case of the waxing and waning of strengths through the period between the late 1940s and mid-1990s in integrated circuit production in the United States, Europe, Japan, and the Republic of Korea, that 'the competitive position of a nation's semiconductor industry hinges upon its relationships with its customers, the companies comprising the electronic system industries, and upon the industrial structure of the semiconductor industry itself, including the processes of evolution and reconfiguration resulting from technological change' (Langlois and Steinmueller 1997: 2).

Although the importance of the role of governments in the governance system is recognised, they argue that 'the actors in this industry's drama find themselves alternately constrained and liberated by the evolution of circumstances over which they, and their governments, have little direct control. These circumstances include the uncertainties of the path of technological change; the conditions and strategies adopted by their customers in the electronic systems industries; the changing needs, interests, policies of other governments; and the strategies of international competitors' (Langlois and Steinmueller 1997: 3). For countries that see the technological revolution in the ICT industry as an opportunity to forge ahead in competition with players in the world market or to meet domestic demand, the lesson is that there is no 'optimal strategy' for competitive success that is independent of time and particular circumstance. Assembling the key capabilities for success in any segment of the ICT industry is highly dependent upon changing synergies and interdependencies between production and consumption.

7.4 TECHNOLOGICAL INNOVATIONS AND THE GLOBAL REACH OF SATELLITE INFRASTRUCTURES

The extremely uneven distribution of telephone mainlines world-wide has led some observers to look to technological innovations in telecommunications as a means of alleviating the scarcity of this resource in developing countries. For countries with very low telephone penetration rates, Low Earth Orbiting Satellites (LEOS) are enticing. The developers of the new systems argue that they 'will foster the very economic development that will fuel the demand for the service' (Gilder 1994b: 7) and that they will 'provide the same high grade of coverage to all parts of the world without any significant investment by developing countries' (Iridium Today 1994: 10).

LEOS are expected to play a key role in extending the reach of the global information infrastructure (GII) and allowing poor countries to join the global information society (Iridium Today 1994). Technological 'leap-frogging' will be feasible with the provision of an 'instant infrastructure' to allow developing countries to avoid building an expensive terrestrial fixed network (see Box 7.2). Others argue that LEO services will be priced beyond the reach of most of those who do not have access to terrestrial tele-

phone services and that this will reduce the revenues available to national public telecommunication operators for investment in the extension of the terrestrial system or geostationary orbit satellite services to rural and remote areas. This section examines the extent to which this innovation in communication technology is part of the system that needs to be assembled to achieve the modernisation of communication networks in developing countries.

LEOS can be classified according to their transmission capabilities. 'Little LEOS' will offer data-only services such as paging, low speed data communication, and cargo and vehicle tracking; 'Big-LEOS' will provide voice telephony in addition to value added services such as fax, e-mail, and other modem data transmissions. These systems are planned for operation by the end of the 1990s (see Tables 7.5 and 7.6).

The larger systems are planned to support 'Global Mobile Personal Communications' (GMPCS). All of the currently planned systems are non-geostationary satellite systems and, because of the low orbits and large number of satellites required to achieve global coverage, investors must commit substantial funds before service can be offered. These systems can provide service directly to end-users. The International Telecommunication Union World Telecommunication Policy Forum has advocated widespread non-discriminatory licensing of GMPCS networks and unrestricted circulation of handsets and other user terminals (Tyler 1997). By February 1997, World Trade Organization negotiations had gone some way to opening market access for satellite services (see Chapter 9).

Because of their low navigational altitudes, typically from 700 km to a maximum of 12,000 km (Medium Orbit Satellites), these satellites will orbit the earth at a very fast speed. A large constellation of LEOS is needed to guarantee that at least one satellite is always above a specific service area. Instead of using fixed ground stations, users with 'wireless' mobile terminals can access commercial satellite systems for voice and data applications (Cochetti 1994). Small hand-held terminals, similar to cellular telephones, will allow use in rural and remote areas.

Proponents of these systems suggest that the LEO services will support: basic telephone and data services to connect isolated villages with large cities using solar powered phone booths, particularly where alternative facilities are impractical or uneconomical; commercial enterprises such as mining, logging, utilities, agriculture, road construction, and long haul transportation; emergency and disaster relief efforts; telemedicine and distance education; and access to Internet and other applications; and government officials visiting rural and remote areas (Kensinger 1996, Cochetti 1994).

The prime movers on the Big LEOS scene are operators who received clearance from the United States Federal Communications Commission in 1995. Licensing the

TABLE 7.5 - LITTLE LEOS APPROVED AS OF JANUARY 1995

Name	Holding company	Number of satellites	Altitude km	Start-up date	Estimated cost to build and launch (US$ million)
STARSYS	General Electric/ CLS France	6 (initial)	1,000	1998	200
ORBCOMM	Orbital Science Corp.	36	775	1998	100
VITA	non-profit	1	1,000	1990	-
	modification	3	800–1,000	1998	-
TELEDESIC	McCaw/Gates/ AT&T	840	695–700	2001	9,000

Note: Teledesic is not a 'little LEO' in the conventional sense. It is designed as a huge (1 Ghz in Ka band) broadband system, an 'information superhighway in the sky'. It will not offer conventional voice telephony, but will focus on the computing market offering video teleconferencing and downloading of audiovisual services, for example, a two-hour feature film is expected to take 16 seconds (Guilder 1994b).
Source: Chenard (1996); Kensinger (1996); US Congress Office of Technology Assessment (1995b).

TABLE 7.6 - BIG LEOS APPROVED AS OF JANUARY 1995

Name	Holding company	Number of satellites	Altitude km	Start-up date	Estimated cost to build and launch (US$ million)
GLOBALSTAR	Loral/Qualcomm	48	1,414	1998	2,200
ICO	INMARSAT	10	10,000	1999	2,600
IRIDIUM	Motorola	66	780	1998	3,400
ODYSSEY	TRW	12	10,355	1998	2,300

Source: Compiled from Chenard (1996), Globalstar (1996), Iridium Today (1996), Rusch and Leventhal (1996).

Mobile Satellite Systems, as the LEOS were designated, involved a negotiated rule-making procedure whereby satellite system operators negotiated frequency coordination with each other and with current domestic users of the radio frequency spectrum. The first request to operate a LEO system was filed by Iridium in 1990 and similar applications from other North American operators soon followed. Over four years elapsed before the domestic licences for the global systems were authorised. However, the process of internal negotiation and coordination meant that the way was paved for a concerted effort to obtain the necessary international frequency allocations.

At the World Administrative Radio Conference of 1992 in Spain a watershed in the telecommunication world was reached. Frequencies were allocated to global wireless technologies, including LEO systems, and a radio frequency spectrum agenda was established emphasising the primacy of mobile radio services over fixed applications (Sung 1992). At the World Radio Conference (WRC) in 1995 additional spectrum was allocated for mobile services. This time, the winners of the month-long round of negotiations held in Geneva were the Big LEO systems (see Table 7.7) (Foley 1995).

The decision-making process in the US and the subsequent allocation of operational frequencies by the

BOX 7.2 - LEO OPERATORS TARGET DEVELOPING COUNTRY MARKETS

Globalstar is a technological and economical business solution for mobile and fixed telephony. It is designed to integrate existing terrestrial telecommunication systems, not bypass them. Globalstar benefits service providers and government telecommunication operators that need low-cost regional and national communications (Globalstar 1996).

Global mobile satellite services will extend domestic telecommunication networks. The increased traffic promises to expand domestic traffic and increase the income earned by national telecommunication operators. Global mobile satellite services will allow every country, and in particular developing countries, to provide instant telecommunication services without the large investment that otherwise would be required to develop a local infrastructure (Iridium Today 1994).

For the first time, Odyssey satellites will provide rural and remote areas of developing countries with the same affordable, modern, reliable telephone service enjoyed by the people in developed countries (Rusch and Leventhal 1996).

International Telecommunication Union have far-reaching implications. The procedures of the Federal Communications Commission provided a model that can be copied or modified to deal with issues and policy options for the introduction of LEO systems. For example, the auctioning of mobile satellite licences, a process initiated in 1992, has been emulated by Australia, Colombia, Ecuador, Venezuela, and India, among others (Chenard 1996).

TABLE 7.7 – FREQUENCIES ALLOCATED TO LEOS

Satellite system	Frequency band (Up/Down links)
STARSYS	-
ORBCOMM	148–150.05/137–138 MHz
VITA	148–150.5/137–138; 400.15–401 MHz
TELEDESIC	18.9–19.3/28.7–29.1 GHz
IRIDIUM	1610–1626.5/1610–1626.5 MHz
GLOBALSTAR/ODYSSEY	1610–1626.5/2483.5–2500 MHz
ICO	1980–2010/2170–2200 MHz

Source: Compiled from Leite (1996); Kensinger (1996).

Decisions emerging from the licensing process in the United States led to that country's claim to 100 per cent of two important frequency bands and appeared to settle *de facto* many matters about how these bands would be used. This had two implications.

▌ First, given the need for replacements to keep the satellite constellations operational (satellites at low altitude have a life-span of 4 to 10 years), international allocations may result in permanent occupation of spectrum effectively precluding the development of other systems in favoured frequency bands.[6]

▌ Second, LEO signals have the potential to interfere with other telecommunication services. Although technical proposals for spectrum sharing are emerging, sharing is not always feasible. For example, the 30 to 300 MHz frequency range used for Little LEOS may cause disruptions to existing low cost applications such as private radio land mobile services for police, taxi and fire brigade usage, and FM broadcasting which also use Very High Frequency bands (US Congress Office of Technology Assessment 1995b). Geostationary telecommunication satellites, the technology currently used for domestic and international telecommunication services, have been protected from harmful interference by the International Radio Regulations. Non-geostationary systems have been put on an equal footing with geostationary systems and developing countries have expressed concern about the issue of interference.[7]

The difficulties of frequency coordination are not the only challenges facing developing countries. To provide seamless mobile service world-wide, systems operators must obtain regulatory approval on a country by country basis. As provision to unserved populations is expected to account for a large part of the market, proponents are strategically courting the developing world for service authorisation.

Two related issues need to be addressed when planning LEOS regulation: interconnection to the public switched telephone network, and bypass of that network. Satellite operators are seeking a regulatory environment which creates a 'level playing field' and reasonable, non-discriminatory access to the domestic public switched telecommunication network (Kensinger 1996). Competition is expected to benefit consumers through lower prices and more innovative services. The operators argue that the market should be allowed to determine which LEO system will prevail. In order to operate in any country, the satellite system operator must obtain approval for the use of the frequencies, the terminal equipment, and the services. To facilitate international roaming, that is, the transborder use of satellite telecommunication, the free circulation of mobile terminals is being actively promoted by operators in multilateral fora and on a regional basis.

Demand for business networks and advanced information services is closely related to requirements for the extension of the national public switched telecommunication network to unserved areas and the accessibility of services for low-income users. Affordability of user terminal equipment and the cost of air time will be crucial factors in the choice of LEO systems. Quality, scope of service, and scalability, are also major considerations. It is unclear whether the competing alternative systems will offer the same quality of transmission world-wide. Other outstanding issues include whether the use of this technology for voice telephony is desirable and whether the systems will be able to increase capacity as needed. The International Telecommunication Union has prepared a checklist of technical and regulatory factors which developing countries need to take into account as they consider the advantages and disadvantages of licensing alternative LEOS services that interconnect with their existing networks (Parapk 1996).

Another concern for LEOS regulation at the national level is the issue of bypass. Bypass refers to the loss of revenue by a national public telecommunication operator due to the 'bypass' of the domestic terrestrial telecommunication network using a satellite-based mobile communication system. Satellite operators argue that access charges for connection to the domestic public switched telecommunication network and the service provision charges that are paid to domestic operators will bring financial benefits to the countries in which they operate. However, some domestic telecommunication operators take a different view because they believe that traffic will be diverted from their networks. Maintaining and extending public access to conventional and advanced telecommunication services requires policies that promote a balance between the internal requirements of developing countries and the technological and economic characteristics of the different LEO systems.

This section has focused on LEO systems as an illustration of the opportunities and problems created by technical innovations in satellite technology. A related set of issues that needs to be considered by developing countries stems from the growing opportunities for the 'dual use' of satellite systems (Gasparini Alves 1996). The military and civilian applications of the 'simultaneous multiple use' satellite systems have implications for national security and for the provision of data used in international observation systems supporting environmental protection, crop production, the management of natural and other disasters, as well as monitoring narcotics legislation enforcement and providing dedicated communication systems to the police and the armed forces. In the future it will be technically feasible for civilian satellites to undertake military missions and for military satellites to provide civilian functions. 'Dual use' considerations arise with respect not just to the data and remote sensing imagery applications but also with respect to telecommunication, broadcasting, global positioning, and other services. Emerging space-competent states include Brazil, India, Indonesia, Pakistan, South Africa, the Republic of Korea, and Israel. A publication by the United Nations Institute for Disarmament Research suggests that with the exception of India and Israel, the capacity of most countries

to develop a high level of autonomy, including indigenous launchers, has been limited by the international Missile Technology Control Regime and similar measures. ... However, this trend has been offset to a high degree by an increase in the availability of commercial launch services ... Thus, access to advanced space capability for many states has actually increased (Steinberg 1996: 33).

Technological innovations affecting future satellite systems raise two main questions. Firstly, there are new issues about the military uses of satellite systems and their impact on international stability and the potential for an arms race in space. Secondly, they raise problems of access for developing countries that do not have direct access to space capabilities for commercial, technological and national security purposes (Gasparini Alves 1996).

7.5 NEW MEDIA SERVICES AND THE BROADCASTING AND CABLE TELEVISION SECTORS

As technologies in the ICT sector converge allowing communication, information, and audiovisual services to be distributed using many different types of networks, the importance of the broadcast and cable industries cannot be overlooked as components of the national information infrastructure that need to be assembled. Recent statistics on the availability of cable television systems and the introduction of new media services such as pay television, are unavailable for most of the developing countries. The country studies which contain limited information provide little basis for international comparisons. However, many developing countries have extensive broadcasting networks and, in some cases, cable television networks have been put in place in the 1990s to support the distribution of information and audiovisual services.

In this section recent developments in Brazil and India provide an indication of the need to introduce policy and regulatory arrangements to address issues including the relationship between telecommunication, broadcast and cable providers, the rules concerning cross-media ownership, the feasibility of providing local or national programming (information and entertainment), and the measures affecting foreign investment in the new networks and services.

7.5.1 INTRODUCING NEW MEDIA SERVICES IN BRAZIL

In Brazil commercial pay television services arrived only in 1991 when several major cable systems were constructed in the cities of Florianópolis and Curitiba and wireless cable services were introduced in São Paulo and Rio de Janeiro. Five years later, in 1996, a Ku-band satellite service was launched by Galaxy Brasil (a subsidiary of Tevecap and affiliate of DirecTV). The delay in the introduction of this new media service has been attributed to the absence of regulatory legislation, the high quality of Portuguese-language programming available on off-air broadcast television, and the extensive geographic coverage of the national broadcast networks.

Four technologies are in use to support the delivery of new media pay television services - satellite, wireline cable, wireless cable metropolitan multipoint distribution systems (MMDS) and the ultra high broadcast frequencies. Ultra High Frequencies (UHF) represent only about 15,000 subscribers. Satellite TV was transmitted using C-Band analogue technology until recently when the launch of the Galaxy Brasil and Net Sat satellites introduced Ku-Band digital systems which are expected to predominate in the future.

Demand for pay television services is significant. Some 85 per cent of Brazilian households have television sets and the average television household watched television for more than four hours per day in 1995. The market for television sets is expected to grow and it is estimated that Brazilian companies will manufacture 9 million sets in 1997 with annual sales increases of at least 50 per cent thereafter. However, the penetration of pay television services is relatively low. At the end of 1996 there were only 1,850,000 pay television subscribers representing only 4 per cent of the potential market. In comparison, the pay television penetration rate is 50 per cent in Argentina and 20 per cent in Chile as a percentage of television households.

Cable television (CATV) services are in operation in Brazil and this market is expected to expand during the 1996-2001 period following the approval of a Cable Act in

January 1995 which is favourable to the introduction of a range of new media 'convergent' services. The Brazilian Ministry of Communication (MINICOM) is responsible for regulating the television industry and granting licences for cable, wireless cable and the Direct Broadcast Satellite services. The licences are granted on a non-exclusive basis for each metropolitan area to one or more companies (with open competition). They are valid for 15 years and are renewable as long as the operators remain within the terms of the licence and agree to meet some technical and economic requirements. Subscription rates and installation fees are not regulated, except in regions where only one operator exists.

In 1991, 101 licences were granted by MINICOM, leaving over 2,000 licensees' bids awaiting approval. In 1995, MINICON authorised operators in the telecommunication and CATV industries - including AG Telecom, TVA and Globosat to begin trials of local multipoint distribution services (LMDS). In 1996, concessions were made to broadcasters to convert their networks into CATV operations. MINICOM has been considering standards for evaluation and award of new licences using new technologies.

There are nine operators of wireless MMDS, the largest with around 200,000 subscribers, or 35 per cent of that total. Compared to wireline fixed cable systems, MMDS is simpler to provide and the prices are lower. Transmissions are sent by microwave to an antennae installed at the subscriber's home. MMDS systems can be implemented more quickly than fixed cable networks and the capital cost per subscriber is about US$ 500 resulting in profitability at lower penetration rates and making it more attractive for low density regions. Fifteen year renewable licences have been granted to MMDS operators for the provision of up to 16 channels at the 2.5 GHz bandwidth and for coverage areas up to a 50 kilometre radius from transmission sites. When licences are granted for more than 16 channels, two must be used for educational and cultural programming.

NET Brasil is the largest operator in Brazil with 400,000 subscribers in many cities. The consortium is owned by Globopar (40 per cent), RBS (18 per cent), Mcom Telecomunicações (31 per cent), and other small shareholders. Globo Grup is the largest media group in the Brazilian market and Net Brasil is expected to dominate the market when cable licences are distributed. In 1996 Globo started offering 'Sky' direct-to-home services and uses PamAmSat-6 to distribute its programming. The aim is to attract 80,000 subscribers in 1997 with the help of Gradiente, a Brazilian electronics company, that has invested US$ 23 million in 'Sky' access products. Multicanal operates CATV services in 18 Brazilian cities and is owned by Mcom and Net Brasil. It maintains a degree of autonomy from Net Brasil with respect to

network development and is focusing its efforts only on proving cable television services.

Although it is the second operator in the market in terms of the total number of subscribers, TVA has led Brazil's MMDS subscribers since 1992 with around 310,000 subscribers in 1996. A partnership between Hughes Communication, Venezuela's Cisneros Goup, Tevecap, and MVS Multivisión has led to the launch of DirecTV services in Brazil, with the exclusion of the North (the states of Amazonas, Pará, Rôndonia, Amapa, Roraima and Acre) where the 'footprint' of the Galaxy Latin America satellite does not reach. TVA has attracted foreign investors and partners to face competition in the Brazilian market. Chase Manhattan bought a 17 per cent interest in June 1994 and TVA has been restructured into six companies, each with a foreign partner. Tevecap, TVA's holding company, is owned by Grupo Abril, ABC-Disney/Hearst Publishing, Falcon Cable, and Chase Manhattan.

Current regulations restrict commercial arrangements between telephone and cable operators, but 'convergent' services are emerging on a small scale in some states. In December 1996, the Ministry of Science and Technology, which regulates Internet use, passed legislation that would allow Internet use over cable television backbone networks. However, some state operators, Telebahia, Telesp, and Telemig, are already working with the largest CATV companies, and the telecommunication operator, Telebras, is installing a network platform for cable services to facilitate transmission of their programmes using the existing telecommunication network.

Emerging convergence operators (those offering a mix of telecommunication voice and data services and information or entertainment services) are likely to become strong competitors to the existing basic telecommunication service provider. Brazil's cable operators are positioning themselves as potential basic telephone service operators and they are designing their networks so that they can be easily upgraded to offer multimedia services, including Internet access and teleconferencing, in addition to basic telephone services.

7.5.2 GROWTH POTENTIAL AND INVESTORS IN INDIAN MEDIA SERVICES

In India a Broadcasting Bill introduced in the Parliament in 1997 is being debated by various stakeholders and the outcome will have a significant impact on the development of satellite broadcasting and cable television in the future. The Bill represents the culmination of the number of issues and concerns that have been raised as a consequence of rampant expansion of cable television services in India. As yet, there are no clear guidelines regarding the provision of cable services although a system of licensing is in place in some states and the Government of India expects cable operators to distribute at least two channels of the state-owned Doordarshan (Indian Television Network). However, no monitoring mechanism is in place to ensure that they in fact carry these channels.

The operation of cable television services in India is relatively simple. A local entrepreneur sets up an earth station antenna and associated equipment in a viable neighbourhood and extends the service to as many households as possible. Approximately 100 to 150 houses can be handled by one operator. The affluent households and hotels usually have their own antennae. Depending upon the number of channels provided a tariff is charged which includes an installation charge of Rs 1000-1500 (US$ 30-35) (in some areas less), and a monthly subscription fee. The subscription fees differ from one state to another depending upon whether the state levies an entertainment tax which, in turn, is passed on to the subscribers. The subscription fees are between Rs 100-150 (US$ 3-5) per month. The cable operator may be independent or a franchisee of a larger group which is usually an extension of the broadcast television network owners, the latter being the growing trend. For example, the popular Zee network owns Siticable which has a number of franchisees.

The number of channels available varies from city to city. Variations arise because a small number of cable operators control the large subscription base in the metropolitan areas. About 25 channels/networks publicise their programming schedules in the newspapers. These channels are in addition to the state-owned Doordarshan which has a primary channel, a national channel, a metro entertainment-based channel, and 14 other channels to cater to different linguistic groups. Thus, in India subscribing to a cable service means having access to multiple channels. The marketing strategy of the television manufacturers is to limit the number of channels the set can provide in order to increase sales of sets as more channels become available.

The growth of the cable industry in India is limited by several factors. From a population of nearly 1 billion there are about 270 million broadcast television viewers with access to a set in their homes. It is estimated that there are about 145 million viewers who do not have television sets in their homes but who watch programmes in other locations. Total viewers are estimated at about 45 per cent of the total population. However as far as cable television is concerned, of an estimated 52.5 million households only about 10 million have satellite television service via their cable operator. When cable services were introduced in the early 1990s all the services were free and many of them continue to be so. There is a trend towards introducing pay television services involving the cable operator rather than the subscriber. The cable operator pays a quarterly rent to obtain the necessary de-scrambling interface to supply the channels, for example, the Star Movie and Discovery channels.

The debate on new media policy and regulation in India centres around the role of the government as simply the licensing authority or as a regulator of content and ownership. Strong lobbying by the foreign television interests advocates a laissez faire policy in all respects. Another group wants collaboration in which Indian companies or individuals have an equal stake in any new ventures. Some are calling for cross-media ownership restrictions, while others lobby for their complete removal. In addition there are strong views concerning the need for content regulation to respond to the sensitivity of the cultural and moral fabric of the country.

Fears of 'cultural imperialism' as a result of imports of foreign programming have been overcome by exploiting different languages as 'cultural screens' (Smythe 1981). The success of many regional language channels especially in South India suggests the presence of this phenomenon. These channels also emerged as anti-centralist moves to avoid imposing one language and one identity on the nation. Some of the regional networks are controlled by the ruling regional political parties and it has been suggested that these network operators may obtain concessions and incentives that will enable them to prosper in the new media services market. The attractiveness of imported programming is also limited by language diversity. Many long-running American soap operas have been dubbed in Hindi to make them more attractive. However, while dubbed cartoons are popular, the popularity of dubbed versions of *Santa Barbara* and *The Bold and the Beautiful* is not very high, although the English versions of these programmes are very popular among the elite in India.

Criticism has been levelled at the cable television industry because, although it offers more channels, they tend to cover the same type of programmes, that is, films, sitcoms, and games shows. There are limited audiences for very good, sensitive programmes. Cable television started in India as a cost effective alternative to watching films using a video cassette player (VCP). With one VCP a cable operator could feed 50 to 60 homes. This practice developed into satellite services during the Gulf War when CNN started beaming its programmes via satellite. In response Doordarshan launched a commercially oriented programming policy that provided viewers with more entertainment programming. In terms of both viewing time and channel expansion, the State network was unable to satiate viewers. The arrival of STAR TV in December 1991 heralded the multi-channel era and cable operators became important as service providers.

At present it is unclear whether the private telecommunication operators will move into the entertainment television business using new technologies to provide value added services. The spread of PCs and the Internet may also affect the growth potential of the cable industry.

Cable television is currently an urban phenomenon catering mainly to the middle classes as potential consumers.

In 1997 foreign interest in the television industry in India was represented by Rupert Murdoch's News Corp which owned 50 per cent of Asia Today Ltd with the Indian partner, Essel Group, which owned the other 50 per cent. The Dow Jones group owned 50 per cent of Asia Business India with Hindujas and TV-18 which both have a stake. Sony owned 80 per cent of Sony Entertainment Television in India and there are merchant bankers and other foreign companies with future investment plans.

As of mid-1997 it was expected that a Broadcasting Authority of India would be created to regulate satellite, cable, and radio channels. Foreign equity interests would be restricted to 49 per cent rather than the 100 per cent which in some cases has emerged in the absence of regulation. Cross media ownership restrictions and other regulatory provisions in place in other countries would be adapted to Indian conditions. A common programme code for all broadcast channels would also be introduced, but the policy framework will depend on a report and the recommendations of a 30-member joint select committee of the Parliament.

7.5.3 DEVELOPMENTS IN ASIAN AUDIOVISUAL MARKETS

Observers have noted that there are two Asias, one rich and the other poor. The rich countries are largely concentrated in East Asia. These include Japan and the newly industrialising countries and, increasingly, the next generation of newly industrialising countries in Southeast Asia. According to Dató Jaafar Kamin, President of the Asia Pacific Broadcasting Union (ABU), the complexity, disparity, and contrasts in the broadcasting systems operating in Asian countries make Asia the most challenging, yet the most promising, region in the 21st century.

Technological change is at the core of the changing scene in information services and audiovisual markets. As technological developments accelerate, new applications proliferate with far-reaching consequences for individuals and institutions, practitioners, and policy-makers, and national and international bodies in the audiovisual production field. The mantra for the new millennium is 'convergence'. To quote Rupert Murdoch: 'The traditional distinctions are breaking down. Five of the world's biggest industries - computing, communications, consumer electronics, publishing, and entertainment - are converging into one large dynamic whole' (see Menon 1996: n.p.). Information gathering, processing, storage, and transmission over telecommunication networks will enable technologically advanced nations to close the 20th century as information societies. In Asia, there are countries, such as Malaysia, that are establishing Multi-Media Super Corridors and much of the action is in information content and new forms of communication.

The telecommunication network is providing the electronic platform for the development of new communication and information services including database access, the Internet, Pay TV, High Definition Television (HDTV), and multimedia. They are all made possible by the digitisation of the information and media content and the introduction of a new variety of interactive services where the interactivity is determined by users.

In Singapore, the Institute of System Science has done pioneering work in the area of virtual reality. Virtual reality can be used today for three basic applications: games, medicines and design walk-throughs. The coming virtual reality revolution is expected to bring about massive changes in the way society communicates, designs, and plays. Anticipated applications range from super telephones to interactive adventures and an infinite 'cyberspace' that contains all the information, machines, and people in the world.

The Internet is having an impact on the news, publishing, and advertising industries. The Internet's fusion of some of the capabilities of traditional media could lead to new modes of usage. The main differences will be interactivity in communication and the facility to time-shift consumption of information. The traditional structure and role of broadcasting is expected to change dramatically in the coming decade. As transmission and programme production benefit from technological innovation and as programming becomes less labour-intensive, stations will require multi-skilled journalists rather than technical specialists. Downsizing and structural changes will radically alter broadcasting in Asia.

As international economic integration expands and technologies advance, government control of the economy is becoming weaker and national regulation is eroding, a good example being international satellite transmissions. The loosening of government monopoly and control of broadcasting witnessed in the past few years will accelerate as changing technology and increasing competition necessitate speed and flexibility in decision-making and higher revenue generation. Corporatisation, privatisation, and competition will continue to be the predominant trends.

Public service programming is likely to suffer in the rush to maximise profits. However, as in the case of Singapore, it may be possible to incorporate national goals in commercial programmes. Regional initiatives to counter foreign programming dominance are also likely to gain support. Broadcasting has grown from a national to a regional activity and is now on the verge of developing an international dimension. This is facilitated by the commercial broadcast stations and networks being under the umbrella of transnational corporations, for example, Zee TV in India. This, in turn, will contribute to a fundamental shift in audience focus away from distinctive national characteristics, facilitating global marketing campaigns by advertisers. New complaints of hegemony, trivialisation, and cultural erosion, could occur as entertainment programmes are designed to promote specific brands. Interactive television provides new opportunities for commercialisation. This phenomenon has already appeared in Asia and it can be expected to spread as television and satellite shopping gain in volume.

The Asia Speaks Out project is being promoted by the Hoso Bunka Foundation (HBF) and ABU. In April 1995 this project was initiated and pursued by various organisations including HBF and ABU. The project is assessing practical means of promoting co-productions and exchanges; better distribution and use of ABU prize-winning programmes; economic means of dubbing/subtitling television programmes and films; cooperation between public and private sector broadcasters; and ongoing research into broadcasting systems, media laws/regulations and aspects of programming, including the effects of television programming on Asian children.

The project represents a positive move, that is, a means to intensify understanding and cooperation among Asian countries. The efforts of similarly oriented organisations, such as the ASEAN Committee on Culture and Information (COCI), where representatives from the seven ASEAN nations meet regularly to initiate and financially support projects in broadcasting and print media development, should also be recognised. Regional cooperation is one way to ensure that some part of the programming content originates in Asia. Examples of such programmes (ongoing or proposed) are *Asia Bagus*, *ABU Hour*, *Asia Now* TV Documentary Competitions and *Asiavision*.

Cooperation in broadcasting could not be achieved without the support and understanding of commercial players such as Star TV and CNN. Their involvement raises policy issues for Asian countries which need to decide between the options of 'open' and 'controlled skies'. Some countries have imposed quotas on the import of foreign programming. Others have stipulated that foreign programmes be dubbed, or at least subtitled, in the national languages. At the moment, these measures seem to have achieved a modicum of success. Private broadcasters and advertisers are beginning to appreciate that their programmes will reach wider audiences if dubbed or subtitled in the national languages of countries such as Thailand, Japan, Indonesia, and Malaysia, where the national language predominates. Ultimately, market forces will determine which foreign programmes survive in such an environment. Those responsible for radio and television programmes will have to meet the challenge of providing Asians with programmes based on Asian values and culture, working with governments to promote this objective.

7.5.4 CONVERGENCE AND THE TRANSITION ECONOMIES

The Polish experience illustrates the way policy measures are being introduced as the country restructures the media industry. The measures parallel many of those that are being implemented across the European Union. Many of the central and east European countries are seeking to rapidly expand the telecommunication infrastructure. Technologies such as cellular communication, digital overlay networks, satellite networks, and wireless in the 'local loop' are being used to supplement core telephone networks. Cable telephony is offering the potential to meet demand and installation offers to sources of revenues from information/entertainment (multimedia) services and telecommunication services.

The number of television homes and the number of those connected to cable television by cable and satellite networks as of 1993 are shown in Table 7.8.

TABLE 7.8 – TRANSITION ECONOMIES CABLE AND SATELLITE PENETRATION, 1989-1993

	1989	1990	1991	1992	1993
TV homes (m)	19.3	20.4	21.5	22.6	24.0
Cable					
Subscribers (m)	0.26	0.34	0.53	0.95	1.31
% of TV homes	1.10	1.70	2.50	4.20	5.40
Satellite					
Receivers (m)	.01	0.03	0.08	0.38	0.67
% of TV homes	–	0.10	0.40	1.70	2.80

Source: Industry estimates by Datamonitor cited in Law (1995).

Cable television is highly developed in Russia where it is estimated that there were some 10 million cable subscribers in 1995 representing 22 per cent of all television households (MDIS 1997). In Moscow until 1996 there were some 80 cable operators serving between 5,000 and 10,000 subscribers and offering six terrestrial channels. In the same year, the operators were required to interconnect their networks to form one network operated by Moscow Municipal Cable Television, which is now planning to upgrade the network. There are plans for Lucent Technologies (US) to install a 30 channel digital network passing 1 million homes by the year 2000 and a further 2.5 million homes by 2006. In January 1997, CellularVision of Russia received permission from the Ministry of Communication to offer telephone service via its Local Multipoint Distribution Services (LMDS) under a 10 year licence to offer television, data transmission, and local and long distance telephone service throughout the country.

In other transition economies, such as Bulgaria, for example, although cable television distribution licences have been granted to private companies since 1994, few new networks have been built and minimal services are provided. In contrast in the Czech Republic there were estimated to be 600,000 cable subscribers in mid-1995 and three operators have begun to offer telephone services over the cable network (MDIS 1997). In Hungary, there were 1.52 million subscribers in 1995 or 40 per cent of television households although many were connected to systems offering less than 15 channels. The largest operator, Kabelkóm, is a joint venture between Time Warner and United Communications International (a United States concern).

These examples suggest that the cable/satellite infrastructure in the transition economies is likely to expand as a service delivery mode. This, in turn, will raise policy issues for existing public broadcasters and government authorities as they seek ways of maintaining the viability of 'public service broadcasting' in the face of an increasing number of commercial operators of service delivery networks. The case of Poland provides an interesting example of the structural changes in the new media markets and highlights the difficulties in producing local content to meet the potential increase in transmission capacity.

The legal set up for Poland's broadcasting sector is constituted by a regulatory authority, the National Broadcasting Council which issues broadcasting licences, and the Broadcasting Act adopted in 1992 which determines quotas for domestic Polish broadcasting stations. The Council differentiates between the quotas for different types of broadcasters and encourages the transmission of domestic productions (Jakubowicz 1996). No longer a monopoly, public television and radio have been separated and are regulated by the Council. The involvement of foreign companies is limited in all areas of broadcasting, production, programme content, and distribution.

Rather than using public funds, Polish Television (state-owned) relies on licence fees and advertising, and operates two national, one satellite, and several local channels. The development of commercial television is challenging the public service Polish Television, but is hampered by a radio frequency shortage due to the absence of an allocation policy. The army has retained the use of many of the higher frequencies and there are technical deficiencies including the underdevelopment of the transmitter network. Small local television stations are struggling financially, but cable and satellite television channels have matured.

Polish cable television via satellite is one of the largest in Europe, reaching 2 to 2.5 million households and offering up to 30 channels. Polish language satellite channels are also increasing in number, the most successful being POLSAT featuring mainly American films and series. In 1990, Chase Enterprises (US) announced a US$ 900 million investment in a national cable network but no further progress was made. Poland already had a black market in satellite television reception and the planned monthly cable subscription charge of US$ 8 was considered too high for the market to bear. Poland's Direct-to-Home satellite television penetration is the third highest in Europe next to Austria and Germany. However, companies such as TCI, Time Warner, Comcast, and US West are said to be considering cable network investment in the future (MDIS 1997).

Polish Television is the largest television production company and buyer of works produced by independent producers. It plays an important role in complementing the Film Production Agency by supporting the majority of film productions. Film distribution takes place via state-owned and leased cinemas and also via privately-owned cinemas. Since American film distributors dominate the Polish cinema market as well as the video market, the Distribution Agency promotes the distribution of Polish and non-commercial films. Policies that protect the domestic market from foreign imported programming are believed to have prevented its dominance. However, insufficient capital is available locally for production and this is regarded as the major limitation to the further development of Polish-owned commercial television.

7.6 Software Development Challenges, Export Markets, and Domestic Capabilities

Software is the driver of the ICT-led economic growth being experienced across the developed world. The market demand for new software solutions to business problems is large (with world sales of software approaching US$ 200 billion per annum) and growing (OECD 1994a). This market is dominated by organisations in developed countries. Nevertheless, many developing countries consider that entry into the software market promises opportunities for economic growth. This section considers the challenges facing governments and institutions in developing countries seeking to enter the software industry. It focuses on policies for stimulating the development of software-related capabilities as a platform for market entry.

Strategies for software market entry are premised on the understanding of software and the nature of software work. Software is both a product and process technology. It affects the production of goods and services especially where production is knowledge or information-intensive. Software is not homogeneous and the main divisions are between systems software, applications packages, and development tools (Hewett and Durham 1987).[8] In the industrialised countries, the range of software 'products' required by a variety of end-users, together with the limitations of transferring expertise between market niches within the industry, has led to a wide variety of software producers operating in separate communities within the industry. These include hardware manufacturers, system houses, software product companies,

FIGURE 7.1 - THE WATERFALL MODEL OF SOFTWARE DEVELOPMENT

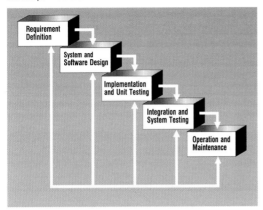

Source: Sommerville (1995).
Reprinted by permission of Addison Wesley Longman Ltd.

consultancies, and dealers. This array of software production activity represents the minority of total software development. The majority is carried out inside businesses in the domestic economy, supporting cross-sectoral production and process activities. As a result, software cannot be treated as a single sector of the economy.

Despite considerable investment, the software development process is mainly pre-industrial, that is, craft-based, and skill intensive, with few economies of scale, and low capital intensity (Brooks 1982). Methods of production are generally *ad hoc* and implicit. Diagrammatic representations of the software development process aim to impose methodological order on apparently chaotic practice. Typically, they represent the software development life-cycle as involving a fragmented set of discrete sequential activities or 'phases' from conception through to eventual obsolescence. Each phase reflects 'discipline-bound' tasks originally performed by different actors, often in different physical locations. For example, the well known 'waterfall model' of software development (Figure 7.1) developed in the late 1960s and early 1970s considers software development to be a linear process (Yourdon 1992). The process is represented as beginning at the 'upper end' with the analysis and specification of system requirements. It proceeds through their translation into a system design and on to the 'lower end' tasks of coded implementation and system testing. The substantial problems of software development practice are reflected in problems with this representation of the process.

For instance, the development of software systems is often paper-based and is not practised in a formal, rigorous manner. It cannot be subjected to automated error checking or mechanically transformed into programming code. For large systems, this also means that it is especially difficult to trace through from requirements to the code. Requirements may (and usually do) change radically over the course of software development. One result of not

taking such changes into account is low quality software where error detection is delayed until the final phase. Requirements specification is the most error prone, and consequently the most costly, phase of the software development process. Time pressures mitigate against thorough testing and problems are left to be sorted out during maintenance. The results of the software development process are not obtainable until coding has been completed. Configuration management, the management of integration between individual system elements or modules, does not typically occur until this time. Problems with integration are left for maintenance. In focusing on performance of a series of atomistic tasks, the fact that software development is a systemic process is often overlooked. Software development work in industrialised countries is highly dependent on skilled labour, has low capital intensity and few economies of scale. The growing maintenance burden contributes significantly to development backlogs which reduce the likelihood of providing timely and effective solutions to competitive business problems. Software is an impediment to the promise of ICT-led growth.

7.6.1 DEVELOPING SOFTWARE CAPABILITIES

Governments and institutions in a number of developing countries have formed policies for stimulating the production of capabilities that are appropriate for entry into the software market. The content of these policy measures reflects the more general industrial policies within the economy as well as the particular understanding of software and software development work that is adopted.

The most common view of software development is a 'machine-centred' one. Software is understood as a technically engineered product - a computer program, an extension of the computer hardware, ultimately concerned with the manipulation and control of hardware states. In this view, the goal is to approximate, as closely as possible, technical engineering practice. This is because the rigour and precision of engineering principles are assumed to impose predictability and control on traditionally *ad hoc* software development practices and result in higher quality, more reliable programs.

This 'discipline-bound', machine-centred, perspective is enshrined in the waterfall model of software development process (see Figure 7.1). Problems with software are defined as technical and are located with technical staff and associated with technical production methods. Alleviating software problems is seen to rely on the development and diffusion of tools, techniques, and methods which urge software professionals toward the adoption of increasingly engineered approaches which facilitate scientific management such as the application of advanced technological support for software development (Cooley 1987).

Policy measures for skill development conceived within this framework focus, for instance, on the provision of training courses in discrete, technical, computer-related skills. Policy instruments which focus on the production of low cost, low value, specialised technical skills for export are short-term solutions to the need to generate foreign exchange. They produce vulnerable industrial structures in the domestic economy which serve as weak platforms for entry into either the domestic or the export software product markets. There is an alternative way to understand the software and the software development process which can lead to enhanced opportunities for entry into the domestic as well as the export markets.

A different, 'context-centred' perspective on the software development process focuses on the need to solve commercial business problems. The aim of system development is to maintain integrity at the interface between the entire information system (software plus hardware) and its operational context.[9] This directs attention to the need to understand the business context and to reflect that understanding in the specification of requirements for holistic system design. For this reason, close relationships between software client and producer should be encouraged although this is difficult to achieve in practice (Easterbrook 1991). It involves discovering a unique representation of the business functions to be supported by the software system. This representation needs to capture the business understanding of the individuals within each business function who will use the system. The representation also needs to be specified through awareness of the way in which it might be affected by system-related constraints (for example, characteristics of the hardware platform).

Individual members of any business enterprise, in different positions in a variety of departments, may put different interpretations on the business context as well as on the tasks that the system needs to accomplish. Each member will tend to have a different understanding of the business context. Reconciling these understanding into one statement of requirements for design involves continuous negotiation and interactive learning (Millar 1996), that is, 'discovery in the context of application' (Foray and Gibbons 1996). Throughout this learning process, software products evolve through negotiation about the salient features of product and context. These mediate the production, interchange, translation, and transformation of system-related knowledge during product design (Millar et al. 1996).

The strategic options for software market entry are different in this 'context-centred' view. Policy-making institutions need to implement measures which give priority to the development of a domestic market for software. The domestic market can provide work, services, and products and make market entry easier. A strategy of entry into a particular segment of the packaged software market may be more successful than attempting to enter the market for systems integration services. This is because systems integration services require the accumulation of a vast range of cross-sectoral business knowledge as well as development practice (Quintas 1996).

A domestic platform can support entry into the export market. Export market success is more likely between countries with significantly similar business contexts. One way in which firms in developing countries might enter the export market is through establishing symbiotic relationships with multinational firms in the domestic economy. For example, the Indian Kale Consultants joint venture with Nixdorf Computers enabled them to export their banking and hospital systems to other countries such as Malaysia, where Nixdorf had an installed base (Schware 1987).

The implications of the 'context-centred' view for capability development are that a broader set of skills and experiences than those gained within the software development waterfall model is required to increase the software development capability of the domestic population. These skills are likely to attract higher value work, but they also require a mix of information system and business-relevant training and experience.

... for countries seeking to start up their own software development activities, it is more advantageous to use professional "generalists" rather than software specialists. Developing countries need a pool of talented and qualified professionals who combine some software experience with education and experience in computer science, engineering, mathematics, construction, manufacturing, utilities, finance and education (Schware 1987: 1254).

This might be achieved by encouraging the provision of joint business and information systems courses at degree/diploma level. Another option may be to encourage business professionals in the domestic economy to develop systems to support their own business practices (as user-developers) through stimulating the diffusion of software development tools.

However, as the experience of the Brazilian software industry has shown, where policies for entry into the domestic software market have been pursued independently of initiatives for export, capability development is only one aspect of stimulating a domestic market for software (Schware 1992). Other critical aspects involve the removal of barriers to capability development. This makes policy measures for capability development focusing on domestic market entry costly in the short term, but such policies are a route to long-term success.

7.6.2 EXPORT MARKET PROSPECTS

Three main strategies potentially enable developing country firms to trade in the world software market (Correa 1996) (see Table 7.9).

▍The export of software development workers (also termed 'body shopping') to perform short-term work overseas at client premises (a predominant strategy in

India and the Philippines). This strategy is low cost and low risk. Workers gain valuable experience and knowledge of foreign markets and software process management techniques. The work is mainly confined to routine and low value added tasks such as programming and there is little exposure to the more creative activities such as design.

▌The export of software development services. This strategy requires the development of local infrastructure and the provision of support for business. It is potentially more profitable than the first strategy and is capable of fostering the development of project management skills. Firms in Chile as well as the governments of Taiwan (Pr. China) and Singapore have adopted this strategy. The export of software development services can be implemented through the development of customised software to client specifications; entry into software subcontracting (or 'outsourcing') relationships with client firms; or joint venture agreements with foreign companies. Of these, entry into the niche, customised software development market including systems integration services is probably the most costly and carries the highest risk. Outsourcing is generally restricted to the basic programming of legacy systems, for example, recoding required in order to fix the Y2K (year 2000) problem (Kelly 1996).

▌The export of software products. Export demands considerable capability in the domestic economy and high levels of capital investment. This strategy carries the greatest risk but it has the greatest potential to generate profit and learning. It may also facilitate the creation and retention of value added in the exporting country and provide entry into the more lucrative value added services market (many Israeli and Chilean firms are pursuing this strategy).

The share of world software production and trade held by developing countries is low and the main reasons are summarised in Table 7.10. It is increasingly recognised that export success in world markets requires the development of a strong domestic base as a platform for growth (NASSCOM 1996):

... countries without a relatively active and up-to-date domestic market for software will find it increasingly difficult to develop a software sector which involves absorbing new technologies for software production, monitoring and analyzing trends in the industry, and using software to solve domestic productivity problems. The cost of developing such capabilities increases rapidly over time, making "catch up" more difficult (Schware 1992: 144).

The strength of this platform depends on the policies adopted to foster software development competencies within the domestic population.

The world market for software is large and expanding. In 1992 the value of world trade in software was US$ 184 billion with annual growth rates averaging between 15 per cent and 20 per cent according to OECD estimates (Schware 1992). The OECD also estimates that with the inclusion of untraded (in-house) software development this figure would be closer to US$ 370 billion. Growth areas include software packages and systems integration services (OECD 1994a). One reason for this may be that firms in industrialised countries wanting to avoid the risk of dependence on in-house systems development staff, are seeking customised solutions by integrating a range of software packages in particular ways.

The software market is dominated by firms in developed countries where the high level of demand for software outstrips the capability of software development professionals to supply it. This is partly because industrialised countries have experienced severe shortages of software professional skills in the employment pool. This has inflated the cost of labour, a dominant input to software development practice. Together with the low productivity of software professionals the high cost of labour has imposed an equally high cost on the software solutions being produced.

Entry into the software market represents a considerable export opportunity for developing countries as long as barriers to market entry remain low.

Since the traded software market is rapidly expanding, technology for software development and production is not proprietary but legally accessible, software development is skill (labor)

TABLE 7.9 – SOFTWARE EXPORT STRATEGIES

Export of work	Export of services	Export of products
Advantages: low entry barriers; low risk; stimulate project management skills; knowledge of foreign market; advantages dependent on partner/client	Advantages: moderate value added; moderate profitability; experience of project management; advantages dependent on partner/client	Advantages: high value added; high potential for profit; encourage the development of technological capabilities; possible basis for entry into value added services market
Disadvantages: low value added; experience limited to programming; disadvantages dependent on partner/client	Disadvantages: moderate entry costs; possibility of marketing costs; requires developed infrastructure; disadvantages dependent on partner/client	Disadvantages: requires high levels of capital, managerial and marketing skills; high risk; force of non-price competition

Source: Abstracted from Correa (1996).

Internal factors	
Market size	Small size of domestic market.
Structure of domestic demand	Low levels of demand for technologically sophisticated products. Weak incentives for technological upgrading. Under-investment in domestic market development.
Firm size	Software firms are small and financially weak. Notable absence of medium-sized enterprises.
Capital markets and financial institutions	Absence of venture capital. Inadequate lending for intangible investments. Poor access to credit for SMEs.
Structure of education and extension institutions	Weak links between R&D institutes and industry. University education relatively unresponsive to needs of industry. Low standards of private training institutes. Poor quality of technology support institutions.
Technical and managerial capabilities	Low information and computer literacy. Poor attitudes to information management. Institutional rigidities and constraints to learning.
Supply of and access to knowledge	Weak presence of ICT multinationals. Poor access to world-wide technology networks. Information asymmetry between local and multinational firms. Weak user-producer interactions. Underdeveloped local consulting industry.
Relative weight of labour costs	High labour costs for packaged software, due mainly to the costs of management, administration and marketing.
Quality standards	Lack of experience with quality standards.
Tools, techniques and methods	Limited diffusion of key software development tools, techniques and methods.
Infrastructure	Lack of appropriate and reliable infrastructure.
Marketing requirements	Marketing limitations constrain developing software for export.
Government policies	Underdeveloped public sector capability as information collector and ICT user. Restrictions on public procurement and information sharing practices. Underdeveloped legal framework for information sharing and intellectual property rights. Lack of partnership between government and business.
External factors	
Mistrust	The 'not-invented-here syndrome'.
Identification of user needs	Problems in establishing the needs of users in different geographical and cultural locations.
Maturity of software industry	Limited - as indicated by developing country participation in the world supply of software packages.
Language barriers in non-English-speaking countries	Difficult to produce good documentation.
Ability to enforce intellectual property rights	Poor - leading to lack of protection.
Marketing costs	High cost of launching a new product in a foreign market. Reluctance of foreign dealers and distributors to commercialise software from small developing country firms.

Source: Abstracted and adapted from Correa (1996); and Hanna et al. (1995).

TABLE 7.11 – SOFTWARE EXPORTS FROM SELECTED COUNTRIES AND TERRITORIES

Country	Year	(US$ m)	Growth rate (%)
India	1990	120	34
Singapore	1990	89	43
Israel	1990	79	39
Philippines	1990	51	32
Mexico	1990	38	30
China	1990	18	43
Korea (Republic of)	1990	15	40
Taiwan (Pr. China)	1987	11	48

Source: Based on Heeks (1996a).

intensive rather than capital intensive and small size is a source of dynamism, it is not surprising to find the interest and expectations raised in some developing countries by the possible development of a local software industry (Correa 1996: 173).

The growing burden of maintenance due to the long-standing software crisis in developed economies, has further stimulated the demand for software professional skills (particularly those related to coding and testing). This has created additional opportunities for developing countries to exploit.

There are a number of developing countries and territories with high growth rates for their software industries (see Table 7.11). While India's software exports consist predominantly of software services, others concentrate on the development of software packages and data entry services (Ramesam 1996).

India's geography places it in time zones almost opposite to most of the western industrialised world so that Indian firms can provide 'around the clock' services via communication links. The Indian computer industry doubled its revenues in the five year period 1990 to 1995 (see Table 7.12).

Although its increased share in the United States software market is impressive (doubling from 0.82 per cent in 1990/1991 to 1.7 per cent in 1994/5) as shown in Table 7.13, the United States was India's major export partner in this period. In addition, the total market share of 1.7 per cent in the United States software market in 1994/95 was an even smaller proportion of the global market.

TABLE 7.12 - GROWTH OF COMPUTER INDUSTRY IN INDIA, 1990-1995 (US$ MILLION)

	1990-91	1991-92	1992-93	1993-94	1994-95
Hardware					
Domestic	436	423	370	490	590
Exports	105	111	52	93	177
Total	541	534	422	583	767
Software					
Domestic	115	140	163	230	350
Exports	128	164	225	330	485
Total	243	304	388	560	835
Maintenance	93	99	90	117	142
Others	210	228	207	233	297
Grand Total	1,087	1,165	1,107	1,493	2,041

Source: NASSCOM (1996).

TABLE 7.13 - GROWTH IN THE INDIAN SHARE OF US SOFTWARE MARKET

Year	US software market (US$ million)	Indian exports to US market (US$ million)	Indian share of US market (%)
1990/91	9,250	76.3	0.82
1991/92	10,400	101.2	0.97
1992/93	11,960	126.6	1.06
1993/94	13,630	180.8	1.33
1994/95	16,080	274.1	1.70

Source: Based on Heeks (1996a).

In the Indian context there are many institutions providing computer education at the degree/diploma level of which there are about 150 universities and regional engineering colleges. The output of trained manpower at degree/diploma level has increased from less than 1,000 in 1983 to about 55,000 in 1995. The Government of India has introduced new courses including a Diploma in Computer Application, Masters in Computer Application, and a Diploma in Computer Engineering. These courses have been very useful in adding technical personnel to the Indian software industry (NASSCOM 1996: 54).

This focus on training has implications for the strategies that India has used to enter the software market. The Indian government has adopted short-term, export-led industrial policies in order to obtain foreign exchange. Indian software suppliers have needed to satisfy clients in other (usually developed) countries. Most Indian software firms have been unable to penetrate the software *product* export market and have been forced to export the software-related capabilities of the domestic population (mainly computer programming skills). The market for software professional skills is complex. Skills involved in performing tasks at the 'lower end' of the software waterfall model have lower value than the skills required to undertake activities at the 'higher end', such as requirements analysis and design. Entry into the systems integration market requires a broader base of general professional skills in addition to those that have been developed in India through its training programmes (Schware 1992).

While India's own software industry has flourished by drawing on the largest English speaking pool of scientists outside the United States (MSF/ITPA 1996), multinational corporations, predominantly from the United States, and some European countries, are making increasing use of this comparatively cheap, trained labour force for offshore project development of their own operations (the comparative salaries of programmers are shown in Table 7.14).

The relatively low cost of the software capability base in India has proved to be well suited to 'body shopping' and the majority of Indian activity in the software export market is achieved through the provision of low value, short-term, off-shore computer programming services (Schware 1992). Increasingly, and on the basis of the market knowledge gained through such arrangements,[10] Indian firms have participated in the export of services from India's own shores. Indian firms have established outsourcing arrangements with organisations in industrialised countries and the National Association of Software and Service Companies (NASSCOM) believes that this movement away from body shopping is positive. However, the distancing of relationships with organisations in developed countries and the removal of opportunities for learning about the operation of markets and businesses in the industrialised country context, could have less positive, longer-term ramifications. The factors affecting India's software exports are the relatively low-skilled IT professionals, mostly on-site work, mainly programming, and predominantly American collaboration, usually with a single collaborator (Ramesam 1996).

Indian software experience is mainly restricted to coding. Competition is generally based on price and is vulnerable

TABLE 7.14 - ANNUAL SALARIES OF COMPUTER PROGRAMMERS, 1994

	US$
India	3,957
Mexico	26,528
United Kingdom	31,247
Hong Kong	34,615
France	45,521
United States	46,600
Japan	51,730
Germany (western)	54,075

Source: d'Orville (1996) citing data from *Der Spiegel*.

TABLE 7.15 - OFFICE RENTS IN PRIME BUSINESS AREAS

City	Rent as % of total cost
Mumbai	92
Tokyo	84
Hong Kong	88
Moscow	88
London	70
Delhi	89
Singapore	78
Beijing	94
Shanghai	78
Paris	82
Hanoi	91
New York City	65
Frankfurt	86
Taipei	87
Buenos Aires	77
Sao Paulo	81
Mexico City	68
Prague	91
Ho Chi Minh City	88
Manila	80
Budapest	90
Kuala Lumpur	75
Istanbul	74
Bangkok	83
Jakarta	65

Source: Based on Ramesam (1996) citing data from *The Economist*.

to fluctuations in the perceived relative cost and value of alternatives (such as the use of software development tools, contractors, permanent staff and so on). For example, the recent 25 per cent per annum increases in the wage levels of Indian programmers, fuelled by high levels of demand in developed countries for time-critical Y2K (year 2000) date changes to existing program code, have generated anxiety about the long-term validity of price based competition (Kelly 1997).

Entry into higher value markets has been precluded for three main reasons: first, lack of maturity and absence of broad software development experience although this is being counteracted by the quality focus of Indian companies (by 1996, 55 Indian firms had ISO 9001 quality assurance accreditation) (Kelly 1996); second, unreliability of the ICT infrastructure; and third, lack of trust arising from cultural conventions of politeness (such as reluctance to impart bad news) and asymmetric interpretations of confidentiality which create problems (Kelly 1996). The extension of training programmes to remove these skill limitations (in requirements analysis and design, for instance) to enter higher value markets is a continuation of the predominant technical perspective. Indian firms seeking to export such skills (especially through outsourcing) are likely to have limited success due to the social and context dependent nature of requirements analysis and design tasks (Millar 1996).

Constraints imposed by a poor telecommunication infrastructure not only limit the export of Indian software over satellite (64kbps) or other communication networks, but also have a negative effect on foreign investment (Tassell 1997). Another limiting factor is the increasing office rents in India as compared to other locations which erodes the cost advantages to foreign inward investors (see Table 7.15).

7.6.4 SOFTWARE CAPABILITIES IN CHINA

The commercial software industry in China emerged when institutional restructuring in the early 1980s enabled its evolution from laboratory research. Until this time, software was embedded in computer hardware and it was not marketable as a separate product. There were few 'software' companies as such. Progress was made in 1988 under the national reform policy 'Torch Programme' which aimed to promote a wide range of new technology business organisations spinning off from R&D institutes. This gave a major a boost to the development of the software industry as shown in Table 7.16.

The development of packaged software has concentrated largely on the localisation of computer languages by re-engineering English languages into Chinese characters. Research on the Chinese software industry indicates that those Chinese software companies who have managed to establish themselves internationally depend on being able to tap all possible sources of technological expertise

TABLE 7.16 - SELECTED SOFTWARE ENTERPRISES IN SHANGHAI

Name	Category	No. of workers	Sales	Exports
Qingming Software Ltd	Sino-Japanese joint venture	over 110	US$ 1.6 million	US$ 1 million
Huatend Software Systems Ltd	Sino-American joint venture	over 140	US$ 11 million	US$ 700,000
Huatend Software Development Ltd	Sino-Japanese joint venture	45	US$ 840,000	US$ 40,000
Yingyeda Electronics Ltd	Solely foreign-owned enterprise	over 900	US$ 5.3 million	US$ 5 million

Note: Sales for Qingming Software Ltd, Huatend Software Development Ltd, and Yingyeda Electronics Ltd have been converted from Yuan RMB to US$ at the period average for 1st quarter 1996 as reported in IMF (1997).
Source: Haiyan (1998 forthcoming) citing data from *China Infoworld*, 23 January.

and fostering specialised competencies to develop complementary innovations compatible with existing systems (Gu and Steinmueller 1998 forthcoming). The software design and development capabilities acquired through the development of sub-systems and components which enhance existing systems ensure the companies' domestic and international competitiveness, although not at levels comparable to India. Along with rising standards of living and family investment in PCs, domestic demand for software has been increasing.

Harnessing these resources, has resulted in internationally competitive products. The progress of the software industry also has been assisted by legal and regulatory adjustments, the establishment of standards institutions, and software engineering centres. The 'Three Gold Project' launched by the Chinese government in 1993, included several priority projects in information technology and this has enhanced the opportunities for the software industry. However, national programmes provide funding for R&D activities to higher education and research institutes. They do not support enterprises directly and many of these firms are primarily involved in marketing and spreading innovative software solutions. This situation is encouraged by unfavourable taxation of software development activities (Haiyan 1998 forthcoming).

7.6.5 MYTHS ABOUT SOFTWARE DEVELOPMENT IN DEVELOPING COUNTRIES

Developing countries became consumers of software in the 1950s and 1960s and some began producing software at this time. Since then, several myths about software development have become part of industry folklore in developing countries with both positive and negative implications for the future growth of production and the future entry possibilities for firms in countries that are beginning to consider a software development strategy (see Boxes 7.3 and 7.4).

Governments, firms, and public sector institutions in developing countries need to overcome vast hurdles if they are successfully to enter the market for software. The

strategic options for market entry which follow from adopting the linear 'machine-centred' view on capability building are limited. They reproduce weak structures and vulnerability in the domestic economy. A wider set of strategic options for market entry follows from the 'context-centred' view of software. The policies for capability development associated with this view are one component of the range of the long-term measures required to capitalise on the potential for domestic and export software market entry.

7.7 INFORMATION CONTENT AND THE NATIONAL INFORMATION INFRASTRUCTURE

The global reach of ICTs through broadcasting, telecommunication, and radio networks in combination with new cable and satellite communication, raises concerns about the sociocultural implications of ICTs. Much of the content of audiovisual and information services originates from a few sources, giving rise to limited cultural diversity. The economic benefits of becoming part of the global information infrastructure can appear to clash with policies designed to protect local sociocultural and religious values. Traditional broadcasting and local programming are among the means of countering cultural and linguistic dominance with local and national cultural values but these avenues are not open to all countries because of the cost involved. Most countries in the developing world have to make choices about the technologies appropriate for delivering information services and audiovisual content. They also need to consider how to involve as diverse a range of content producers as possible so as to include the cultural interests of different races, and genders, and those with disabilities (Matsepe-Casaburri 1996).

Access to information by the majority through the choice of appropriate technology and applications and combinations of old and new in the process as well as access to quality programming in indigenous languages is, however, crucial to bringing people into the information society. For developing countries knowledge and understanding of their past, understanding

BOX 7.3 - THE NEGATIVE MYTHS ABOUT SOFTWARE DEVELOPMENT

1. *'It is computers that matter, not software'*

National policy and the investment strategies of both multi-nationals and aid donors have been overly-oriented to the hardware of information and communication. Yet software is known to be the key to successful, localised information systems. Software services provide developing countries with a good entry point into the ICT production complex. They provide wider externalities and much lower entry barriers than hardware, being less capital-intensive, and more labour-intensive, with a lower rate of obsolescence, and far fewer scale economies.

2. *'Developing countries cannot write software'*

In 1995/96, some US$ 2 billion-worth of software was exported from developing countries, mainly to western markets. Such figures create their own myths but software development is nevertheless pervasive, from the one-person enterprise creating customised databases to Asia's 'software factories' winning multi-million dollar contracts. Software development work is often hidden because it is undertaken in-house, but it is clearly no longer the preserve of just a few developing countries, let alone of just the western nations.

3. *'Piracy is ruining software production in developing countries'*

Piracy accounts for 50 per cent to 90 per cent of software consumption in developing country markets, yet this has not crushed local software production. Quite the reverse. Piracy has expanded the local market by speeding the diffusion of information technology and of software skills. As piracy diffuses standard imported packages, many local software firms have developed capabilities by producing localised versions

through 'reverse functional engineering' (Heeks 1996a). Piracy has stimulated innovation and has also helped the diffusion of software production tools.

4. *'Jobs are being lost in the industrialised countries'*

The globalisation of software production has included outsourcing work to developing countries that was once done in the industrialised countries. However, demand for software labour exceeds supply in the industrialised countries and will continue to do so for the foreseeable future. Many projects which are too small, risky, strategic, complex or high-tech are not outsourced. Therefore, although developing countries may eat into the industrialised countries' demand-supply gap, they will not eliminate it. In addition, industrialised countries retain the most highly-skilled tasks of analysis and design, thus creating an international skill division of labour.

5. *'New technology will wipe out developing country software exports'*

In theory, automation threatens software development jobs and developing countries' low labour cost advantages. In practice, the threat is far off. New technologies - both product and process - have created new skill requirements and new markets that developing countries are seeking to fill. The spread of open systems has reduced entry barriers for developing countries. Techniques such as program modularity and formal methods have increased, not reduced, the opportunities for software outsourcing.

---

their present and participating in their future, will then become more probable and possible (Matsepe-Casaburri 1996: 10).

During the 1970s as the audiovisual content produced in the western industrialised countries began to be exported in increasing quantities concerns were voiced about cultural impacts. Some argued that these media imports would soon destroy indigenous cultures leading to new forms of 'media' imperialism. Others took the view that market forces were working to ensure that the global structure of demand for the media products (films, books, broadcast and radio programming) would reflect the cultural and economic preferences of viewers and readers and that there was no cause for concern.

This debate has continued and in the 1990s there is a need for new assessments.[12] In some countries in the developing world, the terms of access to new ICTs are changing in ways that enable local content production reflecting diverse cultural values, and some countries are exporting their products. Others are viewing a wide mix of local and foreign products and reading a vast range of text-based products that are located on the Internet. Technical, economic, and social conditions are changing rapidly and

these are giving rise to key differences between debates about 'globalisation' or 'transnationalisation' and the media in the 1990s as compared to the models of 'media/cultural imperialism' which characterised the 1970s.

The G7 conference on the Information Society in February 1995 commented on the importance of culture and ICTs as follows:

All participants supported the principle of encouraging cultural and linguistic diversity. In international terms, the recognition and protection of cultural differences is an expression of good will. It is not about creating barriers; it is about tolerance (Bourdeau et al. 1996: 19).

In a 1995 World Bank report it was recognised that the cultural implications of the diffusion of content (broadcasting, educational products, on-line services) in the developing world could be significant and bring positive, as well as negative, consequences.

Culture can be preserved; it can also be destroyed. Intellectual and artistic products of national cultures can be preserved and disseminated with information technology. But creative cultures and societies can also be overwhelmed by the influx of

BOX 7.4 - THE POSITIVE MYTHS ABOUT SOFTWARE DEVELOPMENT

1. *'Developing countries are earning billions from software exports'*

The headline figures on software are deceptive. India, for example, may claim US$ 750 million worth of exports in 1995/96 but this is a gross figure (Dataquest 1996). The majority of this money subsequently leaves the country to pay for: the travel and living allowances of the large number of Indian software workers who undertake their development work in the client's country, not in India; marketing expenses; imports of hardware and telecommunications equipment used for in-India contract components; and repatriation of profits by the many multinational subsidiaries involved in this trade. Net export earnings for 1995/96 were closer to US$ 250 million and are unlikely to have compensated for India's software import bill.[11]

2. *'Developing countries are cheap locations for software development'*

Of course, low labour costs have been at the heart of interest in developing countries as software development sites. The salary of a programmer in country X being one-tenth that of a programmer in America is often quoted. However, such figures ignore well-above-average pay for good developers, a large range of non-salary labour costs, and the fact that labour costs are typically only a minor part of total software production costs. Factors such as skills availability, productivity, trust, labour flexibility, and access to local markets also underlie outsourcing decisions.

3. *'Telecommunication links are transforming the software export trade'*

Over the past five years, most developing country software exporters have invested in a telecommunication link. The image has been promoted of virtual development - clients sitting in the industrialised countries interacting with developers overseas, or even split-site development teams. The reality is more mundane. Fax and e-mail correspondence remain the backbone of communication. The vast majority of contracts still involve extensive periods during which the developers work at the client's site or, more

rarely, the client visits the developers. Telecommunication technology is slowly modifying this trade but has yet to revolutionise it.

4. *'This is a market-driven phenomenon'*

The Department of Defense was a key motivator of the creation of the United States software industry, and all subsequent development in other countries has been state-initiated, state-led or state-promoted. From South Africa to Egypt to India to Singapore the story is the same - 'Cherchez l'état' - in the spheres of financing and marketing, in skills and infrastructure development, in procurement, and in the diffusion of best practice (Heeks 1996b). Selective policy liberalisation - such as removal of software import tariffs - may have a role. However, the elimination of all state interventions and the free play of market forces will lead only to the atrophy of local software-related technological capabilities.

5. *'Software exports drive domestic improvements'*

Export production - mainly based on services, not packages - is a virtual enclave. Any transfer of skills has been one-way: from domestic to export production. Export pressures have thus diverted resources away from domestic-oriented production and have led these resources to create software that benefits companies based in the industrialised countries rather than addressing local needs. Far from assisting, exports are reinforcing weaknesses in the domestic market.

6. *'India is exporting - so can we'*

India's apparent success in software exports has encouraged many developing countries to naïvely believe that they can follow the same path. But they cannot. Added to its inherent linguistic and size advantages, India has spent more than two decades developing the requisite skills, contacts, policies, and infrastructure that are so lacking in many other countries. As a result, it may continue to consolidate its position while squeezing out latecomers. New entrants should therefore eschew the competition and fake glister of exports for the solid effectiveness of domestic software applications.

---

outside information, and sinister uses of information technology, notably computerised weaponry, certainly exist (Talero and Gaudette 1995: 8).

On the one hand, the press tends to see the new ICTs including the traditional broadcast media as well as the Internet, as providing a new milieu in which 'musicians and artists are redefining their work by embracing the computer - and shaking up the world of culture' (Bellafante 1995: 14). On the other, the spectre of the consequences of the pervasive spread of media content and other services which increase the predominance of the English language is raised (Mulligan 1997).

7.7.1 THE CULTURAL INDUSTRIES DEBATE

There is a very wide spectrum of approaches to this debate. Globalisation tendencies are being addressed within the disciplines of political science, economics, and media and cultural studies, with the media frequently being recognised as the key global infrastructure that underpins and facilitates other dynamics of globalisation. Scholars describe this process in various ways. For example, Anthony Giddens identifies five sub-structures of globalisation which he sees as the necessary outcome of modernity (Giddens 1991). The anthropologist Arjun Appadurai discusses five 'scapes' of global interaction, reminding us of the shifting 'ethnoscape' of mobile populations, and the 'disjunctures' between the various scapes (Appadurai 1990). In his recent work this is summed up as 'the joint force of electronic mediation and mass migration is explicitly transnational even post-national' (Appadurai 1996b: 9).

These dynamics pose real and conceptual challenges to nation/state centred models, from 'above' in the emergence of supranational organisations, international law and regulation, etc., and from 'below' in the emergence of new/old ethnicities, new social movements, sub-cultures, etc. The significance of recognising the increasingly multicultural nature of most states is that it profoundly destabilises easy attempts to construct a singular national culture/identity. It renders the possibility of national hegemony over cultural minorities more difficult than previously recognised in international debates.

In the media, there is increasing evidence of technological convergence and overlap in the roles of telecommunication providers, broadcasters, news providers, etc. In broadcasting, there is evidence of increasing conglomeration and ever larger units of supply, especially as those firms with distribution capacity buy up content suppliers (film libraries, old television programming). But there is also the emergence of new media industries outside the historic western industrial centres of cultural production. Examples include telenovellas from Brazil and Mexico; Islamic soap operas from Egypt and Turkey; films from India, China, Iran (Islamic Republic Of), Senegal; cartoons and serials from Japan; international news from Dubai and from the Saudi-financed MEBC based in London (Sreberny-Mohammadi 1995). This material not only circulates internally, within the national production contexts where it often garners bigger and more satisfied audiences than imported programming (Sepstrup and Goonasekera 1994), it also circulates globally, finding unanticipated cross-cultural viewerships (for example, the popularity of the Japanese serial 'Oshin' in Iran (Islamic Republic of)).

Of growing importance are geo-linguistic cultural regions. Access to the global English-language market has long been recognised as a key factor in the comparative advantages of United States audiovisual production. In 1996-97, the growth of Arab-language and Chinese-language media production, among others, is being recognised as evidence of the growing importance of regional media/ culture markets (Sinclair et al. 1996). While all non-western international television exchange perhaps does not yet rival American television exports in viewing hours and revenue, the growth of other media producers is further evidence that many of our conceptual models may have been framed in the very short term. Until recently, the structure and organisation of the media industries have not readily allowed for the development of television (and other cultural) industries beyond the United States or western industrialised countries.[13] It is important to remember that television as an industry (whether commercial or public service) is a post-World War II development, not yet fifty years old and undergoing substantial technological change.

There are many contradictory tendencies in the local, regional, and global audiovisual markets. There is continuing evidence of media globalisation, for example, in large-scale media production and distribution by horizontally and vertically integrated electronic empires. There is the spread of western material and mediated culture. There is the homogenisation argument, for instance, the ubiquity of *The Bold and the Beautiful*, McDonalds, Benetton and blue jeans, Qeche Indians in Guatemala listening to the Beatles; versions of Rambo across South East Asia, etc. There are concerns about commercialisation and cultural degradation that are still powerfully voiced by nations who are trying to defend a national space. There is the traditionalist 'defence' of cultural values against western cultural encroachment in the religion-based policies of the Islamic Republic; there have been attempts to limit audience access by controlling the use of satellite earth stations in China, Saudi Arabia, and Malaysia, for example. However, such controls are often relaxed after a period of time as in the case of Malaysia. Women voice concern about the 'objectification' of women in western programming; and indigenous peoples are concerned about the erosion of their cultural values and ways of life. Such concerns are powerfully collected together in the People's Communication Charter, now signed by a wide variety of concerned groups world-wide (Hamelink 1994).

Not only has the direct, unmediated and overly-national frame of older models (that 'American' or 'western' products impact on national 'southern' audiences) been heavily criticised, not least by Latin American writers like Martin-Barbero and Canclini, but the media production environment is also changing.

There is growing evidence of heterogeneity and media localisation. In media terms, the latter includes the use of alternative media in development processes, for example, Tanzanian women's radio clubs (Lewis 1993); a huge variety of alternative women-made media (Sreberny-Mohammadi 1995); women's global networking (Frankson 1996; Gittler 1996); hybridisation of popular music and growth of 'world music'; 'small' media in political transition, for example, in Iran (Islamic Republic of) (Sreberny-Mohammadi 1994), South Africa, the Philippines, and Poland. Some of these processes reinforce the importance of media as an essential element of civil society, and the importance of considering the political effects as well as the economic impacts of media.

Issues of 'cultural power' remain as groups and new social movements take action to acquire the capacity to represent themselves. The global cultural environment is becoming symbolically enriched even if these groups are not fully empowered in a way that leads to direct practical outcomes. This may also signal a shift away from a model of culture as a bounded or closed space, as in the notion of 'national' cultures, toward a notion of culture as action. It has been suggested that collective identities are action-based and that one action (or culture) does not pre-empt or cancel out another. Individuals and groups can be part of many different forms of action or culture.

The debates about the cultural impact of the new media create problems for analysis. Much research has centred on the national level: that is, on national broadcasters, national cultural products, national audiences, and national policy-making. But in multicultural societies, the singularity of such notions is under review and considerable research from around the world has suggested that national policy-making is patriarchal in relation to women.

Access to media and ICTs is a key issue, and the fact that there are inequalities of access does not provide a sufficient argument for non-adoption in a bid to protect 'national' cultures. Inequality of access to media has gone on for over five hundred years if one thinks in terms of illiteracy in relation to print media (or chirography) and most new technologies have spawned new elites. Cultural creativity is not limited to the western industrialised countries and there are compelling arguments that developing countries should not be left behind in the ICT field. They are likely to find innovative and adaptive ways of re-working and eventually diffusing media and ICTs in ways that become 'localised' (Sreberny-Mohammadi 1996).

There is also a continuing debate about the implications of English language dominance being increased by the wider diffusion and use of ICTs. Evidence seems to confirm such dominance. English-speaking Web sites are estimated to be 85 per cent of the current total whereas Francophone sites constitute only 2 per cent and German sites, due to the high number of English Web sites originating in Germany, amount to an even smaller percentage (Mulligan 1997). Apart from the content of the World Wide Web, a ranking of the world's 50 largest enterprises in global information services, consisting of press, publishing, television, radio and cinema, positioned according to their total media involvement portrays a similar picture; 35 of these enterprises are based in English speaking nations 25 of which are United States-based, and six are in the United Kingdom (Matsepe-Casaburri 1996). There are also concerns about local variations of English which may come to dominate the content of the World Wide Web and other global information services as these economies increase in importance.

Rapid progress in computer translation is continuing and new computer codes, for example enabling accents on letters, allow the display of any language regardless of its alphabet, including Russian, Korean, and Japanese. These developments may begin to alleviate concerns about English language dominance. Demand for translation software is increasing and automated translations are already available on the Web. These applications are reasonably proficient at converting Web sites from one language to another although they are not particularly good at translating prose. The debate about English language dominance which is accompanying globalisation processes must also take into account the effects of localisation. This involves the emergence of 'netizens' who form common language communities. In this case, language constitutes a means of limiting access to information, potentially excluding the non-speakers of the language being used.

Cultural histories influence people's attitudes toward ICTs in many ways and they have a major implication for the willingness of citizens, consumers, and working people to integrate them into their everyday lives (Mansell and Silverstone 1996). The social process of acceptance (or resistance) to innovations in ICTs and services is closely related to varied understandings of the role of information and knowledge in society and the way that they are best communicated. Culture matters considerably in the different effects of the introduction of the same technology within different cultural traditions.

There is empirical evidence for some of these differences. For example, an international comparative study examined the sophistication of statistics about the press in different countries as an indicator of the transparency of national media policies in the early 1990s (Maier-Rabler and Sutterluetti 1992). In Austria, Germany, Switzerland, Norway, Sweden, Finland, the United States, and Canada, there were positive associations between high quality press statistics and countries with a positive attitude towards economic success and extensive civil rights including freedom of speech and access to information for all. The Scandinavian countries (especially Sweden), Canada, and the United States had the most detailed and transparent press statistics. These countries all share the view that information transparency is good. Firms understand that communication of success in business is part of their economic activities. National administrations understand that an active information policy is a tool with which to justify their actions to their citizens. In these countries, information is good in most cases and more information is better because people need information to make informed decisions. In other countries the basic assumption that information is good and that all people should have access to public information is not as widely shared.

Another factor which may play an important role in citizens' perceptions of the importance and benefits of the 'knowledge society' is linked to language and culture. For example, how is the concept of the GII translated in different countries? In the United States the notion of an NII is closely related to issues such as 'making a better world through communication' or 'connecting all people'. In the German language, however, the vocabulary takes on slightly different meanings. For example, the term 'data highway' is translated into 'Datenhighway' or 'Datenautobahn'. The German word 'Daten' is associated with numeric information, numbers and figures. 'Daten' are cold, impersonal information. 'Daten' are used by organisations and 'Daten' are associated with privacy, that is 'Datenschutz' for privacy protection. 'Highways' and the 'Autobahn' symbolise progress and growth and have come to be associated with the strong environmental movement. The term information infrastructure - 'Informationsinfrastruktur' - does not suggest individual concern; it is associated with computers and business needs. In private and everyday communication one does not exchange information, one talks or chats and exchanges knowledge. In general, the behaviour of individual users of networked services must be expected to vary substantially in relation to their specific linguistic, information, and cultural background.

In some countries the idea of the NII is wrapped in social, educational, and cultural benefits. People form the idea that they should be concerned about the introduction of ICTs into their society. They form ideas about individual advantages like access to information, tele-education, some kinds of telecommuting and telework, and of individual disadvantages like isolation, under-qualification, displacement, offshore-production, etc. For example, differences in cultural traditions provide insights into the diffusion and adoption of ICTs within western Europe and the economies in transition in eastern Europe.

A 'protestant-enlightened information culture' is predominant in the United States with its fundamental assumption of 'transparency through information', its high valuation of economic success and its tendency to value the communication of success (Maier-Rabler 1997). Active communication between businesses and the public and/or consumers stimulates competition and is a basic instrument of economic action. There is broad support by the public for political arguments which see the NII as a precondition for international competitiveness.

A 'social democratic-liberal information culture' generally assumes that each citizen is entitled to obtain information from his or her local authority and state, in the broadest sense. Government information policies are justified not in response to explicit demand but by the perception that enhancing knowledge about civil society is beneficial to individuals. Particularly characteristic of the Scandinavian countries is that the value of information derives from the striving for political emancipation of the individual. The constitutional right to information is perceived as a precondition for political order and the constitutional embodiment of the right to information is very sophisticated in these countries.

This perception had a strong influence on the formulation of the American constitution, and especially on the First Amendment (Godwin 1994). Liberalism in the United States represents a hybrid of two cultural traditions. The private sector is familiar with concepts of 'universal service' and 'open access' for all citizens and policy-making seeks a partnership between government and the private sector to enhance the public good. A characteristic of these cultural traditions is active information-seeking behaviour. People develop the capacity to demand information. A high priority is given to curiosity and the ability to formulate good questions. It may be that question-based cultures have advantages in the use of the new ICTs. The attitude to the Internet, for example, is facilitated by a question-based approach rather than an answer-based approach. Without precise questions one cannot find answers in the maze of information available as a result of access to the global information infrastructure.

The history of cultural traditions in the economies in transition seems to engender the perception that people should expect answers from the Internet without formulating questions. In answer-based schools, the advantages of the Internet as an information tool for the education curriculum is fully appreciated by many people. This perception characterises a 'catholic-feudal information culture' where information is hierarchically available; it is passed on by the information 'rich' and there is little or no consensus upon an individual's right to information. Information is exchanged between citizens and individuals via informal paths and the knowledge about these paths and the degree of access to them affects the individual's position in the hierarchical system. The individuals are not really trained to seek out information and there is little expressed demand for certain kinds of information.

Finally, in Europe there is a 'centralist-socialist information culture' which requires a permanent and systematic exchange of information via forms, statistics, and reports which are the instruments of decision-makers. This cultural tradition also involves an information hierarchy, but it is based on rank or position rather than on the strength of the informal paths of communication. People in the former Communist states have been trained to produce precise information and to pass it to central organisations.

Today, these countries have a strong commitment to market-oriented principles. Their training to manage information exchange and to develop skills to communicate gives them advantages for the introduction of ICTs. Completely new digital telecommunication infrastructures in parts of the Czech Republic, eastern Germany, and Hungary, combined with a 'protestant-enlightened information culture' help to foster a positive attitude toward the use of ICTs.

These information cultures do not occur in a pure form but the particular mix of cultures present in different societies is an important factor in whether there is likely to be a strong demand for access to information via advanced ICTs. The cultural development of 'knowledge societies' is often discussed as if 'culture' is a static phenomenon, but cultural integrity is in fact 'continuously evolving' (Wang 1996a: 14). In some developing countries a completely open approach to the import of audiovisual products and information services will be favoured. In others, varying degrees of closure or control will be maintained in order to support indigenous and diverse cultures and social values.

7.7.2 THE EMPIRICAL EVIDENCE ON CULTURAL IMPACTS

National governments and private companies are investing large amounts of money in extending and upgrading broadcasting facilities to capture larger segments of the viewing population. Local programme production capacities cannot keep pace with the expansion of television time, resulting in the import of even more foreign programme material, usually from the industrialised countries, and particularly the United States. In addition, satellite-based national and regional television transmissions are becoming more numerous. Spill-over television programmes or regional and international satellite-based reception are becoming increasingly important and worrying for national and local authorities.

Analysis of the international flow of television programming needs to take these developments into consideration. Research methods and instruments are needed that are capable of capturing the rapidly changing audiovisual scene. The international flow of television programmes has been the subject of studies by UNESCO, including 'Television Traffic - A One-Way Street?' in 1974 (Nordenstreng and Varis 1974), its sequel 'International Flow of Television Programmes' in 1985 (Varis 1985), and 'Import/Export: International Flow of Television Fiction' in 1990 (Larsen 1990). A summary of research on international information flows appeared in 'International Flow of Information: a Global Report and Analysis' in 1985 (Mowlana 1985). In 1994 'TV Transnationalisation: Europe and Asia' was published,[14] presenting two studies of international flows of television programmes in terms of their supply and consumption in five European and four Asia Pacific countries, Australia, India, the Philippines, and the Republic of Korea.

Empirical research on communication flows has concentrated mainly on the supply of national television programming. The proportion of imported output on national channels was analysed as were the countries from which it came. The assumption of most studies was that they have cultural and economic effects in specific countries or among specific groups of viewers. Together with more general 'media imperialism' or 'dependency theories' (Boyd-Barrett 1977, 1982), this assumption was the domi-

nant 'theory' informing the collection of most data on television flows.

'Media Imperialism' theories suggested that a few countries, and particularly the United States, dominate the content of international media to such an extent that they impose their culture, values, and ideologies on the recipient nations. In the early studies of the international flow of television programmes attention did not focus on the consumption of imported programmes or on the effects of this consumption. It was assumed that if there was supply, there would be consumption with, generally, negative effects as a result of the adoption of foreign values and life-styles.

BOX 7.5 - TELEVISION SUPPLY IN THE ASIA PACIFIC REGION

India: More than 95 per cent of programmes were produced within the country with very little input from foreign sources. A high proportion of education programmes was broadcast (about 150 minutes every day). This accounted for 12 per cent of total supply time, but only 4 per cent of total consumption.

The Philippines: Two-thirds of the programmes broadcast were of national origin. During prime time, the proportion of foreign programmes increased to 47 per cent of total supply and most of these were programme series. The national origin programmes fell mostly within the variety/shows/humour/satire categories which accounted for 16 per cent of total broadcasting time. The largest categories of foreign programmes were series and cartoons, comprising 14 per cent and 13 per cent, respectively, of total broadcasting hours. The United States dominated the share of the foreign programming supply in almost every category. The United States alone supplied 92 per cent of total foreign programme broadcasting time to the Philippines. It was estimated that 94 per cent of movies shown on television in the Philippines were of American origin and that a substantial number of the cartoons, information, religious, and games programmes was supplied by the United States. Next to the United States was Japan, which accounted for 4 per cent of foreign programmes in the light entertainment category, followed by Taiwan (Pr. China) as the third biggest programme supplier with 13 per cent of total foreign programming supply - mainly movies, followed by series, variety, and information.

The early studies (Nordenstreng and Varis 1974, Varis 1985) concentrated on one source of programming, that is, the national channels, which at that time dominated television supply (EBU 1989; UNESCO 1989). Today it is necessary to distinguish between three sources of supply and to analyse the corresponding consumption patterns and effects. These sources are nationally-distributed, bilaterally-distributed, and multilaterally-distributed television and are identified as 'national television' (television supplied on strictly national channels), 'spill-over television' (television signals which are distributed terrestrially, in general from neighbouring countries) and 'satellite television'. More recent studies of television flows concentrate on both the supply and consumption of television programmes to understand the cultural implications. Using this approach the 1994 UNESCO study produced the results summarised in Boxes 7.5 and 7.6 (Sepstrup and Goonasekera 1994).

BOX 7.6 - CONSUMPTION OF TELEVISION IN THE ASIA PACIFIC REGION

India: Average daily viewing was about an hour and a half per day, but viewing time varied from 45 minutes on weekdays to four and a half hours on Sunday. Although the viewing habits among age, gender, and education groups did not vary much, the young and educated viewers living in metropolitan areas appeared to be heavier consumers than others and women were likely to watch more television than men. There were only a few foreign programmes and exposure to foreign programmes was comparatively higher among men than women, the young than the elderly, and metropolitan rather than rural people. Of the total number of foreign programmes viewed, three quarters of these were sports programmes.

Korea (Republic of): The average viewing time per day was one hour and twenty minutes. Very little time was spent watching foreign programmes and only 5 per cent of total consumption was devoted to foreign programmes. National programmes dominated total viewing time, especially drama and movies. On average, approximately 27 per cent of the viewing time was spent watching drama/movies of which 89 per cent was of national origin followed by television series accounting for 24.4 per cent of total consumption. National programmes accounted for 91 per cent of series consumption, while foreign programmes occupied only a small portion of the total consumption.

The Philippines : The average viewing time of the Filipinos ranged from 3 to 5 hours a day. Sport was the most popular programme category of the locally produced shows, while among foreign programmes, American drama/movies were preferred the most. Despite the small supply of European programmes, viewing by all groups except children was considerable. Japanese programmes, mainly in the light entertainment category, were mostly watched by children and young viewers whereas Taiwanese programmes were frequently watched by adults and the elderly.

Philippine television has been strongly influenced by United States programmes. In contrast, India seems to be little influenced by United States programmes despite the fact that there is concern in India about the 'cultural invasion' which might occur with the ICT revolution. Koreans consumed very few foreign programmes and nationally produced programmes seem to be more popular. The results of this study suggest that the consumption of programmes can differ significantly from supply patterns and this is so for both domestic and foreign programming. Other studies have examined the globalisation of media in Singapore, Taiwan (Pr. China), and Turkey, for example, where the active role of the audience as the key to the development of local cultural industries has been noted (Wang 1996a). This raises the question as to whether there is a 'saturation point' for foreign television programming supply. This would have major implications for the expected cultural impact of important audiovisual and information content.

Empirical research of this kind consumes enormous amounts of energy, time, and money, and there are substantial problems of comparison stemming from varying country definitions of age, level of education, and urbanisation. Broadcasters' procedures for the collection of national and international statistics are not directly comparable. There is a need for independent studies of television consumption that may be coordinated regionally or internationally, but carried out locally by those who have knowledge of the particular characteristics of national markets.

The idea of the 'Americanisation' of national television in other countries is challenged by recent empirical results. Although the share of United States television programmes on Asian prime-time TV screens is not negligible, there is little understanding about the possible effect of the national, social, and cultural context on the consumption of these programmes. As a result some argue that national and cultural identities are being eroded, while others contend that the central historical elements of national cultures will resist 'external' and/or 'alien' forces (Biltereyst 1996; Sinclair et al. 1996; Skovmand and Schroder 1992).

The potential cultural impact of foreign media programming means that 'cultural identity' will continue to be an important issue in debates on the impact of the international flows of information and audiovisual services (Servaes 1989, 1991; Hamelink 1989). Proficiency in foreign languages and familiarity with other cultures undoubtedly offer ways to bridge cultural barriers, and local communities are separated by 'cultural screens'.[15] These 'screens' may mean that content is appropriated or 'domesticated' in ways that are often not anticipated by the content producers (Silverstone and Haddon 1996).

Cultures form clusters of institutions that have an impact on, and influence, each other thus creating distinctive identities. Cultural identity refers to an inward sense of association or identification with a specific culture or subculture; and an outward tendency within a specific culture to share a sense of what it has in common with other cultures as well as what distinguishes it from other cultures. The social process of cultural formation is the result of an interweaving of the behaviour of groups of people who interrelate and interact with each other. The globalisation process can have 'particularisation' effects whereby minorities acquire new voices. The extent to which local content producers are forced out as a result of competition from foreign producers depends on whether policy-makers engage in active promotion (Wang 1996a). Culture is not static and policy measures are needed to create a favourable environment for local productions.

7.8 CONCLUSION - THE INTERACTION OF GLOBAL AND LOCAL MARKETS

The interaction of global and local markets with the production and consumption of ICTs and audiovisual or information service content is a very important consideration for countries seeking to assemble the components of the their national information infrastructures. The interaction of global and local markets influences consumption patterns in the domestic market. Only a few developing countries have been able to enter the international market for semiconductors and the new mobile satellite operators that are expected to launch services by the end of the decade are based mainly in the industrialised countries. Larger countries such as Brazil are planning to operate their own domestic systems but production of the hardware and electronic system components is likely to occur elsewhere. Even this alternative is beyond the reach of the least developed countries.

Software development and production of information services and audiovisual programming is taking place in some of the developing countries and capabilities are being strengthened in this way. However, in most cases these capabilities are not diffusing throughout the domestic economy. Some observers question whether software export capabilities will grow substantially beyond their current share of the international market. Most suppliers of on-line information services are located outside the developing world as are the main hosts. Developing countries are building broadcast and audiovisual content production capabilities and, despite the increasing penetration of content from external sources, local content is attractive to domestic audiences. A major factor is the availability of content at a cost that is affordable. However, audiences and service users cannot choose to consume information products that are simply absent from the market and it should not be assumed that demand does not exist on the basis of conventional marketing studies.

The international market sets limits and constraints on ICT and service production within local markets. However, production is not the only consideration in building national information infrastructures. Equally important is the active participation of those who consume products and services. The expansion of national and global networks combined with the declining costs of ICTs are opening possibilities for re-engineering, local

maintenance of software, and for the production of information services and audiovisual programming. However, developing countries, and especially the least developed countries, face difficult choices. These countries will need to ensure that the services and programmes that are consistent with their development goals are encouraged and supported by policy measures.

Capability building on the supply side is resource intensive in terms of skills and knowledge. The institutional framework for regulation of communication services, imports and exports of content and technologies, and investment in R&D, is also very important. The factors affecting the assembly of the components of the national information infrastructure are only part of the picture. The conditions under which ICTs and services are accessed are equally important. Policy-makers in developing countries will benefit from recognising that production and consumption are inseparable.

The politics, economics, and sociology of innovation is always skewed and uneven, fought out at the interface of design and domestication. These relationships are themselves complicated by the competing interests within producing and consuming groups as well as those between them ... this relationship must be seen as a dialectical one whose outcome cannot simply be read off from intention or precedent. Technical and institutional innovation, similarly, are processes that must be understood in their essential tensions (Silverstone and Haddon 1996: 71-72).

The implication of these tensions between supply and consumption for developing countries is that the outcomes will not replicate the experiences of the industrialised countries. There are many opportunities for the creative recombination of local capabilities with new ICT goods and services in ways that offer benefits for developing countries.

NOTES

1 Law 8248/91, Decree 792/93 and 1070/94 provided the legislative tools for policy implementation.

2 See Brazil Ministério da Ciência e Tecnologia (1995, 1996a,b); Brazil Secretaria de Política de Informática e Automação (1995).

3 The Korean chaebol, unlike the more familiar Japanese keiretsu, does not have a bank at its core. Consequently, the chaebols always have been heavily dependent upon the largesse of the Republic of Korean government in terms of credit subsidy provision.

4 Governance refers to the process of coordination and regulation of transactions, which is best conceptualised at the level of industrial sectors. The governance structure provides both an institutionalised constraint on firms and an opportunity for implementation of strategy. It matters for the performance of a sector because different modes of governance are conducive to different mixes of cooperation and competition Sako (1994). See also Streeck (1993); Streeck and Schmitter (1991); Campbell et al. (1991).

5 For the market regulation view, see Balassa (1981) and various World Bank publications on Korean industrialisation. For the state regulation view see Deyo (1987) Wade (1990).

6 Communication by the Delegation of the Commission of the European Communities to the US Department of State, Washington DC, June 1994 in International Telecommunication Union (1994).

7 Communication by Pape G. Toure, the delegate from Senegal, representing the Group of African and Arab Countries at the World Telecommunications Policy Forum, Geneva, 21-23 October 1996.

8 Systems software includes the operating system, compilers, debuggers, editors, etc. Applications packages encompass both cross-industry (for example, order processing and accounting systems) and industry-specific (for example, banking and manufacturing systems) software. Development tools include reusable libraries (for example, kernels, mathematical sub-routines, input-output routines, etc.), CASE product clusters (such as analysis and design aids, code generators, programming support environments and IPSEs and applications tools (for example, 4GLs, database management systems, report generators, query languages, spreadsheets, graphics, etc.). Software may be delivered in different modes (standard packages, customised packages) and media (floppy disc, tape, cartridge) and software programmes may be run on mainframe, mini-computers or micros. Programs can be written in a plethora of contrasting programming languages - different generations of which co-exist in time.

9 In contrast, the machine-centred perspective encouraged concentration on maintaining the integrity of individual system components.

10 According to Correa (1996), Tata Computing Services and Tata Unisys Ltd, dominant exporters of Indian software, based entry into this market on earlier service bureau activities with clients in developed countries.

11 Calculated by R. Heeks based on more than 250 interviews with representatives of the Indian software industry including those with all the top and most of the middle software exporters, see Heeks (1996a).

12 Several key references address the role of audiences, the media, political order, and culture in the context mainly of industrialised countries, see for example Cliché (1997); Morley (1989); Dervin and Clark (1989); Schlesinger (1992); Silverstone and Hirsch (1992). Nostbakken and Morrow (1997) take a global perspective.

13 This argument is made by Jeremy Tunstall (1977).

14 Based on reports by Sepstrup and Goonasekera (1994) and Goonasekera (1993).

15 This term was used in the Canada in the context of the debate about the implications of United States broadcast programming reception for Canadian culture, see Smythe (1981).

CHAPTER 8

NATIONAL INFORMATION INFRASTRUCTURE ACCESS – BUILDING SOCIAL AND MARKET VALUE CHAINS

Growing 'access gaps' and the impact of market liberalisation

8. National information infrastructure access – Building social and market value chains

8.1 Introduction – Promoting access to communication infrastructures

This chapter focuses on the strategies being adopted by developing countries to encourage the modernisation and extension of the communication infrastructure. The principal goal is to ensure that the infrastructure is available to a wide range of potential users so that they can access and distribute information from both local and global sources. The diffusion of basic telephone services in many developing countries lags substantially behind the industrialised countries (see Chapter 2). One aspect of current strategies is to improve the accessibility and affordability of the telephone service. Another is to extend the capacity of networks that can be used to access advanced services and applications including the Internet. If a relatively ubiquitous and affordable communication infrastructure is in place it can provide the basis for gaining advantage from the national information infrastructure in ways that are consistent with encouraging new social and market value chains in developing countries.

Under the public monopoly form of communication network supply, the rate of investment in most developing countries has been insufficient to meet these goals for a variety of reasons. In the past, these have included the political motivation to limit access to networks, the perception of access to telephony as a luxury, the use of telecommunication service revenues to contribute to general government funds, and inefficiencies stemming from the structure and organisation of the domestic industry.

There is a very strong association between the rate of investment in the communication infrastructure and economic growth potential. The potential value to firms and citizens of an affordable basic telephone service is now widely recognised, and the use of networks and ICT applications as tools to support both social and economic development is occurring on an increasingly wide scale. The Internet offers new possibilities for communication and for distributing information that can engage many people in creating information resources. Without an adequate communication infrastructure, the promise of the new ICT services and applications simply cannot be delivered.

In this context, there are many who argue for the liberalisation of communication infrastructure and service markets. Market liberalisation is expected to lead to new investment in the infrastructure and, in combination with privatisation and competition, to efficiencies of operation. Many developing countries have, in fact

already begun to liberalise their markets. At the same time, the industrialised countries have been moving away from traditional monopoly supply arrangements. One result of this has been that an oligopolistic form of competition is emerging on the world telecommunication scene. The former monopolists in the industrialised countries are facing competition in their home markets and they are seeking entry into other markets in both the industrialised and developing world. Market liberalisation and new entry into the telecommunication supply market is being accompanied by new regulatory measures. All this has major implications for developing countries.

The first implication is that a combination of competitive pressures, technological innovation, and regulatory policy is being accompanied by 'tariff rebalancing'. This is a process whereby the prices for long distance telecommunication services and business oriented services tend to be reduced and those for local access and usage tend to be increased (depending on the strength of competition in different segments of the market). Once competition becomes effective, price reductions for all services are expected.

Secondly, private, competing network operators are encouraged, with incentives or obligations, to extend their networks and services on an affordable basis to geographic and socio-demographic areas deemed to be marginally profitable or unprofitable. Universal service obligations for basic telephone access (and occasionally access to other services) are being introduced in the form of 'taxes' on telecommunication revenues to fund service extension to unserved areas. Conditions are often placed on licensees to achieve a specified coverage and quality of service in the territories they serve.

As competition is introduced in telecommunication, cable, and satellite markets, the 'convergence' of communication delivery modes is a third focal point for new developments. In some countries, telephone companies are offering entertainment and information services, and cable, satellite, and utility companies are beginning to move into the telephone service market. These developments have an impact on the dynamics of the domestic market and the rate at which the infrastructure is extended and modernised.

In the international market, competition is putting enormous strains on the arrangements used to share the revenues generated by international telecommunication services. Historically, these services were supplied by two national monopoly operators (and transit operators). These mainly state-owned organisations, the Public

Telegraph and Telecommunication administrations, organised an international accounting system within the framework of International Telecommunication Union regulations. International telephone service revenues were shared on the basis of agreements on the costs of supply and the flow of inbound and outbound traffic between countries. With the introduction of competition in some national markets, the traditional system is being called into question. This problem arises especially when the outbound flow of international traffic is substantially greater than the inbound flow. The existing accounting system results in a situation in which United States telecommunication operators' net payments to other countries in both industrialised and developing countries amount to an estimated US$ 5 billion annual transfer of revenues.

It is argued that the costs of international telecommunication service supply have been substantially reduced by the advent of digital networks, high capacity fibre optical links and the use of satellite technologies. Some analysts foresee 'near zero prices' as a result of the greater capacity available for international telecommunication. If the costs of supply to the operators are declining, it is argued, so too should the prices of services. To the extent that prices fail to decline substantially, the operators in countries which benefit in revenue terms from the current arrangements are said to be reaping unfair monopoly profits. The United States Federal Communications Commission and the International Telecommunication Union are negotiating new mechanisms for managing the joint supply of international services. There are also pressures to permit market access so that a single operating company can provide end-to-end services between countries. As a result of the new proposals, the revenues from international telecommunication traffic accruing to many developing countries are likely to be reduced substantially in the coming years.

For many developing countries, however, these revenues after settlement, have been a major source of funds. The changes being proposed are likely to have a major impact on the capacity of these countries to generate internally the investment needed to develop their domestic infrastructures. The capacity costs of raw switching and transmission for communication networks are a relatively small portion of the total costs for the supply of international telecommunication services. The costs of software requirements, producing content, and marketing in response to competition, are an increasing proportion of total service costs. Thus, as the costs of some elements of service provision decline, others are increasing. If new proposals for sharing revenues do not take the increasing cost elements of service supply into account, the telecommunication development aspirations of some developing countries will be jeopardised.

The potential of telecommunication development is substantial. It is likely that most countries will be able to generate revenues from service supply if they can attract inward investment for the extension and modernisation of their networks. This is essential if these countries are to gain leverage from electronic networks to address social and economic development problems. However, market liberalisation, privatisation, and the introduction of regulation are not straightforward processes. There are many difficult policy choices and problems that need to be managed and overcome if the hopes for telecommunication development are to be fulfilled.

This chapter reviews the arguments for investment in telecommunications as a means of enhancing economic development prospects (section 8.2). The meaning of 'universal service' in the context of developing countries that do not have high levels of telephony penetration is considered next (section 8.3). Section 8.4 provides a summary of the measures that are being introduced in the countries and territories with economies in transition in central and eastern Europe, and the Latin American and Asian regions to encourage investment in the communication infrastructure (details of selected country and regional experiences are included in the appendix to this chapter). Section 8.5 highlights some of the patterns that are emerging in different regions and the key issues for developing countries as they attempt to reduce the 'access gap'.

8.2 INCREASING THE RETURNS FROM INVESTMENT

The communication infrastructure is only one part of the national information infrastructure, but it plays an important role as part of a complex technological system. The notion of a technological system is emerging as a substantial advance in the economic analysis of technological change and the determinants of economic growth. Technological systems are made of a variety of subsystems and specific technologies that produce at a maximum level of efficiency only when all the components of the system are in place.

New technological systems emerge in instances where technologies that are more effective and productive than their substitutes provide scope for improvements in productivity as a result of their association with other technologies. New systems also depend on factors such as specific skills and intermediate inputs. When a new technological system emerges a cumulative process of endogenous growth and productivity increases is likely to take place along with the introduction of new complementary technologies and applications with their effects on overall productivity levels.

The complementarity requirements of technological innovations in the ICT sector have an impact on overall levels of productivity and the profitability of each technological innovation. The diffusion and adoption of new complementary technologies is a factor in the implementation of the new technological system and, consequently,

TABLE 8.1 - MULTIPLE BENEFITS OF NETWORK EXPANSION

| Population (% coverage) | Calling opportunities (% of total) | Change with growth | | |
		Population coverage (% increase)	Calling opportunities (% increase)	Calling opportunity multiple
10	1	–	–	–
20	4	100	400	4.0
30	9	50	25	2.5
40	16	33	78	2.3
50	25	25	56	2.3
60	36	20	44	2.2
70	49	17	36	2.2
80	64	14	31	2.1
90	81	12	27	2.1
100	100	11	23	2.1

Source: Melody (1993).

a factor in further improvements in productivity. Only when an appropriate mix of innovations is available can the full beneficial effects in terms of increasing returns and externalities be achieved.

Interrelatedness between new technologies and those embodied in existing capital stocks is a major issue in assessing the rate and effective penetration of new technologies in the economic system (Antonelli 1995). With low levels of interrelatedness, adoption of new technologies is faster and technology blending is easier. Piecemeal addition of new capital goods to existing capital stocks is possible. With high levels of interrelatedness, new technologies can diffuse only with substantial changes in the composition and vintages of the stock of fixed (and human) capital (Antonelli 1995; David 1987; Frankel 1955).

ICTs have high complementary requirements in terms of interrelatedness. They are likely to diffuse widely into the economic systems only when a full set of complementary and interrelated infrastructures has been installed. The levels of technological interrelatedness for advanced telecommunications are very high. Simply adding on digital and software-based telecommunication technologies to pre-existing electromechanical switching and copper or coaxial cables will not allow the full benefits to be gained. The adoption of electronic switching and transmission technologies and optical fibre cables often requires parts of the installed infrastructure to be retired.

The modernisation of switching and transmission equipment is a precondition for the growth of distributed ICT applications. An advanced telecommunication infrastructure is essential to provide universal, reliable, high quality, and low cost services upon which a full array of technological and organisational innovations can be based, for example, flexible manufacturing systems, just-

in-time management systems, distributed data networks, innovative advanced services, and intra- and inter-corporate information flows.

Telecommunication networks are characterised not only by the direct gains from technical improvements and cost reductions. Their value increases as the network is extended. Table 8.1 provides an illustration of this effect for telephony networks. In networks, calling opportunities are determined by the combination of those who can initiate calls, and those who can receive calls. A 10 per cent penetration rate permits only 1 per cent of the potential calling opportunities, because 90 per cent of the participants can call neither one another, nor the 10 per cent who are connected to the network. At 90 per cent penetration, 81 per cent of the potential calling opportunities are possible. As the network is extended, the benefits of expanded calling opportunities increase at a rate more than twice that of the network expansion rate.

Telecommunication networks provide empirical evidence for the notion of network externalities. The incremental introduction of a full array of complementary and interrelated ICT innovations in the production process, and in the firm or public sector organisation, depends on the penetration of advanced telecommunication and computers in the system. High levels of diffusion of advanced telecommunication infrastructure are likely to spread major externalities to downstream sectors - users of telecommunication services - and potential adopters of those technological and organisational innovations, based on this infrastructure and services.

The analysis of the international diffusion of ICTs confirms that investments in infrastructure are crucial. New technological systems, especially those embodied in capital intensive processes, are likely to diffuse faster within the economic system when high rates of economic growth make it possible to increase the flow of investments. Faster rates of adoption, in turn, contribute to increasing productivity rates. The empirical evidence confirms that this dynamic stresses the role of total investments, that is, both gross and net investment. Gross investment plays the essential role of modernising the communication infrastructure of the economy. It makes it possible to supply advanced services to a large number of users. Rates of growth of output and total factor productivity levels appear to be significantly related to the levels of penetration and the rates of growth of both basic telecommunication infrastructure and advanced telecommunication (measured by the share of digital lines of total available lines) as well as to the levels and intensities of output of investments in telecommunications. The econometric evidence confirms that a clear cumulative relationship exists between the rate of modernisation of the telecommunication infrastructure and productivity growth (Kaldor 1957; Salter 1966; Lamberton 1995; Pogorel 1996; Bohlin and Granstrand 1994).

The evidence also confirms that the levels of investment in telecommunications and, therefore, the diffusion of advanced infrastructure, have important impacts on the demand and supply sides of the telecommunication industry. The supply of advanced telecommunication services favours the emergence of a 'network of networks', that is, an array of specialised, complementary, and rival networks that substitute for the more homogeneous networks characterising monopolistic market structures. The demand for telecommunication services is influenced by the demand for data communication. Adoption of new ICTs has significant effects on the organisation of production processes, for example, radically modifying the sequence of production phases, the length of the processes, and the quantitative and temporal relationships between stocks of intermediate goods and final goods. Adopting new technologies enables the composition of economies of scale at batch, department, and plant level to be modified. The adoption of new ICTs makes it possible to modify the organisational relationships between phases of the production process, so that market relations can be strengthened. Hierarchical/bureaucratic types of coordination can be replaced to some extent by a mix of cooperative relationships (Antonelli 1988, 1992).

The economic advantages and the extent to which an economic system can benefit from the development of an advanced telecommunication network are likely to be much larger than the actual marginal economic gains accruing to each adopter. These network externalities apply to a variety of ICT innovations. The productivity arising from the adoption of a single component of the network - as well as of a variety of network-based products and services - is dramatically enhanced by the advantage of being able to network with other computers, firms, and organisations. Networking requires an advanced telecommunication network and network externalities provide the main argument in support of the hopes and expectations that investment in telecommunication networks will spread beneficial effects to users and, ultimately, to the whole economic system.

8.3 THE NECESSARY AND SUFFICIENT CONDITIONS FOR ACCESS

Sub-Saharan Africa has fewer telephones than the city of Tokyo. Sri Lanka has one telephone mainline per 100 people, while Australia has 50. The situation is similar for computers that are needed to access the Internet. There is a greater number of television sets and radios available to people in developing countries but there is an 'access gap' here as well. These are elements of the standard discussion about the 'access gap' and concerns about the 'information rich' and 'information poor'. However, this standard narrative obscures as well as illuminates. Access leading to greater use of ICTs is only part of the story. People must be able to obtain benefits from use and the new networks need to be regarded as providing a basis for accessing intermediate goods and services rather than final goods and services.

This means that it is important to ask what is gained through access to the telecommunication network. The telecommunication network has never provided a single 'product'. Distinctions range from primary use of the network for calling (for example, pay phones) versus receiving calls (for example, 'life-line' services) to voice telephony versus data communication. The differences are reflected in technical features, prices, and the symbolic aspects of the services. Most networks and services have been shaped by economically and politically powerful actors. Access by the less powerful is limited in two ways. First, they have fewer opportunities for physical connectivity to the network. Second, services offered on the networks do not always reflect their needs. If access is to assist in meeting social and economic development goals, both conditions must be satisfied.

In industrialised countries, lower connectivity takes the form of unconnected households within certain demographic groups and lower levels of connectivity to advanced services (Samarajiva and Shields 1990). In developing countries, unconnected households predominate with an overwhelming rural component. When marginal groups do have access to the network, the services are often inappropriate for their needs. Simple network expansion or the provision of more of the same services will not necessarily close the 'access gap', even if teledensity (main telephone lines per 100 people) reaches parity with the industrialised countries.

Several conditions need to be satisfied to ensure that technological design, price, and the symbolic features of networks and services meet users' needs in a way that closes the gap. Cultural factors shape user needs as much as economic and political conditions. There is therefore no universal prescription for closing the gap. Since different user groups have different needs with respect to telecommunication network access, a homogenous package of network-based services suited to all users is not feasible. 'Access' has a significant subjective component that is not fully captured by standard indicators reflecting the quality of service or the penetration rate of telephone lines. These indicators can only document whether the *necessary conditions* for access are being met.

The necessary conditions for access include the physical availability of network connections in various forms including wireless links and pay phones. Indicators such as main lines and cellular connections, settlements with at least one pay phone, pay phone distribution, and prices of services in relation to the cost of living, can be used to judge whether the necessary conditions of access exist. Quality indicators such as time-to-dialtone and failure and repair rates are also components of the necessary conditions of access. A pay phone that does not work most of the time does not provide access. A telephone line that mostly generates busy signals does not provide access.

These indicators are gross indicators because they are usually reported in aggregated form, averaging data for an entire country. It is always useful to disaggregate by geographic area as well as by demographic group. For example, a recent study of network connectivity by census tract in the American city of Camden, New Jersey illustrates the effects of geographical averaging. The city had a household penetration rate of 80 per cent, 14 per cent lower than the United States national average, but in parts of the city centre, the penetration approached 50 per cent. The value of demographic disaggregation is shown by the stark disparity between the teledensity of below 3 for Blacks and 25 for Whites in South Africa (Mueller and Schement 1996).

Ensuring that people's needs for access are met means that *sufficient conditions* for access must also be in place. These conditions are culture and group specific. They are represented by indicators that incorporate subjective responses to telecommunication services. Indicators of subjective satisfaction, complaint rates, 'churn' (the rate of subscribing to and terminating service subscriptions), provide proxy measures of these subjective responses although they require care in interpretation. For example, the complaint rates increased in Mexico after the Telmex privatisation at the same time that other measures of quality increased. Subscribers who were resigned to poor service under the old public monopoly, started to complain because privatisation raised both their expectations and some of their telephone charges. The availability of multiple services, service packages, and pricing options often appears to indicate that the sufficient conditions for access are being met. However, supplier-provided market differentiation is not necessarily responsive to all users' needs and especially not the needs of those who have historically been marginalised.

There is no 'one-size-fits-all' solution to reducing the 'access gap'. Public or private monopolies are not very effective in providing services that are responsive to all user needs. Regulatory mechanisms (including social contracts and other conditions) that involve users in the service provision process may alleviate some of the negative effects of monopoly. Because of network externalities, increasing returns, and path dependencies in the telecommunication industry, perfectly competitive markets are unlikely to emerge and the market cannot easily perform its discovery functions. However, competition is beneficial in providing incentives for innovation and improved performance. It is important that flexible regulatory mechanisms are established to enable and sustain competition which is responsive to all user needs.

Regulatory agencies are needed to emphasise particular measures to reduce the access gap at different stages of network development. In the early stages of network development, for example, when teledensity is less than 10, an emphasis on creating conditions for effective competition and network expansion is often needed. Potential users need to be brought into network planning and design processes. Prices may be given a lower priority in that early subscribers will have the economic and political wherewithal to keep the operators' pricing strategies in check, especially if there is competitive entry. As network penetration increases, subscriber education needs greater emphasis together with the systematic integration of indicators of subscriber satisfaction and the introduction of incentives to operators to consult with, and be responsive to, users.

Most of the information available from case studies of telecommunication liberalisation and investment strategies in developing countries focuses on the necessary conditions that are being addressed in an effort to reduce the 'access gaps'. New indicators are needed to assess whether the sufficient conditions for access are being met.

8.4 COMMUNICATION MARKET LIBERALISATION, REGULATION, AND INVESTMENT

Profiles of market reforms in the economies in transition, the Latin American region, and Asia (see also more detailed accounts in section 8.7 - Appendix) show that the priority being given to introducing reforms is somewhat different in the three regions. Although there are common elements in the movement toward greater reliance on market instruments to encourage developments in the communication infrastructure and services, it is being articulated differently. There are exceptions and differences in the strategies being adopted by each of the countries within these regions. Nevertheless, the Asian countries seem to have achieved an explicit linkage between reliance on electronic commerce, engaging people in creating information resources, and infrastructure investment. Both the economies in transition and the countries in the Latin American region are concerned with telecommunication infrastructure investment and this is not as closely linked with efforts to build capabilities in service content areas.

8.4.1 REFORM IN THE ECONOMIES IN TRANSITION

There has been explosive growth in demand for telecommunication services in most of the economies in transition since the beginning of the decade. Electromechanical switching capacity has restricted expansion and upgrading of public telecommunication networks. By 1994 the waiting list for a telephone line totalled 23 million people and one quarter of the expressed demand was unsatisfied. The models of privatisation and competitive entry differ considerably between these countries. Monopoly supply has been retained in some countries, while in others, full competitive entry in local service markets is being permitted. Regulations are putting conditions on inward investors to increase the penetration rate for telephone services and more competitive tendering procedures are being introduced. Wireless 'local' loops are providing a technological alternative to the fixed infrastructure. Tariff rebalancing has been introduced in some countries with the result that better prices have been achieved during privatisations. Many businesses continue to have access only to a single telephone line, limiting the advanced applications they can adopt to improve decision-making and to gain efficiencies in supply chains. After an initial flurry of privatisation and market liberalisation, problems remain of how to respond to escalating demand and to ensure that competition is effective.

8.4.2 ACCESSING THE INFRASTRUCTURE IN LATIN AMERICA

The emphasis in many Latin American countries in the telecommunication sector is on the expansion of telephony connections from the relatively low base that exists as compared to the average rates of penetration in the OECD area. Privatisation, legislation to accompany competitive entry, the build up of regulatory capabilities, and consideration of how to extend basic telephone services to a greater share of the populations of these countries are often priorities. Investment in advanced facilities, including optical fibre grids, to increase the capacity of backbone networks is occurring but the telecommunication sector continues to be relatively technology driven as the discussion of changes does not focus explicitly on the relationship between the investments in infrastructure and the uses and applications of services. ICT applications including audiovisual programming and interactive service applications tend to be the concern of a separate information technology community. Organisational convergence in policy-making to parallel the technical convergence between information technology and telecommunication technologies is not readily apparent in most of the countries in the Latin American region.

Brazil economic and legal reforms

Brazilian telecommunication services are provided by Telebras, a state-controlled holding company, that had achieved an average telephone density in 1996 of 10.2 lines per 100 population. It has been slow to respond to demand for increased service quality and data speeds. Market liberalisation for telecommunications is part of a structural adjustment plan for the economy as a whole. Reforms have included a change in 1995 to the legal framework for the telecommunication sector which is being implemented on a step by step basis. Since 1996 entry of the private sector into cellular telephony, satellite and data transmission, and value-added services has been opened but there are restrictions on foreign ownership. A General Law of Telecommunications, including a regulatory office, funding instruments for universal service, and preparation of future privatisation measures is under discussion. A 'Program for Recovery and Expansion of the Telecommunications and Postal System' is underway with optimistic plans to generate investment of US$ 75 billion between 1995 and 2003. Tariff rebalancing has increased the basic residential subscription price and the prices of local and domestic long distance calls.

Outstanding issues include measures to foster domestic production and indigenous technological development. External factors, including the reduction of import tariffs and the termination of preferential procurement policies, are expected to dampen demand for locally produced equipment. The establishment of a reliable regulatory body, mechanisms for price control, financing universal services, and selling Telebras based on the best price or strategic benefits are controversial issues. In the short run, the increase in public investment in preparation for privatisation has brought benefits but in the medium term the situation is unclear. A reform schedule that provides guidance to all the players concerned, as well as the customers, continues to be necessary.

Investing in telecommunication in Colombia

Since the establishment of a Telecommunications Development Plan in 1995, the goals have been to achieve universal coverage for telecommunication services through a Social Telephone Service Programme, infrastructure modernisation, and the diversification of available services. As a result of a privatisation process and regulatory measures introduced by the Ministry of Communications, investment in the sector for the period 1995 to 1998 is estimated at US$ 4 billion representing a net growth of 65 per cent over the period 1990-1994. The average telephone density of 14 main lines per 100 inhabitants at the end of 1995 is expected to reach 25 per 100 inhabitants by 2003 and service penetration has grown by 8.5

per cent annually over the past 10 years. Toward the end of 1996, cellular telephony services had 410,256 subscribers, and accumulated revenues of nearly US$ 500 million for six private companies covering three regional cellular telephony territories.

Jamaica's telecommunication regime

The Jamaican Government's approach to market liberalisation has been to introduce regulation across the utility sectors. Responsibility is to be shared between the new regulatory office and the responsible minister. The telephone mainline penetration rate per 100 people in 1995 was 11.6. Regulatory policies have been outlined with respect to licences, tariff setting, interconnection, and network access, and promotion of competition in value added services. However, questions have been raised as to whether the regulatory office will have advisory or mandatory powers. The introduction of competition faces a number of hurdles owing to the position granted to Telecommunications of Jamaica Ltd, a majority-owned subsidiary of Cable & Wireless. In return for providing an efficient and modern network, the company was granted a 25-year exclusive franchise for fixed telephone service, renewable for a further 25 years. Although competition is permitted in the supply of cellular telephone services, Telecommunications of Jamaica has a *de facto* monopoly and has been operating an international call-back service competing with its own wireline services. The government intends to open up competition in services such as electronic mail, teletext, videotex, and circuit switched data, but the legal power to implement this policy awaits industry-specific legislation. Obligations for the monopoly provider of wireline services to interconnect with new market entrants are still to be put in place.

The Mexican telecommunication sector

The telecommunication sector in Mexico has been exposed to many changes including privatisation and liberalisation and by 1995 the telephone main line penetration rate per 100 inhabitants had reached 9.6. The modernisation of the infrastructure began with the installation of digital networks and the launch of the first Mexican satellites in 1980s. The government has initiated a series of policy measures that peaked with the privatisation of Telefonos de Mexico (TELMEX) in 1990. Guidelines were established for the introduction of competition into local, long distance, and international service markets by 1997 as well as satellite, cellular, and value added service markets. An independent regulatory agency to implement regulation was established although licensing remains the responsibility of the Secretary of Communications and Transportation. New legislation permitted 100 per cent foreign ownership of telecommunication operations subject to certain conditions. One of the important goals has been to provide greater legal certainty to investors.

New telecommunication groups are being attracted by the growth of the long distance market with their expected revenues of US$ 20 billion annually by 2000. The regulatory developments have opened the way for the provision of new services and equipment and made the sector more attractive to foreign investors. Nevertheless, there is a high level of uncertainty as the regulatory provisions have yet to be tested.

8.4.3 THE INFORMATION SUPERHIGHWAYS IN INDIA, CHINA, AND THE ASEAN REGION

In contrast to the recent experience of the Latin American region, there appears to be a much stronger focus on telecommunication, information technologies, broadcasting, and multimedia as components of the global information infrastructure in this region. For example, the countries comprising the Association for South East Asian Nations (ASEAN) embraced integration into the Global Information Infrastructure as early as 1995 under the auspices of the Asian Pacific Economic Cooperation (APEC) forum and the Seoul Declaration on the Asia-Pacific Information Infrastructure. The telecommunication and information industry is believed to have a critical role in strengthening market linkages and enhancing trade and investment liberalisation. The Seoul Declar-

TABLE 8.2 - ASEAN REGION POPULATION, LITERACY, AND ICT PENETRATION, 1994

	Total population	Urban population	Literacy rate	Telephones/ 100 pop.	PCs/ 100 pop.	TVs/ 100 pop.
Country	(million)	%	%			
Singapore	3.1	100	91.6	47.3	38.0	15.3
Malaysia	19.2	45	78.5	14.7	23.0	3.3
Thailand	59.4	25	93.0	4.7	19.0	1.2
Philippines	65.2	45	93.5	1.7	12.0	0.6
Indonesia	190.3	31	81.5	1.3	9.0	0.3
Viet Nam	73.0	20	88.0	–	–	–

Note: Data unavailable for Brunei and Myanmar.
Source: Various, as quoted in *Asiaweek*, 8 June 1994; *ITU STARS Database* (1996).

ation aims to facilitate the expansion of an interconnected and interoperable information infrastructure in the region and to promote the exchange and development of human resources within a favourable policy and regulatory framework (APEC 1996). [1]

The ASEAN nations are characterised by relatively high literacy rates but they vary signficantly in terms of the distribution of the urban and rural populations and the density of telephone, computers and television equipment that had been achieved by the mid-1990s (see Table 8.2).

A central issue facing India, China, and the ASEAN member states is securing private sector participation in building the national and regional information infrastructures. Attention is focusing on foreign ownership and management options as well as collaborative arrangements to gain access to networking technologies, fibre optic cable links, and satellite capacity. The expansion of national infrastructures is occurring under varying regulatory environments and in response to the different infrastructure requirements of each of the countries in the wider Asia Pacific region. Observers have emphasised the need for regional cooperation (see Box 8.1).

Telecommunication Policy in India

The policy framework in India is fragmented and there are demands for a more coherent approach to building a supportive national information infrastructure. A national telecommunication policy was announced in 1994 allowing private sector participation in basic services but maintaining the public monopoly on long distance services. The continuing high cost of long distance calls is regarded as a major inhibitor to the international competitiveness of the software industry in India. Since 1997 foreign direct investment is permitted in equity shares up to 49 per cent in the telecommunication industry without government approval. In 1994 the telephone density in India was about 0.8 telephones per 100 inhabitants, lower than China, Pakistan, and Malaysia. To alleviate the 'access gap', the government's strategy is to achieve market liberalisation, global integration, and market-driven growth. The passage of the Telecommunication Regulatory Authority Bill in March 1997 was intended to improve the rural telecommunication network but much of the investment activity continues to be concentrated in urban areas. Tariff rebalancing for the wireline network is being introduced and cellular telephones are available to those who can afford them. The Government has agreed to phase out its monopoly on service supply and to introduce competition by 2004. For rural areas, access depends mainly on public telephones. The business community is seeking investment to extend access to the Internet and to support data networking. There has been some recognition that investment in infrastructure needs to be linked closely with plans for literacy, education, and commerce in other sectors of the economy.

Box 8.1 - Modernising the Asia Pacific regional infrastructure

In 1993, a review of telecommunication development in the Asia Pacific region looked forward to the immense opportunities for new technological developments. Three-quarters of all households did not have access to a telephone and the estimated investment to maintain levels of existing growth was at least US$ 100 billion from 1993 to the end of the century. The cost of achieving a teledensity of 10 lines per 100 inhabitants for the lower income countries, including India and China, was estimated at US$ 400 billion. To achieve significant investment levels countries would need to corporatise their public telecommunication operators, obtain new sources of funding via privatisation, build-operate-transfer schemes, licensing of new market entrants or by freeing the national operator to raise funds on the market. Under these conditions and given threshold levels for investment, the ITU expressed optimism for some countries. It was observed that 'the inequalities within the region, expressed in terms of access to telecommunication services, are likely to persist for the foreseeable future. Some countries have succeeded in catching-up, but elsewhere the gap between the poorest and the richest is widening' (ITU 1993: 23).

Is the superhighway on its way in China?

The global fervour concerning the information super-highway has put the modernisation of China's ICT sector at the top of the political and economic agenda. Many of China's top leaders regard it to be the principal driving force toward economic growth and a particular role is being played by users who 'co-invest' in the telecommunication network. The telecommunication sector has been enjoying a very high annual growth rate since 1989 but demand still cannot be met. The investment strategy includes a fibre optic network linking the eastern provinces with high population densities, and links to other countries in the Asia Pacific region. Cellular networks have been established in urban centres and provincial towns. Although the market continues to be dominated by the Ministry of Post and Telecommunications (MPT) a separation of regulatory functions is in process and most value added services are open to competition. Reforms are being discussed including how and when to open basic telecommunication markets to competition. Whether direct foreign investment should be permitted in telecommunication operators, and the degree of foreign involvement in management, are being debated. A decentralised strategy within the country means that a large number of regional and local models of telecommunication supply is emerging. There are also conflicts between ministries responsible for telecommunication and those with an interest in stimulating production and use of information technologies.

One of the results of the investment strategy in recent years has been the bifurcated nature of telecommunication development between rural and urban areas, coastal and interior areas, and advanced versus rudimentary technological infrastructure availability. These emergent disparities in access to the infrastructure between 1988 and 1994 are shown in Table 8.3.

TABLE 8.3 – EMERGENT ACCESS DUALISMS IN CHINA, 1988-1994

	1988 (million)	1991 (million)	1994 (million)	1988-1994 % increase
Total telephones in China	9.4	15.0	28.9	207
Total urban telephones	7.5	12.2	23.1	210
Total rural telephones	2.0	2.8	5.8	193
Urban teledensity (per 100 people)	2.6	3.97	6.74	
Rural teledensity (per 100 people)	0.24	0.33	0.67	
Coastal region teledensity (per 100 people)	1.21	1.94	3.88	
Central region teledensity (per 100 people)	0.67	0.92	1.66	
Western region teledensity (per 100 people)	0.19	0.72	1.02	
National total teledensity (per 100 people)	0.85	1.29	3.20	
Cellular Subscribers:				
Coastal region teledensity (per 100 people)			0.54	
Central region teledensity (per 100 people)			0.17	
Western region teledensity (per 100 people)			0.09	
National total teledensity (per 100 people)			0.13	

Source: Compiled from State Statistical Bureau (1989, 1992, 1995); Wang (1996b).

Improving the infrastructure and overcoming the low penetration rate of telephones and computers, strengthening local area networks, and producing new information services are likely to take some time despite the rapid rate of investment. China will continue to face major challenges and there will be a need for effective policy and regulation in order to attract the necessary external investors. A telecommunication law covering most of the ICT sector has been in the drafting stage and subject to internal discussion for some years.

Investing in the Asia Pacific regional infrastructure

Since the movement for privatisation and liberalisation became popular in the OECD countries in the 1980s,

investment in the telecommunication sector has received priority in the emerging economies of the Asia Pacific region. Telecommunication was seen as a catalyst for regional development with special emphasis on building regional community networks as a means of ensuring economic growth and the intellectual infrastructure of the region. Countries of the Pacific Rim are investing in a basic telecommunication framework that links such investment to strategies of development in education and training, and boosting their business sectors to participate in global markets. This has led to a healthy partnership between the government and the private sector in promoting innovations and transfer of technology which will help them take advantage of the global information infrastructure.

Some 50 per cent of the world's total output comes from the Asia Pacific region along with 46 per cent of world trade and 40 per cent of world population. It is now recognised that when the economy of a country is expanding, its telecommunication sector grows faster. For example, in China the economy has been growing at 11 to 12 per cent each year, but the telecommunication sector has registered a growth rate of more than 25 per cent annually. Even if the economy is stagnant, as in the case of Viet Nam or Cambodia, the telecommunication sector keeps growing. With 250 million people inhabiting the region there is a booming market for telecommunication equipment and services. However, there is widespread disparity between the availability and affordability of telephones in the lower income and higher income countries of the region. The World Bank estimates that the Asian countries will need US$ 90 to US$ 120 billion to provide basic telephone services to the more remote regions as well as some urban centres.

Although income distributions are highly skewed throughout the region, there has been a substantial rise in a more affluent urban middle class, resulting in greater demand for value added products and services. Many of the potential products and services are being created largely in the developed countries. Policy-makers are becoming more pragmatic in their approach towards investment in the telecommunication sector, leading to greater liberalisation of investment patterns. While investment in infrastructure is a determinant of economic growth, the location and expansion of this infrastructure are equally important. The creation, use, and transfer of knowledge can bring dynamic externalities providing the basis for both incremental and radical innovations. There have been major developments in all the key ICT infrastructure markets.

▌ Fibre optic technology: The rapid deployment of fibre for terrestrial and submarine connectivity has become critical to investment policies. Investors are aiming to enhance telephone line density in their countries, not only for voice connectivity but for programmes of tele-education and telemedicine.

▌ Mobile communication: While submarine systems have many advantages, they only serve coastal regions and need to be augmented by other systems to transmit signals to interior regions and island formations. Mobile communication is attracting the attention of investors around the globe with high annual growth rates in the Asia Pacific region (see Table 8.4).

TABLE 8.4 – CELLULAR TELEPHONY IN THE ASIA PACIFIC REGION, 1994, 1995 (MILLION)

Country	Subscribers December 1994	Subscribers December 1995	Annual growth %
Australia	1,570	3,170	102
Brunei	15	30	107
China	1,570	3,390	116
Fiji	1	2	100
Hong Kong	439	697	59
India	0	29	n.a.
Indonesia	101	188	86
Japan	3,450	8,052	133
Malaysia	568	836	47
Macao	26	40	54
New Zealand	222	356	60
Pakistan	36	53	46
Philippines	193	479	148
Singapore	219	290	33
Korea (Rep. of)	960	1,641	71
Sri Lanka	33	47	48
Taiwan (Pr. China)	584	789	35
Thailand	810	1,274	57
Viet Nam	10	30	194
Others*	26	48	83
Total	10,833	21,441	98

Note: * Bangladesh, Cambodia, Guam, Kyrgyzstan, Laos, Myanmar, Samoa
Source: Global Mobile (1996).

▌ Geostationary satellites (GEOS): The rush for satellite orbital slots over the Pacific Ocean indicates the fast-growing demand for telecommunication and television services. Ever since Indonesia launched its first Palapa series of domestic satellites in 1976, the benefits to users in the region have been clear, leading to large scale investments in this technology over the last two decades. As satellite technology advances into the realm of the higher KU band of the radio spectrum and digital

switches, the Southeast Asian countries are mustering their resources to 'leapfrog' to newer satellite models popularised in the United States.

▌ Very Small Aperture Terminals (VSATs) for satellites: The advantage of VSATs is that they are low cost and portable and can be located on roof tops even in rural areas. These are one-way receiving dishes that are now able to receive Direct-to-Home satellite signals from the new satellites made for this use.

▌ Low Earth Orbiting Satellites (LEOS): The potential for portable LEO systems is considerable because they permit roaming across political and geographic boundaries. However, LEOS require large quantities of radio spectrum.

▌ Internet Access: Most Asian countries have started surfing the Internet with technology provided by industrialised countries. Asian countries want to use the empowering service of the Internet to get their citizens 'onto' the global information infrastructure. Even the small islands of the South Pacific are bidding to obtain their own Internet services.

All forms of global connectivity, from telephone messaging to the Internet, are being embraced by the developing countries in the Asia Pacific region and competition is becoming imperative (Jussawalla 1995a). Few countries have attempted to acquire the benefits of the most advanced ICTs in the past two years as enthusiastically as the economies in Asia (Jussawalla 1995b). The new media are changing the way Asian societies think, work and interact with each other. With the dawn of the 'Dragon Century', Asia is being forged by economic integration, telecommunication technology, and the mobility of information. 'This is not the 'westernisation' of Asia, but the 'Asianisation' of Asia: an exploding market of 3 billion people, half of whom are under the age of 25'. [2]

8.5 EMERGENT ACCESS 'DUALISMS'

Many of those who monitor and forecast trends in the costs and prices of international and domestic telecommunication services are forecasting massive reductions. They argue that a 'bandwidth glut' created by overcapacity in international communication will spill-over into domestic long distance markets. Combined with market liberalisation and competitive entry, the prices for the use of switched and leased network capacity will fall dramatically. 'Near zero' prices for services could be in place by 2005 (Forge 1995). Major price decreases that would produce the forecast 'near zero' prices for communication services (as distinct from raw transmission capacity) on a global basis are unrealistic for many reasons, not least because of the increasing costs of the software that is needed to provide services. Nevertheless, as competitive entry occurs in national markets and oligopolistic competition in the international market takes hold, it is likely that international telecommunication service prices will decline substantially from their current levels.

The prices for telecommunication services are determined by the costs of the two basic components of networks, the core network and the access network. The access network represents a large investment by network operators. A mobile operator's investment is generally significantly lower than that of a fixed network operator. Future trends in prices are affected by reductions in the costs of network investment as new technologies substitute for older less efficient methods of supply. They are also affected by cost savings due to changes in network configuration. The introduction of competition is expected to force retail (end-user) and interconnect (charges to competing operators accessing the incumbent's network) prices down. However, the actual impact is closely linked with whether institutional reforms are introduced alongside privatisation and competitive entry (Melody 1997a).

The impact of privatisation measures and competitive entry in domestic markets is unpredictable. Privatisation generally has been introduced to alleviate demonstrable (and sometimes growing) cost inefficiency. It has been a counter to the unresponsiveness of national public monopolies to business and/or residential consumer demand, the appearance of alternative technologies, and investment requirements for modernisation and extension of networks that far exceed public sector resources. In some cases the proceeds for competitive bidding for ownership of a share of the national monopoly operator have been used to contribute to general government revenues rather than to boost investment in the telecommunication sector. In others, legal private or *de facto* monopolies have been created generating new problems (Melody 1997b).

In practice, the impact of privatisation is unpredictable because public monopoly, private monopoly, and imperfectly competitive markets each have a different set of potential benefits and costs. For instance:

Market failures can lead to divergence between profit and welfare objectives in private firms. Government failure leads to divergence between political/bureaucratic and welfare objectives in state-owned enterprises. Monitoring failure leads to divergence between the objectives of enterprise managers and their principals, whether the principals are private owners or political superiors. The effects of ownership changes on welfare will depend upon the relative magnitudes of these imperfections. As a first approximation, privatization can be viewed as a means of reducing the impact of government failure, albeit at the risk of increasing market failures, and of changing monitoring arrangements (Vickers and Yarrow 1991: 130).

As evidence of the impact of privatisation in different countries around the world accumulates, the World Bank has concluded that only about 15 countries have carried out 'exemplary privatisations' of public utility operations (Melody 1997c). If private monopolists are granted lengthy periods during which competition is not permitted or they retain a substantial share of the market sufficient to enable them to behave as quasi-monopolists, then the imperfections of markets and monitoring through regulation are likely to bring results that do not meet expectations for the development of the telecommunication sector. Unless privatisations in the telecommunication sector are carried out with other major institutional reforms, they rarely ameliorate the 'access gap'.

In developing countries there continue to be substantial barriers to reform, increasing investment and reductions in prices. In addition, current price structures around the world are not highly favourable to encouraging use of advanced network access to take advantage of the Internet. In the industrialised world there are advocates of major changes in pricing structures that would reduce the costs of access and use. For instance, a report by the OECD notes that, 'if the Internet, or similar services, are to play a central role in information infrastructure, the evidence indicates that new pricing structures for the use of communication networks are necessary' (Paltridge 1996: 26).

In developing countries, the problem of affordable access is even greater. For example, analysis of Internet access in Africa shows that dial-up access is too expensive and only affordable by the elite in the capital cities, due to subscription charges and high rates for calls to the service providers (mainly United States-based, followed by France) (Jensen 1996). Low cost dial-up store and forward e-mail services are becoming relatively widespread.

The flexibility available to most developing countries to introduce more attractive prices as they extend their networks in domestic markets is limited by the pressures of declining revenues from international telecommunication service supply. Determining whether there are cost differentials in telecommunication infrastructure supply between developing and industrialised countries is difficult and controversial. In 1988 the International Telecommunication Union commissioned a study in this area. The investigators reported that the required data were extremely difficult to obtain. They were scattered throughout different departments and had to be manually collected from Accounts, Finance, Traffic Revenues, Engineering, and Project Planning & Management as well as from international and domestic operators. The conclusion of this study was that the data were inadequate to allow any conclusive statements about the disparity in costs between developing and industrialised countries (ITU 1988).

The international accounting system for sharing international revenues is based on agreements reached on a bilateral basis among operators and this establishes the costs incurred by each country. Surplus revenues after taking account of incoming and outgoing traffic flows using the

TABLE 8.5 – TELEPHONE CALLBACK IMPACT

	Brazil		Kenya		Philippines	
	With call back %	Without call back %	With call back %	Without call back %	With call back %	Without call back %
Revenue to incumbent operator	22	78	23	77	29	71
Payment to AT&T for ending the call in the US	0	22	0	23	0	29
USA global link	5	0	14	0	18	0
Local representative of USA global link	3	0	4	0	5	0
Price difference kept by customer	70	0	59	0	48	0
	100	100	100	100	100	100

Note: Brazil US$ 2.59 vs. US$ 0.79 per minute; Kenya US$ 3.00 vs. US$ 1.24; Philippines US$ 2.10 vs. US$ 1.10
Source: USA Global Link data cited in *CommunicationsWeek International* (1996), 9 April.

public switched telecommunication network are shared between countries (Stanley 1991, 1997). The costs for most developing countries have been set at a level that the globally operating companies argue is 'above cost'. The impact of changes in accounting 'rates' (the costs agreed as a result of bilateral negotiations) on market developments in very poor countries with small potential telecommunication markets is likely to be very different from that in mature industrialised or emerging service-based economies. For example, both Botswana and Malaysia have been committed to restructuring their telecommunication markets, but the latter has much greater capabilities to build up the services that will generate network traffic revenues (Souter 1997).

The argument that revenue generated by international telecommunication services should not be used to reduce the costs of local telephone access or use, or to contribute to general government revenues, has consequences for developing countries different from those for industrialised countries. In many developing countries few can afford access to telecommunication services at any economically justified price. In the industrialised countries tariff rebalancing has been introduced before privatisation or to encourage competition, but access to telephone service has been almost universal and widely affordable.

The limited extent of local networks in many developing countries means that 'their international traffic per telephone line is above the world average and they are critically dependent on international traffic revenues' (ITU 1995b: 29). Without alternative means of reducing the cost of access to the local network for low income customers, a reduction in international revenue is likely to lead, in the short term, to higher prices for domestic services and reduced accessibility. Reduced international service prices stimulate increased traffic and revenue in the industrialised countries and newly industrialising countries,

especially if they have a significant service sector. However, the lowest income countries understandably lack confidence that reforms in their countries will have the same impact.

The confidence of developing countries in their capacity to generate investment to reduce the 'access gap' is also undermined by the development of bypass services such as callback where a company, usually based in the United States, leases capacity allowing callers to bypass the domestic switched network infrastructure. Table 8.5 shows the estimated impact of callback. USA Global Link, one of the callback operators, argues that callback service provides economic benefits to a developing country even if its public switched network is bypassed. These data show that while there are savings for some customers, there are reductions in revenues for the national public telecommunication operator. Analysis of the patterns of call origination would be needed to assess the overall impact on the economies of developing countries, but the short term impact on the national operator that no longer has access to these revenues is substantial. The introduction of callback and other services as well as satellite based mobile services that may bypass national switched networks represents a threat to many developing countries and especially the poorest ones.

Some developing countries have argued that the internationally operating carriers have a responsibility to promote, or at least not to inhibit, telecommunication development. However, this argument is difficult to sustain when national operators are inefficient when measured by international benchmark standards. Change is desperately needed if telecommunication networks are to support national information infrastructures. Technical and economic assistance to facilitate alternative financing arrangements are needed for network development. The United States Federal Communications

Commission has recognised the need for an adjustment period.

We ... realize that countries will need time to make the adjustments necessary to introduce competitive reforms. We also recognize additional time may be needed to enable US carriers to negotiate for lower settlement charges with their foreign correspondents without forcing undue disruption of both parties' operations. For example, carriers in many developing countries have significantly distorted rate schedules involving cross-subsidies from users of international services to those using domestic services. These carriers also may have substandard telecommunications infrastructure, including low levels of network build out and low levels of network reliability. An immediate shift to cost-based settlement rates thus could create adjustment problems for carriers in these countries while they are trying to rebalance rates and upgrade their network (Federal Communications Commission 1996: 61).[3]

Any period of adjustment leaves developing countries with difficult decisions about the time scale of adjustment, whether negotiations should be conducted bilaterally or through multilateral agencies like the International Telecommunication Union, and the criteria that should be used in negotiations on the costs of service supply.

The World Bank estimates the need for about US$ 40 billion per year to the end of the century for telecommunication investment in developing countries and US$ 10 billion to US$ 15 billion for the economies in transition. This represents twice the annual investment over the period 1990 to 1994. The private sector is expected to generate about 50 per cent of this total, with internal cash generation accounting for about 40 per cent. This leaves about 10 per cent to be funded from official or other lending sources (Bond 1995).

8.6 Conclusion - Market liberalisation and institutional reform

Telecommunication development is as important for developing countries as it is for the industrialised economies. It is critical to securing inward investment, exploiting the export potential of local businesses, and building innovative social and economic communities. The products, services, and models of market organisation in the industrialised countries are often not responsive to developing country needs. A low income, low density, population in central Africa, or a small island state in the South Pacific, will have different problems, priorities and market potential than the major telecommunication markets in the industrialised and newly industrialising countries. Much greater attention needs to be given to these differences in the local context (Souter 1997).

There is a major requirement for institutional reform in developing countries to address information and communication service market development. Communication network operators will need to provide high-quality connectivity for international businesses and low-cost basic voice telephone services for communities where most citizens will not be able to afford a telephone connection. Innovative models of service provision based on pay phones or wireless technologies will be needed. The growth of various forms of arbitrage between countries will mean that international telecommunication revenues will not be sufficient to finance major network development and innovative forms of financing will be called for.

Structural changes through privatisation and/or market liberalisation will need to be accompanied by managerial and organisational reforms. Developing countries often lack the numbers of economists and lawyers required to participate effectively in the international negotiations that affect the outcomes in their national markets. There is a need for skills and training in regulatory reform as well as in the necessary technological knowledge.

'Access' is neither simple to define, nor easy to achieve. National ICT strategies are needed to tackle the new communication 'dualisms' emerging on a global scale and within countries. Key priorities include measures to provide answers to such questions as the following.

▪ What models of infrastructure and service provision will address the 'access gap' in terms of physical access and affordability? What intermediate models of 'universal access' can be introduced? What innovative pricing schemes can be introduced to increase affordability? What priority should be given to access for businesses, citizens, schools, governments, and public service providers?

▪ What are the necessary conditions for access? What network facilities need to be in place and what are the technical design alternatives that will respond to user profiles in developing countries?

▪ What are the sufficient conditions for access? What cultural and social features of using communication services need to be taken into account? What community environments are conducive to using telephones or Internet connections for social or business purposes? What environments attract women rather than men?

▪ What are the necessary institutional reforms? Political and administrative reforms to implement effective regulation of imperfect markets are needed. Investors will want to minimise regulation but they will also seek market stability in order to protect their investments. What incentives and regulations will secure investment that leads to network expansion and modernisation consistent with development plans?

Companies operating as private 'monopolists' are unlikely to move to address the new communication 'dualisms' in the absence of institutional reform. Regulation that focuses on both the economic and social benefits of improved access is essential. Institutional reform is mainly concerned with capabilities. Access to communication networks will not be meaningful for people whose education and training does not permit them to use it effectively. More affordable connections can enable many new social and business activities, but this is only a small part of the 'knowledge societies' vision.

The vision embraces the hope that the infrastructure will enable people to creatively combine the new information available via global and local networks with tacit knowledge. As Sam Pitroda has pointed out, the absence of appropriate institutional reforms can lead to a situation in which telecommunication investment widens, rather than closes, the gap between developing and industrialised countries. Developing countries have often had to depend on unreliable equipment and ICTs have been regarded as a luxury (Pitroda 1993). India, for example, was buying obsolete equipment when the greatest need was to build up technological capabilities to gain a degree of technological independence. In the 1990s extended or 'universal' access is being offered as the promise of a means of achieving a wide range of development goals. Fulfilling the promise, however, will require much more than improved access conditions.

Institutional reform and innovation are needed in the international governance system that shapes the capacity of developing countries to build national information infrastructures. Developments in governance systems that influence the world-wide distribution of capabilities for producing and using ICTs, and the capacity to build new capabilities, are addressed in Chapter 9 (trade in ICT equipment and services) and Chapter 10 (protection of intellectual property, individual privacy, security for international electronic commerce).

NOTES

1 *References to developments in ASEAN in the press include Business Asia (1996); Bright (1996); Chia (1994); Fluendy (1996); Reid (1996); Skillings (1996); and Weiss (1995). See also International Telecommunication Union (1995a); Schenk (1995); and Ure (1995) for analytical discussions.*

2 *Observation by M. Jussawalla, Honolulu, Hawaii, 1997.*

3 *The United States instituted an investigation in the light of estimates of the cost of outpayments for the termination of international services using the public switched network. At least three-quarters of the US$ 5 billion in outpayments was deemed to be a subsidy from American consumers, carriers and their shareholders to foreign carriers (Federal Communications Commission 1996).*

Transformations in the economies in transition

Since the beginning of the transition from planned to market-based economies in 1990 the underdeveloped and obsolete telecommunication infrastructure has posed a major problem for countries in transition to integrate with the rest of the world. Increases in traffic from 1989 to 1994 (see Table 8.6), could barely be channelled via traditional networks of the public telecommunication operators (PTOs). The underdeveloped networks with an average of 14 main lines per 100 inhabitants throughout the region, compared to an OECD average of 45 main lines, have been completely overburdened.

TABLE 8.6 - OUTGOING MINUTES OF TELEPHONE TRAFFIC FROM CENTRAL AND EASTERN EUROPE

	Million minutes		CAGR
	1989	1994	1989-1994
Bulgaria	49.8	82.7	75
Poland	73.1	356.6	48
Russia	57.1	229.2	43
Hungary	89.7	236.6	42
Czech Republic	76.5	157.6	37
Romania	23.8	72.1	33
Albania	17.8	21.4	20

Source: *ITU STARS Database* (1996).

The existing networks produced high fault rates because of the worn switching and transmission capacity. In 1994, around 10 per cent of main telephone lines were connected to a digital exchange as compared to the OECD average of 50 per cent (ITU STARS Database 1995). Electromechanical switching capacity restricted further expansion and upgrading of public networks. Radical telecommunication reforms are required to tackle the crisis in this region. Long-lived stereotypes are being discarded concerning the benefits of public monopoly supply and these countries are introducing competition in network supply (Sadowski 1996). Although, before the introduction of competition, monopoly providers in the industrialised countries progressively met demand, it is evident that even with the best economic incentives, a single provider will be unable to keep up with escalating demand in the economies in transition. Evidence is accumulating that networks have grown faster under competitive market conditions (OECD 1993c; ITU 1995a). New market entry also has accelerated the digitalisation of the telecommunication infrastructure and the need to interconnect the networks of new entrants with the incumbent's

network often requires the digitalisation of switching capacity. There is evidence too that new entry enlarges the market for telecommunication services.

Despite the changes several stereotypes are influencing the market liberalisation process. The task for regulators is a very difficult one. Moving away from a single provider does not necessarily mean a move to the other extreme. There is a threat of 'cherry-picking', if new entrants serve only the most profitable areas. A variety of approaches to network access has been used. Monopoly operators in some countries have been allowed to expand and modernise the public network in conjunction with foreign firms that provide capital as well as technological expertise. In Hungary, the consortium MagyarCom (a partnership of Deutsche Telekom and Ameritech) entered into a joint venture with MATAV, the national operator, in 1993 acquiring a 30 per cent minority stake in the national operator and a dominant position in the Hungarian market for at least 15 years. In exchange, the investors promised to increase the number of main lines by more than 15 per cent a year, pushing the Hungarian public network to 35 main lines per 100 inhabitants by 1999.

In Poland, the introduction of competition in different segments of the telecommunication network began in January 1991. Apart from monopoly provision of international telephone services by Telecomunikacja Polska SA, the Polish national operator, all other areas of the market were opened up to competition. Restricted entry based on the granting of a licence was allowed in the long distance market and full competition was permitted in local markets. Since February 1997, the Ministry of Communications has been discussing interconnection between private networks. Thus, the mobile telephone provider, Plus GSM (Global System for Mobile communications), has sought interconnection of its digital mobile network with the private telephone network of the electricity industry and two petrochemical firms for some 14,000 subscribers. Plus GSM, a joint venture between Airtouch, TeleDanmark, a Polish electricity supplier, and two petrochemical firms, which has been in the market since 1996, argues that interconnection would stimulate network development.

Another factor influencing network growth is the tendering procedures employed by national public telecommunication operators. Some countries continue to underinvest, or invest inefficiently, because they have not employed competitive tendering procedures. In Poland, in 1993 for example, the Ministry of Communications granted exclusive rights for telecommunication equipment supply to three firms: AT&T (in joint venture with Telfa), Alcatel (with Teletra), and Siemens (with Zwut), giving rise to fears that suppliers would have the opportunity to overcharge.

A factor leading to more efficient investment in networks is the use of new digital transmission and switching equipment. In contrast to countries such as Hungary that have begun to upgrade local loops based on fibre optics links, others, like the Baltic States, have begun to implement wireless loops which allow installation of basic telephony at lower investment costs per line (PNE Networks 1993; Sadowski 1996).

The telecommunication tariff structure has also hindered network development. The historical tariff structures proved to be insufficient to raise revenues, especially in countries with high inflation and weak currencies, such as the Ukraine. Those countries that have sold off parts of their national telecommunication operators to raise investment funds, such as the Czech Republic, Hungary, and Latvia, received a much better price after having reformed their tariff structures (Kelly 1995).

In the mid 1990s, the telecommunication infrastructure in the countries in transition continues to present a barrier to providing a basis for catching-up with the western European countries (Chalmers et al.1996; OECD 1994b). A 'catch-up' strategy based on investment in capital intensive and high technology sectors was the optimistic scenario for further economic growth. This requires world market integration, increasing foreign investment, and the adoption of ICTs in offices and throughout the economy. The existence of only one main telephone line for a business does not allow the adoption of more advanced ICTs for office automation. There are problems, for example, if fax machines and telephones have to be operated at the same time. The relatively underdeveloped and obsolete telecommunication infrastructure continues to suggest a pessimistic scenario for office automation (Radosevic 1995).

Nevertheless, there are signs of improvement in the telecommunication infrastructure. In some countries the pace of network growth and digitalisation has been remarkable. In Hungary, for example, digitalisation increased between 1989 and 1994 from one to 41 per cent of main lines connected to digital exchanges. The network in the Czech Republic showed growth from zero to 15 per cent of main lines connected to digital exchanges over the same period. Pro-investment telecommunication policies could help to close this aspect of the 'access gap'.

The impressive growth figures shown in Table 8.7 cannot disguise an underlying dilemma. The pace of structural reform has slowed compared to the first half of the 1990s. The focus has shifted from reforms such as privatisation that were 'easier' to implement, to more challenging reforms requiring a longer time to reach completion (EBRD 1996). In the telecommunication area, regulation

must be implemented and enforced, a difficult challenge for all countries. The management of the continuous implementation of reforms will affect the growth potential of the transition economies, and whether policy-makers and managers in these countries are regarded as having entered into credible commitments to complete the telecommunication reforms.

TABLE 8.7 - GROWTH IN GROSS DOMESTIC PRODUCT (GDP) IN CENTRAL AND EASTERN EUROPE

	Growth in GDP		
	1994 %	1995 %	*1996 %
Czech Republic	2.6	4.8	5.1
Hungary	2.9	1.5	1.5
Poland	5.2	7.0	5.0
Bulgaria	1.8	2.6	-4.0
Romania	3.9	6.9	4.5
Russia	-12.6	-4.0	-3.0
Albania	9.4	8.6	5.0

Note: * Estimated by EBRD
Source: EBRD (1996).

Market liberalisation in Latin American countries

Brazil

Telecommunication services are provided by Telebras through its 28 subsidiaries, - 27 local operators plus the long-distance carrier Embratel. Telebras is responsible for overall planning to coordinate the operations of all the subsidiaries. In December 1996 the Telebras group of companies had 17.7 million lines, of which 14.9 million were fixed lines and 2.8 million were cellular connections representing a 91 per cent share of the total of telephone lines in Brazil (see Table 8.8). A small percentage is in the hands of four independent local operators, one of which, CTBC, is a private-sector company. The average telephone density in Brazil in 1996 was 10.2 lines per 100 population.

TABLE 8.8 - BRAZIL - TELEBRAS PERFORMANCE, 1990, 1996

	1990	1996
Conventional telephone main lines	9,300,000	14,900,000
Cellular subscribers	10,000	2,800,000
Public use telephones	227,000	433,000
Digitisation of local lines	13.9%	55%
Employees	93,000	89,000
Localities served	13,900	20,900

Source: Telebras Annual Reports (various years).

The telecommunication equipment industry included companies with a combined output of around US$ 5.0 billion in 1995. This is a relatively strong presence compared with other Latin American countries and the industry has capabilities that can meet international standards and also adapt products and systems to Brazilian conditions. The majority of these companies are linked to, or maintain agreements with, the world's leading companies facilitating rapid access to the most modern technology. The public sector accounts for 75 per cent of industrial production of equipment and the remaining 25 per cent is absorbed by private sector purchases, with a small proportion of exports.

The structural adjustment plan for the Brazilian economy includes stabilisation of the currency, attraction of foreign capital, privatisation of state-owned companies including telecommunications, and reduction of the fiscal imbalance. Liberalisation reforms have included a change in the legal framework in 1995 so that the Brazilian Constitution no longer prevents private companies from investing in the basic telecommunication sector, and making changes aimed at improving the technical and economic performance of Telebras.

The first measures were proposed at the beginning of Fernando Henrique Cardoso's government in 1995. In August 1995 the government approved an amendment to the 1988 Constitution abolishing the state monopoly on telecommunications and this was interpreted as a move toward the 'flexibilisation' of the Telebras monopoly as distinct from the privatisation or sale of assets. The next step (passed in July 1996) was a 'Minimum Law' allowing entry of the private sector into cellular telephony (where there had been great pressure from the private sector and substantial unmet demand), and into satellite transmission, data transmission (for closed user groups), and value-added services. For three years concessions for cellular telephony (B-band) are to be granted only to Brazilian companies in which at least 51 per cent of the voting capital is directly or indirectly owned by Brazilians. This limits foreign shareholders to 49 per cent of voting capital and 83 per cent of total capital. The new law gives the present concession holders (the public fixed network operators) two years to spin off their analogue cellular divisions into independent companies which may then be privatised.

The market structure of cellular private telephony has 10 geographical areas. Concessions were to be auctioned from April 1997 and many consortia including international operators and large Brazilian enterprises have been formed. Among the foreign players are American and Canadian operators, such as AT&T, BellSouth, SBC, AirTouch, CCII, GTE, and Bell Canada; European companies including Portugal Telecom, France Telecom, STET, Telia, and Mannesmann, and companies from Asia, such as DDI, Hutchinson, and KMT. The

Brazilian partners in the consortia include large enterprises such as banks, and medium and large size construction firms.

At the end of 1996 the government presented a Bill proposing a General Law of Telecommunications, including measures like the establishment of a regulatory office (Agencia Brasiliera de Telecomunicações), a new classification for telecommunication services open to competition, funding instruments for universal service and authorisation for the government to merge the 27 operating companies into regional companies. The government plans to privatise these regional operators as well as the long distance and international carrier, Embratel. The final step will be the opening of the basic services (local and long distance) to competition, but it has not been decided when these measures will be implemented.

The preparation for liberalisation and privatisation has included a far reaching plan, the Program for Recovery and Expansion of the Telecommunications and Postal system (PASTE) which aims to generate investment of US$ 75 billion (from both the public and private sectors). By the year 2003, PASTE is expected to meet the target of 40 million main fixed lines (with a teledensity of 23.2 lines per 100 population) and 17.2 million subscribers to cellular telephony. As a result of this plan, service providers, network operators, and equipment suppliers are experiencing tremendous growth.

The government also introduced rebalancing of telecommunication tariffs at the end of 1995. The basic residential subscription was increased by 513 per cent, and the price of a local call metered unit increased by 67 per cent. The price of the domestic long distance service was raised by an average of 21.3 per cent. This realignment of public sector prices began when inflation was relatively low and the economy was growing at a relatively slow pace. In 1997 other measures were planned, such as the reduction of the installation fee (from US$ 1,100 to US$ 400) and further increases in the tariffs for local services. The new tariffs and expanding markets for services have enabled a substantial recovery of investment. Compared with the average Telebras investments during 1994/95, the growth in 1996 was 49 per cent (see Table 8.9).

TABLE 8.9 - BRAZIL - TELEBRAS INVESTMENT, 1974-1996

Years	Average annual investment US$ billion nominal values*
1974-1982	1.3
1983-1987	1.1
1988-1993	2.5
1994-1995	4.5
1996	6.7

Note: *Current values (unadjusted for inflation)
Source: Telebras Annual Reports (various years).

The following problems are to be expected after liberalisation.

First, protection for the domestic equipment industry and the specification of an adequate mix of local production and imported goods, may require a new policy to foster domestic production and indigenous technological development. The telecommunication equipment market has grown since 1994 and, in 1996 alone, the demand for equipment increased by 43 per cent. However, this boom is unlikely to last due to the ending of the fiscal advantages for domestic production in 1999; the lack of practical mechanisms in the General Law of Telecommunications to boost local production; the privatisation of the Telebras local carriers; the termination of a government purchase policy aimed at the procurement of equipment made in Brazil; and decreases in import tariffs on final equipment.

Second, there is a need to establish a reliable regulatory body that will create confidence for private investors and that is capable of drawing up rules for fair competition, regulating tariffs and establishing conditions for universal service. The establishment of a regulatory body is problematic as Brazil has no experience of this type of governance structure. The government initially announced that it would set up an independent body like the United States Federal Communications Commission but now proposes to establish an authority subordinate to the Telecommunication Ministry.

With regard to the sale of the Telebras companies to international investors, the government will decide whether to look for a good bid or a strategic partner(s). If it is the latter, technology and capital will be important as well as whether the company is based in a country with reciprocal relations with respect to imports and exports. If privatisation becomes a priority for international investors and there is no protection for the domestic industry, there may be losses for Brazilian companies and a decline in the leading-edge activities of their R&D centres. It is likely that the large customers will benefit once competition improves quality and lowers the prices for the services they use. The decisions of the regulatory body will be crucial to whether smaller customers benefit from the planned reforms. Until recently government indecision has meant there was no timetable for the debates and decisions that would enable the technological and economic objectives of privatisation to be met.

Colombia

Traditionally, telephone services were provided by public monopoly firms. TELECOM offered national and international long distance services, while INRAVISION provided national television broadcasting. Local telephone services were offered by local companies based in the main cities. After 1990, this situation changed substantially as a result of the privatisation process, leading to the generation of new value added services and opening basic services to competition. The Ministry of Communications is the regulatory body.

The 1995 Telecommunications Development Plan included measures to address universal coverage of telecommunications and a Social Telephone Service Programme, network investment, and service diversification. Investment over the period 1995 to 1998 is estimated at US$ 4 billion representing net growth of 65 per cent over 1990 to 1994. The pattern of investment is shown in Table 8.10 indicating the remarkable growth rate in investment by the private sector investment estimated at 430 per cent over the period.

TABLE 8.10 - INVESTMENT IN THE TELECOMMUNICATION SECTOR IN COLOMBIA, 1991-1998

	Investment (US$ millions)		Growth	% of GDP	
	1991-94	1995-98	%	1991-94	1995-98
Telecommunication Sector Total of which:	2,662	4,393	65	1.1	1.5
Public	2,290	2,793	22	1.0	0.9
Private	372	1,600	430	0.2	0.5

Source: Ministry of Communications (1995).

From 1995 to 1998 the rate of investment in basic telephone service is expected to decrease while investment in long distance services, social telephone support, and television is to increase (see Table 8.11). Local telephone service revenues comprise the main segment of the industry with a 43 per cent share of total revenues in 1994 of about US$ 1.4 billion (see Table 8.12). By the end of 1996, 80 per cent of the domestic long distance network connecting urban areas was digital with a target of 100 per cent by 1998. The long distance operator, TELECOM, is developing a project to install 3,200 km of optical fibre connecting 26 cities with a first phase to be completed in 1997 interconnecting 13 cities and supporting narrow and broadband services.

At the end of 1995 there were 4.9 million telephone lines representing a density of 14 lines per 100 inhabitants. Basic telephone service is provided by over 30 companies varying in size, coverage, and market. The biggest firm is ETB (Bogota Telecommunications Company) with 1.8 million lines, while the smallest is Teleobando with only 4,600 lines. The three largest cities account for 65 per cent of lines, 12.3 per cent are installed in intermediate-sized cities, and 22.7 per cent in the rest of the country. This distribution follows the concentration of the population in urban areas and the development of industry and commerce in each city.

There was an estimated unsatisfied demand of 1.18 million lines (890,000 corresponding to residential users and

TABLE 8.11 – INVESTMENT BY TYPE OF SERVICE IN COLOMBIA, 1995-1998

Service	1995 %	1996* %	1997* %	1998* %	Cumulative %
Local telephone service	70.9	61.0	56.1	55.7	60.4
Long distance service	13.8	22.1	24.3	24.9	21.6
Value added services	2.5	1.2	1.6	1.0	1.5
Cellular telephone	5.4	4.9	6.5	7.2	6.0
Social telephone service	1.1	5.2	5.1	4.2	4.0
Television	1.6	2.1	2.7	3.1	2.4
Postal service and others	4.8	3.5	3.8	4.1	4.0
Total	100.0	100.0	100.0	100.0	100.0

Note: Estimated *
Source: Ministry of Communications (1995)

TABLE 8.12 – TELECOMMUNICATION REVENUE BY TYPE OF SERVICE IN COLOMBIA, 1994

	Per cent
Local telephone service	43
National long distance	20
International long distance	19
Cellular	12
Other services	6
Total	US$ 1.4 billion

Source: Ministry of Communications (1995).

290,000 to commercial and industrial potential users) in 1996 concentrated mainly in the bigger cities and manufacturing centres. It is expected that the telephone density will grow to 18 lines per 100 inhabitants by 1998 and 25 lines per 100 inhabitants by 2003. The company profiles of 23 of the largest of the 30 or more operators are shown in Table 8.13.

By the end of 1996 cellular service operators had 410,256 subscribers, accumulated revenues of nearly US$ 500 million and estimated monthly revenues of US$ 38 million. The service is offered by six private companies covering three regional cellular telephony territories.

By the end of August 1997 an open competitive market for telecommunications was to have been established. As shown in Table 8.12, 19 per cent of Colombia's telecommunication operator revenues were derived from international long distance telecommunication services. Any change in the international accounting and revenue sharing apparatus could have an impact on these revenues.

Jamaica

The Jamaican Government intends to regulate telecommunications within the framework of an across-industry Office of Utilities Regulation (Girvan 1997). Industry-specific legislation will grant regulatory powers to the Office and enable it to grant licences for specific services (Minister of Public Utilities and Transport 1996). Regulatory policies have been outlined with respect to licences, tariff setting, interconnection and network access, and promotion of competition in value added data services and value added network services. Regulatory responsibilities will be shared between the Office and the responsible Minister, who will retain the power to issue licences.

The evolving regulatory regime is constrained by the terms of the existing exclusive telephone/telecommunication licences held by Telecommunications of Jamaica Ltd, a majority-owned subsidiary of Cable & Wireless.

TABLE 8.13 – LOCAL TELEPHONE OPERATING COMPANIES IN COLOMBIA

Local telephone service	Operators ›200,000 lines	Operators 30,000 – ‹200.000	Operators ‹ 30,000 lines
Number of operators	3	8	12
Telephone density within operational area per 100 inhabitants National average = 14.8	22.4	12.5	9.4
% digital equipment and installations National average = 76.1	68.5	84.7	74.2

Source: Ministry of Communications (1995).

Until the regulatory office is established policy is governed by agreements reached between the company and the Jamaican Fair Trading Commission and a decision from the Jamaican Court of Appeal confirming that the company lies within the jurisdiction of the Fair Competition Act.

A former British colony, Jamaica became an independent state in 1962. Under colonial rule regulation was based on contract law and domestic telephone and external telecommunication monopolies operated through licences issued under the Telephone Act of 1893, and the old Radio and Telegraph Control Act, which remained in force. Prior to 1987 international telecommunication was a monopoly of JAMINTEL, a joint venture between the Government of Jamaica and Cable & Wireless, while domestic telephone service was a monopoly of the state-owned Jamaica Telephone Company. In that year the two companies merged and Cable & Wireless acquired a majority stake in the new company. As part of the agreement, exclusive telephone and telecommunication licences were issued to the company in 1988.

Telecommunications of Jamaica is obliged to provide an 'efficient and modern telephone integrated network' and service to customers on request; to agree minimum standards of service; and to undertake development programmes provided that finance is available for such programmes on reasonable terms. In return the company acquired a 25-year exclusive franchise for wired telephone service, renewable for a further 25 years [1]; and is guaranteed a net rate of return on shareholders' equity. Public government services, radio and news agency services do not fall within the monopoly granted to the company. Telecommunications of Jamaica's wireless telephony licence allows it to operate a cellular service on a non-exclusive basis. The government is committed to honouring the terms of the existing licences by preserving the company's monopoly rights over domestic and international telephone services in any new licences issued under changed legislation. The company has been operating a *de facto* monopoly cellular phone service since 1991 and an international call-back service competing with its fixed network services.

The company's existing licences contain no explicit obligations or rights with respect to network access and interconnection. The Government has declared that its policy will be to open up to competition in services such as electronic mail, teletext, videotex, and circuit switched data. However, the legal power to implement this policy awaits industry-specific legislation. [2]

Legal opportunities to open the market arose as a result of proceedings under the Fair Competition Act. In 1994 Infochannel, an Internet service provider, brought a suit against Telecommunications of Jamaica claiming abuse of the Company's dominant position. The matter was not pursued in the Courts but, as part of an agreement with

the Fair Trading Commission to allow connection to its network of customer-owned equipment, the Company agreed, subject to certain conditions, to provide circuits on a commercial basis to customers wanting to provide value added data services (VADs). [3]

Under its existing licences, Telecommunications of Jamaica is assured of tariffs sufficient to generate a minimum net rate of return of 17.5 per cent, and a maximum of 20 per cent on shareholder equity in its consolidated operations. Since interconnection issues are not covered in the existing licences, price setting does not arise directly and advanced service providers negotiate interconnection rates directly with the company.

In the future, the Government intends that the regulatory office will have the power to determine telecommunication tariffs but it is unclear whether the prerogatives of the Minister will be assumed or whether this implies only an advisory role. Such regulatory powers cannot at present be exercised and any changes must await the enactment of new telecommunications legislation.

In the telecommunication sector, Dunn argues that a 'major consequence of British imperialism on the existing policy and network structure of Caribbean telecommunications is the region's increasing reliance on external capital, technology and management expertise' (Dunn 1995: 201). The current development of the infrastructure may be widening the divide between rural and urban populations. Some observers have questioned the need for a monopoly over telecommunication services, arguing that this hinders the development of internal and international computer-based communications (Girvan 1993). A competitive framework for non-voice, value added services is needed as are competitive access prices to telecommunication facilities and these are not favoured by the current monopoly situation. It has been suggested that a stronger regulatory authority will be needed to divert powers away from the Ministry (Girvan 1994b).

Mexico

The modernisation of the telecommunication infrastructure began with the installation of digital networks and the launch of the first Mexican satellites in 1980s. The privatisation of Telefonos de Mexico (TELMEX) in 1990 was followed in 1997 by the introduction of competition into all areas of the market (Mexico Poder Ejecutivo Federal 1996; Mexico Secretary of Communications and Transport 1995). With the TELMEX privatisation, the company's legal monopoly in domestic and long distance services and its *de facto* monopoly in the local service were maintained until 1997.

One of the first measures taken in preparation for competition was the approval of new entrants in the 'auxiliary' and new service markets. Concessions for cellular telephone services were also granted. The country was divided into nine regions with a duopoly market structure permitting two operators in every region. By 1997 mobile services were available in 170 cities with more than 680,000 subscribers. Competitive entry was also authorised for other mobile services including paging, messaging, and dispatch services using various frequencies.

In 1995, the Mexican Executive adopted the Federal Telecommunications Law establishing a telecommunication regulatory framework including principles for a competitive industry. An independent regulatory agency, the Comision Federal de Telecomunicações, was established to implement the law and promulgate the regulations. The law regulates the use and operation of radio frequencies, telecommunication networks, and satellite communication. The goal is to develop and promote competition to create more diverse and better quality services at affordable prices.

The law widened the scope for private investment including foreign investment within specific parameters. The 1993 Foreign Investment Law liberalised restrictions limiting foreign investment in Mexican companies to 49 per cent, to permit up to 100 per cent foreign ownership of telecommunication operations including cellular telephony and value added services. However, certain other broadcast and telecommunication operations, including basic telephone service, videotex, and packet switched data service remained limited to 49 per cent, with a 30 per cent investment limit for wireline and 40 per cent for wireless services. The 1995 Law stated that the maximum 49 per cent limit (ownership of the capital stock) applied to operations that require a concession, and certain investments continued to require approval by the National Commission of Foreign Investment.

Features of the law include the legal authority to implement rules for interconnection of long distance service providers with TELMEX; a licensing structure and auction process for network service providers; a framework for granting concessions through public bidding to private companies to build and operate private satellites and provide satellite services in Mexico using foreign satellites. However, the control and operations centre for the satellites must be in Mexico and preferably operated by Mexican nationals. Procedures for securing rights to use the radio frequency spectrum bands for radio and television programming distribution are subject to Federal Radio and Television Law.

The new law also permitted foreign investment up to 49 per cent in Mexican holding companies that control geostationary orbital slots, or that use rights to transmit and receive signals in frequency bands associated with foreign satellite systems. Value added services can be provided competitively subject only to registration and from 1995 foreign investors have been able to own 100 per cent of a Mexican enterprise providing value added services in line with the North American Free Trade Agreement

(NAFTA). Concessions to facilities-based operators extend over 30 years and may be renewed for an equal period. No concessions or licences are required to operate private telecommunication networks unless they use radio bands and offer commercial services to the public. Concession holders are prohibited from cross-subsidising services offered by their subsidiaries or affiliates. Tariffs are regulated to ensure that each service category recovers revenues in line with average long run incremental costs.

As a result of all these changes, new telecommunication groups have been attracted by the explosion of the Mexican long distance market with expected revenues of US$ 20 billion annually by 2000.

Market liberalisation in India, China, and the ASEAN Region

India

A study team of the Department of Electronics on National Information Infrastructure of India, in preparation for the 9th Five Year Plan 1997-2002, has stressed that the administration of the ICT sector lacks a unified approach and that plans for literacy, education and commerce must be closely linked to those for telecommunication and information technology (Ramesam 1996). There is a substantial resource gap and private sector investment is needed. The Government has agreed to phase out its monopoly and other restrictions on competitive entry by 2004, in line with the World Trade Organization agreement on basic telecommunication services signed during 1997.

A Centre for the Development of Telematics (C-DOT) was established by the Government in 1984 as the premier R&D organisation for domestic and some foreign manufacturers of telecommunication and telematics equipment. By 1994 a National Telecommunications Policy was announced by the Department of Telecomm-unications (DoT) which maintains the government monopoly on long distance telecommunication services. The aim is to achieve benefits for basic service users and a wider choice of equipment. There has been criticism of the DoT's role as policy-maker, owner, and price setter (Ramesam 1996). The National Telecommunication Policy of 1994 gives highest priority to the development of telecommunication services as part of its economic policy, through foreign direct investment and domestic investment (Petrazzini and Harindranath 1996; Ramanujam 1996). The overall strategy is to achieve market liberalisation, global integration, and market-driven growth.

Guidelines for screening foreign equity proposals by the Foreign Investment Promotion Board were issued by the Industry Minister in January 1997 and foreign direct investment is permitted for equity shares up to 49 per cent without government approval (Nicholson 1997).

FIGURE 8.1 – OPTICAL FIBRE INFRASTRUCTURE ACROSS CHINA

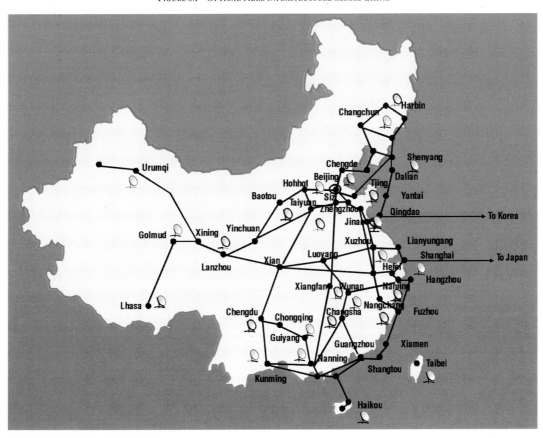

The DoT initiated an agreement on funding for basic telecommunication projects to ensure payment of telecommunication operator debts to financial institutions (Anand 1997; Nicholson 1997). The present regulatory process is complex involving the Ministry of Communications, the Telecommunication Commission, the DoT, the Prime Minister's Office, the Ministry of Finance, and the Congress, but a Telecom Regulatory Authority of India (TRAI) is now being established (Banerjee and Bhattacharya 1996).

In 1994 the telephone density in India was about 0.8 telephones per 100 inhabitants; lower than China, Pakistan, and Malaysia. There was a waiting list of about 2.5 million people and only a very small proportion of villages were connected to the network. The passage of the Telecommunication Regulatory Authority Bill by the Indian Parliament in March 1997 was intended to improve the rural network, but the main activity is directed at the urban centres to provide a wide range of services to industry (Agarwal 1996a,b,c). For people who can afford cellular telephones and telephones located on long distance trains, new services are available. For example, a traveller intending to make a standard rate call within the country is charged Rs 126 per minute and Rs 162 per minute for an international call using a satellite service. Videsh Sanchar Nigam (Overseas Telecommunications Corporation) Ltd collects Rs 120 and 150, respectively, for these calls.

While these new services are being introduced, the role of government continues to be debated. The long waiting list for telephone services, and investor interest in the telecommunication sector, have led to changes in some service tariffs. Rebalancing is bringing reduced prices for long distance users but increases in application fees and metered local service calls mean that some more sections of society are opting out of the race to subscribe. More advanced networks for data communication are provided by the National Informatics Centre Network (NICNET) supporting computing and two-way data communications for government departments and related agencies using satellite earth stations; and INONET, a data network established and maintained by CMC Ltd and the Educational and Research Network (ERNET) providing computer communications to India's academic and research community.

In rural areas, public access depends on the availability of public telephones. In 1997 there were 249,000 village public telephones of which it was estimated that 11,264 are out of order at any given time. Companies are bidding to provide new services in various parts of the country. The business community is arguing for improved Internet services and by the first quarter of 1997 there were 28,000 subscribers to access services with growth to 200,000 subscribers forecast by the end of the year. Although their numbers are small compared to the millions of Internet users world-wide, their role is influential in setting the national information infrastructure agenda in India.

China

China has made major efforts to build up of its national information infrastructure and it is now ranked among the top ten countries in the world in terms of total number of telephones (Paré 1995; Gu and Steinmueller 1998 forthcoming). The telecommunication sector has been enjoying 40 to 50 per cent annual growth rates since 1989 (CMS 1996).

Rapid expansion has been spurred on by additions to the Chinese infrastructure of more than 10 million telephone lines to the public telephone network each year, resulting in a teledensity increase to 6.2 per cent in 1996, up from 1.1 per cent in 1990. The personal computer market has also been growing and in 1996 about 1.6 million PCs were sold, a 40 per cent increase over 1995. Of the 1.6 million PCs, 20 per cent were purchased by residential consumers and a 50 per cent increase in sales was projected for 1997.

Some 128,000 km of optical fibre cables, supplemented by large satellite earth stations in almost every provincial capital, have been added to transform some parts of China into a well-connected nation with a sophisticated infrastructure (see Figure 8.1). Nevertheless, demand cannot be met and the national telephone installation waiting list which reached 5 million in October 1994 has been increasing.

The fibre optic network will link the eastern provinces where the population densities are highest. The goal in the 7th Five Year Plan is to complete seven million kilometres annually of fibre using Synchronous Digital Hierarchy (SDH) technology.[7] There is also investment in domestic SDH manufacturing capability. Submarine fibre optic cables through a joint venture with Cable & Wireless will support a China-United Kingdom submarine system, 51 per cent owned by China's MPT (other links with Thailand, Viet Nam and Hong Kong are being established).

In addition, China has 'leap-frogged' into cellular technology in its urban centres and provincial towns. In 1994, China Unicom (LianTong) was licensed to compete directly with MPT in local and long-distance as well as mobile services creating a duopoly supply structure. In 1997 there were 15 million pagers and imports of one million each year from companies including Ericsson, Nokia, Motorola and Nortel. Cellular services were set up to provide competition with MPT. Three Ministries, Power, Electronics and Transportation, in China set up Unicom (Lian Tong) as a cellular mobile service. In Guangdong province, 1.4 million subscribers are equipped with analogue cellular phones and 1.2 million with digital GSM cell phones. CT2 or one-way telepoint phones are competing with public call offices in this region and are being deployed with pagers.

To further the development of the national information infrastructure, the government has launched a series of 'Golden Projects' (d'Orville 1996). Three of these projects are supporting networks linking government ministries, staff organisations, companies, and the public (Golden Bridge), improving clearance of goods by upgrading customs service communication using a private data network (Golden Customs), and developing the banking, credit and debit card system (Golden Card). These networks are supported by the public X.25 network (Chinapac), a digital leased line network (ChinaDDN), and various private data networks using satellite networks. Implementation of Frame Relay and ATM networks is being planned.

In May 1994, the High Energy Physics Institute of the Chinese Academy of Science became the first user to access the Internet via Japan. Since then, users in China have increased eightfold and by March 1997 there were 12 main networks connected to the Internet, 50,000 users, and 6,000 PCs with access to the Internet. These networks are mainly set up by government, research and education institutions and the Ministry of Electronic Industry (MEI), the State Education Commission (SEC), the Chinese Academy of Science (CAS), and MPT have been authorised since 1996 to connect their networks to the Internet. Any domestic organisation, after minimum background screening, can obtain an Internet Service Provider licence by interconnecting with, or by leasing facilities from, one of the four agency networks.

Reform of the industry structure to accommodate the planned information superhighway has been under consideration by a high level group, the State Council's Leading Group of Economic Informatization, since 1996 (Tan 1995; Mueller and Dougan 1993). In the telecommunication regulatory field, although the sector is dominated by the MPT, separation of regulatory functions from service provision is in process. Most value added services were opened to domestic competition in 1993. It was expected that a new telecommunication law would be passed at the end of 1997, but it was doubtful whether it would be on schedule.

The major challenges for China are associated with software and the need for effective policy and regulation. Decisions will be needed about the extent to which the MPT's regulatory functions are to be separated from service operation; how to open the basic telecommunication service market to competition and whether to maintain a duopoly; and whether the service sector should remain closed to foreign investment. Isolation from the global community could prevent the country from gaining access to advanced technology and management skills as well as to foreign investment. Indirect investment in the service sector by sharing revenues with external operators is allowed, although involvement in operation and management is prohibited.

The emergence of 'communication dualisms' will also need to be addressed. In 1996, the telephone penetration rate had reached 22 main telephones per 100 inhabitants in the cities. But, the nation wide figure was only 6.2 per cent. There are computers in 5 per cent of households in the cities while the national average is only 2 per cent. Interconnecting cities is a policy priority but this leaves the rural areas unconnected. Although there have been discussions about a universal telecommunication service policy, nothing has been implemented. A major question is whether current investment strategies will create new access disparities.

Existing disparities or 'dualisms' are a reflection of the government's development strategy. Dualistic growth is considered to be a transitory phase rather than a development 'problem'. Given the coastal region's superiority over inland areas in terms of infrastructure, capital, technical levels, management skill, and general economic efficiency, the policy holds that the development strategy should focus on providing this region with adequate levels of capital, energy, and foreign currency. Once this region has become sufficiently developed, greater attention would be paid to the central and western regions. The recent Internet explosion in China reflects the same dualistic pattern with the greatest number of paying customers being in Beijing, Guangdong, and Shanghai.

The establishment of new telecommunication services is largely a business phenomenon. The majority of new systems has been installed in government agencies, institutions, and/or cooperatives. Administrative and fiscal reforms since the early 1980s have enabled the pursuit of provincial, local, and private interests at the lower levels in the telecommunications hierarchy. Local interests are increasingly playing a greater role than national actors in promoting network expansion.[5] Decentralisation of decision-making enables users to 'co-invest' in the telecommunication network (Gu and Steinmueller 1998 forthcoming).

Various Provincial Telecommunications Authorities (PTA) and Provincial Telecommunications Bureaux (PTB) are responsible for local infrastructure development. These units have been encouraged to seek investment from local governments and other local interests, and have been permitted to retain a percentage of the revenues they generate for reinvestment. The initial aim

of this policy was to increase the speed of development of local networks, but the result is that the poorer areas have had to make do without telephone services or with cheaper and more rudimentary forms of technology. The wealthier coastal regions and the urban centres have improved access to more advanced technologies. This approach is exacerbating intra-regional differences in the penetration rates of telecommunication services, as well as laying the foundation for the possible emergence of new forms of social and economic stratification.

Decentralisation is resulting in a multitude of regional and local models. The lack of a clear vision regarding how the expansion of telecommunication services should proceed may be significantly impeding central government's ability to effectively shape the direction of infrastructure expansion. The sector is experiencing both inter- and intra-ministerial conflicts, notably between the MPT and the MEI which has a stake in both Unicom and Jitong, MPT's state sanctioned competitors. Incompatible networks, congestion on the existing public telecommunication network, long waiting periods for telephone service, high connection fees, and disparities both between and within regions continue to persist.

Stakeholders in the Asia Pacific region

Throughout the Asia Pacific region government-business partnerships and regional business networks are being encouraged to stimulate investment in the regional National Information Infrastructure. This has led to major changes in the world as we move to the next millennium (Naisbitt 1996). Examples of the new business networks include an alliance between a Southeast Asian carrier, ACASIA Communications, and Infonet of the United States to extend network services world-wide; a Japanese Asia Internet Interconnect Initiative aimed at providing network access through an international satellite link with Indonesia; Telekom Malaysia is leading a new cable network being established in the region; Singapore's Trade and Development Board and National Computer Board have established a Multimedia Interactive Group comprised of both public and private organisations; and Indonesia, Malaysia, and Thailand are considering an international Special Telecommunications Zone (STZ) to attract private sector involvement. Singapore and Malaysia are strongly positioned to influence regional developments while Thailand, Indonesia, the Philippines, and Viet Nam have tended to concentrate their efforts at the domestic level. Table 8.14 highlights the range of inward investors to the region that are striking alliances and partnerships to build the new infrastructures.

Optical Fibre Submarine systems are weaving a web of communications for the Pacific Rim countries with the expectation of lower prices for international direct dialling. There are four TransPacific Cables (TPCs) operating

TABLE 8.14 – REGIONAL ALLIANCES IN THE ASIA PACIFIC REGION

Telecom Operator	Venture	Country	Investment
France Telecom	Lian Tong	China	GSM network in Guangdong
Nynex	Reliance Telecom	India	10% stake in cellular
First Pacific	Escorts Mobile Communications	India	49% cellular operation
Hutchison Telecom	Hutchison Max	India	Mumbai Cellular JV
Shinawatra	HFCL	India	Fixed network with JFCL/Bezeq
Telstra	Modi Telstra	India	Cellular joint venture
US West	US West BPL	India	49% in cellular operation
Distacom	Modicom	India	Cellular joint venture with Motorola
PTT Telecom, NL	PT Telkomsat	Indonesia	17.3%; GSM operator
Nynex	PT Excelcomindo	Indonesia	23%; GSM operator
DeTeMobil	Satelindo	Indonesia	25%; GSM and int. gateway
Cable & Wireless	PT Daya Mitra	Indonesia	KSO consortium
SingTel	PT Bukaka SingTel Int.	Indonesia	KSO consortium
Telstra	PT Mitra Global Telekomunikasi	Indonesia	KSO consortium
US West	PT Aria West	Indonesia	KSO consortium
France Telecom	PT Pramindo Iket Nusantaro	Indonesia	KSO consortium
US West	Bianariang	Malaysia	20% stake in full service network
Deutsche Telekom	TRI	Malaysia	23% stake in cellular/international franchise
PTT Telecom Swis	Mutiara	Malaysia	30% stake in PCN/international operation
Telekom Malaysia	MRCB	Malaysia	Acquired PCN operation
BT	Clear	New Zealand	25% stake
Shinawatra	Isiacom	Philippines	Cellular network
NTT	Smart	Philippines	12% stake in full service network
Cable & Wireless/ Hong Kong Telecom	MobileOne Asia	Singapore	30%; 2nd mobile network & paging
Hutchison Telecom	IntraPage	Singapore	40% of paging operation
Hong Kong Telecom	TTNS	Taiwan (Pr. China)	26% in 2nd network
Deutsche Telekom	Shinawatra International	Thailand	Stake in international operations
Telstra	DGPT	Viet Nam	BCC contracts for international and possibly fixed network

Source: Compiled by M. Jussawalla, Institute of Culture and Communication, East-West Center, Honolulu, Hawaii, 1997.

at full capacity, TPC5 is 90 per cent subscribed, and TPC6 will be installed by the end of 1998. These cables link the west coast of the United States with Japan, the Philippines, Guam, and Hawaii. AT&T is investing US$ 1 billion in a fibre submarine pathway to link Oregon with California, Hawaii, Guam, and Japan. Another US$ 1 billion involves AT&T in the Asia Pacific Cable linking 11 Asian countries and territories including Taiwan (Pr. China) and the Republic of Korea. Southeast Asia is linked to Tokyo by Worldsource and Singapore has two cables linking it with Marseilles through the Mediterranean with a third being installed linking Singapore with Shanghai. FLAG (Fibre Link Around the Globe) involves a large investment by NYNEX and others connecting 12 countries including the United Kingdom and Japan.

Mobile communication technologies are expected to attract some US$ 2.6 billion in new systems in the Asia Pacific

Figure 8.2 – Transponder capacity via satellite

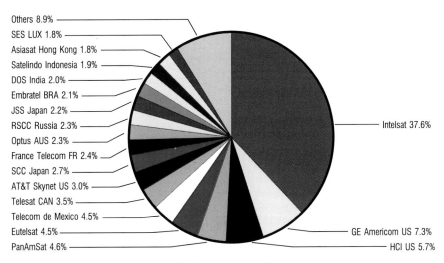

Others 8.9%
SES LUX 1.8%
Asiasat Hong Kong 1.8%
Satelindo Indonesia 1.9%
DOS India 2.0%
Embratel BRA 2.1%
JSS Japan 2.2%
RSCC Russia 2.3%
Optus AUS 2.3%
France Telecom FR 2.4%
SCC Japan 2.7%
AT&T Skynet US 3.0%
Telesat CAN 3.5%
Telecom de Mexico 4.5%
Eutelsat 4.5%
PanAmSat 4.6%

Intelsat 37.6%

GE Americom US 7.3%
HCI US 5.7%

Note: Total transponders = 3,771
Source: World Satellite Communications and Broadcasting Market Survey in *Communications Week International* (1996), 10 December

region by the turn of the century (Euroconsult 1995). The costs of equipment and air time are higher than terrestrial services, and farmers in China, India, and Indonesia prefer to use CT2 mobile systems supplied by Motorola for one-way communication. The expansion of cellular markets is enormous in Malaysia, Singapore, China, the Philippines, and Thailand. In Thailand, Singapore, and Malaysia there is an installed base for GSM standard equipment even though Japan and Korea are pushing for different standards. Singapore has invested US$ 150 million to supply Personal Communication Networks to 160,000 subscribers using a network installed by Nortel with over 100 base stations providing 95 per cent coverage. Indonesia is reviewing tariffs to make use of cellular telephones more economical for users and removing the 25 per cent import duty on cellular equipment. In Malaysia, the Chase Manhattan Bank is leading a consortium of financiers to advance a loan of US$ 667 million to Celcom, the largest cellular telephone company.

Satellites transcend national boundaries and provide a cost effective 'ramp' to the global information infrastructure (Jussawalla 1995a). In 1991 Indonesia privatised its satellite services and created a commercial company, Palapa Pacifik Nusantra, in an orbit with coverage for Hawaii and the Pacific Islands. Its orbital location was contested by Tongasat and after a bitter dispute ending in arbitration by the International Telecommunication Union, the Palapa satellite was moved to the east. Since then satellite wars have erupted in the Pacific because of the lucrative business opportunities for providing data and television programmes. The reason for the boom in the satellite market is the exponential growth of traffic levels over the Pacific Ocean Region, despite the submarine fibre optic

cables. Parking places in geosynchronous orbit have become contentious between countries in the Asia Pacific along with the push from private suppliers like PanAmSat, Asiasat, and APstar (Jussawalla 1994). PanAmSat is the first foreign privately owned satellite to have landing rights in China, India, and Japan. The distribution of transponder capacity world-wide is shown in Figure 8.2 illustrating that new systems have a small share of capacity relative to Intelsat and the other top four players.

As satellite technology advances into the higher KU band of the radio spectrum, the Southeast Asian countries are moving to use the newer systems. Hughes is providing Indonesia with the Direct Broadcast Satellite 601 type satellite for digital video and audio broadcasts. Another new satellite launched for Indonesia is the Garuda. Built by Lockheed Martin, it has a footprint covering parts of Australia. Tongasat had obtained permission for the use of six orbital slots over the Pacific Ocean but Tongasat was sued in the US courts over its use of orbital slots. In 1991 Malaysia introduced its own domestic satellite system and selected Benariang, a small telecommunication service provider, to operate it. The system is called Measat (Malaysian East Asian Satellite). The company advanced US$ 118 million to Hughes to construct the first space segment which was launched in January 1996. US West has invested US$ 1.8 billion in this venture.

The United States, with a population of 250 million, has access to 750 satellite transponders now in use while China with 1.5 billion people has access to only 15 transponders. Despite growing demand, one of the most successful commercial satellite operators in the region, Asiasat, experiencing losses. The causes may be market saturation and cultural and linguistic diversity which deter growth in advertising revenues. Neverthe-less, Rupert Murdoch's Asiasat is trying to gain a foothold in the vast Chinese market. When Asiasat I was launched in 1990, it filled a vacuum for high powered television distribution, telephony, and VSAT networks. It was the first privately owned satellite in Asia. It is estimated that by the year 2000, Asia will have 1,000 new transponders for television and telephone usage. A Japanese satellite system announced in September 1996 as JCSAT 5 will be able to broadcast to Asia and Hawaii with a new satellite built by Hughes Space and Communications.

Very Small Aperture Terminals (VSATs) are expected to grow by a factor of ten by the year 2000. China's investment in VSATs and satellites will grow from US$ 1 billion in 1994 to US$ 2 billion by 2000 according to the Chinese Academy of Satellite Technology (CAST). VSATs adapt to different environments. For example, Russia's Savings Bank has contracted with AT&T Tridom to install two-way communication using VSATs between the head office of the bank in Moscow and its branches in other cities. China's use of VSATs is tied to its investment in Asiasat and in another private consortium, APstar, which has so far launched two satellites both of which failed. The greatest beneficiary of China's demand for satellites is Hughes although Lockheed Martin and Space Systems Loral also manufacture satellites for China. There is a private satellite company in China called Sinosat which has commissioned its satellites from Daimler Benz Aerospace with whom they have a joint venture agreement (Jussawalla 1995b).

Until 1994 there were three regional satellites in the Pacific region - Intelsat, Palapa, and Asiasat. In 1995 these were joined by Thaicom, APstar and PanAmSat. Intelsat's launch of its 708 series was aborted within 20 seconds of the launch by Long March in 1996. Direct to Home (DTH) satellites are becoming very popular in the region. Along with Indonesia's Garuda, another ten such satellites will be launched in the region within the next five years. Both the Republic of Korea and Thailand have their own systems.

Low Earth Orbiting Satellite (LEOS) operators are negotiating access to provide services. In China Globalstar hopes to provide services to remote areas including Ulanbator in Mongolia. China has a large investment in the Iridium system. Other Asian countries that have made investments in Iridium are Japan, Thailand, Singapore, India and Indonesia. China has contracted six launches for the Iridium satellites from the Taiyuan launch centre. Iridium China Limited has its headquarters in Hong Kong and is owned by China Aerospace.

NOTES

1 Unless the government opts to acquire the company after the first 25 years.

2 The features covered in monopoly apply to call forwarding, facsimile, and telex.

3 Agreement between the Fair Trading Commission and Telecommunications of Jamaica Ltd, 21 December 1994.

4 The 7th Five Year Plan identified the development of telecommunications as a national priority.

5 See Rehak and Wang (1996); Triolo and Lovelock (1996); Wang (1996b); Wu (1996).

CHAPTER 9

FRIEND OR FOE?
DEVELOPING COUNTRIES
AND THE INTERNATIONAL
GOVERNANCE SYSTEM

The global information infrastructure –
emerging 'zones of silence'

9.1 INTRODUCTION - GOVERNANCE REGIMES FOR ICTs

A large number of institutions and governance regimes are influencing the emergence of the global information infrastructure (GII) and national and regional information infrastructures around the world. Some of these institutions have a long history of involvement in telecommunication supply or the protection of information. The participants in these institutions are finding it necessary to adapt to rapid changes in global and national markets. Other institutions are relatively new and are introducing new rules, regulations, and procedures that set the framework for the dynamic between competition and cooperation as ICT markets evolve. Historically, many of these institutions included only national government representatives. Today, however, the private sector is increasingly represented in the memberships of these institutions and is able to influence their decisions.

The growing importance of the market as an institutional mechanism that influences the production and consumption of information and ICT hardware and software means that the governance systems operating on a regional or global scale need to be very closely coordinated with the evolving structure of national, regional, and international markets. Governance systems involve the exercise of power and, in many cases, sovereignty. They also involve the maintenance of a bureaucratic and technical apparatus. Governance processes can enable as well as constrain new developments. Governance involves the application of rules in order to influence action.

Governance of science and technology, and especially of ICTs, is the institutional dynamic that leads to the creation, exploitation, and control of technology.[1] Institutional instruments include laws, regulations, treaties, conventions, codes of practice, and standards. The governance problems in science and technology are becoming increasingly international, and the institutional structures of governance are acquiring an internal focus that embraces the industrialised and developing countries. Governance processes are usually understood to involve trade-offs and priorities in order to reduce tensions and to secure economic gains. Frequently, the discussion of international governance is confined to international institutions or 'state actors' taking no account of all the regional, national, and sub-national institutions and organisations with which the international institutions interact. In the ICT sector, this interaction is crucial to the outcomes in the market and for the producers and users of ICT applications. National and regional ICT strategies can be most effective if they take into account, and seek to influence, the governance regimes that are emerging internationally.

Governance regimes emerge as a result of shared ideas and discourses or ways of describing developments in technology and society. Governance is important in terms of understanding where the power to define problem areas for international governance regimes is located. Governance regimes are also culture specific and not all systems work in the same way. Some operate in a conflictual manner while others operate by consensus. Differing cultural perceptions can become destabilising factors in the formation and application of international governance regimes. The implementation of governance decisions is as important as the decisions themselves. For example, decisions may be made that cannot be implemented or enforced because of cost or different perceptions of what the agreed rules mean. All governance decisions incorporate some degree of risk. This can have significant effects upon public and private investment trajectories in research leading to technical innovations, the commercialisation of innovative products and services, and the emergence of capabilities needed to use technology effectively.

In the ICT sector, the speed of technological innovation is making it difficult for international governance systems to work effectively and there are some observers who suggest that government institutions in the ICT sector have a declining role to play (Wriston 1992). Anthony Rutkowski's long association with the communication industry, both at the International Telecommunication Union and in the private sector, has led him to suggest that although the relative importance of the International Telecommunication Union is declining while that of the World Trade Organization (WTO) is rising, for example, there are even bigger changes taking place. In general, 'it is private telecommunications providers themselves that are most responsible for shaping the direction and laying the groundwork for the provision of such services ... these providers are inventing new forms and forums for international cooperation that are more agile, far faster and more focused on immediate needs than those of the past' (Rutkowski 1995: 234).

Others argue that governments and governance institutions with public representatives and often those from the private sector, have a very important role to play in establishing the 'rules of the game' for international and national markets (Hirst and Thompson 1996). In the ICT field, the development of global networking capabilities depends on the working out of complex administrative agreements at national, and regional, and international levels. The workings of governance regimes can influence the dynamics of decision- and rule-making (technology choice and appraisal, the dynamics of negotiation processes and their outcomes), regulation (as a market tool, setting up of a public authority to regulate), the formation of powerful networks leading to technology agreements and treaties (affecting whether innovative capabilities can be built up), the sociopolitical impact of technical change (that is, patterns of trade in ICT products and services), and issues related to productivity such as whether the promise of technologies is fulfilled in terms of what they deliver for employment and the quality of life.

Issues of governance and 'governability' in the ICT area are very closely associated with the recognition that 'knowledge, more than ever, is power. The one country that can best lead the information revolution will be more powerful than any other' (Nye and Owens 1996: 20). This view of the ascendancy of the power of one country over another through competition stands in contrast to the view which regards knowledge and the GII as creating opportunities for using ICTs to contribute to a more equitable distribution of wealth and well being. For example, United States Vice-President Al Gore has promoted the GII in the following way.

Let us build a global community in which the people of neighbouring countries view each other not as potential enemies, but as potential partners, as members of the same family in the vast, increasingly interconnected human family ... We view technology not as an end in itself but as the means through which the GII can realise its potential to improve the well-being of all people on this planet (Brown et al. 1995: 1, 2).

Questions about the role and effectiveness of government, and governance regimes, and particularly at the state or national levels are important for development and the role of ICTs. The World Bank's (1997: i) focus on 'what the state should do, how it should do it, and how it can do it better in a rapidly changing world' is linked directly to issues of power, resources, and capabilities. The Bank's World Development report for 1997 also recognises the important role of international institutions in coordinating the actions of national and regional governments. These institutions embody the norms and rules that are shaping the landscape of the markets for ICTs. Capability in this context means the ability of state institutions to 'undertake and promote collective actions The state's potential to leverage, promote, and mediate change in pursuit of collective ends is unmatched. Where this capacity has been used well, economies have flourished. But where it has not, development has hit a brick wall' (World Bank 1997: 3, 157).

Stakeholders in the ICT sector have different views on appropriate national and international governance solutions (see Table 9.1). International governance regimes affect telecommunication and information technology equipment diffusion and the distribution of producer and user capabilities (for example, trade barriers and market access rules), regulations for telecommunication network and service supply (international service supply, standards agreements for interconnection of networks and terminal equipment). These aspects of international governance are discussed in this chapter. Other aspects of governance are considered in Chapter 10, including the conventions and agreements that set rules for intellectual property protection, implementation of security for electronic commerce transactions, and protection for the privacy of individuals and the social communities who use electronic networks. Table 9.1 shows that in each of these areas, there are different views on the appropriate governance solutions.

The global environment in which the international governance regimes for ICTs operate could become more inclusive, open, and enabling over the next decades, or it could become more exclusive, closed, and restrictive. Decisions with respect to governance issues illustrated in Table 9.1 will influence the outcomes in the global market. If the international environment becomes more open and enabling, there will be opportunities to use ICTs to reduce the growing gaps between the industrialised and the wealthier developing countries, and the rest of the developing world.

The impact of international governance regimes on ICTs capabilities is not a one-way street from the international to the regional, national, or sub-regional. National or regional initiatives can make a substantial difference to the outcomes depending on whether there is a proactive or reactive strategic response to ICT development, acquisition, and use. A report on the scenarios developed by members of the UNCSTD Working Group on IT and Development puts the differences between more optimistic and pessimistic scenarios this way.

The global community has two value systems jostling for power. One is inclusive, open, and enabling with solid attempts to integrate the weak and disadvantaged. The other is exclusive, fractured, restrictive, a Darwinian world, red in tooth and claw, dominated by the strong and powerful for their own ends, with increasing concentrations of technology, wealth, and power and little regard for those left behind. The difference is not simply one between private and public. It is more the difference between cooperation and exploitation.

In turn, national responses range from being complete and positive to being partial, disengaged, and reactive. Some countries have ambitions to learn and create strong policies at home and take a full part in global debates and negotiations. Some want to respond but lack the resources. Others are unresponsive to the challenge. Again, this need not be a split between government and the private sector. Governments must lead, but the whole country must learn. It is also important to realize that being active does not necessarily mean being controlling. And doing nothing is just as much a policy as doing something, except that

TABLE 9.1 – POLICY AND STRATEGIC ACTION TO BENEFIT FROM ICT USE

Issue	Computing/software and information service providing companies	Most communication network operators, larger media companies and publishers	Smaller public and private sector ICT users - 'virtual communities'
Technology diffusion; distribution of producer and user capabilities	Available solutions are inadequate for the challenges of the innovative 'knowledge societies'. New user interfaces are the key to future developments. The infrastructure should provide 'pipes' for delivering information services.	The path to 'knowledge societies' requires coordinated infrastructure development with network interoperability and incentives to generate new information/ programme content.	The necessary computing tools for implementing the innovative 'knowledge societies' are here now. However, telecommunication access must improve. Emphasis should be on user awareness and skills acquisition.
Regulation and ICT policy	Regulators need to prevent infrastructure suppliers from erecting entry barriers and to implement liberal interconnection policies.	Regulators need to ensure that globally competitive companies have the opportunity to construct the GII.	Governments can play a role in ensuring that investment is made in a common national information infrastructure.
Standards measures	The market is moving too fast for *de jure* standards formation. *De facto* standards will emerge and address user needs.	Carefully thought out *de jure* standards in some areas are needed for an integrated and interoperable user environment. In other areas, market competition and market led standards should prevail.	The standards that are needed will be chosen by the user community from a mix of public and private solutions. Standards will 'self-organise' as critical mass of user interest is achieved.
Intellectual property rights (IPR)	A high level of IPR protection in software and multimedia content is essential for the construction of the GII.	IPR protection is necessary for the creation of commercially viable services.	IPR is only one means of stimulating diversity in the availability of services and multimedia content. IPR protection should not limit access; new mechanisms for charging are essential.
Securing electronic networks	Security is an ongoing problem that must be addressed to boost the potential commercialisation of innovative services like electronic commerce.	Existing networks are adequately secure and legislation is sufficient to maintain this security.	Security is needed to create incentives for some new services. Security concerns should not infringe networks as 'open public spaces'.
Social communities and privacy	Concerns about individual privacy, independent of security issues, are unnecessary and will stand in the way of rapid commercialisation of new services.	Suppliers should be indemnified from liability for inadvertent breaches of privacy.	Privacy is a matter of individual choice and should be governed by the cultural and social norms evolving within the NII/GII community.

Source: Modified from Mansell and Steinmueller (1996a).

doing nothing often precludes learning. Most people, and most organizations, learn from their mistakes (Howkins and Valantin 1997: 25-26).

Section 9.2 looks at the types of international and regional institutions that are playing a role in the restructuring of governance for the ICT sector. Section 9.3 turns to the global information infrastructure visions that are spawning initiatives to liberalise markets and invest in infrastructure and services in developing countries. The impact of changes in the ICT governance system on the least developed countries is discussed in section 9.4, followed by a consideration of the tensions involved in strategies to open markets while, at the same time, retaining some control over developments in national or regional markets. The final section (9.5), assesses the likelihood

that the governance system will promote greater equity in the emergent economic and social orders.

9.2 INSTITUTIONS GOVERNING ICTs

In today's international governance system any country that tries to strengthen its national information infrastructure must do so in close interdependence with the global environment. The representatives of governments and the private sectors of developing countries are finding it necessary to negotiate with an increasingly wide range of influential international institutions. These institutions influence ICT investment and producer and user capabilities. They include private and public banks, regional satellite services supply bodies, international regulatory agencies, private sector associations, and a multitude of others. They can make it easier or more difficult for a given country to pursue its national goals by providing or withholding resources.

It has become much more important for decision-makers to be familiar with international regulations and standardisation and other issues that are under discussion in older and newer fora. This section highlights the main responsibilities of several key international institutions beginning with those established early in the history of innovations in communication and information technologies. Early international governance in the ICT sector was provided by the International Telecommunication Union for the infrastructure networks, and by the conventions and agreements for trademarks and the protection of intellectual works (including literary, musical, dramatic, pictorial, photographic, and cinematographic works) were administered by WIPO.

International Telecommunication Union (ITU)

The ITU was founded in 1865 to address the growing need for the international coordination of telegraphy and it became a United Nations specialised agency in 1947 (Codding and Rutkowski 1982). It is now split into three sectors which address specific issues in radiocommunications, standardisation, and development.

The radiocommunications sector ensures the efficient use of the radio frequency spectrum by all services including those using geostationary satellite orbits. It concentrates on spectrum utilisation and monitoring, interservice sharing and compatibility, scientific services, radio wave propagation, fixed satellite services, fixed terrestrial services, mobile services, sound broadcasting, and television broadcasting. The standardisation sector issues recommendations concerning all aspects of telecommunication standards. It concentrates on services and network operation, tariffs and accounting principles, maintenance, protection of outside plant, data communication, terminals for advanced information services, switching, signalling, and human-machine languages, as well as transmission performance, systems, and equipment.

The goal of the development sector is to assist developing countries to advance their telecommunication services to a level approaching that of the industrialised countries. This sector seeks to raise the level of awareness of decision-makers concerning the important role of telecommunication in national economic and social development programmes, and to provide information and advice on policy and structural options. It aims to promote the development, expansion, and operation of telecommunication networks and services; enhance the growth of telecommunication through cooperation with regional telecommunication organisations and global and regional development financing institutions.

This sector helps to mobilise resources to provide tele-communication networks by promoting the establishment of preferential and favourable lines of credit, and cooperating with international and regional financial and development institutions. It promotes and coordinates programmes to accelerate the transfer of appropriate technologies to the developing countries in the light of developments in the networks of the industrialised countries. It encourages participation by industry in the telecommunication sector in developing countries, and advises on the choice and transfer of technology. It offers advice, and carries out or sponsors studies on technical, economic, financial, managerial, regulatory, and policy issues, including studies of specific projects in the field of telecommunication.

World Intellectual Property Organization (WIPO)

WIPO was established in 1967 in Stockholm and became a specialised agency of the United Nations, based in Geneva in 1974 (Monroe et al. 1995). WIPO administers international conventions for the protection of trademarks and copyrights and offers assistance to countries in formulating intellectual property protection. Membership includes signatories to conventions. In the trademarks area there is the Paris Convention for the Protection of Industrial Property of 1883 and the Madrid Agreement Concerning the International Registration of Trademarks of 1981 supplemented in 1989. In the field of copyright there is the Berne Convention Concerning the Creation of an International Union for the Protection of Literary and Artistic Works of 1886 with a series of treaties and amendments up to 1997. Other conventions cover music and broadcasting from 1961 and 1971. There is also a Universal Copyright Convention signed in 1952 which is administered by the United Nations Educational, Scientific, and Cultural Organisation (UNESCO) to provide protection under national laws, for example, the United States did not sign the Berne Convention until 1989. Copyright protects a particular form or expression of an idea rather than the idea itself and is a central mechanism for the governance of access to electronic information by developing countries (issues relating to copyrights are discussed in detail in Chapter 10).

The end of World War II gave rise to the institution of the United Nations System, the World Bank Group, and the Organisation for Economic Cooperation and Development (OECD).

The United Nations system

The agencies of the United Nations system also are actively promoting applications of ICTs in key sectors. The goals are to enhance the capacity of developing countries to meet their basic needs, develop indigenous capabilities, and strengthen their position in the rapidly changing global environment (UNCTAD 1997). Activities are unevenly spread across the agencies. Various agencies are providing advisory services and contributions to national capacity-building which help to support efforts to strengthen national information infrastructures (NII). United Nations agencies are active in ICT policy formulation providing expertise to interested countries or interested parties within countries. As an international body with analytical capacity, the United Nations is in a unique position to identify the policy, institutional, legal, and regulatory governance issues that need to be addressed if developing countries are to create national information infrastructures. Various activities are facilitating access to the GII by establishing networks that can allow users to access information, clients, and resources world-wide.

These activities include (UNCTAD 1997):

▪ Research, mainly on ICTs and development, the ICT revolution, the social and economic impact of ICTs, and the new applications in relation to the specialised areas of competence within the United Nations system.

▪ The application of ICTs in developing countries at national, regional, and community levels often linked to United Nations-sponsored Technical Cooperation Programmes.

▪ Local capacity-building, mainly in terms of upgrading infrastructure, for example, supporting telecommunication upgrading programmes in low-income countries, and facilitating access to ICTs.

▪ Software development focusing on the needs of developing countries.

▪ Facilitating connectivity to global networking.

▪ Creating databases for use by developing countries or the United Nations organisations themselves in planning development programmes.

The United Nations Development Programme (UNDP) sees the information and knowledge revolution as 'a unique opportunity to position itself as an agent of change and leapfrog itself in the process' (d'Orville 1996: 46). ICTs are treated as generic technologies which, together with biotechnology and new materials, are enabling radical changes in techniques and systems of production and distribution. UNDP is developing a four-pronged strategy for the systematic development of communication systems based on innovation, transfer, policy reform, and finance.

The United Nations Educational, Scientific, and Cultural Organisation (UNESCO) was created in 1945 and became active in 1946 with the original purpose of advancing, 'through the educational and scientific and cultural relations of the peoples of the world, the objectives of international peace and of the common welfare of mankind for which the United Nations Organisation was established and which its Charter proclaims'. The influence of UNESCO derives from the experiences of its member states, the conferences, debates, and research, and the assistance available to member states in capacity-building

in the areas of communication, information, and informatics. For developing countries, UNESCO also provides some training and develops arguments concerning cultural rights, 'the right to communicate', and other positions many developing countries support. UNESCO has been emphasising the need for action to address legal and ethical issues in the ICT area, the need for incentives and subsidies to promote services, the problems of maintaining a public domain for information and improving public access, the necessary development of flexible, modular and scalable network designs for developing countries, and the importance of training, research, and cooperation (UNESCO 1996, ITU/UNESCO 1995).

The International Bank for Reconstruction and Development (IBRD), The World Bank Group

The Bank was founded in 1945 to provide low-cost loans to European governments to help them reconstruct their severely damaged economies after World War II. The focus has shifted to promoting development and economic reforms in Africa, Asia, Latin America, and the Caribbean. Associated institutions include the International Monetary Fund (IMF), the International Finance Corporation (IFC), and the Multilateral Insurance Guarantee Association (MIGA). The World Bank provides a variety of resources and services to the ICT sectors of developing countries, including loans, expert advice, and access to its new Information for Development Program (infoDEV). In return for its loans and services, the Bank negotiates economic and institutional conditions that must be met by the borrowing government.

The Bank has been pursuing four objectives for the GII including: widespread and equitable access to communication and information services through accelerated deployment of NIIs and effective integration into international networks; systemic improvements in the functioning and competitiveness of key economic sectors through strategic information policies and systems; and new ways to use ICTs to help resolve the most pressing problems of human and economic development - education, health, poverty alleviation, rural development, and care of the environment.

The World Bank and the ITU, for example, are sponsoring initiatives to ease the transition by developing, and especially the least developed, countries towards innovative 'knowledge societies'. Closely associated with the ITU is WorldTel, an entity designed to raise private sector financing for telecommunication investment (Cane 1997b).[2] Its mission is to encourage the spread of telecommunication services in countries with a telephone density of less than 1 per cent or a telephone service waiting time of more than five years. WorldTel is able to draw on ITU expertise but has to pay for these services. Projects will be implemented on the basis of build-own-operate or build-operate-transfer schemes. The design and preparation of projects is underway following an initial subscription of US$ 50 million, far short of the billions needed to meet its objectives.

The World Bank is developing a knowledge brokering service by using its resources to analyse clients' needs and to tap expertise world-wide. Knowledge brokering is central to building new capabilities within developing countries. The Bank aims to become a long term partner and facilitator for countries adjusting to the need to build knowledge networks and is developing strategic alliances to mobilise knowledge and financing (Talero and Gaudette 1995). The Bank argues that the GII is very real, that market economies are prevailing world-wide and firms are competing on the basis of knowledge, networking, and agility. The result is the reorganisation of society, new social and cultural agenda, new market dynamics and an urgent need to incorporate ICTs into any development programme.

In 1995 the Bank announced the Information and Development Programme (infoDev). This initiative concentrates on mobilising partnerships among private, bilateral, multilateral, NGO and other actors to support activities that are more innovative than traditional bilateral or Bank projects. InfoDev provides money for telecommunications reform, information infrastructure strategies (including national assessments), consensus-building activities, and demonstration projects (World Bank 1996). The Bank defines its role as an honest broker, helping to define the needs of developing countries and matching them with the appropriate resources. The roles expected of governments are suggested in Box 9.1.

Organisation for Economic Cooperation and Development (OECD)

Established in 1961, the OECD originated in the Organisation for European Economic Cooperation (OEEC) that was set up in 1948 to administer Marshall Plan funding in Europe. The OECD's goals are to achieve the highest sustainable economic growth and employment and a rising standard of living in member countries, while maintaining financial stability and thus contributing to the development of the world economy. It aims to assist sound economic expansion in member, as well as non-member, countries in the process of economic development, and support the expansion of world trade on a multilateral, non-discriminatory basis in accordance with international obligations.

The greatest challenge is for the developing countries themselves to understand at the highest political level the benefits that communication infrastructures can provide them and put forward the appropriate framework to facilitate this (OECD 1997a: 84).

The OECD's influence lies mainly in its research and

BOX 9.1 - WHAT SHOULD GOVERNMENTS DO?

Government action is necessary:
As a policy-maker
As a major user of information technology
To compensate for market failures

Governments can:
Improve their own efficiency
Set fair rules of the game
Catalyse infrastructure projects
Push the education agenda
Jump-start the private sector

Source: Extracted from Talero and Gaudette (1995).

statistical analysis, its reputation for superior technical and analytical work and its track record in helping member countries reach consensus on difficult issues. The committees and working groups formed by the OECD monitor developments and policy ideas in their area of interest and accumulate an immense volume of statistics and reports. The groups then pass these data to the Secretariat which processes, compares, and analyses them, and formulates forecasts and policy suggestions. The Science, Technology, and Industry Directorate concentrates on ICT issues through its Information, Computer, and Communications Policy (ICCP) Committee. In addition to specific studies of information technology, telecommunication, and related legal and standardisation questions, the ICCP also addresses issues of technology and policy convergence, diffusion, and impact on the economy and society. The ICCP has working groups and committees centring on telecommunication policies, the economics of the information society, high-performance computing and networking, security, privacy, cryptography, and intellectual property rights, standards, regulation, convergence, and pricing (OECD 1977b,c).

The deployment of satellite technologies in communication networks brought the need for several new international organisations, including the International Telecommunication Satellite Organisation (INTELSAT) and the International Maritime Satellite Organisation (INMARSAT).

International Telecommunication Satellite Organisation (INTELSAT)

Created in 1964, the mission of INTELSAT is to establish a global commercial telecommunication satellite system and organisation. It aims to utilise the most advanced technology with the most efficient and economic facilities, and to offer telecommunication services on a non-discriminatory basis in all areas of the world. INTELSAT has a vast array of satellite services that it makes available to member countries. The two main types of services it distributes are voice/data and video.

INTELSAT resources include a wide variety of high powered satellites in geostationary orbit, earth stations owned and operated by country signatories, and other satellite technologies that allow it to effectively connect any two or more points on the globe. The Organisation's power stems from its ability to establish technical and operating standards for earth stations with which all INTELSAT users must comply.

A key question for the developing countries is whether INTELSAT will continue to be one of the most efficient low cost suppliers of services, or whether new providers will erode its international markets. As the organisation seeks to respond to its clients, it has established regional support centres providing added local geographical focus and support and increased market and business awareness. The Indian Ocean Regional Centre became operational in March 1996 in Mumbai. INTELSAT hopes to work jointly with the Indian signatory to bring services such as direct-to-home (DTH) television to the region and to assist in developing the expanding market for broadcast to cable systems. June 1996 saw the opening of a second regional centre in Singapore. This centre will help meet the exploding telecommunication needs of the Asia region. Regional centres also are to be opened in Africa to satisfy the telecommunication needs of this region.

International Maritime Satellite Organisation (INMARSAT)

INMARSAT, created in 1979, has expanded the scope of its expertise to all mobile users and now offers satellite support almost everywhere in the world, at sea, on land, and in the air.

The following regional organisations have become active contributors to the ICT governance system. Most of the regional groupings explicitly acknowledge the importance of telecommunication infrastructure investment to meet their development objectives. These organisations tend not to stress the importance of information policies to complement network development initiatives.

Latin American and Caribbean Cooperation

The Latin American Integration Association, the Central American Common Market, the Andean Group, the Southern Common Market (Mercosur), the Caribbean Common Market, and the Organisation of Eastern Caribbean States all list the communication sector as an area of mutual interest (UNCTAD 1996a). The Inter-American Social and Economic Council preceded the Inter-American Telecommunications Commission (CITEL) which was established by the General Assembly of the Organisation of American States in 1963 with the goal of using all means at its disposal to facilitate and further the development of telecommunication in the Americas for the purpose of contributing to the development of the region. It organises and sponsors periodic meetings of technicians and experts to study planning, finance, construction, standardisation, technical assistance, maintenance, and other matters related to the use and operation of telecommunication in the hemisphere. The organisation has been instrumental in establishing 'RedHUCyt' which was started in 1991 as a plan to connect member countries to the Internet to support information exchanges among professionals, researchers, and specialists. The programme responds to local initiatives and provides equipment, technical support, and specialised training, and sponsors technical workshops and seminars. Initiatives are being taken to allow regional, as well as national, access to databases (Bourdeau et al. 1996).

Asian cooperation

The Cooperation Council for the Arab States of the Gulf, the Central Asian Economic Cooperation Organisation, and trading agreements in South and South East Asia, including the Association of South East Asian Nations (ASEAN) established in 1967, and the South Pacific Forum established in 1971, all have cooperation initiatives in the ICT sector (UNCTAD 1996a). The Asia Pacific Economic Cooperation (APEC) was formed in 1989 in response to the growing interdependence among Asia Pacific economies to advance Asia Pacific economic dynamism and a sense of community. The Telecommunications Working Group (TELWG) was set up in 1990 and has been meeting regularly to work on human resource development, technology transfer, and regional cooperation, opportunities for on-site visits/observerships/fellowships, and telecommunication standardisation matters. Studies are looking at issues concerning data compilations, electronic data interchange, electronic commerce, infrastructure development, international value added networks (IVANs), and mutual recognition of telecommunication equipment test data. The APEC member countries have agreed to a Japanese proposal to develop an information infrastructure in the Asia Pacific region.

African regional organisations

Cooperation to promote national information infrastructure development culminated in May 1996 with a document representing an ambitious new regional effort in the form of the Economic Commission for Africa's (ECA) Africa Information Society Initiative (AISI). Prepared by a High Level Working Group on Information and Communication Technologies and approved at a ministerial meeting of the ECA, this document provides a planning and implementation framework for African governments. Implementation of the document was the subject of a meeting in Ethiopia in October 1996. The Pan African Information Development System (PADIS) has sponsored conferences, training sessions, and other activities on applying computer/information resources to Africa's development challenges. Its successes demonstrate the importance of the promotional elements of policy at the early stages of these technological changes. The PanAfrican News Agency (PANA), the Pan African Telecommunication Union (PATU), the Regional African Satellite Communications Organisation (RASCOM), and the Union des Radiodiffusions et Télévisions Nationales d'Afrique (URTNA) are also active in promoting infrastructure and service development.

Other regional groupings that are targeting telecommunication development and the information industries include the Arab Maghreb Union, the Economic Community of West African States, the West African Economic Community, the Mano River Union, the Economic Community of Central African States, the Central African Customs and Economic Union, the Preferential Trade Area for Eastern and Southern Africa, and the Southern African Development Community (UNCTAD 1996a).

From the mid-1970s stakeholder organisations with social, political, and economic interests in the expansion of global markets for communication equipment and services began to emerge on the world scene.

The International Telecommunication Users Group (INTUG) was founded in 1974 as an international association linking large, multinational companies that were heavy users of telecommunication services. These companies joined forces to discuss how they might reduce their telecommunication costs as they promoted the introduction of competition within the United States domestic market and began to see the advantages of world-wide market liberalisation. INTUG promotes its users' interests at the international level and ensures that the voice of the business user is clearly heard in national and international policy discussions in fora such as the ITU and other regional groups.

In 1977, the *Institute for International Communications (IIC)* (initially the International Broadcast Institute created in 1968) was set up as a meeting place for Chief Executive Officers of broadcasting organisations to review the impact of new technologies. Today the organisation hosts conferences and workshops on issues in the telecommunication and broadcast sectors fostering debate across the ICT industries and across countries. This Institute also has a small academic membership.

The *International Association for Media and Communication Research (IAMCR)*[3] was founded in 1957 and is an NGO with formal consultative relations with UNESCO. With some 1,500 individual and institutional members around the world, IAMCR members have played an active role in 'free flow of information' debates, and human rights issues, and have produced numerous studies on the social and economic impact of ICTs from a variety of social science and policy perspectives and especially on the implications of ICTs for developing countries.

The *Association for Progressive Communications* (APC) grew out of an earlier organisation, the Institute for Global Communications, founded in 1986, created to serve non-governmental organisations and citizen activists working for social justice, environmental sustainability, and related issues. Composed of a consortium of 21 international member networks, APC today provides communication and information-sharing tools to its members. It offers communication links to over 40,000 NGOs, activists, educators, policy-makers, and community leaders in 133 countries. APC works closely with the Institute for Global Communications which has organisational members including PeaceNet, EcoNet, LaborNet, WomensNet, and ConflictNet.

Various *Standards Development Organisations* (SDOs) including the ITU but extending to largely private standards institutions are influencing what technical standards manufacturers will employ. These include the International Organisation for Standardization (ISO), and the International Electrotechnical Commission (IEC) as well as a large number of consortia emerging around new technical designs and configurations. Some of these have the potential for major international impact, while others concentrate more on national or regional markets. For example, the situation of Asian actors with respect to standards consortia is especially intriguing. Even though Japanese and Korean (Rep. of) firms are key players in many areas of advanced digital applications (particularly in semi-conductors and consumer electronics), as yet no consortium or SDO based in Asia has assumed independent international significance (Hawkins et al. 1995, 1997; Mizumoto 1997).

By the mid-1990s, major changes in network architectures and protocols had enabled Internet accesses to take-off both inside and outside the United States. New forms of governance in this area are emerging. These include *The Internet Society (ISOC)*, announced at an international networking conference in Copenhagen in June 1991. This is a non-governmental organisation for global cooperation and coordination of the Internet and its interworking technologies and applications. It came into being in January 1992 with the goal of facilitating and guiding the evolution and globalisation of the Internet and its technologies and applications. The Society seeks to enhance the availability and use of these technologies on the widest possible scale. The *Internet Assignment Number Authority (IANA)* acts as a clearinghouse to assign and coordinate the use of numerous Internet protocol parameters. There is no consensus among the Internet community on how the governance structure will evolve for the 'domain name system' (DNS).[4] Domain name registrars have monopolies based on their administration of national or generic top level names. They are currently unregulated which impacts on the costs of access to the Internet for industrialised and, more especially, for developing countries (OECD 1997d). Monopoly pricing and infringement of trademarks issues are being considered in the context of whether a new international regime is needed. Developments within this governance regime will have enormous implications for electronic commerce and other aspects of the GII.

With respect to international trade, major changes on the international governance scene have been very visible with the establishment of the *World Trade Organization*.

World Trade Organization (WTO)

The WTO, created in January 1995, built on the foundations of the General Agreement on Tariffs and Trade (GATT) which was established and took effect in 1948. Although the GATT has been in existence for many years the setting up of a formal institution represents the emergence of new processes of governance and new opportunities for negotiation by developing countries. The objectives of the WTO are to raise standards of living, ensure full employment, and encourage growth of real income and effective demand. In order to achieve this, it seeks expansion in production and trade in goods and service. The WTO also recognises the need for positive efforts to ensure that developing countries gain a share in international trade that is commensurate with their economic development. By late 1996, 123 governments had accepted the Marrakech Agreement establishing the WTO, and 31 others had applied for membership.

The power of the WTO derives from its members' agreement to cooperate in solving trade problems and negotiate binding, trade-liberalising agreements. All members have agreed that the WTO is the international, legal, and institutional foundation of the multilateral trading system. It provides the general obligations determining how governments frame and implement domestic trade legislation and regulations. It also provides the foundation for trade relations among countries to evolve through collective debate, negotiation, and adjudication.

The key issues of the WTO are ensuring trade without discrimination, establishing predictable and growing access to markets, promoting fair competition, and encouraging development and economic reform. The WTO is active in the protection of intellectual property rights and the opening up of national telecommunication markets. The WTO agreement on Trade-Related Aspects of Intellectual Property Rights (TRIPS) is a response to global inconsistency in the protection of property rights and the increase of international trade in counterfeit goods. The agreement is concerned with provision of adequate intellectual property protection, effective enforcement measures for those rights, a multilateral dispute settlement mechanism, and transitional implementation arrangements, particularly for developing

countries (see Chapter 10). The key issues in the trade-in-services sector reflect the general goals of the organisation as well as specific barriers to the successful completion of the liberalisation of markets.

Over 90 of the WTO members are developing countries or countries with economies in transition. Because of this large membership, and their increasingly important roles, the needs and problems of developing countries are receiving attention. For example, missions and seminars to address issues such as effective participation in multilateral negotiations and dispute settlements, are conducted in developing countries. The WTO also provides developing countries with trade and tariff data relating to their individual export issues.

Consistent with the formation of the WTO and a move to a more market-oriented system of governance for the ICT sector as a whole, another stakeholder institution in the GII vision was created in 1995. The *Global Information Infrastructure Commission (GIIC)* was established with a base in the United States to strengthen the leadership role of the private sector in the development of a diverse, affordable, and accessible information infrastructure. It also has a remit to promote greater involvement of developing countries in building and utilising a truly global and open information infrastructure. The GIIC facilitates activities and identifies policy options that are intended to foster effective applications of telecommunication, broadcasting, and information technologies and services.

The Commissioners are Chief Executive Officers from leading information and telecommunication companies, and several senior government officials are drawn from the relevant sectors. The GIIC is a private, independent, non-governmental organisation with a three-year mandate, involving leaders from developing as well as industrialised countries. With representatives of countries like Brazil, Indonesia, India, Russia, and Senegal, and with formal participation from senior officials of the World Bank, the GIIC concentrates much of its attention on the developing world. However, rather than focusing on issues only or mainly relevant to developing countries, the Commission addresses key issues of the GII such as electronic commerce, market access, intellectual property rights, and financing from the perspective of the mutual interests of these countries and the industrialised countries (GIIC 1994, 1997).

This brief overview of influential international and regional institutions in the ICT sector illustrates that they are numerous and that they are concerned with the way the ICT infrastructures, and services emerge in national, regional, and international markets. The purposes, effectiveness, responsibilities, resources, competencies, and interrelationships of these international organisations are changing substantially and quickly. This presents daunting challenges to developing countries and especially the least developed countries. New organisations are emerging (especially in the Internet and standards areas), existing ones are changing their missions, some are being rejuvenated, and others are losing relevance and power in ways that may disadvantage certain developing countries. The international governance system for ICTs is moving away from being highly centralised, monopolistic, and state controlled, to being much more decentralised, heterogeneous, independent, and distributed.

At the same time, it is becoming much more important for decision-makers to be familiar with these international regimes and their impact on national and regional developments. These institutions have control over valuable and scarce resources that developing countries can use to design their national information infrastructures. They are important fora where the new 'rules of the game' are being debated and decided by powerful states. They are also sources of influential ideas and proposals that other world actors take very seriously (Wilson 1996a).

Governments, development banks, trade organisations, equipment vendors, and the public all have to reconcile opposing tendencies in the emerging international ICT governance regime. State-led approaches are inconsistent with dominant trends in the global economy. Current trends are toward the introduction of effective national policies and international cooperation to achieve a balance among development, equity, and environment objectives (UNCSTD 1997c). As a result of economic liberalisation and the acceleration of forces of 'globalisation' following the demise of 'East-West' tensions and the opening up of many developing countries, there is a drive to liberalise and open markets to build national information infrastructures. However, there is also a desire to maintain a degree of control over the way in which the people in developing countries will interact with the GII.

The increased diffusion of ICTs is altering systems of production and work organisation affecting employment and international competitiveness which is having major implications for international investment and trade in goods and services for developing countries. New forms of partnership represent emergent governance systems and an opportunity to find 'new forms of technology cooperation which involve two-way relationships, and determined endeavours to share technological knowledge, and to collaborate on R&D, training, manufacturing and marketing' (UNCSTD 1997c: 19; UNCTAD 1995c, 1996b). The next sections examine the visions and the realities of the evolving international ICT governance system with respect to the infrastructure and trade in information technologies.

9.3 GLOBAL INFORMATION INFRASTRUCTURE VISIONS

Concepts of an 'information age' or an 'information economy' that gained in popularity between the 1960s and the 1980s, rarely went beyond sketchy designs and vague action plans. They were addressed mainly to the most industrialised countries. New, bold metaphors emerged in the early 1990s, such as Singapore's Intelligent Island, the Smart Philippines, Malaysia's Multimedia Corridor, Europe's Information Society, the Information Superhighways, and more recently the global information infrastructure (GII). It is not only these metaphors that are bringing about rapid change, it is the high-profile political commitments that are now strongly promoting GII and NII projects around the world.[5] The predominant GII vision was first articulated by the United States but the idea has captured the imagination of people in many other countries. Its construction is being accompanied by the introduction of new governance measures. In the trade and regulatory areas the new measures are intended to prise open national markets. The impact on the strategies and plans of the least developed countries and smaller developing countries cannot yet be measured. Nevertheless, the cost of adjustment to a much more open, liberalised world trading regime will be significant. A major question is whether these countries will secure the benefits of market liberalisation and attract investors to build their national information infrastructures to link with the GII.

The GII is a combination of physical infrastructure and applications of all sorts that flow over high speed communication networks capable of 'seamless delivery of content'. Massive financial investments, a conducive policy/regulatory environment, a trained and available workforce, and a high degree of international cooperation are fundamental to advancing the GII. Since the GII embodies both computers and communication, some countries and companies refer to the Global Information and Communication Infrastructure (GICI). Although 'globalisation' is the hallmark of the new era, eventual realisation of the GII is contingent on most countries implementing ambitious NII programmes.

Infrastructure upgrading and 'build-out' as well as measures to maximise utilisation and reduce bottlenecks in service delivery, are receiving the highest priority in national and regional initiatives for achieving the GII. Essential elements involve fully interactive, non-discriminatory access to services within countries and across borders via voice, data, video, and multimedia. In order for information systems and networks to be sufficiently reliable to be able to maximise their applications, a 'cyber age' governance regime must be in place to cover financial transactions, legal contracts, intellectual property rights, security of commercial information, and information privacy.

The crucial new dimension that undergirds the GII is its wide endorsement and promotion by heads of state and major international organisations. One of the earliest pronouncements on the GII was made by United States Vice-President Al Gore at the International Telecommunication Union development conference in Buenos

Aires in 1994. President Bill Clinton suggested that the G-7 countries should organise an event around this theme. In February 1995, the G-7 organised a ministerial conference on the information society in Brussels, under the aegis of the European Union. The APEC (Asia Pacific Economic Cooperation) regional group also organised a ministerial event on the information infrastructure in Seoul, Korea (Rep. of), later that year (Donovan 1995, 1996a,b). In 'the Americas', the Organisation of American States and other regional groups were considering the importance of GII for their development (Bourdeau et al. 1996).[6]

During the incubation period of the information society's development (1960-1990), the responsibility for most initiatives fell to officials in technical divisions or bureaux, but they had little authority for policy, political power, or influence. A dramatic transition occurred in 1994. Although the European Commission had been carrying out reforms to the telecommunication and information services sector for two decades, this had attracted little notice from the Council of Ministers or heads of state. The reform programmes were re-titled and integrated within a European Information Society (EIS) Action Plan. The Commission's 5th Framework Programme in 1999 will include funding to enhance a 'user-friendly information society'. Quite independently, countries and entities as diverse as the United States, Singapore, the European Union, and Japan have been preparing complementary GII/NII Action Plans.

■ The *United States* sees the NII as a seamless web of communication networks, computers, databases, and consumer electronics to put vast amounts of information at users' fingertips. The NII encompasses equipment such as cameras, scanners, keyboards, telephones, fax machines, computer disks, video and audio tape, optical fibre transmission, microwave sets, televisions, monitors, and printers. The goal of the NII is to link homes, businesses, schools, hospitals, and libraries both to each other and a vast array of electronic inform-ation resources. Growth and productivity with the deployment of NII is estimated to be US$ 300 billion by 2007, an increase of between 20-40 per cent (Cohen 1996a,b).

■ The *European Union (EU)* endorsed a report prepared under the direction of Commissioner Martin Bangemann in 1994 calling for a shift in political direc-tion of the Union financing of infrastructure to the private sector (European Commission 1994). It empha-sised the benefits of liberalising national telecommuni-cation policies and market structures, building an information and multimedia market, giving high priority to intellectual property rights, privacy, legal, and security protection of networks, and media rules to protect plural-ism and competition for the information sector. Further initiatives included the establishment of the European Information Society Forum and publication

by the Social Affairs Directorate (DGV) of a report entitled 'Building the Information Society for Us All' (European Commission 1996d). DGXIII, responsible for telecommunications, the information market, and the exploitation of research, has initiated a large number of trials and demonstration projects within programmes aimed at strengthening European R&D and the involvement of citizens and businesses in the European Information Society (European Commission 1996e; Mansell and Steinmueller 1996a; Bernard et al. 1997).

■ *Japan* has embarked on a Fibre Optic Info-Communication Network connecting every business and household for an Intellectually Creative Society to meet social and economic restructuring in the 21st century. This involves development and introduction of applications in public education, medical care and welfare services, informatising public works, and supporting pilot projects. A shift of perspectives from the goods- and energy-dominated 20th century to intel-lectual creativity based on high-performance info-communications is expected. The government is review-ing restrictions on the interconnection of networks, separate regulations for the telecommunication and broadcasting sectors, and new approaches to universal service and tariffing systems.

■ In *Singapore* the government's IT2000 master plan was adopted in 1991 to transform the nation into an Intelligent Island. The vision called for the creation of an NII that would facilitate information flows within the country and connect Singapore to the rest of the world. The National Computer Board (NCB) is pursuing strategies to make Singapore a global hub for goods, services, capital, information, and people, to generate greater productivity and new business opportunities, to enhance the potential of individuals, to link commu-nities locally and globally, and to improve the quality of life of its citizens.

Since 1994, heads of state from G-7, APEC, EU and OECD countries have been known to discuss such 'techno-policy' issues as interconnection, universal services, gateways, and local loops, and number transport-ability! By the middle of the decade, the GII had become a cornerstone for economic and social development and it is becoming a central element of trade policy. Senior government officials have recognised the importance of the GII to their countries. They are giving higher priority to telecommunication and information technologies, more funds are being directed to applications such as education and medicine, and national initiatives are being pushed at the international level. The World Bank has aggressively promoted telecommunication liberalisa-tion and the privatisation of national operators. The influ-ence of the World Bank in developing countries, recently reinforced by the International Telecommunication

Union, is stimulating governments to reform their markets. GII/NII initiatives have become much more universal in a shorter period of time than almost any movement in memory (European Commission 1997b).

9.4 A DECADE OF TALKS ON TRADE AND GOVERNANCE

The political capital invested by countries to ensure the success of a WTO agreement on basic telecommunication services is a testimonial to the high priority being given to accelerating the GII. Although the GATT has provided a legal international framework for reducing tariffs and promoting trade in goods since the end of World War II, services - including telecommunications - were put on the table only in 1985. The completion of the Uruguay Round talks led to the creation of the WTO, the conclusion of a General Agreement on Trade in Services,[7] a telecommunication annex to the services agreement,[8] and a commitment to negotiate new arrangements for trade in basic telecommunication services. The basic telecommunication services talks commenced in 1994 with thirty 'key' countries and concluded in February 1997 with participation of just over seventy countries.

The agreement on basic telecommunication services not only provides for liberalisation of market access beginning in January 1998, but also substantially opens markets for foreign investment and contains binding regulatory principles. The negotiations covered services involving end-to-end transmission of customer supplied information over public network infrastructures, and using private leased circuits. The commitments of nearly seventy countries, including over forty developing countries and six of the central and eastern European countries, will be phased-in over varying periods of time (WTO 1997b).[9]

Five of the participants in these negotiations, the European Union, the United States, Japan, Canada, and Australia, had leading shares of world telecommunication revenues accounting for 77 per cent of the market in 1995 (WTO 1997c). The European Union, the United States, and Japan were ranked as the world's largest telecommunication markets in terms of global shares by all main indicators except outgoing international traffic (where Japan ranked sixth behind Canada, Switzerland, and Hong Kong). For all of the main indicators (see Table 9.2), the combined shares of the European Union, the United States, and Japan, in 1995 represented well over half of the world total.

Although most of the developing countries participating in the negotiations accounted for lower shares of global telecommunication activity in 1995 than did the United States, the European Union, or Japan, they were still significant players. See the appendix to this chapter for the revenues of participating countries and territories and the commitments they have made to creating new opportunities for market access. Korea (Rep. of), Brazil, Mexico, and Argentina were in the top ten by share of

global revenue. Hong Kong was ranked fifth as a source of international telephone traffic, while Mexico and Singapore were among the top ten. Korea (Rep. of) was fourth in terms of telecommunication investment, with Argentina and India among the top ten. For numbers of telephone main lines, Korea (Rep. of) was in the top five and Turkey, Brazil, India, and Mexico were among the top ten.[10]

TABLE 9.2 - SHARE OF WORLD TELECOMMUNICATION, 1995 TOTALS AS PERCENTAGES

	EU	US	Japan	Total
Revenue	28.3	29.7	15.6	73.6
Main lines	26.1	23.8	8.8	58.7
Investment	27.1	15.6	22.0	64.6
International traffic	35.2	25.3	2.7	63.2

Source: WTO (1997c)

Announcing the agreement on basic telecommunication services, the Director General of WTO noted that market liberalisation could mean global income gains of US$ 1 trillion over the next few decades.

Perhaps most importantly of all from a longer-term perspective, this deal goes well beyond trade and economics. It makes access to knowledge easier. It gives nations large and small, rich and poor, better opportunities to prepare for the challenges of the 21st century. Information and knowledge, after all, are the raw material of growth and development in our globalised world (WTO 1997a: 1).

This is not the only major trade agreement to set the parameters for a new international governance regime. A Ministerial Declaration on Trade in Information Technology Products was signed in December 1996 in Singapore by 28 Governments. The Information Technology Agreement (ITA) provides for the elimination of customs duties and other charges on information technology products through equal annual reductions beginning in July 1997 and concluding in January 2000. The implementation of the agreement required that other countries sign up so that draft schedules could be reviewed at the end of March 1997. The goal was to achieve commitments representing 90 per cent of world trade in information technologies and this goal was met. Countries and territories submitting schedules for tariff reduction by March included Canada, Costa Rica, Estonia, the European Union countries, Hong Kong, Iceland, India, Indonesia, Japan, Korea (Rep. of), Macau, Malaysia, Norway, Romania, Singapore, Switzerland, Thailand, and the United States, Australia, New Zealand, Turkey, Taiwan (Pr. China), and Israel are expected to join.

Although some developing countries are included, many more are not. The impact of this agreement on the least developed countries will be important and they will need to work out how it will affect their initiatives to develop new capabilities in the information technology sector. The relatively rapid preparation and acceptance of the ITA which commits countries to zero tariffs for computers and component imports is an example of the breadth and scope of changes in the international governance regime.[11] The major producers of information technology (hardware and software) and telecommunication technology and services, are moving rapidly to restructure the rules of the game in the global market (WTO 1997a; Dunne 1997).

These two governance instruments promoting trade in information technology products and communication services demonstrate the fullness of commitment to rapidly advancing the GII. The rate at which the GII is constructed depends on the liberalisation of regulatory regimes but it also depends on the capacity of countries to put new rules in place. Deliberate efforts are underway in many developing countries to stimulate private sector innovation and investment. These WTO measures address only some of the measures needed to stimulate their participation in emergent 'knowledge societies'. The diffusion and effective use of ICT applications will be the true indicators of national transformations. At present, there are many bold action pledges, but some of the G-7 pilot projects are said to be under-powered and behind schedule and this may also be the case for similar clusters of APEC and other regional projects. However, with a favourable global economy, a more relaxed international political climate, and uninterrupted leadership at national levels, there is room for optimism for some countries. These changes in the governance system and in the international market for ICTs are giving rise to very substantial challenges for the least developed countries and many smaller developing countries including small island states.

9.5 INTERNATIONAL GOVERNANCE FOR ICTs AND THE LEAST DEVELOPED COUNTRIES

There are two keys to the ability of any country to exploit the potential of ICTs for economic and social development. The first is the availability of a network infrastructure which is essential for the provision of applications. The second is the capability to create and administer an enabling environment and to develop the applications that exploit the infrastructure in ways that are consistent with needs in the local environment. The WTO agreement on basic telecommunication services commits countries to privatise their national public telecommunication operators and to introduce competition in the provision of all services.

Only 13 developing countries that made commitments are represented among the 'top 40' measured in terms of international telecommunication revenues. Table 9.3 shows that there are very great differences among these large operators in terms of their dependence on international

revenues as a proportion of their total revenues, their overall profitability and relative efficiency (revenue per employee). Many of the least developed countries and smaller developing countries are even more dependent upon international service revenues.

As the experience of a country like India suggests, the positive gains expected from liberalisation of the domestic market take time to materialise. For example, in February 1997, Siemens announced that it would terminate some of its telecommunication manufacturing facilities in India because of losses, and the failure of an expansion of telecommunication demand to materialise (Tassell 1997). The company claimed that the increase in telephone lines over the preceding 18 months had been well below target.

The implications of privatisation and market liberalisation for the least developed countries, many of which have not joined the WTO agreement, for inward investment, and the construction of their NIIs, are considerable. These countries are being advised to adopt the same policies as the wealthier countries for three main reasons:

▪ liberalisation and privatisation have been successful elsewhere although most of the evidence is from advanced countries with long established universal services;

▪ investment in telecommunication networks enables greater use of ICTs in support of competitive economic activities;

▪ national monopoly operators normally perform very poorly and this provides a strong incentive for major changes in their ownership and operation.

The issue for the least developed countries is how they can attract both competence and investors at the same time as they achieve some movement toward universal service provision. The major world telecommunication companies are likely to concentrate on their home markets and on opportunities in countries covered by the WTO agreement. The less experienced companies are likely to be the ones investing in the least developed countries. The terms and conditions that will be attractive to them may not be the same as in countries covered by the WTO agreement.

The cost of new technologies, such as wireless in the local loop, is likely to be higher in the least developed than in other developing countries. Alternative ways of providing services in the individual circumstances of these countries need to be devised. The challenge of defining policy and regulatory arrangements that respond to the needs of these countries is great. Hiring external professionals who have built up experience in countries facing similar circumstances and pressures is as important as acquiring the managerial and commercial competence that may be provided by external investors. The models for the least developed countries will need to be adapted from those adopted by countries that have joined the WTO agree-

TABLE 9.3 – PROFILES OF TELECOMMUNICATION OPERATORS IN WORLD TOP 40 BY INTERNATIONAL TELECOMMUNICATION REVENUES, 1995

Rank in top 40 by internat. telecom revenue 1995	Company	Internat. telecom revenues US$ million 1995	% change in international communication revenues in local currency 1994-95	Internat. revenues as % of total revenues	Profit before tax US$ million 1995	Profit as % of total revenues	Revenue per employee	State-owned %
11	Telmex Mexico	1,452	24	27	1,471	27	110,480	0
15	Singapore Telecom	1,287	9	45	1,394	49	270,798	82
17	DGT Taiwan	1,061	19	18	1,467	25	162,979	100
21	Embratel Brazil	771	-5	53	231	16	121,921	100
22	China Telecom	740	57	7	n.a.	n.a.	16,431	100
24	Korea Telecom	706	15	8	736	9	143,474	80
25	Telkom S. Africa	674	25	20	410	12	60,467	100
29	Telintar Argentina	641	-2	100	53	8	954,755	0
31	VSNL India	621	30	48	130	10	459,582	82
32	Rostelecom Russia	584	20	33	505	29	50,119	51
33	PLDT Philippines	575	10	60	271	28	52,017	0
36	Telekom Malaysia	449	17	22	765	37	72,021	75
37	Indosat Indonesia	422	11	92	266	58	202,655	65

Notes: With the exception of Singapore, India, South Africa and Malaysia, whose year end is 31 March, 1996, Taiwan (Pr. China), whose year end is 30 June 1996 and Argentina, year end 30 September 1996, figures are for the 1995 fiscal year. Figures are converted to US dollars at company fiscal year end. Domestic operators are excluded from the ranking.
Source: Adapted from Yankee Group estimates in *Communications Week International*, 25 November 1996.

ment. Innovative approaches to financing and negotiation of conditions for inward investors must be carefully balanced between national priorities and what is acceptable to potential investors.

Another important issue is the ability to develop applications that are meaningful for the people in the least developed countries. In education, for example, the initial focus is often on side-stepping the inadequacies of existing arrangements by experimenting with distance learning and access to external professional competence via telecommunications. Although this is helpful in demonstrating pioneering efforts, major progress cannot be made until the potential is absorbed into local education systems with extensive programmes of training and support. Resources and capabilities are also needed to evaluate technology options; for example, what software can be used, what can be adapted and what needs to be developed for the national market? An uncritical willingness to use what is available on the market, that is, mainly foreign software in English, will eventually bring innovative uses of ICTs into disrepute.

This is an example of the necessity for human resource development. Decision-makers in senior public and private positions need to be well informed about their roles in realising the potential of ICTs, staff must be trained to develop successful ICT applications, opportunities for national companies to enter new markets must be created, and the relationship between national ICT strategies and other sectors, such as education, needs to be carefully considered. The human resource development component of an ICT strategy requires oversight at government and corporate levels. Although it is desirable to have balanced representation across the many stakeholder interests in the public and private sectors, this can be very difficult to achieve.

The movement by African trade negotiators throughout the WTO negotiations over basic telecommunication services – particularly those from the Ivory Coast, Ghana, Senegal, and South Africa – offers insights into their changing perceptions of the benefits and costs of market liberalisation. At its onset, African negotiators pointed out that the proposals for market liberalisation seemed to offer questionable benefits to countries lacking a comparative advantage in telecommunications. Nevertheless, several countries that had been making domestic regulatory changes felt they were in a position to reap the benefits of liberalised global trade in telecommunication services. Over the course of the negotiations, these countries tabled national schedules identifying areas for future market access (see appendix to this chapter).

One of the most marked characteristics of these negotiations was the lack of active participation by representatives of the African states despite the role of supporting funding bodies like the World Bank's infoDev.[12] The International Telecommunication Union (1997) points to several explanations, but perhaps the most accurate is that not all countries have the American AT&T or MCI (Microwave Communications Inc.), or a BT (British Telecom) plus some 150 competitors, as in the United Kingdom, to provide evidence that market liberalisation can bring economic advantages. The indirect economic benefits of liberalisation for an African state are also not likely to be obvious. For example, international telecommunication revenues decline at the outset, new investors may be hesitant to enter the market, public telecommunication operator employment declines, and the technological support for interconnecting national networks with higher capacity networks and new sources of information is not available immediately. Nevertheless, some countries in the African community had taken steps to reform their markets before the WTO negotiations.

For example, in *Ghana* liberal economic principles were introduced, with privatisation in 1974 and significant deregulation in 1987. Other African States had also begun to liberalise their domestic markets over the past decade. The WTO agreement provided an opportunity to codify changes that have been introduced. In Ghana a duopoly structure for facilities-based suppliers of local, long distance, and international public voice telephone services and private leased circuit services is to be maintained. In order to promote universal service, additional suppliers of local services will be licensed to supply under-served population centres, but the duopoly operators will be given first refusal. The exclusivity granted to the duopoly operators will be reviewed by the regulatory body. Competition in data transmission, telex, telegraph, and fax, Internet access (excluding voice), fixed satellite, teleconferencing, trunk radio, telecommunication equipment sales, rental and mobile services, including cellular telephone, mobile data, personal communication, and paging are permitted. Ghana expects to participate in global satellite services through arrangements with licensed public telephone operators. Joint ventures with national companies are required to offer services but there is no specific foreign equity limit.

The *Ivory Coast* was one of the first African states to table an offer to the WTO. Voice telephone service over a fixed network infrastructure, and telex are reserved to monopoly provision until 2005 to be followed by unrestricted competition. Open market access (without a phase-in period) was offered for all other basic telecommunication services including data transmission, all mobile networks and services, video transmission services and satellite services, and earth stations.

The monopoly for telephone service over fixed infrastructure, telex, and Integrated Services Digital Networks in *Morocco* is reserved until December 2001. Foreign equity participation may be limited (level as yet unspecified). There is open market access for packet switched data transmission, and frame relay, and licences for mobile services will be issued by public tender.

Senegal plans to abolish its monopoly on voice telephony, data transmission, telex, fax, private leased circuit services, and fixed satellite services between 2003 and 2006. The authorities will review policy from 2003 with respect to licensing other operators. The number of operators will be limited to three in selected service areas, such as cellular mobile services, including mobile data from 1998. The maximum number of licences for mobile satellite services was to be established in 1997.

South Africa intends to terminate monopoly supply and introduce a second supplier by the end of 2003 in public switched facilities-based services including voice, data transmission, telex, fax, private leased circuits, and satellite services. It will also investigate the feasibility of allowing additional suppliers of public switched services by the end of 2003. Mobile cellular services are to be offered under a duopoly arrangement and foreign investment in telecommunication suppliers is limited to just under one-third.

Even though only a handful of African States decided to participate in the WTO talks, their proposals signal that they are being cautious. Despite commitments to break up monopolies, the dates set for the introduction of competition indicate that they see a need to allow for internal changes and observation of the liberalisation experiment before opening their markets to external companies.

These moves toward market liberalisation, tentative though they are, raise several issues. What measures should be taken to enable the African telecommunication operators to compete against foreign or domestic-owned competitors? What is the likely magnitude of bypass of the national operators' networks by competitors and how much hard currency will be lost? What are the opportunities to provide services that will replace these revenues?

If the majority of African people remain disconnected from the rest of the world as a result of high priced communication services and their lack of access to the GII and its services, such as the Internet, other developing countries are likely to have a similar experience. At current rates of investment, a substantial number of the poorest countries in the world will not see the 'access gap' close within the next 50 years (see Chapter 2). Some governments may choose to give higher priority to investment in clean water and universal education rather than ICTs. But for those choosing to construct the NII, innovative means of opening up and keeping control of network and service development will be essential.

9.6   OPENING UP, BUT KEEPING CONTROL

The forces around ICTs run very strongly both in the direction of opening up markets and keeping them sufficiently closed to enable domestic control over priorities. On the one hand, communication has long been international and open. On the other, telecommunication services were established in a majority of countries after a brief period of competition as entrenched monopolies. Along with the supply of water and electricity, most countries favoured large centralised telecommunication systems. Historically, it was strategically advantageous for countries and corporations to push for openness and linkages between national systems while jealously keeping control of conditions within their borders. There is now a tug-of-war between those wanting to open these systems to competition and to integrate them throughout regions, and those wanting to conserve and protect local ownership and sovereign standards and services (WTO 1997b; Melody 1997c). Can these interests and forces be reconciled?

The pressures for opening up have been building very quickly. In 1989, the International Telecommunication Union drew attention to the need for major structural adjustment in the sector (ITU 1989). The need for restructuring to gain operational efficiencies and to stimulate new service development in national and international markets was stressed. Management practices had to be changed and the workforce needed new skills. Large amounts of capital were vital. Few of the benefits of liberalisation and privatisation of the telecommunication sector can be reaped by developing countries unless measures are taken to plan service development that reflects the characteristics of each country and region. Provisions must be made to extend the infrastructure using the most appropriate mix of technologies, and legislative and regulatory arrangements must encourage the appropriate type and degree of competition in each country.[13]

The cumulative gains from competition between 1997 and 2010 in terms of cost savings and quality benefits for the low income countries have been estimated at US$ 177 billion. Those for the high income countries are estimated at US$ 523 billion (Petrazzini 1996). These estimates are based on models that assume the presence of effective competition and, therefore, the presence of an enforceable governance regime. Development agencies have long argued for the opening of telecommunication and information technology markets, and now they and other organisations are working in concert, with larger pools of private capital to shape the ICT environment in developing countries. The telecommunication sector is particularly attractive. because it requires very large loans. This size has offered 'influence out of all proportion to the size or complexity of the investment'.[14] This influence was intended specifically to bring about privatisation and international competitive bidding and to reduce inefficiency. The development banks have offered a new kind of discipline in the sector, talked directly to governments (particularly in the context of the annual aid donor meetings), provided the legal protection of cross-default clauses, and generally acted as a catalyst to open up markets while helping governments to retain the appearance of control.

9.6.1   OPENING UP, SEEN FROM INDIA

India presents a good example of the contradictory forces which run through the ICT sector. Competition in the Indian telecommunication sector was traditionally heavily managed and not at all transparent. Use of advanced applications of ICTs in the military, police, air-traffic, and nuclear research communities began years ago, followed gradually and unevenly by banks, tax agencies, railways, airlines, etc. After fifteen years of pressure from international agencies and internal interests (buoyed by a vast public demanding more telephones and better service), in the late 1980s the Indian government took steps to permit more open bidding for telecommunication projects. Following the urging of the World Bank in the early 1990s this process became formally transparent and segmented so that markets and contracts in one State were separated from those in others.

India has funded R&D for domestic ICT production for many years, and the sale of telecommunication equipment was one of the prime objectives of this policy. Indian suppliers, for example, rebuilt the telecommunication system of Kuwait after the Gulf War. The domestic market simply could not be protected as it had been in the past.

Seen from the point of view of Indian industrial interests, this opening up bypassed the log-jam around long-term infrastructure capital supplies in the country that were committed to dams, roads, etc., and which international investors were unwilling to touch. Telecommunication, like the power sector, could attract and absorb large quantities of foreign investment precisely when a tide of international capital was available. The idea was 'to promote a quantum leap' in communication, and to have the results of this 'leap' influence other sectors of the economy.[15]

In recent years, competition between international suppliers with their local partners has become fierce. Some licences were sold by auction at higher than anticipated prices, and some by other means, involving large unrecorded transaction costs to influence the decisions. The process of alleged influence-buying involved local and state officials, and agents/consultants, but also people at the top. The large scale of these unrecorded transaction costs came to light in an August 1996 raid on the residence of the former Minister of Telecommunication. Bribery scandals had surrounded international competition in other sectors, for example, automobiles, but there had been little awareness of the scale of influence buying in the telecommunication sector (Crook 1997).

Sensitive to the consequences of bribing senior officials, but not wanting any reduction in services, questions were raised about whether the hidden costs of open competition were being passed on to consumers by the competitors. India has always had strong regional variations, and the telecommunication system and its ailments have reflected these. Advocates of a state-segmented market for telecommunication, pointing to regional needs such as the large computer software industry around Bangalore, have confronted the centralised decision-making system in New Delhi. The contracts themselves have come under scrutiny, and doubts have been voiced about whether the best results have been achieved because of the lack of transparency. There is no doubt that the process was fiercely 'competitive'.

9.6.2 BYPASSING THE OLD WAYS WITH WIRELESS COMMUNICATION

Sri Lanka presents an interesting example of a country moving quickly into wireless communication. By 1997 the government had licensed a fifth cellular radio operator, indicating strong international competition and local popularity of the service. Wireless technology avoided Sri Lanka's slow-to-develop terrestrial fixed system where the waiting period after payment was up to eight years, and was ideal in a dangerous war-torn society. Wireless technologies also enhanced surveillance capabilities for national security. Sri Lanka 'opened up' communication on demand. Although Sri Lanka is a densely populated country with a good wireless morphology, it is unclear whether the country can support all these operators (Schwartz 1996).

Should wireless, because it is potentially a bypass technology, be largely unregulated, or is there a useful role for regulation and management of wireless communication? The radio spectrum is a limited common resource, albeit one that is self-renewing after use. The disadvantages of unmanaged competition are considerable. If funds and licences are provided for too many operators then there may be a loss of benefits accruing to governments in comparison to those if the optimal number of licences were awarded. Missed opportunities include the introduction of beneficial rate structures, establishing new areas of service, promoting local training, and participation in

technical development. In addition, some qualified operators may choose not to invest if too many licences are awarded because of the uncertainty of recovering their investment.

India also auctioned wireless licences, but these are confined to the four major cities where the waiting time for a telephone line has been reduced to one year. With tariffs nine times higher than for fixed telephones, wireless in these Indian cities is not an attractive alternative to waiting a year for a telephone line. The high prices paid for wireless licences in auctions have squeezed service providers who now must wait for a luxury urban market to grow. Rural mobile wireless remains expensive and the rural population is deemed to be too poor to support it.

9.6.3 ZONES OF SILENCE?

In 1984, the widely circulated 'Missing Link' report observed that 'in a majority of developing countries the telecommunication system is inadequate to sustain essential services' (ITU 1984: 3). It was estimated that to achieve its target for all the world's people to be brought within easy reach of a telephone by the 21st century, an investment of about US$ 12 billion a year would be needed. In the intervening period investment has occurred in countries like India and Sri Lanka and some of the missing links are being put in place. However there is also the potential for the emergence of new 'zones of silence' as suggested in Box 9.2.

These zones of silence will only be filled with productive sounds that resonate with local cultures if specific efforts are made to resolve the tensions between opening up and maintaining control over the NII. The two opposing tendencies - opening up and keeping control - are never fully reconciled but remain in constant conflict. The global economy sometimes favours large open structures like the GII. And yet that favouring nurtures the seeds of disfavour. Market opening, competition, decreasing the control of states, and increasing control by corporate intermediaries are the processes of globalisation. But the desire to reassert local control and sovereignty is not extinguished by acceding to openness, and may in fact be increased and amplified by it. This process is built into the structure of the relations between rich nations and regions, and poor ones, and into the interplay of technology, capital, people in markets, and states. No individual would relinquish the pursuit of either tendency, and most would hope skilfully to play one off against the other. Planners and advocates need to be prepared for a continuing contest between these forces which will be visible in the international community whether in the WTO, the ITU or other international bodies, in regional fora, and national groups.

The future is likely to bring a mixed picture in which there is an interplay among various aspects of the visions for the GII. The instability and tensions created within scenarios where there is local success but little global integration may also permit a 'virtuous spiral of diffusion'. Diffusion will bring many benefits for economic and political development and perhaps for cultural development as well. But this 'virtuous spiral' will coexist with two less attractive tendencies. The first is the spread of cybercrime and surveillance. The second is the risk of a continuation in some areas of a sense of futility. These negative outcomes may be avoided as a result of cooperation which emerges in the optimistic visions of the GII. However, this will only occur as a result of active ICT policy measures initiated by national governments and other interested stakeholders.

9.7 CONCLUSION - GOVERNANCE REGIMES FOR INNOVATIVE 'NETWORLDS'

It cannot be assumed simply that the governance system for ICTs that is emerging in the wake of recent developments in international markets and the institutional set up will benefit developing countries and especially the least developed countries. Some developing countries certainly do stand to benefit, and in some cases very considerably. Evidence of the rapid diffusion of infrastructure and services is clear especially in the newly industrialising economies in South East Asia.

For other developing countries, and particularly those least developed and small countries that cannot devote substantial time to monitoring and participating in the developments on the global stage, the greatest need is to establish more effective ways of ensuring that their 'voices' are heard. Changes in markets and governance regimes must take account of their circumstances. Without substantial investment in physical and human capital, some of these countries will be excluded from the potential benefits of ICTs.

In the optimistic 'Networld' scenario developed by members of the UNCSTD Working Group on IT and Development, the principles of equity, open access, and fair competition are features of the new global system of governance. By about 2005, 'the major intergovernmental organizations seek new agendas, new missions, and new sources of revenue ... At the end of the scenario period, poverty and deprivation still remain. But the international system is not only supportive but also knowledgeable' (Howkins and Valantin 1997: 43). National and regional governmental organisations and the private sector work in cooperation to take advantage of many of the benefits of ICTs.

In other scenarios it is much less likely that the investment in people and technologies necessary to enable excluded and marginalised people to benefit from ICTs will take place or, if it does, it is not likely to do so in an open cooperative international environment. The UNCSTD Working Group members who developed the scenarios felt that a 'Netblocs' scenario was most realistic in the

BOX 9.2 - ZONES OF SILENCE IN THE GIS

> Although India's telecommunication system is growing steadily, there is a particular district which is one of the poorest in India, where there are about 300 telephones for one million people (most of them permitting only local calls); there are about five computers (one each on the desk of the chief government officer and the chief of police). This absence of ICT does not cause the poverty - poverty is much older than that - but it reinforces it. As the national system grows and surrounds it, perhaps this district will become, in time, a zone of silence.

next decade. In this scenario, ICTs diffuse rapidly and many people become connected to the GII. Several major groups or blocs emerge based on shared cultures and languages. These include the OECD countries, the newly industrialising countries of Asia, the countries and territories around the Indian Ocean (South Africa, the Gulf States, India, Malaysia, and Singapore), the Francophone countries in Africa, the Latin American countries, and other blocs based on Islam and the Chinese characters, Eastern Europe, and Russia with the former Asian Union of Soviet Socialist Republics. However, the blocs are competitive and divisive and many countries are too poor to maintain any association with a bloc. The countries within blocs are successful in creating innovative 'knowledge societies' reflecting their histories, cultures, and business traditions. However, because of the tensions between them and the exclusion of the poorest countries, the market and the system of governance are very unstable (Howkins and Valantin 1997).

The key element in these two scenarios is that stakeholders and national governments take positive steps to put ICT strategies in place. These strategies set priorities for ICT development and help to ensure that the institutional set up and governance system contribute to capabilities for constructing national information infrastructures.

1   For discussions of ICT governance issues see Mansell (1996a), Hawkins (1992) and Zacher and Sutton (1996).

2   WorldTel is chaired by Mr Satyen Pitroda and advised by NatWest Markets. It aims to raise private sector investment for telecommunication in the developing world and is in active discussion of projects in Bangladesh, Brazil, China, India, Kenya, Mexico, Pakistan, Tanzania, Uganda, and Zimbabwe.

3   The association operates using three official languages and publishes work in these languages. Association Internationale des Etudes et Recherches sur l'Information et la Communication (AIERIC), Associacio Internacional des Estudios de Comunicacion Social (AIECS). Two sections of the association, communication technology policy and the political economy of communication have generated detailed studies of the emerging ICT governance system.

4   A domain name is any name representing any record that exists with the Domain Name System, for example .com, and a domain has name server records associated with it. There may be subdomains or hosts beneath the name.

5   Key issues are discussed in Kahin (1996), Kahin and Keller (1996), Branscomb and Keller (1996), and Kahin and Wilson (1997).

6   In 1995, the GII-Agenda for Action was released in the United States. In February 1995, the G-7 held an information summit and agreed 11 pilot projects to demonstrate the potential of the information society, including projects on cross-cultural training and education, electronic libraries, environmental and natural resource management, global healthcare applications, and maritime information systems. In May 1996 the Information Society and Development Conference (ISAD) was held in South Africa and the GIIC began to talk again of the promise of a 'New World Information Order', a concept abandoned in the 1970s and early 1980s when its use by developing countries made it a target for conflict between the interests of the industrialised and developing countries.

7   General obligations included in the text require transparency in domestic regulation (Art. III) where such regulations do not discriminate among foreign suppliers (Most Favoured Nation rule - Art. II), rules on government procurement (Art. III), guidelines for monopoly provision of services (Art. VIII), as well as a dispute settlement mechanism (Art. XXII and XXIII). In addition to these principles, which apply to regulations governing all services, governments may make specific liberalisation commitments by listing them in national schedules. In this way, governments take on two additional responsibilities. Firstly, they cannot erect further barriers to market access and, secondly, they agree to provide equal treatment for domestic and foreign firms - the national treatment rule.

8   The Annex covers access to, and use of, the public telecommunication and transportation network.

9   The commitments will be annexed to the 4th Protocol of the General Agreement on Trade in Services. The General Agreement on Trade in Services (GATS) consists of 29 articles, 8 annexes, and other schedules of commitments on specific services or service sectors. Obligations include most favoured nation treatment which prohibits members from discriminating amongst themselves, or from treating other members less favourably than any other country, regardless of membership; domestic regulation, the treatment of monopolies, and exclusive service providers and the removal of restrictive business practices. Countries submit exemptions from most favoured nation treatment: for example, the United States exemption on one-way satellite transmission of DTH (Direct to Home) and DBS (Direct Broadcast Satellite) services and digital audio services; Brazil - distribution of radio or television programming directly to consumers; Argentina - supply of fixed satellite services by geostationary satellite; Turkey - two neighbouring countries with respect to fees for transit land connections and use of satellite ground stations; Bangladesh, India, Pakistan, Sri Lanka, and Turkey to permit Government, or Government-run, operators to apply differential measures such as accounting rates in bilateral agreements with other operators or countries; Antigua and Barbuda to extend to nationals of other CARICOM (Caribbean Common Market) member countries treatment equal to its own nationals.

10   Ranks are based on data excluding governments that are not WTO members and applying a single rank for the European Union member states based on their combined total.

11   The ITA covers five main categories: computers (including printers, scanners, monitors, hard-disk drives, power supplies, etc.), telecom products (including telephone sets, fax machines, modems, pagers, etc.), semiconductors (including chips and wafers), semiconductor manufacturing equipment, software (discs and CD-ROMs), and scientific instruments.

12   The Information for Development Program (infoDev) was mandated in early 1995 with the task of helping developing countries integrate fully into the information economy by benefiting from the promise of information technology.3

13   More detailed studies of developing countries are found in Hudson (1992), Petrazzini (1995), and Mody et al. (1995).

14   R.S. Anderson personal communication with Asian Development Bank official, Vancouver, February 1997.

15   R.S. Anderson personal communication with Indian telecommunication investment analyst, Vancouver, February 1997.

9.8   APPENDIX – WTO GROUP ON BASIC TELECOMMUNICATION

TABLE 9.4 – TELECOMMUNICATION REVENUE 1995 FOR WTO MEMBERS WITH OFFERS AS OF 15 FEBRUARY 1997

Country	US$ million	% share of world total	Ranking
United States	178,758.0	29.70	
European Union	170,166.0	28.27	
Japan	93,855.0	15.59	
Australia	11,403.0	1.89	Top Five
Canada	10,689.0	1.78	77
Switzerland	8,889.0	1.48	
Korea (Rep.of)	8,728.0	1.45	
Brazil	8,622.0	1.43	
Mexico	6,509.0	1.08	Top 10
Argentina	6,009.1	1.00	84
Hong Kong	5,113.0	0.85	
India	3,818.0	0.63	
South Africa	3,675.0	0.61	
Norway	3,234.0	0.54	Top 15
Indonesia	2,735.0	0.45	97
Singapore	2,540.0	0.42	
Israel	2,249.0	0.37	
Poland	2,162.0	0.36	
Malaysia	2,097.5	0.35	Top 20
New Zealand	2,091.0	0.35	89
Thailand	2,040.0	0.34	
Turkey	1,674.0	0.28	
Venezuela	1,594.0	0.26	
Chile	1,321.0	0.22	
Colombia	1,213.0	0.20	
Peru	1,139.7	0.19	
Pakistan	1,045.0	0.17	
Philippines	982.0	0.16	
Czech Republic	890.0	0.15	
Hungary	770.0	0.13	
Morocco	659.4	0.11	

Country	US$ million	% share of world total	Ranking
Romania	423.1	0.07	
Ecuador	332.4	0.06	
Slovak Republic	320.5	0.05	
Jamaica	313.6	0.05	
Tunisia	263.2	0.04	
Bulgaria	232.5	0.04	
Sri Lanka	218.6	0.04	
Guatemala	197.2	0.03	
Bangladesh	194.9	0.03	
Trinidad and Tobago	162.6	0.03	
El Salvador	153.3	0.03	
Papua New Guinea	141.4	0.02	
Ivory Coast	138.2	0.02	
Iceland	132.5	0.02	
Senegal	107.5	0.02	
Bolivia (1993)	104.6	0.02	
Mauritius	104.3	0.02	
Ghana	65.0	0.01	
Brunei Darussalam	61.4	0.01	
Belize	37.8	0.01	
Antigua and Barbuda	n.a.	n.a.	
Dominican Republic	n.a.	n.a.	
Dominica	n.a.	n.a.	
Grenada	n.a.	n.a.	
Total	550,375.3	91.44	
World Total	601,900.0	100.00	

Source: WTO (1997d).

As of 1998 – 47 countries permit foreign ownership or control of all telecommunications services and facilities	
1998	Australia (except Vodafone and Telstra), Austria, Belgium (except state-owned company), Chile (except local service), Colombia, Denmark, Dominican Republic, El Salvador, Finland, France (except France Telecom), Germany, Guatemala, Iceland, Italy (except Stet), Japan (except KDD and NTT), Luxembourg, Netherlands, New Zealand (except 49.9% limit in Telecom NZ for any one single foreign entity), Norway, Spain (except Telefonica), Sweden, Switzerland, Trinidad and Tobago, United Kingdom, and United States
1999	Peru, Portugal
2000	Argentina, Ireland, Singapore, Venezuela
2001	Bolivia, Czech Republic
2002	Hungary, Papua New Guinea
2003	Greece, Romania, Slovak Republic
2004	Bulgaria, Mauritius, Pakistan
After 2004	Ivory Coast, Grenada, Brunei, Antigua and Barbuda, Bangladesh, Jamaica

10 countries and territories permit foreign ownership or control of certain telecommunication services	
Brazil	100% for non-public services; 100% for cellular and satellite services after 7/99
Canada	100% for resellers and mobile satellite service providers; 100% for fixed satellite services as of March 2000; 100% for submarine cable licences as of 10/98; 46.7% on all other services.
Ecuador	100% cellular only
Ghana	only in joint venture with Ghanaian nationals
Hong Kong	100% for resale of voice, data and fax, closed user groups
Israel	80% for cellular; 74% for international services; 100% for value added services
Korea (Rep. of)	100% for resale in 2001; 33% for facility providers except Korea Telecom (20%) until 2001, thereafter 49%
Mexico	100% for cellular services; 49% for all other services and facilities
Poland	100% for local wireline (voice and data); 49% for wireless, international and long distance voice/data
Tunisia	Telex, data transmission in 1999; mobile, paging and teleconferencing in 2000; and local service in 2003

10 countries do not permit foreign control
India-25%
Indonesia-35%
Malaysia-30%
Philippines-40% for all services
Senegal-35%
South Africa-30%
Sri Lanka-35%
Thailand-20%
Morocco-unbound
Turkey-49%

53 countries guarantee market access to international telecommunication services and facilities	
1998	Australia, Austria, Belgium, Canada *, Chile, Denmark, Dominican Republic, El Salvador, Finland, France, Germany, Guatemala, Iceland, Italy, Japan, Republic of Korea*, Luxembourg, Malaysia * – through existing suppliers, Mexico, Netherlands, New Zealand, Norway, Philippines*, Papua New Guinea, Spain by 12/98, Sweden, Switzerland, Trinidad and Tobago, United Kingdom and the United States.
1999	Peru
2000	Argentina, Venezuela, Ireland, Singapore, Portugal
2001	Czech Republic, Bolivia
2003	Poland, Greece, Slovak Republic, Romania
2004	Mauritius, Hungary
2005	Bulgaria, Indonesia*
2006+	Turkey, Senegal, Grenada, Thailand, Brunei, Antigua and Barbuda, Jamaica (2013)

6 countries and territories are open for selected international services	
Brazil*	open for all non-public services for closed user groups not connected to the public switched network, but will have legislation covering public and non-public. Must route through Brazilian gateway.
Ivory Coast	analogue cellular, mobile, Personal Communication Service, and non-voice satellite based services, data transmission and private leased circuit services.
Hong Kong	resale of voice, data and fax, call back and closed user groups
Israel	open for switched resale, fax and private networks
Pakistan*	telex and fax
Ghana	closed user groups

(*) countries maintain foreign investment limits below control.

TABLE 9.5 CONTINUED – COUNTRY AND TERRITORY COMMITMENTS – GROUP ON BASIC TELECOMMUNICATION OF THE WTO, 1997

8 countries have limited or no market access commitments for international services	
Colombia	(subject economic needs test), Bangladesh, Ecuador, India (subject to review in 2004), Morocco, South Africa (duopoly), Sri Lanka (duopoly), Tunisia.

42 countries guarantee market access for services and facilities (domestic and international) for satellite service suppliers	
1998	Australia, Austria, Belgium, Chile, Colombia, Denmark, Dominican Republic, El Salvador, Finland, France, Germany, Guatemala, Iceland, Israel, Italy, Japan, Republic of Korea, Luxembourg, Malaysia, Netherlands, New Zealand, Norway, Spain 12/98, Sri Lanka, Sweden, Switzerland, Trinidad and Tobago, United Kingdom, United States.
1999	Peru
2000	Argentina, Canada (for fixed, 1998 for mobile), Ireland, Singapore, Venezuela, Portugal
2001	Bolivia, Czech Republic
2002	Mexico, Bulgaria (all public services by 2004)
2003	Greece, Hungary, Poland, Romania, Slovak Republic
2004 or after	Brunei, Indonesia, Jamaica, Grenada, Thailand, Turkey, Senegal

6 countries and territories guarantee market access for selected services and facilities for satellite service operators	
Brazil	open for all non public domestic and international services for closed user groups not connected to the public network. Requirement to route all international traffic through gateway in Brazil. Brazilian or foreign satellites can be used but preference given for Brazilian satellite supply when they offer better service or equivalent conditions. No foreign ownership restrictions after 7/99.
Ivory Coast	open for all services except fixed voice and telex
Ghana	open for global mobile, open for domestic fixed (excluding public network) through joint ventures with Ghanaian nationals.
Hong Kong	open for mobile satellite services and self provision of external satellite circuits by a company or closed user group. Interconnection to public switched network at Hong Kong end not permitted.
Mauritius	open for GMPCS.
South Africa	will schedule commitments within one year of adopting legislation at national level.

9 countries have no market access commitments for satellite service operators
Antigua and Barbuda, Bangladesh, Colombia, Ecuador, India, Morocco, Pakistan, Philippines.

54 countries and territories guarantee pro-competitive regulatory principles
Antigua and Barbuda, Argentina, Australia, Austria, Belgium, Brunei, Bulgaria, Canada, Chile, Colombia, Ivory Coast, Czech Republic, Denmark, Dominican Republic, El Salvador, Finland, France, Ghana, Germany, Greece, Grenada, Guatemala, Hong Kong, Hungary, Iceland, Indonesia, Ireland, Israel, Italy, Jamaica, Japan, Republic of Korea, Luxembourg, Mexico, Netherlands, New Zealand, Norway, Papua New Guinea, Peru, Poland, Portugal, Romania, Senegal, Singapore, Slovak Republic, South Africa, Spain, Sri Lanka, Sweden, Switzerland, Thailand, Trinidad and Tobago, United Kingdom, United States.

3 countries commit to adopting pro competitive regulatory principles in the future
Brazil, Bangladesh, Mauritius

8 countries adopt some pro-competitive regulatory principles
Bolivia, India, Malaysia, Morocco, Pakistan, Philippines, Turkey, Venezuela

Source: WTO (1997d).

CHAPTER 10

INSTITUTIONAL INNOVATIONS
FOR THE GOVERNANCE OF
INFORMATION SERVICES

Enforcing intellectual property rights
and protecting security and privacy

The international governance system has a very important impact on capability-building and the construction of the national information infrastructure. Chapter 9 looked at the governance system for the underlying communication infrastructure. This chapter looks at the institutional set ups and the 'rules of the game' that are being established for the content and information. It should not be assumed that the governance system for digital information will automatically benefit developing countries. Some developing countries, especially the newly industrialising economies in South East Asia, stand to benefit from the newly negotiated agreements that are shaping global information flows. For other countries in the developing world, the evidence is either ambiguous, non-existent, or suggests that these developments embody the seeds of new processes of social and economic exclusion.

This chapter reviews recent international developments in the area of copyright protection (section 10.2) and electronic commerce (section 10.3). In both cases the interests of the producers and users of information are contrasted. In section 10.4 the implications of the growth in the international markets for information services and the role of the Internet are considered from the perspective of public policy interests in governance, social control, and the protection of personal privacy.

10.2 INTELLECTUAL PROPERTY RIGHTS IN 'DIGITAL' INFORMATION

The shift toward knowledge-based economies has meant that the law and economics of intellectual property rights have changed more in the last five years than in the last two centuries (Acheson and McFetridge 1996). The activities of creating, distributing, and using digital forms of information are of growing importance in the lives of citizens, consumers, and businesses. Intellectual property laws extend the right of property protection to inventions, literary and artistic works, and trade marks. Intellectual property protection attempts to balance society's interest in the disclosure and dissemination of ideas with an exclusive right to control and profit from invention and authorship. It is possible to have too little protection, or too much, and for some people to be disadvantaged while others gain. There are inconsistencies between the goal of achieving the widest possible use of electronic information services and the enforcement of strong intellectual property protection. The social and political choices regarding

the granting of intellectual property rights are made more complex by technical innovations that are making it possible to bring together voice, text, audio, and visual materials within common digital formats and to copy this material inexpensively and accurately.

As networks are increasingly interconnected it is feasible to distribute the world's stocks of information around the globe. The major producers of information products (including software) are becoming very active in seeking strong intellectual property protection and they are calling upon governments to ensure that international conventions and national legislation are updated and enforced. The cost of reproducing electronically encoded information is very low. However, the cost of the 'first copy' of a film, broadcast programme, book, multimedia programme, on-line database, or other information product, is relatively high. The majority of these products are produced in the industrialised countries. Firms and governments have been changing the governance regime for intellectual property protection in response to the pressure from those who stand to gain from stronger enforcement.

The degree to which this regime will be strengthened in any given country depends on its economic circumstances and its perception of the social and economic costs and benefits of greater protection. Some developing countries are heavily dependent on access to information services from external sources. Others are seeking to expand production of information products including software, broadcast programming, films, and databases, for domestic consumption or external markets. They are interested in providing improved protection to local producers. Most countries are signatories to the international conventions that offer intellectual property protection, but some developing countries do not have enforcement institutions in place. Enforcement requires public resources and there are many competing claims on law enforcement expenditure. Policy-makers in developing countries are in a difficult position. They must decide how to respond despite the absence of empirical evidence on the economic costs and benefits of changes in existing policy and practice.

10.2.1 PROTECTING ECONOMIC INTERESTS AND ENCOURAGING INNOVATION

The General Agreement on Tariffs and Trade (GATT) Uruguay Round of negotiations put the relationship between intellectual property protection, economic and social development, and innovations in ICTs, high on the policy agenda (Correa 1998 forthcoming). Over the years, the system of protection which applies to intellectual property has shifted from protection for inventors (authors) toward a system that encourages investors and the commercialisation of information products on an international scale. This shift has accompanied the rapid development of ICTs. Historically, the protection of intellectual property has been said to be necessary in order to create incentives for scientific and technical progress which benefits the public interest.

By granting economic rights to the creator of intellectual works, information would be created and disseminated, and thus a number of other social and economic objectives would be achieved. In this model, not only were other societal goals understood to be furthered fostering the learning environment, these goals were also seen to be mutually compatible and self-reinforcing (US Congress Office of Technology Assessment 1992: 38, 56).

However, as Paul David has argued:

... even if the rhetoric of argument occasionally appeals to notions of justice and equity, modern economic analysis, and its characteristic preoccupation with questions of efficiency, now set the terms for policy discussions about the protection of intellectual property (David 1993: 20).

As the emphasis has shifted to efficiency and away from invention, intellectual property protection has become more concerned with problems arising from the 'misappropriation' of intellectual products, than with the incentives for creative production of information or the social value of *using* information that has been produced.

The Agreement on Trade-Related Aspects of Intellectual Property Rights (TRIPS) was negotiated as an outcome of the Uruguay Round in 1995. A major objective was to establish minimum standards for the protection of intellectual property. Developing countries negotiated for and won a period of grace of four years (the least developed countries, ten years) before the provisions of the TRIPS agreement come into force. However, they were expected to implement some aspects of the agreement concerning market access and the treatment of information products produced in external markets (national and most-favoured-nation treatment). In exchange for the 'grace periods', the industrialised countries obtained transitional periods before they are to comply with obligations in the agriculture and textiles sectors.

TRIPS affects access to computer programs, software development technologies, and commercially available software products. It puts limits on reverse engineering and extends the patent system to protect certain elements of software (for example, translations from one language to another, graphics displays on a computer screen, measurement techniques for the performance of general purpose computers) (Fishman 1994). These developments have major implications for developing countries

as to whether they can access ICTs and learn how to develop them for their own needs. Greater protection means that developing countries must pay the market price for externally produced software. Being without the resources to enforce protection, many developing countries have not implemented national legislation to cope with the ICT revolution. For example, in the field of integrated circuit design very few developing countries have legislation to protect such designs although all World Trade Organization (WTO) members have an obligation to do this. Copyright enforcement affects information services, databases, and the information and software available on the Internet and other networks.

A potential creator of information in a developing country may be a member of one or more social and economic groups. Depending on the group, the creator will have a different perspective on the benefits and costs of the enforcement of intellectual property rights. For example, many individuals benefit from information distributed to the 'public domain', that is, without ownership or owned equally by everyone (Mansell and Steinmueller 1995, 1996b). When people use public domain information they make little or no use of copyright protection. Contributors to the public domain benefit from the dissemination of their work in ways that are indirectly related or unrelated to their receipt of revenue or income. Social groups using the public domain also include users who create information for personal and commercial reasons.

A substantial amount of information provided on the Internet and commercial bulletin board services is non-commercial. Examples of this type of interest in information include the researcher who wants to disseminate scientific data, an individual exchanging political viewpoints, or a teacher sharing insights on education. This group supports the inexpensive distribution of information and again has little use for, or interest in, copyright protection. Citizens and researchers in developing countries may benefit from the growing size of information in the public domain available over international networks. However, they face high charges because of the relatively high costs of software and PCs and telecommunication costs in relation to their incomes. Paying royalties due to copyright holders could put useful information out of their reach regardless of its potential value.

Another group uses copyright protection to control the content of intellectual works, but still benefits from the wide dissemination of copies. Creators in this 'indirect revenue' group are interested in distributing information without direct payment. However, the creators expect that the distribution of information will increase their revenues or income. This group includes businesses that expect certain types of information to improve their positions with investors, the public at large, and customers. Sophisticated ways of exposing individuals to advertising and promotion messages using the Internet are emerging as new sources of revenue for this group. This group has a substantial interest in preventing any alteration to the information provided.

The last group of potential information creators seeks direct control over selling and buying information. Producers in this 'direct revenue' group need a means of protecting the value of information and preventing others from obtaining it without payment. This group is interested in a high level of intellectual property protection. Success for the companies in this group is based on winning a share of existing markets or creating new ones.

These groups have very different interests in the enforcement of copyrights. Information producers in the 'public domain' group simply want to retain some credit for their work. This group comes into conflict, particularly with the 'direct revenue' group, because strong intellectual property protection and enforcement are likely to result in an increase in liability for those who are found to have infringed and in the risk that infringement will be inadvertent or unintended. For individuals and firms in developing countries the cost of infringement increases as intellectual property protection is strengthened. These costs may take the form of trade sanctions, threatened or applied, or costs to individuals or firms of defending themselves against claims of infringement.

For developing countries the choices are to increase the level of monitoring and enforcement to avoid the risk of increased liability, to insure against the risk of liability, to accept the risk and hope to escape legal liability, or to transfer the liability risk to another party. The first two options directly increase the costs of information for the 'public domain' group (mainly citizens and researchers). The second two may lead to higher costs depending on the level of copyright enforcement.

Problems of intellectual property rights infringement could lead to pressures to limit public access to national information infrastructures. The alternative is to monitor users of networks and to introduce enhanced security procedures. Security measures lead to increasing costs and the threat of compromises to user privacy. These implications need to be considered as developing countries alter their current intellectual property laws and institutions. If stronger protection is introduced and enforced it is likely to disadvantage some local users just as it protects domestic information producing firms.

The least developed countries will need to introduce measures to improve conditions of access to existing

sources of scientific, technical, and other forms of electronic information. The options for these countries include:

▌ seeking to negotiate directly with intellectual property rights holders for favourable country-wide licences for software and other services that are deemed to be 'essential'. Essential information may take the form of educational or scientific information, information with regard to health care, the environment, etc., or business information.

▌ attempting to encourage competition between international information suppliers to achieve the most favourable terms for the purchase of rights to information products and services.

▌ considering whether the sanctions for intellectual property right infringement are a sufficient disincentive to their exploiting available knowledge even if, outside their sovereign territory, it is viewed as 'owned property'.

Strategies that promote production capabilities for ICT products and services generally are accompanied by stronger intellectual property regimes. This brings local producers in developing countries who are targeting export markets into conflict with domestic users. Countries that seek to strengthen user capabilities through access to electronic information services will be less enthusiastic about enforcing stronger protection for digital information products. However, the threat of sanctions is considerable. For example, potential users within countries may be denied access to information services. This happened in a case where America On-Line denied Russia access to its services for a period pending the resolution of fraudulent credit card practices.

International organisations providing assistance to developing countries could encourage and support technology assessment programmes to determine whether adequate software solutions and information access conditions are available in the public domain to support applications that are linked with development objectives. If deficiencies are found, development assistance could be linked to measures to reduce the costs. The technical expertise could be oriented towards assisting developing countries to formulate the best mix of proprietary (copyright protected) information to support their development goals and to providing assistance in negotiating licences.

10.2.2 LEGISLATION AND INTERNATIONAL GOVERNANCE

Stakeholders in the 'direct revenue' group, the 'copyright industries' in the United States and Europe, have been major catalysts for the intellectual property rights reform.[1]

In the United States, the Information Infrastructure Task Force 'White Paper' on intellectual property rights of September 1995 recommended the extension of copyright protection in a way that would broaden the definition of reproduction to include temporary storage of works in a computer's random access memory (RAM) (IITF 1995, Kurtz 1996).[2] It was also recommended that transmission should be redefined as a form of reproduction and distribution such that any unauthorised transmission would become an infringement of copyright law. Other recommendations included measures to make on-line service providers and bulletin board operators responsible for monitoring information uploaded on their systems to ensure that this information does not amount to an infringement of the law. Information providers and system operators would be liable to prosecution for infringement if protected material were to be found on their systems (Cavazos 1996). These proposals have not been favoured by all the players in the information or 'copyright' industries, but they indicate the strength of interest in greater protection among some of the members of the 'direct revenue' group.

The existing Copyright Act in the United States permits downloading of legally protected information as long as this is not done for commercial reasons. This is known as the doctrine of 'fair use'. Reproduction with limitations and conditions is permitted for research, teaching and scholarship, comment and criticism, and news reporting. The White Paper pointed to the 'lacuna in the criminal provisions' for such acts and recommended that it become a criminal offence to wilfully infringe a copyright by reproducing or distributing copies with a retail value of US$ 5,000 or more 'regardless of the non-commercial reason for doing so' (IITF 1995: 228–9). The use of technical means of protection, tracking transactions, and licensing is expected to reduce the application and scope of the 'fair use' doctrine. These and other recommendations are being debated by the United States Congress and changes could be incorporated in the National Information Initiative Copyright Act, an amendment to the Copyright Act expected in 1998.

In the European Union legislative measures to strengthen the protection of 'digital information products' include the 1991 directive on the legal protection of computer programs which extended copyright protection to computer software (Council of the European Communities 1991). Europe-wide consultations on the need to introduce legislation to extend greater protection to information delivered by electronic means resulted in the European Commission's 1995 Green Paper on copyright and related rights (European Commission 1995a). A directive on the legal protection of databases was accepted by the European Council of Ministers in February 1996 (European Commission 1995b). This directive applies to all works from non-European Union countries which qualify for protection under the legislation providing that reciprocal treatment is available to European information producers in countries outside the Union. A *sui generis* right of protection for 15 years is available for databases in which there has been a substantial investment in 'obtaining, verification or presentation' of the contents. This language covers telephone directories for example and the right extends to nationals of a member state or companies registered in a member state. Copyright protection for literary, dramatic, and musical works produced by nationals has been harmonised to protect works for the length of the author's life plus 70 years, a term which is longer than the protection available in the United States, that is, the length of the author's life plus another 50 years.

The intergovernmental organisation with special responsibility for intellectual property rights is the World Intellectual Property Organisation (WIPO), a specialised agency of the United Nations. WIPO administers international conventions for the protection of trademarks and copyrights and offers assistance to countries in formulating intellectual property protection (see Chapter 9).[3] In December 1996 the WIPO Diplomatic Conference on Certain Copyright and Neighbouring Rights Questions adopted two treaties, the Copyright Treaty and the Performances and Phonograms Treaty. These treaties are regarded as responses to the challenges of digital technology, particularly the Internet. They provide an exclusive right for authors, performers and producers of phonograms to authorise the making available of their works, performances and phonograms, to the public by wire or wireless means so that they can be accessed via on-demand and interactive services.

The treaties incorporate provisions concerning technical measures of protection and electronic rights management (systems that track and bill for the use of protected material). Attempts to remove or circumvent technical systems of protection or to alter electronic rights management systems in an unauthorised way will now be subject to legal remedies for signatories to the treaties. The treaties leave to national legislation the problem of determining the territorial effect of the exhaustion of rights with the first sale of a copy and the issue of whether parallel imports are allowed (WIPO 1996a). The Treaty on Performances and Phonograms contains other economic rights of performers and producers of phonograms. The treaties were open for signature until 31 December 1997 and will enter into force three months after being ratified by national governments (a process which is not necessarily immediate).

The Conference was unable to reach agreement on the rights of performers in the audiovisual recordings (or fixations) of their performances and called for another session to discuss this issue. Delegates also did not discuss a draft Treaty on Intellectual Property Rights in Databases which would have granted protection to non-original databases.[4] Referred to as the 'basic proposal', this would have created prohibitions for the 'importation, manufacture and distribution of protection-defeating devices' along the lines advocated by the United States Information Infrastructure Task Force. Some firms, including leading providers of information services and computer and electronics manufacturers in the United States, objected to these provisions arguing that they would discourage investment in the multimedia and electronics industries. Agreement would have established a *sui generis* right for databases (similar to the European Union directive on the legal protection of databases), in addition to the protection that databases currently receive (Union for the Public Domain 1996). The 'basic proposal' has generated much controversy among database producers and the academic community. These groups argue that extended protection would mean that the use of data needed to produce their products or academic works would have to be paid for and that this would have a negative impact on the database business and academic research.

Participation by developing countries in the proceedings and negotiations leading up to a major diplomatic conference, such as the 1996 WIPO Conference, is difficult because of the numerous meetings and smaller discussions which help to formulate national or regional positions. Analysis of the representation of developing countries as compared to the industrialised countries at the Conference provides some insight into the degree to which developing country delegations are stretched. Most developing countries have a small number of delegates to monitor and participate in the debates on issues

TABLE 10.1 - WIPO DIPLOMATIC CONFERENCE ON COPYRIGHT, DECEMBER 1996, DELEGATES

Region	No. of participating countries	No. of country delegates	Av. size of delegation	Largest delegation	Number of association delegates			Total delegates
					Number representing private sector companies	Number representing authors, performers, etc.	Other, e.g. education, scientific	
United States, Canada, Australia, New Zealand	4	44	11	32	57	1	0	102
Japan	1	12	12	12	20	0	0	32
Western Europe including European Union	23	120	4.57	9	25	10	2	157
Central and East European Countries	24	75	3.13	7	0	0	0	75
Middle East	5	19	3.80	9	0	0	0	19
Latin America (plus Mexico)	22	89	4.05	11	4	3	0	96
Asia/South East Asia/Asia Pacific	15	82	5.47	14	1	0	0	83
Africa	34	97	2.85	7	2	0	3	102
International Associations	37	–	–	–	50	36	12	98
Total	–	538		–	159	50	17	764

Notes: Eleven international associations could not be assigned to this classification. Largest delegations by country are for United States, Canada, Australia, New Zealand - United States; Western Europe - United Kingdom, and Germany; Central and East European Countries - Russia and Croatia; Middle East - Israel; Latin America (plus Mexico) - Brazil; Asia/South East Asia/Asia Pacific - Indonesia and Thailand; Africa -Tunisia. The European Commission had 15 delegates.
Source: WIPO 1996b.

that will affect their economic interests. In the regional groupings, developing countries were represented by relatively few coordinating institutions. The impact of stronger intellectual property protection will be different for each developing country. Nevertheless, compared to the groups representing the interests of producers, consumers, and scientific and education users of electronic information in the industrialised countries, the developing countries are not well represented. Table 10.1 shows the relative numbers of participants at the WIPO Conference.

African organisations include the Organisation of African Unity with two delegates, and the Union of National Radio and Television Organisations of Africa with three delegates. Ethiopia had observer status. For the Latin American region coordinating institutions numbered only three (Asociación Argentina de Interpretés, Caribbean Broadcasting Union, and the Ibero–Latin-American Federation of Performers). For the Asian region only the Asia Pacific Broadcasting Union was represented. This compares with the 22 associations representing the United States including Internet organisations, the telecommunication and software industries, broadcasters, film and video producers, musicians organisations, and the legal community. Of the 37 international associations with representatives at the Conference a review of the affiliations of delegates suggests that they were mainly, although not exclusively, people from the industrialised countries. A relatively small proportion of these organisations directly represented the interests of the individual creators of information or the science and education establishments with an interest in 'public domain' information.

A simple count of individual participants and coordinating institutions reveals nothing about those individuals' and organisations' competencies. Nor does it reveal the degree to which informal agreements were reached on regional positions. Nevertheless, this analysis highlights the scale of the challenge to monitor and participate in international rule setting in relation to the numerous other claims on people's time and resources in the developing countries.

The developments in the intellectual property protection arena are significant for developing countries who wish to become producers of 'digital products' or to use externally produced electronic information services and products as tools and components of ICT applications. On the one hand, these provisions, together with those in the Agreement on Trade-related Aspects of Intellectual Property Rights (TRIPS), are expected to generate greater incentives for local innovation in developing countries and attract foreign investors. On the other, higher prices for protected technologies and information products and restrictions on their diffusion by imitation or copying could have negative effects. Developing coun-

tries need to 'strike and sustain a balance between the needs of innovative firms and their licensees for protection from easy appropriation of their intellectual property, on the one hand, and the needs of legitimate follow-on competitors and consumers, on the other' (UNCTAD 1996c: 1)

One impact of stronger protection is a reduction of domestic output and employment by firms which have been producing counterfeit copyrighted information products. There could be longer term gains in improved product quality for consumers and users (at higher prices) and gains in employment and wages in other sectors. Some studies have found no relationship between membership of intellectual property rights conventions and treaties and investment in developing countries or technology transfer. However, a survey of potential investors from the United States, Japan, and Germany has shown that the perceived adequacy of the intellectual property protection system in developing countries does have effects on decisions about whether to invest.[5] The beneficial effects of copyright enforcement are expected to accrue mainly to the newly industrialising countries and the larger developing countries. There could be a net cost for the least developed countries where there is little capacity for local development of information services and products (UNCTAD 1996c). These countries need to implement intellectual property protection provisions in a way that promotes 'dynamic competition through the acquisition and local development of technology in an environment which is conducive to growth' (UNCTAD 1996c: 4).

Another impact is the potential for arbitrage among countries with stronger and weaker enforcement regimes. Box 10.1 illustrates the difficulties for enforcement once protected 'digital' products circulate through global distribution networks such as the Internet.

BOX 10.1 – DIGITAL TECHNOLOGIES AND INTELLECTUAL PROPERTY PROTECTION

In November 1996, the popular British rock band, U2, discovered that their new, but unfinished songs, not due for release until the spring of 1997, were being sold on compact discs in street markets, as well as being distributed on the Internet (Harlow 1996; Internet Magazine 1997). Earlier in the same year, illegal copies of Italy's San Remo music festival were on sale within days of the close of the prestigious music festival. They were of better quality and had more songs than the authorised version. Sales of digital intellectual property transmitted on various distribution systems and produced in numerous formats are global. Digital technologies facilitate easy and large scale reproduction of digital information, and rapid transmission and easy access (Tang 1997b). In the case of the U2 incident, it was a Hungarian-based site that was found to be transmitting the songs. When it was closed down by national authorities, new sites sprang up in Brazil, Japan, and France.

As the Hungarian officials sought to enforce existing legislation, the protected material was sent across the network to new sites in other countries. Countries that have not complied with legal obligations to prevent this kind of activity, become potential targets for sanctions (Kahin and Nesson 1995).

10.2.3 CRYPTOGRAPHY AND OTHER METHODS FOR PROTECTION

Enforcement of strengthened protection for intellectual property depends partly on the extent to which technical means can be devised to prevent illegal copying of information products and services. The 'direct revenue' group or the firms representing the 'copyright industry' mainly in the United States have argued that measures need to be adopted to combat copyright infringement (Software Business Alliance 1995). Companies argue that the framework which can provide a legal penalty for infringement of their ownership rights in information will always lag behind the means of distributing and accessing information. Digital content owners are turning to technology to supplement the law and to limit infringement of their rights under existing law.

There are many systems for the protection of intellectual works that are being used by content developers. Electronic copyright management systems to protect works integrate many different techniques to identify their authors, and the owners of rights. They provide information about the terms and conditions for the use of works, provide billing systems, and track the royalties paid to rights holders. *Cryptography* is the most widely used method of protecting information from potential infringement. Information is encrypted so that it is unusable until a 'key' is applied.

Private key encryption involves a pre-established relationship between the user and the source of information before an encrypted document is transmitted. This kind of encryption is limited to a one-off transmission and is regarded as being costly, time consuming, and complex to implement. The 'RSA standard', named after its creators, Rivest, Shamir, and Adleman at the Massachusetts Institute of Technology, is a public-key system whereby the sender uses a public key (belonging to the recipient and available in a directory) to encrypt data. The second key which belongs to the recipient is a private, secret key that is used to decrypt data. To authenticate a message the sender attaches a digital signature that can be verified by the recipient. Another encryption technique links pro-tected material to a computer containing a code that enables the user to view the text and graphics, or listen to music. To gain access, a special key (password or identification number) is needed. CD-ROM publishers use encryption software packages to protect their disks or to limit access to specified groups of users. Software encryption and a unique laser treatment are being used to make copying of CD-ROMs very difficult.[6] For advanced CDs, such as digital versatile disks (DVD), encryption is being used to protect their contents and to segment global markets into regions. For example, separate regional codes are being introduced so that a DVD bought in the United States will not play in France. DVD players are being developed for regions containing circuitry that will recognise disks designed only for a specific region.[7]

Watermarking audio material with a code number does not affect the sound quality of a recording but offers a method of establishing whether the material has been used by a non-licensed user.[8] *Holograms* are being developed which are embedded in CD or CD-ROM packaging or media to authenticate the legitimacy of a copy. Means have been devised to limit the reproduction of digital media by making it impossible, for example, to produce a second generation copy (a recording of a recording). *Fingerprinting* of digital images by embedding originator-specific data-within-data is a potential method of legally demonstrating originality which is attracting the interest of publishers. In principle, all of these methods can be circumvented, but in practice their increasing use is a deterrent to those who might consider infringing copyright.

The use of technical systems for copyright protection is increasingly supported by industrialists and policy-makers. However, a study of the methods of copyright protection adopted by small and medium-sized electronic information publishers in the United Kingdom suggests that their use is not yet widespread (Tang 1995). Many smaller firms view these methods with scepticism and those who are using them have adopted weak encryption techniques. The absence of an agreed industry standard; rising costs of production and customer support; the need to make electronic publications 'user friendly'; the perceived inadequacy of copyright law; and the need to accelerate the 'time to market' of products are factors contributing to the relatively slow take-up of new techniques. There is a cautious attitude toward measures that could result in over-protection and disincentives to the creation of innovative 'digital' products.

Some electronic information publishers claim that companies that are very concerned with copyright infringement should not be in the 'digital content' business. The nature of the business makes products vulnerable to legal and illegal replication. Too much legal or technical protection might harm the growth of the electronic publishing industry. However, if a reliable, easy-to-use and to implement protection system standard were to emerge it is likely that this would stimulate wider acceptance among firms. Cost and acceptability by users are also major determinants of whether a protection method will be taken up industry-wide.

Although none of these methods of protection has been accepted as a standard, encryption is being used to an increasing extent. Until 1997, the International Traffic

Arms Regulations in the United States prevented American firms from exporting encryption techniques. They are now able to do so subject to certain restrictions. Until 1996, France had stringent laws for the use of encryption both domestically and for export, but these have now changed. In addition the Organisation for Economic Cooperation and Development (OECD) developed an initiative to harmonise the use of encryption techniques among its member countries and the OECD Council adopted a set of guidelines in March 1997.[9]

10.2.4 MANAGING OWNERSHIP RIGHTS IN DIGITAL INFORMATION

Digital technologies are making the enforcement of copyright law increasingly difficult. Legislators in some developing countries have begun to introduce reforms in response to the pressures of governments in the industrialised countries and the major software, music, motion picture, and publishing industries (Tang 1997c). 'Antipiracy' or anti-infringement organisations are campaigning to encourage developing countries to update and enforce their copyright legislation. Industry trade associations are increasing their efforts to ensure that available protection is enforced.

The International Federation of the Phonographic Industry (IFPI), representing record producers in more than 70 countries, has been instrumental in shutting down several companies producing illegal compact discs in Bulgaria, Italy, and China. IFPI is involved in the development of technical solutions for the protection of digital content and promotes the enforcement of national legislation and international conventions on intellectual property. IFPI has recommended the adoption of an International Standard Recording Code system which identifies the source manufacturer at the mastering and reproduction levels.[10]

The Business Software Alliance membership comprises the leading software companies. It has filed more than 600 lawsuits world-wide against suspected infringements and has been responsible for closing down several software production facilities in China and Thailand. The Alliance runs education programmes on intellectual property rights in more than 65 countries. Other national organisations also act as collecting societies and they are organised by industry sector representing music, film, video, and publishing. These organisations are collaborating internationally to control counterfeiting and bootlegging of digital information products.

There is concern on the part of those who generate revenues from the sale of electronic information products and services, and national governments, that producers' viability will be eroded if infringement is not stopped or reduced.[11] The United States-based coalition of trade associations, the International Intellectual Property Alliance (IIPA), publishes figures on estimated losses in

revenues to the 'copyright industries' in the United States.[12] The countries on the 'watch list' are shown in Table 10.2 representing an estimated US$ 6 billion in estimated losses to firms in the United States.

IIPA figures for losses including business software are shown in Table 10.3 by region. Deducting US$ 7.2 billion for business software from the total of US$ 14,639 billion leaves some US$ 7.4 billion of losses estimated for the motion picture, records and music, entertainment software, and publishing industries.[13]

Most of the attention of the trade associations and the press focuses on infringement in the developing world. However, there is considerable 'piracy' within the industrialised countries. In 1995, the United States was the second largest country for illegal pre-recorded music sales with US$ 279 million or 29 per cent of total sales just behind Russia with US$ 363 million representing a larger share of total sales in the country of 62 per cent (IFPI 1996). These sales in the United States explain why there is controversy within the country over the need to strengthen existing legislation. In 1994, the United Kingdom was the tenth leading country for illegal sales, with estimated sales of US$ 58 million or 2 per cent of total sales in the country. A decline in the volume of illegal sales in 1995 was attributed to the successful closing down of a major counterfeiting plant in the United Kingdom (IFPI 1996). Table 10.4 shows the estimated illegal sales in selected countries in eastern Europe and in Italy and Greece.

In Thailand copyright legislation, improved enforcement, and pressures from the European Union and the United States, resulted in a reduction in illegal sales in 1995. In 1994 these sales were estimated to be around 33 per cent of total sales and in 1995 the figure dropped to 13 per cent. In the United Arab Emirates enforcement has brought illegal sales down from 33 per cent in 1994 to 18 per cent in 1995.

In the world-wide software market, losses due to illegal sales were estimated at US$ 13 billion in 1995, representing a 9 per cent increase over the US$ 12.2 billion estimated for 1994. Eastern Europe had the highest overall illegal sales as a percentage of total country sales at 83 per cent in 1995, followed by the Middle East and Africa with 78 per cent (Business Software Alliance 1995).

Table 10.5 shows the leading three countries in each major region for illegal sales of software as a percentage of total sales in the country. In the Asia Pacific region, Viet Nam is highest with 99 per cent followed by eastern Europe where Slovenia has the highest rate at 96 per cent. In western Europe, Greece has the highest rate of 87 per cent.

Research has been undertaken in parallel with negotiations by members of the WTO and WIPO. However, there is still very little empirical evidence for the actual

TABLE 10.2 – ESTIMATED TRADE LOSSES TO UNITED STATES COPYRIGHT INDUSTRIES, 1995

	Motion pictures US$ million	Records and music US$ million	Entertainment software US$ million	Books US$ million	Total estimated losses US$ million
Priority foreign country					
China	124	300	1,286	125	1,835
Russia	312	180	189	46	726
Turkey	57	8	87	18	170
Priority watch list					
Brazil	90	70	83	30	273
El Salvador	1	3	22	4	30
Greece	60	6	21	5	92
India	58	10	26	25	119
Indonesia	15	2	83	45	145
Italy	294	128	73	20	515
Korea (Republic of)	17	6	174	25	222
Paraguay	2	20	6	2	30
Saudi Arabia	100	29	53	9	191
Viet Nam	5	6	n/a	7	18
Watch list					
Argentina	49	15	65	7	136
Bahrain	30	10	1	45	45
Bolivia	2	3	33	5	42
Bulgaria	10	105	58	1	173
Czech Republic	8	2	n/a	5	15
Hong Kong	10	5	112	2	129
Lebanon	44	n/a	n/a	2	45
Pakistan	10	5	n/a	30	45
Philippines	26	3	14	70	113
Poland	39	10	73	14	135
Romania	20	16	63	2	101
Thailand	29	5	73	32	139
Taiwan (Pr. China)	29	5	105	6	145
United Arab Emirates	5	n/a	n/a	1	6
Venezuela	30	5	51	23	109
Total Estimated Losses	**1,542**	**1,042**	**2,852**	**592**	**6,028**

Note: Numbers may not add due to rounding.
Source: Adapted from IIPA (1996).

Table 10.3 – Losses to United States software, entertainment, and publishing industry by region, 1995

Country	Motion pictures US$ million	Records and music US$ million	Business software US$ million	Entertainment software US$ million	Books US$ million	Total estimated losses US$ million
Asia	514	349	2,756	2,002	377	6,017
Middle East and Mediterranean	248	54	180	100	104	686
Latin America and Caribbean	289	226	836	359	129	1,847
Canada	22	18	270	n/a	n/a	310
Africa	11	25	171	n/a	60	267
Eastern Europe and Russia	464	363	534	396	73	1,830
Western Europe	710	245	2,451	286	41	3,683
Total	2,267	1,280	7,217	3,093	783	14,639

Note: Numbers may not add due to rounding.
Source: Adapted from IIPA, as cited in *Financial Times*, 10 February 1997.

economic impact on developing countries of changes in the international intellectual property rights regime.[14]

Developing countries account for only a small proportion of the world production of software. India is at the forefront but had a share of the United States software market in 1994–95 amounting only to 1.7 per cent (Heeks 1996a). Estimates of illegal sales and their potential economic harm to producers mainly in the industrialised countries are provided by governments and the private sector both of which have substantial economic interests in stronger protection.

Table 10.4 – Europe's music sales, 1995

Country	Illegal sales as % of annual total	Legal sales (US$ million)	Illegal sales (US$ million)
Romania	85	4	22
Bulgaria	80	2	6
Russia	73	83	222
Latvia	54	2	3
Italy	33	44	22
Greece	26	8	3

Source: Adapted from IFPI (1996).

The Special 301 provisions (Section 182) of the Omnibus Trade and Competitiveness Act of 1988, obliges the United States Trade Representative to identify countries that should be placed on the 'watch lists' shown in Table 10.2. These countries are deemed to be denying adequate and effective protection to United States intellectual property rights holders and to be preventing fair and equitable market access to producers of intellectual property. They are regarded as countries whose policies and practices have the greatest actual, or potentially adverse, impact on the economic interests of American producers. They are also believed not to be entering into negotiations in good faith and to be failing to make significant progress in bilateral or multilateral negotiations (US Congress 1988; IIPA 1996). A range of instruments is available to impose sanctions including the withdrawal of preferential tariffs and the imposition of import quotas.

Problems of measuring the economic value of information make it difficult to assess the claims about the economic impact of changes in the international intellectual property rights regime and the national responses to these changes. Strong enforcement of software protection could result in higher prices and more limited access to leading software packages for people in the least developed countries. Scientific research requires software models and tools in fields such as biotechnology, environmental protection, and agribusiness. Moves to eliminate private copying by citizens and to remove 'fair use' provisions that enable reproduction for scientific and educational purposes would raise new barriers to accessing electronic information. This would occur at the same time that the global information infrastructure is creating the potential for the wider distribution of information at very low cost.

If strengthened intellectual property rights regimes restrict access to information for developing countries, there are likely to be costs. An alternative argument suggests that firms in the industrialised countries will be more likely to enter into partnerships with better exchanges of codified information and tacit knowledge with a country that has a reasonable record of enforcing intellectual property protection. Strong protection regimes are expected to attract direct foreign investment by multinational firms. However, 'many factors influence direct foreign investment decisions, and there is little systematic empirical evidence to support or contradict the assertion that the insecurity of intellectual property exerts powerful adverse effects among these, except, possibly in the cases of the chemical and pharmaceutical industries, and in choices about the location of overseas R&D facilities' (David 1995: 17).

TABLE 10.5 – INFRINGEMENT RATES BY REGION

Region/Country	1994 %	1995 %
Western Europe		
Greece	87	86
Spain	77	74
Ireland	74	71
Eastern Europe		
Slovenia	96	96
Bulgaria	94	94
Russia	94	94
Latin America		
El Salvador	97	97
Paraguay	95	95
Guatemala	94	94
Middle East/Africa		
United Arab Emirates	92	92
Bahrain	92	92
Kuwait	91	91
Asia Pacific		
Viet Nam	100	99
Indonesia	97	98
China	97	96
North America		
Canada	46	44
United States	31	26

Source: Compiled from Business Software Alliance (1995).

Despite the absence of independent evidence on the impact of changes in the intellectual property rights regime internationally, it is clear that changes will affect the costs of producing and using electronic information. They have an impact on the economic feasibility of combining external and indigenous information resources within developing countries to further development goals.

In principle, the wider distribution of publicly accessible information should enable people in developing countries to make more informed choices about ICTs and enhance the use of these technologies to support development goals and to alleviate poverty. Simply accessing digital information does not build the capabilities to transform it into useful knowledge. Nevertheless, there is a belief that the diffusion of greater quantities of information will produce new knowledge. The 'new growth theory' is rekindling interest in the transfer of technological knowledge (Romer 1986). The new models recognise that the transfer of knowledge is affected by the intellectual property protection regime. These models give rise to insights into the hypothetical impact of changes in the intellectual property regime. They do not capture the actual impacts because they cannot model the potential for building capabilities to use the new sources of information. As Paul David suggests, 'borrowing capabilities' may be one of the strategic core competencies needed by organisations in developing countries. In order to 'learn to borrow' organisational and technological competencies in the ICT field will be needed as well as better access to electronic information. The combination of these and other factors may enable developing countries to monitor the scientific and technological knowledge frontier more effectively and to learn from the failures and successes of others (David 1995).

10.3 ELECTRONIC COMMERCE – INTRODUCING A GOVERNANCE SYSTEM

Electronic commerce is regarded in the United States, and increasingly in Europe and some of the newly industrialising countries, as a prerequisite for the conduct of business in the 'knowledge societies' of the future. Countries that do not implement electronic business networks will almost certainly find themselves disadvantaged in the conduct of trade and in their financial affairs.

Electronic commerce refers to a very wide variety of ways of doing business over networks. It is defined generally as 'all forms of commercial transactions involving both organisations and individuals, that are based upon the electronic processing of data, including text, sound and visual images. It also refers to the effects that the electronic exchange of commercial information may have on the institutions and processes that support and govern commercial activities' (OECD 1997e: 20). It includes activities that may be replaced by electronic media such as the exchange of documents, telephone calls, faxes, etc. It also includes standards for the procurement of manufactured goods by governments and the private sector. It increases the potential for firms and individuals to participate in global electronic marketplaces (Ferné 1996: 2).

Electronic commerce raises issues about intellectual property protection, the introduction of electronic money or e-cash, the protection of individual privacy, as well rules with respect to advertising, prevention of fraud, the treatment of 'seditious' material, technical standards for electronic payments, security service infrastructures (public key authorities and trusted third parties), the role of electronic catalogues, and many technical issues concerning high speed networking and digital object and data interchange (moving beyond text-based electronic data interchange protocols).

As more transactions take place using advanced public and private networks including the Internet the competitiveness of firms is becoming much less a function of their size in terms of tangible (physical) assets or capital and more related to their capacity to manage information supply chains - links between suppliers and customers (Eliasson 1990).[15] Electronic commerce is emerging as a way of reducing transaction costs and of supporting all the elements of commercial transactions potentially without human intermediation.

Today, however, electronic commerce is a long way from the vision of a completely virtual market. To enable such an environment to work there is a need for a governance regime, just as there is in the case of commercial activity in physical goods. There is also a need to build a technical and service infrastructure that can sustain the volume of commercial transactions that will move into 'cyberspace' in the 21st Century. For example, a bank may have about 10 million electronic transactions per day and a major retailer may be processing total annual transactions worth more than US$ 10 billion (OECD 1997e). These volumes of commercial activity are present in some industrialised countries today. They involve enormously complex interactions with both known and unknown parties. The need for new ways of managing the trust that is implicit in market transactions is growing.

For example, if electronic commerce is to expand, trust needs to be established between parties. Buyers and sellers need to be able to prove that the content of electronic information has not been altered and that the owner, originator, and recipient can be linked to that information. This calls for a way of establishing the integrity, authentication, and non-repudiation of information (like company letterheads, written signatures, and seals on paper documents). This involves data integrity and access control. Another element in the establishment of trust is the confidentiality of information, ensuring that only those authorised to read information can do so. Confidentiality is important because documents can be copied so easily (EURIM 1997).

The policy challenge in these areas is to provide a balance between the ability to combat fraud, terrorism, and other criminal activities while providing opportunities for businesses and citizens to use the new technologies. To achieve this balance in a single country would be a major challenge. However, electronic commerce is global. Any citizen or business with access to an affordable network and the capabilities to work with software and services can engage in electronic commerce. Incompatible rules and standards for electronic commerce create barriers to the flows of information and 'lock out' potential participants from 'cyberspace' markets (Leer 1996). The international flows of transactions make it imperative that cooperation between governments and the private sector is increased. There is a need for ongoing attempts to reach consensus on the rules and standards for the new kinds of markets that are emerging (Mizuno 1997).

Establishing trust on a business-to-business basis is difficult. However, creating rules that will effectively establish norms for consumer protection and ensure that people's privacy is not damaged by electronic commerce is even more crucial. As the Internet has become more pervasively accessible, the volume of commerce on the network is also growing. Although transactions in most cases are not handled completely on the network, there are trends in this direction (see Box 10.2).

BOX 10.2 – SECURING ELECTRONIC TRANSACTIONS

Singapore took its first step into secure electronic commerce in April 1997. The world's first Visa Card purchase on the Internet using the Secure Electronic Transaction (SET) protocol involved cardholders and merchants using special software called 'digital certificates' providing a means of electronic identification and ensuring confidential information was sent in a secure code across the Internet. The transaction was unusual because it relied upon several different vendors' technologies (National Computer Board 1997a).

There are differences of opinion on how fast electronic commerce will grow. World trade involving computer software, entertainment products (motion pictures, videos, games, sound recordings), information services (databases, on-line newspapers), technical information, product licences, and professional services (businesses and technical consulting, accounting, architectural design, legal advice, travel services, etc.), is growing rapidly and now accounts for well over US$ 40 billion worth of exports in the United States alone (IITF 1996).[16] If new rules and standards are put in place between buyers and sellers, electronic commerce would become easier for those with access to global infrastructures. Commerce on the Internet could reach US$ 5 billion by the turn of the century growing on the 1995 base estimated at US$ 200 million (IITF 1996, OECD 1997e).[17]

The global information infrastructure, including the Internet, is likely to bring profound changes in the traditional model of relationships between buyers and sellers (IITF 1996). Use of the Internet, intranets (intrafirm), and extranets (interfirm) could lower transaction costs and facilitate new types of commercial transactions. The Internet was launched in the 1960s as a network funded and run by the Department of Defence in the United States and its Advanced Research Project (ARPA). It was intended as a means for scientists and military personnel to exchange information. In the 1980s the National Science Foundation in the United States was given the responsibility for further developing a highly decentralised network. The network uses protocols, Transmission Control Protocol/Internet Protocol (TCP/IP), that are less sophisticated than those used in proprietary corporate data networks or those supporting traffic on the public switched telecommunication network. Nevertheless, these protocols are open. They support interoperability between virtually any computer user who seeks to connect and transmit information.

TCP standardises the exchange of data, while IP allows different systems to recognise one another in the network. The advantage is that each existing network can retain its own architecture. By 1989 in the United States, the Internet had been opened to commercial users and this began to occur elsewhere as governments received increasing pressure from the private sector. By the mid-1990s Internet hosts were flourishing in most of the industrialised countries. Although a relatively small proportion of Internet traffic is generated by developing countries, growth is taking off in most regions where there is a reasonably well developed telecommunication infrastructure.

Box 10.3 - Private Internets and electronic commerce

'There are two main types of risk that need to be addressed: securing core business systems against malicious attack once they are opened up to external customers; and ensuring security from a business point of view, allowing a company to be sure it is doing business with a genuine customer or supplier and that both have committed to a transaction The lure of the Extranet is that it will potentially widen the number of partners with which a business can carry out e-commerce. The danger is that it will deal with companies with which it has had no previous relationship and thus will need to authenticate those companies and their communications in some way' (Chappell 1997: 14).

At the same time that public access to the Internet has been increasing, traffic growth and the lack of security of the Internet have led to the emergence of 'extranets'. Extranets based on a leased network infrastructure will provide 'internet-like' services to the corporate world, but they will be provided with security guarantees. These networks are only beginning to be put in place by companies like IBM who want to provide services to help companies with 'customer relationship management' (Chappell 1997). Services will provide supply chain partners with Web access to data from corporate systems. At a more sophisticated level they will offer assistance in building new applications using software development technologies like Java to create wholly new electronic environments. The premium offered by the extranet, as compared to the Internet, that will be accessible to most users once the underlying infrastructure is extended, is risk reduction (see Box 10.3).

The emergence of extranets is similar to the process which occurred when private corporate networks using capacity leased from telecommunication infrastructure operators offered premium services to larger companies that were not supported by the public network. These networks were built in the 1970s and 1980s to bypass the public switched telecommunication network. In those countries which had relatively inexpensive prices for leased lines were available (terrestrial or satellite which were available even at higher prices in developing countries to overcome the absence of adequate infrastructure), large multinational companies have been able to reorganise and introduce distributed working practices. This is one factor which has enabled them to locate business activities (such as software development and data processing) around the world.

In developing countries similar developments should be expected for Internet (public) and extranet (private) services as firms seek security and advantages for their customers. The other advantage of these developments for larger firms is that they are likely to be subject to self-regulation. Governments and regulatory authorities will find it increasingly difficult to regulate private networks provided by companies with no territorial presence within their borders.

10.3.1 Towards new principles of governance

The interest of developing countries in electronic commerce varies widely based on their current capacity to participate in electronic communication. Governments and businesses in the industrialised countries are concerned that some governments in the developing countries will seek to regulate the Internet and network-based transactions. If governments levy taxes and duties, restrict the types of information transmitted, or control standards development, it is feared that a fragmented global electronic trading regime will emerge. The United States perspective on the need for a new set of rules and codes of conduct in the electronic commerce field relies on a market-oriented approach and several key principles have been outlined (see Box 10.4).

As the Internet becomes more attractive as a support infrastructure for electronic commerce, the need to evolve new governance systems is becoming evident in many areas. An example is the system used to assign 'domain names' to host computers such as the popular '.com'. With increasing demand, the number of available top level domains is becoming a relatively scarce resource. The allocation and administration of names is handled by a private company in the United States that has a virtual monopoly and is authorised to charge fees for domain name registrations. In May 1997, WIPO established an arbitration and mediation centre for dispute settlement among parties. This new governance institution will administer procedures for settlement of disputes concerning Second Level Domain names. A Memorandum of Understanding on the generic Top Level Domain Name Space of the Internet Domain Name system has been agreed. The Memorandum is open for signature but it is unclear whether this international initiative will resolve the tensions and conflicts that have arisen over the present administrative apparatus (WIPO 1997). It is also unclear how it will affect developing countries as they seek to register a growing number of sites.

As the Internet becomes increasingly commercially oriented, issues are raised with respect to customs and taxation of traded goods and services in 'electronic space'. When electronic media such as the Internet are used, there are no fixed geographical routes of trade as there are in the case of physical trade in goods. The structure of the Internet would make it difficult to levy taxes when products or services are delivered electronically. Nevertheless, some consideration is being given to new modes of taxation and the industrialised countries have expressed concerns that some developing countries will look to the Internet and electronic commerce for new sources of public revenues (see Chapter 12).

The United States is advocating that the WTO should declare the Internet a tax-free environment. In Europe, individual country positions vary, but by mid-1997 there appeared to be a view on the part of the European Commission that while no major changes in the principles of taxation should be considered, it would be premature to declare the Internet a 'tax-free zone'.

The industrialised countries seek to establish a 'uniform commercial code' for business conducted over the Internet. The aim is to build a uniform legal framework for electronic commercial transactions world-wide. Steps in this direction have been taken by the United Nations Commission on International Trade Law (UNCITRAL) which has developed a 'model law on electronic commerce' for international contracts in electronic commerce. This document establishes rules and standards for electronic contract performance, defines what constitutes valid electronic writing and an original document, and provides for the acceptability of electronic signatures for legal and commercial purposes. It also defines a procedure for the admission of computerised evidence into the courts and arbitration proceedings. However, all countries would need to implement this framework to achieve harmonisation of global electronic trading.

Box 10.4 - PRINCIPLES FOR ELECTRONIC COMMERCE

> ▮ The private sector should lead.
> ▮ Governments should avoid placing undue restrictions on electronic commerce.
> ▮ Where government involvement is needed, its aim should be to support and enforce a predictable, minimalist, consistent, and simple legal environment for commerce.
> ▮ Governments should recognise the unique qualities of the Internet.
> ▮ Electronic commerce over the Internet should be facilitated on an international basis.

Source: IITF (1996).

Negotiation will be needed to encourage governments to recognise and accept official electronic communications (that is, contracts, notarised documents, etc.). New institutional procedures for authentication, establishing electronic registries, promoting the development of dispute resolution mechanisms, and establishing rules in connection with licensing and transfer of rights in software and electronic data will be necessary.

Cryptography provides the means for securing networks in order to establish a basis for trading. Until recently cryptography was rarely used outside the military and government context but commercial pressures for its use are increasing. Governments aim to retain the ability to intercept and read communications in order to protect national security and they try to limit the availability of cryptography. The policy issue is whether the use of cryptography should be controlled, by whom, and in what manner. There is a need for an internationally acceptable, practical, and commercial framework. Business demands for adequate levels of secure information and the requirements of national security and law enforcement are potentially in conflict in all countries.

The essence of cryptography is that the sender uses an encryption key as input to a conversion routine (or algorithm) which makes the digital message being stored or transmitted unintelligible. This can be restored to its original form only by someone possessing the corresponding decryption key and algorithm. This technique is being widely used in the financial services industry, for example, to protect fund transfers and personal information, during the withdrawal of cash from an Automatic Teller Machine. It is also being used in consumer products designed to control access to pay TV systems. Cryptography is essential for electronic commerce because it provides a solution to the requirements for integrity, authentication, non-repudiation, and confidentiality (EURIM 1997).

Some governments are proposing the use of Trusted Third Parties (TTP) to provide certification for public encryption keys but this requires a high degree of trust in the TTPs. TTPs must be respected nationally and internationally. Most governments prevent product suppliers from selling products outside their national boundaries by using the strongest methods of cryptography.

Apart from the issue of establishing trust in electronic commerce, issues highlighted by the OECD discussions include consumer protection, competition, financial and payment systems, taxation, intellectual property rights, legal safeguards against criminal activities, dispute settlement mechanisms, and other requirements relating to the regulation of electronic infrastructures.

As a matter of urgency, governments need to clarify the legal definitions, practices and structures that pertain to commercial activities in an electronic environment, and to seek multilateral agreements on critical legal matters, especially the laws regarding residency, agency, liability, auditability, control of databases, unauthorised use of databases and data protection (OECD 1997e: 16).

The OECD (1997e) recommends that,

▌ Electronic services infrastructures (including telecommunications, television, and data networks) must converge to support electronic commerce applications.

▌ Measures may be needed to ensure that proprietary standards do not create entry barriers.

▌ No country should be able to enforce national encryption policies on firms in other countries and national data protection laws should be harmonised to ensure that public confidence in electronic trading systems is not destroyed.

▌ Physical transport systems should be coordinated to complement efficiencies gained as a result of the introduction of electronic commerce.

▌ Industry and government cooperation is essential in promoting electronic commerce and there should be a dynamic international dialogue on the harmonisation of electronic commerce and electronic administration principles.

▌ Governments should adjust existing laws (including intellectual property protection) and regulations to apply to 'intangible' as well as 'material' products, and agree on policing and enforcement.

▌ Approaches to taxation based on principles relating to the source and destination of products and residency of companies should be maintained rather than suggestions for taxing the process of data exchange.

The positions of developing countries on these issues and their interests in the outcomes are important for future access to the new 'virtual' trading routes of knowledge-based societies.

10.3.2 DEVELOPING COUNTRY ACCESS TO VIRTUAL TRADING ROUTES

The participation of developing countries in the current discussions is important to ensure that the electronic commerce systems they develop are compatible with those in the industrialised countries. However, the principles of doing business on networks, that is, the rules for 'cybercommerce', also need to be consistent with their development goals. Changes in the electronic trading regime are likely to have a very significant impact on trade throughout the developing world (Mansell and Hawkins 1992). The new 'virtual' trading routes are being designed using architectures that can favour either open access or closure to a select membership of traders (Mansell and Jenkins 1992a).

The French historian, Fernand Braudel, observed that

The division of labour on a world-economy scale cannot be described as a concerted agreement made between equal parties and always open to review. It became established progressively as a chain of subordinations, each conditioning the other. Unequal exchange, the origin of inequality in the world, and by the same token, the invariable generator of trade, are long-standing realities (Braudel 1984: 48).

Electronic commerce networks are being established progressively and designs with respect to networks, standards, interoperability, access arrangements, as well as the procedures that enable trust to be established, are being dealt with step-by-step (Mansell 1996b). They are being established most quickly in the industrialised and newly industrialising countries. For example, Singapore has heavily promoted the use of electronic data interchange (a component of electronic commerce) for several years (Mansell and Jenkins 1992b). Brazil also has considerable experience in the banking and financial services sectors having introduced automation in the 1960s (Cassiolato 1996).

However, many developing countries have only just begun to use ICTs to address financial management at the macro-economic level. They are not well positioned in a world in which every small and medium-sized business and consumer seeks to do business using a network. UNCTAD has supported a large number of projects with implications for electronic commerce initiatives (UNCTAD 1997). A Debt Management and Financial Analysis System (DMFAS) has been designed to assist developing countries in recording and monitoring external debts. The system provides a basis for learning about the institutional, legal, and administrative issues concerning debt management and financial flows. Disbursement requests and payment orders are generated automatically, and reports are standardised to adhere to World Bank requirements. This is a precursor to fully-fledged electronic trading.

A Measures Affecting Service Trade (MAST) programme also initiated by UNCTAD provides information on laws, regulations, and international trade in service commitments. The system is intended to assist developing countries in regional and multilateral negotiations and to enable sharing of country experiences in institutional and national reforms and the regulation of trade in services. The Trade Point Initiative launched in 1992 involved the implementation of 'one-stop shops' for traders. These physical places provide an access point to PCs and networks where this is appropriate. Traders can engage in electronic transactions such as customs clearance. They can obtain information about foreign trade institutions, chambers of commerce, banks, and insurance companies. The trade points are either connected electronically to distant networks, or the electronic information is assembled under one roof using stand-alone technologies. Trade related information is available from local and remote international databases.

UNCTAD's Trade Analysis Information System (TRAINS) provides information on international trading conditions. These innovative services are providing some people with experience of the potential of electronic commerce, but they are very distant from the leading experiments with electronic cash, virtual trading, and secure transactions that are on the verge of becoming a reality in the industrialised countries, and in some of the wealthier developing countries.

Other systems developed by UNCTAD are the Automated Systems for Customs Data (Asycuda) and the Advance Cargo Information System (ACIS), which are global information systems for customs transit. The system aims to reduce transport costs which for landlocked countries in West Africa can amount to more than one quarter of the value of the goods as compared to about 5 per cent on average for goods in the industrialised countries. The information system allows goods to travel through different countries with minimum frontier checks. Regional schemes are being developed. The system is important because some of the poorest countries depend on customs payments for between 40 and 80 per cent of their revenues. Fraud, corruption, and administrative errors can reduce these revenues significantly. The new systems automate the necessary information exchanges and the Asycuda system, now in use in more than 70 countries throughout the world, costs only about US$ 2 million to install compared with the US$ 50 million for commercial systems (Financial Times 1997; Mansell and Jenkins 1992a).

Electronic commerce promises enormous gains to developing countries if it becomes pervasive. However, for those businesses and citizens who are left out of this new arena of trade, there is a great likelihood of complete exclusion. This should be of substantial concern since it would represent exclusion from the equivalent of the waterways, air transport, rail and road transport systems, that historically have provided the basis for trade in physical goods.

10.3.3 THE SOCIAL DIMENSIONS OF ELECTRONIC COMMERCE

In the industrialised countries and in some of the developing countries, electronic commerce is leading to practices of 'red-lining' or 'apartheid' marketing. Data are generated as a result of electronic transactions and these are used to target socio-demographic groups with products and services tailored to their demand profiles. Those who are deemed unable to pay are simply excluded from these offers (Ratan 1995).

The targeting of products and services to consumers around the world is relying on the generation of telemetadata or transaction generated information (Samarajiva 1996). These data are transmitted as part of the set-up, transmission, billing, and management of a message sent through a publicly accessible telecommunication network. Billing data, call pattern data, and 'intelligent' network databases used to support services, are examples (Sayers 1997). These data are generated by the public (citizens and businesses) and they include routing information, origin and destination identity, time of calling, whether a call invokes special services as well as 'simple' transmission (Arthur D Little 1991).

The volume of these data is growing rapidly with the diffusion of digital telecommunication networks and especially mobile services which generate large amounts of these data. Users of the data include network operators (to provide of value-added services and to manage network service provision), law enforcement agencies who gain access to, for example, surveillance and marketing agencies.[18] Users of information face problems of searching and filtering information of value to them in ever more complex electronic network environments. This is generating a demand for guides and directories to electronic information and services. Direct marketing agencies are flourishing in some countries. They use electronic services to track consumption patterns. The 'red-lining' practices of direct marketing agencies threaten to exclude poorer localities in developing countries creating one community of citizens and businesses who transact business using electronic networks and another that is excluded.

National information infrastructure development enables electronic commerce but it also raise issues for data protection and the privacy of individuals. The codes of conduct and legal restrictions on the uses of transaction generated information about businesses and citizens within countries, and by people outside countries, are only beginning to be considered.

There are theories suggesting that money laundering, for

example, increases with the liberalisation of cross-border capital movements as a result of more open markets and greater volumes of cross-border trade. The liberalisation of financial markets, globalisation of the financial sector, and the spread of electronic networking also are challenging the international law enforcement system. It has been estimated that world-wide money laundering could reach a value of US$ 100 billion a year. Much of this would be controlled by a small number of criminal syndicates (German 1995). Money laundering is likely to grow as greater use of electronic commerce occurs.

In addition, the Internet and computer bulletin boards provide information about how to commit crimes. Enforcement of laws, and evidence requirements, differ between countries. Various countries are entering into mutual legal assistance treaties concerning criminal matters, and reciprocity under these treaties has major resource implications. The United States Defense Science Board has urged its government to expend US$ 3 billion on military defences against information warfare (Branegan et al. 1997).

ICTs provide the technologies for encryption as well as electronic surveillance. Criminal issues and surveillance issues are beyond the scope of this report because little information on these activities is in the public domain.[19] Nevertheless, 'cybercrime' is an issue that cannot be ignored by developing countries.

10.4 GLOBAL INFORMATION INFRASTRUCTURES, PRIVACY, AND SOCIAL CONTROL

Cultural and social considerations become very significant as developing countries address the impact of the Internet and electronic commerce on business conduct and on everyday life. Understanding that 'sociability' proceeds differently in different 'knowledge societies' is fundamental to understanding that different countries and regions in the world will seek to nuance the rules and standards governing the new 'cyberspace' transactions in different ways. As Francis Fukuyama writes,

In any modern society, the economy constitutes one of the most fundamental and dynamic arenas of human sociability. There is scarcely any form of economic activity, from running a dry-cleaning business to fabrication of large-scale integrated circuits, that does not require the social collaboration of human beings ... economic activity represents a crucial part of social life and is knit together by a wide variety of norms, rules, moral obligations, and other habits that shape society (Fukuyama 1995:6,7).

The social capital that gives rise to capabilities to interact in a beneficial way with electronic media is informed by religion, tradition, history, and the intermingling of these aspects of societies with new experiences. This report does not address the details of cultural shaping of electronic business or the everyday environment. This is partly a reflection of the lack of systematic information that exists and partly a reflection of a bias in what is generally reported in studies of the diffusion and use of ICTs. Chapter 2 of this report emphasises that available indicators simply do not capture the social capabilities that are vital to the effective use of these technologies. The case studies of approaches in the developing countries tend to focus on cultural and social issues in the context of audience interaction with entertainment or educational programming. They leave the culture of work, the workplace, and business conduct on one side. An exception to this is work on business groups and alliances which considers culture in the context of learning and the transfer of knowledge through new kinds of partnerships (Amsden 1994; Whitley 1992).

One project that examined the use of ICTs by commercial banks confirmed the considerable difficulties that arise when the introduction of ICTs is considered without any attempt being made to examine the nature of the information and knowledge production itself. The study found that while Japanese, American, and British-owned commercial banks have made very large investments in computer systems and networks which facilitate intra-organisational communication, the usage of these networks and systems to automate the manipulation of data was significantly constrained. Confidential customer data, although in principle available electronically, was strictly controlled with availability being dependent on 'negotiated access' taking place at the inter-personal level (Credé 1997a,b).

In the Internet context there are very large differences in the initial approaches to governments' roles in managing issues of social control and the new norms for business conduct. In the United States in 1995, for example, the Privacy Working Group of the Information Policy Committee of the Information Infrastructure Task Force adopted principles for providing and using personal information. It noted the need to further develop the technical means to improve user privacy in the Internet. Design principles for technology and services should enable the individual user to control, and acquire feedback on, the use of personal details without having to reveal their identity when personal data are not needed. Once such principles become part of the design features of software and hardware, they raise issues of compatibility with the designs of other international initiatives.

Social concerns about the protection of personal data are linked closely with European Union-wide initiatives to protect minors and human dignity from harmful and illegal content on the Internet and in audiovisual and information services (European Commission 1996f,g). The Commission is urging cooperation among the member states to enforce existing legislation and encouraging the development of self-regulation. It is also encouraging the introduction of filtering software and rating systems and has recognised the need for an international discussion of the need for a convention on harmful and illegal content. The Commission seeks a balance between ensuring the free flow of information in the market place and guaranteeing protection of the public interest.

In Austria, Germany, France, and the United Kingdom, legislation has either already been adopted or is proposed defining the legal responsibilities of Internet host service providers such that they are liable only for an item of content hosted on their server when they can reasonably be expected to be aware that it is *prima facie* illegal, or fail to take reasonable measurers to remove such content once the content in question has been drawn clearly to their attention.

The attention of the press and the legal profession has focused on attempts, especially by Asian countries, to explicitly manage their citizen's access to the Internet. Singapore is an often cited example of a country that is seeking to become a pioneer in ensuring that Internet access is widely available while managing access to certain types of information. Singapore has been proactive in taking advantage of ICTs while maintaining regulatory control. The Singapore government has made Internet access technologically and economically feasible. In July 1996, the Singapore Broadcasting Authority (SBA) Class Licence Scheme came into effect and provision of 'computer on-line services' by Internet Service Providers (ISPs) was deemed a 'licensable' broadcasting service. This is an automatic licence but licensees must comply with Internet Content Guidelines. These apply to ISPs and content providers and they prohibit a large variety of material (Millard 1997).

The three Internet Service Providers (ISPs), SingNet, Pacific International, and Cyberway, are owned by a government-linked company. In 1996 the personal computer penetration rate per 100 population had reached 35.8 per cent and there were an estimated 38,376 Internet hosts in July 1996. The model being adopted is to ensure that Internet access is only provided through proxy servers that are capable of blocking banned sites. The three Internet Service Providers are licensed to provide services directly to consumers as well as institutions (PNE Networks 1997). The aim is to block access to some sites to protect children from illegal content, but also to ensure that electronic commerce is able to flourish for business.

Since the ISPs are not foreign-owned, pressures can be applied to deny access or to block certain undesirable sites. Singapore is not the anomaly. Viet Nam's leadership has also extended regulatory control to the Internet using a model similar to that of Singapore, and this model has also influenced China's attempts at regulation. In Malaysia, the Multimedia Super Corridor is expected to provide an infrastructure that enables experimentation with alternative technical means of blocking access to undesirable information.

Box 10.5 - Attempts at Internet control

China

In September 1996, the Chinese government blocked access to more than 100 sites, including American newspapers, the Tibetan information network and the Taiwanese government. Internet users in China are required to register with the police.[20]

Myanmar

Heavy sanctions have been imposed on unauthorised use of the Internet, as the government claims that dissidents are using it to campaign against the government. Possession of a computer with networking capability is an offence that can lead to a custodial sentence of 7 to 15 years. Neither of the two ISPs provide service to the general public.

Viet Nam

The Viet Nam government has drafted regulations that require both ISPs and users of the Internet to register with authorities and to report any 'illegal activities or damaging information they may come across'. ISPs are obliged to allow monitoring of Internet traffic by the government, and from the users' point of view, those who send or receive data regarded as harmful to national security or social order will be held liable. The government was allowing a small academic and scientific network, NetNam, to operate, but has also established a new network which is owned by Viet Nam Post and Telecommunication (Millard 1997).

These attempts are meeting with varying degrees of success (see Box 10.5). This is likely to have an impact on the extent to which local access providers are attracted to provide service on a commercial basis as well as the extent to which public institutions promote the use of the Internet as a source of information which can facilitate the provision of their own services (Millard 1997).

The material available on the Internet that is of concern to legislators, regulators, and parents can be classified into two categories: illegal material and offensive material. Material is illegal when it violates an individual right protected by criminal or civil law. Child pornography and racism are examples. Offensive material does not violate any law but may offend the values and feelings of others. Various forms of censorship and jamming are based on the premise that there is a need or duty to protect society or individuals from certain types of information (Smith System Engineering Ltd 1997).

Content filtering and scanning technologies can be integrated with a computer's operating system. These technologies can routinely inspect programs running on computers for suspicious features and raise alarms. Illegal material exchanged between cooperating subscribers is likely to be encrypted and can be removed to other systems to be decrypted (see Figure 10.1).

FIGURE 10.1 – INTERNET CONTENT CONTROLS

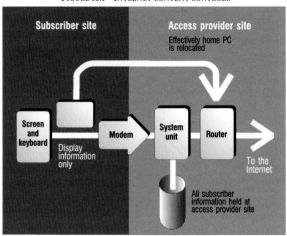

Source: Smith System Engineering Ltd (1997).

Any new governance regime, whether open or closed, with respect to the management of global networks, has significant social consequences. The growing population of users of the Internet is coming to represent an increasingly broad range of people although user profiles still point to the predominance of the young affluent male population. More people may seek (or be deemed to need) protection. More people will also seek to influence or profit from information that is illegal or offensive. As the Internet becomes more representative of society there will be an increase in the visibility and opportunity for contact with behaviour that most individuals regard as deviant. The social impacts of this contact may result in greater levels of tolerance or a greater desire to avoid contact with these groups.

Efforts to regulate the material transmitted over the Internet are stimulating debate about the availability of inappropriate and illegal material in other formats (including those that are non-electronic). Efforts to control access to such material on the Internet and to disrupt or deter the formation of networks supporting illegal activity are likely to spill over into broader social efforts to discourage such behaviours. It is difficult to predict the extent to which 'knowledge societies' will become more intolerant as a result of exposure.

The Internet is already creating social norms and customs that will be affected by regulatory systems. For example, users who abuse the tolerance of others on the Internet are often sought out for retribution, for example, they may receive hundreds of e-mails jamming the ordinary use of their systems ('flamed') or may be the subject of other even more harmful direct action (Thompsen 1996).

National cultural norms and legal standards vary. What is offensive or illegal in one country may not be so in another. Some of the international conflicts over content issues may by alleviated by promoting 'good neighbour'

policies in the export of undesirable and illegal content. Intergovernmental coordination for exchanging complaints about inappropriate or illegal material could be organised. This policy would be effective with regard to material that is inappropriate or illegal in both the country originating and that receiving the complaint.

The range of options for regulation by the government or industry self-regulation include greater reliance on user choice or on measures to protect users. It is unclear how great international cooperation will be in implementing user authentication to enable a high level of user responsibility. Services exist to make e-mail and other communication anonymous. A high degree of user responsibility does little to restrain the availability of illegal or offensive inappropriate material via the Internet and other delivery modes (see Table 10.6). Attempts to maximise subscriber protection retain the ability of users to control their own actions. However, they expand the social and private responsibility for control of Internet access points. This approach reinforces user authentication procedures and provides a means to deny access to illegal material.

Direct regulation of Internet access points has to be supported by access providers. It is unlikely that measures to protect users will be implemented uniformly. If certain countries are excluded, access providers are likely to block access to all identifiable sites in that country. If protection is extended to measures to deal with encrypted information then monitoring all uses of ICTs capable of modifying information, for example, personal computers, will be necessary. This is an extremely intrusive form of surveillance and raises issues of state control of information dissemination. The extent to which this can be implemented given the stocks of information is also questionable.

Economic and social benefits and costs are associated with different approaches to the management of the Internet.

TABLE 10.6 – INFORMATION CONTENT DELIVERY MODES

Type of architecture	Users	Intermediaries	Infrastructure networks	Multimedia services and material
Digital TV	Terminal: TV & set top box	Broadcasters, cable television operators	Narrow or broadband network	Satellite, cable, radio
Video-on-Demand (VOD) system (closed architecture)	Terminal: TV & set top box	Cable television operators, satellite television suppliers	Broadband network	Services and material put out by VOD system operator, text, fixed image, video, sound
Proprietary on-line services (closed architecture, highly interactive services)	Terminal: PC & modem	On-line service hosts	Proprietary network, leased line networks	Services and material by VOD system operator, material loaded by users (e-mail, BBS, chat lines), text, fixed image, video, sound (sound and animated image development)
Internet (open architecture)	Terminal: PC & modem	Internet host servers Internet access providers	Full Internet Access network	Services and material by VOD system operator. Material loaded by users (home page, WWW, e-mail, BBS, Chat lines), text, fixed image, video, sound (sound and animated image development)

Source: Adapted from European Commission (1996f).

The decentralised use of ICTs is a central feature of network architectures. It is necessary to centralise access to ICTs to achieve control of illegal or inappropriate material. Strong controls also run the risk of reducing the effectiveness of the Internet as a medium for commercially encrypted messages, that is, electronic commerce.

10.5 CONCLUSION – SOCIAL EQUITY AND EFFICIENCY CONSIDERATIONS

This chapter has illustrated that a new governance regime is emerging to coordinate the development of electronic commerce. The institutions and practices that historically have governed the intellectual property protection regime are being modified to address the interests of producers and users of digital information. In both cases, public policy initiatives are intertwined with private sector initiatives. The main participants in these negotiations of the rules for the 'new world information order' (Cowhey and McKeown 1993) are representatives of people in the industrialised countries, but the developing countries are also represented in these fora. The social and the economic impact of these developments is considerable. For some developing countries there are opportunities to immediately begin constructing national information infrastructures and to combine indigenous capabilities with the opportunities created by the new order for ICTs. For others, substantial investments in human capabilities and in the underlying infrastructure are necessary before widespread benefits can accrue to anyone and especially those in remote and rural areas.

The transition to innovative 'knowledge societies' will be very difficult for the least developed countries. These countries have few resources to avert the risk that they will be excluded from the potential benefits of ICTs. Nevertheless, it is clear that the creative use of ICTs can enable some people in these countries to improve their circumstances. In order for this to happen the institutional framework that provides the governance of ICTs and services must be favourable to attracting investment and to developing the necessary skills.

The world information order has changed dramatically since the 1970s. Larger changes ought to occur. The objective should be to tap the potential of a revolution in digital information technology for consumers and producers in the private and public sectors. This technological revolution is going to upset many traditional market positions and practices on a global scale. It is not simply a matter of new winners and losers, although these will be very numerous, or of changing national advantages in global competition. Change also implies the reordering of many public and commercial institutions as we discover new ways of doing things and new goals to be fulfilled (Cowhey and McKeown 1993: 113-4).

The 'reordering' of public and private institutions involves people and organisations at the community, national, and international levels. Their decisions affect the dynamics of the balancing of social and economic interests in information products and services. They influence whether it is possible to develop information products and services for domestic use and export markets and whether it is feasible to import and use the necessary technologies and information services. Social equity and efficiency are equally important considerations as policy-makers and corporate decision-makers plan the most effective means of building national information infrastructures. Chapter 11 takes up the issue of the measures that decision-makers at the national and regional level can take to complement policy developments in the international context.

1. The 'copyright industries' refers to the producers of inform-ation products who seek protection on behalf of the creators or themselves in order to benefit from sales. The term was used initially in the United States, but has since been used more widely by the OECD and the European Commission.

2. The Information Infrastructure Task Force (IITF) was established to address a range of issues including intellectual property rights. The Working Group on Intellectual Property Rights was chaired by the Commissioner of United States Patents and Trademarks, Bruce A. Lehman, who also led the United States delegation at the WIPO Convention on Copyright in December 1996. Placing data in RAM is regarded as a copyright infringe-ment according to the law in the United Kingdom.

3. For example, the Berne Convention Concerning the Creation of an International Union for the Protection of Literary and Artistic Works of 1886.

4. The Protocol to the Berne Convention for the Protection of Literary and Artistic Works is sometimes referred to as the Global Information Infrastructure Treaty.

5. See Mansfield (1995) for the results of this study and Maskus (1993), Ferrantino (1993), Primo Braga (1996), Maskus and Penubarti (1995) for other empirical assess-ments of studies on the expected impacts of intellectual prop-erty protection regimes and introduction of market access provisions.

6. This system is embedded in CD-ROMs at the mastering stage. Each CD-ROM has a unique locking code which prevents products from being copied by a CD-Recordable machine.

7. The video industry is looking at a method developed by Thorn EMI UK known as Visually Embedded Coding (VEC) which inserts and retrieves invisibly encoded information. These invisible identification codes can be retrieved using a VEC decoder (Multimedia Association News 1995; Fox 1996).

8. Thorn EMI UK has developed the Identification Coding Embedded (ICE) system that allows inaudible codes to be embedded in audio material. ICE decoders identify audio files and search for ICE codes. P. Tang, personal communi-cation with David Monteith, a member of the development team for ICE and VEC, Central Research Laboratory, EMI, 29 May 1996.

9. The OECD Recommendation of the Council Concerning Guidelines for Cryptography Policy was adopted on 27 March 1997. It is a non-binding agreement that sets out eight principles for policy (trust in cryptographic methods, user choice, market-driven development, standards, protec-tion of privacy and personal data, liability, international cooperation) (OECD 1997^f).

10. The code system is the basic identifier of the recording indus-try and is recognised by the International Organization for Standardization. With Philips Consumer Electronics, IFPI has introduced an identification programme - Source Identification Code - for CD manufacturing plants.

11. The methodology for calculating the estimated value of illegally copied products is not made public by industry asso-ciations.

12. The eight organisations are: the American Film Marketing Association, the Association of American Publishers, the Business Software Alliance, the Interactive Digital Software Association, the Information Technology Industry Council, the Motion Picture Association of America, the National Music Publishers' Association, and the Recording Industry Association of America. The IIPA represents more than 1,350 American companies producing and distributing copyrighted works in various formats.

13. In 1995 sales of illegally copied pre-recorded music were estimated at US$ 2.1 billion. This represents illegal sales of 955 million units comprised of 866 million cassettes (68 per cent), 85 million CDs (31 per cent) and 4 million long playing records (1 per cent) (IFPI 1996). The top 10 terri-tories with illegal sales were Russia, the United States, China, Italy, Brazil, Germany, Mexico, India, Pakistan, and France.

14. For work in the economics field see Correa (1995); David (1993); Siebeck (1990); UNCTAD (1996c).

15. See also Denison (1985) and Abramovitz and David (1996).

16. Survey of private services transactions, Bureau of Economic Analysis, United States Department of Commerce, November, 1996 cited in IITF (1996). The estimate covers 1995 and does not include transactions between affiliated companies which could add as much as $47 billion in additional exports.

17. Internet Commerce, American Electronics Association/ American University, September 1996 cited in IITF (1996).

18. Marketing 'agents' such as computer software 'intelligent agents' are programs which can carry out tasks automati-cally from a specification. The agent carries out a set of tasks more or less regardless of outcome, unless selectivity is pre-set.

19. For a review of the issues surrounding the governance of the use of encryption technologies, see, Wehn (1996) and Mansell and Steinmueller (1996c).

20. See A.P.-Dow Jones News Service, 15 February 1995. The Ministry of Post and Telecommunications was made the sole provider of connections of Chinese computers with inter-national networks.

CHAPTER 11

NATIONAL ICT STRATEGIES FOR
KNOWLEDGE-BASED DEVELOPMENT

What processes are needed?

11.1 INTRODUCTION - PROMOTING NATIONAL ICT STRATEGIES

The ICT revolution is a massive challenge for politicians and for the business sector. It is redefining, sometimes abolishing, the 'borders' between industries, and revealing the inadequacy of existing political and economic institutional structures. Key trends in the governance activities of international organisations are setting the framework for the development of national and regional ICT strategies (see Chapters 9 and 10). The trends include the continuing powerful role that these organisations play both in implementing and enforcing current rules and in deciding upon the new rules and regulations to reflect the technological, commercial, and political shifts in ICT and service markets. The leading international organisations are reshaping themselves to increase their responsiveness and flexibility in the face of dramatic market changes. The growing power of private sector organisations in shaping emergent 'knowledge societies' is expressed through private sector consortia that are setting international standards, through organisations like the Global Information Infrastructure Commission, and through established institutions like the International Telecommunication Union and the World Bank which are becoming more open to private sector partnerships (Wilson 1996a).

Box 11.1 - COORDINATION ACTION BY THE G-7 COUNTRIES AND DEVELOPING COUNTRIES

- Integrated systems to meet people's basic needs (using ICTs as tools and focusing on rural areas)
- Universal access (for all sectors of society)
- Innovation to develop appropriate applications and content
- Human resource development
- Support for business, and particularly small and medium sized enterprises
- Support for good governance
- Promotion of cultural heritage
- Infrastructure development (using appropriate technology and linked with universal access goals)
- Special assistance for countries with special circumstances

Source: ISAD Conference (1996a,b).

An international consensus has emerged on the urgent need for developing countries to prepare national ICT strategies to provide a framework to govern the allocation of resources among different groups of users and sectors and to establish priorities (Harfoush and Wild 1994). There is also consensus about the necessity to focus on the financial measures needed to reduce the gap between the developing and the industrialised countries in their capacity to reap the potential benefits of the global information society (GIS). The Information Society and Development (ISAD) conference held in South Africa in 1996 called for coordinated action by the G-7 countries and the developing countries to promote the use of ICTs (see Box 1.1).

Participants in the conference emphasised the need to prepare national and regional inventories of existing ICT projects; to ensure that the appropriate national or regional institutions are set up to provide for the coordination of ICT strategies; and to promote widespread dissemination of relevant information. This chapter offers a practical guide to the responses on the new consensus on the importance of the global information infrastructure and emerging national information infrastructures in developing countries. Section 11.2 focuses on some of the strategies that are already in place. Section 11.3 emphasises the need for integrated ICT strategies and the importance of coordinated action to maximise the positive contributions of investment in the technologies and in capability development. Section 11.4 looks at what steps are necessary to mobilise resources to develop the national information infrastructure. This section offers guidelines for policymakers and stakeholders in the business community to assist in devising ICT strategies that will be effective and responsive to development priorities (see also Annex 3). Section 11.5 provides further guidelines on measures that can be taken to improve the efficiency and to mobilise resources for building national information infrastructures. In section 11.6 the immediate actions which can be taken by the policy and business communities are outlined.

11.2 HARNESSING ICTs FOR DEVELOPMENT

Some of the national ICT strategies summarised in this section are being implemented in countries that have achieved a relatively high level of telephone penetration on an aggregate national basis. For example, Bermuda, Singapore, Malta, Taiwan (Pr. China), and the Republic of Korea have penetration rates exceeding 40 main telephone lines per 100 population. These countries are succeeding in addressing the 'telephony access' problem although there are problems of uneven distribution of access. They face continuing challenges in terms of building ICT-related capabilities within the labour force and ensuring that the communication infrastructure is managed in a way that brings benefits both to the economy and to society as a whole. Malaysia, Jamaica,

Mexico, and South Africa (with telephone penetration rates of between 9 and 16 in 1995) either already have, or expect to have, modern backbone networks in place by the end of the century. They face the challenge of encouraging inward investment to provide services to meet business requirements in urban areas and of extending access to the urban and rural poor. They also have to encourage capability-building and put new legislative and regulatory frameworks in place.

In Indonesia, Viet Nam, and Ethiopia which each have telephone penetration rates of less than two per 100 in habitants, the differences in their capacity to address the crucial financing issue are dramatic. Taking investment in the telecommunication infrastructure as an example, Indonesia experienced an increase in investment of 42 per cent between 1990 and 1994.[1] Ethiopia saw investment decline by 29 per cent over the same period. These disparities in the capacity to attract investors to build national information infrastructures clearly call for different kinds of approaches to the role of ICTs in the development process. The emphasis on strategies aimed at producing or using ICTs and services is changing in each country.

The emphasis in each of these countries on entry into international equipment and service markets as compared to that given to the diffusion and use of ICTs in the domestic economy also varies considerably.

Six of the countries in this sample are aiming to become either global or regional hubs for electronic services: Bermuda, Singapore, Jamaica, Malaysia, Malta, and Thailand.

Bermuda

Bermuda is a small country which describes itself as the 'Information Island of the 21st Century' (Sculley 1997). Its hope is to become a global electronic hub for storing, processing, and disseminating digital information. Teleports and submarine optical fibre cables link the island to global networks. The Bermuda Stock Exchange intends to launch an offshore electronic stock exchange and discussions are underway about the establishment of a Catastrophy Risk Exchange. Internet World Wide Web services are providing background information about business opportunities for potential investors. The aim is to become 'the Switzerland of data' for corporations, and a centre for the electronic sale of offshore financial derivatives as well as a major distributor of electronic software. The country faces several barriers to achieving these goals including the relatively high cost of telecommunication services and the need to provide appropriate training to upgrade the ICT-related skills of the local population.

Singapore

Singapore's 'Intelligent Island Vision' is embedded in the IT2000 master plan (National Computer Board n.d.a,b,c, 1996, 1997b). This strategy aims to ensure that

ICTs are pervasively used in every aspect of professional and personal life. The vision calls for computers and other information appliances located in homes, offices, schools, and factories to be linked by a broadband network built, owned, and operated by an industry consortium. The Singapore ONE network will provide access to public sector services and facilitate (inter) government transactions. Singapore is bidding to be a global 'centre of excellence' for science and technology, a high-value location for production, and a strategic node in global commerce, communication, and information networks. The IT2000 strategy has been developed by the National Computer Board (NCB) in collaboration with private sector stakeholders. NCB is responsible for implementing more than sixty sectoral applications and the key goals of the strategy are summarised in Box 11.2. In July 1996 the government launched the Local Industry Upgrading Programme (LIUP) involving multinational and local companies to nurture the local ICT industry and encourage industry collaboration. The NCB provides a 'one-stop-shop' to assist in the identification of local collaborators and projects and in formulating the terms of collaboration.

BOX 11.2 – IT2000 GOALS IN SINGAPORE

- ▌ Create an IT culture
- ▌ Plan IT human resource development
- ▌ Nurture the IT industry
- ▌ Evolve an information infrastructure
- ▌ Deploy IT2000 flagship projects
- ▌ Exploit IT in government

Source: Adapted from National Computer Board (n.d.a).

Jamaica

As the size of the international information services market grows, opportunities for Jamaican businesses are expected in the creation and distribution of content using on-line services (Bennett 1995; Patterson 1995; Commonwealth Secretariat 1988; Girvan 1994c). The information processing services industry has been slow to take off because of the dualistic structure of the industry where some firms have much greater access to financial resources than others. This is the result of a number of factors: preferential treatment by foreign investors, higher than estimated costs of marketing, the need to develop a suitably trained work force, and the high costs of access to the Internet. Obstacles to the procurement of loans indicate the need for greater involvement of banks in providing financial support for the ICT industry. The establishment of a government body that would focus on the development of the ICT sector and support public institutions in their use of ICTs has been recommended.

ICTs are not being exploited to their full potential because decision-makers have yet to become completely convinced of the need for investment in ICTs. Recommendations also include the development of ICT services and an 'IT park', measures to encourage venture capitalists in the development of 'digital' content publishing, human resource development, and the telecommunication infrastructure. Other recommendations include measures to update the general legal framework for competition policy and legislation for the ICT sector. The government and the private sector have been criticised about the lack of ICT policies and forward planning. For example, the local industry depends upon government computerisation projects to generate revenues, but frequently these projects are given to overseas consultants. Software and value-added products and services are often imported from the industrialised countries and most local companies are active only in the hardware and pre-packaged software segments of the market where the primary focus is on software development and product enhancement. Trained personnel with ICT-related skills do exist, but there are major deficiencies at management level. Initiatives in the ICT sector need to be complemented by measures to strengthen the competitiveness of firms and to implement development objectives.

Malaysia

An ICT policy was introduced in Malaysia in the early 1980s and planning is the responsibility of numerous committees, including the National Consultative Committee on Information Technology (NCCIT) formed in 1988 (Raman and Yap 1996; Shariffadeen 1994a,b, 1995; Baharuddin et al. 1994; Karthigesu 1996; Hashim 1996). The country's strategic approach to ICT planning and management includes establishment of the National IT Council (NITC) which provides advisory and consultative assistance. The Council is expected to ensure that the social implications of ICT are considered along with the need to develop human and technical capabilities. The national strategy is linked to the Vision 2020 development policy which emphasises that the ultimate purpose of development should be for human development. Projects include the Malaysian 'Multimedia Super Corridor' incorporating a new airport and 'intelligent' multimedia cities to attract investors, and use of computers in education. A Multimedia Development Corporation has been established to coordinate the development of Malaysia's own 'Silicon Valley'. The goal is to create an environment that will attract investment and highly skilled knowledge workers. Potential investors include the Nippon Telegraph and Telephone Company, Shell, Reuters, and Oracle (Kynge 1997). Skills, values, and knowledge are accorded great importance. Policies are being designed to treat people as 'learning individuals' and to ensure that ICTs play a facilitating role. The strategy emphasises the need to prepare Islamic countries for the information revolution.

Malta

Malta is implementing a National Strategy for Information Technology. In 1992 the Malta Council for Science and Technology (MCST), the advisory body to government on national science and technology policies, organised a national conference entitled 'Vision 2000: Developing Malta as Regional Hub through Communications Technology'. This led to the commissioning by Government through MCST of a study involving over 100 experts and practitioners from various sectors to develop a national strategy for ICT (Camilleri 1994a,b,c). The study combined a macro-perspective on likely political scenarios influencing economic and ICT strategies with a micro-perspective on ICT issues in education and human resource training, business, and telecommunication infrastructure development. The strategy was presented to the Government in 1994 and set in motion recommendations in several general strategic directions and related initiatives in the education and telecommunication sectors. A review of the National Strategy for Information Technology was carried out in early 1997 and one of the major recommendations was the establishment of a National Commission for Information Technology (see Box 11.3).

BOX 11.3 - NATIONAL COMMISSION FOR INFORMATION TECHNOLOGY, MALTA

The Commission is focusing on seven major areas:
▌ Nurturing an IT culture
▌ Promoting the development of skills in ITs
▌ Encouraging investment in state-of-the-art telecommunication services
▌ Aiding the effective use of IT in Maltese organisations
▌ Promoting an indigenous export-oriented IT industry
▌ Helping to widen the use of IT to enhance government information services
▌ Bringing about sectoral cohesion through IT

Source: Balzan and Vella (1997).

In July 1997, this Commission was set up with a chairperson from the private sector, and comprises representatives of the academic, private, and public sectors. Its main objectives are to keep the national IT strategy updated, to take responsibility for the implementation of certain parts of the strategy, and to coordinate the work of public and private organisations involved in this strategy.

Malta's IT strategy takes into account the multiple dimensions of IT including the technological, economic, spatial, occupational, social, cultural, and legislative. The approach stresses the importance of private sector involvement and investment for successful implementation of the strategy. It aims to stimulate markets for ICT services and goods and to achieve effective deployment of ICTs in all sectors. It is also concerned with the development of the necessary skills and infrastructure. The role of government is to provide market guidance and targeted incentives for the country's small and medium sized enterprises.

Thailand

Thailand's ICT strategy includes measures to encourage investment in an equitable national information infrastructure. It emphasises investment in the skills base to increase literacy and good governance. Thailand's goal is to become a regional hub in South Eeast Asia for financial services, manufacturing, commerce, transport, tourism, and human resource training. The telecommunication network is digital with optical fibre and satellite links between the major cities, but there are problems in extending access to rural areas. Although the telephone penetration rate reached one for every ten people in 1996, only about a third of the population in the largest cities had benefited as many tambons (sub-districts) and almost all the 60,000 villages were without public telephone services. The country also faces a shortage of skilled people, the estimated shortfall being close to 10,000 in skills in software and telecommunication engineering fields in 1996. Investment in ICTs to provide public services lags behind the private sector. The Five-Year Rural Thailand Communications Expansion and Modernisation Programme, an independent telecommunication regulatory authority, and a School Informatisation Action Programme are among the recent government measures. This last aims to achieve a PC density in all state schools of at least one for every 80 primary school children, and one for every 40 secondary school children. The IT2000 policy supports ongoing policy research, and the local ICT industry (Durongkaveroj 1996).

Indonesia, Korea (Republic of), Mexico, and Taiwan (Pr. China) all have mixed strategies that emphasise both ICT producer and user capabilities with an outward orientation toward the emerging international market opportunities in hardware and services production.

Indonesia

There is a five-year development plan which includes the telecommunication sector. It is being opened to private sector participation in order to increase telephone density and improve services in rural areas (Idris 1996). The telecommunication infrastructure is seen as vital to the country's economic and social development. Mobile satellite technology will extend access to the infrastructure but a 'Universal Access Fund' is being established to reduce the costs for individual subscriber lines in public areas. Television broadcasting is the main infrastructure for disseminating information, education, and entertainment because of its wide coverage of rural and urban areas.

The Republic of Korea

A 'Blueprint' for an information society has been launched designed to develop and promote the use of the national information infrastructure, strengthen competition in the ICT industry, support firms in the broadcasting sector, improve the quality of services, and establish good practice in ICT usage. There is a plan to establish a National Backbone Computer Network (1997-2000). A committee addresses potential trade friction with countries such as the United States and regions such as the European Union as the country builds its capabilities to address external markets for ICT goods and services (National Computerisation Agency 1996).

Mexico

The Instituto Nacional de Estadistica Geografia e Informatica is responsible for formulating national ICT policies. A strategy is in place to promote the development and use of these technologies which are regarded as a 'strategic factor' for development. Policies emphasise the uses of ICT and country-specific ways of integrating them within the economy and society. Emphasis is on active rather than reactive policies, fostering the initiatives of collaborative groups. ICTs are included in the Plan Nacional de Desarrollo 1995-2000 to ensure that the government will promote mechanisms to coordinate, develop, and supervise new initiatives at the national level (Guerra Benitez 1996).

Taiwan (Pr. China)

A National Information Infrastructure Steering Committee was established in Taiwan (Pr. China) following recognition of the importance of ICTs for economic growth (Institute for Information Industry 1995). Government plans stress the role of ICTs in education and training, the exploitation of ICT applications, the promotion of computer literacy programmes, the development of a high capacity telecommunication network, and R&D in fields including distributed databases, electronic data interchange, and geographical information systems. Legislative measures are in preparation or under discussion, with respect to universal network access, equipment standards, intellectual property rights, and other areas. The aim is to support a competitive national information infrastructure that will contribute to human and cultural development.

South Africa, Viet Nam, and Ethiopia

The ICT strategies in South Africa, Viet Nam, and Ethiopia represent cases of generic strategies to build capabilities for using ICTs but from extremely different starting points in terms of the capacity to attract investor interest.

South Africa

The 1994 South Africa Reconstruction and Development Programme established ICTs as a high priority sector that should be closely linked with measures to meet the basic needs of the population.

The use of information technology provides a major challenge in linking basic needs with information highways in innovative ways that improve the capacity of industry to successfully reintegrate into world markets. Southern Africa could lead the way in providing this link so vital to the developing world (South African Government 1994: 17).

A 1996 White Paper on Science and Technology observed that South Africa needed a national policy to facilitate integration into the global information society (Hodge and Miller 1998 forthcoming). A research and technology foresight programme was introduced to help reach consensus among stakeholders and to ensure that national R&D policies would be aligned with the country's development goals. In the same year a Telecommunications Bill was passed establishing a Universal Service Agency to fund network access using revenues from the licence fees levied on the telecommunication operators. The Bill also outlined the conditions for phasing out the national public telecommunication operator's fixed line monopoly over the next six years. A National IT Forum has been launched to provide an ongoing forum for debate among representatives of government, the private sector, labour and community organisations, and the academic community.

Viet Nam

A national programme for ICT development was initiated in 1993 in Viet Nam. It stressed the use of ICTs by government agencies as well as links between the development of ICTs and economic and social policies. A National Programme on Information Technology Steering Committee was established in 1994 and this led to the IT-2000 programme which emphasised education and training, R&D, and the development of a data communication network. Institutions and enterprises in all sectors are encouraged to participate and the programme provides a framework to coordinate activities between the Ministry of Science, Technology and Environment and other ministries such as the Ministry for Heavy Industry. The use of ICTs by the government and strengthening economic activities, skills, and R&D capabilities are stressed. A major goal is to produce hardware and software for the domestic market and subsequently for the world market. Tax incentives, investment assistance and shared cost schemes are under consideration to encourage the private sector which has been slow to promote the ICT sector. Policies and guidelines on foreign investment, technology transfer, and intellectual property rights protection also need to be strengthened (Dieu and Le 1995, Vietnamese Association for Computing 1994; Vu 1995).

Ethiopia

The National Economic and Social Infrastructure Policy in Ethiopia emphasises the telecommunication infrastructure, and coverage in remote places. The science and technology policies for the agriculture, health, manufac-turing, minerals, water, energy, and geo-information sectors acknowledge the importance of using ICTs to support information collection, analysis, and dissemination. A coherent approach taking account of basic infrastructure requirements and human resource needs, is required.

Many other developing countries are in the process of making fundamental changes to their national information infrastructures (Wilson 1996b). The changes involve cooperation between a wide range of individuals in the public and business sectors and new partnerships between these individuals, the non-governmental organisations (NGOs) that are becoming increasingly active in the ICT area, and between groups of citizens. As governments move to put new strategies in place they need to balance the conflicting priorities of these individuals and organisations. Among the most crucial issues are the dynamically changing relationships between:

▮ public and private ownership and control;

▮ monopoly and competition;

▮ national and foreign enterprise ownership and control;

▮ strong regulatory procedures and the removal of controls;

▮ the introduction of sophisticated ICTs and programming or information content from abroad and measures to protect the national cultural heritage;

▮ measures to develop universal access to networks, and the role of financing to address a rapidly changing competitive market;

▮ intellectual property rights provisions to reward and protect the creators of content, and measures to encourage the use of intellectual property to educate and inform as many people as possible;

▮ the need to build indigenous scientific and technological capacity and technology and to attract the latest leading-edge technology from abroad.

Developing countries are in very different positions with regard to each of these issue areas. Some countries are taking measures to restructure their markets to promote ICT production capabilities while others are concentrating on export markets (Ramani 1998 forthcoming). Some countries are giving priority to capabilities for using ICTs while others are focusing on hardware and software production skills and training. Short-term priorities often mainly involve public and community services and strategic plans to attract foreign investors into the telecommunication sector. ICT strategies need to forge strong links between the ICT sector and development goals. This requires an integrated approach with broad participation by all stakeholders.

11.3 INTEGRATING NATIONAL ICT STRATEGIES

ICT policy overlaps with four well-established policy

FIGURE II.I - POLICIES FOR SHAPING INTEGRATED ICT STRUCTURE

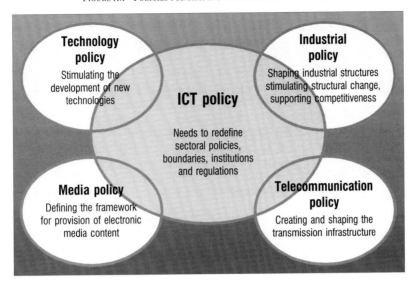

fields: technology, industrial, telecommunication, and media policy (see Figure 11.1).

Technology policy tries to stimulate the economy by fostering innovation. Industrial policy is about growth and employment. It tries to stimulate the emergence of new industries in order to secure future growth. It often attempts to slow down the exit of firms from declining industries in order to protect jobs. Telecommunication policy seeks to secure the provision of communication services, and media policy provides the framework for the development of the audio-visual sector. With the convergence of ICTs, these separate policy domains are proving inadequate and it is not unusual for turf wars to hamper the formulation and implementation of new policies that cut across existing policy domains. Technology policies aimed at stimulating R&D have tended to target manufacturing technologies rather than services. The telecommunication equipment industry has been the concern of telecommunication, technology, and industrial policies but these are frequently not well coordinated.

Many countries have separate ministries for technology, industry, telecommunication, and the media (Meyer-Stamer 1996). Restructuring to integrate existing ministries in order to bring competencies together is very difficult and can lead to an intensification of turf wars. Planning for the future of ICT development cannot be left entirely to the state or to the market. Neither approach on its own is politically acceptable or responsive to the emerging ICT 'paradigm' (Freeman 1987). An early failure to shape ICT development and use through the coordinated participation of all the stakeholders in government, industry, civil society, and the science and technology community, means that the trajectories of ICT development will become more entrenched.

Economic and social development involving the diffusion and use of ICTs is highly 'path dependent' (David 1975, 1985). Once a particular path of development of a software system, a telecommunication network, or an ICT-based process control technology has begun to gather momentum it can prove very resistant to radical changes in direction. This does not mean that there are no opportunities to shape the trajectory of ICT diffusion and use in developing countries. However, it does mean that the longer decision-makers delay the introduction of strategies that affect investment in ICTs, the more likely it is that particular designs and architectures of systems and applications will become fixed. This will make it more difficult to tailor ICT products and services to the specific needs of developing countries. A failure to take early steps using coordinated ICT strategies also increases the costs of shifting the trajectory of ICT development. A failure to shape the structure of ICT production and use, can severely restrict future policy options.

Technological innovation is not a once-and-for-all event. The innovation process in the ICT sector is continuous and it emerges as a result of interactive learning. During this process there are many 'degrees of freedom' and opportunities to shape the direction of the development of new ICT applications if the capabilities are available in the producer or user community (Mansell 1996c). If the ICT selection process is uncoordinated and anarchic, there is a risk that high costs will be incurred in terms of abandoned technological development paths and foregone opportunities for economic development.

National ICT strategies involving a process of participatory, interactive learning, and planning are emerging as an alternative to either state planning or market lotteries for constructing national information infrastructures. In

FIGURE 11.2 – ACTORS IN SHAPING INTEGRATED ICT STRUCTURE

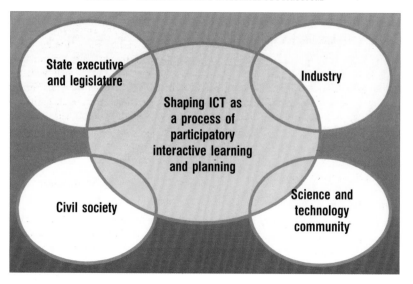

fact, the development of large technical systems has rarely been left entirely to market forces. These developments have been shaped by political factors, for example, the post war experience in nuclear energy. However, in this case, and in other large system developments, the shaping of the technological trajectory involved a relatively small set of actors from certain branches of the state executive, industry, and science and technology. There was little direct involvement of citizens or other representatives of civil society. It is debatable whether it was sensible to leave these technology selection decisions to a limited set of actors in the light of their far-reaching consequences.

Very large ICT systems will facilitate, as well as constrain, the development of 'knowledge societies' for many decades to come. Opportunities to shape the trajectory of the development of this system in the developing countries can be created by involving a wide set of actors, and especially by including representatives of civil society (see Figure 11.2). Consensus conferences and future-oriented workshops are helpful in creating an environment for interactive learning involving actors from a country or region as well as international participants. These fora help to build bridges between the knowledge of people in existing ministries, the business sector, NGOs, labour organisations, etc.

Using new fora and other innovative legislative and regulatory instruments to create new coalitions of resources is preferable to leaving the trajectory of ICT diffusion to the market or to attempting to use a heavily centralised governance structure to direct the path of development. These approaches give rise to opportunities to establish new governance systems that are responsive to innovations in ICTs and to development priorities (Meyer–Stamer 1997).

Consideration can be given to people's expectations for the delivery of services, the plans and architectures for the delivery of transmission, switching, computing, and software with appropriate training, and whether to develop or reconfigure hardware and software in the national market or to 'buy in' products and systems from external sources. These opportunities can also create an environment for the ongoing assessment of people's information needs and their changing capacities to use electronic information and ICT applications effectively (Aksoy and Goddard 1990).

A better understanding of the role and impact of ICTs within specific development contexts is needed. A major ingredient for this is the presence of a mechanism for ongoing policy review, assessment, and monitoring (Akhtar 1995). To design and implement a national or regional ICT strategy requires consideration of several major issue areas. Guidelines can be followed to ensure that strategies are developed that help to harness ICTs to priorities for sustainable development. The next section highlights these areas, suggests guidelines for decision-makers, and illustrates what can be done to mobilise investment and expertise.

11.4 GUIDELINES FOR NATIONAL ICT STRATEGIES

The United Nations Commission on Science and Technology for Development (UNCSTD) Working Group on IT and Development concluded that ICTs offer huge potential for creating economic and social benefits for all citizens. The application of these technologies also has the potential for widening the gap between the rich and the poor. If the benefits are to outweigh the risk of a widening gap, governments, the business sector, and civil society must work together. Key considerations in the design and implementation of an ICT strategy include the following.

Producing and using ICTs for social and economic advantage

Although there are risks, the production and use of ICTs can result in very considerable social and economic benefits. In order to avoid the risks, strategies need to create a dynamic relationship between the technological and human resources devoted to producing, maintaining, and using ICTs. The profiles of country strategies are likely to differ and the specific targets of national ICT strategies should be expected to change over time.

Developing human resources for effective national ICT strategies

ICTs are changing rapidly and new applications are being created daily resulting in continuous change in skills requirements. Fortunately, these technologies also contribute new means of acquiring those skills. ICTs provide the means for enabling lifelong learning and for more widespread education which can lead to an improved quality of life. National ICT strategies need to encourage governments, businesses, and civil society to complement one another by using ICTs to enhance skills, formal education, and informal learning processes.

Managing ICTs for development

The introduction of ICTs requires new forms of organisation. These organisational changes need to be identified and implemented by informed managers. People are needed who can act as intermediaries and who can coordinate, integrate, and disseminate information drawn from scientific and technical research, and practical experience about the production and use of ICTs. The management of ICTs for development demands people who are knowledgeable about the technical, social, and economic goals and a combination of ICT applications that support national development priorities.

Accessing ICT networks

There are risks of social exclusion if businesses and citizens do not have access to an adequate national information infrastructure. Legislative and regulatory frameworks can help to promote the efficient use of private investment to extend and upgrade the national information infrastructure in line with development priorities. The national information infrastructure needs to be integrated with the emerging global information infrastructure in a way that maximises the benefits and minimises the risks. The design of the infrastructure also needs to encourage ICT development that is responsive to the needs of different goups, including the poorest sectors of the population and specific communities, such as women's groups.

Promoting and financing investment in ICTs

Market mechanisms alone are unlikely to be sufficient to generate adequate financial resources to enable developing countries, and especially the least developed countries, to upgrade their national information infrastructures. Governments can experiment with two-way investment partnerships between local and foreign firms. The new ICT applications can generate positive spin-offs throughout the economy but this requires a coalition of resources from the public and business sectors. This mechanism could be more fully exploited by developing countries (UNCSTD 1997c).

Creating and accessing scientific and technical knowledge

A failure to build a national information infrastructure is likely to handicap the scientific and technical research communities in developing countries. Capacity building involves the accumulation of scientific and technical knowledge to enable assessment, selection, application, adaptation, and development of ICTs so that they contribute to sustainable development. Expertise within, and external to, developing countries needs to be coordinated and strengthened. Improved 'early warning' of new technical, market, policy, and regulatory developments is feasible if networks of expertise are coordinated.

Monitoring and influencing the 'rules of the game'

The international governance system for the global information infrastructure is strongly influenced by the governments and private sector stakeholders in the industrialised countries. The rules in areas such as standards, intellectual property rights, security, privacy, regulation, and trade are changing and they have important implications for the strategies adopted by developing countries. Developing countries need to share information and strengthen their participation (through national or regional fora) in establishing these rules. The new rules also need to be monitored so that steps can be taken to minimise any negative impacts they may have.

The Guidelines of the UNCSTD Working Group

The UNCSTD Working Group on IT and Development generated a generic set of guidelines that can be used by national governments and other interested stakeholders to assist them in developing their own national ICT strategies. The guidelines and a summary of the conclusions and recommendations of the Working Group are included in Annex 3.

11.5 COALITIONS OF RESOURCES FOR BUILDING CAPABILITIES

In order to build a capability in ICTs and develop a national information infrastructure, developing countries will have to mobilise and pool large amounts of investment and expertise. Action is required in three closely inter-related areas.

First, developing countries should seek to create a market-friendly environment (that is, one conducive to the regulatory and business environment) and to formulate an explicit national or regional ICT strategy. This involves providing a coherent framework that secures an efficient and a socially balanced allocation of scarce resources. Without this strategy, it will be very difficult to build powerful coalitions of resources for ICT sector producers and users or to mobilise substantial funds from international investors and financial institutions, and the donor community.

Second, it is necessary to ensure that any existing ICT strategy explicitly addresses the question of financing. There need to be operational guidelines on how to raise and combine public and private funds from domestic, regional, and international sources. Very few national ICT strategies meet this requirement. Finance strategies are needed to systematically explore possibilities of exploiting the principle of self-funding by building ICT projects into existing programmes and refocusing existing expenditure. Mechanisms for coping with initially high investment costs and foreign exchange constraints, and accommodating the needs of rural areas and non-commercial users in sectors such as education and health, are also needed.

Third, given the complexity of developing an ICT strategy and linking the question of financing to the process of planning and implementing the national information infrastructure, existing governance processes need to be reviewed and eventually adjusted. In line with initiatives in industrialised and newly industrialising countries, developing countries may seek to complement the market mechanism and decentralised decision-making structures with institutional frameworks that encourage participatory planning procedures.

If action is taken along these lines, there will be scope for even the least developed countries to build a capability in ICTs and develop a national information infrastructure. Financial resources and expertise have to be mobilised to:

▮ formulate a national ICT strategy and monitor its implementation

▮ build and operate the telecommunication infrastructure

▮ promote the production, maintenance, and development of ICTs

▮ promote computer literacy

▮ promote the application of ICTs in fields such as education, health, public sector management

▮ support the agriculture, the manufacturing, and natural resources industries, and the services sector.

Forming powerful coalitions of resources in these areas is not just a question of mobilising and pooling funds and

expertise. Building ICT capabilities also requires efficient utilisation and management of funds and intellectual resources. Guidelines for efficient use of financial resources, mobilising and attracting new resources, and managing the formation of new coalitions of resources are outlined below.

11.5.1 GUIDELINES FOR SECURING EFFICIENT RESOURCE USE

A market-friendly environment is the key to the rapid development of ICTs and the national information infrastructure. The infrastructure cannot be developed simply by adopting a market-driven approach. Given the existence of market failures and the need to combine efficiency and equity considerations, a national ICT strategy that complements the market mechanism is required. A strategy involving key decision-makers in the public and private sectors as well as users of ICTs might aim to achieve the following.

Integration of development policies: ICTs are a tool for the development of other social and economic sectors. They need to be planned and developed as an integratal part of each country's overall development strategy (ITU 1995c).

Building indigenous capabilities: The ICT sector needs to be treated as a profit sector like other sectors in the economy. A strategy of building national (indigenous) capabilities can be based on a clear medium- to long-term vision. This vision should focus on the areas where indigenous capabilities are needed and on the hardware and software components and skills that must be imported. A failure to define national strengths and weaknesses in ICT production, maintenance, and development can result in overly import-dependent development. It can lead to lost opportunities to generate economic growth, export earnings, and jobs. Insufficient mastery of ICTs and a weak absorptive capacity for foreign technology can also result from a failure to build capabilities in key areas. Clearly justified 'make or buy' decisions are important for all countries and especially for the smaller and least developed economies.

Balancing private profitability and social welfare: Building a capability in ICTs requires a focus on businesses and user groups with sufficient ability to purchase products and services and the willingness to do so. An exclusive focus on commercial viability is unlikely to be sufficient for the promotion of social and economic development. ICTs are an important tool to increase the productivity of firms and of organisations providing social services such as education and health. ICT applications can also help to promote growth in remote areas. ICT applications should be addressed to the needs of sectors and regions where short-term financial returns on investment are low but the social welfare returns are high. Private profitability must be balanced against social welfare considerations to avoid the development of two-tier 'knowledge societies'

FIGURE 11.3 – AFRICA TELECOMMUNICATIONS OWNERSHIP

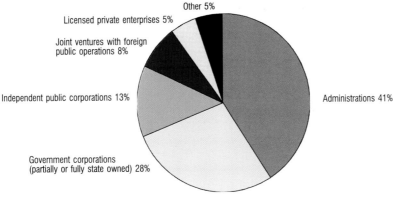

Source: *Communications International*, July 1996.

where the divisions between the 'haves' and 'have nots' are reinforced. In addition, building 'knowledge societies' is likely to involve cumulative effects and increasing returns that must be considered in the allocation of both private and social investment.

Exploiting economies of scale and cooperation: ICT systems generally are scalable offering scope for a step-by-step approach to building the national information infrastructure. However, an incremental approach to ICT development, production, or use may result in wasted resources. For example, if the telecommunication network is designed only from a national perspective, this may lead to higher costs than a design that is integrated with a regional, continent-wide, or international network. Regional and international cooperation may also result in cost effective solutions in the production of ICTs and in human resource development and R&D activities. Cooperation may also open up new possibilities for smaller countries.

Emphasising economies of harmonisation: The harmonisation of technical standards (network interfaces and protocols) is of critical importance for the rapid emergence of an efficient national information infrastructure. The potential of networks can be maximised when network interconnection and service interoperability are feasible for national, regional, and international services (OECD 1996b; UNECA 1996b). Interconnection and interoperability encourage competition and stimulate market growth by reducing transaction costs and allowing the exploitation of economies of scale and scope.

Exploiting economies of joint use: The investment costs of installation of networks may be shared by different user groups leading to a possible reduction in user charges when the network becomes operational. Savings can also be achieved by permitting the interconnection of private and public networks. The use of public access points, telekiosks, and multi-purpose telecentres are examples of ways in which economies of joint use can be exploited to

enable wider public access to the national information infrastructure at a reasonable cost.

Exploiting economies of joint production/economies of scope: There is a potential for considerable savings if large scale investment programmes for the national information infrastructure can be linked to other major projects such as the construction of roads, railways, canals, or electricity links. The management skills for large scale projects are likely to be common to some extent, resulting in lower costs in this area as well as in construction of physical plant.

Exploiting economies of coordination: In the competition for finance and support, project proposers and funders often seek to preserve the specific technical characteristics of their projects. If similar projects are implemented using different technical standards, this is likely to dilute resources and reduce the funds available for better quality, self sustaining projects (Jensen 1996b). Project planners and sponsors need to cooperate to avoid developing competing and overlapping ICT projects.

11.5.2   GUIDELINES FOR MOBILISING AND ATTRACTING RESOURCES

Bold strategies for building a capability in ICTs set targets and define clear investment requirements (ITU 1995d). National ICT strategies should explicitly address questions of financing. Many ICT strategies consist mainly of a collection of principles. Figure 11.3 shows the ownership arrangements for public telecommunication operators in Africa in 1996. The number of joint ventures with foreign companies and private operators marks a change from the public monopoly ownership structure of the past. Figure 11.4 shows the diversity of sources of financing for infrastructure development that has occurred with the change in ownership structure. In this complex stakeholder environment general principles will not succeed in mobilising investment in the telecommunication or

FIGURE II.4 - SOURCE OF INVESTMENT CAPITAL FOR INFRASTRUCTURE

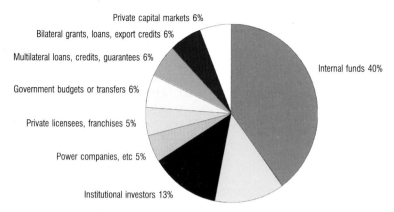

Private capital markets 6%

Bilateral grants, loans, export credits 6%

Multilateral loans, credits, guarantees 6%

Government budgets or transfers 6%

Private licensees, franchises 5%

Power companies, etc 5%

Institutional investors 13%

Internal funds 40%

Joint ventures or consortia partners 13%

Source: *Communications International*, July 1996.

other areas of the ICT sector. Success in mobilising and attracting resources will require very clear strategies.

The mobilisation and attraction of domestic and external financial resources necessary to ensure that ICT projects are financially sustainable may involve the following steps.

Focusing on self-funded programmes or projects: Programmes and projects in the ICT field should be based on the principle of self-funding whenever possible. They should be financed by user charges or by other mechanisms that generate a regular cash flow, for example, advertiser-supported models. In principle, revenues should be sufficient to cover getting-started investment requirements, maintenance, ongoing R&D, up-grading costs, debt servicing, and operating costs.

Targeting commercial users: Self-funding implies a focus on users with sufficient ability and willingness to pay for ICT products and services in the first instance. Users in sectors such as banking, insurance, trade, transport, tourism, and the media are likely to be able to afford the costs and be willing to pay for applications which are responsive to their requirements. Programmes aimed at broadening the market for commercial applications in the education sector, and for small- and medium-sized enterprises, and micro-enterprises, are very important in building the potential market.

Accommodating commercial users in remote areas: Self-funding is unlikely to be feasible for programmes and projects in rural and remote areas although there may be some users in these areas with the ability and willingness to pay for ICT products and services (World Bank 1994). The costs of building the 'last kilometre' of the national information infrastructure are high. This means that finance for the extension of services to remote areas must come from government sources or from the introduction of price structures that assume a contribution of revenues to the costs of network development in low density traffic

areas. For example, a (small) surcharge can be included in the prices for service in commercial centres with high traffic densities. Rapid advances in wireless communication technologies are likely to improve the prospects for building commercially viable infrastructures in remote areas using the self-funding principle.

Accommodating non-commercial users: In sectors such as health, education, government funded R&D, and government administration, the ability of users to pay for ICTs is very weak. There is a need to earmark adequate public funds to finance ICT use in these sectors and to attract financial resources from other domestic and foreign sources. To maintain financial requirements at realistic levels it is important to ensure that non-profit ICT users are organised and operate in a business-like manner (Jensen 1996b).

Refocusing existing expenditure: There are always competing claims on scarce resources and this is particularly so in the least developed countries. The potential for refocusing existing financial resources can be exploited by ensuring that public expenditure contributes to financing ICTs in targeted sectors and institutions including schools, universities, R&D centres, and government agencies.

Building ICTs into existing programmes and projects: Development programmes and projects often do not explicitly consider the benefits of the cost-effective use of ICTs. However, the absence of an adequate telecommunication infrastructure means that some basic needs projects in rural areas, and in sectors such as education and health, are limited in their use of ICTs (ITU 1995c). The feasibility of integrating ICTs into programmes for accelerating social, economic, and rural development should be explored systematically.

Coping with high initial investment costs: Prices charged to users are important in recovering investments and financing operating costs, but other sources of finance generally are needed for projects involving high initial investment costs. The sources of funding that can be tapped and combined include: the profits of network operating companies, equipment supplier credits; loans from domestic, regional, and international financial institutions; domestic and foreign equity investment; medium- or long-term credit from national, regional and international venture capital funds for infrastructure development; public funds and domestic bonds; concessions from multilateral, regional, and bilateral donors; and grants from international donors especially for the least developed countries (ITU 1996a).

Innovative financing mechanisms such as build-operate-transfer (BOT) schemes have been implemented successfully in countries such as Thailand and Indonesia to extend rural telecommunication networks. Other financing schemes that may be feasible include build-operate-own (BOO), rehabilitate-operate-transfer (ROT) or build-lease-transfer (BLT) arrangements (ITU 1996b). Full use of a variety of financing mechanisms often requires the use of complementary instruments such as guarantees for investors and creditors covering commercial and political risk by national governments and international financial institutions.

Coping with foreign exchange constraints: If there is no local ICT production capacity the costs of imported components may be as much as 80 per cent of total investment costs for telecommunication infrastructure projects and comprise close to 100 per cent of the total project costs for components such as interactive terminal equipment, computers, or software. For developing countries with large trade deficits or weak international financial standing, the import costs of the information infrastructure will be prohibitive. There are no short-term solutions to overcome this constraint and the active involvement of the international donor community will be needed especially in the least developed countries for an extended period. During this period, these countries can begin implementing policies to attract foreign investors by introducing economic, structural, and regulatory reforms and begin to develop endigenous capabilities in targeted areas.

Although the resource requirements for building a capability in ICTs are large, a wide range of financial strategies and instruments can be combined drawing upon domestic, regional, and international resources to create powerful coalitions of resources for developing national information infrastructures.

11.5.3 GUIDELINES FOR MANAGING THE FORMATION OF COALITIONS OF RESOURCES

Mobilising and pooling resources for building capabilities in ICTs requires adequate management capabilities and decision-making processes. Neither a top-down nor a very decentralised approach to decision-making is likely to be sufficient. Participatory planning procedures offer a promising approach to capability development in the management area.

In operational terms this approach may call for the establishment of a body (advisory council, national committee) at the highest political level to oversee the development of a coherent ICT strategy. Mission-oriented task forces in fields such as telecommunication infrastructure, computer literacy, and human resource development, and the application of ICTs, may also need to be established to act in an advisory or advocacy capacity, to provide guidance and coordination functions and need not necessarily replace existing decision-making processes. Government and public agencies, project managers, professional organisations, and financial institutions can participate, together with ICT user groups, to ensure that strategies and ICT programmes are responsive to development needs.

11.6 TAKING ACTION NOW

Developing countries need to develop their own strategies by drawing creatively on experience to configure their technical and human resources to invest in ICTs in a way that achieves the greatest social and economic benefits at the lowest cost. The preceding guidelines provide a framework for the issues that developing countries need to consider in formulating ICT strategies. Each society has its own distinct social and economic context. Therefore, the design of a new ICT strategy, or the improvement of an existing one, involves a distinctive learning process for domestic and other participants (Avgerou and Mulira 1996). This section outlines some practical steps that can be taken by policy-makers and business people in the short-term to minimise the risk of exclusion from the 'knowledge societies' of the future.[2]

11.6.1 MONITORING AND INFLUENCING THE GII

Given the importance of a systematic and integrated national ICT strategy, the many local, national, regional, and international organisations need improved coordination of their actions. Since these organisations have the capacity to advance or retard developing country interests, government officials need to maximise the interest of these organisations in their priority needs and to ensure that evolving strategies are consistent with development goals (Wilson 1996a,b). The measures that might be considered include:

▌ Assigning clear administrative responsibility for tracking key issues within the senior ranks of government.

▌ 'Mapping' the environment, and deciding which agencies will produce the most usable, relevant information about what a country needs, and then tracking developments in those organisations. Institutional monitoring needs can be given priorities so that some important agencies are covered very well, and others less so.

- Giving the responsible officials the necessary technical and material resources to gain full access to the global networks for 'virtual participation'.

- Creating a 'Virtual Forum' of monitors who are assigned responsibility to track important global debates and developments occurring around the GII and its institutions, and to report on their relevance to developing countries.

- Pressing for greater coordination of current efforts to create regional marketing and information centres. These can be coordinated with other regional bodies, including non-telecommunication bodies.

11.6.2 STEPS FOR MANAGERS IN DEVELOPING COUNTRIES

Vision, leadership, and promoting organisational change

The biggest ICT challenges that developing country governments face are not technical. The technology is available for most of what governments want to do (Wilson 1996b). The challenge, especially for the least developed countries, is to exercise vision and leadership and to promote organisational change. The most successful ICT producing and using countries are those best able to combine Vision-Leadership-Organisational Change to serve national interests. The least successful countries lack one, two or all three elements. Focusing only on the production or acquisition of technology is not sufficient. National and regional leaders must have a vision of ICT uses.

Vision

In the ICT sector the most practical step for a government is to create a vision - being visionary is practical in today's rapidly changing world. ICTs can be put to many uses. Long-term vision is required to select the most important technologies and applications for a particular country. This requires a vision of the desired future, and a clear sense of how ICTs could serve that future and help to realise it. Visions must be strategic and have the capacity to recognise what can be changed and what cannot. Having a vision means being proactive, rather than reactive. Government decision-makers must believe that new things are possible, for example, that in today's world comparative advantage actually can be created using ICT.

Developing a national vision involves setting clear priorities. The most difficult challenge for policy-makers in developing a positive forward-looking vision is to recognise that governments do not have all the answers. ICTs are mostly driven by private suppliers responding to private demands for goods and services.

Leadership

The essence of leadership means articulating the vision of what ICTs can do, sharing that vision with others, and creating incentives that mobilise people to change their behaviour, in accordance with a shared vision, as they move toward their chosen futures. This means mobilising resources so people can adjust their vision, and develop new patterns of resources to meet new patterns of opportunities and challenges.

Organisational change

One of the greatest barriers to the successful development and application of ICT is organisational change. To achieve government vision and leadership requires the creation of an effective, flexible, and authoritative unit close to the top of government. This unit should be empowered to press these changes and to create opportunities for producers and users to offer and implement innovative products, services, and applications. A crucial barrier to diffusion is an organisation's capacity to absorb a new technology. The introduction of hardware and software into a plant or office is relatively easy. Effective use of ICTs requires a profound transformation in the internal organisation of the firm and its interconnections with markets and suppliers. The successful absorption of ICTs requires technical capabilities and also effective planning and organisational capabilities (Hanna et al. 1995).

Decision-makers need to be able to address each of the following points and this requires substantial leadership and organisational change.

Convergence and big disputes over the true meaning of ICTs

In any revolution, there are always very serious and sustained conflicts over the meaning of the changes. Such conflicts occur within government between competing agencies, and between government and social groups, each seeking to impose its own interpretation. The stakes are high - new directions in public policy, professional status, and control of resources. The 'ICT Revolution' is no exception.

Such conflicts are inevitable because ICTs challenge the definition of the problem, who gets what resources to solve it, and whose career will be advanced. Most countries start the ICT revolution with a tendency to define the problem as entirely a telecommunication problem. Another misconception is to think the computer problem will be solved by placing cheap, stand-alone computers on desks in government departments. Better answers emerge through widespread discussions between governments, the private sector, and other stakeholders, and across government units. One description of the answer is convergence.

A truly national, visionary, and strategic perspective recognises that convergence unites telecommunication technologies, computers, and software to create networks that can enable citizens to be more knowledgeable, better off financially, and better served by governments and firms, and to make their businesses more competitive internationally.

Government needs to learn to 'do new things' to 'win' globally and locally

Being proactive in the face of the ICT revolution is essential. Governments need to make a proactive response to global information infrastructure-global information society developments. They should avoid excessive or heavy-handed interference in new ICT markets (OECD 1996b).

'The trillion dollar global deal'

The 1997 basic telecommunication services agreement commits some developing countries to a major restructuring of their national telecommunication policies including ownership of facilities, access to networks, pro-competition regulatory policies, and national information infrastructure approaches. The outcome of these negotiations is intended to be technology-neutral. It is very important for officials in the least developed countries to understand this deal. These changes constitute a telecommunication strategy and a foreign investment strategy.

The least developed countries should not get too 'hyped up' about the ICT revolution

Despite the sense of urgency, the least developed countries have the time to approach their visions and policies in a deliberate and careful manner. Government officials should beware of the hype. Success requires substantial organisational change, and because organisational change is very difficult, changes should be accomplished by careful thinking about financing and ICT policy. They should not be rushed. Much of the hype comes from self-interested vendors based in the industrialised countries and officials of the least developed countries should be especially wary.

Short-term expenditure on ICTs will compete with expenditure on other very important social needs such as transport and medical care. In the medium and long-term, investment in ICTs will contribute to expanding the coverage and quality of health care services and improving transport resulting in reduced competition for resources. That is little consolation for the official who must live in the short-term. In the short-term ICT expenditure may be a zero-sum affair.

The 'gap' - there is no 'convergence' on the horizon without action

The prophets of the ICT revolution argue that a 'gap' between the information 'haves' and 'have nots' can be prevented. There already are huge gaps such as the GDP per capita 'gap' between most of the least developed countries and the industrialised countries. One study has noted that at present rates of growth in the industrialised countries and Brazil, it will take about 487 years to close this gap (Pritchett 1996). At current rates of investment, it will take more than 50 years to close the existing telephone penetration 'gap'.

Identifying and measuring the right thing

There are a variety of ways of mapping and measuring the quantitative and qualitative changes associated with the ICT revolution. Most experts believe they are incapable of capturing the wide range of services and products now available to developing countries. There is little agreement on what the new indicators should include. New metrics are needed for 'knowledge societies' that capture usage rates and the capacity to use ICTs effectively for development, rather than only the availability of hardware and services.

11.7 CONCLUSION – SUSTAINABLE DEVELOPMENT SHOULD BE THE GOAL

The goal of a national ICT strategy is to serve the consumer and citizen. What is good for them is good for everyone including the producers of the products and services. When competition is intense, investment should rise and prices should drop producing useful and desirable information. Decision-makers often slip into an overly technocratic approach that ignores the consumer and the citizen. Consumer 'demand pull' and citizen needs should be shaping the ICT revolution. Instead of beginning with the most sophisticated users, the strategies of national planners could be designed for women and for the marginalised people in urban areas and rural villages. If national ICT decision-makers were to gear deliberations toward what people in these areas need each morning when they rise, cook, want medical attention, seek crop prices, need weather forecasts, and seek education and jobs for their children, their ICT strategies would be more balanced.

The ICT revolution presents the least developed countries with a double challenge. They must assign qualified and able people to keep abreast of the latest developments in the ICT field while they assign scarce human, organisational, and financial resources to meet the needs of rural and marginalised people. Decision-makers who take the initiative to develop coherent guidelines for national or regional ICT strategies that reflect their development needs will take a major step toward building ICT capabilities that enable people to benefit from these technologies.

NOTES

1   *Based on ITU STARS Database (1996), three-year averages for 1990–92 and 1992–94.*

2   *The International Federation for Information Processing (IFIP) is a multinational federation of organisations with technical committees covering a broad range of computing themes like information systems, education, and communication. One of these deals with computers and society and its mandate is to collect, exchange, and disseminate experiences of developing countries and to develop criteria, methods, and guidelines for the design and implementation of culturally adapted information systems. A set of papers on these topics is published in Roche and Blaine (1996).*

CHAPTER 12

INNOVATIVE 'KNOWLEDGE SOCIETIES'-CONSEQUENCES OF ICT STRATEGIES

The benefits, risks, and outcomes

Some developing countries have been investing heavily in the human and technical components of their national information infrastructures. Some of these countries already have national ICT strategies in place. This chapter considers the hopes and expectations associated with ICTs. New investment strategies are expected to stimulate economic growth and create new opportunities to achieve a more equitable distribution of wealth both on a global basis and within countries. The positive outcomes of ICT strategies should begin to be visible in new sources of employment and the potential for new ways of working and organising the production of manufacturing and services. The possibilities of enriched communication and shared understanding of cultures should be enhanced and new knowledge should be available about how to address a wide range of social, economic, and environmental problems. Factors contributing to social exclusion should start to decrease and the competitiveness of firms should be strengthened. Investment in ICTs should help to reduce poverty and enhance the possibility of sustainable development.

There is a risk, however, that the diffusion of ICTs and the transition to knowledge-based development will exacerbate existing social and economic problems. The creation of new jobs could be counterbalanced by the loss of jobs in traditional sectors. The social and cultural infrastructure which enables a positive working environment and community-based activities may not support the new requirements of 'knowledge societies'. Instead of being empowered by ICTs, disadvantaged or excluded groups, including women, the unskilled, and disabled, may be further marginalised.

This chapter looks first at the potential contribution of ICTs to economic growth (section 12.2) and then at their impact in terms of job creation and the growing tradability of services. These two areas have major implications for the distribution of economic resources on a global basis. This aspect is examined in section 12.3. Sections 12.4, 12.5 and 12.6, respectively, look at the experience of teleworking as an example of the 'global' impact of ICTs, women's use of ICT applications to gain greater control over their lives, and the contribution of unions to the education, training, and re-training that will be necessary to cope with major changes in skill requirements.

12.2 ICT INVESTMENT AND ECONOMIC GROWTH

Fifty years ago ICTs were inaccessible to most of the world's population. Long distance telephone services were manu-ally operated and employed thousands of 'operators'. Banks and insurance companies employed people who performed arithmetical calculations. In the richer countries, households were more likely to have a radio than a telephone and, in the poorer countries, the radio was a luxury, even for those receiving electricity supply. The world has changed enormously with respect to the availability and diversity of ICTs. A small minority of people is still unaware of the telephone. A larger, but still modest, minority is unaware of the television, and the broadcast media have enabled most of the world's population to see images of computers and communication satellites.

The seemingly relentless advance of technology and its ever wider diffusion suggest that people find value in it and wish to incorporate it into their lives to the extent that they can afford it and it can be made comprehensible and useful for their purposes. New markets are created, new jobs are created, and new ways of organising the workplace and other social institutions are emerging. The process of transformation accompanying the spread of ICTs is profound. ICTs bridge distances in time and space, contribute to the productivity and diversity of human activities, and foster new forms of human relationships.

These transformations are ultimately processes of development and growth, of evolution, and the flowering of new potentialities and alternatives. These transformations are also capable of producing massive dislocations as established competencies and habits are replaced by new ones. For some people, this process will be destructive, destroying their means of livelihood, threatening their values and ways of life, and creating a world in which they feel incompetent. For others, however, the transformations made possible by ICTs are creating new and exciting opportunities.

These alternatives of progress and exclusion run as two threads through this report's examination of the role of ICTs in building 'knowledge societies'. For those who welcome the new world there are many positive indications that ICTs will become more pervasive and influential in the everyday lives of the world's peoples. In the case of people who feel they may be harmed or who feel threatened by these developments, there is considerable evidence to suggest that they could be right. There are real issues of choice about the rate and direction of ICT developments in the coming years.

For many, the spread of ICTs will bring about new opportunities for economic growth. New markets, new products, and new services are being created bringing with them new sources of revenue. There is considerable evidence that ICTs contribute to economic growth. Much of this contribution will come about through their capacity to increase productivity, to create more economic output with the same or fewer inputs. Over the long term, measured in terms of human generations (twenty or more years), the principal determinant of economic growth is the ability to expand productivity. Neither increases in labour nor material inputs are capable of expanding economic output as rapidly as improvements in productivity. Simon Kuznets, one of the creators of economic growth accounting, explained modern economic growth in exactly these terms (Kuznets 1993).

Productivity growth improvements ensure that the contribution of ICTs to long term economic growth will be sustainable. The significance of ICTs is that as they increase in capability they fall in price. They require very large investments in skills and major transformations in organisations, but ultimately they contribute more to the production of goods and services than alternative tools for producing those goods and services.

Another distinguishing feature of ICTs for economic growth is the generality of their application. Like other general purpose technologies, such as the internal combustion engine and electrical power, the production of ICTs, while a significant source of growth, has a smaller impact than the *use* of ICTs on economic growth. This can be compared with the development of the internal combustion engine whose use as a means of locomotion, to augment human and animal power, had far greater impacts on economic growth than the production of internal combustion engines themselves. Similarly, the use of electricity makes a larger contribution to economic growth than does the production of electrical power. Economic growth is created by adding value to the input. For ICTs, it is knowledge that is added and it is the quality and variety of that knowledge which determines the extent of their contribution to economic growth.

12.3 ICTs, A PLUS OR MINUS FACTOR IN EMPLOYMENT?

The impact of ICTs on employment and the distribution of the different kinds of low and high-skilled jobs in the 21st century are the subjects of widespread and inconclusive debate and research. Comparison of the gains and losses in employment as a result of ICTs is difficult as numerous empirical studies confirm.[1] The naive view of ICTs as simply a process of automation and job destruction has its counterpart in the equally naive view of ICTs as a purely positive source of new employment. The OECD countries have seen their unemployment rates edge upwards in recent years.[2] In the United States, however, over eight million new jobs were created between 1993 and 1996. Of these 60 per cent were in professional and technical occupations, resulting in an upgrading of the overall occupational profile. Manuel Castells has argued that, at least for the United States, the problems are related not so much to overall unemployment as to selective unemployment (Castells 1996a,b). In Europe, the European Commission has concluded that:

… in the short and medium term, temporary job destruction by ICT cannot be excluded. But the opportunities they present can be grasped if structural changes are made in companies, in education and training systems and in society at large (European Commission 1996h: 4).

It is to be expected that growing use of ICTs in developing countries also will bring the need for structural adjustment as the patterns of employment change.

12.3.1 PRODUCTIVITY GROWTH AND THE NEW INFORMATION SERVICES

The impacts of ICTs on employment are associated with their impacts on productivity growth and output growth, particularly with respect to the new information service sectors. The degree of impact depends on the rate of growth of new services which, in turn, depends upon their responsiveness to market needs and on the distribution of productivity gains throughout the economy.

Productivity gains include the overall counter-inflationary effects of falling costs and prices in microelectronics, computers, and telecommunication which make it possible to substitute new configurations of labour and equipment for old ones. In addition, organisational improvements and other, more dynamic, learning effects that yield efficiency improvements on the shop floor, production, planning, or administrative levels, make it possible to reduce or to redeploy labour inputs. In attempting to assess the employment creation and destruction effects of ICTs it is therefore no longer possible to distinguish many of the direct negative and positive effects from the indirect effects. The direct effects represent the new jobs in producing and delivering new products and services as much as the old jobs being replaced by new ICT equipment. The indirect effects occur as the result of the redeployment of labour and the reconfiguration of market demand throughout the economy.

Both direct and indirect employment effects are likely to be substantial and will undoubtedly further intensify the structural transformation of 'knowledge societies'. The rise of entirely new industries, such as the software industry, the electronic computer industry, the microelectronics industry, and the video cassette recorder and television industries, in the second half of this century, has brought about new employment opportunities. All of these industries only barely existed before 1950 but now employ millions of people. As new information and communication service sectors emerge they can similarly be expected to provide new employment opportunities. However, their capacity to do so will depend very much on whether the appropriate regulatory environment exists for the emergence of new markets, and on the macroeconomic climate.

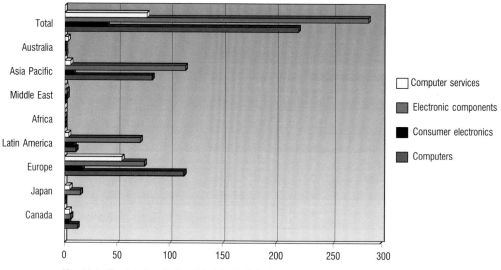

FIGURE 12.1 - EMPLOYMENT IN MAJORITY-OWNED UNITED STATES AFFILIATES ABROAD, 1993 (THOUSANDS)

Note: Asia Pacific excludes Australia, Australia includes New Zealand and South Africa.
Source: OECD (1997c).

ICTs make it possible to acquire, store, and transmit information in common formats. Software methods are regularly devised to translate this formatted (or codified) information across different hardware and software systems, making it widely accessible. In this sense, ICTs, and related software systems, are becoming truly 'global' technologies. With international data communication and the compactness and durability of modern storage media, stored information is increasingly bridging time and distance. This allows organisations to locate the relatively routine activities associated with the acquisition and processing of information, wherever in the world the

advantage is greatest. In this more transparent global world, greater trade in these activities is feasible. It is a world in which economic incentives allow countries to converge more rapidly and which brings about more equitable development on a world level. This is clearly advantageous.

In employment terms, Figure 12.1 provides an example of the jobs generated in the ICT sector by affiliates of American majority-owned companies outside the United States. In 1993, Europe had the largest share of these jobs in computers but the Asia Pacific region had the largest share of jobs relating to electronics compo-

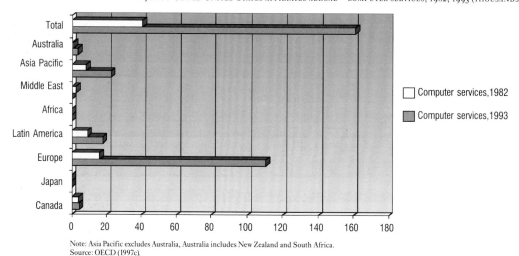

FIGURE 12.2 - EMPLOYMENT IN MAJORITY-OWNED UNITED STATES AFFILIATES ABROAD - COMPUTER SERVICES, 1982, 1993 (THOUSANDS)

Note: Asia Pacific excludes Australia, Australia includes New Zealand and South Africa.
Source: OECD (1997c).

FIGURE 12.3 - EMPLOYMENT IN MAJORITY-OWNED UNITED STATES AFFILIATES ABROAD - ELECTRONICS COMPONENTS, 1982, 1993 (THOUSANDS)

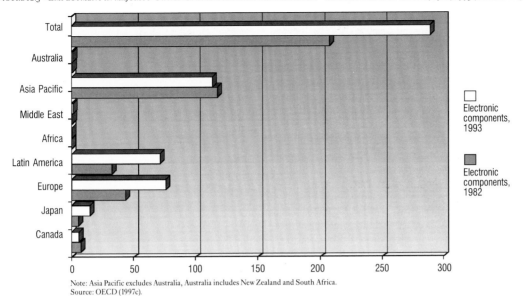

Note: Asia Pacific excludes Australia, Australia includes New Zealand and South Africa.
Source: OECD (1997c).

nents. Computer services jobs were located mainly in Europe, an area now being targeted by many of the newly industrialising companies.

Figures 12.2 and 12.3 show how the patterns of employment for regions can change over a decade. Europe claimed more than 50,000 jobs of United States affiliates from 1982 to 1993 in computer services (Figure 12.2), and increased its share of jobs in electronics components (Figure 12.3). The share of the Asia Pacific region in electronics components fell slightly and Japan's increased (Figure 12.3). These three figures show that the Middle East and the African region failed to build capacity to attract these kinds of jobs over the decade.

ICTs contribute to economic transparency insofar as they bring the cost advantages of alternative locations, international capital mobility, and international 'outsourcing' of particular activities to the forefront. For example, activities such as software development, processing health insurance claims, and maintenance of customer databases, outsourced by North American companies, have generated 3,000 jobs in total in Barbados, the same number as those employed in growing sugar cane. Certain routine activities that were outsourced in the early 1980s were either replaced by optical character recognition technology, or the jobs have been moved to low-cost Asian locations. Barbados is moving into back-office work which requires more highly skilled workers. This move is most definitely facilitated by the workers' knowledge of technologies and processes accumulated during the earlier wave of outsourcing.

ICTs facilitate a globalisation process that not only leads to direct employment impacts but also to technological and knowledge spill-overs. This could help industrialising countries to 'catch up' with many obvious economic and social benefits. The extent of this 'catching up' is dependent on many factors, such as the political, cultural, economic, and social infrastructure, and the capability of the country to benefit from technological spill-overs and accumulated technology. Not all countries will be equally well positioned to catch up in all industries. This ability will depend on 'created' and 'natural' assets including the availability of skilled human capital and information infrastructures.

12.3.2 TRADABILITY OF SERVICES AND THE DISTRIBUTIONAL IMPACTS

ICTs allow for increased tradability of services activities, particularly those most constrained by the geographical or time proximity of production and consumption in the past. By bringing in a space or time/storage dimension, ICTs are making possible the separation of production from consumption in a large number of activities, thereby increasing the possible trade of such activities.

The new ICTs offer the potential not just to collect, store, process, and diffuse enormous quantities of information at minimal cost, but also to network, interact, and communicate across the world - the world becomes a 'global village'. The time/storage and space dimenions of the new technologies are likely to bring about the further opening up of many service activities, increasing both their domestic *and* international tradability. As in the case of the telephone, it is likely that the 'new' emerging computing and other electronics manufacturing sectors ultimately will be relatively small compared to the growth and size of new information and communication services sectors. But the definition of the services sectors will blur, as more and more of the traditional 'physically present' service activities become 'info-type' service activities.

ICTs have effects other than bridging time and distance. They also make it possible to tighten linkages in supply chains, and to reorganise the logistics of product design, production, and delivery. However, in more traditional production processes, typical of industrial production but also common in traditional service sectors such as transport, and wholesale and retail trade, these linkages and logistics effects may dominate and the impact of ICTs could be exactly the reverse. Many of the most distinctive characteristics of the new ICTs are directly related to the potential for linking networks of component and material suppliers, thus allowing for reductions in costs of storage and production time - typified by the so-called just-in-time production system. At the same time, the increased flexibility associated with ICTs allows for a closer integration of production with demand, thus reducing the firm's own storage and inventory costs, that is, just-in-time selling. Both features clearly work in opposition to the features of ICTs that reduce the constraints of time and distance. In so doing, they might reduce the 'tradabiity' of a number of intermediate storage and inventory activities and enhance the value of *local* production activities.

On balance, ICTs are likely to increase trade in services as well as manufacturing. The competitiveness of service enterprises, as for manufacturing, will be determined increasingly by the business and macro-economic environment in which they operate and by the extent to which they are individually competitive. Thus, it may be expected that service industries will become increasingly dependent on cyclical swings, foreign demand, import competition, and foreign investment.

How, and in what way, do new ICTs impact on productivity growth in the service industry? The sector is huge and there are many different ways that the potential improvements in efficiency can be analysed and categorised. Market segmentation, types of applications, modes of delivery, and levels of commercial viability vary considerably from one service to another. However, there are some key elements that are common to most service providers. First, the use of ICTs affects a company's internal processes by providing opportunities to improve the efficiency with which organisations carry out their more internally focused functions (for example, inter-enterprise communication including electronic data interchanges and extranets, document handling, workflow, and data warehousing). Second, ICTs offer new delivery mechanisms that customers find more convenient (for example, call centres and interactive data exchange). Companies are restructuring their businesses around key processes that are customer-facing and concerned with how the customer receives the service.

ICTs are concerned with 'informatisation', the essence of which is increased memorisation and storage, speed, manipulation, and interpretation of data and information. This will continue to increase the possibilities for 'codifying' many human skills. This is not to deny the importance of the 'tacit' part of knowledge. On the contrary, as more knowledge becomes codifiable, the tacit knowledge is likely to become even more crucial. Thus, the ability to codify relevant knowledge in creative ways as well as the competence to select relevant information and to use it efficiently will become a more important source of demand for skilled labour. By the same token, an increasing number of routine skills will become completely codifiable and their importance will be dramatically reduced.[3] As the largest part of employment involves routine tasks, there is increasing concern about the distributional implications of 'knowledge societies' for employment patterns. Box 12.1 suggests the potential for new opportunities in countries with an appropriately skilled labour force.

Research on the impact of ICTs on employment falls mainly into two categories. The first emphasises the long term structural adjustment of the labour force to productivity enhancing technological change. The second focuses on the likelihood of technology-induced unemployment or high costs of labour adjustment to technological change (Cyert and Mowery 1987). Many attribute the impact of innovation and technical change in the ICT sector to the speed up of changes and the failure of adequate adjustment in the organisation of work, training, and education (Freeman and Soete 1994). But there are differing views on whether this factor is a primary cause of the mismatch between the labour force that is available and the jobs that need to be done in both the industrialised and developing countries (Cyert and Mowery 1987).

It is clear that apart from case studies on the impact of ICTs in the developing countries, there is very little basis from which to project the actual outcomes of the present moves towards 'knowledge societies'. Some see the relatively youthful workforce as a major advantage to developing countries, as young people can be educated and trained, and are enthusiastic. However, problems will arise as this young workforce is recruited by developed countries, thus depleting developing countries of an important portion of their workforce. The intellectual capacity present in developing countries has to be realised as a result of policy measures (Patterson 1995). Another study of the growing potential of outsourcing work from industrialised to developing countries, suggests that the 21st century may see the beginnings of reverse migration patterns. Developing countries may start to attract skilled workers who seek a lower-cost environment in which to live using ICTs as a basis for teleworking (Forge 1995).

Essential to all the forecasts of employment generation associated with ICTs as well as the scale and pervasiveness of projected job losses is the training, retraining, and life-long learning opportunities for all workers. Employment policies need to be integrated closely with policies in other areas, and increasing emphasis given to the organisational, political, and cultural aspects of the workforce.

There is a growing belief, and some evidence, that the use of new ICTs will continue to reduce the relative demand for unskilled workers, while increasing the relative demand for skilled workers. In Europe, the rise in structural unemployment over the last two decades stems in part from the growing educational and occupational 'mismatch' between job losses and new employment opportunities. Many such changes in the demand for new skills are a direct result of the introduction of the new ICTs.

Many studies have concluded that the spread of computers and the increasingly problem-solving nature of many jobs may underlie the non-neutral nature of ICTs which are said to have increased the demands for skills (Rees 1994, Senker and Senker 1990). This is because, overall, ICT-based new technologies tend to require lower levels of traditional skills and higher levels of abstract and synthetic reasoning abilities. They thus seem to both increase the skill content and the share of high-skill jobs and to reduce the skill content and the share of low-skill jobs, leading to an upgrading of the skills requirements in the workforce as a whole.

The global trading environment is being shaped by interdependence in the economic sphere, growing interdependence and interconnectedness in the technological sphere of ICTs, and growing government commitment to the design and implementation of new strategies to promote innovation and the diffusion of ICTs. The boundaries between technology, trade, and employment policies, are blurring (Cassiolato 1996). Significant changes are occurring in the composition of international trade. OECD countries are modifying the structure and organisation of the production of goods and services. The international diffusion of new ICTs is a central premise of emergent 'knowledge societies'. But in the absence of widespread diffusion significant parts of the world's population will continue to be excluded.

One consequence of the growth in the importance of advanced ICTs is the increasing difficulty of monitoring the flow of information across national boundaries and the problems of valuation of knowledge and software or intangibles.

The new wealth of nations has a capital base of knowledge and software. The new resource of the information age is information itself: in home, educational, entertainment or industrial applications (Cordell and Ide 1994: 10).[4]

Confronted with the accompanying widespread use of various forms of information and computer technologies, skill 'mismatches' are likely to be much more pervasive and general, raising questions about the inherent 'skill bias' of new ICTs. While these distributional concerns point to the crucial need to broaden education and training for all groups in society, they also raise fundamental questions with respect to possibly excluded groups, such as unskilled or routine skilled labour.

BOX 12.1 – IBM BUILDS GLOBAL HIGH-LEVEL SKILL SOFTWARE TEAM

In February 1997 IBM announced plans to establish a 'round-the-clock' development cycle using software programmers in China, India, Belarus, and Latvia to build Internet software components using the Java programming language, 'JavaBeans'. The project links teams of programmers from Tsinghua University in Beijing, the Tata Group in Bangalore, the Institute of Computer Science in Minsk, and the privately-owned SWH Group in Riga. Teams consist of more than 30 software programmers coordinated by a slightly smaller IBM team in Seattle. IBM hopes to cut both development cost and time by tapping into these offshore resources (Taylor 1997).

Building on the suggestion of James Tobin, the 1981 Nobel Prize winning economist who proposed a tax on foreign exchange transactions, there have been suggestions about ways of ensuring that an adequate tax base is maintained as services become a larger share of world trade. In Europe, the question being raised is whether and how to develop 'redistribution' policies to preserve the social welfare system within an increasingly global environment. A 'bit tax' (or transmission tax) has been proposed as one possible solution to be researched in order to distribute the benefits of the emerging information society more equally (Cordell and Ide 1994; European Commission 1996d; Cordell et al. 1997). To avoid distortions it has been suggested that if such a tax were implemented, it should be done on a world-wide basis (Soete and Kamp 1996; Ward 1996). For developing countries, an important issue is the feasibility of re-distributing revenues generated by a 'bit tax' to enable network access for excluded groups.

The issue of taxation according to traditional principles is also being explored by the industrialised countries in the light of the growth of electronic commerce activities.[5] Different countries are proposing varying methods of determining the electronic commerce income tax base. There are problems in imposing retail sales taxes on electronic transactions as well as in determining the value added by electronic commercial inputs. The problems of harmonising the tax rules continue to be discussed (Becker 1997). If changes are introduced to ways of generating public sector revenues in the wake of electronic commerce and increases in the tradability of services, the impacts on information-intensive services supply and access in developing countries could be substantial.

The teleworking army will grow to 200 million world-wide by year 2016 (mainly in the industrialised countries) (Nairn 1997b: Financial Times).

Cybercommuter: Ishasal lives in California, works in Malaysia - This 28 year old entrepreneur runs a 50 person media technology firm that is helping to build the Malaysian Multimedia Super Corridor. He has dinner around midnight in Santa Monica, California, before going to work in Malaysia via the Internet (Branegan et al. 1997: 30, 37).

The first quotation suggests that distance working is likely to produce jobs primarily in the industrialised countries in the foreseeable future. The second quotation highlights lifestyle issues. This 'cybercommuter' works at night. The United States is home to 24-hour shopping malls and many forms of entertainment that enable social communities to operate at any hour. Most other societies do not have these amenities to accommodate the social needs of 'cybercommuters'. The social infrastructure is an important part of the working environment, and policy measures, in areas outside the immediate concerns of ICT policy, will be affected as the structure and nature of employment change.

BOX 12.2 - EXPORTING LOW-LEVEL WHITE COLLAR TASKS

SwissAir has relocated its revenue accounting processes near Mumbai Airport in India. With telecommunication links to Switzerland, 1 million flight coupons a month can be processed with payroll cost savings between 20 and 25 per cent of Swiss costs per person. Together with improved business practices and better software systems, only 100 people are required which is half the number formerly employed in Zurich (Forge 1995).

BOX 12.3 - SERVICES EMPLOYMENT AND THE NEEDS OF SMALLER FIRMS

UNIDO's Information Technology Services for Industry (ITSI) programme offers software packages that are customised to the needs of SMEs in developing countries. Centres of excellence in software development are being established to support the production and dissemination of ICTs that are relevant to industrial processes and UNIDO offers technical expertise. The United Nations University International Institute for Software Technology uses its expertise in software development to respond to the software needs of developing countries cooperating with software specialists in developing countries reflect local linguistic and cultural conditions (UNCTAD 1997).

If international telecommunication costs continue to decline, telecommuting or teleworking could result in a shift of certain jobs away from the industrialised countries to lower-cost high-skilled developing countries. Teleworking includes home-working, satellite centre working (where an office provides the facilities for work at a distance from the firm), telecentre working (where an office is shared by several firms), distance group working, and teleservices such as telesecretarial and telemaintenance services (see Box 12.2).

Evidence of shifts in the structure of employment toward teleworking in developing countries must be estimated on the basis of projected growth in the industrialised countries and from illustrations of outsourcing.[6] No comprehensive estimates of the scale of teleworking activity in developing countries has come to light although some countries may be collecting statistics.

The teleworking jobs that are being exported involve high-level, creative, and professional skilled work as well as low-level information processing and clerical tasks. These jobs require access to the new forms of 'electronic capitalism', for example, reliable telecommunication links. It is forecast that new jobs are likely to grow in areas such as biomedicine, aerospace, and semiconductor design, first in the newly industrialising countries and then in the economies in transition. Services jobs are more likely to migrate to offshore trading zones where countries, for example, in the Caribbean region, are becoming financial services 'back-offices' for Wall Street in the United States (Forge 1995).

Speculation about the restructuring of employment and unemployment patterns is being fuelled by investment in national information infrastructures and in education in some of the developing countries. The importance of low wage costs in attracting new jobs cannot be ignored but some countries are seeking to compete with the industrialised countries on the basis of quality in high-skill areas. So far, outsourcing of jobs in the services sector is occurring mainly in accounting, airline ticketing, data processing, healthcare record processing, insurance claim processing, credit card handling, toll-free telephone services, and some aspects of software development.

According to *The Economist*, most strategic decision-making roles are being retained in the industrialised countries.

With an average Indian programmer's salary being less than a third of his American counterpart's, Indian firms reckon they can undercut American firms by 40% or more, even after allowing for telecoms and other costs of such long-distance work. But although India has become the world's favourite software job shop, it has yet to prove that it can come up with software products of its own (Anderson 1996: 15).

A new set of 'leap-frogging' opportunities is expected for the economies with highly trained knowledge workers (Reich 1991). Industry observers argue that China and countries in east Asia will be the major beneficiaries of the new knowledge-based occupations (Bond 1995). The 'end of geography' as a factor in the location of jobs is expected to enable countries like Singapore, Barbados, and Mauritius, for example, to become world-class exporters of services.

The Internet is the most recent network development to generate employment. New information-intensive 'virtual' enterprises are being created generating jobs in data entry and processing fields, software development, and on-line selling (Hénault 1996). OECD studies suggest that national information infrastructure development in the industrialised countries should have a positive impact on employment (OECD 1996d). Similar employment benefits are expected for developing countries if they invest in the necessary technical and human infrastructure. The growth of telemarketing services suggests that there are opportunities for employment in some developing countries. In Mexico, for example, new entrants in the telecommunication sector, direct satellite broadcasting companies, banks, and other sectors are seeking to provide telemarketing services to companies mainly based mainly in the United States and Canada. Call centres are also being located in Jamaica at the new Digiport International Teleport where employees work for about US$ 2 per hour compared to the US$ 10 per hour rate in the United States (TeleProfessional International 1997).

Small and medium-sized enterprises (SMEs) are expected to provide jobs as ICTs become more widely diffused and the Internet offers relatively inexpensive connectivity to locations around the world. Smaller firms are forming communities - a concept at the heart of the Internet since its inception (Armstrong and Hagel 1996). These new electronic communities are expected to generate economic value by charging user fees for their services or by charging fees for downloading information. They may also generate income on a per transaction basis, from advertising, and by positioning themselves to take advantage of the growing need to provide links in information 'value chains' between stakeholders in the market. Virtual communities of smaller firms can contribute to capability building by establishing an environment that is conducive to generating economic value. The example in Box 12.3 illustrates how economic value can be created by using ICTs.

These opportunities offered by ICTs are extremely unevenly distributed in the developing world. Where there have been initiatives in some of the least developed countries, they have not been documented systematically. In Africa, for example, a study in 1996 by the Council for Scientific and Industrial Research reported that no conclusions about the importance of ICTs for employment in the region could be reached on the basis of available evidence (Council for Scientific and Industrial Research 1996). There was no detailed information about the current situation. This was due both the absence of projects focusing on employment and difficulties in obtaining information about relevant projects. The study suggested that the majority of development programmes that were using ICTs to boost employment were at an early stage.

12.5 THE GENDER IMPLICATIONS OF ICTs

In her introduction to Boserup's (1989) review of the role of women in economic development, Swasti Mitter discusses the tendency for women to be excluded from decision-making fora which affect both their home lives and their participation in the paid workforce. She points to the fact that women are 'ghettoized in low paid, unskilled and semi-skilled jobs' (Mitter in Boserup 1989: 3). ICTs offer the potential for new forms of communication among women, innovative modes of participation in the workforce, and for building highly-skilled competencies. However, these technologies also have the potential to work against women's initiatives to contribute to social and economic development. As Janet Momsen points out, there has been a realisation that 'development plans must be rethought from the start so that women's abilities, rights and needs are taken into account at every stage' (Momsen 1991: 104).

Are planning processes leading to the production and use of ICTs achieving this goal? It is not possible to estimate the net employment impact of ICTs on women's manufacturing employment in the developing world. However, case studies at the sector and country levels are showing that the diffusion of ICTs alters production patterns in both the formal and informal sectors of economies in developing countries (Mitter and Rowbotham 1995). In the services sector, women have experienced gains in highly skilled employment involving ICTs. But they have also experienced the 'deskilling' phenomenon. In addition, although some women are entering work, for example, in the software development field, conditions in terms of contracts, wages, training, health, and safety are often very poor.

Although women share some common difficulties arising from their dual roles as mothers and workers, policy-making with regard to the gender-related aspects of ICTs needs to consider that women do not form a homogeneous category within any society. The employment prospects for women in developing countries vary according to their class, backgrounds, and age groups. These factors determine the opportunities that may arise or be lost to them. The advent of ICTs, whether in manufacturing or the services industries, is accompanied by a demand for cheap but highly skilled labour. Although faced with these changing skill requirements and the need for continuous upgrading of skills, few women have access to the relevant education and training. Most are confronted by obstacles to enrolment in formal training institutes. These obstacles include a mixture of cultural barriers, cost, and the inflexibility of hours of training which cannot be reconciled with their family and working lives (Mitter 1995).

Two distinct categories of initiatives to strengthen women's position in relation to achieving the benefits of ICTs and to reduce polarisation between them can be identified:

▌ those taken by women themselves in using ICTs as tools of social and economic empowerment;

▌ those taken by national and international agencies to ensure that women do not become excluded from the benefits of the emerging 'knowledge societies'.

The evidence gathered from the developing world so far is optimistic about the future but there are still substantial barriers to women being able to benefit from ICTs (Mitter and Rowbotham 1995). Some women at the grass-roots level, even in extremely poor countries, have managed to use ICTs to improve their businesses, reproductive health, and basic human rights. The examples are few and far between because the technology is new and mainstream research has taken little account of the initiatives of non-governmental organisations (NGOs) in the developing world. The limited case studies at the micro-level documented by the United Nations University Institute for New Technology (UNU/INTECH) in co-operation with NGOs in the developing world, highlight an important feature. The sustainability of women's initiatives in 'knowledge societies' depends on an enabling environment which can be created through the efforts of national policy-makers, donor agencies, and United Nations bodies.

There is a very strong link between gender-related initiatives at micro- and macro-levels. There is also a need for new alliances in civil society. This interdependency is particularly evident in the experiences of Sub-Saharan Africa, one of the poorest regions of the world. The average citizen has limited, and often very expensive, access to innovative technologies. Even so generic applications of ICTs have reduced the cost of communication and made it possible for women to collect and disseminate information within and beyond their national boundaries.

The power of ICTs in creating such an environment has been visible since 1992, for example, in the communication centres in Accra in Ghana. These centres have simple set-ups with fax, telephone, copy machine, and a computer service. They serve the business needs of the owners as well as the centres' clients. These centres, now numbering between 50 and 60, are owned almost exclusively by women, and serve many women clients. Until the restructuring of the government-owned telecommunication company in 1991, telephone calls were expensive. The cost of sending an e-mail was US$ 18 on average, and the average monthly salary of a professional woman was approximately US$ 25. After restructuring of the telecommunication sector, the cost of e-mail tumbled to about US$ 1.10. Still high by most standards, this dramatic reduction in cost opened up new channels of business communication nationally and internationally especially when organised on a collective basis. In a society where there has been a long tradition of women traders, ICTs now offer to women especially, new scope for business ventures. Redundancy payments from the retrenchment during structural adjustment, together with repatriated funds from overseas relatives, have provided start-up capital and new ways of generating a livelihood. A word of caution is important here - similar successful initiatives in Nigeria are reported subsequently to have been taken over by men.

SangoNet in South Africa is another example of a grass-roots initiative committed to expanding women's participation by using ICT. This network is the African partner of the Alliance for Progressive Communications (APC), a consortium of 21 member networks dedicated to serving NGOs and citizens working for social equality, economic justice, and environmental sustainability. The SangoNet website contains information about women's projects and campaigns in South Africa including those related to reproductive rights (Marcelle 1998 forthcoming).

ICTs, by enhancing the communication power of the NGOs, also helps to defend the dignity and rights of women activists. Thus, for instance, Drik, an NGO in Dhaka, Bangladesh, acts as the leading, though unofficial, e-mail provider through Drik Tap. It is linked with TOOLS, a Dutch-based NGO. In a country where computers cost as much as half a year's salary, and a modem costs more than a cow, Drik Tap serves as an electronic post office. The ease of communication gives activists, including women activists, a chance to have their voices heard more effectively both inside and outside the country. There is a bleaker side to these developments for women as a result of the use of an ostensibly democratising technology. Bulletin boards often are dominated by men and are used to send messages that are anti-women, and pornographic. It is very difficult to implement regulatory measures to control this behaviour.

The APC and its Women's Networking Support Program exemplify the way in which ICT could be used to make women's roles more visible in public arena. At the World Conference on Women in Beijing in 1996, the APC provided Internet connections and electronic information services to participants in both the NGO and official government conferences. This enabled women to have 'hands on' training in using some of the services and, for many of them, this was their first contact with computers. It also allowed news from the conferences to be disseminated to women who were unable to attend enabling their 'virtual participation'.

In the emerging 'knowledge societies', access to communication is becoming the key tool for social inclusion. A focus on the efforts of women and their use of ICTs is very important because their knowledge is necessary not only to ensure that women gain their rightful share of the social and economic benefits of ICTs, but also because women's initiatives can provide a model for improving the opportunities for other marginalised groups that traditionally have been denied equitable access to employment, property, political rights, and education.

Gender equality in science and technology for development was the United Nations Commission on Science and Technology for Development's theme from 1993 to 1995. This work drew attention to the gendered relationships that emerge with the diffusion and use of advanced ICTs (Marcelle and Jacob 1995; IDRC Gender and Information Working Group 1995). The results were incorporated in a 'Declaration of Intent on Gender, Science, and Technology for Sustainable Human Development' (Gender Working Group UNCSTD 1995) (see Box 12.4).

The UNCSTD recommended that governments adopt the Declaration as a means of orienting policies and encouraged by this, several governments have set up *ad hoc* committees in their countries to address gender-related issues. The International Federation of Institutes for Advanced Study (IFIAS) is undertaking a survey of the use of ICTs by African women, the barriers to using these technologies, and strategies to facilitate women's access to ICTs. The aim is to compile an inventory, and case studies, to highlight the gender related issues (Huyer 1997). Other initiatives include United Nations sponsored seminars on the participation of women in manufacturing and gender awareness training. Research on the impact of new technologies on women's industrial work in Asia and entrepreneurial opportunities for women in the Asia Pacific region has been carried out (Mitter and Rowbotham 1995) and was extended into 1997. Regional workshops involving NGOs and government bodies have been held in Bangladesh, China, India, Indonesia, Malaysia, the Republic of Korea, and Sri Lanka (UNCSTD 1997d).

Policy measures continue to be necessary to reduce the risk of exclusion of women from the benefits of ICTs. A recent study of women's experience of ICT-related employment reports that,

… women are as excluded now as they have always been from the formal endeavour of designing and shaping information technologies. They are marginal to the professional echelons of this work, and more and more, given the hostility of the IT workplace culture to women, they are electing not to enter it. This is the pattern in all countries of the world, even those which have a relatively strong record of women's participation in IT professions (the Nordic countries, for example). On the other hand, the menial and extremely hazardous work of assembling IT systems is almost exclusively female, and much of it is consigned to women who live and work in desperate poverty in the non-developing countries of the Third World (Webster 1996: 177).

There are signs of change in the policy debate about the gender implications of ICTs and other technologies, and there are signs of positive change for some women. But the reality of continuing poverty despite the opportunities of work associated with ICTs is extremely slow to change.

BOX 12.4 - GENDER, AND SCIENCE AND TECHNOLOGY FOR SUSTAINABLE HUMAN DEVELOPMENT

All governments agree to work actively toward the following goals:
1. To ensure basic education for all, with particular emphasis on scientific and technological literacy, so that all women and men can effectively use science and technology to meet basic needs.
2. To ensure that men and women have equal opportunity to acquire advanced training in science and technology and to pursue careers as technologists, scientists, and meet engineers.
3. To achieve gender equity within science and technology institutions, including policy- and decision-making bodies.
4. To ensure that the needs and aspirations of women and men are taken into account equally in the setting of research priorities, and in the design, transfer, and application of new technologies.
5. To ensure all men and women have equal access to the information and knowledge, particularly scientific and technological knowledge, that they need to improve their standard of living and quality of life.
6. To recognise local knowledge systems, where they exist, and their gendered nature as a source of knowledge complementary to modern science and technology and valuable for sustainable human development (UNCSTD 1995).

Another study drawing on the experience of Malaysian women is more optimistic finding that ICTs combined with industrial restructuring have yielded some positive impacts. However, this has not been a uniform experience. This study acknowledges that a small group of women, mainly graduates, has managed to make inroads into information processing jobs creating positive opportunities for women. When women have been provided with opportunities for training they have adapted quite easily to the employment offered by new technologies. However, the employment situation of the majority of women in Malaysia is still concentrated in the low-skilled or semi-skilled areas and this situation is replicated in other Asian countries. The case studies show that women workers form the majority of clerical workers, and data entry, and production operators. Their lack of start-up technical skills makes them vulnerable in a changing labour market (Ng Choon Sim 1998 forthcoming).

The quality of working life needs to be taken into consideration when assessing the benefits of employment associated with ICTs (see Box 12.5). 'Information workers' often must begin travelling early in the morning, returning to their homes around 7.00 p.m. Although in some cases unions are attempting to improve conditions for women workers, there are suggestions that a record of union participation can mean that employment opportunities are not available (Women Working World-Wide 1991 cited in Webster 1996).

In the Penang Free Trade Zone, there is an apparent labour shortage and companies are transporting workers from Kedeh state by bus. The companies say they need young women aged 18-25 because they are more dextrous than men at the fine work on the production line. They also believe that young women from the country will be less likely to join unions, especially on a national scale. Although women are available for the work in Penang, they are not considered suitable because they are married with children, and have poor eyesight due to having already worked in the microelectronics sector (Women Working World-Wide 1991 in Webster 1996: 51).

Conferences on the role of women in science and technology for development such as the July 1997 symposium on 'women, science and development - from indigenous knowledge to new information technologies' have been organised under the auspices of the Pacific Science Association and the Gender, Science, and Development Programme of the International Federation of Institutes for Advanced Study. The integration of women's knowledge into development planning and the gender dimensions of ICTs in Asia and the Pacific region have been discussed.[7]

12.6 PLANNING FOR THE TRANSFORMATION OF WORK

Labour unions around the world representing unionised workers in the ICT sector are recognising that many traditional jobs, especially in the installation and maintenance of telecommunication networks, will be eliminated as advanced technologies are introduced and markets are opened to competition. However, it is also expected that new jobs will be created in the design and provision of network services and multimedia products. There is a growing need for detailed employment studies so that the staffing impact of new ICTs can be understood and plans for re-education, re-training, and re-skilling can be put in place. Some of the expected changes involve (Darlington 1997):

▌ Changes in the *nature of jobs*: Traditional boundaries between jobs in the segments of the ICT sector will disappear. The telecommunication engineer, the broadcasting technician, and the software specialist will have increasingly similar computer-related skills.

▌ Changes in the *structure of work*: The standard working week will become less common with more people working part-time, more flexible hours and shifts to short term flexible contracts.

▌ Changes in the *structure of organisations*: The growing presence of relatively autonomous units and project teams (that is, the flexible firm or network organisation) will characterise the sector, and outsourcing of some aspects of business will become more common.

▌ Changes in the *location of jobs*: Various forms of teleworking that is, from home, a 'hot desk', or a neighbourhood centre, will bring flexibility, but also problems of isolation and exploitation. The potential for outsourcing via teleworking from industrialised countries to developing countries, and between countries in developing regions will present increasing challenges for the enforcement of labour contracts and the quality of working life.

Union responses to the changing employment and working conditions include research to monitor the impact of innovations in ICTs; communication with memberships to discuss the implications of these changes and plan new ways of responding to members' needs; recruitment in new entry companies; and cooperation across the boundaries of the sector and the use of ICTs to help in exchanging information and experiences around the world. Participation as a key stakeholder in the formation of national ICT strategies is also vital.

An important cause of unemployment in the ICT industries is the 'downsizing' of public telecommunication operator workforces as a result of privatisation and increasing competition. For example the British Telecom workforce was reduced by 42 per cent between 1990-1995. Market restructuring is accompanying the liberalisation trends in developing countries. A review of these trends around the world suggests that the impacts on the size of the workforce often take about five years to materialise after initial measures to open markets to competition. This lag may create a 'window of opportunity' for some developing countries to initiate training and re-training schemes through government-industry partnerships and with the involvement of all stakeholders including union representatives (Mansell and Tang 1996).

12.7 CONCLUSION - THE SOCIAL AND ECONOMIC INTERESTS OF DEVELOPING COUNTRIES

Investment in a highly skilled labour force is helping to create new employment opportunities in some of the developing countries. However, it is unclear whether people who are already socially or economically excluded from the workforce are benefiting from ICTs. In the absence of systematic empirical data little can be said about the costs of transition to economies in which knowledge-based production is increasingly central. For those without opportunities for skills upgrading, changes in employment patterns lead to a greater risk of exclusion from the workforce.

As the least developed countries assess their strengths and weaknesses in the light of the job creation potential of ICTs, the conditions of employment, and the capacity of the social infrastructure to support the new workers, need to be considered. On the one hand, information-related service jobs are associated with the dislocation of family and community life and threats to the health of workers especially for women. On the other, new types of employment and modes of work organisation can be highly beneficial, leading to improved quality of life and greater economic resources.

The relationship between investment in education and training, and the kinds of jobs that will need to be done in knowledge-based societies, must be fully understood. Initiatives to generate empirical information on changing patterns of employment, training requirements, and the quality of the work environment, could be launched by international agencies and the private sector in cooperation with national governments.

The increased tradability of services will depend on whether continuing innovation in ICTs enables more knowledge to be codified in digital formats. However, tacit knowledge which enables people to produce or use information creatively, will remain an essential issue as efforts are made to harness ICTs to development. Research is needed on how far ICTs will reduce barriers to the redistribution of work and job opportunities around the world. These programmes would need to give special emphasis to the needs and requirements of women and other marginalised groups.

Notes

1 See particularly, Jaffe and Froomkin (1968), Freeman et al. (1982), Freeman and Soete (1994), National Commission on Technology, Automation and Economic Progress (1966), and Michael (1962: 5) who argues concerning the impact of computers, 'Using these machines does not merely involve replacing men by having machines do tasks that men did before. It is as John Diebold (1959: 3) says, a way of "thinking as much as it is a way of doing. ... It is no longer necessary to think in terms of individual machines, or even in terms of groups of machines; instead, for the first time, it is practical to look at an entire production or information-handling process as an integrated system and not as a series of individual steps".'

2 Especially in the European Union, where unemployment rates in the majority of countries have been in excess of 10%, see OECD (1996d), European Commission (1996h).

3 It is interesting to observe that, in contrast, despite the proliferation of cookery books there is still a highly paid skill called being a 'master chef' and this illustrates that some human tasks might never become codifiable. This explains why the idea of ICT as a 'skill biased' technical change, does not really capture the complexities of the de- and re-skilling processes, see in more detail (OECD 1996e).

4 See arguments about the 'resource' and 'product' character of information and ICTs and their impact on institutions and organisations (Melody 1981, 1985).

5 Multi-jurisdictional taxation of electronic commerce was the subject of an April 1997 symposium hosted by the International Tax Program of Harvard University (Becker 1997).

6 Most of the evidence is from the United States or Europe, see Culpin (1996). For an overview of the development of tele-services and telework in Europe, see Richardson (1998 forthcoming), Reardon (1998 forthcoming), and Narendran and Walker (1996).

7 Organised by Nancy D. Lewis, and Titilia Naitini, SPACHE, conferences in Germany were also planned in 1997. International Federation of Information Processing (IFIP) Conference on Women, Work and Computerisation, Bonn, 24-27 May and the JANUS Project: New Learning Technologies and Women, organised by the Women in Global Science and Technology Network of the Canadian Congress for Learning Opportunities for Women (CCLOW), 21-22 March 1997.

CHAPTER 13

TOOLS FOR BUILDING 'KNOWLEDGE SOCIETIES'

Options for development

13.1 INTRODUCTION – COMBINING SOCIAL AND TECHNOLOGICAL CAPABILITIES

This report stresses the fact that the industrialised countries are becoming knowledge-based societies. It raises questions about the role that ICTs are likely to play in building innovative 'knowledge societies' in the developing world. A central conclusion is that ICTs can make a major contribution to sustainable development but that this opportunity will be accompanied by major risks. For example, the least developed countries face enormous risks of exclusion because they often lack the economic and social capabilities needed to take advantage of innovations in ICTs. The developing countries will need to find ways of combining their existing social and technological capabilities if they are to benefit from the potential advantages of ICTs. These technologies enable innovations in the methods used to acquire and generate knowledge that is relevant to solving specific development problems.

From the topics covered in this report five main conclusions emerge about the potential role of ICTs in developing countries: 1) ICTs can be employed as tools for development, but their effective use requires investment in a combination of technological and social capabilities; 2) although domestic production can contribute to development goals, most countries will obtain greater returns from investments in the capabilities to *use* these technologies; 3) the capabilities for mobilising these investments and bringing them into effective use differ among developing countries; 4) ideally, these investments in capabilities should be undertaken simultaneously, but when they cannot be undertaken in this way, investment in social capabilities should receive priority; and 5) new partnerships or coalitions are needed to address a variety of coordination, investment mobilisation, and social problems in these countries. These conclusions indicate why the Working Group on IT and Development of the United Nations Commission on Science and Technology for Development recommended that developing countries should establish national or regional ICT strategies.

13.2 TOOLS FOR KNOWLEDGE-BASED DEVELOPMENT

Chapter 11 contains practical guidelines for decision-makers in the public and private sectors. These guidelines cover a range of issues that need to be considered in reaching decisions about an effective ICT strategy. Many of these issues involve choices about how to improve upon the availability of the 'tools' for knowledge-based development. The experiences and capabilities of developing countries in producing and using ICTs are very different. It is therefore unrealistic to focus exclusively on the use of ICTs, or on their domestic production, in a 'source book' of this kind. Somewhat greater emphasis has been given to the policies and strategies that are likely to create opportunities for the use of ICTs in sectors of the economy where they have the greatest potential to be effective. If these opportunities are to be exploited, it will be necessary for many countries to develop the capabilities to adapt, maintain, customise, and re-configure existing 'ICT solutions' to specific requirements.

As industrialised countries have discovered, measures of the extent of use of any specific technology are not effective indicators of the development of knowledge-based societies. ICTs are capital goods that can improve productivity and raise quality through their intermediate use in the production of goods and services. Without new skills, investments in other equipment, and organisational change, the potential of these technologies cannot be realised. This means that it is very important to focus on the complementary aspects of ICT use and to recognise that decisions about *how* ICTs are developed and incorporated in social and economic activities are crucial to their effectiveness.

The decisions taken by developing countries about their ICT strategies cannot be isolated from international developments. Chapters 9 and 10 have shown that the options available to developing countries are strongly influenced by international governance institutions which establish rules on trade, intellectual property rights, and the operation of international telecommunication networks. These institutions are largely dominated by decision-makers from the industrialised countries, although the representation of developing countries has increased in recent years.

Although international developments may constrain certain choices, many of the applications of ICTs in developing countries illustrated in this report, especially in Chapters 5 and 6, show that people are capable of taking action to use these technologies to achieve better outcomes in their lives. The challenge for developing country decision-makers is to create policy frameworks that encourage, support, and release peoples' capacities to use ICTs for producing useful knowledge and other resources.

The fact that many of the technological developments and initial ideas about applications occur in the industrialised world sometimes suggests that developing countries should 'wait and see' whether these applications will prove to be useful to them at a later stage. It is very important to develop strategies to harness innovations in ICTs to development goals. Special attention needs to be given to modifying the technologies and applications to support these goals. Innovations are needed to transform 'digital' information into useful knowledge on the shop floor, in schools, in agriculture, in non-profit-making community initiatives, in commercial, and in government activities. Investment in education and training and in some areas of ICT-related R&D, is necessary to make this transformation. Little can be accomplished even when these technologies are available 'off the shelf' (Wade 1990), if this capability-building process is not undertaken.

Difficult decisions and formidable coordination challenges are involved in initiating or sustaining this capability building process. For the policy-maker or private sector investor, there are often apparently intractable conflicts over investment in ICTs *versus* investment in other sectors. Policy-makers operate in a political world in which their capacity for action is highly constrained both by established practices and the urgent development problems that need to be addressed. Private sector investors, quite appropriately, seek a reasonable return on their investment. Without this, in the face of increasingly competitive markets, they will go out of business.

Investment in ICTs competes with other investments necessary for addressing development goals. This competition has sometimes suggested that there is an 'either - or' question to be resolved before substantial investments in ICTs or related capabilities can be decided upon. A key message of this report is that combining existing social and technological capabilities is likely to produce spin-offs in terms of social and economic value. The tensions created by competing investment priorities will not disappear. However, it is more productive to view the use of ICTs as an enabler of development and a source of skills and capabilities that can make a contribution in many different development contexts, than as an isolated sector for investment. This is a strong argument for establishing an effective ICT strategy.

To take advantage of the scope for action created by advanced microelectronics-based ICTs, decision-makers in developing countries can benefit from what has already been learned about innovation and the use of new technology. This 'source book' is intended to bring together some of the recent literature in this area. A particularly important theme in this literature is that new technologies are incorporated into people's lives through individual and organisational learning, adaptation, accommodation, and resistance. These processes create many opportunities to harness ICTs to development objectives.

Studies of innovation and technological change suggest four particularly relevant insights: 1) success depends on *continuous* investment in both the technological and the social infrastructure, 2) organisational change and flexibility go hand-in-hand with new modes and methods of *learning* which are essential to using new ICT applications effectively, 3) the capabilities to develop and use *tacit knowledge* (or local experience) are as important as the new techniques for accumulating 'digital' information, and 4) the innovation and diffusion of new technologies like ICTs is never smooth or uninterrupted. Historical practices and routines, and the occurrence of social, economic and political events, make the process of innovation highly *unpredictable* and therefore uncertain. Decisions about ICTs will have to be taken without a high degree of assurance that the results will be beneficial.

These insights suggest that knowledge-based development involves learning how to reconfigure existing technological and social capabilities and to restructure institutional arrangements to create incentives for continuous learning. Shulin Gu argues, for example, that in China the national innovation system is successfully combining indigenous and external capabilities to strengthen the contribution of ICTs to the country's development process (Gu 1995, 1996). Knowledge-based development is an intricate process of weaving together the social and technological components to create a national information infrastructure.

In this weaving process, some combinations of tacit knowledge, 'digital' information, network components, and other social, cultural, and economic resources yield more positive social and economic outcomes for developing countries than others. The challenge for policy makers, business managers, workers, and citizens, in developing countries is to integrate (and combine) human and technological capabilities in productive ways. There are no hard and fast rules and each country will follow a distinctive path. National and regional ICT strategies can provide a framework for identifying and selecting those pathways and establishing priorities for progressing along them. Strategies for building national information infrastructures must be more than statements about what might be done. They must be action-oriented and appropriately funded.

13.3 PROSPECTS FOR SUCCESSFUL ICT STRATEGIES

A successful ICT strategy involves a dynamic accumulation of skills and knowledge that has a major impact on development goals and aspirations. The prospects for a major impact differ depending on the level of resources that can be committed, the coherence of the policy framework in which the strategy is embedded, and the social capabilities of the country attempting to implement the strategy. The countries that have been successful in the past in addressing development problems are also likely to have success in their development of an ICT strategy. For other countries, an ICT strategy will be as great or a greater challenge than strategies in other areas, and the prospects of success are not as good. The least developed countries face the very difficult challenge of defining a strategy that can make the most effective use of extremely limited resources to achieve their objectives.

13.3.1   THE NEWLY INDUSTRIALISING COUNTRIES

In the First Tier countries and territories, Hong Kong, the Republic of Korea, Singapore, and Taiwan (Pr. China) access to ICTs is rapidly converging to levels that have been attained in the industrialised world and these countries are actively engaging in the knowledge-based development process. The Second Tier countries (Indonesia, Malaysia and Thailand) are 'catching up' reasonably quickly. For these countries, sustaining 'knowledge societies' involves three issues in addition to maintenance of their current rates of investment.

First, for all these countries, sustaining progress toward knowledge-based societies will depend on how tensions are resolved and opportunities are developed as a result of the interaction between their cultures and modes of social organisation and those which are becoming predominant in the emerging global information society. Second, these countries share with the industrialised world the problems of increasing the flexibility of their institutional infrastructures to cope with important governance issues, including intellectual property protection, the security of commercial information, and the protection of individual privacy. Third, all these countries face the challenge of matching their export-oriented goals for ICT products and services with the development of opportunities for broader domestic use of ICTs. For example, they will need to introduce policies and regulations that enable them to produce competitively priced, high-quality ICT-related products and services that are attractive to people in their own countries as well as overseas. The long-term success of ICT strategies in these countries, and in the region as a whole, is likely to hinge on whether they can realise their goals of becoming regional 'hubs' or centres for highly sophisticated ICT applications and for problem-solving expertise.

13.3.2   THE LARGER MIDDLE INCOME COUNTRIES
          AND SOME SMALLER ISLAND COUNTRIES

The larger developing countries, some of the wealthier island economies, and the countries with economies in transition, are moderately well-positioned to harness ICTs to their development goals. Their current strengths and weaknesses differ as measured by the INfrastructure, EXperience, Skills and Knowledge indicators (see Chapter 2). They generally have not achieved a very wide spread of infrastructure 'tools' and, therefore, their prospects are only moderately good in terms of developing effective ICT strategies. However, in most cases they have a base of accumulated social and technological capabilities upon which to build their national information infrastructures. Like the newly industrialising countries, this group of countries also will need to address the three issues mentioned above.

For both of these groups of countries, ICT strategies cannot be expected to eradicate poverty over the next decade, and there is a risk that new policies and investment in ICT applications will introduce new forces of exclusion. Some people will be left out and others will be excluded because resources cannot be extended to provide training, retraining, and lifelong learning opportunities to everyone. ICT strategies will not overcome all the 'dualities' of development.

For these developing countries, building innovative 'knowledge societies' involves initiatives in two major areas - developing the underlying ICT infrastructure, and creating conditions that will encourage the build-up of social capabilities in selected areas.

Developing the underlying ICT infrastructure

ICT investments are enabled and accelerated by rapid economic growth. The First Tier newly industrialising countries have adopted an export-led strategy for the production of ICTs and are beginning to show indications of increasing domestic ICT use as well. In many of the middle income countries, the absence of significant production capabilities has not slowed down their investment in ICTs. However, it presents severe problems in mobilising the accompanying investment in other types of technical infrastructure and in the social capabilities to fully employ the ICT infrastructure investment. In both groups of countries, the diffusion of the telecommunication infrastructure is 'catching up' with the industrialised countries. The rates of investment will need to be maintained, and in some cases increased, if the 'one telephone - one household' model of the industrialised countries is to be replicated. Even if alternative models are introduced, sustaining current rates of investment will depend heavily on trade, on whether privatisation strategies are handled well, and on the effectiveness of the new regulatory institutions.

Investment in both the telecommunication infrastructure and information technology products and services, will occur increasingly in a commercial framework where returns are expected to be competitive with alternative investments. It will also take place in a context where markets are becoming more open to global suppliers. The ICT users in these countries are very heterogeneous and their needs and requirements for the ICT 'tools' vary considerably. Regulatory measures will need to be sensitive both to the social uses of the ICT infrastructure and to business needs.

Choices will have to be made about the priorities for promoting access to ICT infrastructures for the scientific and technical research community, for businesses, citizens and community groups, schools, government departments, and public service providers. The process of arriving at a decision about the definition and implementation of 'universal access' to the national information infrastructure will need to involve suppliers and the representatives of the many user communities.

Developing the social capabilities for knowledge-based development

Investment in the ICT infrastructure needs to occur in parallel with investment in the social capabilities arising from the institutional and social infrastructure, including education and technical knowledge, as well as the political, economic, cultural, and social institutions of developing countries. As innovative 'knowledge societies' emerge, this infrastructure will continually change involving new approaches to education, new types of jobs, new modes of cultural expression, the formation of new social networks, and changes in market relationships.

To build social capabilities, requires an understanding of a country's strengths and weaknesses in the key areas that must be combined to enable knowledge-based development. Experience and skills are needed to develop social capabilities. The First Tier industrialising countries may have experienced substantial spill-overs from their participation in ICT production, partly because of their investment in the technical education necessary to achieve their positions in export markets. Many of the middle income countries (particularly the economies in transition) have achieved a high level of technical education. At present, the available models are inadequate to explain how experience and skills support knowledge development. In addition, the available aggregate data do not reflect the variety or nuances of the distribution of skills and experience within developing countries. The aggregate indicators are inadequate for specifying *how* experience and skills can best be strengthened to produce substantial spill-overs for the rest of the economy. This means that new measurement techniques and indicators will be needed to establish links between skills, experience, and knowledge generation in the use of ICTs in developing countries.

Although there is uncertainty about the best mix of investment in infrastructure and social capabilities, it is very clear that a range of new skills is needed to use ICTs to participate in knowledge-based development. Specialised skills are needed, as are generalised learning, and information and communication skills. The latter two appear to have 'a more enduring value, enabling individuals to adapt to changing patterns of demand.' (Freeman and Soete 1994: 156). There is a risk that those who gain access to skills and training, and especially young people, will move on to more highly paid jobs in other countries. But there is also some, still very limited and anecdotal, evidence that a combination of teleworking, increased tradability of services, and inward or return migration, will help to stem the outward flow of capabilities. On the basis of evidence so far, this possibility is unlikely to provide solutions to unemployment in the short-

or medium-term for most developing countries. Substantial risks will be borne by some workers, and in many cases, shared unevenly between men and women. However, for some developing countries, the new forms of distance working and increasing trade in high value added services will create new employment opportunities.

The newly industrialising countries, the middle income, and wealthier smaller island countries have varying capabilities for developing knowledge-based societies. Nevertheless, there will be a continuing need to guard against unbalanced growth and to take steps to ensure that 'zones of silence' do not grow in size or emerge in new areas within their societies.

13.3.3 CHOICES FOR THE LEAST DEVELOPED COUNTRIES

For the least developed countries, the prospects for creating a comprehensive ICT strategy addressing the range of issues discussed above are extremely limited. Limitations in resources, previous experience, and existing infrastructure, combine to severely constrain the options for these countries. The challenge is to focus or 'target' strategies toward outcomes that can be affordably achieved and that will sustain movement toward fulfilling their development objectives.

All forms of ICT infrastructure are spread thinly and unevenly in the least developed countries. On the one hand, this means that lack of access will continue to be a substantial problem reflecting the very limited investment resources of these countries. On the other hand, the constraints to access challenge decision-makers to ensure that ICT strategies result in the more intensive and effective use of what is available. This may be achieved by designing new ICT systems that will play a key role in building the national information infrastructure in a country. For example, systems for the distribution of medical knowledge, systems for disaster assistance, coordination of environmental protection, and the supply of carefully designed resources for education, are applications where the benefits may justify the costs of implementation even in the very low income countries.

With regard to ICTs that are more widely diffused in wealthier countries, such as telephones and personal computers, the least developed countries face enormous challenges. These countries are generally unattractive destinations for foreign investment because of their poverty and their very limited capabilities for mobilising domestic resources for investment in these technologies. These resources are likely to become even more limited given proposals for changes in the international telecommunication governance system that will reduce the inward flow of foreign currency from international telecommunication services.

One response in these circumstances is to develop sites where telecommunication and computing services are adequate to sustain international business. Responses can be drawn from the experiences of other developing countries (and the rural or remote regions of some of the industrialised countries) where ICTs are being introduced to empower local community groups. For example, the introduction of 'telecottages' in parts of Asia and Africa is helping to broaden access to a variety of ICT 'tools' and information. Community networks are being introduced with public access points in locations such as schools, libraries, community centres, or churches. A 'one-stop-shop' concept is being introduced in South Africa where basic development information, statistics, and transactions relevant to citizens, are being computerised and made accessible via kiosks and terminals located in communities. Even these initiatives are likely to present major financial challenges due to the costs of developing the social, as well as the technological capabilities. Ways will need to be found to ensure that these initiatives are not 'one-off' demonstration projects that terminate when programme funds are exhausted or with the departure of key people.

13.4 BUILDING ON STRENGTHS THROUGH COORDINATED ACTION

Investment in the accumulation of technology and skills does not guarantee that strategies for building innovative 'knowledge societies' will be effective or coherent. Even strategies that are developed with care and pursued intensively may become ineffective if priorities are not established or there are unexpected pressures in the external environment. If ICT strategies are to be effective, they need to be institutionalised and perpetuated. This means that it is necessary to create 'virtuous circles' of positive reinforcement and incentives for the participating actors to maintain their commitment. These processes of reinforcement require the establishment of effective coordination mechanisms.

Some models of development primarily emphasise the need for market-led development. In these models, the market provides the primary means of coordination with a limited role for governments to facilitate this coordination process. Other stakeholders, such as citizens groups, women's groups, non-governmental organisations, and labour organisations are involved mainly through their representation in the political processes that underlie regulation and government programmes. The degree of their involvement varies, and generally occurs after most of the significant technological design decisions have been made and after the education and training curricula that provide a basis for learning have been established. Entrepreneurial activity is expected to mobilise the necessary resources for growth, and growth is expected to improve economic and social conditions.

This model plays a very important role in countering the bureaucratic inertia and inefficiency of many govern-

ments. However, the coordinating capabilities of markets are limited. They suffer from imperfections arising from the uneven distribution of resources, and from the different capacities of market players to exploit market power or mobilise government regulation in their interest. In addition, in the highly uncertain environment of rapid technological change, markets may deliver coordination solutions that do not address important social objectives. Therefore, market-led development cannot always be relied upon to deliver the financial, technological, and social resources necessary for building innovative 'knowledge societies'.

A 'new' development model is emerging that recognises many of the deficiencies of the older model. This newer model focuses on partnerships among stakeholders in the knowledge-based development process (Talero and Gaudette 1995). New partnerships are being forged within developing countries between public sector organisations and the business sector. Firms are becoming networked across the world with partners in industrialised and developing countries. Business groups are diversifying into the production of ICTs in many developing regions, often with the explicit promotional efforts of governments. There are many instances where they are also successfully entering information services, and audiovisual and multimedia software markets for entertainment and education products. Governments and firms are working more closely with users in their local communities to create a greater awareness of the possible contributions of ICTs to their activities. In these cases, governments are playing a vital role, not only in facilitating market-led initiatives, but in initiating the process of capability-building and in coordinating the actions of a large number of interested stakeholders.

Much of the activity in these new partnerships has been undertaken with a renewed commitment to making positive and constructive changes. At this stage, little is known about which initiatives are likely to be most successful or whether these partnerships enhance or detract from other initiatives in developing countries. These new partnerships are encouraging new 'coalitions of resources' and they are introducing mechanisms for financing the build up of ICT-related social and technological capabilities in some developing countries.

For the least developed countries knowledge-based development is likely to be feasible only if initiatives are taken to develop new models justifying investment in their national information infrastructures. The greatest need for these countries is to devise models that will enable limited investment in human and technical capabilities to have an *enduring* catalytic effect in addressing priority development needs associated with poverty and environmental problems. For example, in the development of infrastructure, considerable attention needs to be given to the problem of negotiating the best arrangements for the investment that is undertaken. This may involve a greater commitment to traditional technical training and to a new set of skills for managing the institutional, regulatory, and technological dimensions of the ICT selection process. The options for developing 'digital' information resources also could be addressed. These might include, for example, negotiating directly with intellectual property rights holders for favourable country-wide licences. Such negotiations can be pursued for software (for example, operating systems) or services (for example, remote sensing satellite services) that are deemed to be 'essential'. This strategy may encourage competition among international information suppliers to achieve favourable terms for supplying their products in some countries. In realising the spill-overs from investment, the new partnerships, and new approaches to negotiation, explicit consideration will need to be given to how the benefits can be distributed as broadly as possible throughout these countries.

13.5 CONCLUSION

There are opportunities for all countries in the coming years to make the best use of the potential offered by ICTs to support their leading development goals. This applies to the goals of improving the quality of life and environmental sustainability of industrialised countries. It also applies to the goals of alleviating poverty and contributing to sustainable development in the least developed and developing countries. Exploiting these opportunities requires reflection on the experience that has already been accumulated in the use of ICTs. It also requires renewed commitment to learn from each others' failures as well as successes. Many of the hopes for the social and economic contributions of ICTs will not be realised, or will be realised in unexpected ways that could be disconcerting or destructive. National and regional ICT strategies can provide a framework for strengthening the likelihood of positive outcomes and minimising the risk of negative outcomes.

To exploit these opportunities effectively, it will be necessary to consider the development of the 'tools' for transforming information, experience, and skills into useful knowledge. Some countries will be particularly advantaged in realising gains from these opportunities while others are likely to be bypassed. Even in those societies that have the least advantage, however, innovative use of ICT 'tools' may provide a starting point for the development of innovative 'knowledge societies'.

Assembling the 'tools' is only part of the task facing countries as they design new or improved national ICT strategies. Measures must be taken to assemble the human capabilities and related technologies to make the best use of the new opportunities offered by ICT. This assembly process will be market-led in many instances, but to achieve certain social objectives and to reduce the extent of exclusion, public initiatives will also be needed. The purpose of this 'source book' is to provide access to some of the resources necessary for achieving these goals.

ANNEXES

We are very grateful to many people around the world for their support, encouragement, and contributions to this report. Members of the United Nations Commission on Science and Technology for Development (UNCSTD) Editorial Board gave their time to comment on three drafts of this report, and many provided materials. The Instituto Colombiano para el Desarrollo de la Ciencia y la Tecnología (COLCIENCIAS) hosted in Cartagena, Colombia, the first meeting of the UNCSTD Working Group on IT and Development where the conceptual framework of the project was developed. The National Centre for Software Technology (NCST) in Mumbai, India, hosted a meeting of the Working Group on IT and Development, where the decision was taken to produce this 'source book'. The National Commission for Science and Technology and the Office of the Prime Minister of Jamaica, hosted a meeting of the Editorial Board. We are grateful to Dr Chaparro, Dr Ramani, and Dr Ventura for their respective personal contributions to the organisation of these meetings.

We thank all the members of the Editorial Board for ensuring that special attention is given in this report to the potential benefits and risks of ICTs for smaller countries and the least developed economies.

The secretariat of the United Nations Conference on Trade and Development (UNCTAD) provided substantive and logistical support throughout the project

We also wish to acknowledge the support of George Waardenburg, Fernando Chaparro, and Geoffrey Oldham.

Many other people and institutions contributed materials and portions of the text. We thank all those listed in Annex 2 for permitting us to edit, alter, and in some cases extend, their contributions.

We thank the United Nations University Institute for New Technology (UNU/INTECH), Maastricht, and the International Development Research Centre (IDRC), Ottawa, for giving us access to a large number of pre-publication papers which they had commissioned. Particular thanks go to John Bessant, José Cassiolato, Carlos Correa, Bengt-Åke Lundvall, and Ernest Wilson for permission to draw extensively on their work. Professor Charles Cooper, Director of UNU/INTECH, made substantial contributions to UNCSTD's work on IT and Development, and Ludovico Alcorta was involved in the preparation of an early outline for the report.

Professor W. Edward Steinmueller prepared the analysis in Chapter 2 assisted by Dr Richard Hawkins of the Science Policy Research Unit (SPRU). Professor Steinmueller and Dr Hawkins also contributed in many other ways to the chapters of this 'source book'. Vladimir Quintero of COLCIENCIAS helped with the formulation of the indicators in Chapter 2. Peter Morris of Brighton offered his expertise in the presentation of the graphics. Former and current SPRU postgraduate students contributed with much enthusiasm and we especially thank Michael Albu and Jenny Gristock for their work. Janet France, Pam Strange, and Gail Ross-Wham, SPRU Graduate Studies Office staff, ensured that students' needs were very ably met while Robin Mansell was involved in the preparation of this report.

Cynthia Little, Secretary to the SPRU Centre for Information and Communication Technologies, served as sub-editor. Without her skills and extremely hard work in a very short time, this 'source book' would not exist.

Every effort has been made to trace the owners of copyright material. We take this opportunity to offer our apologies to any copyright holders whose rights we may have unwittingly infringed.

We are entirely responsible for the views expressed in this report and for any errors or omissions. The report does not necessarily represent the official views of any organisation or institution.

We hope that this report will be a helpful resource for a very wide range of people.

Professor Robin Mansell
Uta Wehn
Editors
Science Policy Research Unit
University of Sussex, Brighton

Erika Alfaro-Gallaga, *DPhil Research Student, Science Policy Research Unit, University of Sussex, UK*

Robert S. Anderson, *Professor, School of Communication, Simon Fraser University, Canada*

Christiano Antonelli, *Professor of Economics, Department of Economics, University of Turin, Italy*

Ana Carolina Arroio, *DPhil Research Student, Science Policy Research Unit, University of Sussex, UK*

Martin Bell, *Senior Research Fellow, Director of Graduate Studies, Science Policy Research Unit, University of Sussex, UK*

Roger Blamire, *National Council for Educational Technology, London, UK*

Jean-Claude Burgelman, *Professor and Director of Studies on Media, Information and Telecommunication, Free University of Brussels, Belgium*

James Cowie, *Independent Consultant, Oakton, Virginia, US*

Roger Darlington, *Head of Research, Communications Workers Union, London, UK*

Ümit Efendioglu, *Research Assistant, United Nations University Institute for New Technologies, Maastricht, The Netherlands*

Luiz Fernando Ferreira Silva, *National Council for Science and Technology, Ministry of Science and Technology, Brazil*

Christopher Freeman, *Professor Emeritus, Science Policy Research Unit, University of Sussex, UK*

Michael Gibbons, *Honorary Professor, Science Policy Research Unit, Secretary General, Association of Commonwealth Universities, London, UK*

Jaz Gill, *Research Fellow, Bradford University, UK*

Norman Girvan, *Professor and Director, Consortium of Graduate School of Social Sciences, The University of the West Indies, Jamaica*

Richard Hawkins, *Research Fellow, Science Policy Research Unit, University of Sussex, UK*

Richard Heeks, *Institute for Development Policy and Management, University of Manchester, UK*

Wolfgang Hillebrand, *German Development Institute, Berlin, Germany*

Karol Jakubowicz, *Chairman, Supervisory Board, Polish Television, Warsaw, Poland*

Meheroo Jussawalla, *Research Associate/ Economist, Institute of Culture and Communication, East-West Center, Honolulu, Hawaii, US*

Raphael Kaplinsky, *Professor, Institute of Development Studies, University of Sussex, UK*

S. Ran Kim, *Research Fellow, Sussex European Institute in association with Science Policy Research Unit, University of Sussex, UK*

Xielin Liu, *National Research Centre for Science and Technology for Development, China*

Ursula Maier-Rabler, *Department of Journalism and Communication, University of Salzburg, Austria*

Robin Mansell, *Professor of Information and Communication Technology Policy, Science Policy Research Unit, University of Sussex, UK*

William H. Melody, *Professor and Chair of Economics of Infrastructure, Delft University of Technology, The Netherlands*

Loh Chee Meng, *Deputy Director, Policy Research and Survey Unit, National Computer Board, Singapore*

Vijay Menon, *Secretary-General, Asian Media Information and Communication Centre, School of Communication Studies, Nanyang Technological University, Singapore*

Jörg Meyer-Stamer, *German Development Institute, Berlin, Germany*

Jane Millar, *Research Fellow, The Open University, Milton Keynes, UK*

Swasti Mitter, *Professor, United Nations University Institute for New Technologies, Maastricht, The Netherlands*

David Mundy, *Institute for Development Policy and Management, University of Manchester, UK*

Paula Murphy, *Regulatory Affairs, ICO Global and Part-time Professor, Cambridge University, UK*

Parantha Narendran, *Consultant, Ovum Ltd, London, UK*

Elsa Neira, *Director of the Electronics, Telecommunication and Informatics Program, COLENCIAS, Colombia*

Daniel J. Paré, *DPhil Research Student, Science Policy Research Unit, University of Sussex, UK*

G. Russell Pipe, *President, Transnational Data Reporting Service, Inc., Information-Communication Consultancy Service, Burke, Virginia, US*

Auliana Poon, *Managing Director, Caribbean Futures Ltd and Editor & Publisher, Tourism Industry Intelligence, Trinidad*

Vladimir Quintero, *Advisor to the Director, COLENCIAS, Colombia*

Sankaran Ramanathan, *Head, Special Projects, Asian Media Information and Communication Centre, School of Communication Studies, Nanyang Technological University, Singapore*

Bert Sadowski, *Associate Professor, Department of International Business Strategy, University of Maastricht, The Netherlands*

Rohan Samarajiva, *Associate Professor, Department of Communication, Ohio State University, US*

B. P. Sanjay, *Professor of Communication and Dean, Sarojini Naidu School of Communication, University of Hyderabad, India*

Ingrid J. Schenk, *DPhil Research Student, Science Policy Research Unit, University of Sussex, UK*

Jan Servaes, *Professor and Dean, Faculty of Political and Social Sciences, Director, Research Centre on Communication for Social Change, Catholic University of Brussels, Belgium*

Luc Soete, *Professor of International Economics and Director, Maastricht Economic Research Institute on Innovation and Technology, University of Maastricht, The Netherlands*

David Souter, *Executive Director, Commonwealth Telecommunications Organisation, London, UK*

Annabelle Sreberny-Mohammadi, *Professor and Director, Centre for Mass Communication Research, Leicester University, UK*

Edward Steinmueller, *Professor of the Economics of Technical Change and Innovation, and Director of Studies - Technology and Development, Science Policy Research Unit, University of Sussex, UK*

Zixiang Tan, *Assistant Professor, School of Information Studies, Syracuse University, US*

Puay Tang, *Research Fellow, Science Policy Research Unit, University of Sussex, UK*

Qing Wang, *Lecturer, Science Policy Research Unit, University of Sussex, UK*

Uta Wehn, *Research Officer, Science Policy Research Unit, University of Sussex, UK*

Thomas G. Whiston, *Senior Research Fellow, Science Policy Research Unit, University of Sussex, UK*

Ernest J. Wilson III, *Professor and Director, Center for International Development and Conflict Management, University of Maryland, Senior Advisor, Global Information Infrastructure Commission, US*

Marcio Wohlers de Almeda, *Professor of Economics, State University of Campinas, São Paulo, Brazil*

Simon Zadek, *Research Director, New Economics Foundation, London, UK*

The United Nations Commission on Science and
Technology for Development (UNCSTD), Third
Session, Geneva, 12 May 1997 received the Report of the
Working Group on Information Technology and
Development. This Annex contains extracts from
'Elements of the resolution of UNCSTD adopted at its
12–16 May 1997 session with reference to ICT and
Development'; the Executive Summary of the Report of
the Working Group; the Guidelines prepared by the
Working Group for national ICT strategies; and the list of
members of the UNCSTD Working Group and lead tech-
nical institutions.

ELEMENTS OF THE RESOLUTION OF UNCSTD
ADOPTED AT ITS 12–16 MAY 1997 SESSION

Information and communication technologies (ICTs) for development

1. Recommends that each developing country and
   country in transition establish a national ICT strategy
   taking into account, *inter alia*, the guidelines proposed
   by the UNCSTD Working Group on Information
   Technology and Development; where such strategies
   already exist, they could be reviewed in the light of
   these guidelines;

2. Recommends that action be taken by national
   Governments to establish a task force or commission
   or to ensure that an existing entity be charged with
   the design of the national ICT strategy;

3. Invites countries, in order to facilitate the exchange of
   experiences among them at the international and regional levels, to prepare a report on their ICT strategies
   for the next session of the Commission in 1999; this
   report should include the priorities of each national
   ICT strategy, the mechanisms for updating, and the
   procedures for implementing the strategy; to enhance
   the value of the reports, consideration might be given
   to the organisation of workshops, all of these to be
   financed from extra-budgetary resources;

4. Invites relevant bodies of the United Nations system to
   assess their capability to provide assistance and
   promote cooperation in the ICT area and to suggest
   areas in which they are best able to assist developing
   countries and countries in transition in the design
   and implementation of their national ICT strategies;

5. Requests the secretariat of the Commission to synthe-
   sise the results of these assessments and, within
   existing resources, to hold an inter-agency meeting in

cooperation with the Commission to review this
synthesis;

6. Invites governments, the public and business sectors,
   academia, and NGOs in industrialised countries to
   engage in technological cooperation activities with
   counterparts in developing countries and countries in
   transition in order to facilitate their access, encourage
   the use, production, and development of ICTs and to
   ensure their effective participation in building the GII;

7. Requests the UNCSTD to identify an independent
   institute to prepare a study for the next session of the
   Commission on new forms of resource generation,
   involving ICTs, which may support social and
   economic development priorities.

EXECUTIVE SUMMARY – REPORT OF THE UNCSTD
WORKING GROUP ON INFORMATION TECHNOLOGY
AND DEVELOPMENT

In some parts of the world, ICTs are contributing to revolutionary changes in business and everyday life. Other parts
of the world, however, have hardly been touched by these
technologies. There is little question that their social and
economic potential is enormous, but so too are the risks
that those without the capabilities to design, produce,
and use the new products and service applications may
be disadvantaged or excluded from participating actively
in their local communities and in the global information
society.

The UNCSTD decided to address the IT and Development topic at its third session in May 1997. Its Working
Group's review of the evidence regarding the implications
of ICTs for developing countries and countries in transition led it to conclude that there are substantial indicators
that the new technologies are transforming some sectors
of society. There is a very great risk, however, that if
effective national ICT strategies are not put in place, the
capacity building that is needed in order to benefit from
these technologies may not occur.

The Working Group has concluded that governments and
other stakeholders must be called upon to design new
roles for the public and business sectors to enable ICTs to
be harnessed to economic, social, and environmental
development goals. It therefore recommends that:

▎ Each developing country and country in transition
  establish a national ICT strategy. Where such strategies
  already exist, they should be reviewed to ensure that
  they take note of the guidelines proposed by the
  UNCSTD Working Group;

▎ Immediate action be taken by national governments to
  establish a task force or commission or to ensure that

another entity is charged with establishing the guidelines for national ICT strategies. Reviews should be undertaken over a six-month period and a report should be prepared by each government outlining the priorities of its national ICT strategy, the mechanisms for continuous updating, and the procedures for implementation of the components of the strategy. Progress on the implementation of this recommendation should be reported to the next session of the Commission in 1999;

▪ Each agency of the United Nations system review the financing, production, and use of ICTs for social and economic development in their area of responsibility. This review should monitor the effectiveness of new forms of partnerships in the ICT area, and address the capability of each agency to provide technical assistance in that area. This needs to happen so that the United Nations system can be in the forefront in helping developing countries and countries in transition to implement their national ICT strategies.

Furthermore, the Working Group recommends that UNCTAD prepare a study for the next session of the Commission on the implications of new forms of revenue generation, focusing especially on those involving ICTs which may support social and economic development priorities. In particular, it should report on the implications for developing countries and countries in transition of the ongoing discussions and studies on a 'bit tax'.

Also, the Working Group suggests guidelines that should be noted by national governments, other stakeholders, and the agencies and organs of the United Nations system. These are intended to help developing countries and countries in transition design new roles for the public and business sectors so as to enable ICTs to be harnessed to economic, social, and environmental development goals.

GUIDELINES FOR NATIONAL ICT STRATEGIES

The Working Group's suggested guidelines for national governments and agencies and organs of the United Nations system are set out in the following sections. Effective national ICT strategies aimed at national capacity building for the NII will involve many stakeholders from the public and business sectors, and the guidelines encourage new partnerships in many instances. Multinational companies, the governments of the OECD countries and those of the newly industrialising countries, regional groupings, bilateral donors, and multilateral and regional financial institutions, will need to provide external resources which can be combined with domestic resources through strengthened national ICT strategies. All devel-

oping countries and countries in transition should note these guidelines in developing and strengthening their national ICT strategies.

There is considerable potential for producing and using ICTs for economic and social development. The following guidelines were developed by the UNCSTD Working Group. They are not meant to be comprehensive but are illustrative of measures which will need to be addressed in developing a national ICT strategy.

Producing and using ICTs to social and economic advantage

ICTs have huge potential for creating economic and social benefits for all citizens. They also have the potential for widening the gap between rich and poor. To ensure that the benefits outweigh the disadvantages, it will be necessary for governments, the business sector, and civil society to work together. The following guidelines indicate some of the ways in which this can be achieved.

Suggested guidelines

National governments and other stakeholders should ensure that:

▪ ICTs are used to satisfy the basic needs of all the population and that their production and use contributes to economic and social objectives;

▪ Technology assessment procedures and methodologies are introduced to help identify and select key ICT production sectors and to promote key user initiatives. Feasibility, cost-effectiveness, and the expected contribution to development priorities should be included as explicit selection criteria. Evaluation methods should also be strengthened;

▪ Particular attention is given to promoting innovations in ICTs, especially in hardware, which can be implemented in ICT systems that are used in areas without, or with unreliable sources of, electricity and under difficult climatic or geographical conditions;

▪ Measures to promote and strengthen the social and cultural diversity of content accessed via the NII and to stimulate the production of indigenous content in selected areas are included in national ICT strategies;

▪ Measures are taken to provide access to public information of relevance to citizens and community groups. Such measures might include promoting public awareness of ICT applications and the potential of databases, as well as ICT demonstration projects;

▪ Where appropriate, ICT applications are used to encourage interactive relationships between governments, local authorities, and citizens, and within citizen groups.

Developing human resources for effective national ICT strategies

The new ICTs are changing rapidly and new applications are being created daily. These changes lead to continuing changes in skill requirements. Fortunately, they also provide new ways of creating those skills. They provide the means for enabling lifelong learning and for improved education, which itself can lead to improved quality of life. A national ICT strategy should devise ways in which governments, businesses, and civil society can complement each other in using the new technologies to enhance skills and education in a continuing way. Lifelong learning must also apply to the informal sector.

Suggested guidelines

National governments and other stakeholders should ensure that:

▪ The use of ICTs is encouraged at all levels of the formal education sector and, where appropriate, special attention is given to literacy, training, language skills, and primary education;

▪ Education and training programmes include scientific and technical skills, policy analysis skills, and innovation management skills relevant to the effective production and use of ICTs, and incorporate specific plans for curriculum revision to introduce professional knowledge that is relevant to both the production and the use of ICTs in support of development goals;

▪ Curriculum revisions include training in methods of technology assessment, in creative approaches to ICT development, and in maintenance and adaptation to local conditions, as well as training in evaluating the viability and sustainability of export-oriented strategies and complementary measures;

▪ Curriculum revisions take into account the need for gender-specific training and education regarding the design and application of ICTs;

▪ Measures are introduced to address job creation and working conditions which will contribute to sustainable livelihoods and the promotion of new skills acquisition through new forms of ICT-based interactive learning;

▪ The job creation potential of ICTs is explicitly addressed through employment measures linked closely with education and training policies.

Managing ICTs for development

The evidence from the introduction of ICTs into development programmes suggests that successful programmes require new organisational forms. Successful management requires that these organisational changes be identified and implemented. The changes accompanying the diffusion of ICTs create the need for people who can act as intermediaries able to coordinate, integrate, and disseminate new information about the production and use of ICTs drawn from relevant scientific and technical research and the practical experience of ICT implementation in a variety of organisational settings. The management of ICTs for development requires that knowledgeable people and ICT applications be combined in ways that support national development priorities.

Suggested guidelines

National governments and other stakeholders should ensure that:

▪ Measures are taken to improve the 'management of change' in all organisational settings;

▪ Mechanisms are introduced to compare the management processes adopted in different countries and to assess their strengths and weaknesses;

▪ The process of customising ICTs for more effective use, especially by the least developed countries, marginalised groups in rural areas, and women, is given special attention;

▪ Measures that encourage continuous organisational learning-by-doing, learning-by-using, and learning-by-interacting are included in national ICT strategies.

Accessing ICT networks

There are risks of social exclusion if businesses and citizens do not have access to an adequate NII. The NII needs to be designed so as to manage those risks. Regulatory frameworks can help to promote the efficient use of private investment to extend and upgrade the NII in line with development priorities and to ensure integration with the GII. They can also be used to encourage the development of an NII that is responsive to the needs of different users, including the poorest sectors of the population and specific communities such as women's groups.

Suggested guidelines

National governments and other stakeholders should ensure that:

▪ Clear plans are devised for regulatory frameworks for telecommunication, broadcasting, and cable television. Regulatory frameworks should ensure that minimum standards are in place to achieve network interoperability within countries and GII connectivity;

▪ Regulatory measures are devised to address bottlenecks impeding effective competition, created by unfavourable market structures;

■ Regulatory measures take account of national social and cultural priorities as well as economic efficiency considerations in licensing domestic and foreign operators;

■ Universal service measures and related policies are developed, and measures to ensure that suppliers take account of a wide range of user needs are evaluated and introduced;

■ Special attention is given to street-side 'kiosks' in rural and some urban areas to provide access to networks and services that are responsive to people's needs. National ICT strategies should include measures to explore innovative financing arrangements involving public and business partnerships.

Promoting and financing investment in ICTs

Market mechanisms alone are unlikely to be sufficient to generate adequate investment funds for developing countries and countries in transition that are seeking to upgrade their NIIs. Governments are experimenting with two-way investment partnerships between local and foreign firms that lead to new ICT applications and generate spin-offs throughout the economy. However, these initiatives require a pooling or coalition of resources from the public and business sectors and this mechanism has yet to be fully exploited.

Suggested guidelines

National governments and other stakeholders should ensure that:

■ Plans are introduced that encourage a coalition of resources to initiate ICT production in key areas and to provide a basis for experimental and commercial ICT applications;

■ Innovative financing arrangements are considered that bring together financial and human resources as well as technical contributions 'in kind' to provide seed capital for innovative projects;

■ Priority is given to measures to attract foreign investors to ensure the development of the NII, including the telecommunication infrastructure, ICT applications involving software development, and human resource training. Such measures may include new forms of revenue generation and public and business partnerships to strengthen national capabilities in manufacturing, and the adaptation and customisation of ICTs;

■ The implementation of innovative pricing schemes is encouraged, leading to stimulation of demand for commercial services and exploration of means whereby the most marginalised groups in society can access and use the NII.

Creating and accessing scientific and technical knowledge

If developing countries and countries in transition are unable to build their own NIIs or be part of the GII, they will be handicapping their scientific and technical research communities. Capacity building in the ICT field involves the accumulation of scientific and technical knowledge that enables the assessment, selection, application, adaptation, and development of ICTs in ways that contribute to equitable and sustainable development. The coordination of, and access to, expertise within, and external to, developing countries and countries in transition need to be strengthened. Improved 'early warning systems' regarding new technical, market, policy, and regulatory developments are also needed.

Suggested guidelines

National governments and other stakeholders should ensure that:

■ Science, technology, and innovation policies are formulated in the light of the new opportunities generated by ICTs;

■ Measures encourage and facilitate the establishment of R&D networks linking ICT production and use to priority development issues;

■ Collaboration among science and technology research groups involved in the development and application of ICTs in developed and developing countries is encouraged;

■ Plans are developed and implemented for the dissemination of information on R&D networks, including promotion of the use of ICTs to support these networks, for example, the establishment of World Wide Web pages on the Internet;

■ Special attention is given to ensuring close interaction with end-users and particularly with marginalised and special interest groups in rural areas;

■ Explicit measures are taken to encourage 'knowledge broker' organisations that facilitate the generation and application of scientific and technical knowledge by combining locally relevant expert advice with information acquired through using ICT applications.

Monitoring and influencing the 'rules of the game'

The international agreements, regulations, and protocols governing the GII are influenced to a large extent by the governments of the industrialised countries and companies based in those countries. The 'rules of the game' particularly apply in areas such as standards, intellectual property rights, security, regulation, and trade.

Developing countries and countries in transition have inadequate resources to participate fully in setting these rules, and they may be disadvantaged as a result.

Suggested guidelines

National governments and other stakeholders should ensure that:

▌ Mechanisms are put in place to strengthen participation in multilateral and regional fora involving the public and business sectors;

▌ Measures are taken to support monitoring and analysis of developments in these fora that affect the potential for the production of ICTs in the national context;

▌ Special attention is given to monitoring and analysing the impact of developments in international or regional fora that affect the transfer, customisation, and use of ICTs in domestic markets;

▌ The emerging 'rules of the game' are assessed particularly to ensure that new competitive and cooperation opportunities are recognised and initiatives taken to benefit from them.

Guidelines for the United Nations system and ICTs and development

On behalf of the UNCSTD Working Group, a review was conducted by UNCTAD of the ICT-related activities of the agencies of the United Nations system. These agencies play an important role in facilitating the development of national ICT strategies and in supporting practical programmes for ICT production and use. Six broad areas of current activity were identified: the application of ICTs in developing countries at national, regional, and community levels, often linked to United Nations-sponsored technical cooperation programmes; local capacity-building, mainly in terms of upgrading infrastructure, including supporting telecommunication network upgrading programmes in low-income countries, and facilitating access to ICTs; research, mainly on ICTs and development, the ICT revolution, the social and economic impact of ICTs, and ICTs in relation to the specialised areas of competence within the United Nations system; facilitating connectivity to global networking; software development focusing on the needs of developing countries and countries in transition; and creating databases for use by countries or the United Nations organisations themselves in planning development programmes. Support is provided through advisory services and contributions to national capacity building, which help to facilitate efforts to strengthen NIIs. United Nations agencies are active in ICT policy and strategy formulation, providing expertise to interested countries or interested parties within countries.

These activities vary from one agency to another and in-depth reviews will be necessary to assess fully the extent to which each agency's activities adequately address the needs and requirements of developing countries and countries in transition. Nevertheless, as an international body with analytical capacity, the United Nations is in a unique position to identify the policy, institutional, legal, and regulatory changes needed to create a national ICT strategy. Its activities can also facilitate access to the GII by helping to establish networks which allow users in developing countries and countries in transition to access information, clients, and resources world-wide.

The UNCTAD review revealed considerable differences in the way, and the extent to which, individual agencies are using ICTs to improve their internal efficiency. There is a need to optimise the use of these technologies in technical assistance programmes in order to help developing countries and countries in transition to gain access to the GII. The ICT development lessons need to be learned from each agency's experiences and this knowledge needs to be disseminated more widely.

The adoption of national ICT strategies by developing countries and countries in transition will lead to changed development priorities and needs. The United Nations system will need to ensure that it is in a position to respond to requests for assistance in these new activities.

Suggested guidelines

The agencies and organs of the United Nations system should:

▌ Review their own use of ICTs in achieving greater efficiency in their operations. United Nations system use should match that of the business sector and national governments;

▌ Review their own capabilities in using ICTs for development activities relevant to their mandates, and upgrade these capabilities as necessary in order to support national efforts to strengthen local ICT capabilities;

▌ Implement measures that enable the wealth of knowledge and experience within the United Nations system regarding the use of ICTs for social and economic development to be systematised and disseminated in a much more vigorous way. A percentage of the resources for each project should be devoted to learning the development lessons and to disseminating this knowledge.

REPRESENTATIVES OF STATES' MEMBERS OF THE
WORKING GROUP AND LEAD TECHNICAL
INSTITUTIONS

Representatives of member States:

Professor Dr B.M. Rode	Austria
Dr V.A. Labounov	Belarus
Mr Luk Van Langenhove	Belgium
Ms Renate Stille	Brazil
Mr A. Gonzalez	Chile
Mr Wang Shaoqi	China
Dr F. Chaparro (Co-chair)	Colombia
Dr Eugenia Flores	Costa Rica
Mr Shume Tefera	Ethiopia
Dr Wolfgang Hillebrand	Germany
Dr V. Ramesam	India
Dr Arnoldo K. Ventura	Jamaica
Mr R.H. Manondo	Malawi
Ms Jennifer Cassingena Harper	Malta
Mr Espen Rønnenberg	Marshall Islands
Mr Garro Gado	Niger
Professor R.A. Boroffice	Nigeria
Mr Hilal Raza	Pakistan
Dr Marina Ranga	Romania
Professor Messanvi Gbeassor	Togo
Professor G. Oldham (Co-chair)	United Kingdom
Mr R. Mteleka	United Republic of Tanzania

Lead technical institutions

Institute for New Technologies (INTECH), United Nations University, The Netherlands

International Development Research Centre (IDRC), Canada

Instituto Colombiano para el Desarrollo de la Ciencia y la Tecnología (COLCIENCIAS), Colombia

Science Policy Research Unit (SPRU), University of Sussex, United Kingdom

TABLES

Tables continued

FIGURES

BOXES

ADDRESS: An identifiable location. A location within memory. A location of a node within a network. A reference to a particular point within a computer or network environment. A way of identifying a network, subnetwork, or node.

BACKBONE: A generic term that is used to refer to a set of nodes and links connected together comprising a network.

BANDWIDTH: The range of frequencies transmitted effectively on a channel, that is the difference between the highest and lowest frequencies transmitted across a channel.

BIT/BYTE: All computer data is composed of electrical pulses called bits (binary digits). Each pulse represents a single digit of data. A group of eight bits is called a byte. Bytes are measured in units of a thousand, thus kilobytes.

BITNET: A world-wide network connecting more than 1,000 academic and research institutions in more than 40 countries. It is a store-and-forward, email-based network with limited connection to the Internet.

BIT RATE: The rate at which bits are transmitted through a network, typically in seconds.

BROWSERS: Browsers can be used to view World Wide Web documents prepared in hypertext markup language (HTML).

BULLETIN BOARD: A system with a computer, modem, and telephone line that acts as a central point for information exchange. It can be used for electronic mail and for storing files that can be downloaded.

CD-ROM: Compact disc/read-only memory. A high density storage medium on which electronic data are etched and read by a laser beam.

CELLULAR TELEPHONE SERVICE: Communication service using mobile telephones with radio waves as the transmission medium. The service provider's computer equipment switches the radio frequencies as the caller moves from one geographical district (or cell) to another.

CHANNEL: A link between two terminals over which the users at each end can communicate with each other.

DESKTOP PUBLISHING (DTP): Publishing by means of a personal computer. DTP synthesises the capabilities of typesetting, graphic design, book production, and platemaking into one integrated, cost-effective hardware and software configuration.

DIGITAL SIGNAL: An electrical signal made up of discrete pulses coded to represent information.

DIGITAL SWITCH: A device for making switched connections between circuits to establish transmission paths for digital data transmission. Connections are made by processing digital rather than analogue signals.

DYNAMIC RANDOM ACCESS MEMORY (DRAM): Lower cost main memory than other types of computer short-term memory (or the electronic 'work space') in which software programmes and data reside while they are active.

ELECTRONIC DATA INTERCHANGE (EDI): Enables computers of different types to send and receive information directly. Rather than communicating directly, a trusted third-party service provider usually acts as a store-and-forward mailbox to guarantee and provide backup facilities.

ELECTRONIC MAIL: Computer-based messaging. The transmission of letters and messages from computer to computer over a network.

FIBRE OPTIC CABLE: A type of transmission medium replacing coaxial cable in many regions. Fibre optic cable is made of thin filaments of glass or plastic through which a light beam is transmitted carrying information as pulses of light.

FIDONET: Computerised bulletin board service that uses dial-up telephone lines and high-speed modems to transmit electronic messages.

FILE TRANSFER PROTOCOL (FTP): Allows users to exchange files between their workstations and remote computers connected to the Internet.

HARD DISK: A hardware component of a computer used for storing software, applications, and data. It has a higher capacity and faster speed than a floppy disk.

HOMEPAGE (WEB PAGE): A page of information accessible through the World Wide Web. The page can contain a mixture of graphics and text, and embedded references to other pages.

HOST: Any device on a Transmission Control Protocol / Internet Protocol (TCP/IP) network that has an Internet Protocol address. Also any network-addressable device on any network.

HYPERTEXT MARKUP LANGUAGE (HTML): The language used to create World Wide Web pages specifying font size and colour, background, graphics, and positioning.

INTERFACE: A specification of rules by which interaction between two separate functional units operates to conform with overall system requirements. An interface specification may include logical, electrical, and mechanical specifications.

INTERNET: A collection of computer networks connected together spanning the globe. Provides access to computers, electronic mail, bulletin boards, databases, and discussion groups, all using the Transmission Control Protocol/Internet Protocol (TCP/IP).

INTERNET SERVICE PROVIDER: Organisation or a business providing access to the Internet.

INTERNET PROTOCOL (IP): The particular part of the Transmission Control Protocol/Internet Protocol (TCP/IP) suite of protocols that handles routing of data.

INTEGRATED SERVICES DIGITAL NETWORK (ISDN): A set of standards defined by the International Telecommunication Union that defines a type of digital telecommunication service allowing the integrated transmission of voice, data, and still pictures in digital form.

KBPS, MBPS: Kilobits per second, megabits per second. Refer to units of data volume and are measures of the speed of transmission of digital data.

LOW EARTH ORBITING SATELLITE (LEOS): Low altitude orbiting micro-satellites which require only a small transmitter and lightweight tracking aerial to connect with the satellite.

LOCAL AREA NETWORK (LAN): A method of connecting computers, peripherals, and communication equipment within a restricted locality, such as a building or university campus.

MAILING LIST: Internet users in a group devoted to a particular topic.

MODEM: A device that converts digital signals into analogue signals and vice versa, linking a computer or a terminal to an analogue telephone. The term modem is a contraction of modulator/demodulator.

MULTIMEDIA: Combination of many media using, for example, sound, pictures, and text.

NETWORK: A collection of computers and related devices connected in such a way that users can share software and hardware (for example, printers) and communicate with each other.

ON-LINE: The 'state' of being connected, either via a modem or a dedicated line, to a distant database or to another computer using a network.

PUBLIC SWITCHED TELEPHONE NETWORK: Includes the telephones, local lines, exchanges, and the long distance transmission facilities that make up a network.

SEMICONDUCTOR: In electronics, a material with a conductivity midway between an insulator and a good conductor. The conductivity is sensitive to temperature, radiation, and the presence of impurities.

SMART CARD: Single chip-based plastics cards. Memory cards only store values while 'intelligent' cards have a central processing unit to manage several applications and can provide password restriction.

SOFTWARE: The applications, data, and operating systems associated with computer systems.

SWITCH: Switching equipment directs communication traffic to alternative transmission routes.

TELNET: The Internet standard protocol for a remote terminal connection service used for logging into and searching other computers connected to the Internet.

TRANSMISSION CONTROL PROTOCOL/INTERNET PROTOCOL (TCP/IP): A full-time, interactive Internet connection protocol.

TRAFFIC: The data on a network backbone at a given period of time.

USENET: A large collection of electronic discussion groups each centred around a particular topic and usually referred to as Newsgroups. These are accessible through a World Wide Web browser rather than email-based mailing lists.

VERY SMALL APERTURE TERMINAL (VSAT): A type of terminal used to receive satellite signals.

VIDEOTEX: Generic term for a two-way information retrieval service using a specialised visual display terminal or a personal computer running special software.

WIDE AREA NETWORK: A data communication network that spans any distance.

WORLD WIDE WEB (WWW): An Internet service that organises information using hypermedia. Each document can contain embedded references to images, audio, or other documents.

4GL	Fourth Generation Language
ABU	Asia Pacific Broadcasting Union
Acacia	IDRC initiative for Communities and the Information Society in Africa
ACASIA	Southeast Asian Carrier (Acasia Communications)
ACIS	Advanced Cargo Information System
AISI	African Information Society Initiative
AMIC	Asian Mass Communication Research and Information Centre
AMT	Advanced Manufacturing Technologies
APC	Association for Progressive Communications
APCTT	Asia and Pacific Centre for Transfer of Technology
APEC	Asia Pacific Economic Cooperation
APII	Asia Pacific Information Infrastructure
ARPA	Advanced Research Projects Agency
ARSENATE	Fidonet network supported by Canadian International Development Agency (CIDA)
ASEAN	Association of South East Asian Nations
ASIC	Application Specific Integrated Circuits
ASYCUDA	Automated System for Customs Data
ATM	Asynchronous Transfer Mode
ATT	Advanced Transport Telematics
BLT	Build-Lease-Transfer
BNDES	Brazilian National Bank for Social and Economic Development
BOO	Build-Operate-Own
BOT	Build-Operate-Transfer
BT	British Telecom
BTEC	Business and Technical Education Council
C-DOT	Centre for the Development of Telematics
CABECA	Capacity Building for Electronic Communication in Africa
CAD	Computer-Aided-Design
CAGR	Compound Annual Growth Rate

CALS	Computer-Aided Acquisition and Logistics Support
CAM	Computer-Aided-Manufacturing
CARICOM	Caribbean Common Market
CAS	Chinese Academy of Science
CASE	Computer Aided Software Engineering
CAST	Chinese Academy of Satellite Technology
CATV	Cable Television
CCLOW	Canadian Congress for Learning Opportunities for Women
CD-ROM	Compact Disc-Read Only Memory
CDMA	Code Division Multiple Access
CEE	Central and East European (countries)
CERNET	China Education and Research Network Project
CICC	Centre for International Cooperation in Computerisation
CIM	Computer Integrated Manufacturing
CITEL	Inter-American Telecommunications Commission
CMC	Computer Maintenance Corporation
CNC	Computer Numerical Control
CNPq	National Council for Scientific and Technological Development (Brazil)
COCI	Committee on Culture and Information
COLCIENCIAS	Instituto Colombiano para el Desarrollo de la Ciencia y la Tecnología (Colombia)
COPINE	Cooperative Information Network Linking Scientists, Educators, Professionals, and Decision-Makers in Africa
CoPS	Complex Products and Systems
CREAD	Inter-American Distance Education Consortium
CRNet	Red Nacional de Investigación de Costa Rica
CRS	Computer Reservation System
CRT	Computer Reservation Terminal
CTI	Foundation Technological Centre for Informatics (Brazil)

DBS .... Direct Broadcast Satellite

DFH............... Dong Feng Hong (China's satellite)

DMFAS........... Debt Management and Financial Analysis System

DNC............... Direct Numerical Control

DNS............... Domain Name System

DoT............... Department of Telecommunications (India)

DRAM............ Dynamic Random Access Memories

DSTI .... Directorate for Science and Technology (OECD)

DTH .... Direct to Home (satellite)

DTT............... Digital Terrestrial Television

DVD............... Digital Versatile Discs

EBRD............. European Bank for Reconstruction and Development

ECOSOC......... Economic and Social Council (United Nations)

EDI .... Electronic Data Interchange

EDP .... Electronic Data Processing

EDUNET .... Education Support Trust Network (Pakistan)

EIS................. European Information Society

EMIS.............. Education Management Information System

ENRIN .... Environment and Natural Resource Information Networks

ERNET........... Educational and Research Network

ESA................ European Space Agency

ESANET .... Eastern Southern African Network

EURIM........... European Informatics Market

FINEP .... Financing Agency for Studies and Projects

FLAG .... Fibre Link Around the Globe

FM................. Frequency Modulation

FMS............... Flexible Manufacturing Systems

FTZ .... Free Trade Zone

GATS .... General Agreement on Trade in Services

GATT............. General Agreement on Tariffs and Trade

GDP............... Gross Domestic Product

GEO............... Geostationary Orbit

GICI............... Global Information and Communication Infrastructure

GII................. Global Information Infrastructure

GIIC .... Global Information Infrastructure Commission

GIS................. Global Information Society

GIS................. Geographic Information System (Chapter 5)

GLOB-TED .... Global Technology and Economic Development

GMPCS .... Global Mobile Personal Communication Service

GNP .... Gross National Product

GNSS.............. Global Navigation Satellite System

GPS .... Global Positioning System

GRID............. Global Resource Information Database

GSM............... Global System for Mobile Communications

HBF .... Hoso Bunka Foundation (Japan)

HCI .... Heavy and Chemical Industries

HDTV............. High Definition Television

HEO .... High Earth Orbiting Satellites

HF .... High Frequency

IAMCR........... International Association for Media and Communication Research

IANA .... Internet Assignment Number Authority

IBRD .... International Bank for Reconstruction and Development

ICCP .... Information, Computer, and Communication Policy Committee (OECD)

ICE................. Identification Coding Embedded (Chapter 10)

ICE................. Integrated Circuit Engineering (Chapter 7)

ICT................. Information and Communication Technology

IDC .... International Data Corporation

IDRC .... International Development Research Centre

IEC................. International Electrotechnical Commission

IFC................. International Finance Corporation

IFIAS .... International Federation of Institutes for Advanced Study

IFPI .... International Federation of the Phonographic Industry

IIC	Institute for International Communication
IIPA	International Intellectual Property Alliance
IITF	Information Infrastructure Task Force (US)
IMF	International Monetary Fund
IMRP2	Integrated Production Management Systems
infoDev	Information for Development Program (World Bank)
INFOTERRA	Global Environmental Information Exchange Network
INMARSAT	International Maritime Satellite Organisation
INTELSAT	International Telecommunication Satellite Organisation
INTUG	International Telecommunication Users Group
IP	Internet Protocol
IPR	Intellectual Property Rights
IPSE	Integrated Project Support Environment
ISDN	Integrated Services Digital Network
ISO	International Organisation for Standardization
ISOC	The Internet Society
ISP	Internet Service Provider
IT	Information Technology
ITA	Information Technology Agreement
ITSI	Information Technology Services for Industry
ITU	International Telecommunication Union
IVANS	International Value Added Networks
LDC	Least Developed Countries
LEOS	Low Earth Orbit Satellite
LIS	Land Information System
LIUP	Local Industry Upgrading Programme
LMDS	Local Multipoint Distribution Services
LRIC	Long Run Incremental Cost
MANGO	Microcomputer Access for NGOs (Zimbabwe)
MAST	Measures Affecting Service Trade
MCI	Microwave Communications Inc

MCST	Malta Council for Science and Technology
MEI	Ministry of Electronic Industries (China)
MEOS	Medium Earth Orbit Satellite
MIGA	Multilateral Insurance Guarantee Association
MINICOM	Ministry of Communications (Brazil)
MOS	Metal Oxide Semiconductor
MPT	Ministry of Posts and Telecommunications (China)
MSC	Multi-Media Super Corridor
NAFTA	North American Free Trade Agreement
NASSCOM	National Association of Software and Service Companies (India)
NCB	National Computer Board (Singapore)
NCCIT	National Consultative Committee on Information Technology (Malaysia)
NCET	National Council for Educational Technology (UK)
NCVQ	National Council for Vocational Qualifications (UK)
NDPCAL	National Development Programme in Computer Assisted Learning (UK)
NGO	Non-Governmental Organisation
NGONET	(Global information broker service for Southern NGOs)
NIC	Newly Industrialising Countries
NICNET	National Informatics Centre Network (India)
NIE	Newly Industrialising Economies
NII	National Information Infrastructure
NIS	National Innovation System
NITC	National IT Council (Malaysia)
NLS	oN-Line System
NVQ	National Vocational Qualification
OAS	Organisation of American States
ODA	Overseas Development Agency
OECD	Organisation for Economic Cooperation and Development
OEEC	Organisation for European Economic Cooperation
OEM	Original Equipment Manufacturers
OTA	Office of Technology Assessment (US)

PADIS .... Pan African Development Information System

PADISNET .... Pan African Documentation Centre Network

PANA .... Pan African News Agency

PASTE............ Program for Recovery and Expansion of the Telecommunications and Postal System (Brazil)

PATU .... Pan African Telecommunication Union

POS................ Point-of-Sale

PQLI .... Personal Quality of Life Index

PTA................ Provincial Telecommunications Authorities (China)

PTB .... Provincial Telecommunications Bureaux (China)

PTO .... Public Telecommunication Operator

PTT .... Post, Telegraph, and Telecommunication administration

R&D .... Research and Development

RAM .... Random Access Memory

RASCOM .... Regional African Satellite Communications Organisation

RINAF............ Regional Informatics Network for Africa

ROCE .... Return on Capital Employed

ROT .... Rehabilitate-Operate-Transfer

S&T .... Science and Technology

SADC............. Southern African Development Community

SBA................ Singapore Broadcasting Authority

SCT .... Secretary of Communications and Transportation (Mexico)

SDH................ Synchronous Digital Hierarchy

SDNP .... Sustainable Development Networking Programme

SDO............... Standards Development Organisations

SDZ .... Special Telecommunications Zone

SEA-ME-WE ..... South East Asia, Middle East, Western Europe (undersea cables)

SEARCC.......... South East Asia Regional Computer Confederation

SEC................ State Education Commission (China)

SITA............... Société Internationale de Télécommunications Aéronautiques

SME............... Small and Medium-sized Enterprises

SPRU .... Science Policy Research Unit

STARS .... Socio-economic Time-series Access and Retrieval System

STNCR .... Educational Telecommunications Network of Costa Rica

STZ .... Special Telecommunications Zone (Indonesia, Malaysia, and Thailand)

SWIFT .... Society for Worldwide Inter-bank Financial Telecommunications

TCP................ Transmission Control Protocol

TELMEX.......... Telefonos de Mexico

TELWG........... Telecommunications Working Group

TPC................ TransPacific Cables

TQM................ Total Quality Management

TRAI .... Telecom Regulatory Authority of India

TRAINS .... Trade Analysis Information System

TRIPS............. Agreement on Trade-Related aspects of Intellectual Property Rights

TTP................ Trusted Third Parties

UN .... United Nations

UN INSTRAW ... United Nations International Research and Training Institute for the Advancement of Women

UNCED .... United Nations Conference on Environment and Development

UNCITRAL ...... United Nations Commission on International Trade Law

UNCSTD.......... United Nations Commission on Science and Technology for Development

UNCTAD.......... United Nations Conference on Trade and Development

UNDP.............. United Nations Development Programme

UNECA .... United Nations Economic Commission for Africa

UNEP .... United Nations Environment Programme

UNESCAP .... United Nations Economic and Social Commission for Asia and the Pacific

UNESCO .... United Nations Educational, Scientific, and Cultural Organization

UNIDIR .... United Nations Institute for Disarmament Research

UNIDO .... United Nations Industrial Development Organization

UNITAR .... United Nations Institute for Training and Research

UNU/IIST........ United Nations University International Institute for Software Technology

UNU/INTECH.. United Nations University Institute for New Technologies

UNU/ZERI....... United Nations University Zero Emissions Research Initiative

URTNA .... Union des Radiodiffusions et Télévisions Nationales d'Afrique

USTR .... United States Trade Representative

UUCP............. Unix to Unix Copy Program

VADS .... Value Added Data Services

vBNS.............. Very-High-Performance Backbone Network Service

VCP .... Video Cassette Player

VCR .... Video Cassette Recorder

VEC .... Visually Embedded Coding

VITA .... Volunteers in Technical Assistance

VLSI.............. Very Large Scale Integration

VOD................ Video-on-Demand

VSAT.............. Very Small Aperture Terminal

WARC............. World Administrative Radio Conference (ITU)

WEDNET .... Women's project network for management of natural resources (Africa)

WIPO .... World Intellectual Property Organization

WMO .... World Meteorological Organization

WRC .... World Radio Conference (ITU)

WTO.............. World Trade Organisation

Y2K................ Year 2000

BIBLIOGRAPHY

ABRAMOVITZ, M. (1986) 'Catching Up, Forging Ahead, and Falling Behind', *Journal of Economic History,* Vol. 46(2), pp. 385–406 and reprinted in Abramovitz, M. (1989) *Thinking About Growth,* Cambridge: Cambridge University Press, pp. 220–242.

ABRAMOVITZ, M. AND DAVID, P.A. (1996) 'Technological Change and the Rise of Intangible Investments: The US Economy's Growth-Path in the Twentieth Century' in Foray, D. and Lundvall, B.-Å. (eds) *Employment and Growth in the Knowledge-based Economy,* Paris: OECD, pp. 35–60.

ACHESON, A. AND MCFETRIDGE, D. (1996) 'Intellectual Property Rights in a Global Knowledge-Based Economy' in Howitt, P. (ed.) *The Implications of Knowledge-based Growth for Micro-Economic Policies,* Industry Canada Series, No. 6, Calgary: University of Calgary Press, pp. 239–243.

ADAM, L. (1996) 'Electronic Communications Technology and Development of Internet in Africa', *Information Technology for Development,* Vol. 7, pp. 133–144.

ADLER, N.J., BRAHM, R. AND GRAHAM, J. (1992) 'Strategy Implementation: A Comparison of Face-to-Face Negotiation in the People's Republic of China and the United States', *Strategic Management Journal,* Vol. 13(6), pp. 449–466.

AGARWAL, S.M. (1996a) 'Telecom With or Without MNCs?', *The Hindustan Times,* 4 July.

AGARWAL, S.M. (1996b) 'Telecom Services - How to Privatise', *The Hindustan Times,* 8 November.

AGARWAL, S.M. (1996c) 'Unanswered Questions', *The Hindustan Times,* 27 July.

AJAYI, G.O. (1995) 'Electronic Communication - Internet Connectivity in Africa', paper presented at the International Conference on Information Technology Management, Obafemi Awolowo University, Ile-Ife, Laos, 16–17 November.

AKHTAR, S. (1995) 'Building South-North Bridges on the Information Superhighway - Towards a Global Agenda for Collaborative Research and Action' report of a Workshop on the Role and Impact of Information and Communication Technologies in Development, Information, and Decision Support Centre (IDSC) Regional Information Technology and Software Engineering Center (RITSEC), Cairo, 12–13 January.

AKSOY, A. AND GODDARD, J.B. (1990) 'Mobilising Information Resources for Economic Development', report for the World Bank, Centre for Urban and Regional Development Studies, University of Newcastle upon Tyne, October.

ALEMU, E. (1996) 'IT Access and Application in Ethiopia: From National and Sectoral Development Policies Perspectives', commissioned by COLCIENCIAS as a background paper for the UNCSTD Working Group on IT and Development.

AMBROSE, W.W., HENNEMEYER, P.R. AND CHAPON, J.-P. (1990) 'Privatizing Telecommunications Systems - Business Opportunities in Developing Countries', Washington DC: The World Bank and International Finance Corporation.

AMERICAN ELECTRONICS ASSOCIATION/AMERICAN UNIVERSITY (1996) 'Internet Commerce', September.

AMSDEN, A.H. (1989) *Asia's Next Giant: South Korea and Late Industrialization,* Oxford University Press: New York.

AMSDEN, A.H. (1994) 'Why Isn't the Whole World Experimenting with the East Asian Model to Develop? Review of the East Asian Miracle', *World Development,* Vol. 22(4), pp. 627–633.

ANAND, S. (1997) 'DoT, FIs Resolve Thorny Issues of Telecom Projects', *The Times of India,* 21 January.

ANDERSON, C. (1996) 'The Importance of Being American' in 'A World Gone Soft - A Survey of the Software Industry', *The Economist,* 25 May, pp. 24–27.

ANG, J. AND PAVRI, F. (1994) 'A Survey and Critique of Impacts of Information Technology', *International Journal of Information Management,* Vol. 14, pp. 122–33.

ANNAN, K., Secretary General of the United Nations (1997) 'Secretary General Stresses International Community's Objective of Harnessing Informatics Revolution for Benefit of Mankind' in United Nations Commission on Science and Technology for Development 'Inter-Agency Project on Universal Access to Basic Communication and Information Services', 3rd Session, Geneva, 12 May, E/CN.16/1997/Misc.3.

ANTONELLI, C. (1995) *The Economics of Localized Technological Change and Industrial Dynamics,* Boston: Kluwer Academic.

ANTONELLI, C. (ed.) (1988) *New Information Technology and Industrial Change: The Italian Case,* Boston: Kluwer Academic Press.

ANTONELLI, C. (ed.) (1992) *The Economics of Information Networks,* Amsterdam: North Holland.

APEC (Asia Pacific Economic Council) (1996) 'Ministerial Meeting on the Telecommunications and Information Industry', Gold Coast, Australia, 5–6 September 1996, and Seoul, Korea (Rep. of) 29–30 May 1995, http://www.apecsec.org.sg/coastdecl.html

APPADURAI, A. (1990) 'Disjuncture and Difference in the Global Cultural Ecumene', *Public Culture,* Vol. 2(2), pp. 1–24.

APPADURAI, A. (1996) *Modernity at Large*, Minnesota: University of Minnesota Press.

ARMSTRONG, A. AND HAGEL, J. (1996) 'The Real Value of On-Line Communities', *Harvard Business Review*, Vol. 74(3), pp. 134-141.

ARTERTON, F.C. (1987) *Teledemocracy: Can Technology Protect Democracy?*, London: Sage.

ARTHUR D. LITTLE (1991) 'Telecommunications Issues and Options 1992-2010', final report to the European Commission, Directorate General XIII/D2, October, pp. 15-21.

AUSTRALIAN COMPUTER SOCIETY AND THE AUSTRALIAN COUNCIL FOR COMPUTERS IN EDUCATION (1996) 'Australian National Report on the Development of Education: 1994-1996', Carlton Vic. Curriculum Corporation.

AVGEROU, C. AND MULIRA. C. (1996) 'A Study of a University Admission System in Uganda' in Roche, E.M. and Blaine, M.J. (eds) (1996) *Information Technology, Development and Policy: Theoretical Perspectives and Practical Challenges*, Aldershot: Avebury, pp. 229-244.

AZEVEDO DE PAULA GUIBERT, A. (1998 forthcoming) 'The Brazilian Telecurso 2000: An Experience with Applications of Communication Technologies to Vocational and Continuous Education' in Mitter, S., Bastos, M.-I. and Bartzokas, A. (eds) *Europe and Developing Countries in the World Information Economy: Trade, Distance Education and Regional Development*, London: Routledge and Tokyo: UNU Press.

BAARK, E. (1986) 'The Context of National Information Systems in Developing Countries: India and China in a Comparative Perspective', Research Policy Institute, University of Lund, Sweden.

BAHARUDDIN, S., AHMAD, A., BOKHARI, A. AND HASSAN, M. (1994) *Malaysian Development Experience - Change and Challenges*, Kuala Lumpur: National Institute of Public Administration.

BALASSA, B. (1981) *The Newly Industrializing Countries in the World Economy*, New York: Pergamon Press.

BALZAN, R. AND VELLA, G. (1997) 'A Review of the National Strategy for Information Technology', Office of the Prime Minister, Government of Malta.

BANERJEE, P. AND BHATTACHARYA, S. (1996) *Advanced Telecommunication in India - Regulation and Strategies*, New Dehli: Har-Anand Publications.

BARGELLINI, M. (1997) 'Distance Learning: Opportunities and Problems', *The IPTS Report*, Vol. 16, pp. 29-34.

BARROS, L.A. (1998 forthcoming) 'Network Applications to Education in Brazil: Helping to Integrate Segments of the Population into the Information Society' in Mitter, S. (ed.) *The Cyber-Economy and the Developing World: The Question of Exclusion and Inclusion*, London: Routledge and Tokyo: UNU Press.

BASTOS, M. (1998 forthcoming) 'Learning with Telematics: Opportunities and Challenges to Students, Teaching Institutions, Enterprises and Governments' in Mitter, S., Bastos, M.-I. and Bartzokas, A. (eds) *Europe and Developing Countries in the World Information Economy: Trade, Distance Education and Regional Development*, London: Routledge and Tokyo: UNU Press.

BEAMISH, J. (1984) 'Joint Venture Performance in Developing Countries', unpublished PhD Dissertation, University of Western Ontario, Ontario, Canada.

BECKER, L. (1997) 'Multi-Jurisdictional Taxation of Electronic Commerce', Harvard University 1997 Spring Symposium, Cambridge MA.

BELLAFANTE, G. (1995) 'Strange Sounds and Sights', *Time*, Spring, p. 14.

BELLAMY, C., RAAB, C., DUTTON, W.H. AND PELTU, M. (1996) 'Innovation in Public Service Delivery' in Dutton, W.H. (ed.) *Information and Communication Technologies: Visions and Realities*, Oxford: Oxford University Press, pp. 265-282.

BENNETT, I. (1995) 'National Industrial Policy Information Technology Sector', Draft Report, Planning Institute of Jamaica, 9 May.

BERG, C. (1998 forthcoming) 'Kidlink - Global Network for Youth' in Mitter, S., Bastos, M.-I. and Bartzokas, A. (eds) *Europe and Developing Countries in the World Information Economy: Trade, Distance Education and Regional Development*, London: Routledge and Tokyo: UNU Press.

BERNARD, J., CATTANEO, G., MANSELL, R., MORGANTI, F., SILVERSTONE, R. AND STEINMUELLER, W.E. (1997) *The European Information Society at the Crossroads*, report prepared for the Advanced Communications Technologies and Services (ACTS) Programme, European Commission, Directorate General XIII, by the FAIR Project Consortium, July.

BERNDT, E.R. AND MALONE, T.W. (eds) (1995) 'Guest Editors' Introduction to Special Issue - Information Technology and the Productivity Paradox: Getting the Questions Right', *Economics of Innovation and New Technology*, Vol. 3, pp. 177-182.

BESSANT, J. (1991) *Managing Advanced Manufacturing Technology*, London: Basil Blackwell.

BESSANT, J. (1996) 'Learning to Use Advanced Manufacturing Technology', commissioned by UNU/INTECH and COLCIENCIAS as a background paper for the UNCSTD Working Group in IT and Development.

BESSANT, J. AND CAFFYN, S. (1997) 'High Involvement Innovation through Continuous Improvement', *International Journal of Technology Management*, Vol. 14(1), pp. 7-28.

BESSETTE, G. (1996) 'Empowering People through Information and Communication Technology: Lessons from Experience', paper prepared by the International Development Research Centre, Ottawa, Canada.

BEZANSON, K. AND SAGASTI, F. (1995) 'The Elusive Search: Development and Progress in the Transition to a New Century', Ottawa, Canada: International Development Research Centre and Lima, Peru: GRADE, mimeo.

BILTEREYST, D. (1996) 'The Cultural Imperialism Thesis and Qualitative Audience Research - More than Revisions and Cultural Populism?', *Communication*, Vol. 22(2), pp. 2-13.

BLAMIRE, R. (1996) 'Information Rich and Information Poor: Avoiding a New Divide in Britain', based on a presentation to an Action for Children Seminar, by the National Council for Educational Technology (NCET), London, December.

BLAU, P. (1964) *Power and Exchange in Social Life,* New York: Wiley.

BOHLIN, E. AND GRANSTRAND, O. (eds) (1994) *The Race to European Eminence: Who are the Coming Tele-service Multinationals?,* Amsterdam: North-Holland, Elsevier Science.

BOND, J. (1995) 'Role of Governments and International Financial Institutions in Developing Information Infrastructure', The World Bank, Washington, DC, November, mimeo prepared for a presentation in Bangkok.

BOON, J.A. (1992) 'Information and Development: Towards an Understanding of the Relationship', *South African Journal of Library and Information Science*, Vol. 60(2), pp. 63-74.

BOSERUP, E. (1989) *Women's Role in Economic Development,* London: Earthscan Publications Ltd.

BOURDEAU, J.,VAZQUEZ-ABAD, J. AND WINER, L. (1996) 'Information and Communication Technologies for Generating and Disseminating Know-How', draft paper submitted to the Department of Scientific and Technological Affairs, Organisation of American States, January.

BOWDEN, D. AND BLAKEMAN, K. (1990) *IT Strategies for Information Management*, London: Butterworths.

BOYD-BARRETT, J. (1977) 'Media Imperialism: Towards an International Framework for the Analysis of Media Systems' in Curran, J., Gurevitch, M. and Woollacott, J. (eds.) *Mass Communication and Society*, London: Edward Arnold, pp. 116-135.

BOYD-BARRETT, J. (1982) 'Cultural Dependency and the Mass Media' in Gurevitch, M., Bennett, J., Curran, J. and Woollacott, J. (eds.) *Culture, Society and the Media*, London: Methuen, pp. 174-195.

BRADY, T. (1990) 'In-House Development and Growth of the Software Industry', *CICT Working Paper No. 12*, Brighton: SPRU.

BRANEGAN, J., COLMEY, J., ELSHAM, R., MacLEOD, S. AND THOMPSON, M. (1997) 'The Networked Society', *Time*, 3 February, pp. 30-37.

BRANSCOMB, L.M. AND KELLER, J.H. (eds) (1996) *Converging Infrastructures: Intelligent Transportation and the National Information Infrastructure*, Cambridge MA: MIT Press.

BRAUDEL, F. (1984) 'The Perspective of the World', *Civilisation and Capitalism 15-18 Century, Vol: III,* London: Collins

BRAUN, E. AND MACDONALD, S. (1982) *Revolution in Miniature: The History and Impact of Semiconductor Electronics*, 2nd edition, Cambridge: Cambridge University Press.

BRAZIL MINISTÉRIO DA CIÊNCIA E TECNOLOGIA (1995) 'Plano Plurianual 1996-1999', Ministério da Ciência e Tecnologia, Brasília, DF, July.

BRAZIL MINISTÉRIO DA CIÊNCIA E TECNOLOGIA (1996a) 'Relatorio de Atividades MCT - 1995', Ministério da Ciência e Tecnologia, Brasília, DF, July.

BRAZIL MINISTÉRIO DA CIÊNCIA E TECNOLOGIA (1996b) 'Relatorio Estatistico 1985-1995', Ministério da Ciência e Tecnologia, Brasília, DF, March.

BRAZIL SECRETARIA DE POLÍTICA DE INFORMÁTICA E AUTOMAÇÃO (1995) 'Qualidade no Sector de Software Brasileiro', Ministério da Ciência e Tecnologia, Brasília DF.

BRIGHT, J. (1996) 'Infonet partners with ACASIA', *Telecommunications* [International Edition], Vol. 30(11), November, pp. 17-20.

BROOKS, F. (1982) *The Mythical Man-Month*, London: Addison-Wesley Publishing Company.

BROWN, R., IRVING, L., PRABHAKAR, A. AND KATZEN, S. (1995) 'The Global Information Infrastructure - Agenda for Cooperation', Information Infrastructure Task Force, Washington DC, February.

BUCKLEY, P.J. AND CASSON, M. (1988) 'A Theory of Co-operation in International Business' in Contractor, F.J. and Lorange, P. (eds), *Cooperative Strategies in International Business,* Lexington, MA: Lexington Books, pp. 31-54.

BUHALIS, D. (1995) 'The Impact of Information Telecommunications Technologies on Tourism Distribution Channels: Implications for the Small and Medium-sized Tourism Enterprises' Strategic Management Marketing', unpublished PhD thesis, Surrey University.

BUSINESS ASIA (1996) 'Telecoms Zone?', *Business Asia*, Vol. 28(11), p. 11.

BUSINESS SOFTWARE ALLIANCE (1995) *Piracy Study*, http://www.bsa.org/piracy/piracy.study95/piracy95.html

BUTCHER, N. AND PEROLD, H. (1996) 'Technology Enhanced Learning Investigation (TELI) in South Africa: A Discussion Document', report of the Ministerial Committee for Development Work on the Role of Technology that Will Support and Enhance Learning, 31 July.

BUTLER, R. (1983) 'A Transactional Approach to Organizing Efficiency: Perspectives from Markets, Hierarchies and Collectives', *Administration and Society*, Vol. 15(3), pp. 323-362.

BUTLER, R. AND GILL, J. (1996) 'Co-operation and Trust Across Boundaries: Perspectives from Malaysia, Japan and Britain', paper presented to the 13th Annual Conference of the Euro-Asia Management Studies Association, Chuo University, Tokyo, 15-17 November.

BUTLER, R. AND GILL, J. (1997) 'Trust in the Dynamics of Joint Venture Formation and Operation', paper presented to the LMHV Moet Hennessy Louis Vuitton Group Conference on Partnerships and Joint Ventures in Asia, Fontainebleau, 7-8 February.

BYRON, L. AND GAGLIARDI, R. (1996) 'Communities and the Information Society: The Role of Information and Communication Technologies in Education', report prepared for International Development Research Centre, Ottawa, UNESCO International Bureau of Education (IBE).

CAMILLERI, J. (1994a) 'A National Strategy for Information Technology for Malta', Office of the National Strategy for Information Technology, University of Malta, October.

CAMILLERI, J. (1994b) 'A National Strategy for Information Technology for Malta - Summary & Recommendations', Office of the National Strategy for Information Technology, University of Malta, October.

CAMILLERI, J. (1994c) 'A National Information Technology Unit - A Proposal', Office of the National Strategy for Information Technology, University of Malta, October.

CAMPBELL, J., HOLLINGSWORTH, J. AND LINDBERG, L. (1991) *Governance of the American Economy*, Cambridge: Cambridge University Press.

CANE, A. (1997a) 'A Ringing Endorsement', *Financial Times*, 18 February.

CANE, A. (1997b) 'Spreading the Word', *Financial Times*, 19 March.

CASSIOLATO, J. (1992) 'The Role of User-Producer Relations in Innovation and Diffusion of New Technologies: Lessons From Brazil', unpublished DPhil Thesis, Science Policy Research Unit, University of Sussex.

CASSIOLATO, J. (1996) 'Experiences of Application of Telematics in Services Firms in Brazil' commissioned by UNU/INTECH and COLCIENCIAS as a background paper for the UNCSTD Working Group on IT and Development.

CASTELLS, M. (1996a) 'Relationships of Advanced Information Technology, Economic Organisation and the Social Structure of Cities', paper prepared for the MIT Colloquium on Advanced Information Technology, Low-Income Communities and the City, Cambridge MA, March.

CASTELLS, M. (1996b) 'The New Business World: Networks and Firms', The ILO Enterprise Forum, Geneva, 8-9 November.

CAVAZOS, E. (1996) 'System Operator Liability', paper presented at the 5th OECD Workshop on the Economics of the Information Society, Seoul, 22-23 October.

CHALMERS, J., CUTHBERT, H., DU PRE GAUNT, J. AND RICHARDSON, B. (1996) 'Telecommunication Survey', *Business Central Europe*, September, pp. 45-64.

CHAPPELL, C. (1997) 'The Extranet Dimension', *IT Consultant*, April, pp. 13-21.

CHATAWAY, B. AND COOKE, A. (1996) 'Measuring the Impact of Information on Development: Related Literature, 1993-1995', http://www.idrc.ca/books/focus/783/chataway.htm

CHENARD, S. (1996) 'The New Mobile Satellite Systems: Looking at the Risk Factors', Mobile Satellite Communications Global Conference, London, 17-19 June.

CHIA, A. (1994) 'Convergence: Impact and Issues for the Media', *Media Asia*, Vol. 21(3), pp. 126-130.

CHO, D.-S. (1994) 'A Dynamic Approach to International Competitiveness: The Case of Korea', *Journal of Far Eastern Business*, Vol.1(1), pp. 17-36.

CHRISTODOLOU, A. (1992) 'Commonwealth Cooperation, Reality or Myth?', Broady Lecture ICDE Conference Bangkok, cited in Laaser, W. (1998 forthcoming) 'Technologies for Distance Education in Developing Countries' in Mitter, S., Bastos, M.-I. and Bartzokas, A. (eds) *Europe and Developing Countries in the World Information Economy: Trade, Distance Education and Regional Development*, London: Routledge and Tokyo: UNU Press.

CLARK, P. AND STAUNTON, N. (1989) *Innovation in Technology and Organization*, London: Routledge.

CLICHÉ, D. (ed.) (1997) *Cultural Ecology: The Changing Dynamics of Communications*, London: International Institute of Communication.

CMS (THE BUSINESS INTELLIGENCE SERVICE) (1996) 'China Telecoms 2000', June.

COCHETTI, R.J. (1994) 'Mobile Satellite Services: An Overview of Major GEO, LEO, MEO and HEO Systems', *Via Satellite*, Vol. 11, pp. 26-36.

COCKBURN, C. (1985) *Machinery of Dominance: Men, Women, and Technological Knowhow*, London: Pluto Press.

CODDING, G.A. AND RUTKOWSKI, A.M. (1982) *The International Telecommunication Union in a Changing World*, Dedham MA: Artech House.

COHEN, R.B. (1996a) 'An Economic Model of Future Changes in the US Communications and Media Industries', Vertech, Washington DC.

COHEN, R.B. (1996b) 'The Impact of Audio Visual Industries on the US Economy', Vertech, Washington DC.

COHEN, W. AND LEVINTHAL, D. (1990) 'Absorptive Capacity: A New Perspective on Learning and Innovation', *Administrative Science Quarterly*, Vol. 35(1), pp. 128-152.

COLLET, S., LIE, R., NEUCKENS, F. AND TERSTAPPEN, I. (1996) 'Workshop Summary Report' on an International Summer Seminar on (Tele)communication Policies in Western Europe and Southeast Asia: Cultural and Historical Perspectives, Bruges, 29 August-1 September.

COMMONWEALTH SECRETARIAT (1988) *Information Technology in Government - The Caribbean Experience*, Georgetown, Barbados: Commonwealth Secretariat.

COOLEY, M. (1987) (revised edition), *Architect or Bee? The Human Price of Technology*, London: The Hogarth Press.

COOPER, C. (1998 forthcoming) 'An Outline for Policy Analysis on Access to Information Technology' in Cooper, C. (ed.) *Information Technology Policy and National Economic Development*, London: Routledge and Tokyo: UNU Press.

CORDELL, A.J. AND IDE, T.R. (1994) 'The New Wealth of Nations: Distributing Prosperity', paper prepared for the Annual Meeting of The Club of Rome, Buenos Aires, 30 November - 2 December.

CORDELL, A.J., IDE, T.R., SOETE, L. AND KAMP, K. (1997) *The New Wealth of Nations - Taxing Cyberspace*, Toronto: Between the Lines.

CORREA, C. (1998 forthcoming) 'Implications of Intellectual Property Rights for the Access to and Use of Information Technologies in Developing Countries' in Cooper, C. (ed.) *Information Technology Policy and National Economic Development*, London: Routledge and Tokyo: UNU Press.

CORREA, C.M. (1996) 'Strategies for Software Exports from Developing Countries', *World Development*, Vol. 24(1), pp. 171-182.

CORREA, C.M. (ed.) (1995) 'Special Issue on the Management of International Intellectual Property', *International Journal of Technology Management*, Vol. 10(2/3).

COUNCIL FOR SCIENTIFIC AND INDUSTRIAL RESEARCH (1996) 'The Use of Information and Communication Technologies in the Health Sector in Sub-Saharan Africa', International Development Research Centre, 31 August.

COUNCIL OF THE EUROPEAN COMMUNITIES (1991) 'Council Directive of 14 May 1991 on the Legal Protection of Computer Programs', Council of the European Communities, 91/250/EEC, OJ L122/42, Brussels, 14 May.

COUTINHO, L., CASSIOLATO, J. AND SILVA, A. (1995) *Globalização, Telecomunicações e Competitividade*, Campinas: Papirus.

COWHEY, P.F. AND McKEOWN, M.M. (1993) 'The Promise of a New World Information Order' in Institute for Information Studies (ed.) *The Knowledge Economy: The Nature of Information in the 21st Century*, Annual Review of the Institute for Information Studies 1993-1994, A Joint Program of Northern Telecom Inc. and The Aspen Institute, pp. 89-116.

CREDÉ, A. (1997a) 'Information Society Security: Trust, Confidence and Technology', *FAIR Working Paper No. 26*, Brighton: SPRU.

CREDÉ, A. (1997b) 'Technological Change and the Information Society: An Examination of Credit Risk Assessment and Cash Handling Procedures in Commercial Banks', unpublished DPhil Thesis, Science Policy Research Unit, University of Sussex.

CRONIN, B. AND McKIM, G. (1996) 'Markets, Competition, and Intelligence on the World Wide Web', *Competitive Intelligence Review*, Vol. 7(1), pp. 45-51.

CRONIN, F.J., COLLERAN, E.K., HERBERT, P.I. AND LEWITZKY, S. (1993) 'Telecommunication and Growth - The Contribution of Telecommunications Infrastructure Investment to Aggregate and Sectoral Productivity', *Telecommunications Policy*, Vol. 17(9), pp. 677-690.

CROOK, C. (1997) 'Men from the Ministry', in 'Survey of India', *The Economist*, 22 February.

CULPIN, I. (1996) 'The Importance of Telework for European Employment and Business in a Global Context', paper prepared for the UNU/INTECH International Workshop on Europe and the Developing World in the Globalised Information Society: Employment, Education and Trade Implications, UNU/INTECH, Maastricht, 17-19 October.

CYERT, R.M. AND MOWERY, D.C. (eds) (1987) *Technology and Employment: Innovation and Growth in the US Economy*, Washington DC: National Academy Press.

D'ORVILLE, H. (1996) 'Technology Revolution Study - Communications and Knowledge-Based Technologies for Sustainable Human Development', (Final Report), United Nations Development Programme, New York, 30 April.

DALY, J.A. (1997) 'The Contribution of ICT Tools to Sustainable Development', Rockville, Maryland, mimeo.

DANOWITZ, A.K., NASSEF, Y. AND GOODMAN, S.E. (1995) 'Cyberspace across the Sahara: Computing in North Africa', *Communications of the ACM*, Vol. 38(12), pp. 23-28.

DARLINGTON, R. (1997) 'The Information Society: A Challenge for Trade Unions', Communication Workers Union, London, March.

DATAQUEST (1996) 'The Dataquest Top 20', *Dataquest* (India), Vol. 14(13).

DAVID, P.A. (1975) *Technical Choice, Innovation and Economic Growth*, Cambridge: Cambridge University Press.

DAVID, P.A. (1985) 'CLIO and the economics of QWERTY', *American Economic Review*, May, pp. 332-337.

DAVID, P.A. (1987) 'Some New Standards for the Economics of Standardization in the Information Age' in Dasgupta, P. and Stoneman, P. (eds) *Economic Policy and Technological Performance*, Cambridge: Cambridge University Press, pp. 206-239.

DAVID, P.A. (1993) 'Intellectual Property Institutions and the Panda's Thumb: Patents, Copyrights and Trade Secrets in Economic Theory and History' in Wallenstein, M., Mogee, M. and Schoen, R. (eds) *Global Dimensions of Intellectual Property Rights in Science and Technology*, Washington DC: National Academy Press, pp. 19-61.

DAVID, P.A. (1995) 'Rethinking Technology Transfers: Incentives, Institutions and Knowledge-based Industrial Development', paper prepared for presentation at the British Academy/Chinese Academy of Social Sciences Joint Seminar on Technology Transfer, Beijing, 5-6 April.

DAVID, P.A. AND BUNN, J. (1988) 'The Evolution of Gateway Technologies and Network Evolution: Lessons from Electricity Supply History', *Information Economics and Policy*, No. 3, pp. 165-202.

DAVID, P.A. AND OLSEN, T. (1984) 'Anticipated Automation: A Rational Expectations Model of Technology Diffusion', *Technological Innovation Program Working Papers No. 2*, Center for Economic Policy Research: Stanford University.

DAVID, P.A. AND STEINMUELLER, W.E. (1988) 'The ISDN Bandwagon is Coming - Who Will be There to Climb Aboard?: Quandaries in the Economics of Data Communications Networks', presented at the OECD Tokyo/Osaka Workshop on Information Technology and New Growth Opportunities for the 1990s, 11-17 September, published (1990) *Economics of Innovation and New Technology*, Vol. 1(1-2), pp. 43-62.

DE CUELLAR, J.P. (1995) *Our Creative Diversity: Report of the World Commission on Culture and Development*, Paris: UNESCO Publishing.

DE OLIVEIRA, A. (1991) 'The Key Issues Facing the Electricity Systems of Developing Countries: Synthesis Report of the Cooperative Programme on Energy and Development', Report EUR 13461 EN, Luxembourg: Office for Official Publications of the European Communities.

DENISON, E.F. (1985) *Trends in American Economic Growth*, Washington DC: The Brookings Institution.

DEPARTMENT FOR EDUCATION (1996) 'Schools On Line Phase 1 Final Report', London: Department for Education.

DEPARTMENT OF EDUCATION (1996) 'Technology Enhanced Learning Investigation in South Africa - A Discussion Document', report of the Ministerial Committee for Development Work on the Role of Technology that will Support and Enhance Learning', Pretoria, 31 July.

DERVIN, B. AND CLARK, K. (1989) 'Communication as Cultural Identity: the Invention Mandate', *Media Development*, Vol. 36(2), pp. 5-8.

DEYO, F. (ed.) (1987) *The Political Economy of the New Asian Industrialism*, Ithaca: Cornell University Press.

DIEBOLD, J. (1959) *Automation: Its Impact on Business and Labor*, Planning Pamphlet No. 106, Washington DC: National Planning Association.

DIEU, P. D. AND LE, N. H. (1995) 'Vietnam's IT-2000 Program: Challenges ahead', *I-Ways*, Mid-Year, pp. 19-20.

DJEFLAT, A. (1998 forthcoming) 'The Globalised Information Society and its Impact on the Europe-Maghreb Relationship' in Mitter, S., Bastos, M.-I. and Bartzokas, A. (eds) *Europe and Developing Countries in the World Information Economy: Trade, Distance Education and Regional Development*, London: Routledge and Tokyo: UNU Press.

DOHLMAN, E. AND HALVORSON-QUEVEDO, R. (1997) 'Globalisation and Development', *The OECD Observer*, No. 204, pp. 36-39.

DONOVAN, T.G. (ed.) (1995) 'GIIC Asia Regional Meeting', *I-Ways*, Year End.

DONOVAN, T.G. (ed.) (1996a) 'Africa Adopts Information Infrastructure Strategy', *I-Ways*, Second Quarter.

DONOVAN, T.G. (ed.) (1996b) 'Global Electronic Commerce China Forum', *I-Ways*, First Quarter.

DORDICK, H.S. AND WANG, G. (1993) *The Information Society: A Retrospective View*, Newbury Park, CA: Sage Publications.

DRAKE, W.J. (ed.) (1995) *The New Information Infrastructure: Strategies for US Policy*, New York: Twentieth Century Fund Press.

DRUCKER, P. (1993) *The Post-Capitalist Society*, Oxford: Butterworth Heinemann.

DRUCKER, P. (1994) 'The Age of Social Transformation', *The Atlantic Monthly*, November, pp. 53-80.

DUMORT, A. AND DRYDEN, J. (eds) (1997) *The Economics of the Information Society*, Luxembourg: Office for Official Publications of the European Communities.

DUNN, H.S. (1995) 'Caribbean Telecommunications Policy: Fashioned by Debt, Dependency and Under-Development', *Media, Culture & Society*, Vol. 17, pp. 201-222.

DUNNE, N. (1997) 'US Senators Seek to Change IT Pact', *Financial Times*, 20 February.

DURANT, F. (1997) 'Information for Policy Formulation: Latin America and the Caribbean', Uruguay, IDRC Regional Office for Latin America and the Caribbean.

DURONGKAVEROJ, P. (1996) 'Social Equity & Prosperity: Thailand IT Policy into the 21st Century', report by the National Information Technology Committee and the National Electronics and Computer Technology Centre, http://www.nitc.go.th/itplan/itplane.html

DUTTON, W.H. (ed.) (1997) *Information and Communication Technologies: Visions and Realities*, Oxford: Oxford University Press.

EASTERBROOK, S. (1991) 'Negotiation and the Role of the Requirements Specification', Cognitive Science Research Reports 197, University of Sussex, Brighton, July.

EBRD (European Bank for Reconstruction and Development) (1996) *Transition Report 1996, Infrastructure and Savings*, London: EBRD.

EBU (European Broadcasting Union) (1989) *EBU Statistics - Origin of Television Programmes*, Vol. 10, part 3, Grand-Saconnex: EBU.

ECONOMIC COMMISSION FOR AFRICA (1996) 'Exploiting Information Technology to Accelerate Socio-Economic Development in Africa: An Action Plan', 31st session of the Commission/22nd meeting of the Conference of Ministers, Addis Ababa, Ethiopia, 6-8 May.

EIAK (Electronics Industry Association of Korea) (1989) *Thirty Years' History of the Electronics Industry*, Seoul: EIAK, (Korean).

EIAK (Electronics Industry Association of Korea) (1995) *Korean Electronics Industry*, Seoul: EIAK, (Korean).

ELECTRONIC BUSINESS ASIA (1997) 'No Title', *Electronic Business Asia*, March, p. 72.

ELIASSON, G. (1990) *The Knowledge-based Information Economy*, Stockholm: Almquist & Wiksell International.

ELSEVIER (1996) *Yearbook of World Electronics Data*, Amsterdam: Elsevier.

ENOS, J. (1996) 'Human Skills and Institutions for Information-Sharing: The Challenge to Least Developed Countries', commissioned by UNU/INTECH and COLCIENCIAS as a background paper for the UNCSTD Working Group on IT and Development.

ERNST, D. (1997) 'Partners for the China Circle? The Asian Production Networks of Japanese Electronics Firms', *Working Paper No. 97-3*, Aalborg Danish Research Unit for Industrial Dynamics (DRUID), Aalborg University.

ERNST, D. AND O'CONNOR, D. (1989) *Technology and Global Competition, The Challenge for Newly Industrializing Economies*, OECD: Paris.

ERNST, D. AND O'CONNOR, D. (1992) *Competing in the Electronics Industry, The Experiences of the Newly Industrialising Economies*, OECD: Paris.

EURIM (European Informatics Market) (1997) 'Promoting Secure Electronic Free Trade', EURIM Briefing No. 16, London, May.

EUROCONSULT (1995) 'Asia Pacific Satellite Communications and Broadcasting in the Year 2000', EuroConsult, Paris.

EUROPEAN COMMISSION, (Bangemann Group) (1994) *Europe and the Global Information Society: Recommendations to the European Council*, High Level Group on the Information Society, Brussels: European Commission.

EUROPEAN COMMISSION (1995a) 'Green Paper on Copyright and Related Rights in the Information Society', COM(95) 382 final, Brussels, 19 July.

EUROPEAN COMMISSION (1995b) 'Legal Protection of Databases', OJ C288/14, Brussels, July.

EUROPEAN COMMISSION (1996a) 'Information Society Forum Theme Paper', Brussels, June.

EUROPEAN COMMISSION (1996b) 'Report of the Task Force "Educational Software and Multimedia"', Luxemburg, European Commission.

EUROPEAN COMMISSION (1996c) *Green Paper on Living and Working in the Information Society: People First*, Brussels: European Commission.

EUROPEAN COMMISSION (1996d) 'Building the Information Society for Us All: First Reflections of the High Level Group of Experts', Interim Report, Directorate General V, Brussels, January.

EUROPEAN COMMISSION (1996e) 'Communication from the European Commission to the Council, the European Parliament, the Economic and Social Committee, and the Committee of the Regions on "Europe at the Forefront of the Global Information Society: Rolling Action Plan"', Brussels, 13 December.

EUROPEAN COMMISSION (1996f) 'Communication to the European Parliament, the Council, the Economic and Social Committee and the Committee of the Regions: Illegal and Harmful Content on the Internet', Brussels, European Commission COM(96) 487.

EUROPEAN COMMISSION (1996g) 'Green Paper on the Protection of Minors and Human Dignity in Audio-visual and Information Services', Luxembourg, European Commission, INFO2000.

EUROPEAN COMMISSION (1996h) *Information Technologies, Productivity and Employment*, Brussels: Directorate General III - Industry.

EUROPEAN COMMISSION (1997a) 'Telematics Applications Programme - 1996 Monitoring: Part A - Report of the External Monitoring Panel', Brussels, March.

EUROPEAN COMMISSION (1997b) 'The Information Society and Development: The Role of the European Union', Communication from the Commission to the Council, to the European Parliament, to the Economic and Social Committee, and to the Committee of the Regions, July.

FAULKNER, D. (1995) 'The Management of International Strategic Alliances', paper presented to the Academy of International Business Conference, University of Bradford Management Centre, Bradford, 7-8 April.

FEDERAL COMMUNICATIONS COMMISSION (1996) 'Notice of Proposed Rulemaking on International Settlement Rates', IB Docket No. 96-261, Washington DC, 19 December.

FERNÉ, G. (1996) 'Electronic Commerce and Procurements - Government as a Smart Buyer', paper prepared for the 5th OECD Workshop on the Economics of the Information Society', Seoul, Republic of Korea, 22-23 October.

FERRANTINO, M.J. (1993) 'The Effect of Intellectual Property Rights on International Trade and Investment', *Weltwirtschaftliches Archiv*, Vol. 129(2), pp. 300-331.

FERREIRA SILVA, L.F. (1996) 'US Cold War Foreign Policy and Satellite Communication: The Case of Earth Station Network Build-up in Brazil and Argentina' unpublished DPhil Thesis, Science Policy Research Unit, University of Sussex, Brighton.

FINANCIAL TIMES (1997) 'Data Exchange Backed by World Bank', *Financial Times*, 17 March.

FISHMAN, S. (1994) *Software Development: A Legal Guide*, Berkeley CA: Nolo Press.

FLEURY, A. AND HUMPHREY, J. (1992) 'Human Resources and the Diffusion and Adaptation of New Quality Methods in Brazilian Manufacturing', report presented to Instituto de Pesquisas Economicas Aplicades (IPEA), Brasilia.

FLORES, E. (1996) 'The Relationship between Culture, Education, and Information Technology', commissioned by COLCIENCIAS as a background paper for the UNCSTD Working Group on IT and Development.

FLUENDY, S. (1996) 'Markets Call for Freedom', *Far Eastern Economic Review*, Vol. 159(42), pp. 38-44.

FOLEY, T. (1995) 'WRC Backs Broadband Satellite Plan', *CommunicationsWeek International*, 27 November, p.155.

FORAY, D. AND GIBBONS, M. (1996) 'Discovery in the Context of Application', *Technological Forecasting and Social Change*, Vol. 53, pp. 263-277.

FORAY, D. AND LUNDVALL, B.-Å. (1996) 'The Knowledge-based Economy: From the Economics of Knowledge to the Learning Economy' in OECD, *Employment and Growth in the Knowledge-based Economy*, OECD Documents, Paris:OECD, pp. 11-32.

FORGE, S. (1995) 'The Consequences of Current Telecommunication Trends for the Competitiveness of Developing Countries', report prepared for infoDev, Industry & Energy Department, The World Bank, Washington DC.

FOX, B. (1996) 'Hidden Watermark Traps Picture Pirate', *New Scientist*, 4 May, p. 18.

FRANKEL, M. (1955) 'Obsolescence and Technical Change in a Maturing Economy', *American Economic Review*, Vol. 45, pp. 296-319.

FRANKSON, J. (1996) 'Women's Global Faxnet', *Journal of International Communication*, Vol. 3(1), pp.102-110.

FREEMAN, C. (1987) *Technology Policy and Economic Performance: Lessons from Japan*, London/New York: Pinter Publishers.

FREEMAN, C. (1994) 'The Economics of Technical Change', *Cambridge Journal of Economics*, Vol. 18(5), pp. 463-514.

FREEMAN, C. AND HAGEDOORN, J. (1994) 'Catching Up or Falling Behind: Patterns in International Interfirm Technology Partnering', *World Development*, Vol. 22(5), pp. 771-780.

FREEMAN, C. AND PEREZ, C. (1988) 'Structural Crises of Adjustment, Business Cycles and Investment Behaviour' in Dosi, G., Freeman, C., Nelson, R., Silverberg, G. and Soete, L. (eds) *Technical Change and Economic Theory*, London: Pinter, pp. 38-66.

FREEMAN, C. AND SOETE, L. (1994) *Work for All or Mass Unemployment: Computerised Technical Change into the 21st Century*, London: Pinter Publishers.

FREEMAN, C., CLARK, J. AND SOETE, L. (1982) *Unemployment and Technical Innovation*, London: Pinter Publishers.

FREEMAN, C., SHARP, M. AND WALKER, W. (eds) (1991) *Technology and the Future of Europe: Global Competition and the Environment in the 1990s*, London: Pinter Publishers.

FREEMAN, C., SOETE, L. AND EFENDIOGLU, U. (1995) 'Diffusion and the Employment Effects of Information and Communication Technology', *International Labour Review*, Vol. 134(4-5), pp. 587-603.

FREUND, B., KÖNIG, H. AND ROTH, N. (1997) 'Impact of Information Technology on Manufacturing', *Technology Management*, Vol. 13(3), pp. 215-228.

FRIEDMAN, A.L. (1990) 'Four Phases of Information Technology: Implications for Forecasting IT Work', *Futures*, Vol. 22(8), pp. 787-800.

FRISCHTAK, C. (1990) 'Specialization, Technical Change and Competitiveness in the Brazilian Electronics Industry', *OECD Development Centre Technical Paper No. 27*, Paris: OECD.

FROTSCHNIG, A. (1997) 'Smart is beautiful', *The IPTS Report*, Vol. 13, pp. 11-19.

FUKUYAMA, F. (1995) *Trust: The Social Virtues and the Creation of Property*, Harmondsworth: Penguin.

GALLIVAN, J. (1997) 'A Bit More Backbone', *The Independent*, 25 February.

GASPARINI ALVES, P. (ed.) (1996) *Evolving Trends in the Dual Use of Satellites*, New York/Geneva: UNIDIR.

GENDER WORKING GROUP, UNCSTD (United Nations Commission on Science and Technology for Development) (eds) (1995) *Missing Links: Gender Equity in Science and Technology for Development*, Ottawa and London: International Development Research Centre in association with Intermediate Technology Publications and UNIFEM.

GERMAN, P. M. (1995) 'Information Technologies and Transborder Criminal Activities', notes for presentation to the symposium on Information Technologies and International Relations, University of British Columbia, 13 January.

GIBBONS, M., LIMOGES, C., NOWOTNY, H., SCHWARTZMAN, S., SCOTT, P. AND TROW, M. (1994) *The New Production of Knowledge: The Dynamics of Science and Research in Contemporary Societies*, London: Sage Publications.

GIDDENS, A. (1991) *Modernity and Self-Identity: Self and Society in the Late Modern Age*, London: Polity Press.

GILBERT, J, NOSTBAKKEN, D. AND AKHTAR, S. (1994) 'Does the Highway go South?', *Intermedia*, Vol. 22(5), pp. 9-10.

GILDER, G. (1994a) *Telecosm*, New York: Simon & Schuster.

GILDER, G. (1994b) 'Telecosm Ethersphere', *Forbes*, 10 October.

GILL, J. AND BUTLER, R. (1996) 'Cycles of Trust and Distrust in Joint Ventures', *European Management Journal*, Vol. 14(1), pp. 81-89.

GILLESPIE, A. AND CORNFORD, J. (1997) 'Telecommunication Infrastructures and Regional Development' in Dutton, W.H. (ed.) *Information and Communication Technologies: Visions and Realities*, Oxford: Oxford University Press, pp. 335-351.

GIRVAN, N. (1993) 'Telecommunications Policy and the TOJ Controversy: A Comment' in CACR/JIE Forum on Telecommunications Policy, Kingston, Jamaica.

GIRVAN, N. (1994a) 'Information Technology for Small and Medium Enterprises in Small Open Economies', paper presented to the Meeting on Information Technology Policies for SMEs in Latin America and the Caribbean, 6-8 December 1993, revised January 1994, Montevideo, Uruguay.

GIRVAN, N. (1994b) 'Submission on the Telecommunications Bill by the National Commission on Science and Technology', Jamaica, mimeo.

GIRVAN, N. (1994c) 'Information Technology for Small and Medium Enterprises in Small Open Economies', report prepared for International Development Research Centre, Consortium Graduate School of Social Sciences, Jamaica.

GIRVAN, N. (1996) 'Exclusion, Learning, and Information Technology: Some Lessons from the Caribbean', paper presented at the UNU/INTECH Workshop on the Information Revolution and Economic and Social Exclusion in Developing Countries', Maastricht, 23-25 October.

GIRVAN, N. (1997) 'Regulation of Telecommunications in Jamaica' in Lewington, I. (ed.) *Utility Regulation International 1997*, London: Centre for the Study of Regulated Industries and the Privatisation International Publishing Company, pp. 329-331.

GISL LTD. (1996a) 'Forestry', http://www.gisl.co.uk/forestry.htm

GISL LTD. (1996b) 'Land Information Systems', http://www.gisl.co.uk/lis.htm

GITTINGS, B., HULTON, N., PARK, G., PLACE C., RIDEOUT, T., ANDERSON, H. AND CHERRY, B. (n.d.) 'Geographical Information Systems in Practice - Research Case Studies', http://www.geo.ac.uk/home/research/purple.htm

GITTLER, A. (1996) 'Taking Hold of Electronic Communications', *Journal of International Communication*, Vol. 3(1), pp. 85-101.

GIIC (Global Information Infrastructure Commission) (1994) 'Global Information Infrastructure Commission', Washington DC: GIIC.

GIIC (Global Information Infrastructure Commission) (1997) 'GII to Unite World in Information Society', Washington DC: GIIC, 26 February.

GLOBAL KNOWLEDGE '97 (1996) 'Draft Conference Programme, Global Knowledge '97: Knowledge for Development in the Information Age', 18 December.

GLOBAL MOBILE (1996) 'Wireless Bloc', *Communications-Week International*, 18 March, p. 30.

GLOBALSTAR (1996) 'Wireless Communications for the World', San Jose, Globalstar.

GODWIN, M. (1994) 'Sex and the Single Sysadmin: The Risks of Carrying Graphic Sexual Materials', *Internet World*, March/April, http://www.eff.org

GOONASEKERA, A. (1993) (ed.) 'A Survey of Transnationalization of Television in Four Asian Countries', Asian Mass Communication Research and Information Centre (AMIC), Singapore, report submitted to UNESCO, Paris.

GRANOVETTER, M. (1985) 'Economic Action and Social Structures: the Problem of Embeddedness', *American Journal of Sociology*, Vol. 91 (November), pp. 481-510.

GRIFFITHS, J.-M. (1996) 'Analysis of Issues and Concerns', Appendix to McConnell, P., 'Measuring the Impact of Information on Development: Overview of an International Research Program', Ottawa, International Development Research Centre.

GU, S. (1995) 'A Review of Reform Policy for the S&T System in China: From Paid Transactions for Technology to Organisational Restructuring', *UNU/INTECH Working Paper No. 17*, Maastricht, January.

GU, S. (1996) 'Toward an Analytical Framework for National Innovation Systems', *UNU/INTECH Discussion Paper No. 9605*, Maastricht, April.

GU, S. AND STEINMUELLER, W.E. (1998 forthcoming) 'China's National Innovation System Approach to Participating in Information Technology: The Innovative Recombination of Technological Capability' in Cooper, C. (ed.) *Information Technology Policy and National Economic Development*, London: Routledge and Tokyo: UNU Press.

GUERRA BENITEZ, R.M. (1996) 'IT Policy in Mexico', http://www.ncb.gov.sg/nii/96scan3/MEXICO.html

HAGGARD, S. AND MOON, C.I. (1986) *Industrial Change and State Power: The Politics of Stabilization and Structural Adjustment in Korea*, paper prepared for the American Political Science Association.

HAHN, J.H. (1993) 'Creating High-Technological Competitiveness: A Case of the Semiconductor Industry', unpublished PhD Dissertation, University of Exeter.

HAIYAN, G. (1998 forthcoming) 'Software in China: Opportunities It Creates and Challenges It Faces' in Mitter, S. (ed.) *The Cyber-Economy and the Developing World: The Question of Exclusion and Inclusion*, London: Routledge and Tokyo: UNU Press.

HALL, J.W. (1987) 'Bridging the Technology-Pedagogy Gap' in Smith, P. and Kelly, M. (eds) *Distance Education and the Mainstream*, London: Croom Helm, pp. 44-56.

HAMELINK, C. (1989) 'The Relationship between Cultural Identity and Modes of Communication' in Anderson, J. (ed.) *Communication Yearbook. Volume 12*, Newbury Park: Sage, pp. 417-426.

HAMELINK, C. (1996) *Trends in World Communication: On Disempowerment and Self-Empowerment*, Penang: Third World Network and Southbound.

HAMELINK, C.J. (ed.) (1994) 'People's Communication Charter', *IAMCR/AIERI Newsletter*, June.

HAMILTON, S. (1995) 'Draft Report on Information Technology to the Government of Jamaica/United Nations Development Programme', National Industrial Policy Planning Institute of Jamaica, 1 March.

HANCOCK, A. (1997) 'Hidden Treasure' in Cliché, D. (ed.) *Cultural Ecology: The Changing Dynamics of Communications*, London: International Institute of Communication, pp. 88-102.

HANNA, N., BOYSON, S. AND GUNARATNE, S. (1996) 'The East Asian Miracle and Information Technology: Strategic Management of Technological Learning', *World Bank Discussion Papers No. 326*, Washington, DC: The World Bank.

HANNA, N., GUY, K. AND ARNOLD, E. (1995) 'The Diffusion of Information Technology', *World Bank Discussion Papers No. 281*, Washington, DC: The World Bank.

HARFOUSH, N. AND WILD, K. (1994) 'National Information Management Project - South Africa', report of the preparatory missions, sponsored by the International Development Research Centre, Johannesburg.

HARLOW, J. (1996) 'Rock Band U2 Ripped off by Cyberspace Burglars', *The Times*, 7 November, p. 5.

HARVEY, M. AND GAVIGAN, J. (1996) 'Agile Enterprises', *The IPTS Report*, Vol. 3, pp. 14-19.

HASHIM, R. (1996) 'At the Crossroads of Terrestrial and ET: Henceforth the Malaysian Television Broadcasting?', paper presented at the International Workshop on a Comparative analysis of (Tele)Communication Policies in Western Europe and Southeast Asia: Cultural and Historical Perspectives, Bruges, Belgium, 29 August - 1 September.

HAWKINS, R. (1992) 'The Doctrine of Regionalism: A New Dimension for International Standardization in Telecommunication', *Telecommunications Policy*, Vol. 16(4), pp. 339-353.

HAWKINS, R. (1996) 'The Global Research Village - Background Document', paper prepared for the Conference on The Global Research Village, OECD and Danish Ministry of Research and Information Technology, Snekkersten, Denmark, 13-14 June.

HAWKINS, R. (1997) 'Emerging Technology Clusters for New Electronic Services', *FAIR Working Paper No. 19*, Brighton: SPRU.

HAWKINS, R., MANSELL, R. AND SKEA, J. (eds) (1995) *Standards, Innovation and Competitiveness: The Politics and Economics of Standards in Natural and Technical Environments*, Aldershot: Edward Elgar Publishers.

HAWKINS, R., MANSELL, R. AND STEINMUELLER, W.E. (1997) 'Green Paper - Mapping and Measuring the Information Technology, Electronics and Communications Sector in the United Kingdom', report prepared for the Office of Science and Technology, Technology Foresight Panel on Information Technology, Communications and Electronics, Brighton: SPRU.

HE, F. (1997) 'Present Developmental Situation and Strategies of the China Communication Industry', *China Communications*, January, pp. 56-64.

HEBENSTREIT, J. (1992) 'Where Are We and How Did We Get There?' in Hebenstreit, J., Levrat, B., Bork, A., Walker, D., Poly, A., Gorny, P., Batanov, D., Lewis, R., Lally, M. Hall, N., Sylla, F., Fakhro, S., Lasso, M. and Gwym, R. (1992) *Education and Informatics Worldwide. The State of the Art and Beyond*, London and Paris: Jessica Kingsley Publishers, pp. 9-67.

HEEKS, R. (1996a) *India's Software Industry: State Policy, Liberalisation and Industrial Development*, New Delhi: Sage Publications.

HEEKS, R. (1996b) 'Promoting Software Production and Export in Developing Countries' in Roche, E. and Blaine, M. (eds) *Information Technology, Development and Policy*, Avebury: Aldershot, pp. 77-94.

HEEKS, R. AND SLAMEN-McCANN, A. (1996) *Discussion Paper No.44: Job and Skill Impacts of New Technology in the East Asian Electronics Industry*, Manchester: Institute for Development Policy and Management.

HÉNAULT, G. (1996) 'Employment and Income Generating Activities Derived from Internet Access', report prepared for the International Development Research Centre, Ottawa, September.

HENNART, J.F. (1988) 'A Transaction Costs Theory of Equity Joint Ventures', *Strategic Management Journal*, Vol. 9(4), pp. 361-374.

HENNART, J.F. (1989) 'Can the 'New Forms of Investment' Substitute for the 'Old Forms'?: A Transaction Costs Perspective', *Journal of International Business Studies*, Vol. 20(2), pp. 211-234.

HEWETT, J. AND DURHAM, T. (1987) *Computer-Aided Software Engineering: Commercial Strategies*, London: OVUM Ltd.

HICKS, D.M. AND KATZ, J.S. (1996) 'Where is Science Going?', *Science, Technology and Human Values*, Vol. 21(4), pp. 379-406.

HILLEBRAND, W. (1996) *Shaping Competitive Advantage: Conceptual Framework and the Korean Approach*, London: Frank Cass.

HIRST, P. AND THOMPSON, G. (1996) *Globalisation in Question*, Cambridge: Polity Press.

HOBDAY, M. (1994) 'Technological Learning in Singapore: A Test Case of Leapfrogging', *Journal of Development Studies*, Vol. 30(4), pp. 831-858.

HOBDAY, M. (1995) 'East Asian Latecomer Firms: Learning the Technology of Electronics', *World Development*, Vol. 23(7), pp. 1171-1193.

HOBDAY, M. (1998 forthcoming) 'Product Complexity, Innovation and Industrial Organisation', *Research Policy*.

HODGE, J. AND MILLER, J. (1998 forthcoming) 'Information Technology in South Africa' in Cooper, C. (ed.) *Information Technology Policy and National Economic Development*, London: Routledge and Tokyo: UNU Press.

HOFFMAN K. AND KAPLINSKY, R. (1988) *Driving Force: The Global Restructuring of Technology, Labor and Investment in the Automobile and Components Industries*, Boulder CO: Westview Press.

HOFSTEDE, G. (1980) 'Motivation, Leadership, and Organisation: Do American Theories Apply Abroad?', *Organisational Dynamics*, Summer, pp. 42-63.

HOLDERNESS, M. (1998 forthcoming) 'The Internet: Enabling Whom, When and Where?' in Mitter, S. (ed.) *The Cyber-Economy and the Developing World: The Question of Exclusion and Inclusion*, London: Routledge and Tokyo: UNU Press.

HOLLINGSWORTH, J. AND STREECK, W. (1994) 'Countries and Sectors: Concluding Remarks on Performance, Convergence, and Competitiveness' in Hollingsworth, J., Schmitter, P. and Streeck, W. (eds) *Governing Capitalist Economies: Performance and Control of Economic Sectors*, New York: Oxford University Press, pp. 270-300.

HONG, S.G. (1992) 'Paths of Glory: Semiconductor Leapfrogging in Taiwan and South Korea', *Pacific Focus*, Vol. 7, pp. 59-88.

HONG, S.G. (1997) 'From Regulation to Deregulation: A Case of Korean Telecommunications Policy', paper prepared for the 1997 National Conference on the American Society for Public Administration, Philadelphia, PA, 26-30 July.

HOWELL, T., NOELLERT, W. AND MACLAUGHLIN, J. (1988) *The Microelectronics Race*, Boulder, CO: Westview Press.

HOWKINS, J. AND VALANTIN, R. (1997) *Development and the Information Age: Four Global Scenarios for the Future of Information and Communication Technology*, Ottawa: International Development Research Centre.

HUDSON, H. (1992) 'Developing Countries' Telecommunications: Overcoming the Barriers of Distance' in Froehlich, F.E. (eds) *Encyclopaedia of Telecommunications*, Vol. 5, New York: Marcel Dekker, pp. 351-368.

HUMPHREY, J. AND KAPLINSKY, R. WITH DHATTA, R. CHANDRASEKHAR, RANGARAJ, N. AND SARAPH, P. (1998 forthcoming) *Globalisation, Competition and Industrial Transformation in India*, New Delhi: Sage Publications.

HUYER, S. (Project Leader) (1997) Women in Global Science and Technology, IFIAS, Toronto, Canada.

IDRC (International Development Research Centre) (1996) 'Communities and the Information Society in Africa: A Canadian Initiative for the Millennium' (Draft Working Document), International Development Research Centre, Canada, 4 July.

IDRC (International Development Research Centre) (n.d.) 'Existing IDRC Program Initiatives (PIs) and the "Communities and the Information Society in Africa" Initiative', Preliminary Note, International Development Research Centre, Canada.

IDRC GENDER AND INFORMATION WORKING GROUP (1995) 'Information as a transformative tool' in Gender Working Group, United Nations Commission on Science and Technology for Development (eds) *Missing Links: Gender Equity in Science and Technology for Development*, Ottawa and London: International Development Research Centre in association with Intermediate Technology Publications and UNIFEM, pp. 267-293.

IDRIS, N. (1996) 'Telecommunication Policies and Deregulation for Better Telecommunication Services in Encouraging High Economic Growth and Rural Development in Indonesia', paper presented at the International Workshop on a Comparative Analysis of (Tele)Communication Policies in Western Europe and South-East Asia: Cultural and Historical Perspectives on the Convergence Issue, Bruges, Belgium, 29 August - 1 September.

IFPI (International Federation of the Phonographic Industry) (1996) *Pirate Sales 1995*, IFPI: London.

IIPA (International Intellectual Property Alliance) (1996) *1996 Special 301 Recommendations*, Washington DC: IIPA.

IITF (Information Infrastructure Task Force) (1995) *Intellectual Property and the National Information Infrastructure*, The Report of the Working Group on Intellectual Property Rights, Washington, DC.

IITF (Information Infrastructure Task Force) (1996) 'A Framework for Global Electronic Commerce', Draft, Washington DC, 11 December.

IMF (International Monetary Fund) (1997) *International Financial Statistics*, Vol. L(6), Washington DC: IMF.

INFORMATION HIGHWAY ADVISORY COUNCIL (1995) *Connection, Community, Content: The Challenge of the Information Highway*, (Final Report), Ottawa: Ministry of Supply and Services.

INSTITUTE FOR INFORMATION INDUSTRY (1995) 'From Vision toward Reality: NII Movement in ROC', summary of a speech by General Kuo Yun, Vice-Chairman and President of the Institute for Information Industry (Taiwan, Pr. China) at the Global Information and Software Society Internet Conference (GISSIC), http://www.ncb.gov.sg/nii/96scan1/rocnii.html

INSTITUTE ON GOVERNANCE (1996) 'Information and Communications Technologies (ICTs) and Governance: Linkages and Challenges', International Development Research Centre, Canada.

INTEGRATED CIRCUIT ENGINEERING (1995) *Status 1995*, Scottsdale: ICE.

INTEGRATED MANUFACTURING LAB RESEARCH (n.d.) 'Research', http://kingkong.me.berkely.edu/research

INTERNATIONAL TELECOMMUNICATION UNION (1984) *The Missing Link: Report of the Independent Commission for World-wide Telecommunications Development*, Geneva: International Telecommunication Union.

INTERNATIONAL TELECOMMUNICATION UNION (1989) 'The Changing Telecommunication Environment: Policy Considerations for the Members of the ITU', report of the Advisory Group on Telecommunication Policy, Geneva: International Telecommunication Union.

INTERNATIONAL TELECOMMUNICATION UNION (1993) 'Asia-Pacific Telecommunication Indicators', Geneva: International Telecommunication Union.

INTERNATIONAL TELECOMMUNICATION UNION (ed.) (1994) *The Changing Role of Government in an Era of Telecom Deregulation - Global Mobile Personal Communications Systems* (GMPCS), Report of the Third Regulatory Colloquium, Geneva, 9-11 November.

INTERNATIONAL TELECOMMUNICATION UNION (1995a) *World Communication Development Report: Information Infrastructures*, Geneva: International Telecommunication Union.

INTERNATIONAL TELECOMMUNICATION UNION (1995b) *Telecommunication Indicators for the Least Developed Countries*, Geneva: International Telecommunication Union.

INTERNATIONAL TELECOMMUNICATION UNION (1995c) 'The Africa Green Paper, Telecommunication Policies for Africa', Draft, Geneva.

INTERNATIONAL TELECOMMUNICATION UNION (1995d) 'Plans or Platitudes?' in International Telecommunication Union, *World Telecommunication Development Report 1995: Information Infrastructures*, Geneva: International Telecommunication Union, pp. 46-48.

INTERNATIONAL TELECOMMUNICATION UNION (1996a) 'Africa Telecommunications Finance Colloquium', report prepared for the Colloquium, Abidjan, Ivory Coast.

INTERNATIONAL TELECOMMUNICATION UNION (1996b) 'Arab States Telecommunications Finance Colloquium', report prepared for the Colloquium, Amman, Jordan.

INTERNATIONAL TELECOMMUNICATION UNION (1997) *World Telecommunication Development Report 1996/97: Trade in Telecommunications; World Telecommunication Indicators*, Geneva: International Telecommunication Union.

INTERNATIONAL TELECOMMUNICATION UNION AND UNESCO (1995) 'The Right to Communicate - At What Price? Economic Constraints to the Effective Use of Telecommunications in Education, Science, Culture and in the Circulation of Information', CII-95/WS/2, Paris, UNESCO, May.

INTERNET MAGAZINE (1997) 'Rattle and Hum over U2 Bootleg', *The Internet Magazine*, January, p. 7.

IRIDIUM Today (1994) *Iridium Today*, Vol. 1(1).

IRIDIUM TODAY (1996) 'Reaching a Global Objective', *Iridium Today*, Vol. 3(1).

ISAD (Information Society and Development) (1996a) 'Chairperson's View Concerning Ideas Emerging from the Fora Discussions on Global Information Society and Development', ISAD Conference, Midrand, South Africa, 13-15 May 1996.

ISAD (Information Society and Development) (1996b) 'Chair's Conclusions', ISAD Conference, Midrand, South Africa, 13-15 May 1996.

JAFFE, J. AND FROOMKIN, J. (1968) *Technology and Jobs: Automation in Perspective*, New York: Frederick A. Praeger Press.

JAIKUMAR, R, (1986) 'Post-Industrial Manufacturing', *Harvard Business Review*, Vol. 64(6), pp. 69-76.

JAKUBOWICZ, K. (1996) 'Improving on the West - The Native Way: Poland' in Directorate General X, Directorate D and Directorate General IA, Directorate B, (eds.) *The Development of the Audio-visual Landscape in Central Europe since 1989*, Luton: John Libby Media, pp. 121-152.

JAMES, J. (1994) 'Microelectronics and the Third World: An Integrative Survey of the Literature' in Cooper, C., Fransman, M. and James, J. (eds) *Technology and Innovation in the International Economy*, London: Edward Elgar and Tokyo: UNU Press, pp. 149-230.

JENSEN, M. (1996a) 'Bridging the Gaps in Internet Development in Africa', International Development Research Centre, Ottawa, 31 August.

JENSEN, M. (1996b) 'African Regional Symposium on Telematics for Development', Draft Discussion Paper for UNESCO/UNECA, Geneva, p. 30.

JUSSAWALLA, M. (1994) 'Who Owns the Orbit?', *Asian Communications Journal*, November, pp. 27-29.

JUSSAWALLA, M. (1995a) 'Satellites Bid for the GII' in Jussawalla, M. (ed.) *Telecommunications: A Bridge to the 21st Century*', Amsterdam: North Holland Elsevier, pp. 286-288.

JUSSAWALLA, M. (1995b) 'The Enabling Power of the Internet: Winners and Losers' in Jussawalla, M. (ed.) *Telecommunications: A Bridge to the 21st Century*, Amsterdam: North Holland Elsevier, pp. 195-207.

JUSSAWALLA, M., LAMBERTON, D. AND KARUNARATNE, N. (eds) (1988) *The Cost of Thinking: Information Economies in Ten Pacific Countries*, Norwood NJ: Ablex.

KAHIN, B. (ed.) (1996) *Building Information Infrastructures - Issues in the Development of the National Research and Education Network*, New York: McGraw-Hill.

KAHIN, B. AND KELLER, J. (eds) (1996) *Public Access to the Internet*, Cambridge MA: MIT Press.

KAHIN, B. AND NESSON, C. (eds) (1995) *Borders in Cyberspace*, Cambridge MA: MIT Press.

KAHIN, B. AND WILSON III, E.J. (1997) *National Information Infrastructure III Initiatives: Vision and Policy Design*, Cambridge MA: MIT Press.

KALDOR, N. (1957) 'A Model of Economic Growth', *Economic Journal*, Vol. 67, pp. 591-624.

KAMBOURAKIS, G. AND NOTTAS, M. (1996) 'Pericles Network, System Concept and Development', National Technical University of Athens, mimeo.

KAPLAN, D. (1996) 'Comment on the paper by Andrew Davies (Innovation and Competitiveness in Complex System Industries: The Case of Mobile Phone Systems)', paper presented at the International Workshop on Europe and the Developing World in the Globalised Information Society: Employment, Education and Trade Implications, Maastricht, UNU/INTECH, 17-19 October.

KAPLINSKY, R. (1988) 'Industrial Restructuring in LDCs: The Role of Information Technology', paper prepared for Conference of Technology Policy in the Americas, Stanford University, December.

KAPLINSKY, R. (1994) *Easternisation: The Spread of Japanese Management Techniques to Developing Countries*, London: Frank Cass.

KARTHIGESU, R. (1996) 'Asian Social Values and Global Liberalism: Attuning State Policies to the Convergence of Telecommunications Technologies in Malaysia', paper presented at the International Workshop on a Comparative Analysis of (Tele)Communications Policies in Western Europe and South-East Asia: Cultural and Historical Perspectives on the Convergence Issue, Bruges, Belgium, 29 August-1 September.

KELLY, S. (1996) 'The Jewel in the Crown', *Computer Weekly*, 22 August, pp. 22-23.

KELLY, S. (1997) 'Firms Pay Higher Price for Indian Programming Skills', *Computer Weekly*, 23 January, p. 2.

KELLY, T. (1989) 'The Marriage of Broadcasting and Telecommunications', *The OECD Observer*, No. 160, October-November, pp. 16-18.

KELLY, T. (1995) 'If the Telecommunications Industry is So Successful, Why is It Unable to Reduce the Waiting List for Telephone Service?', Geneva, TELECOM '95, Strategies Summit, Resourcing for Growth, 6 October.

KENSINGER, K. (1996) 'Status Report on Regulation of Global Mobile Satellite Communications by the US Federal Communications Commission', Mobile Satellite Communications Global Conference, London, 17-19 June.

KILLING, J.P. (1983) *Strategies for Joint Venture Success*, New York: Praeger.

KIM, H.K. (1991) 'Industrial Structural Policy and New Definition of the State-Firm Relationship in the Semiconductor Industry' in Min, K. (ed.) (1993) *The State and Public Policy*, Seoul: Beum Moon Sa, pp. 410-446 (Korean).

KIM, S.G. AND RO, K.K. (1995) 'A Strategic Technology Management Model Under Different Technology Acquisition Modes Between Developing Countries: The Case of Telecommunication in Korea and China', *International Journal of Technology Management*, Vol. 10(7/8), pp. 767-776.

KIM, S.R. (1998 forthcoming) *Nationales Innovationssystem und Sektorale Entwicklung: eine Industriepolitische Analyse des Entwicklungsprozesses der Koreanischen Halbleiterindustrie*, Berlin: Edition Sigma Verlag and Wissenschaftszentrum Berlin.

KLUZER, S. AND FARINELLI, M. (1997) 'A Survey of European Cities' Presence on the Internet', *FAIR Working Paper No. 31*, Milan: Databank Consulting.

KNIGHT, P.T. (1995) 'The Telematics Revolution in Africa and the World Bank Group', paper prepared for AFRISTECH'95, Symposium on Information Superhighways: What Strategy for Africa?, Dakar, 12-15 December.

KOREAN SEMICONDUCTOR INDUSTRY ASSOCIATION (1993) 'Development Process of the Semiconductor Industry', *Semiconductor Industry*, Vol. 3, pp. 2-30, (Korean).

KURTZ, L.A. (1996) 'Copyright and the National Information Infrastructure in the United States', *European Intellectual Property Review*, Vol. 18, pp. 120-126.

KUZNETS, S. (1973) 'Modern Economic Growth: Findings and Reflections', *American Economic Review*, Vol. 63, pp. 247-258.

KYNGE, J. (1997) 'Flocking to the Cybercity', *Financial Times*, 19 May.

LAASER, W. (1998 forthcoming) 'Technologies for Distance Education in Developing Countries' in Mitter, S., Bastos, M.-I. and Bartzokas, A. (eds) *Europe and Developing Countries in the World Information Economy: Trade, Distance Education and Regional Development*, London: Routledge and Tokyo: UNU Press.

LALL, S. (1995) 'Science and Technology in the New Global Environment: Implications for Developing Countries', *Science and Technology Issues*, in collaboration with the UNCTAD Secretariat, UNCTAD/DST/8, United Nations: New York and Geneva.

LAMBERTON, D. (ed.) (1995) *Beyond Competition: The Future of Telecommunications*, Amsterdam: Elsevier.

LANGLOIS, R. AND STEINMUELLER, W.E. (1997) 'The Evolution of Competitive Advantage in the Global Semiconductor Industry: 1947-1996' in papers for the DRUID (Danish Research Unit for Industrial Dynamics) Seminar, Skagen, 1-3 June, forthcoming in Mowery, D. and Nelson R. (eds) *Sources of Industrial Leadership*.

LARSEN, P. (ed.) (1990) 'Import/Export: International Flow of Television Fiction', *Reports and Papers on Mass Communication, No 104*, Paris: UNESCO.

LAW, C.E. (1995) *Telecommunications in Eastern Europe and the CIS: Prospects and Markets to 2000*, A Financial Times Management Report, London: Financial Times.

LEER, A.C. (1996) *It's a Wired World - The New Networked Economy*, Oslo: Scandanavian University Press and Brussels/Luxembourg: European Commission, Directorate General XIII.

LEIPZIGER, D.M. (1987) *Korea: Managing the Industrial Transition*, World Bank (Country Study), World Bank: Washington, DC.

LEITE, F. (1996) 'Global Mobile Personal Communications', paper prepared for TELEXPO'96, São Paulo, 26-29 March, p. 4.

LEONARD-BARTON, D. (1995) *Wellsprings of Knowledge: Building and Sustaining the Sources of Innovation*, Boston MA: Harvard Business School Press.

LEVIN, L. (1996) 'Report to the IDRC on the Use of Information and Communication Technologies in Sub-Saharan Africa in the Area of Governance', report prepared for International Development Research Centre, Ottawa, 31 August.

LEWIS, P. (1993) 'Alternative Media: Linking Global and Local', *Reports and Papers in Mass Communication No. 107*, Paris: UNESCO.

LOS ALAMOS NATIONAL LABORATORY (1996) 'TeleFlex', http:www.acl.lanl.gov/TeleMed/teleflex.htm

LUNDVALL, B.-Å. (1992a) 'Introduction' in Lundvall, B.-Å. (ed.) *National Systems of Innovation: Towards a Theory of Innovation and Interactive Learning*, London: Pinter Publishers, pp. 1-19.

LUNDVALL, B.-Å. (ed.) (1992b) *National Systems of Innovation: Towards a Theory of Innovation and Interactive Learning*, London: Pinter Publishers.

LUNDVALL, B.-Å. (1996a) 'Information Technology in the Learning Economy - Challenges for Development Strategies', background paper for the UNCSTD Working Group on IT and Development.

LUNDVALL, B.-Å. (1996b) The Social Dimension of the Learning Economy, *DRUID Working Paper No. 1*, Aalborg: Department of Business Studies, Aalborg University.

LUNDVALL, B.-Å. AND JOHNSON, B. (1994) 'The Learning Economy', *Journal of Industry Studies*, Vol. 1(2), pp. 23-42.

MACDONALD, G. (1997) 'Britain's Interactive Education Industry: A Scenario', Independent consultant, East Sussex, mimeo.

MACHLUP, F. (1962) *The Production and Distribution of Knowledge in the United States*, Princeton: Princeton University Press.

MAIER-RABLER, U. (1997) 'Information Cultures within Western Civilisation: The American-European Differences Regarding New ICTs', prepared for the International Communications Association Conference, Montreal.

MAIER-RABLER, U. AND SUTTERLUETTI, E. (1992) 'Pressestatistik im internationalen Vergleich', Forschungsbericht, Salzburg.

MALERBA, F. AND BRESCHI, S. (1995) 'Technological Regimes and Sectoral Innovation Systems: Schumpeterian Dynamics and Spatial Boundaries', paper prepared for the Conference on the System of Innovation Research Network, Soederkoeping, Sweden, 20-22 January.

MANSELL R. (1996a) 'Network Governance: Designing New Regimes' in Mansell, R. and Silverstone, R. (eds) *Communication by Design: The Politics of Information and Communication Technologies*, Oxford: Oxford University Press, pp. 187-212.

MANSELL, R. (1996b) 'Public Access and Closed Network Membership: Electronic Trading Networks in Europe' in Noam, E. and NíShúilleabháin, A. (eds) *Private Networks Public Objectives*, Amsterdam: Elsevier, pp. 195-208.

MANSELL, R. (1996c) 'Communication by Design?' in Mansell, R. and Silverstone, R. (eds) *Communication by Design: The Politics of Information and Communication Technologies*, Oxford: Oxford University Press, pp. 15-43.

MANSELL, R. AND HAWKINS, R. (1992) 'Old Roads and New Signposts: Trade and Policy Objectives in Telecommunication Standards' in Klaver, F. and Slaa, P. (eds) *Telecommunication: New Signposts and Old Roads*, Amsterdam: IOS Press, pp. 45-54.

MANSELL, R. AND JENKINS, M. (1992a) 'Electronic Trading Networks and Interactivity: the Route Toward Competitive Advantage?', *Communications & Strategies*, 2ème Trimestre, No. 6, pp. 63-85.

MANSELL, R. AND JENKINS, M. (1992b) 'Networks, Industrial Restructuring and Policy: The Singapore Example', *Technovation*, Vol. 12(6), pp. 397-406.

MANSELL, R. AND SILVERSTONE, R. (eds) (1996) *Communication by Design: The Politics of Information and Communication Technologies*, Oxford: Oxford University Press.

MANSELL, R. AND STEINMUELLER, W.E. (1995) 'Intellectual Property Rights: The Development of Information Infrastructures for the Information Society', Final Report for the STOA Programme of the European Parliament, MERIT, University of Limburg, The Netherlands, 17 October.

MANSELL, R. AND STEINMUELLER, W.E. (1996a) 'The Way Forward: Socio-Economic and Policy Issues & Advanced Communication Technologies and Services', *FAIR Working Paper No. 2*, Brighton: SPRU.

MANSELL, R. AND STEINMUELLER, W.E. (1996b) 'Intellectual Property Rights in the Information Society', *Science and Public Affairs*, Autumn, pp. 18-21.

MANSELL, R. AND STEINMUELLER, W.E (1996c) 'Securing Electronic Networks', *FAIR Working Paper No.7*, Brighton: SPRU.

MANSELL, R. AND TANG, P. (1996) 'Technological and Regulatory Changes Affecting Multinational Enterprises in Telecommunications: Aspects of the Impact on the Workforce', *Multinational Enterprises Programme Working Paper No. 78*, Geneva: International Labour Office.

MANSFIELD, E. (1995) 'Intellectual Property Protection, Direct Investment and Technology Transfer: Germany, Japan and the United States', *Discussion Paper No. 27*, Washington DC: World Bank and International Finance Corporation.

MARCELLE, G. (1998 forthcoming) 'Creating an African Women's Cyberspace' in Mitter, S. (ed.) *The Cyber-Economy and the Developing World: The Question of Exclusion and Inclusion*, London: Routledge and Tokyo: UNU Press.

MARCELLE, G. AND JACOB, M. (1995) 'The "Double Bind" - Women in Small and Medium Sized Enterprises' in Gender Working Group, United Nations Commission on Science and Technology for Development (eds) *Missing Links: Gender Equity in Science and Technology for Development*, Ottawa and London: International Development Research Centre in association with Intermediate Technology Publications and UNIFEM, pp. 243-265.

MASKUS, K.E. (1993) 'Trade-related Intellectual Property Rights', *European Economy*, No. 52, pp. 157-184.

MASKUS, K.E. AND PENUBARTI, M. (1995) 'How Trade-related are Intellectual Property Rights?', *Journal of International Economics*, Vol. 39(3/4), pp. 227-248.

MATSEPE-CASABURRI, I. (1996) 'Socio-Cultural Values in IT: Confronting the Legacy of the Past to Meet the Promise of the Future', *Intermedia*, Vol. 24(6), pp. 8-10.

MBEKI, T. (1996) 'The Information Society and the Developing World: A South African Perspective', Draft 5, Version 5.1, April.

MCKINSEY & COMPANY (1996) *Connecting All of America's K-12 Schools to the National Information Infrastructure*, Report prepared for the US National Information Infrastructure Advisory Council, Palo Alto CA: McKinsey and Company Inc.

MDIS PUBLICATIONS LTD (1997) *Telecommunications in Central and Eastern Europe*, Volumes I and II, Chichester, West Sussex: MDIS Publications Ltd.

MELODY, W.H. (1981) 'The Economics of Information as Resource and Product' in Wedemeyer, D.J. (ed.) *Proceedings of the PTC'81 Pacific Telecommunication Conference*, Honolulu: Pacific Telecommunications Council, pp. C7-5-9.

MELODY, W.H. (1985) 'The Information Society: Implications for Economic Institutions and Market Theory', *Journal of Economic Issues*, Vol. XIX(2), pp. 523-539.

MELODY, W.H. (1993) 'Improved Telecommunication: Catalyst for Development?', paper for the Pacific Telecommunications Forum Seminar, Suva, Fiji, 28-30 September.

MELODY, W.H. (1995) 'Telecommunication Policy Options for Developing Countries: Adapting Reforms to Local Conditions', presentation to ITU Telecommunications Policy-Legislation and Regulation Seminar, Bangkok, 21-24 March.

MELODY, W.H. (1996) 'Toward a Framework for Designing Information Society Policies', *Telecommunications Policy*, Vol. 20(4), pp. 243-259.

MELODY, W.H. (1997a) 'Network Cost Analysis: Concepts and Methods' in Melody, W.H. (ed.) *Telecom Reform: Principles, Policies and Regulatory Practices*, Lyngby: Technical University of Denmark, pp. 215-246.

MELODY, W.H. (1997b) 'Privatisation: A Story of Successes, Failures and Regrets', *Intermedia*, Vol. 20(3), pp. 14-17.

MELODY, W.H. (ed.) (1997c) *Telecom Reform: Principles, Policies and Regulatory Practices*, Lyngby: Technical University of Denmark.

MENON, V. (1996) 'How Communications are Changing: Visions for the Future', presented at the General Conference of the Commonwealth Broadcasting Association, Kuala Lumpur, Malaysia, 26 August.

MENOU, M.J. (1993) *Measuring the Impact of Information on Development*, Ottawa: International Development Research Centre.

METCALFE, J. (1986) 'Technological Innovation and the Competitive Process' in Hall, P. (ed.) *Technology, Innovation and Economic Growth*, Southampton: Camelot Press, pp. 35-64.

MEXICO PODER EJECUTIVO FEDERAL (1996) 'Programa de Desarrollo del Sector Comunicaciones y Transportes 1995-2000', Poder Ejecutivo Federal, Mexico City.

MEXICO SECRETARY OF COMMUNICATIONS AND TRANSPORTATION (1995) 'Ley Federal de Telecomunicaciones', Mexico Secretary of Communications and Transportation, Mexico City.

MEYER, J.-A. AND BERGER, M. (1996) 'The Computer-Integrated Curriculum: The German Experience', *Computers in Education*, Vol. 27(2), pp. 129-139.

MEYER-STAMER, J. (1996) 'Das Internet als Beispiel dezentraler Techniksteuerung - Konsequenzen für Technologiepolitik in Deutschland' in Kleinsteuber, H.J. (ed.) *Der 'Information Superhighway', Amerikanische Visionen und Erfahrungen*, Opladen: Westdeutscher Verlag, pp. 139-147.

MEYER-STAMER, J. (1997) 'Knowledge-Driven Development. Key Issues in Creating an Innovation-Oriented Environment to Support Industrial Competitiveness in Advanced Developing and Post-Communist Countries', Berlin, German Development Institute.

MICAS, C. (1997) 'Industrial Alliances in the New Digital Information Era: The Strategic Path' in Dumort, A. and Dryden, J. (eds) *The Economics of the Information Society*, Luxembourg: Office for Official Publications of the European Communities, pp. 65-75.

MICHAEL, D.N. (1962) *Cybernation: The Silent Conquest*, Santa Barbara CA: Center for the Study of Democratic Institutions.

MICHEL, J.H. (1997) 'A New Approach to Development', *The OECD Observer*, No. 204, pp. 33-35.

MILES, I. (1996) 'Service Firms and Innovation - Telematics and Beyond', commissioned by UNU/INTECH and COLCIENCIAS as a background paper for the UNCSTD Working Group on IT and Development.

MILES, I. AND CONTRIBUTORS (1990) *Mapping and Measuring the Information Economy*, Boston Spa: British Library.

MILLAR, J. (1996) 'Interactive Learning in Situated Software Practice: Factors Mediating the New Production of Knowledge During iCASE Technology Interchange', unpublished DPhil Thesis, Science Policy Research Unit, University of Sussex.

MILLAR, J., DEMAID, A. AND QUINTAS, P. (1996) 'Product-in-Context: A Framework for Research into Trans-Organizational Design and Innovation', Open University Business School report to the UK Design Council, October.

MILLARD, C. (1997) 'Local Content Filters and the 'Inherent Risk' of the Internet', *Intermedia*, Vol. 25(1), pp. 21-22.

MILLER, R., HOBDAY, M., LEROUX-DEMERS, T. AND OLLEROS, X. (1995) 'Innovation in Complex Systems Industries: The Case of Flight Simulation', *Industrial and Corporate Change*, Vol. 4(2), pp. 363-400.

MINISTER OF PUBLIC UTILITIES AND TRANSPORT (1996) 'Telecommunications Policy: A Framework', Kingston, Jamaica, January.

MINISTÉRIO DA CIÊNCIA E TECNOLOGIA (1996) *Relatório de Atividades MCT-1995*, Brasilia: MCT.

MINISTRY OF COMMUNICATIONS (1995) 'National Development Plan for the Telecommunications Sector', Colombia, 18 January.

MINKES, A.L. (1995) 'Managers as Entrepreneurs: A View from Asia', *Technovation*, Vol. 15(3), pp. 177-182.

MITCHELL, W.J. (1995) *City of Bits: Space, Place, and the Infobahn*, Cambridge MA: MIT Press.

MITTER, S. (1993) 'New Skills Requirements and Appropriate Programmes for the Enhancement of Participation of the Female Labour Force in Industry in Selected Economies of the Asia-Pacific Region' in ESCAP, UNDP and ILO Report, *Promoting Diversified Skill Development for Women in Industry*, Volume 1, New York: United Nations, pp. 21-98.

MITTER, S. (1995) 'Who Benefits? Measuring the Differential Impact of New Technologies' in Gender Working Group, United Nations Commission on Science and Technology for Development (eds) *Missing Links: Gender Equity in Science and Technology for Development*, Ottawa and London: International Development Research Centre in association with Intermediate Technology Publications and UNIFEM, pp. 219-242.

MITTER, S. AND EFENDIOGLU, Ü. (1998 forthcoming) 'The Information Revolution, New Modes of Employment, Trade and Work Organisations' in Mitter, S., Bastos, M.-I. and Bartzokas, A. (eds) *Europe and Developing Countries in the World Information Economy: Trade, Distance Education and Regional Development*, London: Routledge and Tokyo: UNU Press.

MITTER, S. AND ROWBOTHAM, S. (eds) (1995) *Women Encounter Technology: Changing Patterns of Employment in the Third World*, London/New York: Routledge with UNU/INTECH.

MIZUMOTO, T. (1997) 'Structural Weaknesses of Information and Communication Technology Standardization in Japan', *Keio Communication Review*, Vol. 19, pp. 19-37.

MIZUNO, Y. (1997) 'The World of Electronic Commerce', Executive Advisor NEC Corporation.

MODY, A. AND DAHLMAN, C. (1992) 'Performance and Potential of Information Technology: An International Perspective', *World Development*, Vol. 20(12), pp. 1703-1719.

MODY, B., BAUER, J.M. AND STRAUBHAAR, J.D. (eds) (1995) *Telecommunications Politics - Ownership and Control of the Information Highway in Developing Countries*, Mahwah, New Jersey: Lawrence Erlbaum Associates.

MOMSEN, J.H. (1991) *Women and Development in the Third World*, London/New York: Routledge.

MONROE, K.A., ROHLS, A.F. AND MERDINGER, M. (1995) 'International Overview of Trademarks and Copyrights' in Campbell, D. and Cotter, S. (eds) *International Intellectual Property Law: New Developments*, Chichester: John Wiley & Sons published under the auspices of the Centre for International Legal Studies, Salzburg, Austria, pp. 5-31.

MOORE, M. (n.d.) 'An Introduction to Telemedicine', http://ab.edu/~moore_m/telemedicine/telemedicine_introduction.htm

MORLEY, D. (1989) 'Changing Paradigms in Audience Studies' in Seiter, E., Borchers, H., Kreutzner, G. and Warth, E.M. (eds) *Remote Control: Television, Audiences and Cultural Power*, London/New York: Routledge, pp. 16-43.

MOULTON, D. (1996) 'Realidad Virtual y Applicaciones C3. Simulacion', paper prepared for VII Jornadas de Electrónica Militar, Madrid, 1-2 October.

MOWLANA, H. (1985) 'International Flow of Information: A Global Report and Analysis', *Reports and Papers on Mass Communication, No. 99*, Paris: UNESCO.

MSF/ITPA (Manufacturing, Science and Finance Union/Information Technology Professionals Association) (1996) *The Outsourcing of IT Services - Leading Edge or Bleeding Edge? A Guide for Members*, London: MSF Information Technology Professionals Association, MSF/ITPA 158/6/96.

MUELLER, M.L. AND DOUGAN, D.L. (eds) (1993) 'China Telecommunications and Information Industry Forum (CTIIF): Briefing Paper', Centre for Strategic and International Studies (CSIS) and Chinese Academy of Social Sciences (CASS), Beijing, China, 8-11 November.

MUELLER, M.L. AND SCHEMENT, J.R. (1996) 'Universal Service from the Bottom Up: A Study of Telephone Penetration in Camden, New Jersey', *The Information Society*, Vol. 12(3), pp. 273-292.

MULLIGAN, M. (1997) 'Parley-Vous Lingua Franca?', *Financial Times*, 6 January.

MULTIMEDIA ASSOCIATION NEWS (1995) 'Electronic Tagging and the Problem of Digital Copyright', *Multimedia Association News*; Vol. 1(12).

MUNDY, D.H. AND NYIRENDA, P.B. (1995) 'Guidelines for Policies and Standards', Proceedings of the Workshop on Regional and National Standards and Guiding Policies for Development of Information Systems and Networking Infrastructure in SADC, Gaborone, Botswana.

MURPHY, P. (1993) 'Education and Development: The Contribution of Distance Education', ICDE Standing Conference of Presidents, Lisbon.

MYTELKA, L.K. (1995) 'Information Technologies and the Restructuring of Production' in Summary of Proceedings of a Symposium on Information Technologies and International Relations, Department of Foreign Affairs and International Trade, Ottawa, 13 January.

NAIDOO, J, MINISTER OF POST, TELECOMMUNICATIONS AND BROADCASTING (1996) 'Why I Won't be Serving Cappuccino in Cyber-Cafes', speech on the occasion of the introduction of the new South African Telecommunications Bill, 30 October.

NAIRN, G. (1997a) 'A Crucial Year Ahead for the "Net"', *Financial Times*, 8 January.

NAIRN, G. (1997b) 'Teleworker Army Will Grow to 200 Million World-wide by Year 2016', *Financial Times*, 8 January citing Jack Nilles.

NAISBITT, J. (1996) *Megatrends Asia: The Eight Asian Megatrends that are Changing the World*, London: Nicholas Brealey.

NARAYAN, J. (CMC Ltd) (1997) presentation to the UNCSTD Working Group on IT and Development, Lonavla, January.

NARENDRAN, P. AND WALKER, S. (1996) 'Manchester: A Case Study of a Telematics Programme', paper prepared for the UNU/INTECH International Workshop on Europe and the Developing World in the Globalised Information Society: Employment, Education and Trade Implications, UNU/INTECH, Maastricht, 17-19 October.

NASS, C. (1987) 'Following the Money Trail: 25 Years of Measuring the Information Economy', *Communication Research*, Vol. 14(6), pp. 698-708.

NASSCOM (National Association of Software and Service Companies) (1996) 'Software Industry in India, 1996 Strategic Review', New Dehli, NASSCOM.

NATIONAL COMMISSION ON TECHNOLOGY, AUTOMATION AND ECONOMIC PROGRESS (1966) *The Employment Impact of Technological Change*, *Appendix Volume II, Technology and the American Economy*. Washington DC: Government Printing Office, February.

NATIONAL COMPUTER BOARD (1996) *IT Focus - Newsletter of the National Computer Board*, Aug./Sep, NCB, Singapore.

NATIONAL COMPUTER BOARD (1997a) 'Secure Electronic Commerce Takes Off', *IT Focus*, NCB, Singapore, p. 2.

NATIONAL COMPUTER BOARD (1997b) 'Yearbook 1995-1996', NCB, Singapore.

NATIONAL COMPUTER BOARD (n.d.a) 'Transforming Singapore into an Intelligent Island', NCB, Singapore.

NATIONAL COMPUTER BOARD (n.d.b) 'IT2000 - Singapore Unlimited', NCB, Singapore.

NATIONAL COMPUTER BOARD (n.d.c) 'Singapore ONE - One network for everyone', NCB, Singapore.

NATIONAL COMPUTERISATION AGENCY (1996) 'The Korea Basic Plan on Informatization Promotion', Seoul.

NATIONAL RESEARCH COUNCIL (1996) *Bridge Builders - African Experiences with Information and Communication Technology*, Washington: National Academy Press.

NCET (National Council for Educational Technology) (1996) 'Dyslexia and IT', http://www.ncet.org.uk/info-sheets/dyslexia.html

NCET (National Council for Educational Technology) (1997) 'Visual Impairment and IT', http://www.ncet.org.uk/info-sheets/visual.htm

NELSON, R. (ed.) (1993) *National Innovation Systems: A Comparative Analysis*. Oxford: Oxford University Press.

NG CHOON SIM, C. (1998 forthcoming) 'Making Women's Voices Heard: Technological Change and Women's Employment with Special Reference to Malaysia' in Mitter, S. (ed.) *The Cyber-Economy and the Developing World: The Question of Exclusion and Inclusion*, London: Routledge and Tokyo: UNU Press.

NICHOLSON, M. (1997) 'India Widens Range of Industries Open to Foreign Investment', *Financial Times*, 22 January.

NONAKA, I. AND TAKEUCHI, H. (1995) *The Knowledge Creating Company*, Oxford: Oxford University Press.

NORDENSTRENG, K. AND VARIS, T. (1974) 'Television Traffic: A One-Way Street? A Survey and Analysis of the International Flow of Television Programme Material', *Reports and Papers on Mass Communication, No. 70*, Paris: UNESCO.

NOSTBAKKEN, D. AND AKHTAR, S. (1995) 'Does The Highway Go South? - Southern Perspectives on the Information Highway', report of Pre-Conference Symposium of the International Institute of Communication on Southern Country Interests, Tampere, Finland, 3-4 September 1994, International Development Research Centre, February.

NOSTBAKKEN, D. AND MORROW, C. (eds) (1997) *Cultural Expression in the Global Village*, Ottawa: Southbound Publications and International Development Research Centre.

NYE, J.S. AND OWENS, W.A. (1996) 'America's Information Edge', *Foreign Affairs*, Vol. 75(2), pp. 20-36.

OECD (1992) *Technology and the Economy: The Key Relationships*, Paris: OECD.

OECD (1993a) *IT Diffusion Policies for Small and Medium Sized Enterprises*, Paris: OECD.

OECD (1993b) 'Usage Indicators - A New Foundation for Information Technology Policies', Paris: DSTI/ICCP.

OECD (1993c) *Communications Outlook 1993*, Paris: OECD/ICCP.

OECD (1994a) *Information Technology Outlook, 1994*, Paris: OECD/ICCP.

OECD (1994b) *Telecommunication Indicators for Economies in Transition*, Paris: OECD.

OECD (1996a) 'Measuring What People Know: Human Capital Accounting for the Knowledge Economy', Paris, OECD/DSTI/ICCP.

OECD (1996b) 'Global Information Infrastructures - Global Information Society (GII-GIS): Statement of Policy Recommendations made by the ICCP Committee', Paris, OECD/GD(96)93.

OECD (1996c) 'Information Infrastructure Convergence and Pricing: The Internet', OECD/GD(96)73, Paris.

OECD (1996d) *OECD Employment Outlook - The OECD Jobs Strategy: Technology, Productivity and Jobs Creation*, Paris: OECD.

OECD (1996e) *Employment and Growth in the Knowledge-based Economy*, Paris: OECD.

OECD (1997a) 'Information Infrastructures: Their Impact and Regulatory Requirements', Committee for Information, Computer and Communications Policy, Paris, OECD/GD(97)18.

OECD (1997b) *Communications Outlook 1997, Vol. 1 and 2* (Regulatory Annex), Paris: OECD.

OECD (1997c) *Information Technology Outlook 1997*, Paris: OECD.

OECD (1997d) 'Internet Domain Names: Allocation Policies', Working Party on Telecommunications and Information Services Policies, DSTI/ICCP/TISP (97)2, Paris, April.

OECD (1997e) *Electronic Commerce: Opportunities and Challenges for Government*, Paris: OECD.

OECD (1997f) 'A Consensus on Cryptography', *The OECD Observer*, No. 207, August/September, pp. 14-15.

OLDHAM, G. (1997) *A Decade of Reform - Science and Technology Policy in China*, Report of the IDRC/SSTC Science and Technology Review Mission to China, Ottawa: International Development Research Centre.

PALTRIDGE, S. (1996) 'How Competition Helps the Internet', *The OECD Observer*, No. 201, August-September, pp. 25-27.

PARAPK, J. (1996) 'Policy and Regulatory Issues Raised by the Introduction of Global Mobile Personal Communications by Satellite (GMPCS)', Revised Report by the Chairman, World Telecommunications Policy Forum, Geneva, 21-23 October.

PARÉ, D.J. (1995) 'Ideology, Administration, and Dualism: An Analysis of Telecom Development in the People's Republic of China', unpublished Masters Thesis, University of Guelph, May.

PARKHE, A. (1993), ' "Messy" Research, Methodological Predispositions, and Theory Development in International Joint Ventures', *Academy of Management Journal*, Vol. 18(2), pp. 227-268.

PATEL, I. (1997) 'Distance Tele-Education: A Panacea for Education?' in Cliché, D. (ed.) *Cultural Ecology: The Changing Dynamics of Communications*, London: International Institute of Communication, pp. 103-123.

PATTERSON, P.J. (1995) 'Information Technology and Development in Jamaica' in United Nations Conference on Trade and Development (eds) 'Information Technology for Development', *Advanced Technology Assessment System Bulletin*, Issue 10, New York and Geneva: United Nations, pp. 9-15.

PELTON, J.N. (1991) 'Technology and Education: Friend or Foe?', *Research in Distance Education*, Vol. 3(2), pp. 2-9, cited in Laaser, W. (1998 forthcoming) 'Technologies for Distance Education in Developing Countries' in Mitter, S., Bastos, M.-I. and Bartzokas, A. (eds) *Europe and Developing Countries in the World Information Economy: Trade, Distance Education and Regional Development*, London: Routledge and Tokyo: UNU Press.

PERDIGAO, J. (1997) 'Internet: From Hyper-links to Interactive-Multimedia', *The IPTS Report*, Vol. 12, pp. 26-33.

PEREZ, C. (1983) 'Structural Change and the Assimilation of New Technologies in the Economic and Social System', *Futures*, Vol. 15(4), pp. 357-375.

PEREZ, C. (1988) 'New Technologies and Development' in Freeman, C. and Lundvall, B.-Å. (eds) *Small Countries Facing the Technological Revolution*, London: Pinter Publishers, pp. 85-96. .

PEREZ, C. AND SOETE, L. (1988) 'Catching Up in Technology: Entry Barriers and Windows of Opportunity' in Dosi, G., Freeman, C., Nelson, R., Silverberg, G. and Soete, L. (eds) *Technical Change and Economic Theory*, London: Pinter Publishers, pp. 458-479.

PETERS, P.E. (1996) 'General Information about the Internet II Project', Washington DC: Coalition for Networked Information.

PETRAZZINI, B. (1995) *The Political Economy of Telecommunications Reform in Developing Countries: Privatization and Liberalization in Comparative Perspective*, Westport CT: Preager Publishers.

PETRAZZINI, B. (1996) *Global Telecom Talks: A Trillion Dollar Deal*, Washington DC: Institute for International Economics.

PETRAZZINI, B. AND HARINDRANATH, G. (1996) 'Information Infrastructure Initiatives in India' http://www.ncb.gov.sg/nii/96scan4/india1.htm

PISANO, G. (1996) *The Development Factor: Unlocking the Potential of Process Innovation*, Boston MA: Harvard Business School Press.

PITRODA, S.G. (1993) 'Development, Democracy, and the Village Telephone', *Harvard Business Review*, Vol. 71(6), pp. 66-79.

PNE NETWORKS (1993) 'Tuning into Local Radio's Potential', *PNE Networks*, October, pp. 39-42.

PNE NETWORKS (1997) 'Regulating the Internet: Less is Best', *PNE Networks*, July/August, pp. 35-38.

POGOREL, G. (ed.) (1996) *Global Telecommunications Strategies and Technological Change*, Amsterdam: Elsevier.

POIRIER, R. AND DESCHÊNES, L. (1990) *Typologies and Economic Analyses of New Information Technologies: Avenues of Research*, Lavalle, Quebec: Canadian Workplace Automation Research Centre, Organisational Research Directorate.

POLANYI, M. (1966) *The Tacit Dimension*, London: Routledge and Kegan Paul.

POON, A. (1987) 'Information Technology and Innovation in International Tourism - Implications for the Caribbean Tourist Industry', unpublished DPhil Thesis, Science Policy Research Unit, University of Sussex.

PORAT, M. (1984) *The Information Economy: Definition and Measurement*, Washington, DC: Department of Commerce.

PRIESMEYER, K. (1997) 'What are VOXEL-MAN-Atlases?', http://www.uke.uni-hamburg.de/Institutes/MDM/IDV/VOXEL-MAN.htm

PRIMO BRAGA, C.A. (1996) 'Trade-related Intellectual Property Issues: The Uruguay Round Agreement and its Economic Implications' in Martin, W. and Winters, A. (eds) *The Uruguay Round and Developing Countries*, Cambridge: Cambridge University Press, pp. 341-379.

PRITCHETT, L. (1996) 'Forget Convergence: Divergence Past, Present, and Future', *Finance and Development*, June, pp. 40-43.

PUNDIT, J. (1995) 'Wired to the Rest of the World', *Financial Times*, 10 January.

QUINTAS, P. (1995) 'Software Innovation in the Context of Complex Product Systems', Working Paper, CENTRIM-SPRU-OU Complex Product Systems Project, The Open University Management School, Milton Keynes, May.

QUINTAS, P. (1996) 'Software by Design' in Mansell, R. and Silverstone, R. (eds) (1996) *Communication by Design: The Politics of Information and Communication Technologies*, Oxford: Oxford University Press, pp. 75-102.

RADOSEVIC, S. (1995) 'Science and Technology Capabilities in Economies in Transition: Effects and Prospects', *Economies of Transition*, Vol. 3(4), pp. 459-478.

RAMAN, K.S. AND YAP, C.S. (1996) 'From a Resource Rich Country to an Information Rich Society: An Evaluation of Information Technology Policies in Malaysia', *Information Technology for Development*, Vol. 7, pp. 109-131.

RAMANI, S. (1998 forthcoming) 'National Infrastructure Required to Promote IT Applications' in Mitter, S., Bastos, M.-I. and Bartzokas, A. (eds) *Europe and Developing Countries in the World Information Economy: Trade, Distance Education and Regional Development*, London: Routledge and Tokyo: UNU Press.

RAMANUJAM, J. (1996) *Information Infrastructure Development in India*, New Delhi: Department of Telecommunication, http://www.ncb.gov.sg/nii/96scan4/india2.html

RAMESAM, V. (1996) 'National Information Infrastructure (NII) Profile of India', commissioned by COLCIENCIAS as a background paper for the UNCSTD Working Group on IT and Development.

RATAN, S. (1995) 'A New Divide between Haves and Have Nots?', *Time*, Spring.

REARDON, G. (1998 forthcoming) 'Externalising Information Processing Work: Breaking the Logic of Spatial and Work Organisation' in Mitter, S., Bastos, M.-I. and Bartzokas, A. (eds) *Europe and Developing Countries in the World Information Economy: Trade, Distance Education and Regional Development*, London: Routledge and Tokyo: UNU Press

REDDY, P. (1996) 'New Technologies and Technological Capability-building at the Enterprise Level: Some Policy Implications', United Nations Conference on Trade and Development, *Science and Technology Issues*, UNCTAD/DST/11, United Nations: New York and Geneva.

REES, G. (1994) 'IT and Vocational Education and Training in Europe: An Overview' in Ducatel, K. (ed.) *Employment and Technical Change in Europe: Work Organisation, Skills and Training*, Aldershot: Edward Elgar Publishers, pp. 92-112.

REHAK, A. AND WANG, J. (1996) 'On the Fast Track', *China Business Review*, March-April, pp. 8-13.

REICH, R.B. (1991) *The Work of Nations: Preparing Ourselves for 21st-Century Capitalism*, New York: Simon & Schuster.

REID, E. (1996) 'Strategic Planning for Cutting Edge Communications: The Internet', *Media Asia*, Vol. 23(4), pp. 198-207.

RICHARDSON, R. (1998 forthcoming) 'Teleservices and the Relocation of Employment: Evidence from Western Europe' in Mitter, S., Bastos, M.-I. and Bartzokas, A. (eds) *Europe and Developing Countries in the World Information Economy: Trade, Distance Education and Regional Development*, London: Routledge and Tokyo: UNU Press.

RIM Lab (n.d.) 'Laboratory for Robotics and Intelligent Manufacturing (RIM Lab)', http://deis58.cineca.it/ernet/ernetbook/node58.htm

ROBERTS E. (1980) 'New Ventures for Corporate Growth', *Harvard Business Review*, Vol. 58(4), pp. 134-142.

ROCHE, E.M. AND BLAINE, M.J. (eds)(1996) *Information Technology, Development and Policy: Theoretical Perspectives and Practical Challenges*, Aldershot: Avebury.

ROFFE, P., ANING, K. AND TESFACHEW, T. (1995) 'Overview' in United Nations Conference on Trade and Development (eds) 'Information Technology for Development', *Advanced Technology Assessment System Bulletin*, Issue 10, New York and Geneva: United Nations, pp. v-x.

ROMER, P. (1986) 'Increasing Returns and Long-Run Growth', *Journal of Political Economy*, Vol. 98(5), pp. 1002-1037.

ROODE, J.D. AND du PLOOY, N.F. (1994) 'A Bill of Rights for the Information Age Which Recognises the Third World', Department of Informatics, University of Pretoria.

ROTTER, J. (1967) 'A New Scale for the Measurement of Interpersonal Trust', *Journal of Personality*, Vol. 35(December), pp. 651-665.

ROWAN, G. (1997) 'The Internet-Not Exactly Main Street For Doing Business', *Globe and Mail* (Globenet), 18 February.

RUSCH, R. AND LEVENTHAL, N. (1996) 'Outer Space & World-wide Market Access: Regulatory Issues for Mobile Satellite Service. An Odyssey Perspective', Presentation to the International Bar Association, Berlin, 24 October.

RUTANEN, P. (1996) 'Learning Societies and GII/GIS', paper for the Second Annual Conference of the David L. Lam Institute for East-West Studies, Institutional Strategies for the Internationalisation of Higher Education, Hong Kong, 25-27 November.

RUTKOWSKI, A. (1995) 'Multilateral Cooperation in Telecommunications' in Drake, W. (ed.) *The New Information Infrastructure: Strategies for US Policy*, New York: 20th Century Fund, pp. 223-250.

SADOWSKI, B. (1996) *Back to Monopoly: Opportunities and Constraints for Public and Corporate Networks in Post-Unification Germany*, Aldershot: Avebury.

SAKO, M. (1992) *Prices, Quality and Trust: Inter-Firm Relations in Britain and Japan*, Cambridge: Cambridge University Press.

SAKO, M. (1994) 'Neither Markets nor Hierarchies: a Comparative Study of the Printed Circuit Board Industry in Britain and Japan' in Hollingsworth, J. Schmitter, P. and Streeck, W. (eds) *Governing Capitalist Economies: Performance and Control of Economic Sectors*, New York: Oxford University Press, pp. 17-42.

SALTER, W.E.G. (1966) *Productivity and Technical Change*, Cambridge: Cambridge University Press.

SAMARAJIVA, R. (1996) 'Consumer Protection in the Decentralized Network' in Noam, E. and NíShúilleabháin, A. (eds) *Private Networks Public Objectives*, Amsterdam: Elsevier, pp. 287-306.

SAMARAJIVA, R. AND SHIELDS, P. (1990) 'Integration, telecommunication, and development: Power in the paradigms', *Journal of Communication*, Vol. 40(3), pp. 84-105.

SAMSUNG ELECTRONICS CO. (1994) *Twenty Years' History of Samsung Electronics Co.*, Seoul: SEC, (Korean).

SANATAN, R. AND MELODY, W.H. (1997) 'Adapting to a Global Economy: Implications of Telecom Reform for Small Developing Countries' in Melody, W.H. (ed.) *Telecommunication Reform: Principles, Policies and Regulatory Practices*, Lyngby: Technical University of Denmark, pp. 327-335.

SAUNDERS, R. WARFORD, J. AND WELLENIUS, B. (1983) and (1994) *Telecommunications and Economic Development*, published for The World Bank by Baltimore MD: Johns Hopkins University Press.

SAYERS, D. (1997) 'The Erosion of Privacy and Security in Public Telecommunication Networks: The Growing Significance of Telemetadata in Advanced Communication Services', *FAIR Working Paper No. 13*, Brighton: SPRU.

SCHAAN, J.L. AND BEAMISH, J. (1988) 'Joint Venture General Managers in LDCs' in Contractor, F.J. and Lorange, P. (eds) *Co-operative Strategies in International Business*, Lexington MA: DC Heath and Company, pp. 279-299.

SCHENK, I.J. (1995) 'The State and Economic Growth in a Changing Global Political Economy: A Case Study of Singapore', unpublished Masters Thesis, University of Guelph, May.

SCHLESINGER, P. (1992) *Media, State and Nation: Political Violence and Collective Identities*, London: Sage Publications.

SCHONBERGER, R.J. (1986) *World Class Manufacturing: The Lessons of Simplicity Applied*, New York: The Free Press.

SCHULER, D. (1996) *New Community Networks: Wired for Change*, New York: Addison-Wesley.

SCHWARE, R. (1987) 'Software Industry Development in the Third World: Policy Guidelines, Institutional Options and Constraints', *World Development*, Vol. 15(10/11), pp. 1249-1267.

SCHWARE, R. (1992) 'Software Industry Entry Strategies for Developing Countries: A "Walking on Two Legs" Proposition', *World Development*, Vol. 20(2), pp. 143-164.

SCHWARTZ, R. (1996) *Wireless Communications in Developing Countries*, Boston: Artech House Publishers.

SCULLEY, A.B. (1997) 'Bermuda - The Information Island of the 21st Century', speech given by Chairman of the Bermuda Stock Exchange at the Annual Dinner of the Institute of Directors, London, January.

SENKER, J. (1995) 'Tacit Knowledge and Models of Innovation', *Industrial and Corporate Change*, Vol. 4(2), pp. 425-447.

SENKER, J. AND SENKER, P. (1990) *Technical Change in the 1990s: Implications for Skills, Training and Employment*. Report to the Training Agency, Brighton: Science Policy Research Unit, University of Sussex.

SENKER, P. AND SENKER, J. (1994) 'Information Technology and Skills in Manufacturing and Construction' in Ducatel, K. (ed.) *Employment and Technical Change in Europe: Work Organisation, Skills and Training*, Aldershot: Edward Elgar, pp. 58-77.

SEPSTRUP, P. AND GOONASEKERA, A. (1994) 'TV Transnationalization: Europe and Asia', Reports and Papers on Mass Communication, No. 109, Paris: UNESCO.

SERVAES, J. (1989) 'Cultural Identity and Modes of Communication' in Anderson, J. (ed.) *Communication Yearbook. Volume 12*, Newbury Park: Sage, pp. 383-416.

SERVAES, J. (ed.) (1991) 'Europe 1992: Impact on the Communications Environment', *Telematics and Informatics* (special issue), Vol. 8(3), pp. 127-232.

SHAPIRO, S.P. (1987) 'The Social Control of Impersonal Trust', *American Journal of Sociology*, Vol. 3 (November), pp. 623-658.

SHARIFFADEEN, T.M.A. (1994a) 'Strategic Planning and Management of Information Technology in Malaysia', paper prepared for International Conference on Information Technology '94, Kuala Lumpur, Malaysian Institute of Microelectronics Systems.

SHARIFFADEEN, T.M.A. (1994b) 'Information Technology and Development - Malaysian Development Experience', National Institute of Public Administration, Kuala Lumpur.

SHARIFFADEEN, T.M.A. (1995) 'Moving Towards More Intelligent Use of Human Intelligence', paper presented at Infotech Malaysia '95, Putra World Trade Center, Kuala Lumpur, 1-3 November.

SIEBECK, W. (ed.) (1990) 'Strengthening Protection of Intellectual Property in Developing Countries: A Survey of the Literature', *Discussion Paper No. 112*, Washington DC: World Bank.

SILVERSTONE, R. AND HADDON, L. (1996) 'Design and the Domestication of Information and Communication Technologies: Technical Change and Everyday Life' in Mansell, R. and Silverstone, R. (eds) *Communication by Design: The Politics of Information and Communication Technologies*, Oxford: Oxford University Press, pp. 44-74.

SILVERSTONE, R. AND HIRSCH, E. (eds) (1992) *Consuming Technologies: Media and Information in Domestic Spaces*, London: Routledge.

SILVERSTONE, R. AND MANSELL, R. (1996) 'The Politics of Information and Communication Technologies' in Mansell, R. and Silverstone, R. (eds) *Communication by Design: The Politics of Information and Communication Technologies*, Oxford: Oxford University Press, pp. 213-227.

SINCLAIR, J., JACKA, E. AND CUNNINGHAM, S. (eds) (1996) *New Patterns in Global Television. Peripheral Vision*, Oxford: Oxford University Press.

SKILLINGS, J. (1996) 'Technology Could Bolster Networks, Connect Remote Areas', *Computerworld*, Vol. 30(38), p. 65.

SKOVMAND, M. AND SCHRODER, K.M. (eds) (1992) *Media Cultures: Reappraising Transnational Media*, London: Routledge.

SMITH SYSTEM ENGINEERING (1997) 'Feasibility of Censoring and Jamming Pornography and Racism in Informatics', draft report prepared for the European Parliament, STOA, July.

SMYTHE, D. (1981) *Dependency Road: Communications, Capitalism, Consciousness, and Canada*, Norwood NJ: Ablex Publishers.

SNODDY, R. (1997) 'Digital Radio for Africa Nears', *Financial Times*, 21 April.

SOETE, L. (1985) 'International Diffusion of Technology, Industrial Development and Technological Leapfrogging', *World Development*, Vol. 13(3), pp. 409-422.

SOETE, L. AND KAMP, K. (1996) 'The "Bit Tax": The Case for Further Research', Maastricht: MERIT, University of Maastricht, 12 August.

SOFTWARE BUSINESS ALLIANCE (1995) *Piracy Study*, http:www.bsa.org/piracy/piracy.study95/piracy95.html

SOMMERVILLE, I. (1995) *Software Engineering*, 5th Edition, New York: Addison-Wesley, p. 9.

SOUTER, D. (1997) 'The Perspective of Commonwealth Developing Countries', remarks prepared for a European Union seminar on International Accounting Rates and Developing Countries, by the Commonwealth Telecommunications Organisation, January.

SOUTH AFRICAN GOVERNMENT (1994) 'Reconstruction and Development White Paper' quoted in Hodge, J. and Miller, J. (1997) 'Information Technology in South Africa - The State of the Art and Implications for National I/T Policy', paper prepared for the Telecom '97 8th Biennial Conference on Telecommunications in South Africa, Midrand, 24-26 March.

SREBERNY-MOHAMMADI, A. (1995) 'The Global and the Local in International Communication' in Curran, J. and Gurevitch, M. (eds) *Mass Media and Society*, London: Edward Arnold, pp. 171-203.

SREBERNY-MOHAMMADI, A. (1996) 'Globalization, Communication and Transnational Civil Society: Introduction' in Braman, S. and Sreberny-Mohammadi, A. (eds) *Globalization, Communication and Transnational Civil Society*, London: Hampton Press, pp. 1-20.

SREBERNY-MOHAMMADI, A. (1994) 'Women, Media and Development in a Global Context', UNESCO, and presented as (1995) 'Women, Media and Development in a Global Context', UNESCO International Symposium: Women and the Media-Access to Expression and Decision-making, Toronto, Canada, February.

STANBURY, W.T. (1995) 'New Information Technologies and Transnational Interest Groups', notes prepared for a presentation to the symposium 'Information Technologies and International Relations' sponsored by the Department of Foreign Affairs and International Trade in cooperation with the Institute of International Relations, University of British Columbia, 13 January.

STANLEY, K.B. (1991) 'Balance of Payments, Deficits, and Subsidies in International Communications Services: A New Challenge to Regulation', *Administrative Law Review*, Vol. 43(3), pp. 411-438.

STANLEY, K.B. (1997) 'International Settlements in a Changing Global Telecom Market' in Melody, W.H. (ed.) *Telecom Reform: Principles, Policies and Regulatory Practices*, Lyngby: Technical University of Denmark, pp. 371-391.

STATE STATISTICAL BUREAU (1989) *China Statistical Yearbook 1989*, Beijing: China Statistical Information and Consultancy Service Centre.

STATE STATISTICAL BUREAU (1992) *China Statistical Yearbook 1992*, Beijing: China Statistical Information and Consultancy Service Centre.

STATE STATISTICAL BUREAU (1995) *China Statistical Yearbook 1995*, Beijing: China Statistical Publishing House.

STAVIS, B. AND GANG, Y. (1988) 'Babcock and Wilcox Beijing Company Ltd', *China Business Review*, July-August, pp. 10-12.

STEINBERG, G.M. (1996) 'Satellite Capabilities of Emerging Space-Competent States' in Gasparini Alves, P. (ed.) *Evolving Trends in the Dual Use of Satellites*, New York/Geneva: UNIDIR (United Nations Institute for Disarmament Research), pp. 31-56.

STEINMUELLER, W.E. (1996) 'The U.S. Software Industry: An Analysis and Interpretive History' in Mowery, D.C. (ed.) *The International Software Industry*, Oxford: Oxford University Press, pp. 15-52.

STONE, M.B. AND MENOU, M.J. (1994) 'The Impact of Information on Development', *Bulletin of the American Society for Information Science*, Vol. 20(5), pp. 25-26.

STREECK, W. (1993) *The Governance of Industry: Upgrading Industrial Policy in Europe*, Wisconsin: University of Wisconsin.

STREECK, W. AND SCHMITTER, P.C. (1991) 'Community, Market, State - and Associations?: the Prospective Contribution of Interest Governance to Social Order' in Thompson, G., Frances, J., Lezacic, R. and Mitchell, J. (eds) *Markets, Hierarchies and Networks: The Coordination of Social Life*, Sage: London, pp. 226-241.

SUNG, L. (1992) 'WARC-92: Setting the Agenda for the Future', *Telecommunications Policy*, Vol. 16(8), pp. 624-634.

TALERO, E. AND GAUDETTE, P. (1995) 'Harnessing Information for Development: A Proposal for a World Bank Group Vision and Strategy', Washington DC, The World Bank, October.

TAN, Z. (1995) 'China's Information Superhighway @ What Is It and Who Controls It?', *Telecommunications Policy*, Vol. 19(9), pp. 721-731.

TANG, P. (1995) 'Intellectual Property Rights and the Internet: The Future Needs Work', *Intermedia*, Vol. 23(4), pp. 22-25.

TANG, P. (1997a) 'Electronic Access to Public Information: Government On-line', *The IPTS Report*, Vol. 14, pp. 12-19.

TANG, P. (1997b) 'Multimedia Information Products and Services: A Need for 'Cybercops?'' in Loader, B. (ed.) *Governance of Cyberspace*, London: Routledge, pp. 190-208.

TANG, P. (1997c) 'The Use of Copyright as a Measure of Innovation: Software Applications in the Digital Age', *Intellectual Property Quarterly*, Issue No. 1, pp. 71-91.

TANG, P., POWELL, D. AND VON TUNZELMANN, N. (1997) 'The Development and Application of New Information Technologies in the Next Decade', Final Report for the Committee on Research, Technology Development and Energy, European Parliament, March.

TASSELL, T. (1997) 'Foreigners Cool Plans to Invest in India', *Financial Times*, London, 25 February.

TAYLOR, J., BELLAMY, C., RAAB, C., DUTTON, W.H. AND PELTU, M. (1997) 'Innovation in Public Service Delivery' in Dutton, W.H. (ed.) *Information and Communication Technologies: Visions and Realities*, Oxford: Oxford University Press, pp. 283-299.

TAYLOR, P. (1997) 'IBM Builds Global Software Team', *Financial Times*, 18 February.

TECHNOLOGY FORESIGHT PANEL ON MANUFACTURING, PRODUCTION AND BUSINESS PROCESSES (1995) *Technology Foresight: Progress through Partnership: Manufacturing, Production and Business Processes*, Vol. 9, London: HMSO.

TECHNOLOGY FORESIGHT PANEL ON TRANSPORT (1995) *Technology Foresight: Progress through Partnership: Transport*, Vol. 5, London: HMSO.

TEECE, D. (1981) 'The Market for Know-How and the Efficient Transfer of Technology', *Annals of the American Academy of Political and Social Science*, Vol. 458 (November), pp. 81-96.

TELEPROFESSIONAL INTERNATIONAL (1997) *TeleProfessional International*, January/February.

THE ECONOMIST (1996) 'World Economy Survey', *The Economist*, 28 September-4 October.

THE QUALITY OBSERVER (1996) 'Using Technology to Achieve Manufacturing Excellence: Cutting-Edge Applications of Technology Nominated for 1996 Computerworld Smithsonian Awards', http://www.thequalityobeserver.com/Man-ex.htm

THEOBALD, R. (1996) 'Who Said We Wanted an Information Superhighway?', *Internet Research: Electronic Networking Applications and Policy*, Vol. 6(2/3), pp. 90-92.

THOMPSEN, P.A. (1996) 'What's Fuelling the Flames in Cyberspace? A Social Influence Model' in Strate, L., Jacobson, R. and Gibson, S.B. (eds) *Communication and Cyberspace: Social Interaction in an Electronic Environment*, Cresskill, NJ: Hampton Press Inc., pp. 297-315.

THOMPSON, J.D. (1967) *Organizations in Action*, New York: McGraw Hill.

THULSTRUP, W.E. (1994) 'Scientific Research for Development', Informal Working Paper, World Bank, http://www.worldbank.org/html/hcovp/phnflash/hcwp/hrwp024.html.

TIFFIN, J. AND RAJASINGHAM, R. (1995) *In Search of the Virtual Classroom: Education in an Information Society*, London: Routledge, citing Reidar Roll, pp. xv-xvi.

TRIOLO, P.S. AND LOVELOCK, P. (1996) 'Up, Up, and Away - With Strings Attached', *China Business Review*, November-December, pp. 18-29.

TSANG, E.W.K. (1995) 'The Implementation of Technology Transfer in Sino-Foreign Joint Ventures', *International Journal of Technology Management*, Vol. 10 (7/8), pp. 757-766.

TUNSTALL, J. (1977) *The Media are American: Anglo-American Media in the World*, London: Constable.

TYLER, M. (1997) 'Satellite Phones - Open Skies, Yes, But Open Markets, Maybe', *Intermedia*, Vol. 25(1), pp. 34-36.

TYSON, L. AND YOFFIE, D. (1991) 'Semiconductors: From Manipulated to Managed Trade', *BRIE Working Paper No. 47*, Berkeley, CA.

UNCSTD (United Nations Commission on Science and Technology for Development) (1995) 'Information Technologies for Development: An Issues Note', prepared by UNCTAD Secretariat, 2nd Session, Geneva, 15 May, E/CN.16/1995/9, 16 March.

UNCSTD (United Nations Commission on Science and Technology for Development) (1997a) 'Report of the Working Group on Information and Communication Technologies for Development', prepared for the 3rd Session, Geneva, 12 May, E/CN.16/1997/4, 7 March.

UNCSTD (United Nations Commission on Science and Technology for Development) (1997b) 'Action Arising from the Second Session - Implementation of and Progress Made on Decisions taken at the Second Session of the Commission, including Follow-up Work on Technology for Basic Needs, Gender and Sustainable Development, and Coalition of Resources', prepared by UNCTAD secretariat for UNCSTD 3rd Session, Geneva, 12 May, E/CN.16/1997/8, 7 March.

UNCSTD (United Nations Commission on Science and Technology for Development) (1997c) 'Consideration of Ways and Means of Commemorating in 1999 the Twentieth Anniversary of the Vienna Conference on Science and Technology for Development', Note by the UNCTAD Secretariat prepared for UNCSTD 3rd Session, Geneva, 12 May, E/CN.16/1997/7, 11 March.

UNCSTD (United Nations Commission on Science and Technology for Development) (1997d) 'Implementation of and Progress Made on Decisions Taken at the Second Session of the Commission, Including Follow-up Work on Technology for Basic Needs, Gender and Sustainable Development, and Coalition of Resources', Note by the UNCTAD secretariat, Item 4, UNCSTD 3rd Session, E/CN.16/1997/8, 12 May.

UNCTAD (United Nations Conference on Trade and Development) (eds) (1995a) 'Information Technology for Development', *Advanced Technology Assessment System Bulletin*, Issue 10, New York and Geneva: United Nations.

UNCTAD (United Nations Conference on Trade and Development) (1995b) *The Least Developed Countries - A Statistical Profile -1995*, New York and Geneva: United Nations.

UNCTAD (United Nations Conference on Trade and Development) (1995c) 'Technological Capacity Building and Technology Partnership: Field Findings, Country Experiences and Programmes', UNCTAD/DST/6, Geneva.

UNCTAD (United Nations Conference on Trade and Development) (1996a) *Handbook of Economic Integration and Cooperation Groupings of Developing Countries*, New York and Geneva: United Nations.

UNCTAD (United Nations Conference on Trade and Development) (1996b) 'Exchanging Experiences of Technology Partnership', UNCTAD/DST/15, Geneva.

UNCTAD (United Nations Conference on Trade and Development) (1996c) 'The TRIPS Agreement and Developing Countries', prepared by the UNCTAD Secretariat, New York/Geneva: United Nations (UNCTAD/ITE/1).

UNCTAD (United Nations Conference on Trade and Development) (1997) 'Review of the Activities of the United Nations System in the Area of Information Technology and Development', paper prepared for the United Nations Commission on Science and Technology for Development, Geneva, January.

UNECA (United Nations Economic Commission for Africa) (1996a) 'Exploiting Information Technology to Accelerate Socio-Economic Development in Africa: An Action Plan', United Nations Economic and Social Council, Geneva, 24 April.

UNECA (United Nations Economic Commission for Africa) (1996b) 'The African Information Society Initiative (AISI)', Addis Ababa.

UNESCAP (United Nations Economic and Social Commission for Asia and the Pacific) (1997) 'Regional Economic Cooperation as a Means for Developing and Promoting New Advances in Information Technology for Industrial and Technological Applications in Asia and the Pacific', paper prepared for the Steering Group of the Committee for Regional Economic Cooperation, 9th Meeting, 4-6 February, Chitose City, Japan, United Nations Economic and Social Council, E/ESCAP/SREC(9)/2, 2 January.

UNESCO (United Nations Educational, Scientific and Cultural Organization) (1989) *World Communication Report*, Paris: UNESCO.

UNESCO (United Nations Educational, Scientific and Cultural Organization) (1991) *World Development Report*, Geneva: UNESCO.

UNESCO (United Nations Educational, Scientific and Cultural Organization) (1995) *Statistical Yearbook '95*, Lanham MD: UNESCO Publishing and Bernan Press.

UNESCO (United Nations Educational, Scientific and Cultural Organization) (1996) *Information and Communication Technologies in Development: A UNESCO Perspective*, Report prepared by the UNESCO Secretariat, CII-96/WS/6, Paris: UNESCO, December.

UNESCO (United Nations Educational, Scientific and Cultural Organization) (1997) *World Information Report 1997/98*, Geneva: UNESCO Publishing, edited by Courrier, Y. and Lange, A.

UNION FOR THE PUBLIC DOMAIN (1996) 'Proposals to Regulate the Public's Rights to Use Information Stored in "Databases" ', http://www.public-domain.org/database/database.html

URATA, S. (1997) 'International Technology Transfer by Japanese Multinationals in East Asia', School of Social Sciences, Waseda University, Tokyo, mimeo.

URE, J. (ed.) (1995) *Telecommunications in Asia: Policy, Planning and Development*, Hong Kong: Hong Kong University Press.

US CONGRESS (1988) Special 301 provisions (Section 182 of the Omnibus Trade and Competitiveness Act of 1988) 19 U.S.C. 2242, Washington: DC.

US CONGRESS OFFICE OF TECHNOLOGY ASSESSMENT (1992) *Finding a Balance: Computer Software, Intellectual Property and the Challenge of Technological Change*, Washington DC: OTA.

US CONGRESS OFFICE OF TECHNOLOGY ASSESSMENT (1995a) *Global Communications: Opportunities for Trade and Aid*, Washington, DC: US Government Printing Office, pp. 13-14.

US CONGRESS OFFICE OF TECHNOLOGY ASSESSMENT (1995b) *The 1992 World Administrative Radio Conference. Technology and Policy Implications*, Washington DC: US Government Printing Office.

US DEPARTMENT OF COMMERCE (1996) 'Survey of Private Services Transactions', Bureau of Economic Analysis, November.

VALANTIN, R. (1995) 'Information and Communication Technologies for Development: Some Principles and Lessons from IDRC Experience', *Information Technology for Development*, Vol. 10, pp. 540-544.

VAN DE DONK, W., SNELLEN, I. AND TOPS, P. (1995) *Orwell in Athens: A Perspective on Informatization and Democracy*, Amsterdam: IOS Press.

VARIS, T. (1985) 'International Flows of Television Programmes', Reports and Papers on Mass Communication, No. 100, Paris: UNESCO.

VICKERS, J. AND YARROW, G. (1991) 'Economic Perspectives on Privatisation', *Journal of Economic Perspectives*, Vol. 5(2), pp. 111-132.

VIETNAMESE ASSOCIATION FOR COMPUTING, ENGINEERING TECHNOLOGY AND SCIENCE (1994) 'Electronic and Information Technology in Vietnam', a report to the Ministry of Science, Technology and Environment', Hanoi.

VON HIPPEL, E. (1988) *The Sources of Innovation*. Oxford: Oxford University Press.

VU, X.H. (1995) 'The Vietnamese Information Technology Plans', Viet Nam USA Society, November, http://www.ncb.gov.sg/nii/95scan7/1.html

WADE, R. (1990) *Governing the Market: Economic Theory and the Role of Government in East Asian Industrialization*, Princeton, NJ: Princeton University Press.

WANG, G. (1996a) 'Beyond Media Globalisation: A Look at Cultural Integrity from a Policy Perspective', Seminar in (Tele)Communications Policies in Western Europe and Southeast Asia: Cultural and Historical Perspectives, Bruges, Belgium, 29 August-1 September.

WANG, J. (1996b) 'Walking and Talking', *China Business Review*, March-April, pp. 13-17.

WANGWE, S., SEMBOJA, H. AND NZUKI, M. (1998 forthcoming) 'The Information Revolution and Economic and Social Exclusion in Developing Countries: The Case of Tanzania' in Cooper, C. (ed.) *Information Technology Policy and National Economic Development*, London: Routledge and Tokyo: UNU Press.

WARD, J., GRIFFITHS, P. AND WHITMORE, P. (1990) *Strategic Planning for Information Systems*, Chichester: John Wiley and Son Ltd.

WARD, M. (1996) 'All the World Shall be Taxed', *New Scientist*, 20 July.

WEBSTER, J. (1996) *Shaping Women's Work: Gender, Employment and Information Technology*, London: Longman.

WEHN, U. (1996) 'International Governance of Cryptography', *FAIR Working Paper No.9*, Brighton: SPRU.

WEISS, E. (1995) 'South East Asia: The Expanding Telecom Economies', *Telecommunications* [International Edition], Vol. 29(10), pp. 117-125.

WHISTON, T.G. (1992) *Education and Employment for a Sustainable World*, Volume 18 of 'Global Perspective 2010: Tasks for S&T', Commission of the European Communities, Brussels.

WHISTON, T.G. (1994) *Research Policy in the Higher Education Sector of South Africa*, Pretoria: Foundation for Research Development.

WHISTON, T.G. (1997) 'Information Technology in a Global Context: Developing Country Needs and Challenges - Towards a Theoretical Framework', Science Policy Research Unit, University of Sussex, mimeo.

WHITLEY, R. (ed.) (1992) *Business Systems in East Asia: Firms, Markets and Societies*, London: Sage.

WILLIAMS, F. (1997a) 'US, EU Vie for Credit on Telecoms', *Financial Times*, 17 February.

WILLIAMS, F. (1997b) 'IT Accord to Scrap Tariffs by Year 2000', *Financial Times*, 27 March.

WILLIAMS, F. (1997c) 'UNCTAD Tries to Beat Customs Fraud', *Financial Times*, 5 August.

WILSON III, E.J. (1996a) 'Mapping the Global Information Infrastructure', commissioned by COLCIENCIAS as a background paper for the UNCSTD Working Group on IT and Development.

WILSON III, E.J. (1996b) 'Managing Change in the Information Technology Sector: Scenarios and Strategies for the Future', commissioned by COLCIENCIAS as a background paper for the UNCSTD Working Group on IT and Development.

WIPO (World Intellectual Property Organization) (1996a) 'WIPO Press Release No. 106', Geneva, 20 December, http://www.wipo.org

WIPO (World Intellectual Property Organization) (1996b) List of Participants, CRNR/DC/INF.2, 20 December 1996.

WIPO (World Intellectual Property Organization) (1997) 'WIPO Press Release No. 110', Geneva, 2 May, http://www.wipo.org

WOMACK, J., JONES, D. AND ROOS, D. (1990) *The Machine That Changed the World*, New York: Rawson Associates.

WOMEN WORKING WORLD-WIDE (1991) *Common Interests: Women Organising in Global Electronics*, London: Women Working World-Wide.

WORLD BANK (1993) *The East Asian Miracle: Economic Growth and Public Policy*, A World Bank Policy Research Report, New York: Oxford University Press.

WORLD BANK (1994) 'Telecommunications Sector Strategy. Background and Bank Group Issues', Joint World Bank/IFC Seminar, Washington, DC, p. 25.

WORLD BANK (1997) *The STATE in a Changing World*, New York: Oxford University Press published for the World Bank.

WORLD BANK, INFODEV (1996) 'The Role of the World Bank - An Objective and Experienced Third Party', http://www.worldbank.org/html/fpd/infodev/background4.html

WORLD TRADE ORGANIZATION (1997a) 'Ruggiero Cites Progress in the Information Technology Agreement', Press Release 69, Geneva, 13 March.

WORLD TRADE ORGANIZATION (1997b) 'Informal Background Document for Information Purposes - Data on Telecommunication Markets covered by the WTO Negotiations on Basic Telecommunications', Geneva, 17 February.

WORLD TRADE ORGANIZATION (1997c) 'Negotiating Group on Basic Telecommunication Services', Geneva, 17 February.

WORLD TRADE ORGANIZATION (1997d) 'Press Statement by the Director General at the close of the Negotiations on Basic Telecommunications', Geneva, 15 February.

WORLDVIEW (1997) 'Worldview in Brief', Worldview International Foundation, http://www.worldview.no/worldview.info.html

WRISTON, W. (1992) *The Twilight of Sovereignty: How the Information Revolution is Transforming our World*, New York: Scribner & Sons.

WU, C. (1995) 'Integrated Manufacturing Autonomous in Information Age' in Zhu L. (ed.) *Cross Centuries*, Shenyang, China: Liaoning Education Publishing House, pp. 146-151.

WU, W. (1996) 'Great Leap or Long March: Some Policy Issues of Development of the Internet in China', *Telecommunications Policy*, Vol. 20(9), pp. 699-711.

YOURDON, E. (1992) *Decline and Fall of the American Programmer*, New Jersey: Prentice Hall Inc.

ZACHER, M.W. AND SUTTON, B.A. (1996) 'Mutual Interests, Normative Continuities, and Regime Theory: Cooperation in International Transportation and Communications Industries', *European Journal of International Relations*, Vol. 2(1), pp. 5-46.

ZHAO, P. AND GRIMSHAW, D.J. (1991) 'A Comparative Study of the Application of IT in China and the West: Culture and Stages of Growth Model', *Warwick Business School Research Papers No. 32*, Coventry: Warwick Business School Research Bureau.

ZIMAN, J. (1994) *Prometheus Bound: Science in a Dynamic Steady State*, Cambridge: Cambridge University Press.

INDEX